I0727808

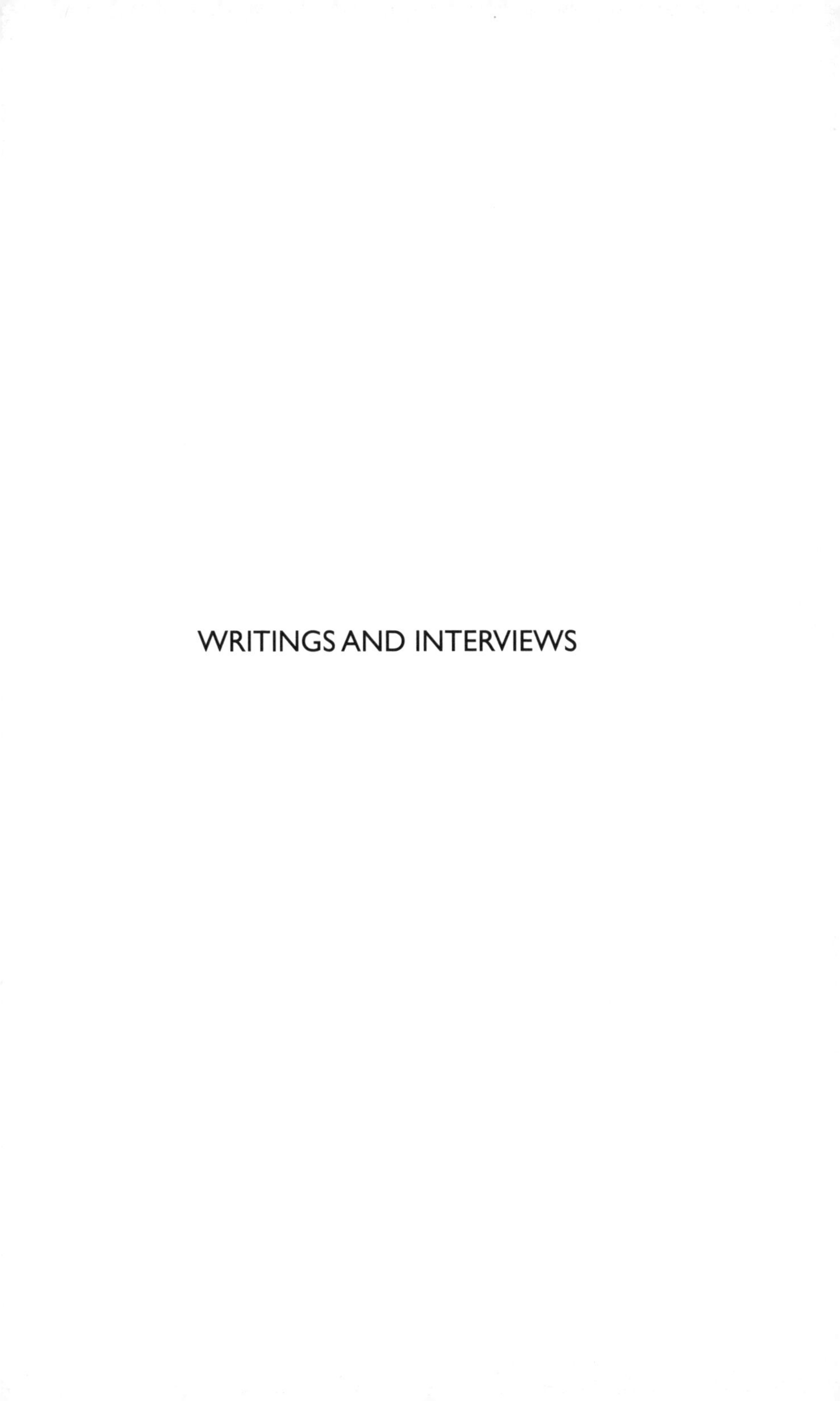

WRITINGS AND INTERVIEWS

MARC CAMILLE CHAIMOWICZ

WRITINGS AND INTERVIEWS

Edited by Alexis Vaillant

Sternberg Press

INTRODUCTION

"I'm working more closely to the way writers might in that they establish certain parameters of sensibility and then elaborate new work to look at different aspects of their central concern."
—Marc Camille Chaimowicz, as told to Dan Fox, *frieze*, October 2008.

The first piece of writing that Marc Camille Chaimowicz published was in 1971. For his solo exhibition "Assumptions—Specific Work-Pieces" at Vaughan College, University of Leicester, he conceived a fourteen-page collage [III. 1] documenting his early stages as an artist. Aiming to contextualise his exhibition, this self-publication, including art jokes, press clippings, and political news of the time, is a Xerox that draws a portrait of the artist as a young man. Fifty years later, when Chaimowicz was eventually invited to do "an exhibition in a museum in the country of [his] birth," as he put it, he wrote "an open letter" to the museum director [III. 29] that describes, room by room, the exhibition he imagined. Written half a century apart, these two pieces bear unstated intentions which show that if writing is one thing, behaving as an artist through writing is quite another. While the first piece was primarily intended to promote the artist's exhibition longer than the amazingly short two-week run in Leicester, the latter—an attempt to start a dialogue with a museum director around a retrospective—was also designed to answer potential questions from museum staff and journalists alike on behalf of the artist, who knew he would not be present in person during the preparation of the exhibition or at the opening in November 2022. As Chaimowicz aptly noted in 2009 [I. 13], "You never really write just for yourself." To highlight such links between Chaimowicz's intuitive and speculative aesthetic thinking and the context in which his "work-texts" and interviews were published, as well as to foster their historicisation, I have written introductory remarks, published below before the interview or text to which it relates.

While some anecdotes circulate about Chaimowicz's mind's eye as a writer, the background and stories behind his writings and interviews have never been told in detail until this book was undertaken. Collecting the stories behind these texts took some time. Between March 2021 and April 2024, I met regularly with Marc Camille at 9 a.m. online. Intertwining memories and *bon mots*, our conversations could vary greatly in length. Depending on mood and topic, some lasted a few minutes, others an hour. Each time, Chaimowicz appeared seated in front of a curtain of his own design. Combining floral and geometric motifs in shades of purple, yellow, pink, blue, and orange, printed on a cream background, this vibrant curtain obscuring the daylight happily gave us the impression that the seasons were all the same: a sunny morning in the company of the artist. Occasionally, Ginger and Amber, two ponies from the nearby Vauxhall City Farm that the artist can see from his apartment, cheerfully interrupted our conversations. Chaimowicz had noticed that these rather staid animals could run at full speed to devour their daily meal, which, by coincidence, was served around the same time as our conversations. Typical of Chaimowicz, these entertaining interruptions eventually led us into lively digressions, some of which are recounted throughout this book. It also emerged from these conversations that Chaimowicz's writings and interviews could be seen as just one of several modes of expression he has chosen, with none taking precedence over the others.

Spanning fifty years of artistic development, these writings are unmistakably diverse. Ranging from commissioned articles to book designs, spontaneously written texts, and illustrated theory, Chaimowicz's heterogeneous body of writings, therefore, needed an editorial framework. As a result, the seventy-four entries in this volume are divided into three parts consisting of:

— [I] TRANSCRIPTS OF INTERVIEWS

— [II] CRITICISM

— [III] TEXTS

Within each of these parts texts are arranged chronologically. While the first two parts bring together classic types of writing, such as interviews and art reviews, the third part presents a diversity of formats and styles, ranging from collage to artistic statement, press release, essay, and book chapter, to name but a few.

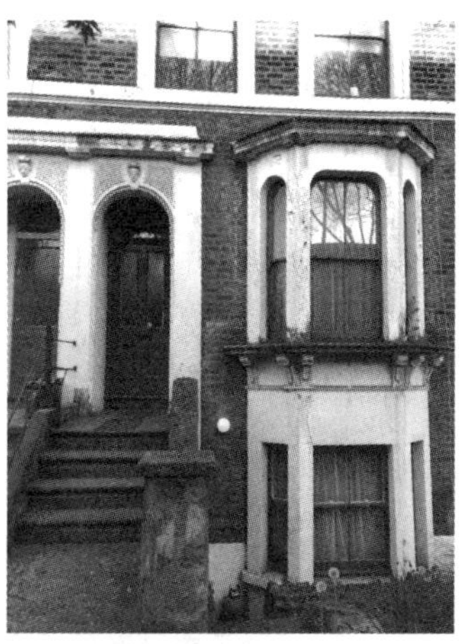

Approach Road, Bethnal Green, London,
24 April, 2021

Spanning post-May 1968 to post-Covid 2023, Chaimowicz's writings interact with five decades of artistic and social concerns. Stemming from post-modernism and post-minimalism, his early written works and interviews are motivated by 1970s Conceptualism, addressing, from the outset, the political role of the artist in relation to the construction of the self. In his texts of the 1980s and early 1990s, Chaimowicz developed a transdisciplinary approach to culture that is visible in his work. While activating mechanisms of de-hierarchisation, essential at the time, he aimed to dissolve the modernist boundaries of "sculpture" and "painting," "artist" and "designer," "fine" and "applied" arts, in both his work and his writings. This process of de-hierarchisation provided him with the space to formalise ordinary aspects of everyday life, on the one hand, and to embrace the "feminised" realms of applied arts and interior design, on the other, while ensuring that there was, as he said, "no intended hierarchy of importance" between them, something his writings of the period underscore.

As for the writings produced after 2000, most interfere with the artist's major projects, such as "re-visitations" of his lost 1970s environments and exhibitions reflecting his key curatorial and publication projects, all of which attracted a new generation of culture mavens and style savants wondering about this "new young artist" probably because, as Chaimowicz had sensed it and later told Lauren O'Neill-Butler in 2009, "they presumed youth behind the work."

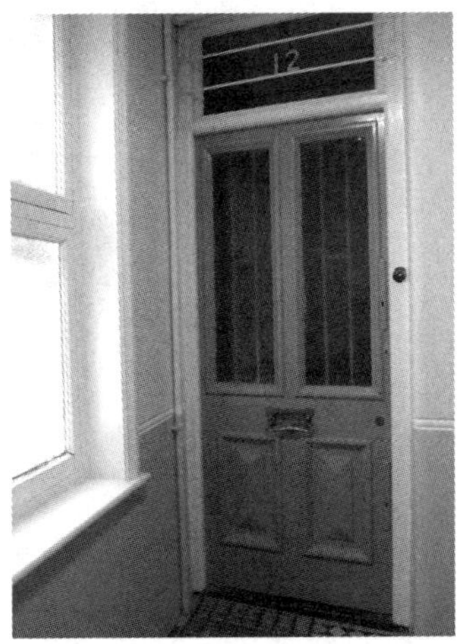

Hayes Court, Camberwell, London,
2 April, 2023

Legendarily reluctant about interviews, Chaimowicz gradually became more cordial towards this format when interviews could take place under "civilised conditions," as he put it in the early 2000s. Thanks to his involvement in interview editing, as well as the striking creativity of several role models who inspired him, such as Diana Vreeland, Jean Genet, and Andy Warhol, he became more confident towards interviewers. He was surprised to find out in 2023 that an interview was simply a few questions sent to him by email. This, compared with Alastair Mackintosh's 1972 interview under the influence of marijuana, amused him greatly. Most of the interviews reproduced in this volume have been originally written, tape-recorded, edited, and illustrated by Chaimowicz. It is important to know that until the end of 2008, the artist had no personal laptop and that doing an interview with him was, in most cases, possible only via regular mail, or a fax machine when it was turned on. Corrections could, sometimes, be added at the last minute by SMS.

Although numerous texts by Chaimowicz can be considered critical, it is remarkable that the artist was actually involved in the press as a performance correspondent and occasional critic between 1976 and 1980. Indeed, Chaimowicz reported on performance in every issue of *Studio International* from January 1976 through March 1977, and subsequently contributed occasional exhibition and book reviews to *Art Monthly* and *Flash Art* between 1977 and 1980. His columns accurately describe the cultural context of performance art, as well as the London art scene of the time. The language used by Chaimowicz is typical of criticism, and the photographs documenting his texts are in most cases his own. Oddly, these texts were written at a time when the artist was distancing himself from performance and video, as well as from criticism. It is therefore essential to read them bearing in mind that, at the time, Chaimowicz was living partially secluded in a studio/apartment on Approach Road, London, and had just published his first artist book: *Dream, an Anecdote by Marc Camille Chaimowicz Dreamt in the Winter and Remembered in the Spring of 1977* [III. 5]. During this time, as Kirsty Bell described in 2015, "the Approach Road interior became a potent site of transformation, where Chaimowicz could play out alternative notions of cultural identity, expand ideas of creative activity, and establish an androgynous zone for its production." Moreover, as he told Kirsty Bell in 2011 in a phone conversation, "Trying to live well became the priority."

Like other artists of his generation, Chaimowicz did not make clear-cut distinction between the different aspects of his artistic activities and, in particular, between the productions of performance, installation art, photography, and writing, through which one can see his flâneur "art of looking." Linked to the artist's dandy lifestyle, this "art of looking" is in no way cut off from the reality of the world, something his writings are emblematic of. Despite their great diversity, these writings have something in common.

Moderating one another, they explore the transmissive qualities of ideas, situations, and storytelling enclosed, where connections can occur years later. Together, these reveal the artist's unique way of writing and speaking (which includes, among other things, compressed hyperboles, the frequent use of ellipses, signifying that "there's no end point in ideas") and vividly convey the artist's original, wide-ranging thoughts on art and culture, the luxury of life, "private-active and public-passive" inclusion, and the real possibility of setting a new template for an expression of queerness through writing. As a result, the reader quickly perceives affiliations and affinities from one text to the next, making this volume a vivid network of lineages, as well as a mind map and toolbox.

Marc Camille Chaimowicz was born in post-war Paris, where he spent the first eight years of his life together with his parents and sisters. His mother, Marie Tailhardt, a French Catholic, was at the time an apprentice with the couturier Maison Paquin, Paris. His father, a Polish Jew who emigrated to Paris in the 1930s, was a mathematician. In the mid-1950s, the family moved to England. Not speaking a word of English, Chaimowicz found himself isolated among children his own age. In 1963, he began studying art. First, at the Ealing School of Art, then at the Camberwell School of Art, London, from which he graduated in painting, definitively freed from the turmoils of a solitary adolescence. In the spring of 1968, he spent several weeks in Paris, where he witnessed first-hand *les événe-ments*, of which he would say in 2000, "It was from there that I dealt, in my own manner, with the Culturally Urgent." At the same time, he was admitted at the Slade School of Fine Art, London, graduating in 1971. Chaimowicz then moved to London. He lived first in a squat (1970–74), then in a two-storey studio/apartment in a vacant building, which he transformed into an art project (1974–79), and in a top-floor Victorian apartment in Camberwell (1979–2017), finally in Vauxhall Pleasure Gardens, in an innovative art building with, at last, an elevator. The texts in this volume were written in these places, most of them in English. For him, "using this language was easier because it is more objective and distant than French which is linked to my mother." However, regularly speaking two languages at once placed him on the edge of a hybrid language, from which charming linguistic oddities sometimes emerged. This linguistic duality is probably linked to Chaimowicz's work being perceived in France as English, whereas the British see it as European.

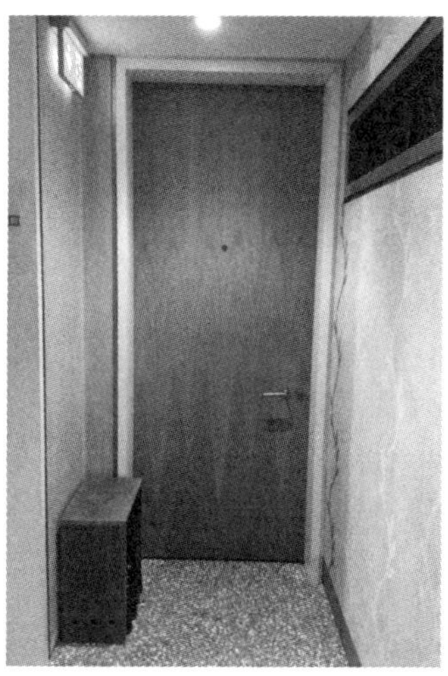

Entrance to the artist's apartment in Tyers Street, Vauxhall, London, 5 April, 2022. As mentioned by the artist, "the door handle, incidentally, is the 'Basel' designed by Roger Diener in 1981 and fabricated by Glutz."

The texts collected in this volume can also be seen as part of a broader history that is characterised by the eruption of language that began early in the twentieth century, exploded on the conceptual art scene, and is still evident today in contemporary art. While artists' writings often combine aesthetic, artistic, intellectual, and political intentions, they are often difficult to classify. An essential source for the study of their work, they usually respond to the specificity of a personality and that of an artistic approach that articulates unknown sites of consciousness, experience, and communication. Chaimowicz's "text-works" and interviews are linked to the visual part of his art. However, the artist didn't write just for himself in the form of an autobiography or diary. Although significant, his correspondence is not as daily as Flaubert's, which would have made Chaimowicz a writer-artist. Instead, his relationship with the written word tends towards a condensed form that gets to the point in terms of what it aims to convey. Instinctive and speculative, rather than theoretical, this use of language enables Chaimowicz to communicate his artistic positions, accompany an artwork or an exhibition, and sometimes, develop a work on the verge of literature in book form.

With approximately two written contributions a year since 1971, the seventy-four entries gathered in this volume inform us about the artist's work and life, while also bearing witness to the writer behind them. Together, they crystallise the radical, self-taught autobiography of a particular sensibility. Influenced by the works of Proust, Flaubert, Genet, Duras, Beckett, and Gide, among others, Chaimowicz, it seems, had a keen sense how concentrated, direct and indirect writing might reach out and suggest the broadest "impressions" without losing a sense of the specific. As Walter Benjamin puts it in "The Consumption of Everyday Life," the flâneur "reads the world from its physiognomy, the surface of things." In Chaimowicz's case, not only from the surface of art, but also from that of architecture, interior design, literature, editing, and writing. However, this is not to be taken lightly. As Chaimowicz remarks, "Writing is probably the only profession where you can't whistle while you work. But I'm not a jobbing writer!"

Sigmund Freud once noted that all writing is autobiographical. This is probably true of most of Chaimowicz's prose. In this respect, after Walter Benjamin, Chaimowicz is less a writer in the novelistic sense than a storyteller: someone who works the events of his own experience so that his readers can in turn integrate them into their own. In a way, Chaimowicz has applied to himself Benjamin's idea that "in fact, one can go on and ask oneself whether the relationship of the storyteller to his material, human life, is not in itself a craftsman's relationship, whether it is not his very task to fashion the raw material of experience, his own and that of others, in a solid, useful, and unique way [...] The storyteller is the figure in which the righteous man encounters himself." (from *The Storyteller: Reflections on the Works of Nikolai Leskov,* 1936).

In response to this way of working, Chaimowicz has often favoured collaborations, both technical and human, in his projects. One thing he really appreciates is that his work surreptitiously changes whoever accompanies it. In this respect, Chaimowicz exclaimed "Bingo!" when I told him this book made me not only the storyteller and editor of his "text-works" and interviews, but also, quite unexpectedly, the potential candidate for his biography. He was so delighted to hear that. So, by extension, when I came to the word count, he was bewildered that a race could exist between us, which he ignored until I told him: "105,346 words for you, 70,289 words for me." Indeed, almost two books in one. What we are left with is an unusually strong sense of interiority as well as a great desire for a lack of closure, both of which might best be appreciated, as the artist suggested in light of the book's proportions, "from a daybed!"—surely the best place to enjoy the ongoing process of reading his writings, now.

Alexis Vaillant
Lisbon, 21 May, 2024

Note: Enthused by this publication project from the outset, Marc Camille Chaimowicz was involved in every stage of its development, approving both the text and graphic design, before passing away on 23 May, 2024. The book is dedicated to his memory.

This is the first collection of writings and interviews by Marc Camille Chaimowicz. Among the seventy-four entries in this volume, four of them are published here for the first time. The first is an English translation of the interview that Philippe Cuenat conducted with the artist in French in 1987 [I. 4]. The second is a letter that the artist emailed to Wolfgang Tillmans on 9 December, 2013 [II. 12]. The third, a text about "object species," was written in English and published only in French in 1996 in an exhibition brochure [III. 17]. The fourth is a two-page text that was exhibited at the South London Gallery, London, in 2006 [III. 21]. The other seventy entries were previously published between 1971 and 2023.

These writings are divided into three parts, consisting of [I] TRANSCRIPTS OF INTERVIEWS, [II] CRITICISM, [III] TEXTS, within which the entries are chronologically organised and numbered in square brackets. Two of them include subentries, the numbering of which includes a lowercase letter, also in square brackets. This numbering system has been used throughout the publication.

Several names, keywords, works, and exhibitions are recurrent in Chaimowicz's writings. To emphasise them, the number of the text in which they are mentioned appears in square brackets in the introductions. Somewhere between a mental map and an index, this referencing system follows the evolution of the artist's practice as well as key people in his writings and work.

Each text by the artist is contextualised by an introduction. Based on research into Chaimowicz's personal archives as well as weekly conversations with him over Skype between 2020 and 2023, these introductions include numerous quotations from the artist. To avoid the proliferation of footnotes the quotations are without citation; any other quotation is referenced accordingly.

Every effort has been made to preserve Chaimowicz's writing style and creative use of line spacing and page placement. The texts appear here as they were originally published, with minor edits made to standardise style and spelling. The texts are reproduced without illustrations. When the artist selected them, they are described in the introductions accordingly. The same applies when the design is initially the work of the artist. However, to make their visual specifications easier to access, the following entries [III. 1, 2, 3, 12, 15, 24, 28] are reproduced in facsimile.

At the end of the volume, a comprehensive bibliography includes editorial information for each entry, including subsequent reprints and translations.

CONTENTS

[I]

TRANSCRIPTS OF INTERVIEWS

Featuring introductions by Alexis Vaillant

Three Approaches: Alastair Mackintosh Examines the Career of Marc Camille Chaimowicz

Alastair Mackintosh

(1973)

Founded in 1966 in London by American editor and curator Mario Anthony Amaya, and published and distributed by Hansom Books, Art & Artists *was one of the few contemporary art magazines printed in London in the early 1970s. Edited at the time by British artist and editor Colin Naylor, the magazine had many contributors, including the London-based art and music critic Alastair Mackintosh. Mackintosh, interested in the work of Marc Camille Chaimowicz, suggested that* Art & Artists *feature an interview with the artist, arguing that Chaimowicz's pioneering performances and installations had attracted a lot of attention in London. Among the works Mackintosh mentioned to* Art & Artists *was* Celebration? Realife, *Gallery House, London (30 March–15 April, 1972) [III. 2, 3, 4], and* Shoe Waste? Piece *[III. 1, 3], which Chaimowicz described at the time in these terms: "I bought many, many second-hand shoes which I painted silver to enhance their value and to give them distance as objects. A friend and I would transport these shoes in large bags and drop them off at different points in the city. It was quite exciting. To my mind these clandestine operations were meant to target an uninitiated public." In early June 1972, Chaimowicz began a three-week artist-residency at the Serpentine in London. During his residency, Chaimowicz conceived* Enough Tiranny, *a floor-based "scattered environment" [I. 14], which would be presented from 1–23 July that same year, as part of the group exhibition "Summer Show 4." Given the artist's topicality in 1972 and the acclaimed reception of his performances and installations, the magazine accepted Mackintosh's proposal.*

In early July 1972, having seen the installation at the Serpentine, Mackintosh went to the artist's home to conduct the interview. From the beginning of the discussion, Chaimowicz noticed "there was a certain conflict of interest" regarding their positions. It was clear, according to the artist, that "Mackintosh had been trained to interpret works of art from a formalist position," which would leave any assessment of Enough Tiranny *incomplete. Consisting of "ponds, fountains, oriental silver carp, TV, flexible sound and lighting," the installation exceeded a strictly formalist interpretation. Conceived, moreover, "as a direct response to the political situation in Northern Ireland"—which was made tangible by the newspapers scattered across the floor and the acronym I.R.A. included in the title—the installation was far removed from any formalist concerns. Nevertheless, considering that "any concession to the Mackintosh approach was OK since he was learning from the artists, and his interest in music—another part of his life—was also a reason why he got so involved," Chaimowicz continued with the interview. After a while, as both smoked, the "chat" gradually disintegrated under the effect of marijuana.*

After a sixteenth-month radio silence, the interview was finally published in December 1973 in Art & Artists. *It was introduced by a "very personal" two-part text by Mackintosh—"Fiction" / "Criticism, Formalist"—which is not reproduced below, and illustrated with shots of the artist's latest projects. A headshot of Chaimowicz was reproduced on the cover, highlighting a figure that would soon be considered "one of the first artists in the UK to merge the realms of performance and installation art." In this photograph, the artist is performing* Genug Tyrannei *("random audiences in various situations") at the Second Art Fair in Graz in the autumn of 1972. In a kind of cross-dressed homage to Jean-Luc Godard's* Pierrot le Fou, *his face is partially in make-up to the neck. The artist wears a dark grey Borsalino hat and a black and white geometric-patterned silk scarf tied loosely around the neck. He is smoking, in a glamorous fashion, a cigarette. Like other shots of Chaimowicz from the period, and as Alastair Mackintosh wrote in a later article, it "reveals the star potential of Chaimowicz's image as an artist." In the same piece, Mackintosh drew parallels between Chaimowicz, Andy Warhol, and Lou Reed ("Art Is Everything That Is Already Something Else . . .",* Art & Artists, Summer 1974*).*

Chaimowicz never heard from Mackintosh again, until a few years later, he received a phone call from Mackintosh's girlfriend who said, "… Are you seated? Well, … Alastair is dead… He died of happiness… You know, he was so relaxed… yogaing… that everything just stopped." Chaimowicz was initially shocked by Mackintosh's untimely death. Later, however, as time passed, he confessed, "Actually, Alastair was so entranced that he forgot to breathe… Very à bout de souffle, indeed!"

A.V.

· · · · · · · · ·

Marc Chaimowicz: A chat more than an interview, maybe.

Alastair Mackintosh: *OK… Your work has this very sexual element (i.e. to do with the sexes) and when it works best it is because of an "edge-city" balance.*
Edge-city … that's nice…

… between the masculine and feminine, and you're also involved in this political or social aspect of things, which—because of the way it has grown up—has a very masculine feel to it. How do you find these two aspects relate? Do you have problems there?
Yeah … Problems do come up. But it works on two levels. On the one hand there are problems that crop up accidentally, and on the other there are problems that seem essential to me, in a way that's why they crop up … that's where my energy comes from … if I look around there are so many disconcerting things about. Equally a few adventures are bound to lead to the occasional problem … if I get into some of the things we've discussed it means going out on a bit of a limb, rejecting a lot of the standards I was conditioned with, new standards are not always clear. Painting was constrictive but also reassuring because I could refer to a tradition for a bit of

guidance … very comfy, really. To leave art and life standards for some discoveries is bound to give rise to problems. I'm looking for something a little more real. Really I think my best work is to do with the best parts of my life. It's when I'm not sure what I'm doing; some adventure, a few thrills, it's a kind of assault course and there's treasure at the other end. It's very much like being on the streets.

But I get the impression that you look for problems. It has an almost masochistic element.
I think maybe it has sensuality, but I don't think it has much masochism … Regarding the balance you mention. I hope it exists with other factors too: hard and soft, tragedy-comedy, etc. … but about the sexual elements, I see it more as an attempt at synthesis, a redefinition rather than a balance. After all I see nothing inherently interesting in sexual balance between male/female whether in art or people because that's a rather smug acceptance of terms within current society, which I find unacceptable in that it implies "masculine/feminine" stereotype roles. I mean current society distorts all human relationships and balance implies norms, and I reject current sexual norms as repressive, restrictive, and boring. For example, male sexuality has for ages been defined in terms of virility and power; that's a main support of our current society … most art is defined, produced, and controlled by men; it's very male and that is possibly one of the reasons it's mostly so boring. Equally female sexuality has been defined in terms of submission, constantly repressed and though that's changing we've not yet witnessed its potential. Relationships of domination and subordination are tyrannical … and Genet's most probably right, the oppressor is oppressed by the role. Anyway, I reckon a lot of people are becoming pissed off with the tyranny perpetuated by stereotyped gender roles; it's just that it's not evident in the establishment art world because of its essentially conservative nature. A lot of art seems chaste and impersonal, lacking in sensuality.

It's that English thing that joy is somehow inferior to sorrow.
Yes … Art should be something you do when you're happy, not unhappy. When I was at the Slade … that was one time I went through a "serious" phase, it may have been valuable, a lot of thinking which was probably essential. I was doing a lot of organisational work, and I stopped painting and began to seek what I felt to be a more relevant approach. But often there's a split … I was at a political meeting recently and because of the rhetoric and the formality of the meeting, I couldn't relate to the issues … I think the issues were in fact absent, the meeting as a form with procedures, etc., took over. It was strangely unreal and I kept daydreaming. The issues were not coming through. In the Artists Union, say, that sometimes comes up; meetings can go on too long or the interesting issues become obscured because of arrogant abstractions or a split between content and form … these are minor points maybe because presumably we can resolve them individually, but collective cultural behaviour is something that has not yet been solved.

Perhaps that's because artists still have too narrow a view of what art is. I've noticed that you're very interested in style, and style could be seen as a non-art way of saying art things … although most artists don't seem to know too much about that.
That's interesting … maybe it's a problem of the specialist again … painting is very difficult to do; formally I have a lot of respect for painting … that's partly why I gave it up, it was too much hard work … well that was one reason … but most art has become so highly specialised and speculative that it has to be done with an enormous amount of seriousness and self-denial, a lot of professionalism, and a kind of American thing, a business-type life-style, the nine-to-five artist. Maybe the specialist loses out quite a lot by becoming limited and exclusive.

It's interesting that you use the word "serious" as something other than what your work is. What do you mean by that?

Well. It's quite a subtle point ... say the seriousness of getting a big studio, beautifully equipped and staring at blank canvases for days waiting for inspiration. I'm exaggerating, but even so that kind of activity, which is perpetuated by our culture, implies a self-righteous arrogance and often-chauvinist behaviour. In my piece at Gallery House or the Serpentine I found it much less alienating to be present all the time, to be changing things, putting some care into the piece and to be chatting to the guests interested in chatting, in a relaxed way. It allowed for occasional collaboration and for feed-back and it meant the reverse process to mystification—because I was vulnerable and open to criticism. It was refreshingly real; discussing art in that context was OK, and that's pretty rare ... I'm not involved in "funny" art, or humour as such; I'm not anti-serious, just skeptical of pomposity and arrogance. I'm more interested in art coming out of a total approach to life than living totally for art and losing touch. Looking good or having a really good time with my girl, say, should benefit my art indirectly rather than distract from it. A few years ago I was much more schizoid than I am now, which wasn't a good thing. I'd be going to work, say, and I'd dress down and apply myself to it ... I'd put out my serious teaching side ... and in the evening I'd become somebody else. It's OK when you've got control over your fantasies but most often it's the world outside that dictates deviancy. It's good when things change ... resting since Christmas has been very positive for me. I've been pretty busy thinking, etc., and feeling pretty confident in a quiet sort of way. But I've lost a lot of ambition, which was a kind of class problem, because I went to a rough school for years—a really useless secondary modern boys' school in West London, and I had to develop an aggression just to get out of that. I used to be pretty aggressive, at least when necessary.

I would say that people find your work not so much aggressive as spikey, just a little bit dangerous.
Hopefully ... it would be nice if it were so. The more recent stuff

should have that slightly icy quality ... although the last time I used barbed wire was in *Sweetness*, a piece at Sigi Krauss' Gallery in 1971. More recently there's been some softness too, flowers, lighting, water, it depends what you see.

Mirrors, you use mirrors a lot.
Mirrors are very hard. They're hard on two levels ... Firstly, like I was saying, it's the very worst parts of the work that I often like the best ... pushing it a bit ... you can't use candles in art, you know, the candle has been over-used so much, it has become a total cliché. And you can't use mirrors ... really; I'm just using those, sometimes getting away with it, other times possibly not. Also, there's a formal or functional reason to play with and fragment the room; big mirrors are like paintings, they can personalise space. The other bit? ... well, they are very private.

Private?
They confront you ... they do strange things.

Now that you've slipped by default out of that whole ambition thing, and now that you're involved in strategies like "can I get away with doing something that's been worked to death anyway?" where do you see yourself in relation to what else is going on, where do you see yourself in the art world?
Well, I don't know. I've been quite active and fairly mobile over the past few years, but I've not come across the "art world." Maybe it's because I don't sell, most probably it's yet another myth ... a competitive con. I'd rather see the Artists Union or a parallel develop successfully whereby artists and other interested cultural workers might interrelate in a concrete manner ... change a few things.

It seems to me the problem for you is what you can do that is moral...
Without being orthodox or boring. Yeah.

Without being boring. Right.
That's the issue. I think I'd quite like to be a second-rate artist, but do it quite well. I got bored with all the stuff we're brought up with, like being the best or the first or the most important and increasingly I'm happy to take from here and there once in a while and say "look, I'm part of a European tradition and my work's OK," maybe it's quite amazing—but I certainly don't have the arrogance nor the naivety of saying this is new, or that my definition of art is the important one. Because I am sure there are lots of other definitions that are fine, and that's what I mean by second rate. I'm probably more ambitious but I'm also more confident than I was … confidence gives me time for a little bit of this and a little bit of that.

In what way are you more ambitious?
Maybe to the extent that I'm more committed.

To what?
Well, I'm doing less art these days—but I'm more committed to what I do—and to living generally, to doing things at the right time and with totality … with a more private sort of pleasure and ambition I guess … I'm not into that anti-art stuff at all; being an artist is all right, it's the best thing I could do.

How has this change manifested itself?
I've been lazing around more; I mean I used to laze around a lot, but I was always conning myself that I was doing something important. Now I work best when it's a pleasure, when I'm enjoying it. Society and education never allow for that.

That's true … there is always this thing about art students having to work hard.
It was always so serious. When I was on a diploma course, you had to suffer, and I got into that quite well. I really suffered and was quite good at angst … but really it's very sad. It's closely linked up

with failed staff, aggressive and distorted behaviour. Institutions seem to repress creativity and ignore or reject the possibility of reaching the so-called pleasure principle by promoting a work ethic. No wonder so many students become cynical or don't make the grade … anyway there shouldn't be that split, that either/or. Extremes are often destructive. One of the reasons I've often used aluminum paint is that apart from its reflective qualities, its softness, it is symbolic of synthesis rather than black or white, it's not clear-cut.

I get the impression from what you say that something appeals to you if it is done well within its own standards. Something that is done badly, even if the standards are the best in the world, doesn't appeal to you. Now … how do you know when you are doing well?
It's a very close thing. I think it has to do with working at something really hard but not too hard. Most people, when they work at something, or the way they live, they are a bit out of sync. Because either they try too hard and it shows—a bit too desperate maybe—or else they don't try quite hard enough—they are a bit dilettante. If I do anything (I suppose this would be one criterion, feedback's another) the criterion would be to do something very well without putting myself out too much. The potential of faith, sincerity, and intuition is based on the amount of preparation done … the readiness, you know?

Would you say that your work has a subject looking at, for instance, what you have done over the past year?
I think the world … definitely the world … things around me. There's a few lines in a Godard film, *Pierrot le fou*, where Belmondo in his traditional role of those years is at a party and he asks the American director, Samuel Fuller, who plays himself, what cinema is about and Fuller says, "Film is like a battleground, it's about love and about hate and action and death, in a word, emotion," something like a six word list. It's a pretty good film. Godard is

criticising the tradition of Symbolism and yet was fascinated by that tradition … maybe he respected it formally. For me, though my work has existed in temporary, specific situations and that implies a critical approach; I nevertheless have a fascination and empathy for a lot of the European tradition. I can get off on Picasso.

The trouble with tradition is that it becomes very self-regarding and pompous.
Oh sure, a lot of it is shit for many reasons, but the whole tradition does include Colette and a few others … the thing is that a society's culture reflects that society, as does its politics to a large extent, right? That's maybe why it's difficult for many mainstream artists to identify their interests as societal or collective. The straight left has that same problem. It perpetuates dogmatism, hierarchy, and paternalism. There are groups that get away from that, using a bit of humour and imagination, but they tend to be new tradition groups like, say, women's movements and Gay Lib, etc.

The same is true in art. Most of the radical stuff is fine on paper and then fails at square one, because it is so serious and boring.
Yeah. But many artists are now reacting against, say, the frequent impersonality of Minimalism and working in a more expansive and complex way towards people art or celebration rather than rhetoric. Art should celebrate without abstaining from taking a critical stand … that's another fine balance. Art can elevate the "moral" and aim for magic.

So how does that apply to where you go next?
I've been putting more effort into domesticity, the quiet life. That's maybe to do with checking that male concept of achievement in the outside world and of course, it's a logical extension of the workrooms of last year. They were highly domestic in terms of my being there ten hours a day, in terms of care and attention, hosting, etc. … eventually the two should blend, but I can't really speak

for the future. I'm hoping though that these directions may help with ideas I have for working with a few other people—relating to other people workwise has so far been a disappointment. It's been too impersonal and with too much compromise. So far the only collaborations I've been satisfied with have been the things I've done with Sue Madden—maybe that's because my approach to the work is as physical, emotional, personal, and sensory as is our relationship. Now though with care and caution, I think the occasional project with a number of people may work … we'll just have to wait and see.

[I. 2]

Interview

Ben Jones

(1976)

Founded in London in January 1976 by British editor and sculptor Ben Jones, together with British artist and painter James Faure Walker, Artscribe *was conceived as an attempt to re-establish a Greenbergian agenda in contemporary art. Published primarily on a bi-monthly basis, the magazine was initially promoted as "a showcase of new British and American abstract modernist painting and sculpture that was intelligently visual and mostly local." For their first issue, Ben Jones invited Marc Camille Chaimowicz to do an interview.*

Given the modernist aims of the journal, Chaimowicz felt that beyond Jones' interest in his work, "they probably thought it would be interesting to post an interview with someone from another *world." A few days before New Year's Eve, Jones and the artist met in a café near Shaftesbury Avenue, somewhere in London's "theatre land", in the West End district. Chaimowicz, who did not know Jones personally, had been perceptive about the editorial context of this interview. Indeed, he said, "Ben Jones was cold, asking questions and taking notes." As a result, the interview was over in fifteen minutes. "It was like speed dating," the artist said, "as usual, a meeting with no further development." Under these circumstances, it is not surprising that the artist was not asked to proofread the interview before publication.*

Published in Artscribe *a few weeks later, the introduction to the interview began as follows: "The artist recently showed an installation and gave an accompanying performance at the new AIR Gallery, and started this month as a performance editor with Studio International." Both the "installation" and "accompanying performance" mentioned in this introduction refer to "Inaugural Show" (22 October–11 November, 1975) at AIR Gallery, London, which featured the work of eleven artists, including Chaimowicz, Nat Goodden, James Griffin, Harvey Hood, Micheal Kenny, Stuart Mealing, Richard Rome, Kerry Trengove, Shelag Wakely, and Rhonda & David Whitehead. An extension of the Artist Information Registry founded in 1968 at St. Katharine's Dock in London, the AIR Gallery had recently moved to 125–129 Shaftesbury Avenue, London, and "Inaugural Show"—a nod to the "Inaugural Show" at Gallery House, London, where Chaimowicz presented* Celebration? Realife *[III. 3] from 30 March through 15 April, 1972—was their first exhibition project in this location. As an "artists' co-operative," AIR Gallery selected exhibitions collectively. Relying on a panel of three artists from the co-operative including David Leverett, Liliane Lijn, and Barry Martin, a guest-selector was also involved in the process. For "Inaugural Show," the guest-selector was Caroline Tisdall, art critic for* The Guardian. *Invited to participate in the exhibition, Chaimowicz accepted the invitation, noting, however, that he had no work available for the show. In two weeks, he conceived an installation whose "title was so long that no one could remember it," he said. The work,* We Chose Our Words With Care, That Neon-Moonlit Evening; It Was As If We Were, Party To A Wonderful Alchemy *was presented at AIR Gallery. As described by Jean Fisher in* Past Imperfect. Marc Camille Chaimowicz 1972–1982 *(Liverpool: Bluecoat Gallery et al., 1983, p. 27) the work was installed...*

"[…] *on a pre-existing raised platform situated at one end of the room. A grey curtain physically separates this space from that of the viewer, although visual access is provided through a number of triangular holes cut in the fabric. On looking through these holes, one has different views of an architecturally organised space illuminated by theatrical red, green and yellow spotlights. The triangularity of the holes is echoed by a stepped pyramid towards one corner and an architectonic arch-like structure that leans at an angle and bisects the space from near the foreground to the top far corner. A fox fur is draped over the steps of the pyr-amid, and various items including vases of irises and roses and a smaller pyramid stand on the floor. These cast shadows on the walls and the faces of the sculpture. Three fountains in a pond to one side provide the ambient sound in the piece."*

In addition to this, three printed ephemera pieces were pinned to the grey curtain, including the invitation card to the "Inaugural Show," a picture of a fox in a forest, and a photo of a wooden bench. Afterwards, the installation lay dormant until it was reconstructed in 2008, as part of the exhibition ". . .In the Cherished Company of Others. . ." at De Appel, Amsterdam, and Mu.ZEE, Ostende [I. 11].

The "accompanying performance" referred to in the introduction of Artscribe is Sur les Marches du Palais, *in reference to the red carpet at the Cannes Film Festival, and was a pretty static ten-minute event in which British film director Sally Potter and Caroline Tisdall were involved. On 22 October at 7:15 p.m., while Potter was playing the violin, Tisdall, who had been asked by the artist to "do whatever art critics do in their milieu that is standing silent, was looking around." For his part, Chaimowicz sang* There Are Four Corners to My Bed, *a lullaby his mother taught him as a child.*

If the participation of Chaimowicz in "Inaugural Show" was an alibi for the interview to begin, the artist nevertheless took advantage of it. Indeed, in discussing the expectations of the audience during a performance—"The zoo-like problem of being expected to do a turn"—the artist anticipated one of the key themes in his performances between 1976 and 1982 [I. 3; III. 8, 11].

Published as double-page spread in the first pages of Artscribe, *the interview included three illustrations that Chaimowicz submitted to the journal, including a headshot of the artist wearing white makeup with a fluffy fox fur in an androgynous pose, a photo of "Marc posing in AIR," and a detail of the artist's installation at AIR Gallery.*

A.V.

· · · · · · · · · ·

Ben Jones: *How did you arrive at your AIR show?*
Marc Chaimowicz: Well, there was a specific invitation to show. The other artists were to show existing work, I didn't have any, so they said, "Would you like to do something for the show?" and suggested the stage … so the synthesis was between the ideas that I develop, notes, drawings, photos, etc. A little like doing exercises, like keeping trim, and the actual stage area, and two weeks or so to prepare. For a number of reasons I'd not shown, apart from one short performance at Garage in 1974, since 1972, so I was quite excited. I decided to construct a piece; the stage was influential too in quite what would occur, although certain elements of the installation, like the arch and pyramid, were already from a repertoire of ideas. Everything including the fountain was made specific to the perspective within that space, and I wanted it to be beautiful. As well as the installation, there was a performance (twice) and graphics.
At Gallery House and the Serpentine I had full control of the space, but at AIR there was the challenge of showing in a mixed show. I decided to produce a fairly cautious, polite statement, as I did not want to intrude on the other artists, and the curtain was a factor within that awareness. Controlled and fairly subtle use of theatre lighting was another, as it blocked the outside from within and vice versa.

The items on the stage, a most suitable context, I thought, led one to interpret the situation, if you like, the story. Would you say there is something pictorially realistic in that premise?
Yes … There are obvious uses of symbol, if not archetypal then universal; flowers, water, both visual and audible, The Fox, The Moon, The Pyramid, which like the fallen Arch is both a formal and symbolic thing. Which would often enough, I think, have been seen in a quasi-sexual way. Flowers have their own interpretations. The piece was to have been sensual, to sight, hearing, and smell. But I'm not sure what you mean by premise? I like your

use of the word story, I love stories, and I am quite happy that the installation may have been "read" though there's no logical narrative to it. There are external references, say, fire was the candles, water the fountains, earth the cacti, and coloured light, air. It's not describing anything, tho' it might stimulate fantasy, it simply is … I would like to be indecisive in that sense.

What responses have you had?
Varied, I've sold a few things that were on the wall, which is always nice. The installation was pretty expensive, and also that friends have said things, which is OK.

I must say I was a little disappointed with the repeat performance on the second evening, knowing something of your own resources. Did that have something to do with our own expectations from the performance?
Absolutely, the issue of repetition is interesting, as to whether someone like myself can develop a repertoire that is repeatable or not. The second one was different from the first, in that I was more nervous. People had given up time for the second one, whereas the first one was a regular opening, with something extra happening called a performance. There are very real pressures with performance. With the zoo-like problem of being expected to do a turn. Whereby the first-generation performance people, including myself, turned to performance originally to broaden the definition, to experiment, to work in a more visionary way. What seems to be happening in the current gallery situation might cancel those wishes, might constrain creative energy. I've also been aware in performance of real-time and have only ever presented short pieces, which might account for what is seen as a slight piece, but then a whisper may be louder than a shout … and equally the concept of a boy singing a love song that his mum taught him, within a whole sexist superstructure, has, I think, real implications which are related to the graphics … you know the song and Sally

on violin was offered with tenderness and without amplification
… some puzzles can best be solved obliquely.

*The show was decidedly decadent—I mean, I sensed "the ball was
over," is that a fair observation?*
It's an interesting one; it's certainly true of our time, if not of my
works specifically. I've always wanted my work to be of its time.
And certainly the reality I live in has changed quite a lot in the
past five years; I was having lunch at Overton's and looked up and
noticed chicken wire on the windows.

*Who do you feel in sympathy with, or who else is around who is doing
anything close to your own perspectives?*
Music and conversations and books are probably the most direct
influences. I love lots of artists, young and old. But often I prefer
the drawings of, say, Cocteau, than a lot of recent work, and I
often like the artists more than the art they do. You mentioned
Beuys, and I still find him a giant, a very magical and acute figure.

You trained as a painter; if you have, why did you stop?
There's already so much, too much, that has been said on this issue,
and training sounds as though I'd been in the army or something …
No, if at art school I "trained" as anything at all it was as an artist,
which is still what I am. The reasons I no longer paint are manifold;
anyhow I found it brought on the strangest antisocial traits in me,
which I didn't particularly want to develop. I now have a studio, so
in part I suppose I am returning to a private relationship to work,
but also the material; the "stuff" can take many forms.

The first item I ever saw of yours was the Random Landscape
Approximation *nearly seven years ago. I took comfort at the AIR
gallery in sensing your consistency. You're still throwing up a situation,
a little surreal, a little nostalgic, unsettling nevertheless, where your
own presence is never quite defined.*

Thank you.

Do you still look at paintings?
Well, of course I spend a lot of time looking at art, days in weeks, and it can be fabulous. Equally the English attitude of ignoring most things maybe feeds back on its culture and produces lots of small-minded and parochial results.

And art magazines?
I read art mags and other glossies and of course *The New Musical Express*. London has fewer mags than other art capitals. That's again affecting the culture our city produces. Anyhow they are not very imaginative, I'd quite like to see artists' homes and families or lovers, etc., but they are very product orientated.

What are you doing next?
I'd like to work more with sound, maybe do some tapes. There are maybe a few things in Europe soon and a show in London. Also Anthony Howell is developing a showing structure in Maida Vale, and I'll probably be involved in that in January. The most specific thing is my studio/flat in Bethnal Green. I'm working towards a public piece there, and I'll open it to the public most probably on long weekends. Opening the studio will mean I have autonomy, I can do what I like, when I like—I wish galleries would open, say, 2 p.m. till midnight. At the AIR show the working people couldn't see the work because it closed at 6 p.m. Lastly I've long had a fantasy to hold a show for the night people of London, people who only live at night. Opening up a studio or gallery at night times, but that may best be central.

Is your name Russian?
No, my Christian name is French, as is my mother. My surname is Polish, as is my father. My childhood years were spent in Paris…

Is that relevant?
Probably, it seems to take years to understand one's past, or roots, i.e. cultural, racial, class, etc. … friends say there is a European aesthetic to my work—singing a song in French that my mum taught me is simply one specific example of this.

Where do you buy your clothes?
Well, some are made up, but my favourite are often finds, occasional gifts. That is, they have a history of sorts, rather than being off the peg.

What after-shave do you use?
Normally I use Vaseline Intensive Care herbal cream then cologne, and Boots No. 7 night cream, of course.

Performance Is Like a Perfect Day: Interview with Marc Chaimowicz

Helena Kontovà

(1978)

Published in Flash Art *eleven years after the launch of the magazine in Rome in 1967 by the Italian editor and publisher Giancarlo Politi, "Interview with Marc Chaimowicz" was conducted by Helena Kontovà in Milan, on 31 May, 1978, the day after* Doubts… A Sketch For Video Camera and Audience *was performed by the artist at Studio Cannaviello, Milan. At the time on tour in Europe, this performance of about fifteen minutes is described in* Past Imperfect. Marc Camille Chaimowicz 1972–1982 *(Liverpool: Bluecoat Gallery et al., 1983, p. 18) by Jean Fisher as follows:*

> *"At first we see an empty chair illuminated by a cold blue spotlight, and facing part-way between a video-monitor and a large projection of an image of a pair of closed interior double doors. The artist enters and, seated on the chair with his back 3/4 to the audience, begins to swing a silvered pendulum to and fro. The video camera, positioned to one side, relays the artist's black and white image on the monitor so that it is visible both to himself and to the audience. The artist then leaves the space and a pre-recorded videotape of ten minutes duration is played back on the monitor. This tape, coloured in soft pastel hues, presents five narrative sequences depicting domestic activities in an interior space: writing, cleaning the face in a mirror, taking tea, looking out of the window, and lying on a bed. The first part of the performance is accompanied by the relaxing and contemplative sound of Brian Eno's* Discreet Music. *This is contrasted in the second part by two tracks from Lou Reed's* Coney Island Baby: *'Nobody's Business' and 'Coney Island Baby.'"*

In 1978, Helena Kontovà was new to Flash Art, *which she had joined to develop the English edition. When she heard that Chaimowicz would soon be in town, she contacted Studio Cannaviello to schedule an interview with him the day after his performance. "It was difficult to say no," he said. Although they did not know each other,*

Chaimowicz identified her as soon as she walked into the café, and thought, "She seems overdressed for the late '70s." On the day of the interview, the artist was exhausted and eager to return to London. The previous week, Chaimowicz had been travelling back and forth between Bologna, where an art fair was being held, and Milan, where he was preparing his performance, in the company of Caroline Tisdall's "energetic" ex-boyfriend, Angelo Bozzalla, an Italian art critic and historian whom the artist knew from London. However, as Chaimowicz recalled, "The situation was made comfortable. I was able to talk about art in general, but from a personal point of view, and I can remember that I ended up saying performance is like a perfect day…"

At the end of the 1970s, performance was a significant part of contemporary artistic practice. Attentive to this trend, Kontovà's meeting with the artist was an opportunity for her to talk about it directly with a producer. However, probably indifferent to the artist's fatigue, and obviously unable to appreciate his words and moderate the discussion accordingly, she eagerly and expectantly pressed Chaimowicz. This tension is discernible in the transcript of the interview. Finally, whether this meeting with Kontovà was a good or bad memory for the artist proved inconsequential, as he said later, "On May 31, 1978, we mostly shared a Campari as well as many misunderstandings."

Published in the early pages of Flash Art, *Chaimowicz's performance-focused interview reproduced below was illustrated accordingly, including performance shots from* Table Tableau *(1974),* Doubts… A Sketch for Video Camera and Audience *(1977–79), and* Shift *(1978).*

A.V.

··········

Helena Kontovà: *If you were to make a short statement on your work, how would you describe yourself?*
Marc Chaimowicz: Average … normal. But there's a difference between me and my work. It's very difficult for me to describe myself.

You once said, "Art is my life, lived with less compromise and more intensity." How does this relate to other notions of life as art, like, for example, the "life is art" idea expressed by Fluxus?
I think the problem with "life is art" is that it's just a concept; it remains an idea. And ideas are important only at the beginning, they don't mean much at the conclusion. Artists surely have ideas at the beginning, but it's what they do with the idea that is important. Of course, my art begins with my experience, but it always gets intensified, becomes a little bit sharper, clearer, idealised. It has to do with the relationship between the ideal and the real; the kind of dialectic that art is always ahead of and relates back to.

Do you mean that art is more advanced than life?
Yes.

In what sense?
It's better.

That's very subjective.
Yes. It begins with a subjective experience. But objectivity is a myth … the only experience I can attempt to reach is my own. This, then, is of course qualified, but it's personal. If you remember the video piece you saw yesterday at Cannaviello, the part about public and private: in a way, the activity is very mundane; it's normal things, like someone cleaning his face, or having a cup of tea, or looking out the window. But it's how it's done that matters—it's not what you do but how you do it; mundane activities

get elevated to possibly an archetypal level. Things get done very consciously, in a very precise way, and that's what I mean about more intensity and less compromise.

The "private" was a film shown on a TV monitor, the "public" was you sitting on a chair with a pendulum in your hand. The "private" was a kind of set of idealised images, beautiful colours, delicate shapes, flowers, and you in a nearly narcissistic pose. On the contrary, your "public" was reserved and static, monotonous. It seemed to me as though you were trying to say that in public you can't be yourself, you can't quite feel comfortable. Isn't this somehow a rather strange attitude for someone who does performances?
I don't know … there was a paradoxical structure inherent in the piece, as well as a questioning of this current form and its resultant expectations…

Your work seems to have some deliberately mysterious qualities. Can you comment on this?
Thank you. As to whether it's deliberate, that's difficult. It's not possible to wake up in the morning and say, "I shall do art that is mysterious," because if you do that you make very self-conscious art. So it's not deliberate. All I can hope to do is to be conscious of what's inside and what's outside.

I noticed when I saw photographic documentation of your work that you use light and darkness and similar contrasts, which in our culture can be considered mysterious. I wondered if maybe you deliberately create this sort of effect.
I think it's very good that you feel this, because I like to deal with the relationship between the visible and the invisible. The reason I cannot be very analytical about my work is that although I have my own interpretation and my own ideas about my work, I think artists are usually liars. They delude themselves.

If that's the way it is, do you still want to go on with this interview?
Yes. [Laughs. Pause.] Yes, because I respect your approach. I suppose I've refused interviews on occasions when, as can happen with any dialogue, there was a lack of basic empathy or rapport—they can be disastrous. But it seems to me you and I have got on OK so far!

I'd be interested, anyway, in your own interpretation of your work.
What was interesting in Vienna [Vienna Performance Festival, 1978] was that in a very Germanic sort of way, before every performance they gave out an information sheet, and I had the text available, but insisted that the text be handed out *after* the performance. If the text is handed out before, people will become lazy, they will read the text and use it as an explanation. But I would prefer they interpret it for themselves. If they read the text beforehand, it preconditions the piece; the piece was very evocative. I'm in favour of a free interpretation rather than a dogmatic tradition. So if someone else says it's about beauty and birth, then I say OK. I have my own favourite I might prefer, but the artist has to respect his public, and I'm not interested in making a direct statement. For me, art is not direct; it's indirect, oblique.

Let's turn to the performance you did yesterday. I didn't understand your role in this piece, how you functioned as a part of the whole.
Well, the title of the piece is *Doubts... A Sketch for Video Camera and Audience*, and so the piece was meant to be a critique as well as being affirmative. It was about the relationship between reality, physicality, and now. And that's what I mean about private-active and public-passive. In a way it's a reaffirmation in favour of prudence in the context of the current situation, where everything has to be public. I don't agree with that. What's interesting about Italy is that it reminds me of Catholicism; the doors—it's a Catholic image.

*I would say that your work is really about your private life, that it con-
sists of very private images that you present to the public, but I don't
feel that your art is about the "dialectic" between private and public
as you once wrote (see* Flash Art *no. 80/81, Feb/April 1978). I think
private and public are antagonists in your pieces.*
You're probably right. I'm not a logical person. When I write, my
attempt is to be clear and logical, but I'm an intuitive person and
my thinking is speculative.

*Do the photos you make merely document your performances. Or can
they be seen as images as well?*
My performances are not photogenic—it's that simple. Some
people make very bad performances and very good photographs.
I don't believe one can document performance, really, because
by definition performance travels through time. I am, however,
interested in working with photographs as a primary reality; like
in a gallery, the pieces on the wall, not as performances but as
a separate thing. The problem with me is I don't really believe
in defining art according to form, I'm more interested in an atti-
tude-based approach rather than a form-based approach. And that
was the trouble with the magazine (*Studio International*, where
I wrote for several years), and maybe your magazine, too. It's
forced, because in reality all you have is good art and bad art. So
in my art I just try to be very conscious of whatever I'm working
on. If I'm working on a book, I try to understand what a book is; if
I work on studies, I try to understand studies; and in performance
I'm both within the performance and outside of it. So photographs
of the performance are for me just documentation, and the photographic studies are specifically located elsewhere.

*In the video of yours I saw yesterday, everything was so soft and deli-
cate, with such beautiful and sweet colours—in a way, one might even
say there was a bit of kitsch. Does this kind of criticism bother you?*
My hope is that my work is about purity; I'm not interested in

kitsch very much. I think, however, that people often confuse the work with the person. It's a cultural problem, but in a way it's their problem, not mine: they expect art to be like Klaus Rinke, sort of hard and black and white, whereas I'm fascinated by certain taboo subjects, culturally. Both these terms are so relative … we live in a basically puritanical climate. In resisting reductionism, I was faced with aesthetic questions about beauty, pleasure, etc.

Do you use symbols in your work, and if so what kind?
I think we have no other choice unless we deal with the abstract, and as soon as you start to deal with things that are recognisable, they of course have the possibility of a symbolic role, but I'd prefer to use the word "metaphor" or "allegory." I think the problem with a symbol for me is that it's fixed and closed. I like your use of the word "images," because there is a very consistent recurrence of images for me: like the window, or the closed door. I prefer to use very open, evocative symbols or metaphors because that enables free interpretation.

Do you have your own interpretations of the metaphors you use?
Yes.

For instance, is there any metaphor in your gestures, like the use of the pendulum?
Yes. My own linguistic reference to the pendulum is coding for synthesis. I think the society we live in is full of contrasts: it's very destructive, it's schizophrenic, it's either yes or no, black or white, men or women. For me, I don't like those extremes, I prefer synthesis: grey or silver, it's not yes or no, or it's yes *and* no, Kierkegaard's "either/or."

How do you challenge male roles in your life and art?
One way possibly is to try to work towards an eternity of these extremes; another way I suppose is to develop most of my work

from my home, because home is traditionally a non-male context, it's private, internal. The outside word is the male world traditionally, which is bad, but I think the point was made in the context of vulnerability.

Do you think the public is necessary for a performance or can you perform alone and record it?
I think that's an academic question in a way. If there's a public, then there's a performance. It's a circular question for me. The book, for example, is a good answer to your question because it's an allegorical anecdote, which occurs without an audience, but eventually gets prepared for the public. Performance has to do with real time, so I suppose by definition performance has to have a public audience even if it's only one person. I think it's really a question for art historians.

Some performers repeat their performances. How do you feel about this?
With the performance we saw yesterday, the history of it in a way has to do with the problems I've had before with going to an alien unknown situation, and sometimes it's a nightmare. You go to a gallery or museum and there are horrible people, or the space is terrible, or the lighting equipment doesn't work. So partly the historical *raison d'être* for repeating was to overcome that. I said to myself, OK, I don't like to compromise, and often these public situations are compromised, so I bring my own life in London with me in my bag on videotape. That's one of the reasons I repeat at least a few times, because I want it to be perfect, and I couldn't succeed otherwise. I usually do one new piece a year. I don't think doing something new just for the sake of it is very interesting.

Caroline Tisdall has suggested (in Studio International *volume 192, no. 982 July/Aug. 1976) that neither you nor Stuart Brisley is interested in the international avant-garde. Could you comment on that?*

I think that's a projection—people who write tend to project. I'm interested in art and in wide cultural references. I like to travel and I like art, so I am interested in the avant-garde, just as long as it doesn't become too obscure. I think avant-garde is a fabrication, really. I suspect that the avant-garde died a few years ago and now what matters is whether people can do art in this kind of time and whether it's effective. But I think the point was made about avoiding careerist-type games and that leading to compromise, which was argued, didn't do.

Why do you think the avant-garde has died, and how are things different as a result?
Well, maybe the term has a different meaning here, but there is surely a developing feeling that "the dream is over," that the avant-garde became cannibalistic, has devoured itself; and the term "radical" implies getting back to roots, to reassess in basic thresholds of cultural roles, activities, and functions—it implies: going back one step in order to go forward.

Do you think a performer must present himself in his performances?
Again, I think it's a problem for art historians … for instance, Acconci is doing a lot of exhibitions now, but people don't know what performance is, I think of Acconci as an artist. People go to see the Acconci show and are very disappointed because he's not there. What he's done is he's sent a long letter diagramming the chairs swinging, or whatever. Today, performance is becoming very fashionable and cheap. Ten years ago nobody was interested and we risked our own careers; no students all wanted to do performance.

What do you think of the future performance in terms of art history?
I suspect that what's important is the demand for the public. It sees that one or two artists are ahead and most of the others follow. If the demand continues, then there'll be a lot of medium artists; if the demand doesn't continue, they'll find something else.

Meanwhile, the good artists will continue to do performance, but I don't think it will be very widespread because it's a very difficult thing to do.

How would you define performance?
Dear me … [laugh] … I don't have an answer to that one. It can be like a temporary truce between the ideal and the actual. I suppose it's like a perfect day, when everything is fabulous and you feel good … but don't put this in the magazine!

[I. 4]

Impressions:
Interview with Marc Camille Chaimowicz

Philippe Cuenat

(1987)

In 1984 AMAM (the non-profit organisation campaigning for the creation of a Museum of Modern Art in Geneva since 1973, now Amis du MAMCO) invited Chaimowicz to create an exhibition project at the Musée d'Art et d'Histoire, Geneva. Chaimowicz brought together "Six Works," which gave the exhibition its title. Including a screen, a pendulum, a diptych, a scarf, a drawing, and a bottle, the exhibition was presented in a large room of the museum from 3 May to 17 June, and then at Le Consortium, Dijon, from 25 June to 28 July [I. 5]. On the occasion of these exhibitions, a 36-page catalogue entitled Marc Camille Chaimowicz Genève-Dijon 1984 *was produced by AMAM. The book, with a print run of only 800, was designed by Chaimowicz in collaboration with Hendel Teicher, curator of the exhibition in Geneva.*

Given the interest in both the exhibition "Six Works" and his broader practice, Chaimowicz thought, "Why not stay longer in this part of the world?" As the recipient of a Hille Fellowship in 1985, the artist was thus able to stay in Geneva over the winter and spring of 1985–86. As a Hille Fellow, an artist's studio located on the island in downtown Geneva was made available for his stay, where he lived for ten months. "It was like being on a boat," he reflected. "I stayed there with the intention of doing nothing, being free from commitments, and living in a kind of timeless void." One day while walking, Chaimowicz dropped by the Centre genevois de gravure contemporaine (Centre d'édition contemporaine; CEC since January 2001). By chance, he met the new co-directors of the space, who cordially invited him to develop a project with them.
Founded in 1966 in Geneva, the Centre genevois de gravure contemporaine was a printmaking workshop, producing engravings and lithographs with the assistance of engravers working on site. In 1985, young Swiss artists Paul Viaccoz, Anne Patry-Chenu, and Marie-Claude Ruata took over the direction of the venue with the intention of refreshing its institutional profile. Over the autumn of 1985, Chaimowicz began working there. After a few weeks, he noticed,

*"Engraving represents something extremely ambivalent that is neither an original nor a reproduction. This ambivalence sheds light on problems such as signature and mediation." A few months later, the artist had produced twenty-six copies of a six-page portfolio, including four watercolour-enhanced prints, a cover text entitled "PERHAPS * REGRETS * SOMETIMES * HAUNTED" [III. 12] and a colophon page; as well as thirteen etchings, and a large engraving titled* La Fin de l'été. *Crafted in collaboration with the technicians working on site, these engravings and etchings were subsequently signed by the artist. A complete set was thereafter framed and presented in the gallery space together with a copy of the portfolio, from 13 November, 1986 to 6 January, 1987, in conjunction with the exhibition "Marc Camille Chaimowicz. Œuvres récentes," Galerie Eric Franck, Geneva (13 November, 1986–3 January, 1987).*

At the same time, the editorial board of Faces, Journal d'Architecture *was preparing its spring issue. Founded in 1985 as part of the former Institute of Architecture of the University of Geneva, the journal's intention was in "pursuing theoretical and critical research on contemporary architectural and artistic productions while questioning, more broadly, the notion of modernity." Faces, published four times a year, had a specific theme for each issue, in addition to recurring sections such as archives, forums, readings, and routes, including features on artists and exhibitions. Because Paul Viaccoz was on the editorial board, and Anne Patry-Chenu was a close friend of one of the editors, the projects developed by the Centre genevois de gravure contemporaine were known to the journal. Interested by the new dynamics of the institution, the editorial staff decided to dedicate part of its next issue to the Centre genevois de gravure contemporaine. Among the contributions published in this section was the interview with Chaimowicz conducted by the Swiss art historian Philippe Cuenat.*

In 1986, Philippe Cuenat was still a student at the University of Geneva. Although a few of his published texts and his master's thesis on the French artist Christian Boltanski had been well received, his visibility as an art critic was still modest. As he reflected later, "Since I was one of the few people in the circle of the Centre genevois de gravure contemporaine who was genuinely interested in the etchings of Marc Camille Chaimowicz, I was offered to interview the artist in Faces." When Cuenat met with the artist to further prepare for the discussion, his enthusiasm was so palpable that Chaimowicz exclaimed, "Let's do the interview right away!" Conducted in French in November 1986 in the exhibition space of the Centre genevois de gravure contemporaine, the interview was subsequently edited by Cuenat, proofread by the artist, and published in Faces over the spring of 1987. Translated into English by Martyn Back in 2022, the interview is published below in English for the first time.

As Cuenat wrote in his introduction:

> "Unlike Cézanne, who sought the means to achieve certainty and a form of verification in painting—'I owe you the truth in painting, and I shall tell it to you' (Letter to Émile Bernard, 23 October 1905)—Marc-Camille Chaimowicz offers the viewer a fiction that involves supposing that the distance between I and you can only be resolved in infinite intimacy. The fictional approach he develops by claiming that aesthetic form and intuition are by definition unverifiable and superior to any kind of legitimising authority nonetheless possesses its own ethical dimension, which prompts him to hold back on making statements as a creative subject, instead delegating his powers to others in areas of expertise that he only appears to master. This has resulted in a series of personal projects where the artist as a single creative figure is constantly eclipsed—as in the aptly titled performance Partial Eclipse [III. 8, 11c]; in more emblematic works where he plays hide-and-seek with the viewer, for example Les Paravents [III. 7]; and in more impersonal projects carried out with 'technicians' in the tra-

dition of the applied arts: furniture, textiles and wallpaper. Engraving, which lies halfway between these two types of 'creation,' raises a number of problems due to the different methods it involves, the collaborative work it entails, and the specific genealogy it possesses. Marc Camille Chaimowicz was to gain first-hand experience of these issues as a summer guest of the Centre genevois de gravure contemporaine."

A quotation from Ludwig Wittgenstein's posthumous Philosophical Investigations *(1953) was jointly selected by Chaimowicz and Cuenat, and placed accordingly at the beginning of the interview. If, as the artist said in retrospect, "this quotation somehow reflects the pretentiousness that runs through the discussion," it could just as well function as a tag or beacon regarding self-reflexivity in contemporary art in the late 1980s. Focusing on the artist's etchings and engravings from 1985–86, this interview was illustrated accordingly.*

Considering this interview appeared in a theoretical journal on architecture, Cuenat admitted retrospectively: "The publication in Faces *of a six-page interview with Marc Camille Chaimowicz dealing with etchings in the Neo-Geo, Post-Fluxus and Post-Conceptual context of the visual arts in the mid-1980s in Geneva, may seem like a real feat today!"*

A.V.

• • • • • • • • •

The essential thing about private experience is really not that each person possesses his own exemplar, but that nobody knows whether other people also have this or something else. The assumption would thus be possible—though unverifiable—that one section of mankind had one sensation of red and another section another.
—Ludwig Wittgenstein, *Philosophical Investigations*

Philippe Cuenat: *Over the summer you stayed for a long time at the Centre genevois de gravure contemporaine. I think it would be useful to talk about the work you did there and the dialogue you established with specialist engravers—in particular Paul Viaccoz. Given the complexity of the final result and the very wide variety of techniques you used for these etchings, two questions come to mind: How much did you know about engraving and how did you start working in this medium?* Marc Camille Chaimowicz: I knew nothing at all. Twenty or so years ago I did a bit of linocut at art school, but that's all. However, I've always been fascinated by anything that's printed: I'd already done some designs for fabrics, two of which were produced at Jean-Louis Lhopital's studio in Lyon in 1984, and a silk square produced by the AMAM [Association pour un Musée d'Art Moderne in Geneva / Non-profit organisation for a Modern Art Museum in Geneva] in a limited edition of 300, as well as some designs for wallpaper. But all that is far away from engraving, and getting into it was quite a leap for me. It was all the more difficult because at that time I had to get used to the possibility of working again … In 1985, following the publication of *Café du Rêve*, a substantial book that took four years to complete, I did several exhibitions relating to the same themes—intimate interaction, fictional connections, absence, nostalgia, identity, and the correspondence between different media. I then felt the need to step outside my space, to escape from my studio, my apartment, my city, my language… So I went to Geneva during the winter of 1985–86 with the intention of doing nothing, being free from commitments, and living in a kind of timeless void … in particular due to the serious risk there is in this business of producing things for the sake of it, of giving in to self-aggrandisement and careerism. I clearly and consciously disengaged myself from the rationale that the more you work, the more commissions you get. That being said, I did some work, some drawings, but with no particular aim in mind; they represented a kind of intimate, private activity in a neutral setting. Then I left Geneva for Australia, and the contrast between leaving in the snow and arriving in the middle of the Australian summer caused a kind of thaw to happen. This is an effective metaphor because it explains that I was able not only to get back to work but also to commit to the project at the Centre de gravure when I returned to Geneva, a project that had been well prepared but which implied a number of risks. These ranged from my almost complete lack of experience as an engraver to the prospect of working in close collaboration with someone I didn't know very well, not to mention the moral obligation this kind of invitation entails: if I was being invited to stay for such a long period, it was because they were aiming at, or hoping for, an exhibition, which was far from being a foregone conclusion for me because I prefer to see the result before deciding whether it's presentable or not.

So engraving was an experimental process for you in every possible way.
Absolutely. Working in a place like the Centre de gravure, learning about the medium and developing a dialogue represented a range of probabilities and a number of unknown quantities to which I had to try to respond. Establishing a dialogue required a very precise kind of discipline where the main challenge was the specific nature of the medium—in this case, engraving. When you're trying to be disciplined in this way, there's always the hope that you might escape from yourself; one of the things that motivate the creative process is its heroic dimension, because on the

other hand you have the fact that it's never actually possible to escape from yourself completely, the fact that it's destined not to happen. What I hope for with the aesthetic I develop in my work is to spark an awareness of this specificity: a way of feeling it and respecting it. And within the constraints of the collaboration, for example the fact that I would meet with Paul Viaccoz at a set time every day to talk about specific problems, I saw an almost psychoanalytical discipline whose purpose was to reveal aspects of the subconscious. There's an alchemical relationship with the process of engraving that reveals itself gradually, step by step, almost without our knowing it. Sometimes at the printing stage, when I saw the result, I would tell Paul that the plate was a complete mess and that it couldn't be saved, and he always replied that in engraving everything can be reworked and transformed, that everything is reversible. To a certain extent, I wasn't sufficiently aware of these properties to understand what engraving was really about. That's why I quickly understood that I couldn't take much away from Paul's proposal, which was to teach me technique. I don't think it would have done me much good to become, at best, a second-rate engraver when I had the opportunity to work with someone who was so immensely talented. This probably points to a problem that deserves further investigation. I remained absolutely dependent on technical collaboration, on a relationship with someone like Paul, and I have a great deal of respect for certain aspects of the collaboration, including the personality and artistic qualities of the other person. Such an interaction, when it works out well, symbolises my connection with a particular practice and its history. Passing an engraved metal plate on to someone who will then ink it and print it is an aesthetic act: you reach the absolutely magical moment when that person cranks the press, and you suddenly become aware of being part of a practice that has lasted for centuries.

At that moment, did you have the impression that it was a similar

experience to your work in textiles, in particular your work with Jean-Louis Lhopital?
No, not at all …

In an interview with Michel Nuridsany, you said, "the ideal process is to design a project, then forget about it and see it carried out by someone else whose practice is highly refined": Doesn't this apply to engraving?
The timeframe where engraving is concerned is shorter, and it's a very different process. There's less exterior intervention, and printing only takes a few minutes instead of several months. Also, in my relationship with the applied arts, the connection is essentially mechanical and the dialogue is purely technical and determined by what is or isn't possible; it doesn't relate to the content of the work. But in Geneva, the dialogue went much deeper: it involved a reciprocal acknowledgment of the work and personality of each person, and also a charm offensive with regard to the milieu of engraving, which is quite closed and surrounded by a somewhat mythical aura. So we had to begin by developing a shared language that was most often based on tacit agreement and on gestures rather than words. I had to familiarise myself with the profession, with all its traditions and habits.

More generally, but still in relation to the problem of mediation, do you identify with Lawrence Wiener's statement that the artwork can be "made by someone else"—in other words, inasmuch as you rely on others to carry out your projects, do you feel any affinities with Conceptual art?
Paradoxically, I'd say both yes and no. If we're only talking about the moment when the motivations behind a piece of work begin to operate—about our relationship to the work rather than the work itself—I think the answer is yes. But I'd immediately add that, as an artist, I feel free from moral criteria, responsibilities and the so-called need to justify oneself and explain the reasons behind

what one creates. There is no didactic intention at all in my work; I'm interested in how the artist integrates into society, but I don't claim to play a political role: I can hardly see myself publishing manifestos or becoming some kind of William Morris. So I'm not really drawn towards theoretical statements such as Wiener's.

And yet as soon as you do work that is not only for yourself, you have to think about the question of the reception of an artwork and, by the same token, address the question of the real or symbolic existence of the Other. Personally, I try to build a relationship based on the idea of winning each other over: something that's essentially private. The only responsibility I make myself assume in a piece of work arises from the existence of the other person and the contract I seek to establish with that person; but it's all very intimate and exclusive, especially as very often my work is based on questions of identity that are never resolved. From an artistic standpoint—and although I doubt whether it's still possible to make art nowadays—this quest for identity in a direct relationship with another person is of special interest to me.

To a certain extent, the fact that I delegate certain problems and certain responsibilities means I can avoid feeling claustrophobic and anxious. For several years, I thus decided to return to a practice in which a less exclusive alternative might emerge; this is what my research in the field of applied arts focuses on. By definition the work is shared out, and several people intervene quite extensively from the start. The relationship with the finished work is also transformed because it no longer addresses "the other person" exclusively, but "other people": you move from an investigation of the name, about who's who and who I am, to something that exists outside the name: anonymity, namelessness, lack of identity. And I think that's a model for certain situations… What fascinates me in this model is the fact that we buy textiles or wallpaper based on taste alone, knowing nothing about the person who designed them, whereas in our profession, in the art world, these questions always interfere: I know that if I see a drawing signed by Matisse my reaction will not be the same as if I see more or less the same drawing signed by someone else. The name of the artist is part and parcel of the artwork, and this phenomenon seems to me to be the source of a trend that worries me a little because it is becoming a cultural constraint.

The applied arts touch on a myth, a taboo: the artist who is free to do what he wants and who, as such, has come to symbolise freedom. On the other hand, collaborating with a technician or a manufacturer demands a very precise sense of discipline: constraints regarding materials, colours, manufacturing timeframes, and so on. For example, the problems we've had with the glass for the small piece of furniture currently being made in Lyon are not yet completely resolved. Here, the artwork exists outside the categories proposed by Wiener: in order to exist, it not only *can* but it *must* be made by someone else, because it entails something specifically industrial, an expertise that I do not need to acquire and that allows me to propose a model of communication from the start.

In a section of the text Partial Eclipse, *you wonder about the meaning of transposition, and you say: "…it is impossible to transpose one's reality into another without the very process of transposition affecting that reality […] an idea subjected to change is never again the same idea, […] its purity is violated, spoilt… ." Does the intervention of another person in a work not increase the risk of this happening?*
That text concerns my most exclusive work on identity, not on the issue of applied arts; it testifies more to an ideal of communication that I try to discern at the metaphysical level.

Where engraving is concerned, I am wary of the phenomenon that has led certain artists to reproduce their works almost literally on a smaller scale to make them easier to distribute. Engraving is not a reduction, still less a simplification. You can't go from thirty colours to three with impunity: the work loses all of its value. Personally, I have adopted the opposite stance, which doesn't necessarily mean that I agree with engraving but that I try to understand its specific characteristics; throughout my stay [in Geneva], I tried to incorporate the techniques and qualities specific to etching. In the beginning, some conditions such as the choice of format, the number of prints and their dimensions seem very abstract to me; you have to free yourself from all that to be able to work. One day, I was given a little metal plate and an engraving point, and I had to cope on my own; the result was *A Search*, my first, extremely simple engraving, which we initially didn't think would be produced as an edition given that it didn't correspond to the decisions made at the outset. Then things evolved and the pace changed, especially when I abandoned drawing for brush and ink; when you explore a medium, you get close to a kind of visualisation of the subconscious.

In A Search *and* La Fin de l'été, *the very free but also very spare graphic style recalls the inner concave side of a folding screen: its intimate, private side. It puts one in mind of a special moment where we search for a sign or a paradigm. We see patterns of variations that give us the impression of witnessing the emergence of a piece of writing: its abstract origin.*

Yes, that corresponds to what's beautiful and useful in the metaphor of the thaw: the magical moment when things become possible again. The questions one asks at that moment, especially about the specific nature and relevance of a medium, spark a renewal. After *Café du Rêve,* which was conceived as a very carefully written book, crafted in a very precise way with deliberate rhythms and contrasts between the different parts, I had the idea of a meaningless narrative. This might be the origin of another work that began with the portfolio and could become a new publication that would be more substantial than the portfolio—perhaps another book. What I liked about the portfolio was the opportunity it gave me to reintroduce myself to something I thought I was no longer able to do, at least for a few years, namely to write a new text—quite a short one, but a text all the same—and to relate it to four engravings.

The aim of *Café du Rêve* was to produce a book that was not founded on the myth of the artist but would help to redefine the framework in which an artist can work and reach out to an audience. The next book, however, could be a fully-fledged artist's book that would play on a certain tradition: it would be printed on fine paper and produced in a very limited edition, which would allow me to insert a watercolour—something more artisanal, much more tactile, sensual, and intimate. From this point of view, engraving may well have been very useful to me because it represents something extremely ambivalent: an engraving is neither an original nor a reproduction. This ambivalence sheds light on problems such as signature and mediation.

In the relationship you establish with writing, it seems that you are very often exploring the limits of legibility, for example using effects of superimposition and saturation of space in Café du Rêve. *In engraving, your narrative tends towards something elliptical: there is a sense of discontinuity from one sign to the next. Might these constraints applied to reading be a way of establishing a dialogue with the viewer?* Absolutely. If I had to ascribe a place to engraving in my artistic work, this is where it would be: alongside the special contract I try to establish with each viewer.

And as regards what one might call a dislocation of writing? In the words of the portfolio—the word "perhaps" for example—there are gaps, sometimes with an abstract form intruding into a string of letters [P/e^vaPs], which might be said to resemble the treatment of letters in certain English-language manuscripts.

I hadn't made that connection, but it's worth looking into. In this particular case, the word itself would ideally be looked at through the gap: it would then clearly mean "perhaps", and this might be the correct way of writing it. This word is ambiguous, anxious, without purpose: in my view, it had to be written as it is here. Moreover, all these words—*haunted, sometimes, regrets, perhaps*— are words encountered by chance … overheard in the street, in London or elsewhere, or heard in conversation. Although they remain in the memory, there's something serendipitous and crazy about them: they seem like accidents or attempts at writing. Moreover, engraving inevitably raises the question of the dislocation of writing because it involves a reversal at the printing stage; and I was fascinated to know whether this is connected to the reason why we write with our right or left hand.

I've always been sensitive to this problem because although I'm left-handed I was forced to write with my right hand. The left hand generally creates a strange, more emotional relationship. So instead of laboriously writing with my left hand, instead of copying my right hand with my left, I made myself upturn the logic of the whole process by writing in reverse with my left hand, from right to left. The left hand is the right hand in reverse: its mirror image.

Can this be applied more generally to the use of space; can it help us to understand works such as the Paravents [Screens], *which are articulated on both sides?*
It's still too early to establish a precise role for this phenomenon. All I can do is connect it to an ambivalence that seems to be essential in all my work: the creation of an in-between state, a dialectical form…

Or a space of interactions? In the exhibition "Four Rooms," you combined objects of different origins, some designed by you, others borrowed from Eileen Gray and Aalto; in one of the Innuendo *pieces, you refer openly to Jasper Johns.*

In that particular *Innuendo*, it's a way of establishing that painting has always been a dialogue with what came before. Using allusions and referring to Jasper Johns or others reflects my desire to recall the cultural dimension of painting.

In "Four Rooms," the problem is much more complex. In a way, this work is a defence and revaluation of the modern mind, but this perception of history is obviously out of sync, as shown by *Desk on Decline*. This piece acts on two levels, and it ended up being the symbol of the exhibition because it lies at the heart of the debate between functionalism and non-functionalism: it fully expresses the ambiguity between art and applied art. This piece is rooted in the anxiety I felt as I wrote *Café du Rêve*: a writer's block that this piece of furniture in decline aims to symbolise. But I wanted to make it possible for this seemingly non-functional object, which is probably impossible to classify except perhaps as a sculpture, to tip back to the horizontal position. A technical solution had to be found: a system of counterweights. Now all you have to do is give it a push so that it assumes its functional position, allowing you to sit at the desk and use it in the normal way. Even the drawers can be used.

Do you feel close to the idea of décor as Broodthaers redefined it in the early 1970s: "the idea of the object reinstated with a real function, which means that it is no longer itself considered as a work of art?"

First of all, I think that idea needs to be qualified today: the historical and artistic context has changed a great deal, and this has modified not only our way of understanding the problem but also the form and function that the notion of décor per se is able to embrace. For Broodthaers, the polemical aspect of such a statement had to be justified with respect to the almost universally shared rejection of anything that might recall historic décor and its role in the perception of an artwork. I think it's necessary to think about the environment in which an artwork is shown, and the museum, as far as the artist's resources allow, is no exception.

Also, these questions seem to me to be very often insoluble or at least impossible to boil down to a single point of view; asking them again in the same way, using the same terms as Broodthaers, is impossible: this would be giving in to a kind of academism, and most importantly it would be to neglect the irony that was essential in his work. What I take away from all this personally is a renewed awareness: the fact that nobody escapes from historic décor, from a social and cultural climate that determines not only the real function of the object but also its value. I prefer a form of skepticism to criticism; I think today the artwork finds its own place in its décor, most often by accident, as in a collage. But this suits me because, as in the applied arts, it allows me to escape from questions of identity and signature. In a way, it assumes that the aura of the work no longer emanates from the artist or their personality, but from the décor. This is also one of the reasons why I no longer really believe in the validity of environments or installations that claim to control and motivate their entire space. I'm currently more interested in producing singular works.

Is it from this perspective that we should understand the transformation of the Paravents? *The first folding screens you made in 1979 were intended to be very narrative, they had photographs on them referencing the sphere of intimacy; in your latest screens, these photographs have been replaced by window-like openings. It seems to me that you've abandoned projections of private life for projections of the behaviour of the viewer. We seem to have moved from a symbolic definition of the screen to its actualisation, a real experience that makes use of different viewpoints, effects of parallax, a direct and more individualised awareness of the body, and thus a phenomenology of perception. Without going so far as to say that the body becomes the subject of perception, I'm tempted to compare these screens with the work of Richard Serra, whose finality is often a visualisation of behaviour.*

Why not? Our sensibilities are obviously very different. Serra is probably much more focused on this kind of speculation on space than I am. But attitudes are often more interesting than forms.

Interview with Marc Camille Chaimowicz

Jean-Michel Roudier and Éric Troncy

(1994)

Chaimowicz's relationship to Burgundy began in 1984. While installing his solo exhibition "Six Works" [I. 4] at the Musée d'Art et d'Histoire, Geneva (3 May–17 June, 1984), he was contacted by Éric Colliard, Xavier Douroux, and Franck Gautherot (later dubbed "The Three Musketeers" by Chaimowicz), the co-directors of a newly established art centre in Dijon, Le Consortium, who invited him to spend the day with them in Dijon.

At that time, Chaimowicz's work was gaining visibility in France. Catherine Thieck, the director of the powerful Galerie de France in Paris, had just invited him to do a solo show at the gallery the following year—"Café du Rêve" (9 May–15 June, 1985) [III. 11]— and a troop of private art collectors and writers were following his work. As the artist recalled, "I was aware that part of the cultural project of Le Consortium consisted in presenting overseas artists for the first time in France with a specific project." During the meeting, the availability of "Six Works" after its presentation in Geneva was discussed with the artist, who detected that beyond "Six Works," the co-directors of Le Consortium were interested in introducing his work in Dijon before Paris—he had to be quick. Therefore, the Swiss exhibition came at the right time. Although "the proposal was very last minute," Chaimowicz thought, "Why not take it?" The meeting with the museum's co-directors had been "inspiring," and the wine tastings "excellent!" However, before confirming the exhibition tour with them, he proposed that "Six Works" in Dijon be related to the production of a label, either a wine from Burgundy or mustard from Dijon. The co-directors of Le Consortium immediately made the connection with Dijon-based French artist Michel Verjux, who had contacts with several winemakers of the Region. A couple of days later, the production of a wine label for a Mercurey red, classified as Premier Cru, *was confirmed and Chaimowicz went to Dijon by train immediately on the Sunday following his first meeting with the co-directors of Le Consortium. On the train, however, he panicked, realising that his exhibition would open in Dijon only a week after it closed in Geneva, but "gradually relaxed … as the day passed." As a result, the exhibition was officially programmed in Dijon (25*

June–28 July, 1984), and the wine label for a wine piece (i.e. 228 litres) of Mercurey red by Mellenotte-Drillien 1982 (one of the greatest winemakers in Burgundy) was crafted and glued on 304 bottles.

Surprisingly, no one from Le Consortium came to see "SixWorks" in Geneva. Since Chaimowicz could not be present in Dijon between 17 to 24 June for the installation of his exhibition at Le Consortium, he came up with the following proposal: that his fellow artist Balthasar Burkhard, with whom he "had excellent conversations at night in Geneva," would take care of the installation of the exhibition instead of him. "Everyone loved the idea of having Balthasar curate for my first exhibition in Dijon," said Chaimowicz. "It worked so well that when I arrived at the opening, I was surprised by my own work. That is luxury, isn't it?" This playful approach to curating and exhibition making laid the foundation for a long-standing relationship between the artist, Le Consortium, and the Burgundy Region.
Ten years later, Chaimowicz was again invited by Le Consortium to create an exhibition in Dijon. Entitled "Peintures & Objets" (10 September–15 October, 1994), and co-produced by Le Quartier in Quimper, where it was later presented (22 October–31 December, 1994), the show brought together works produced by the artist between 1988 and 1994. Conceived with the intention of highlighting the multiple facets of Chaimowicz's recent production, it combined craft and decorative elements with paintings and objects [I. 6].

A few days before the opening, Éric Troncy and Jean-Michel Roudier invited Chaimowicz to do an interview in Documents sur l'art. *Co-founded in Paris in 1992 by the French critics and curators Nicolas Bourriaud and Troncy, together with artists Philippe Parreno and Liam Gillick,* Documents sur l'art—*whose title alludes to Georges Bataille's* Documents *(1929–31)—provided a forum that reflected the artistic and curatorial currents generated by Troncy and Bourriaud that was key for artists and art producers of the time. Combining interviews, theories, essays, and reports, this black and white contem-*

porary art magazine, published in French and English until 2000, invited an artist to contribute to each issue as a "guest-editor," curating a section of about forty pages of the publication.

It was planned that Troncy, then editor-in-chief of Documents sur l'art, *and Roudier, an independent curator then based in Burgundy, would meet with Chaimowicz on 11 September at Le Consortium, and subsequently have lunch with him at the Casino self-service. The three had already collaborated with each other. Troncy and Roudier had co-organised the acclaimed group project "Ozone" at APAC, Nevers (14 October–16 December, 1989) and Roudier had developed several projects with the artist in different contexts, including the exhibition "Marc Camille Chaimowicz 1986–1990, To Give and To Take Meaning … Fine and Applied Art," Musée de Cosne-sur-Loire (13 July–16 September, 1990). By mutual agreement, they decided that the interview would focus on the relationship between performance, installation, and furniture in the artist's work.*

On the day of the meeting, Chaimowicz was late. He had to leave Dijon earlier than expected and had little time to spare. As a result, the interview was done quickly. Tape-recorded, it was subsequently transcribed and translated into English for publication. Chaimowicz did not hear from Troncy and Roudier afterwards, though he came across a copy of Documents sur l'art *and discovered the interview a few months later. What struck him as he read the interview was, he recalled, "probably on account of a massive hangover, there's a certain degree of urgency that runs through the whole discussion." Flipping through the magazine, he found out that in addition to the interview, a few pages were devoted to his performances from 1972 to 1982, including* Celebration? Realife *(1972),* Table Tableau *(1974),* Fade *(1976),* Doubts *(1977), and* Partial Eclipse *(1980). At first surprised, Chaimowicz quickly admitted, "It didn't really matter… I was in good hands anyway!"*

A.V.

Éric Troncy: *What in the 1970s led you to do these performances?*
Marc Camille Chaimowicz: A sort of cultural claustrophobia. Too great a love for painting that made the very idea of painting impossible. I was quite attracted by French nineteenth and twentieth century painting, and also, maybe unfortunately, Renaissance painting, Tintoretto and Veronese. But I was also attracted by Gorki and Johns. Retrospectively, I think in the beginning of the 1970s, it seemed necessary to place oneself in cultural spaces that had not yet been named, and where I felt free to give shape to my own needs. What is shocking is that very quickly, some of us have been recuperated by cultural agencies. We were sent like cultural ambassadors to represent Britain at various Biennials and that had a name: performances, and installations. At the beginning, they weren't called happenings, a term that applies rather to New York activities and to Fluxus, a movement that always worried me because it was too anarchical with political tendencies that led its protagonists to place themselves vis-à-vis the public.

Jean-Michel Roudier: *Can one establish a link between the happenings and the rock scene of the same period: the first Roxy Music concerts, Bowie's touring of Ziggy Stardust and his glittery spirit, which the elements used (fur, Disco-balls) and transvestite's gear seem to refer to?*
Quite, and if it is important to remember painters that interested us, you mustn't forget that at the Beaux-Arts, the things that were most important to me weren't the visual arts, but rather things related with Godard's films or rock concerts, at the beginning of a new culture, if not "counter-culture." Female personification is prior to this, simply with Oscar Wilde and Shakespeare. Sexual ambiguity is actually closely associated with an English sensibility; external characters like Lou Reed later used it, more than Bowie actually. In 1968, I was preparing my degree and I was very attracted by what happened in Paris. It seemed at least to me very pressing to go and check it out, which my teacher wasn't too con-

vinced about. It wasn't even a political problem, but a school one. If I could simply think of taking a leave to go to Paris and run wild, it would automatically mean that I wasn't serious. For me, being serious was precisely to go and check it out, and not simply achieve one more small painting. But I was besides sufficiently immersed in the context, I was going out very late, I used drugs and was under therapy. The 1960s and 1970s weren't just happy days … particularly if you take yourself seriously, which the practicing of art involves. Some friends wanted me to sing but as with happenings, I had a certain reticence about work in actual time. I need a critical distance, which the visual arts do offer.

É.T.: *A performance like* Celebration? Realife *seems to deny this since physically present, you served tea to visitors.*
It was to outline the boring and alienating aspect of contemporary art. I wanted to narrow the distances between the spectator and the creator. But these performances were very short. What was the real failure at the beginning of structuralist cinema and video projects was the length of these very boring pieces. On the other hand, if we waited for an audience to cross a city to be at eight at a happening that would only last five minutes, that wouldn't do either. Generally, I repeated the performance two or three times till it would be achieved according to my own standards then I'd stop. Ten years later, I felt I had said the most essential of what I could have said, and using this activity and its institutionalisation seemed too absurd. There were specialised magazines on the subject and even classes at university. I performed one in Italy, in an atmosphere where collectors play a great part, and a spectator even tried to grab a few relics of the performance, putting them in a box and asking me to sign an autograph on it. I was stunned. This cultural reflex was so remote from my own needs developed in the project that I realised performance art wasn't necessarily the best solution. It had to produce an ulterior form, cinema or rock concerts, as was the case with Laurie Anderson. Though, to my

mind, her concerts were too heavy going, too professionalised. As a general rule, the idea of signing an activity, then leaving so that the spectator should be able to place himself in relation with the work (a painting or a piece of furniture) seems more practicable.

É.T.: *Can you be more precise about your present interest in decorative or useful objects?*
Some years ago, the most sensible question was probably about the object's status. This most Duchamp-esque question has been broadly treated, which means today the urgency, as it were, is elsewhere; for instance, in the questioning of the role(s) of the artist of our time. Why be an artist, what to do, or who is it for? There's also the need for an object because I can't find it in the real world. *Café du Rêve* was, too, a way of seeing how a book could be done, set, and seen. Namely, it was conceived like a record, whose every chapter was a song. The production of objects and elements of furniture, finally, force you to take into account criteria already defined by Adolf Loos, who, I hope, I remain faithful to, and who was roughly much less bigheaded than Josef Hoffmann, who he at the end opposed. For Loos the artist was above all free, with eventually some accounts to give to God. On the contrary, architects and craftsmen still according to his views have to engage in a hierarchy of responsibilities relative to clients, material, or techniques. I feel if you engage in this aspect of the practice, which is subcontracted to others, you ought to care about these responsibilities that are economic among other things. With Eileen Gray for instance, the violent break between the works of her earlier years and those of her later years can be explained by the understanding of the inadequacy of a production of unique objects extremely well-done destined to a rather well-off clientele with a culturally and economically troubled background. I feel, like herself later on, engaged in what is almost the contrary of painting: a refined production, though in series, and inexpensive.

J-M.R.: *Does the making of furniture, earthenware, and cloth correspond with the pursuance of a Utopia? For there is, ironically, no economic viability in this production, contrary to Starck's objects for example. It remains a kind of artistic gesture.*

É.T.: *The relation to the decorative function is rather badly regarded in contemporary art. There still remains this most engrained idea that decorative objects aren't "art."*
I feel it is high time one should question this taboo, among so many others. We were talking of sexual ambiguity, but it has meaning so long as there should be a social taboo. During my student years, the teachers directed their best pupils towards painting, those that were less good towards modelling, then the even less good towards textile, the graphic arts, and, at the bottom of the scale, ceramics. Besides, female students tended to be geared towards the applied arts and male ones towards sculpture and painting. So the decorative aspect interests me, but not only on the pictorial level. My past work was connected with the attempt at establishing a personal aesthetic, very subjective, and to shift it into the public ground. Nothing original actually. My work remains open to various interpretations. In fact, I am a painter who thinks. And if you paint today, you can but only think about it.

Conversation with Marc Camille Chaimowicz

Alain Coulange

(1995)

The interview reproduced below was first published in Peintures & Objets, *the catalogue of a solo project across two exhibitions—one at Le Consortium, Dijon (10 September–15 October, 1994) and the other at Le Quartier, Quimper (22 October–31 December, 1994). Dedicated to the artist's mother, who passed away in 1994, this 88-page bilingual (French and English) publication, illustrated in colour, was released in 1995, after the exhibition tour mentioned above. Spanning the artist's production from 1988 to 1994, the book was produced to highlight recent directions the artist had taken in his practice. Conceived by Chaimowicz together with Franck Gautherot (co-director of Le Consortium), the publication includes three texts commissioned from Stuart Morgan, Xavier Douroux, and Jean Rosen. The acclaimed Welsh-born, London-based art critic Stuart Morgan considered the notion of being "camped in life," which in his words "means existing on a cusp between definitions the world makes and which the artist can choose to revise." Douroux, co-director of Le Consortium, contextualised the artist's recent paintings in relation to his furniture/sculpture. Rosen, a researcher and ceramic specialist based in Burgundy, looked at the earthenware produced by the artist in Quimper and Nevers at the turn of the 1990s. Crystallising the moment when the artist was, as Morgan put it, "reveling in the opportunity to extend the limits of the stylistic definition, even of object recognition," these texts echo the idea that one of the great strengths of art is its willingness to leap into the unknown, regardless of the materials the artist uses.*

Also included in this publication is the interview reproduced below. Conducted by French writer and art critic Alain Coulange, the exchange highlights the way Chaimowicz has played off distances with his own work while developing new facets of his production, particularly in the late 1980s, being committed to various artistic fields simultaneously. The interview was later translated for publication into English by Nissim Marshall, whose translation is reproduced here.

At the time of the interview, Coulange was working as a State official representing contemporary art in Burgundy for the Ministry of Culture. He was also known for his publications mixing history, fiction, contemporary art, photography, and philosophy. Intrigued by this kind of cultural crossover, and fascinated by "the way Alain Coulange was handling both the French language and himself as a writer," Chaimowicz was always happy to speak with him when he was in Dijon. As a result, when Douroux suggested to the artist that Coulange interview him for the catalogue Peintures & Objets, *his proposal was well received by the artist.*

However, despite their mutual enthusiasm for the interview, it was a particularly slow process. Although Chaimowicz and Coulange met several times between June and August in Burgundy, no basic structure for a text was ready by the end of the summer. In order to speed up the process, they decided to record the conversations. As stated in the catalogue, it took four months to complete the recordings, which were made on the following dates in "Dijon, 1, 13, 19, 25, 27 September; 15, 16 October; 13, 18 November; 14, 15 December."
Once these conversations were transcribed, Chaimowicz had access to a computer for the first time in his life. Amazed by the flexibility of the machine, he reflected, "I've discovered new ways of doing text montage." Echoing his textual compositions, which for the most part combine text, image, and pattern, the possibilities of the computer immediately fascinated him. "Writing itself was becoming a montage," he said. As a result, Chaimowicz admitted in retrospect, "The editing of the interview conducted by Alain Coulange became the slowest and highly crafted one I've ever made." As he stated later, "The most interesting interviews are fictions; they are reconstructed in order to seem alive." And yet, his enthusiasm for the potential of the computer as a machine for "writing as montage" did not become an addiction. Indeed, the first computer that Chaimowicz bought dates back around the end of 2008.

A.V.

Alain Coulange: *Is it wise or even useful to speak of the origin, or do you feel that the work evinces it adequately?*
Marc Camille Chaimowicz: Origin. What a peculiar word. Can we not speak of origins? Our origins are fantasies. We reconstruct them. My origins lie very far away from me.

Yet they exist?
They emerge slowly and occasionally. For instance, in the exhibition at Le Consortium in Dijon and at Le Quartier in Quimper, I showed the *Warsaw Suite*. This work revolves around painting and indirectly incorporates my view—or what could be my view—of Poland.

Have you returned there?
For this project, I visited Warsaw three times. I managed to talk about it a little—not much really—with my father, who attended the university there. *Warsaw Suite* is a fiction around what could have been Poland. We never discussed it at home. My father told me a few stories about his mother, about his far off life in Poland before the war.

So, finally, where are your origins?
My origins are rather here in France: French culture, painting and its discovery. Is it necessary to speak of origins? When looking at a Giotto, surely the important thing is to "register" what the painter has signed. We ought to be able to envision a measure of autonomy for the works. Aren't the origins present in the work? The question contains its own answer.

What is your culture?
My culture is mainly Anglo-French. There's such a tremendous difference between these two countries that it's really difficult to try to articulate a cultural conception nourished by such different traditions. The vicinity of these two traditions generates misunderstandings, conflicts, mistrust, as well as mutual fascination.

I feel constantly split between the two.

What is your language?
I think I've constructed a language for myself, which is necessarily a mixture of French and English. More specifically, I speak a triangular language between English, French, and drawing. I speak English fluently. French culture offers me a language that I haven't quite mastered: I miss the nuances; I'm to some extent weakened. It's the price you have to pay.

What distinctions do you draw between the two languages?
Unlike English, French is a language that I have *heard*: it's the language of my mother, my first language. Closer, because connected with my childhood: French rejuvenates me, feminises me. It's not a language of the exterior, of power. It's my interior language, directly associated with creativity.

Which are the first works, meaning artworks that you first saw?
Rather than speaking of artworks, I prefer to speak about what affected me sensorially. I think about details, objects, interiors.

Details associated with childhood?
In London, I missed the perception that I had preserved of my early years in the 14th arrondissement in Paris, and of Malakoff, the suburb where my grandmothers lived: the very lively climate of a sort of backdrop, sounds, images … Perhaps these memories are connected with my taste for a certain French painting, epitomised by Bonnard or Matisse.

In the beginning, were you aware of any direct relationships? And if so, which?
When I attended art school, I was more interested in literature, cinema, and music. I accepted no models. So the relationships are rather vague.

Anyway, which works attracted you the most, what type of art?
Firstly, a fairly intimist art, especially Hockney, and then Hamilton, Johns. In England in the 1960s, many students opposed the examples of our tutors by a taste for American art, more precisely for the New York School. These references were certainly interesting, but not close enough to my needs. I gradually felt the need, beyond questions of form, to grapple with the challenges associated with cultural content.

What approaches did you adopt?
This reflection led me into ephemeral works, revolving around installation and performance. I found other forms of expression stifling. I was looking for markers that were neither English nor American.

How were your early works received?
It's certainly no accident if my work was received in France as the expression of an English sensibility and in England as very European. Since England did not consider itself an integral part of Europe, I was considered an artist who was different—one of a kind. Rather a strange position to find oneself in.

Just when, in what circumstances, did you decide to practice art, to be an artist?
I went through a number of difficult years of introversion. I found myself in a country called England, in an environment that I couldn't contact because in the beginning, my English was non-existent. For a delicate eight-year-old, this was a serious problem. Faced with these difficulties, I tended to withdraw into myself. Lacking fluency in the language, I failed my exams. I was saved by art school where I met other young people who had interests and problems that resembled my own; I discovered that I wasn't that abnormal or strange after all.

What characterised this period?
It was a giddy and intense period of my life, which often led to social embarrassments! On a spiritual level, these years were very important: I succeeded in perceiving and understanding things more simply. I felt that I was faced with a very simple choice: either I merged with a sort of subculture, or I developed in myself a "belief" centred on the practice of art. Art school offered me a framework in which I could start to realise my potential.

So you associated the practice of art with the notion of belief quite early?
The art schools that I attended in succession—the Ealing School of Art, Camberwell School of Art, and finally an M.A. at the Slade School—enabled me to come back to a certain kind of belief, in the rudimentary sense of *believing in something*. Making art enabled me to redefine myself in spiritual and cultural terms. It was a vital need. However, I didn't adopt the forms of belief that my teachers proposed. I tried to develop my own.

The violence stemming from this rebellious period seems to have been absorbed, dissolved in your work. At least it no longer appears as violence. Your art isn't socially committed. Visually it rather reveals certain elegance, distinction, refinement.
Quite right. Yet the question of violence is very complex. It concerns the role of the artist, his status, the areas that he invests in. As for myself, perhaps my rebellious period isn't unrelated to my taste, my interest, for example, in the applied arts. As for elegance, it isn't innate: as with Yves Saint Laurent, Eileen Gray, or Matisse—to mention three very different examples—it is, by definition, hard won, the fruit of a long struggle.

Let us briefly return to your formative years. At art school, at least in the final phase, how did you perceive the future? How did you work out your final choices, which, I presume, determine the framework of your current practice?

At the Slade School, I was accepted in the Painting School. This was lucky, but painting was actually less and less what I wanted to do. I was going through a crisis. My tutor understood this. He was a true "gentleman." He wavered between comprehension and incomprehension, accepting my commitment but not the types of response that I proposed. He obliged me to make choices, for instance, between theatre and socio-political activity. I talked to him about the world surrounding painting, which was becoming increasingly formal, increasingly alienated from content, from the values that I cherished.

Did your tutors, in as much as you could then tell, believe in your artistic ability? Were you encouraged to continue working towards the practice of art?
My teachers felt, it seems to me, that I was rather talented yet somewhat lost. They saw me as someone who was searching for a means of expression, a form that I had obviously not yet found. Very likely, these highly distinguished people were fascinated by this young man who apparently did nothing, in the sense that he produced little. Undoubtedly he gave them the impression that he lacked ambition. At the same time, the pupil demonstrated a degree of "commitment" by which he managed to win them over. Their support was discreet and their tolerance was great.

What did this commitment involve?
To stake his territory, the young man made a picture. As it turned out, this painting wasn't that different from the ones he made later. The canvas, in several parts—like my polyptychs today— was spread on the floor. This was a way to play the game, to earn acceptance in a painting class. Starting with the presence of this canvas, the student reflected, argued, read. And mostly, he looked. He went through moments of silence, probably the most important of this period, concerned more with life—his own— than with a studio life.

What was the point?

In reality, the young man was trying to reconstruct the world in his own fashion—something a few young people still manage to do—hoping to give it meaning in an existential climate dominated by meaninglessness. Invited to a glass of sherry at Sir William Coldstream's, the Head of the School, he enjoyed the privilege of testing the impertinence of his ideas twice monthly.

On the whole, can we identify a point of view, a position concerning the school of art as an institution?

The student questioned traditional values and, above all, the absolute priority assigned to the actual practice of painting and drawing. For him, this purely formalistic activity could only lead to isolation, to an increasingly alienated expression of reality. He was drawn to Rauschenberg's proposition, which said something like: "To work in the gap between life and art …"

What brought you to performance art?

At the same time, I was involved in "mysterious" activities. I had bought many, many second-hand shoes, which I painted silver to enhance their value and to give them distance as objects. A friend and I would transport these shoes in large bags, and drop them off at different spots in the city. On bridges, for example. It was quite exciting. To my mind, these clandestine operations were meant to target an uninitiated public.

Were you aware of similar practices in other countries?

At the time, we were far less well informed than we are today. Later on, someone told me about Kaprow, about "happenings" in New York, and about Fluxus. Fluxus naturally led me to the work of Beuys, who was still virtually unknown in Britain, and in France too, I imagine.

Were these mysterious activities in that they were spontaneous, instinctive?

Did they prove satisfying?
These actions were instinctive but considered obsessional rather than impulsive. Little by little I realised that the Fluxus attitude—with its anarchic dimension, close to Dada, its confrontational character—didn't coincide with my desires, my needs, my way of living. I found the official frameworks insufferable. And I didn't find the street—the public space—suitable either. So I decided to work at home.

At home, that is to say Approach Road, *what did you do?*
I performed small rituals with objects that I felt to be pertinent, evocative of certain alternatives. This practice was closely related to behaviour. I wasn't in the real desert, but in a desert that I had myself constructed.

Did these rituals gradually become organised, structured?
A ritual is always structured.

Xavier Douroux has written that your performances create a moment "of the affirmation of the essential of [your] acceptance of the real as it is." How do you feel about that?*
My performances affirmed privacy. They were virtually anti-performances.

What do you mean by "affirm privacy?"
It means to claim the sacred or the intimate. Often, you only saw my back. For me, it was a way to refer to my own life, hence effectively to accept the real as it is, by framing it more intensively, and without any compromise.

Was that the time when you were asked to present performances abroad?
Curiously, my efforts were recognised rather quickly. I enjoyed a sort of success for which I was unprepared. I was invited—often—

with two other artists of my generation to Paris, Vienna, Canada, and elsewhere. Stuart Brisley displayed tendencies closer to the Vienna School, with a lot of suffering and violence. His presence was counterbalanced by that of Bruce McLean, a sort of clown, very much in tune with art world jokes, and by my own presence. As for myself, I stood for refinement and "sensibility," a more "Proustian" side. This trio suited the British Council.

What did this mode of expression represent for you?
I accepted its necessity intellectually. I was drawn to the ephemeral, by alternative venues—hotel lobbies, stairways, private spaces—rather than by the places where contemporary art was normally exhibited. All this was rather positive. I also liked the shortness associated with performance and the fact that after the action, these moments disappeared, no longer existed. I often presented the same piece in several situations, till the time came when the problems raised had all more or less been resolved.

At what time, and for what reasons, did you stop performing?
The very restlessness that in the early '70s had prompted the need to define new activity, was rekindled ten years or so later: I felt the need to construct, abandoning transience, something that would have its own time. So I stopped performing. Above all, I realised that the very idea of an alternative activity was a contradiction.

What do you mean?
I'm thinking of Marcuse, about his idea that everything is absorbed by capitalism. Philosophically speaking, the idea of the alternative does not exist. Later on, French philosophers spoke about appropriation, and the advertising circles quickly understood the phenomenon of quotation and absorption. I didn't want to operate in a ghetto. It therefore then seemed to me that working in real time implied positioning oneself, in terms of the dominant forces, such as music, cinema, and theatre.

How did you feel about this renunciation?
I considered it a "failure." The concept interests me. One cannot hope to reach certain maturity without accepting these painful moments, which remind us that most of the finest ideas end badly.

Can you think of precise examples in the field of art or art history?
Matisse was ever searching for an ideal of happiness, and yet his finest works were made when he was bedridden and suffering from rheumatism. The most outstanding churches were often built after extremely violent religious wars. Periods of transition are often ambiguous and bring about compromise. One can also cite Surrealism, which produced few interesting works and which, today, constitutes a convincing example of the concept of "failure."

Looking back today, how do you feel about the performance period?
A crucial moment that many artists had to pass through, an opening, which sometimes allows vital encounters, like those of Johns, Rauschenberg, and Cage. Today, for me, that chapter is closed.

But what have you personally retained from that experience?
From the activity falsely called "performance," I retain a strong commitment to questions of content. This realisation occurred at the time of a general deterioration in the visual arts: sculptors after David Smith, and painters after Johns, were at a loss. The real advantage of that period was that performance art, conceptual art and, later on, some new painting, led to a repositioning of questions of content in practice itself.

Can we go on to talk about what came after the performance period?
During the performance period, I also worked on installations. My research into questions of content and the concept of privacy continued with photographic montage. This new vocabulary was developed in small formats, which I called "studies" and, at a larger scale, on boards placed on the floor, giving the impression

of a fragile and informal presentation.

How did you use photography?
I tried to construct narratives. I placed myself resolutely outside actual time so as to offer the other greater latitude of reading and interpretation.

Isn't this the work that was associated in particular with Here and There *that you showed at ARC in 1979?*
Quite right. In fact, I find this to be the most resolved piece from this period. It enabled me to pursue my research into subjectivity in a different way. *Here and There* orchestrates decorated panels overprinted with details of still lives, interiors, and portraits.

Can you tell us just what's happening, for you, between "here" and "there?"
This piece is based on a presumption: that the artist and the viewer never see the same thing. "Here" meant my private space (Approach Road), and "there," the exhibition space (The Hayward Gallery, then ARC). The opposite undoubtedly held for the viewer. In any case, the idea was to transfer an idealised reality from one place to another.

Could you tell us more about this interior in which you lived, Approach Road?
The place consisted of two floors of a condemned Victorian terrace. A sort of legal squat intended for the use of artists as studio cum residence. In this exile of his choice, the young man I was speaking of began to build his oasis with whatever came to hand. As he came closer to himself, he became more sensitive to his environment. A vital need to rebuild was gradually aroused. Unsatisfied with the possibilities offered by the then current decorative trends, he decided to approach the question of décor differently. Thus began his engagement in the field of the applied arts.

Over and beyond the question of the décor, what precisely were the challenges?
I organised the space to deal with questions related to identity, to gender (masculine/feminine, etc.), and to politics. The 1970s were deeply politicised. My select political position was summarised in the formula: "Personal is political." I subscribed to the idea that our internal behaviour can have a political dimension.

This singular position deserves some clarification.
The more I developed my thinking, the more alienated I felt by the gap between my internal quest and the reality of my immediate environment. To design my living space differently became for me a vital, physical necessity. I felt the need to overthrow the traditional (masculine) view, which consists of treating domestic aspects with contempt.

Did you assess the dangers of this highly internalised behaviour?
Such a process could in fact provoke a cut-off from the exterior, from the social. This attitude temporarily enabled me to perceive my environment more intensely, to be more sensitive to the aesthetics of things. Thus I began to feel an interest, for instance, in wallpaper. In 1975, I did my first works with this medium, using a stencil. For me this meant responding simultaneously to an internal need and a visual need: the wallpaper that I wanted to see did not exist.

As an artist, weren't you also interested in dabbling in a so-called "decorative" practice?
The challenge was to realise myself, hence by extension—even if I wasn't resolutely turned outward and hadn't yet claimed the social identity of an artist—to assume the creation of a wallpaper through what I myself wanted. And besides, grappling with a major taboo wasn't at all unpleasant!

Did you receive people at Approach Road *to show them your work?*

Not at the outset. Later on I invited friends to tea, two or three at a time. I needed to break my isolation and to check whether I was on the wrong track. Notwithstanding, my interior didn't become a "literary salon." The invitations were quite ritualised.

Was this when you published your first book Dream, an Anecdote?
Yes. That modest object was very important to me. Writing and its relationship to the photographic image enabled me to externalise my internal concerns. It represented the re-transcription of a dream I had in *Approach Road,* in which this place is destroyed and rebuilt.

Any connection between the publication of the book and your meeting with Nigel Greenwood?
At the time, a number of people began to show an interest in my work, including Caroline Tisdall, who's well-known for her work on Beuys. She mentioned me to Nigel Greenwood, who was inaugurating his gallery and showing Gilbert and George. Nigel, in deciding to publish *Dream, an Anecdote,* showed that he understood my work.

So, did Nigel Greenwood come to Approach Road?
He asked to see my work, but paradoxically, I had no idea what to show him. I didn't have many "objects" to present! I repeatedly postponed the meeting, and this bothered him. One day he called me and asked, "Who's chasing whom?" and decided to visit me the following day.

What did you show him?
The *Studies* that I mentioned earlier. He decided to take them right away and we crossed London together to Chelsea, where his gallery was located. On arrival, I found the place to my taste, as it was within a flat. Nigel hung my little frames on the gallery walls, and that's how we began working together.

Besides Gilbert and George, what was he showing in that period?
A very important painter of the time, John Walker, well-known in the English-speaking countries, but unknown in France. Joël Fisher, the Bechers … Nigel was highly cultivated and very knowledgeable about art history. He was the first to exhibit Marcel Broodthaers in England.

What impact did the meeting have on your work?
At specific moments, certain individuals play a decisive role, a bit as if the artist were momentarily "adopted," as if this "temporary adoption" enabled him to achieve what he couldn't do alone.

You were then asked to participate in the exhibition "Four Rooms?"
Yes, with Anthony Caro, Richard Hamilton, and Howard Hodgkin. The Arts Council had contributed generously for each of us to construct an interior. I perhaps put more of myself into the project than the others, whose careers were already well advanced. I created a fabric and a wallpaper, both of which were edited, two stained-glass windows, three or four pieces of furniture. I added a rug and a lamp by Eileen Gray. I also installed a set of slides to crystallise a sort of narration between two persons. Michael Regan, the organiser, had the brilliant idea of putting together an unusual exhibition venue, the department store, Liberty's.

For you, this exhibition appears to have been decisive.
The particular setting of "Four Rooms" enabled me to imagine an "alternative" model: I realised that I could assume a certain social role by occasionally embracing the area of the applied arts. The exhibition also travelled a great deal.

So the field of the applied arts became for you a privileged area of work, of experiments?
In fact, for the last ten years or so, I've had the opportunity to do at least one project every year in a variety of areas. I thus suc-

ceeded in investigating crafts as varied as earthenware, joinery, textile printing, glass, etc.

Far from the solitary occupation of the studio artist?
Collaboration with specialists brought me solutions that I couldn't alone realise. The price of this engagement is the acceptance of compromises—other taboos—connected with materials, with techniques and technologies, with financial desiderata, and naturally with individuals, with the concomitant risks of tension, of misunderstanding. When these collaborative undertakings were terminated, a return to the studio became a need and—not at all negatively—a pleasure. Both adventures nourished one another.

We haven't really talked about—or have only touched on—painting?
In a certain way, painting speaks for itself, sparing us the trouble. Truth in painting, as in anything connected with art, cannot be conceived outside an ethic. My painting developed on a register, which incorporated refinement and false modesty, craftsmanship and impulse. It's difficult to tell just how to perceive it. It's tremendously ambivalent. You cannot quite believe your eyes. In a diptych, the dialogue established between each part of the work—between pleasure and concern, in a manner of speaking—can become complex, or even hermetic. Culturally speaking, painting can no longer stand-alone. How to redefine it in relation to other practices or techniques, such as installation, for example? *Warsaw Suite*, which we spoke of earlier on, is established and "functions" in this mode.

In this light, the conceptual and formal importance of this work emerges and prevails…
Warsaw Suite displays many aspects. The trend today is to invite artists to work *in situ*. To take up the challenge proposed by the institutions that have bigger and vaster spaces. I decided to occupy the walls with easel paintings. As a painter, I cannot produce in too short a time. As a result, I had to develop a specific mode of

presentation. This work stands at the focal point of the questions concerning a work and its presentation.

So this work is really quite emblematic…
Quite right. It shows where and how my preoccupations are crystallised: between speculative research and decorative solutions, the conceptual and the sublime, anxiety and grace. Didn't Saint Augustine suggest that "beauty is unity in variety"…¿

* "Marc Camille Chaimowicz: éloge d'un Nabi" in *Chaimowicz, Rideau de scène*, Bourgoin-Jallieu: Théâtre Jean Vilar, Musée Victor Charreton, 1992.

Marc Camille Chaimowicz Interviewed at Cabinet on 26 July, 2000

Michael Archer, William Furlong, Martin McGeown, and Andrew Wheatley

(2000)

On 26 July, 2000, a roundtable discussion with Chaimowicz was organised at Cabinet, located then in Northburgh Street, London. The conversation took place near the artist's exhibition "Celebration? Realife Revisited 1972–2000" that was on view at the gallery from 9 June to 29 July. Moderated by English writer, artist, and publisher William Furlong, with the British critic and art writer Michael Archer, this twenty-eight minute tape-recorded interview was made available from Audio Arts, *Volume 19, numbers 1 & 2, September 2000. Archer was subsequently commissioned by Polly Staple, at the time co-editor of* Untitled, *to edit the interview for reading. Co-founded in the Spring 1993 in London by John Stathatos and Mario Flecha following the demise of Artscribe the previous year,* Untitled, *a twenty-page tabloid folded in loose sheets and folded over, was a British art magazine, which Flecha edited until 2006. The interview with Chaimowicz was published in issue #23 of* Untitled, *in the Autumn / Winter 2000.*

Conceived as a "spoken magazine," Audio Arts *(1973–2007) was created with the intention of documenting contemporary artistic activity by recording artists' voices in a free and unmediated way. Launched in 1973 in London by Furlong with Barry Barker, a British curator who left* Audio Arts *shortly after he was appointed Director of Exhibitions at the ICA in the same year, this "magazine of contemporary art on cassette tape" was a continuous publication for over thirty years. Purchased from Furlong in 2004 by Tate, the archive was later digitised and made available online through the Tate website. As with all* Audio Arts *magazine editions and supplements, the issue with that recording can be heard there.*

Furlong, Archer, and Chaimowicz met in 1977. At that time, Archer was the first editorial assistant with whom Furlong worked with regularly. The two had met at Whitechapel Gallery, London, when the exhibition "Nine Works for Tape / Slide Sequence" was presented (first staged in September 1977 at the Battersea Arts Centre and subsequently at the Whitechapel Gallery, from 21 September to 23 October).

In this capacity, Archer participated in the recording, editing, and production of numerous issues of Audio Arts, *including the one produced in conjunction with the exhibition, where a new work by Chaimowicz was presented. Responding to this exhibition, Chaimowicz also wrote an article in* Art Monthly *no. 13, December/January 1977 [II. 7]. Chaimowicz was a fan of the unmediated immediacy characterising* Audio Arts, *whose mission was, as Archer wrote in* Art Monthly, *no. 35, April 1980, to "disseminate as much information first-hand to as many people as possible."Therefore, twenty years later, their roundtable at Cabinet was a reunion of sorts.*

Also present that day were the co-directors of Cabinet, Martin McGeown and Andrew Wheatley, who contributed to the discussion by talking about their own perspective on the work and their reasons for wanting to show it again in 2000. For his part, McGeown was fascinated by Celebration? Realife, *which he had discovered in magazines when he was a teenager, a few years after the installation was first exhibited in 1972 in Birmingham [III. 2], and then in London [III. 3, 4]. McGeown was able to speak about the installation in great detail even though he had not seen it in person. Therefore, when he and Wheatley co-founded Cabinet in 1991, both stimulated by the interactions between creative disciplines, Chaimowicz's groundbreaking post-Pop environment from 1972 was already on their radar. When Wheatley and McGeown met with the artist a few years after the gallery was founded, Chaimowicz understood the lasting impact that his installation had on another generation.*

In the mid-1990s, Chaimowicz often visited Cabinet, whose program and artistic community were appealing to him in addition to the changing name of the gallery, which, as Martin McGeown mentions, "has on occasions and continues to be called by the following names CABINET, THE CABINET, THE CABINET GALLERY, CABINET GALLERY, CABINET LONDON, depending on mood and context." However, despite mutual interest and admiration, it took eighteen months for McGeown and Wheatley, together with British curator and artist Matthew Higgs, "an invigilator of the mid 1990s" according to McGeown, to convince the artist to "revisit" his cult installation-performance piece from 1972.

When Chaimowicz eventually agreed to return to the piece, it took a while for the process to be completed. As Chaimowicz stated, "They had to reconstruct something which was partly forever lost and whose surviving components had lay dormant within cardboard boxes for 28 years." As described in Celebration? Realife Revisited *(London: Koenig Books Ltd, 2005, p. 91):*

> *"The latter version was reconstructed by the artist with the assistance of Martin McGeown and Andrew Wheatley of the Cabinet Gallery over a period of two years which involved the identification of the original lighting specifications based on documents both written and visual which the artist had retained. It also involved research through the artist's archives in order to locate many of the original contents of the piece. However it also includes a variety of elements which have been added and which are therefore specific to these particular works and date of its reconstruction. It was at this juncture that the verb 'Revisitation' was incorporated."*

There was interest and curiosity about this approach to reconstructing the work. During a trip to Dijon, Chaimowicz spoke about it to Xavier Douroux (co-director of Le Consortium, Dijon). Although the work was conceived by Chaimowicz in 1972 as a finished piece, and retired almost immediately after it was presented and thus precluding its potential future and preservation, the artist admitted that revisiting it collectively fascinated him. While describing the process and situation to Douroux, Chaimowicz emphasised the difference between "remake as collaboration, and revisitation as autonomy." Thrilled by the story and its potential, Douroux suggested that Chaimowicz revisit the

installation twice at the same time, which he did, restaging the instal-
lation and duplicating it. Re-titled Celebration? Realife Revisited
1972–2000, the two versions of the revisited installation were pre-
sented concurrently over the summer of 2000 at Cabinet, London, and
at the School of Fine Arts, Dijon (7 July–16 September, 2000) as part
of the annual program I Love Dijon, *conceived by Le Consortium.*
Two years later, two permanent collections, the FRAC Bourgogne,
Dijon, and the Migros Museum für Gegenwartskunst, Zürich, acquired
them both.

When the opportunity was given to include the interview in
Untitled, *Chaimowicz remarked that "I prefer not to take part in*
the editing but rather follow its transformative aspects, from tape
to print." Flipping through Untitled #23 *a few months later,*
Chaimowicz declared, "The illustrations are excellent!" Indeed, in
addition to the black and white juxtaposed shots of the original and
revisited installation, there was the 1973 cover of Arts & Artists
featuring the artist performing Genug Tiranney in Graz *[I. 1], as*
well as the invitation card announcing the exhibition at Cabinet,
which can be seen as a part of the revisitation of Celebration?
Realife. *During a meeting at the gallery, McGeown noticed the*
artist had a copy of Marcel Proust's Remembrance of Things
Past *in his coat pocket. Attracted by the distinctive blue and red*
fleur-de-lis motif used for so long on British dust jackets of C.K.
Scott Moncrieff's translation of Proust, McGeown immediately made
a connection with revisiting of Celebration? Realife. *After dis-*
cussing Proust together, McGeown suggested that the artist use the
same design for the invitation card of the exhibition "Celebration?
Realife Revisited 1972–2000," which Chaimowicz welcomed.
Commenting further on the collective decision to appropriate this
design, Archer wrote in Artforum, *Volume 39, no. 4, October 2000:*

> *"Nowadays Proust's title is more straightforwardly trans-*
> *lated as* In Search of Lost Time, *but Moncrieff's*

Shakespearean Remembrance of Things Past *is perhaps a more appropriate epigraph in this instance. Whatever the case, though, the revisiting of* Celebration? Realife *is a Proustian event. In making the work again after nearly thirty years, Chaimowicz has accomplished the task of pulling the past into the present rather than merely taking a retrospective look at his own history. [...] In looking back at his own work, Chaimowicz has refashioned a wholly contemporary reflection on personal and social responsibility."*

A.V.

· · · · · · · · ·

Michael Archer: *Marc, this show, which you have called "Celebration? Realife Revisited," also has a date in its title: 1972 to 2000. Are there very great differences for you between doing it now and doing it then? Is there much difference in terms of the material that you have used, for example?*

Marc Camille Chaimowicz: The differences are more perceptual than material. The title is symptomatic of a proactive working relationship that I insist on with agencies or galleries. That is perhaps why I have not shown much in London for a long time: I wasn't able to make those connections. One day when I walked into Cabinet, Andrew noticed that I was carrying a volume of Proust. Martin was then able to make connections in terms of his love of Proust, my perceived love of Proust, and the fact that we were dealing, in representing this piece, with compacted time. That led to the wonderful invitation card, which is a replication of the Proust cover with the original artwork by Enid Marx. I would love to take credit for that, but it was actually Martin's idea. I then suggested another oblique cultural reference, a word taken from Dylan's *Highway 61 Revisited*, a seminal album of that time. So there are already two implicit cultural references in the packaging of the piece.

M.A.: *You are not, then, simply looking backwards in order to recall something that happened nearly thirty years ago. What happens here is much more a Proustian pulling of the past right into the present such that this work, even though it has this history, is absolutely contemporary and is taking place right now.*

M.C.C.: Well, I hope so. It came out of quite lengthy bar room discussions between Martin, Andrew, and I. There are times in my subjectivity in which I need to reconnect with the outside world and I tend to do so almost in a Boltanski-like way, by hanging out in the shadow lands and quite often just finding things. There was a gut instinctual aspect to the original piece that I was able to reconnect with. The low culture side of the piece seemed more viable as a matter to deal with after twenty-eight years than might have been the case, say, fifteen years ago. So I think timing was critical.

M.A.: *And this low culture accumulation of things that you are refer-ring to includes things like strings of really cheap beads and masks from newsagents, Party masks.*

Carnival.

M.A.: *Glitter, fake glamour, or add-on glamour perhaps.*

Trash culture. Then as much as now there was a relatively prim-itive or at least childlike attraction, a magpie-like attraction to things that glitter. A kitsch interest, one more to do with that part of one's subjective self that maintains a sense of delight in the inci-dental. It's obviously relative to the neighbourhoods in which I hang out. In that sense it is a South East London kind of piece. Oddly enough, I think I was living in Camberwell in 1972 and I'm back in Camberwell now and I don't think Camberwell has changed very much. The very concept of the studio was anathema at that time, so the streets—notably at night—were material for the need to contest the dominant cultural values. What now has to be taken into account is how much that marginal position has gradually been acquired by the dominant culture. The piece now has a much more aesthetic feel about it. Whereas in 1972, I was self-consciously attempting to question alienation between the viewer and the maker, for example, by being present in the piece and inviting them to talk and to participate, that is no longer as necessary. At that time there was an intellectual attempt to bring a kind of caring side to art making. It was implicitly a questioning of practice. Because there has been such a cultural shift the piece paradoxically has perhaps become much more autonomous. It is now welcoming in itself rather than needing the agency of the maker.

M.A.: *One of the important elements to the installation is the way it offers elements and possible identities that are absolutely not fixed, in terms of gender, attitude, position, or whatever. An aspect to this is the way that you draw on the pop culture of the time, represented here through the CDs that are available for playing—Bowie with his androgyny, Janis Joplin having on the one hand a very aggressive, but on the other a very feminine aspect to her, the Stones, and so on. Was that very important for you at the time?*
It was, at the time there weren't any pluralistic options so one always had to make choices. I remember at art school one of the staff asking, "Does any of us work to music?" and one of the staff replying, "Well I always work to music but it's classical of course." Even there, there was a kind of hierarchy, was there not? It seemed to me that my generation was fortunate to be party to a radicality that was actually more prevalent in popular culture than in my area. Bringing in that music with its implications of, say, the drug culture, did by default annex a very wide range of youth, I suppose, who would not necessarily be particularly involved in high art however radical it may be. I think that was symptomatic of the other artists present in the context of the first showing of *Celebration? Real Life*. However immaculate the pedigree of Gustav Metzger or Stuart Brisley might have been, the implication is that they were rigorous in the sense that there was no compromise

in their position. This meant by definition that they were actually quite exclusive. By contrast my piece was quite inclusive, and music was a very good metaphor for that.

M.A.: *I am interested in the question mark in the middle of the title:* Celebration? Realife.

It's going back a long time, but typographically it is crucial. It has been kept and I think it has held its import. I presume it dealt with the dilemma that any artist has if they are attempting to step outside of normal boundaries. The moment you question the frame, as it were, that questioning could so easily cause it to implode, such that there would be no artifice left because it could so easily lead one into the literal. The piece wasn't evidently about real life, it was a fiction. It just happened that many of the constituent parts were of the everyday, but it was almost as though one was tripping without the agents, so there was a transformation. The question mark was a metaphor for that gap between art and life.

M.A.: *That's very much a part of many of the things that one finds in there: the camera as a reflective or a distancing device, the mirror, the mirror balls refracting and reflecting, and so on. One is never simply in one place within this space.*

Hopefully not. What I found very moving about Gustav's interjection at the Whitechapel conference on '70s art was that what he remembered most were the smells. Smell is perhaps the most elusive of all the senses and it is probably the least common within our practice. In an almost blind-like way he primarily recalled the smell of the heat coming from the theatre spots, the candles, and the flowers. Also, daylight was controlled in 1972 as it is in 2000, and again—except in film screenings—that's relatively rare. It is not that this piece isn't about light—there is a lot of light there— but it is artificial light, and so that again I suppose is a kind of distancing agent. Mirror globes are two a penny nowadays and they have become incorporated into mainstream youth culture, but in 1972 the only places that used them were dance halls like the Hammersmith Palais.

M.A.: *Does doing the piece now sit very comfortably for you with the other things that you are engaged in at present?*
Surprisingly so. Some things have understandably had to be reviewed. We fantasise, for example, about the technical possibility of somebody wishing to acquire the piece for their own pleasure, which would have been anathema to me in 1972. In that sense time plays its part in terms of how a work that hasn't changed all that much in the visual sense will have changed in how it's received and perceived. I think it has acquired a kind homogeneity that it lacked then. But what's been really interesting has been the problematic of reconstructing a piece from then that wasn't contained. It is evident that a maker of objects can straightforwardly summon up work from thirty years ago by making a few phone calls, whereas we had to do a lot of thinking and looking, archiving a number of relatively blurred photographs. It was a much more active mental game.

William Furlong: *I'm very interested in this process of how work travels through time, Marc. 1972 was a very particular moment that some of us have a hazy recollection of. What has changed in the meantime is what's around all this. Now we go to any art school degree show and we see installations with lights, with mirror balls, maybe with sound, with controlled lighting. The context is so very different that the kind of susceptibility, the kinds of expectations now make the work acceptable and readable. It becomes almost part of a territory of practice that's been adopted by so many. The work hasn't changed, but what surrounds it has in terms of prevailing culture and practices.*
I think that the awkwardness of the piece in 1972 is in retrospect perhaps its strength. It was problematic; people didn't know how to handle it. They didn't even know whether they were allowed to walk into the piece or not. There was no critical framework

through which to witness or enter it. At that time, if one was questioning painting or sculpture, the options tended to be dry and conceptual. Because it was so sensual and seemingly without boundaries, it was quite difficult. It was a problematic piece for the art world, and probably easier for the non-initiated who could simply enjoy it as experience.

Andrew Wheatley: I think it is its historical pedigree that actually makes it radical now. In as much as it has received such positive reaction from a very different generation of artists. Part of the excitement and revelation for us is that we brought it to two if not three generations of artists who are mid their own practice and are coming to this piece twenty-eight years later. Our knowledge of *Celebration? Realife* was mediated through art journals. At St Martins, they then had a great collection of *Studio International* and other magazines, but of course he was a figure that I wasn't necessarily aware of as someone active then in the '80s. It was that that first interested us. I think it was very important for Marc to witness someone's reaction to the work in real time, in the late '90s, and for us to argue the means by which it negotiates its way into current consciousness. Whilst we can argue the ways in which it is prescient of much that has come after it in terms of a practice that's common, I believe there are artists that have adopted its inherent formalism as a strategy, whereas that wasn't the case when Marc first showed *Celebration? Realife*. It wasn't about making strategic decisions; it was the only possible action that Marc could enact in 1972. Now I think it is its provisional nature that is almost shocking to artists who are half Marc's age.

Martin McGeown: There is a mixture of motives behind re-presenting this work, some of which are really quite selfish or subjective. I had originally encountered it in documentation maybe two or three years after the event at the same time that I began to look at art. I was also listening to music, which is in fact the music that is featured in the piece. So these interests of mine were in many ways reflected in the piece and I guess were a part of Marc's thinking. As a teenager I was unable to reconcile these interests in what we've been taught to think of as high and low culture, but here was something that was seemingly bringing them together. I have always been fascinated by the nature of documentation, especially from that period in the '70s when it was considered very important because there was so much temporary installation, performance, and conceptual art. The documentation of this piece was very rich and I guess looking at it was like looking at album covers, in that you could scrutinise them endlessly for all sorts of clues. There was always the thought, "Wow, I would really love to have seen this piece," and then you end up running a gallery and the opportunity to do so is there. It is interesting for galleries to deal with things that are really quite personal from the point of view of the gallerist. Galleries very rarely do that and curators don't either. Curators do things which are about what they think people will need to see, and dealers tend to deal with things that they think people need to own, whereas gallerists—I'm paraphrasing Dave Hickey here—are looking for the marriage of desire and esteem. It is interesting that a gallery should in that sense admit to all sorts of desires in terms of the presentation of work and that those desires are not necessarily to do with the market, or with a theoretically appropriate position that they feel they ought to adopt. Of course I believe that both those things are apparent in this work but they are there as the accidental fallout of desire.

[I. 8]

**1000 Words:
Marc Camille Chaimowicz Talks
About *Jean Cocteau*, 2003**

As told to Michael Archer

(2004)

A few days after the opening of the exhibition "Jean Cocteau," Chaimowicz received a phone call from the London-based critic and writer Michael Archer. Back from Norwich, Archer wanted to discuss the exhibition, which he had found "very interesting." The project, conceived by Chaimowicz, featured Marcel Breuer, Stephen Buckley, Enrico David, Cerith Wyn Evans, Alberto and Diego Giacometti, Tom of Finland, Isokon, Marie Laurencin, Paulina Olowska, Nadia Wallis, and Andy Warhol, and was hosted by British curator Lynda Morris at the Norwich Gallery, Norwich School of Art & Design (11 September– 25 October, 2003). Since the interview at Cabinet in 2000 [I. 7], Chaimowicz had not heard from Archer and was "quite surprised" to learn that, in addition to his interest in the Norwich exhibition, he wished to propose an article on it to Artforum. *A frequent contributor to* Artforum, *both as a writer and editorial consultant, Archer thought it appropriate to feature Chaimowicz's new work,* Jean Cocteau (2003) *in the magazine's influential "1000 words" section. Archer had to conduct an interview with the artist to gather his words, from which he would then write a text* as told by *the artist.*

"By choice and for practical reasons," recalled Chaimowicz, "the interview was done at the Royal Festival Hall, a few days after Michael's phone call." Tape-recorded, the interview was subsequently edited by Archer and emailed to the magazine, along with installation shots. The feedback was immediate. The artist said, "Michael had to fight with a proof-reader! While that person from Artforum *was trying to slick the text, Michael insisted on keeping it as close to my way of speaking as possible," which, by definition, the as-told-to format is supposed to reflect, and which, in the end, "Michael Archer quite successfully achieved."*
Introducing the "1000 words" on Jean Cocteau, *Archer wrote the following:*

"After moving from his native Paris as a boy, Marc Camille Chaimowicz spent the remainder of his youth in the some-

what less exciting surroundings of English new-town suburbia, before going on to art school. His family's move, coming as it did in the aftermath of World War II, was felt as a bizarre wrench that continues to inform his work. He now divides his time between London and Dijon. With a deep interest in France's modernist literary legacy yet equally alive to subtle shifts in the terrain of contemporary pop culture, Chaimowicz has, since the early '70s, defied straightforward categorisation in his pursuit of the beautiful. The sexually ambivalent sensibility that suffuses his environments, installations, and performances seduces the viewer into reflection and reverie. Visually rich and precisely observed, the objects and images he designs, makes, and gathers from elsewhere propose connections, set up oppositions, and trace narratives in a dense play of puzzle, metaphor, and interpretative accessibility.

*As far back as 1976 Chaimowicz paid homage to Jean Cocteau in Fade, performed at London ACME Gallery. * Complex Lighting, a faux-Cocteau backdrop, and disappearing figures referenced to the French polymath's films, particularly* Orpheus (1949). *In his current project,* Jean Cocteau, *installed at the Norwich School of Art and Design's gallery last fall and traveling to Angel Row, Nottingham, in May, Chaimowicz has furnished an imaginary apartment for the poet-filmmaker, and artist, the fortieth anniversary of whose death fell last year. Alongside his own furniture, carpets, ceramics, and sculptural structures, including a double staircase dedicated to the late critic Barbara Reise, Chaimowicz has incorporated period pieces from Breuer and Isokon together with works by Enrico David, Paulina Olowska, Tom of Finland, Cerith Wyn Evans, Warhol, Giacometti, Marie Laurencin, and others, to construct a space which is almost usable yet thoroughly dreamlike."*

Chronologically wise, this double-page article was written to coin-

cide with the first exhibition of "Jean Cocteau." However, from 2004 onwards, some of the elements that were originally featured in this museum-like installation were reshuffled [I. 11, 12]. Indeed, in addition to the queer and quasi-domestic creations of the artist permanently presented, works by other artists were not available at each presentation of the installation and had to be replaced. Among them, for example, was a portrait by Andy Warhol, which had to be loaned from a collection based in the city where the installation was presented. The two bronze lamps by the Giacometti brothers, originally part of the installation, were permanently replaced in 2004 with their colour photographs mounted on plywood.

Additionally, the dates of the piece began to incorporate the year of the installation's presentation, which was regularly exhibited and thus partly rearranged between 2004 and 2014. Therefore, when this 260 × 552 × 1012 cm installation was finally purchased by Fiorucci Art Trust in 2014, it not only gained its final title and date—Jean Cocteau... (2003–2014)—but also resolved issues of authorship and funding related to the artworks featured in the installation, including, for example, like praying (faded fax) *(2005) by Wolfgang Tillmans [II. 12].*

Both a fictional three-dimensional portrait and a "furnished interior that obliquely references [Cocteau's] poetics" as Chaimowicz put it in the text below, Jean Cocteau... (2003–2014) *flirts somewhere between the theatricality of an established yet queer figure in French literature and the reality of a famous writer, socialite, filmmaker, and artist, none of whose works were actually included in the installation. With the absence of Cocteau's work in this theatrical yet fantasy study-cum-bedroom that nevertheless references him, Chaimowicz may have represented his desire to have someone to share the illusion of reality with over time.*

** From 1976 to 1981, Acme operated from a converted banana* *warehouse in Covent Garden, London. It showed work from emerging artists, or those whose work in installation and performance was difficult to accommodate elsewhere. Chaimowicz performed* Fade *with the British editor and artist Colin Naylor (approximately fifteen minutes), on 18–19 November, 1976. As described by Jean Fisher in* Past Imperfect. Marc Camille Chaimowicz 1972–1982 *(Liverpool: Bluecoat Gallery et al., 1983, p. 16):*

> *"The piece was specifically conceived and built for the space, its structure was linear and developed through four stages. Around the room are carefully arranged matriarchal symbols: flowers, fruit, vegetables, a fountain, and a small statue of Madonna illuminated by a candle, the whole spot lit by coloured lights. In the center, against the end wall, is a large stylised line drawing of an Annunciation, framed by scaffolding and behind gauze. This is the artist's homage to Jean Cocteau (whose dynamic sprang from sexual conflicts). Towards the front of the especially erected ramp are two tastefully ornate chairs. The two performers enter to the romantic sound of Mahler's Fifth Symphony. They sit down, and then at intervals stand, walk towards the Annunciation and back again. The difference in the movement of the two figures reflects the male/female pattern running through the rest of the environment. The 'courting' finally comes to consummation with the figures entering the scaffold frame of the Annunciation. At this point, oblique light, projecting a red diagonal cross, transforms the gauze veil into an opaque screen obliterating them at their point of communion. Eventually the figures re-emerge to continue their pacing and the Annunciation is restored to view. When the performers finally leave the ramp, the gauze screen metamorphoses once more into an image of the artist, with his back to the viewer, silhouetted against the window of this studio."*

A.V.

A year ago, Lynda Morris, director of the Norwich Gallery, reminded me that in the '70s, I had taken her to one of London's best-kept secrets, a mural commissioned from Cocteau by the French for their Catholic church in London, Notre-Dame-de-France. It's a little miracle, very competent, very assured—Cocteau at his best. The project then slowly emerged through dialogue with Lynda. I'd never before developed such a complex dialectic between my own practice and the appropriation of other's people work in order to construct what is, by default, a kind of portrait. I found the experience liberating. That end wall in my installation, for example, with a Warhol, a Stephen Buckley, and the Giacometti lamps: one can stand back and exclaim with joy as to how fabulous it looks, because one's not burdened by the responsibility of one's own ego.

I accept that in France the jury is still out on Cocteau. His blatant disengagement from the body politic is problematic. He made some mistakes out of naïveté, I think. For instance, he supported the work of Arno Breker only because he was, at that point in his own career, reassessing the neoclassical. I think the ambivalence with which Cocteau was regarded had a lot to do with the fact that he came from a very well-to-do background. This would have been socially disadvantageous for someone trying to associate himself with the avant-garde. The modernist establishment—André Breton, for one—was very critical of him. It's presumed this was because of Cocteau's sexuality, but then Gide was critical of him as well, so he was forever stuck in the middle. And I think one can extend that problematic into Cocteau's practice. The work is very erratic. His painting for example, is dire. One has to recognise that, and I briefly comment on it by including artists—Buckley, Nadia Wallis—who have a real feel for painting. I like the idea of labyrinthine possibilities of interpretation and, in a way, a kind of intellectual puzzle in the project. For example, we commissioned Wallis to do a site-specific curtain painting for the show, and as we know, Cocteau was highly involved in the sociability of practice, in commissioning, in exchange, in collaboration.

We deliberated at length about which Warhol to use. Warhol evidently has a place as a kind of surrogate descendant, a symbolic distant relation of Cocteau's, and yet the "Electric Chair" is so incongruous to the Cocteau's sensibility. If nothing else, it's so American. But Cocteau did have a fascination with death. As an ambulance driver during World War I he initially saw the Belgian front as a kind of Wagnerian scenario, but seeing death for the first time, he became imbued with the reality and horror of the day-to-day. Then there was the tragic loss of his young protégé, Raymond Radiguet, which led to a physical decline in Cocteau as well as a spiritual crisis. Warhol therefore becomes more relevant. And then the eye goes, one hopes, from the "Electric Chair" on the far wall to the foreground, where on the rug there is a copy of a 1963 Warhol portrait of Cocteau commissioned by Pierre Berger for *Libération*.

In parallel to dealing with Cocteau, I'm also dealing with a subjectively loaded kind of fiction, a sort of fantasy about that which is Parisian. This has to do with the reclaiming of what I felt had been taken from me in my formative years. If somebody in his early childhood is removed from a particular cultural environment and then has to process that relatively brutal displacement, that person is liable, is he not, to fantasise? During World War II, Cocteau was advised by many of his friends to flee Paris. To his credit he said: "I am Parisian and here I'll stay," with all that that implied. He gives specificity to something that in me is nebulous and yet perpetual and powerful. It's a real pleasure to give materiality to this active inner life, to realise a fictional interior that is both a proposal for habitation and a mindscape.

The ease with which Cocteau could move from one area to another is fascinating to me, as I was educated in an art school tradition wherein something was meritorious only if it was hard-gained. He provides a bridge to the Proustian world of the salon, and yet toward the end of his life he's not just helping out gutter angels like Piaf, he's also fascinated by somebody like Jean Genet, partly because Genet could do what he could never do in writing, which is to be explicit. There's a kind of disappointment, is there not, in what Cocteau did and what we presume him to have done. He was the reverse of the bland figures behind the sophisticated and coherent practices we encounter today. In his case, the persona was more resolved, refined, and complete than the results.

Interview with Marc Camille Chaimowicz

Jackie Hatfield

(2004)

In 2003, British video artist Stephen Partridge, then Professor of Media Art and Associate Dean of Research & Enterprise at the Duncan of Jordanstone College of Art & Design, University of Dundee, submitted a proposal to the Arts and Humanities Research Council outlining plans to locate, digitise, and preserve British artists' video from the 1970s and 1980s. Working closely with LUX (the UK's largest collection of films and videos made by artists with over 5000 works from the 1930s to the present day) and FACT (the UK's leading organisation for the support and exhibition of art, film, and new media), Partridge, Jane Prophet (co-investigator, 2004–05), and the late Jackie Hatfield (project researcher) launched "REWIND: British Artists' Video of the 1970s and 1980s" in 2004, warning of the danger that "many of the films and videos from the 1970s and 1980s might disappear because of their poor technical condition and obsolescence." At the time, their aim was "to address the gap in historical knowledge of the evolution of electronic media arts in the UK." To do so, they decided to recover and restore the earliest tapes, conduct interviews, and collect ephemera associated with seminal works. At the same time, REWIND assembled written documentation on the history of each work, seeking ways to exhibit the artworks once they were preserved and documented. Based in Scotland at Duncan of Jordanstone College of Art & Design, University of Dundee, this research project lasted four years (2004–08). Supervised by Partridge, REWIND collected 450 single screen works and documentation of installation works, which were remastered on Digital Betacam and as high-quality files on disk, and subsequently made available for future research. From the beginning of this project, the artists approached to participate were selected by the project team and by an advisory group of influential artists. Most of the artists solicited agreed to be video interviewed. The filmed interviews were subsequently transcribed and posted online. Today, these video interviews (some of which are audiotaped only) and transcripts are available online via the REWIND database section.

Early in the process, Dr Jackie Hatfield contacted Chaimowicz for an interview. Hatfield, who passed away in 2007, was at the time a renowned young British researcher and academic specialising in "Expanded Cinema." As a member of the REWIND team, Hatfield was convinced that Chaimowicz's luminous and pragmatic insights into performance, video, community, and collaboration in the UK in the 1970s would help encode the fledgling research platform. She travelled to Hayes Court, the artist's home in Camberwell, London, and interviewed "Marc C Chaimowicz" on 21 November, 2004 about performance and video in the UK at the turn of the 1980s. Tape-recorded, this was one of the first interviews conducted as part of REWIND.

At that time, Chaimowicz's work was gaining momentum throughout Europe. Indeed, Celebration? Realife Revisited *(1972–2000) was regularly exhibited and attracted much attention.* Partial Eclipse, *the artist's final performance from 1981 [III. 8] was revived that year at Galerie Giti Nourbakhsch, Berlin. And* Jean Cocteau *[I. 8; II. 12], which was exhibited that year in Nottingham, marked an important step in the recognition of the artist's unique approach to curating and curated portraits.*

The interview was subsequently made available online, including a link to its transcription. Reproduced below, this transcript has been slightly edited for readability, brevity, and clarity by Hatfield together with the artist. For editorial reasons, several questions were removed from the transcript, as they seemed redundant to the artist's responses. This transcript is divided into four parts. First, the artist talks about performance and video in the 1970s. Second, he explains notions of community and collaboration in the context of the 1970s, including his role as a performance reporter with Studio International *[II. 1, 2, 3, 4, 5, 6]. Third, he discusses the traditional institutional boundaries that loosened in the late 1970s in relation to new interests and ideas. Finally, he concludes with a discussion about interdisciplinarity, which helped reshape part of the cultural landscape at the turn of the 1980s. Conducted twenty-five years after the time depicted, the interview provides additional context to Chaimowicz's written chronicles and critical texts, collected in the second part of this publication. In retrospect, the artist conveys the pervasive atmosphere of dissolution that characterised the 1970s, while capturing the essence of a period when he distanced himself from both performance and performance writing.*

A.V.

· · · · · · · · ·

Marc Camille Chaimowicz: There was one piece for example involved—actually anchored in video—a video dependent piece, which I seem to recall being shown at the Biennale des jeunes artistes in Paris. So what is that? That's a kind of institutional context. And then there was a video, an autonomous video piece that was shown, I think at '78 at the Hague Annual within part of an installation. So that again is an institution. So there were either institutions or else festivals and in the late '70s, I started working with the private sector with a gallery, the Nigel Greenwood Gallery and a number of works would have been shown there. In Italy, i.e. the Cavallino, was kind of unique in a sense because Gabriella ran the gallery program but Paolo, her brother, was highly engaged, and I suspect still is, he works exclusively in video, so there was a parallel activity going on within the walls of the Cavallino Gallery in Venice. So although it was the private sector and I think that Paolo wasn't remotely interested in dealing with art or making money from art, he was essentially somebody highly engaged and committed to video based practice and happened to work from within the private sector but it felt more like a Foundation, really, because it wasn't profit driven. So I guess those will be the three areas.

You see, this is very interesting because earlier on I talked a bit about, in my mind, the highly enlightened, editorial engagement of Richard Paul in the 1970s when he took over the editorship of *Studio International*. Richard did two things; first he decided he would run a number of thematic issues, a number of which have become great reference work in their own right. That was pretty unusual and I suspect in retrospect still remains unique in terms of you know *Art Monthly*, *International Art* magazine in that each magazine, each issue was devoted to a specific issue. He was also quite committed to what I suppose would then have been known as "New Activities" or "Experimental Work" or whatever, anything that wasn't painting and/or sculpture. So, I think he felt as a good journalist would, that his audience needed to be sensitised to radical practice and so part of that procedure would have been in terms of devoting a whole issue to performance art for example or a whole issue to video art. Both of those issues are now seen as reference points. But then in parallel to that, that would have been a features part of the magazine, there was also a "review" section and in the "review" section he decided that there should be a regular column, written by specialists in these new fields on the basis that most critics and most journalists simply didn't have the grassroots understanding of what the issues were or even who the people were or where the action took place. A lot of it was alternative underground or, you know, emergent. As I recall he invited I think four or five people to each run this monthly column. Video was rightly run by David Hall, Malcolm Le Grice in Experimental Film, Michael Neiman did Experimental Music, I did Performance.

Jackie Hatfield: *So performance and video tended to be very closely linked?*
I can imagine, yes. It also, in a sense, it wasn't as alienating, it wasn't as butch as film would have been then because film was as we all recall was very ... seemed very technical. And also it was more expensive with the exception of ... I mean that's perhaps one

of the reasons why David Larcher was so fascinating, was that he had a kind of lightness of touch and kind of autonomy in terms of how he redefined his own usage of presumably what we would view was 16mm, then he was processing it himself which I found very painterly and there would be a whole reel of Larcher where there was almost no recognisable element which would then be countered by the whole reel of documentary-like work. So I think that the slow time base of his work gave him a kind of breadth that was untypical but ordinarily, you are absolutely right, I would have found film too cumbersome.

So Marc, could you talk about where the fixed boundaries were coming from, because you talked earlier about the fact that there were these kind of institutional boundaries that the artworks and the artists were working across. So could you talk about where were those boundaries coming from?

Well it would seem to me that they were primarily originating in the academies, in the art schools. I mean until the mid-1970s students had to make choices from the very outset so you would apply to do a first degree to the School of Painting or the School of Sculpture. The art schools inherently also perpetuated a kind of hierarchy of values which now would seem to us absurd, in which the noble art of "painting" was at the very top of the apex and the humble craft based practices, the applied arts, as in the department of ceramics or textile for example, was at the bottom of the pile. There was also an implicit gender divide whereby the applied arts would tend to be peopled by female students, and painting and sculpture by male students. But the hierarchy was so ineptly rigid that if you were perceived as a very gifted young student then you were presumed to go off and study painting, if you were not quite so fine or sensitive perhaps a little more manually minded then you would be sent off to carve stone or whatever, thus to study sculpture. So the institution was largely responsible, the institution, the Academy was largely responsible for perpetuating those rigid kinds of categories. But beyond that in terms of the world of the museum for example, likewise, there would be the curator of painting, the curator of sculpture. Then within that, within those autonomous fields of practice there'd be further sub-divisions whereby there'd be forever a kind of mistrust and a climate of rivalry between, for example, figurative painting versus abstract painting. Then within that there'd be further categories between, say, romantic kind of figuration, which was derivative of say Delacroix—I could have included somebody like Francis Bacon who was opposite the Expressionists and then the kind of Neo-Classic's tradition of figurative painting from Paul Cézanne through to Sir William Coldstream. It actually meant that the creative potential, which is probably inherent in most students and can come through in an artist able to master their own relative freedom of practice as with say Picasso or Matisse or Bonnard, they are actually bobbing about between earthenware, painting, sculpture, collage, and graphic work, you know. I mean there has been some great graphic work done by any number of these people but graphics was again seen as a lower art form. But I think that, ironically perhaps, even within the field of, within the hopefully more enlightened area of say video there would have been inevitably a kind of conscious or otherwise perpetuation of those kinds of categorisations, so there'd be the purists and there'd be the romantics and there'd be the structuralists and the others. There'd be someone like Sally Potter, say, who was interested in narrative and would have had to find a different field, in which to work, which happened in her case to be experimental cinema.

What about art and language and a little bit about how some artists would not be seen to write because art and writing are separate?
Of course that's absolutely true. Writing was, I mean even within the English formal, within the kind of post Coldstream tradition which, I suppose, held its kind of gods Kossoff or Auerbach in which, you know, you did kind of suffer, perpetuate the work

ethic and so there'd be myths, there'd be these great myths that spread within the activity, wherein Auerbach maybe had one day's holiday per year. The idea which would have been, I suppose, disapproved of and seen as prone to a kind of Parisian sort of dilettantism really, you know the kind of dandy-like figure of Charles Baudelaire, for example, who happened to be a regular prose writer and brilliant critic, nonetheless in England that was highly disapproved of, you had to commit yourself fully to one area of activity and you are either fully engaged in the subjective nature of making work, or in the so called objective nature of critiquing work, and so you cannot be both a critic and a maker. It wasn't until Art & Language, for example, that the implicit dialectic between the two was recognised wherein they would propose that theory was practice and practice could be theory. So I would say that between them there was probably a greater body of radical questioning and re-evaluation between say '72 and '82 than maybe any other decade. A very wide range of criteria was being questioned.

So what happened in the UK where suddenly—in the 1960s—you get this kind of polarity?
Well yes, it's a good point. Someone like Brian Eno for example, who is even now highly regarded by people a lot younger as someone who is critically, culturally quite aware, I think suffered quite a lot from being seen as dilettante because he was working between pop music, i.e. popular culture and highbrow practice, i.e. experimental music, and intermittently wished to promote himself as a visual artist with his light box installations. He was very involved in theory and cybernetics and very interested in sciences. In a way he is a kind of very good example of the kind of universalist. But that's always been disapproved of as I think maybe there is a kind of Protestantism perhaps. I mean we know England is not a Catholic culture, and I think it does mistrust someone who, they would either see as dilettante or a jack-of-all-trades and both imply

the presumption that you have to fully devote yourself to one thing, you know, you have to focus in. I think that's presumably a kind of manifestation of the work ethic which is inherently quite puritanical and it would nonetheless engage a very wide range of people who may, for example, wish to redress the dichotomy between work and life, or, i.e. between the professional and the private or the domestic and the professional or whatever. And so, you know, that's why to our generation we were so awestruck by Joseph Beuys who had elegance and fluidity in his ability to move from botanic and the natural sciences to sculpture and on to politics and sociology. He was very engaged with say the Green Party, one of the founding members of the Green Party, so he is engaged also in environmental issues, and yet he is in parallel almost kind of organically and inherently engaged in making the most beautiful watercolours and drawing and objects and installations. So there is a project, a Beuysian project that is almost free of boundary, some kind of antithesis to the earlier model. Whether or not the work is accessible or meaningful or important it was, I think, to a number of people in the 1970s a kind of revelation. Because as you say it wasn't unique, I mean it was actually a reassessment and a way of perpetuating a continuum that went right back to the turn of the century, in a way, to Duchamp.

But even then, you know, we mustn't forget that institutions are forever resistant for all kinds of reasons wherein they don't have either the will or therefore the need to recognise that kind of, that kind of fluidity. So given that the canon of art history doesn't recognise that those ways of working by default will remain seen as marginal.
But then you see in those days the term "performance" didn't exist. They were called events or happenings, from Kaprow you know. And I was also working with things. I was placing things in terms of reassessing how to work with the real rather than to transcribe to real through a camera or through a brush. I was actually

dealing with… I was bringing matter into the work. And we used to call those environments and then they later became known as installations. But then it took only about ten years for those activities to become in their own manner increasingly institutionalised. So you got art schools running performance modules and you got the word installation becoming a kind of passé party in terms of publishing silly books on. So again the problem we'd highlighted earlier on in terms of how formalism insidiously can appropriate a very wide range of work re-emerges on a kind of regular basis and so some, the term installation is by default absurd, it means nothing at all and yet it's now a kind of …

Norm?
A norm, yes.

And a medium in itself.
That's right; it's become a medium, a force in itself. But that would have been why I was drawn to time-based work. Well I have to say that I was never all that happy in that way of working. I mean intellectually it seemed the right way to work, I am glad I did what I did and hopefully there is one or two pieces that may've been of some, of some worth. But temperamentally I'll always find ploys wherein I was showing my back to the audience or to the camera or working in darkness with the use of slides, I wasn't extrovert enough to really enjoy that kind of "look-at-me" nature of much of that work. So it was a kind of relief to move away from it after about ten years.
So, I think in that sense community remains kind of urgent. But then of course it led me to question the premise of collaboration but I found that more so in terms of skills, really, whereby I enjoyed working with industrialists or with carpenters, or with cabinet makers, or with people who can make things for me because I am actually working with their skills rather than attempting to do what they do better than myself. So that's another kind of com-

munity I suppose but that still implies dialogue. Which is maybe more to do with materials than ideas. So, I suppose, dialogue is something that we kind of, we all directly or indirectly yearn for is it not; really cultural practice is about dialogue, is it not? Even if it may just be a dialogue between two colours. So I think that certainly the video work was very often looking at those questions, certainly questioning the dialogue between the maker and the viewer.

A Certain Simplicity of Means, True Luxury of Life: 7 Questions For Marc Camille Chaimowicz

Catherine Wood

(2006)

Domeniek Ruyters, editor-in-chief of Metropolis M, invited
Chaimowicz to be interviewed by a person of his choice for the
magazine. Ruyters was intrigued by Chaimowicz's recent projects,
including "Jean Cocteau" in Norwich [I. 8] and "MARC CAMILLE
CHAIMOWICZ" at the Kunstverein für die Rheinlande und
Westfalen, Düsseldorf (11 September–6 November, 2005), and he
was eager to contextualise the forthcoming presentation of the artist's installation Celebration? Realife Revisited 1972–2002
[I. 7] as part of the group exhibition "Raw, Among the Ruins,"
which I co-curated with Dutch curator and professor Lisette Smits
at Marres, Utrecht (11 March–20 May, 2007). To further support
his invitation, Ruyters mentioned to the artist that this interview
would be an opportunity to announce his recently confirmed large-
scale exhibition at De Appel, Amsterdam [I. 11]. Usually resistant
to this type of publication, Chaimowicz hesitated. He had experienced a kind of harassment in Zürich where someone claiming to
work for Tema Celeste, he said, "was desperately texting me stupid
questions," the day after the opening of his exhibition "Zürich Suite"
(8 April–11 June, 2006) at the Migros Museum für Gegenwartskunst
[III. 22]. At that time Chaimowicz thought that he needed a break
from the press. However, considering Ruyter's invitation in relation
to his future exhibition in Amsterdam, he decided to participate,
believing that Catherine Wood would be the right person for it,
which "she gladly accepted." Wood was the Curator of Contemporary
Art and Performance at Tate Modern, London, and a frequent contributor to Artforum and frieze. She had recently published "an
excellent text" in the monograph produced for the exhibition "MARC
CAMILLE CHAIMOWICZ" in Düsseldorf [I. 16] and was therefore
up to date with the artist's projects. Chaimowicz was sure that an
interview with Wood would take place under "civilised conditions."

In September 2006, Wood travelled to interview the artist at his
home in Hayes Court, Camberwell, London. Sitting in the living
room, their meeting took place, as expected, in "civilised conditions."

Recorded on tape, the discussion was then transcribed by Wood and mailed to Chaimowicz, who gave the green light by phone a few days later. Finally, Wood emailed the text to Ruyters who thanked her in return. However, when the artist received a complimentary copy of the magazine in the mail, he was surprised to discover that not only were two different shots from 1977 of the artist in Approach Road juxtaposed on the cover like a vintage collage, but also that the interview was framed by the issue's theme: "Comeback."

To contextualise her "Seven questions for Marc Camille Chaimowicz," Wood wrote a two-paragraph introduction that read:

> *"Marc Camille Chaimowicz's extensive body of work from the past thirty or more years inhabits a variety of forms: from oil paintings to performance tableaux to environments that include adapted furniture and fabrics of his own design. Chaimowicz's installations occasionally incorporate carefully placed found objects that draw upon the tradition of still-life painting and integrate text, photography or slide projections within these sculptural arrangements.* Approach Road, *produced from 1975–79, was a major project developed in the artist's East End home and studio that experimented with a synthesis of the realms of art and domestic life. Early work such as* Celebration? Realife *staged at Gallery House, South Kensington in 1972 was radical in its presentation of what appeared to be the scattered detritus from a party as a form of installation and involved the live presence of the artist who slept in one of the rooms and invited visitors to join him for coffee and discussion.*
>
> *Making—in the form of painting, sculpture and design—has always been central to Chaimowicz's practice. But in distinction to the gestural and explicitly masculine work ethic of abstract and expressionist painting prevalent during his formative years as an art student in London, he deliberately chose*

not to separate out the working process and the art object from the processes and objects of everyday life. Approach Road *represented for Chaimowicz both a living space that offered essential solitary retreat, and an ongoing work in its own right; giving the artist the space to formalise ordinary aspects of everyday life, at the same time as dissolving the boundaries of 'fine art' to embrace the 'feminised' realms of applied art and interior design. In the intervening thirty years, Chaimowicz's body of work has accumulated gradually and has been consistently re-ordered in a manner that perpetuates a bittersweet dialogue between past and present. Chaimowicz continues to reject art as a privileged and separate sphere, treating the decorative potential of art as a form of camouflage necessary to his survival as much as it is a pleasurable aesthetic 'flourish' laced through everyday activity."*

Among the illustrations Wood and Chaimowicz selected for the magazine was a rarely seen 1998 shot of the artist's studio at The British School in Rome. As in a still life, several small papier-mâché sculptures rest on the artist's worktable amidst tools and papers. Behind a long lily flower hangs crafted paintings of varied sizes, each inch of which is filled with unexpected turns and a richness of detail that unifies the nature of their contents. Finally, a shelf holds a few publications next to which are small sculptures covered with newspaper and painted over.

A.V.

• • • • • • • • •

Catherine Wood: *Your work grafts the space of dreaming or fiction —the imagination—with practical reality, as is epitomised by the way in which you have decorated your house and the simplicity of your approach to certain things I have noticed: you have screen printed your own wallpaper, your phone number is listed in the telephone directory, you take the bus (even when—as was the case before your recent performance in* Partial Eclipse—*the Tate offers you a taxi!)*

Marc Camille Chaimowicz: A certain simplicity of means may afford me the true luxury of time! … and it is perhaps because I am prone to reverie that I all the more seek some anchorage with the external world … taking the 36 bus can rudely bring one down to earth! This "grafting of fiction with reality" is perhaps a sophist device … what led to a conscious domestic aesthetic began in the pictorial—from concept—as a means by which to negotiate that which is unpalatable, or indeed vulgar about the everyday—and resulted, in loop form, towards a new reality … which became my home and in turn a catalyst and a resource for work.

One of your earliest exhibitions was held in the luxury department store, Liberty's, on Oxford Street in a show called "Four Rooms" with Howard Hodgkin, Richard Hamilton, and Anthony Caro. It seems to me that there was a real logic to your work in this context that maybe was not relevant for the other artists, with the possible exception of Hamilton. Are you comfortable to trace a trajectory that links this moment to your recent decision to participate in a feature about your home in The World of Interiors*?*

Having earlier worked on textile designs—as a way of questioning implicit hierarchical values, which relegate the applied arts to a lowly order—this was a timely project. I nonetheless recall certain reservations regarding Liberty's; with its house style and the Arts and Crafts legacy … which Paul Nash has cryptically identified as suffering from "a certain Medieval malaise" … I was however thrilled, through the aegis of the Arts Council, to have the opportunity to extend maquettes, notably for furniture, to that of the functional prototype as well as realising fabric for Warner and wallpaper for Coles.

More recently, conceding to a photo shoot by James Mortimer, the doyen and, with Min Hogg co-founder of that illustrious magazine, was irresistible! I did not so much participate, however, as surrender and feel somewhat distant to the result … which feels like elsewhere … but given that in the symbolic act of giving one is then freed of the gift as a process of formalisation it may the better enable me to distance myself from the risk of atrophy … finally, if one is to summarily venture on occasion onto the "high street," it is probable that it will be towards High End … and it has in each case been illuminating to measure viability according to criteria set outside of art world practice.

Your engagement with ideas of "hospitalit" and participation was evident in your practice in works such as Celebration? Realife *in the 1972 Gallery House exhibition in South Kensington well before these ideas became familiar in contemporary art practice through the work of those artists who have been characterised in terms of "relational aesthetics." Do you see any common ground between your work and the practice of that generation of artists, i.e. Liam Gillick, Rirkrit Tiravanija, and others?*

One cannot now imagine how parochial the London art scene was in the 1970s … there was a barrage of conservative and often reactionary values to contest. It would seem that an agenda, which I hope to have helped establish, has gained some critical currency and in this sense my work sits more easily in the current climate … as if then one can but try to forward key questions …

London is now more internationalist and aware and I enjoy much work from emerging generations … though fraught with risk I remain taken by the premise of collaboration, both directly and in proxy, as can occur with exhibition orchestration or when curating or commissioning the work of others, as with *Jean Cocteau* and, more recently, working with young artists in France.

Jean Fisher wrote: "As the sentimental nature of many of the objects provoked a sense of the residue of an attachment—discarded or half-remembered feelings—so their scattered arrangement on the floor suggested the residue of pleasure, a party abandoned, or the memory of childhood play, or the street bric-a-brac of a Parisian flea market." [Jean Fisher, "Celebration? Realife" in Past Imperfect. Marc Camille Chaimowicz, 1972–1982, (Liverpool: Bluecoat Gallery et al., 1983, p.9)] *The interplay between past and present is a strong theme in your work. I noticed recently that you had made a series of objects when you were on a residency in Rome that comprised ordinary things covered over with layers of newspaper so as to form miniature sculptures that were both formal objects and miniature documents of the time—even the specific day—on which they were made. Would you agree that these illuminate your practice in the sense that making objects always involves some kind of "fossilisation" of the present that works against the "practice of everyday life" in a lived sense? How do you deal with that perpetual tension?*

For me the fulcrum, when at the British School at Rome, was that of existing in suspended time and mostly outside of language. Housed and fed, I was free from "the practice of everyday life." Its very location is removed from the heartbeat of the city … a daily ritual became that of drifting, and in the manner of urban beach combing … of finding detritus. Some were then qualified, perhaps in the manner of "journals." It was most perceptive of you to have identified that which seems to me not fully formed … they have not been shown, their status is ambiguous; the mute becoming anecdotal … their destiny is perhaps ideally to be held in the palm of one's hand, as is found treasure.

Gender is complicated in your work: you have spoken of the idea of "decorative" arts being associated with the feminine as opposed to the "heroic" tradition of expressionist painting—but you are always drawn to these complications, to "grey half-tones" rather than black and white, male-female. In what way is this a political attitude?

But surely, from the moment we query inherited values, gender is complicated! And the one certainty is that it is hardly black and white … because that polarity is both archaic and redundant … In *Tenderness* (1973), a participatory project with pupils from Highbury Girls School with whom I later travelled to Rugby Boys School, the artist was extending the questioning of gender issues to that of class … how successful, however, is a moot point! I can nonetheless recall that these two events were examples of experiments in use as attempts to make some sense through practice… The dilemma and challenge is how to deal with issues partially rooted in the socio-political realm whilst avoiding the piousness and dogma of "political art", which in itself can veer back towards a certain patriarchal tyranny. The review of gender stereotypes was central to *Table Tableau* (1974) that proposed a static image of vulnerability and lament, the embodiment of passivity and thus demasculinised … Arising from critique, this work had grown feeling constricted by values inherent in the dominant culture… Although hopefully visually eloquent and accompanied by a commissioned violin soundtrack the piece was mute yet, in retrospect, perhaps prefaced *Partial Eclipse* (1980) in which the protagonist acquires a voice by which to articulate (his) subjectivity and muse upon a relationship—a subject itself then outside of the masculine norm. *Table Tableau* had, in one version, been re-enacted as a private ritual by which to initiate *Approach Road* (1975–79) which in turn attempted to reclaim the once considered peripheral or minor spheres of the domestic and the decorative. This nourished a subsequent repertoire of work including *Partial Eclipse* … Built on a conditional dilettantism, paradox became the creative method, ambiguity its means. Inclusive and built on the conscious choice of diversification … it was perhaps an oblique means with which to redress negatively biased gendered sensibility?

Your furniture pieces such as Desk on Decline *or* Arch *appear to me as hieroglyphic forms that propose an alternative mode of living.*

To what extent were you designing these objects so as to be able to live with them, in a personal sense, and to what extent are they sculptures that are to do with representing your aesthetic?
Arch was once intrinsic to the furbishment of my sitting room in *Approach Road*. As well as indexing history and implying mental travel its role was perhaps to query function. The date, in that it has both a functional and a non-functional mode (rendered manifest when exhibited) negotiates this duality ... it was conceived at a time when I was attempting to work with text and therefore as metaphor for the condition implicit to that practice.

You have spoken of there being periods of more visibility and less visibility for your work throughout your career: What has this meant for your practice?
Beyond involuntary moments in which other facets of one's life take priority ... and which can in themselves in turn also nourish practice. Self-elected periods of withdrawal and reflection can refresh ... especially so if crafting a practice on the subjective—as was the case with *Approach Road*. The dynamic of stopping in order to move forward can generate insight ... what is later required is to formalise these towards a certain possible autonomy.

"…In the Cherished Company of Others…" by Marc Camille Chaimowicz: A New Work Is a Retrospective, of Sorts

Dan Fox

(2008)

A few days after seeing the group exhibition "Paris-London: Le Voyage Intérieur" in January 2006, Ann Demeester, then the Director of De Appel, Amsterdam, called me to talk about it. Impressed by the show's focus on contemporary decadence after Joris-Karl Huysmans' novel À Rebours *(Against Nature, 1884), which I co-curated with the British curator Alex Farquharson at Espace Electra / EDF-Foundation, Paris (15 November, 2005–5 March, 2006), Demeester suggested I think about developing a project at De Appel "based on the one in Paris." I thought of Chaimowicz immediately. Firstly, the dialogue initiated with the artist around the preparation of the exhibition "Paris-London: Le Voyage Intérieur" in which several of his works were presented, was far from over. Secondly, I was convinced that the design of his fictional interior for* Jean Cocteau *(2003) [I. 8]—"a proposal for habitation and a mindscape," as the artist put it—could be extended and expanded. To discuss this further, I met Chaimowicz in London in early May 2006.*

Chaimowicz had reserved a table for two in a wonderfully labyrinthine private club in Soho, located in a black brick mansion where daylight barely penetrates. Over zucchini flowers and white wine, he described his roles in Jean Cocteau *(2003): simultaneously art director, stage designer, visual artist, and curator. Echoing this, it seemed appropriate that in addition to a selection of works by him, numerous architectural models and artworks made by a select group of artists whom Chaimowicz felt synergy with might be presented together. Fearful of retrospectives, he said:*

> *"There's something that increasingly worries me about major solo retrospectives. They seem kind of false because the implication is that the work emerged from a complete vacuum as if the external world does not exist … I think in that sense the title '…In the Cherished Company of Others…' hopefully implies that, although we might choose to court solitude to a high degree, we should never find ourselves fetishising the sadness of isolation, conceptual or otherwise."*

With this in mind, the group of artists selected for the exhibition was as follows: Richard Artschwager, Atelier E.B, Nairy Baghramian, Joseph Beuys, Tom Burr, James Lee Byars, Enrico David, Émile Guy, Michael Krebber, Jason Meadows, Clémence Meunier, Jozef Peeters, Loïc Raguénès, Gerrit Thomas Rietveld, Elsa Schiaparelli, Lily van der Stokker, and Amikam Toren. Presented over three floors, the exhibition included a modified rear entrance using an unknown ancient spiral staircase with a thin metal handrail repainted in tangerine colour by the artist. This exhibition, both a group show and a survey exhibition, was the last to be presented in the historic building of De Appel in Nieuwe Spiegelstraat, Amsterdam (5 July–7 September, 2008), after which it toured at the Mu.Zee, Ostende (28 September–15 December, 2008).

Curious about the project, the British writer, musician, and frieze *editor Dan Fox was keen to speak with Chaimowicz. Having worked with him before, Fox was aware that the artist had no computer, so the best way to reach him was by post. Fox wrote a letter to the artist introducing the "questionnaire" he intended to publish in* frieze. *Always interested in Fox's projects, Chaimowicz replied to him promptly, and invited him to Hayes Court, in Camberwell, London, to discuss this "questionnaire" further. When Fox walked in the apartment, Chaimowicz noticed, "Dan was affected by the domestic environment." Initially surprised, the artist recalled that a few years earlier, "Dan had written a text in part about this apartment without seeing it directly," which might explain why the interior of this apartment seemed so uncanny. Entitled "Close Watch," this text by Fox that was published in* frieze, *no. 88 (January / February 2005), deciphers the artist's yearning for a place never lived in but rather dreamt of.*

Following Fox's distracted entrance into Chaimowicz's home, they both sat down in the artist's iconic canary yellow and red kitchen and immediately began discussing the exhibition in Amsterdam. Their conversation lasted several hours and was recorded on a voice recorder. Once the discussion was transcribed, Fox thought they needed to continue. They met again, but "this time more briefly!" said Chaimowicz. When the second transcript was complete, Fox mailed it to the artist, who annotated it and sent it back to him. Upon receiving it, Fox called the artist and asked questions that resulted in a third draft. With a looming deadline, they both met in Central London to finalise the text together, yet they had so much to share that day that the transcript proved impossible to complete. Close to the deadline, Fox hastily emailed the fourth draft of the interview to frieze, *and the "questionnaire" was finally published in the "Features" section, which included the following endnote: "Marc Camille Chaimowicz spoke to Dan Fox."*

It is this version that is reproduced below. Hand-annotated by Marc Camille Chaimowicz and partially edited by Dan Fox together with the artist, the fourth draft that was passed on to frieze *in 2008 remains unpublished to this day. This text in limbo, as Marc Camille Chaimowicz presupposes, might be today "located on Dan's external hard-drive, probably in the same condition as it was in 2008…"*

A.V.

•••••••••

Dan Fox: *How does "…In the Cherished Company of Others…" relate to your earlier work?*

Marc Camille Chaimowicz: That's a big question, but the negotiation of an answer is a metaphor for my working method and that's why it's interesting. The choice I made from the early 1980s to tentatively establish a broad arena within which things might get made has enabled me to develop a wide vocabulary both in terms of issues and materials to work with. I'm working more closely to the way writers might in that they establish certain parameters of sensibility and then elaborate new work to look at different aspects of their central concern. Notably, someone like Gustave Flaubert, who entrusted his sensibility to that which he knew well, which, therefore, meant he wouldn't really step outside of it. Some of his works may deal with the specificity of revolutionary France but he would still site his provincial bourgeoisie within that revolutionary moment, so there is continuity. Establishing my sensibility by questioning self-censorship was quite a radical gesture at the time because it was frowned upon and seen as dilettantism. It went against the morality of the period which was based on terms like "commitment" and "rigour"—which is such an ambiguous word and yet has been a key term for such a long time that it features in probably every art school report ever—but which can actually be tyrannical and constrictive. "…In the Cherished Company of Others…" at De Appel is a retrospective of sorts but a very associative one that includes the work of other artists, such as Richard Artschwager, Tom Burr, Michael Krebber. When reconfigured for the Mu.ZEE in Ostend it will also index the museum itself designed by Gaston Eysselinck and built in the 1950s. Inevitably there may be misunderstandings and surprises arising. It's seemingly the case with something like the De Appel show where the exhibition can become the work even though, in terms of its constituent parts, it might largely be a question of re-presenting any number of pre-existent pieces. What is specific, therefore, is the choreography between works. An implicitly slow time base exists within my work, so there's a built-in, perpetual reassessment. There's a term the French have, *la boucle*, which means "the belt" but has more resonance in French, implying a circularity. To give a specific example, I'm thrilled to have been invited to do a solo show at the Vienna Secession next year. This gives me a fifteen month lead-in time, but more to the point, beyond the august tradition the Secession has, it may also solicit a response that takes into account the fact that I was living there twenty years ago, and is likely to produce a project that will have, in all probability, a twenty to twenty-five year time base. In my book *Café du*

Rêve (1985) there's a chapter entitled "Letter from Vienna," and I'm thinking that it might be interesting as a kind of solipsistic exercise to answer, two decades later, my own letter. Of course, whether I will actually show work from that period is still open to question.

Who, if anyone, commissioned the work, and how did the context it was to be exhibited in influence its creation?
The mechanics of the invitation came from the curator Alexis Vaillant, who I worked with on two previous occasions. I presume that the director of De Appel, Ann Demeester, prefers to invite guest curators—although I can't be certain. Anyhow, Alexis contacted me. As a result of conversations I'd had with him, we first thought of doing the show in three parts, with each part probably being autonomous within each of the three floors of De Appel. We then thought it would be interesting to contextualise my work, which isn't that well-known in the Netherlands, with key pieces from the early to mid-twentieth century "golden age" of Dutch architecture and design through furniture and architectural maquettes. Then we thought we'd bring in other artists, but the floor plan changed in that we chose not to use the top floor, which is awkward. This made the project more compact. From that we thought it would be more interesting for us and more vital for the viewer to integrate works by others throughout the project. We proposed a different route from De Appel's problematic entranceway via a charming eighteenth century spiral back staircase, which was colour-coded by painting in a soft peachy orange the handrail that led people upstairs. We gave ourselves two weeks and forfeited some possible space, which we preferred to hold in reserve, simply to store excess work that we may or may not have had the need to call upon.

How long did the work take to complete?
This relates to the earlier issue of how one defines a work and how it evolves over time. At De Appel we included *Jean Cocteau*, built into which is an implied protocol that changes and mutates

with each showing, partly for logistical reasons but also because it makes it that much more vital to reconstruct. The piece was originally shown at Norwich Art Gallery in 2004, and came out of a very informal conversation with Lynda Morris. She reminded me that I'd talked of Cocteau with her many years ago. I'd actually taken her to see work by him and had then elaborated on my interest, which in retrospect was to do with how B-list people can be more interesting than A-list. Although Cocteau is a highly thought of figure I guess I'd been drawn to him in an intuitive way by the fact that he pre-dates great *bricoleurs* such as Andy Warhol, so I was more attracted to him as a symbol of a certain sensibility than by the actual work he produced; the fact that he was able to apparently effortlessly pop about from one practice to another seems like a commitment on his part that he would have been penalised for by the dominant figures around. He was socially very active and had the broadest address book, which I found intriguing. He was close to Jean Genet but also to Winston Churchill, Coco Chanel, and Elsa Schiaparelli—that's very Warholian. So from that Lynda and I picked up a conversation we'd had twenty years before and I suggested we might investigate the possibility of doing a kind of portrait in absence of any of the work by the person being portrayed. That was the point at which the work became more malleable. That is, of course, consciously recognised by the fourth showing of *Jean Cocteau*, at De Appel, now perhaps a microcosm of the whole show in that it is self-contained as "a work" with its own guest-list of artists.

Did the work change during the making of it?
The principle of any given project is to establish that element of chance, to a certain extent, which happens when working with others. What was interesting in Amsterdam was not just bringing in the work of others but that I was co-curating a show with Alexis and there were times when decisions were made in my absence which I never would have thought of taking but was very happy about,

so it set up a certain gamesmanship. There were instances when he would go off to lunch and by the time he'd come back I would have set up something else, a dynamic he'd never quite imagined. I find in the way I work there'll be a delay, because there's a distance in terms of concept, realisation, and geography. I'm entrusting things to someone else, there's no chance of me validating its production, yet with all the risks that implies it does also enable me the significant pleasure of hopefully being pleasantly surprised by something I've probably generated in a small maquette or non-professional technical drawing. In a way it's the very antithesis of studio practice whereby you often spend an inordinate amount of time in front of the work to the point that you know it too well, really.

How did the title of the work come about?
There's something that increasingly worries me about major solo retrospectives. They seem kind of false because the implication is that the work emerged from a complete vacuum as if the external world does not exist. Take a distinguished show such as Cy Twombly at Tate Modern: imagine if there was just one little flag by his friend Jasper Johns in that exhibition, it would galvanise the show. I think in that sense the title "…In the Cherished Company of Others…" hopefully implies that, although we might choose to court solitude to a high degree, we should never find ourselves fetishising the sadness of isolation, conceptual or otherwise.

Is the finished work what you expected it to be before it was made?
Prior to the installation of *Jean Cocteau* at De Appel I got a great text message from Alexis which just said: "Electric Chair OK." But until the piece was couriered in I didn't know which Warhol it would be. It's rare, is it not, to be literally surprised by one's own work? Beyond that there's also the people who have been consistent in *Jean Cocteau*: the guests, notably Warhol, Enrico David, and Paulina Olowska. Both Enrico and Paulina have come up with quite different proposals which have an impact on what one sees. If the work was

to eventually settle in a collection, one would have to build in a detailed protocol as to how that mutability can be recognised with the evolution of the piece. It's also manifest in material terms; for instance, the lamp stands by the Giacometti brothers, which we were able to borrow from the Sainsbury Centre for Visual Arts for the first two showings but are now no longer available. My solution was to theatricalise the visual by having full-size colour, actually very grainy, photo enlargements of them simply stuck onto plywood. A vindication of circumstance echoing Cocteau's way with bricolage. I've heard a rumour that, for the showing in Ostend, we may get a Marie Laurencin drawing, actually of Jean Cocteau, which would be great! It's true that there's much time spent on negotiation but there are moments of delight. The fact that *Jean Cocteau* changes in each specific showing avoids boredom. In a sense it's an ideal scenario in that there isn't the anxiety associated with new work, given that it isn't yet proven, but equally there is a degree of surprise. We should resist the tyranny of linear time for one which is much more elusive, labyrinthian, gracious, and, once understood, perhaps even kindly. Once we recognise that it can fold in on itself—wherein, for example, recent events can seem distant and more distant ones seem closer—we then have a greater fluidity of means. With *For MvdR* (2008) at the 5th Berlin Biennial, although I responded specifically to the site of the Neue Nationalgalerie, and worked for the first time on sheets of polished granite and marble, I was nonetheless able to call upon a personal grammar of means—that of the provisional leaning of decorative panels, which I first developed in Vienna in 1982. That I've been invited to prepare a show for the Secession next year will imply the likelihood of extending that procedure of possibilities … and so the future will, in all probability, fold itself into the past, the better then to accommodate the present.

[I. 12]

A Personal Grammar of Means

Roger Cook

(2009)

*Established in the early 2000s, the annual Frieze Art Fair was cre-
ated "to bring the world's top contemporary art galleries to London's
Regent's Park." Since the inaugural Fair in 2003, Frieze Projects has
pursued a curatorial program, inviting artists to produce works specifically responding to the context of the Fair, while the Frieze Talks
program has brought leading cultural and artistic figures to the
stage. As part of Frieze Talks 2008, Chaimowicz and Roger Cook,
a British artist, art historian, model with the London agency So
Damned Tough, which featured him on the catwalk for Issey Miyake
in the 1980s, and film extra as Jesus Christ in Derek Jarman's* The
Garden *(1990), were invited by the Frieze Foundation to give a
public lecture at the Fair in the afternoon on Thursday, 16 October.
As it was announced in the program, Chaimowicz was supposed to
talk about his practice "from the 1970s to the present in relation
to the Deleuzian notion of 'the fold' and the particular reflexive
dynamics that characterises his work." This public conversation was
recorded, and subsequently transcribed and edited by the British
publishing consultant and editor Rosalind Furness for publication
in* Frieze Projects & Frieze Talks, 2006–2008, *the second publication to report on the Fair's events.*

*To accompany the conversation between Chaimowicz and Cook,
selected slides from the artist's recent exhibitions and Olivier
Messiaen's* Catalogs of Birds *"books" were projected. None of these
images were subsequently included in the Frieze publication.
Discussing Gilles Deleuze's concept of "the fold" publicly was not
something the artist felt immediately comfortable with. However,
Cook had a method to facilitate this. As Chaimowicz said, "Roger
would suggest a topic for me to consider until the time came. A
perspective that was driven by him and that only a great complicity
between two persons could make entertaining in the context of an
art fair." From then on, as the conversation progressed, their pleasure was palpable. When Cook passed away in September 2021,
Chaimowicz remembered his longtime dandy friend:*

"I first met Roger Cook in the Fine Art Dept. of the University of Reading where Roger was a tenured, Senior Lecturer, (who had his very own study!), and I was initially but a sessional part-time Visiting Lecturer … I can recall that we were soon drawn to one another, I supporting his fledgling interest in theory and he, my then radical visual art practice. Roger was perceived, by some conservative other staff, as controversial: his flamboyance and the fact that he was then also a successful fashion model was frowned upon, (which I however saw as a bonus) … as was the fact that he had—oh sacrilege— stopped painting! And so, within the minefield of Academia we were each supportive of one another and what began as professional fellowship soon developed to that of a great friendship … Roger was older than me and when he was retiring from the Dept. he invited me to design a gift, which was to be made in our workshops. Aware of his passion for scholarship I designed an adjustable bookstand on which was engraved Pour mon frère fictif … "

A.V.

· · · · · · · · ·

Roger Cook: *Today, I'm in conversation with the artist Marc Camille Chaimowicz. The invitation to talk about Marc's work is very timely, because he currently has two exhibitions on: "…In the Cherished Company of Others…" at the Mu.Zee in Ostend, which was previously at De Appel in Amsterdam, and "Some Ways By Which To Live" at FRAC Aquitaine Bordeaux.*

Marc was initially recognised for his performance work in the 1970s and went on to be included in the seminal exhibition "Four Rooms" in 1984 alongside the three knights of the realm: Richard Hamilton, Howard Hodgkin, and Anthony Caro. When you invited me to share a platform with you at Tate Modern eight years ago, it seemed appropriate to consider your work in relation to Gilles Deleuze's notion of "the fold" from his book The Fold. Leibniz and the Baroque *(1988). So we discussed your work in relation to four folds: the temporal fold, the performative fold, the material aesthetic fold, and the cultural fold. One of the things that has characterised your practice from its inception is what we might call the reflexive dynamics of its becoming, for which the fold is the perfect image. This reflexive dynamics arose partially from the specific reflexivity of the historical moment. You entered the field at a prescient moment in the development of advanced practice in the late 1960s and early 1970s when painting and sculpture were undergoing radical transmutation—sometimes thought of as the postmodern moment. Ploughing your own furrow first as a student at Ealing Art College on an advanced foundation course, and then at Camberwell College of Arts, where there was a rigid and reactive tradition of representational painting from the model, you went on to the Slade School of Fine Art where, contrary to what one might expect, you were encouraged by Professor Sir William Coldstream to follow your own dictates in relation to the new productivity and performativity that was emerging under the influence of earlier, partially eclipsed forms of avant-garde cultural production. As a result of the impact of Dada, neo-Dada, Fluxus, and Pop, the rigid segmentations of the resolutely autonomous art represented by painterly painting and heavy metal sculpture began to refold performatively into the field of the everyday from which we now understand they can only ever be relatively separated. There was also the vital political question of the relative—and it can only ever be relative—autonomy of art in relation to the field of power. Viewed from a Deleuzian perspective, the 1960s and early 1970s can be seen as an intensely transformative time of a peculiar sort. John Rajchman, in his wonderful book, a philosophical reflection on architecture,* Constructions *(1998) describes it as a time of "perplication," appropriating the conceptual invention by which Deleuze defines the cross-foldings that occur "during the untimely moments that redistribute what has gone before while opening up what may yet*

be to come." The French word for fold is "pli," which is present in a number of words—implicate, explicate, replicate, duplicate, multiplicate, complexity, perplexity, reflexivity—that seem highly appropriate in relation to Marc's practice, since it is characterised by its multiplicity. The work that best exemplifies this "perplicating" moment is the one for which you have become best known: Celebration? Realife.
Could you say something about this extraordinary moment when you entered the art world in the 1970s?

Marc Camille Chaimowicz: I presented *Celebration? Realife* in 1972 at Gallery House in London. It was a remarkable experience. The gallery building had been acquired by the Goethe Institute, but was standing empty whilst planning permission was being negotiated. During that time, the London-based German gallerist Sigi Krauss, who had introduced a number of interesting artists onto the scene when running a little gallery in Covent Garden, was offered the space, which I think had more square footage than any other gallery in London during this time. Myself, Stuart Brisley, and Gustav Metzger did the inaugural show. The conditions were very intense. We had to clean the building; we had to paint it; there was no funding. Nonetheless, it was one of those high points of youth in which a person in their twenties somehow brings together the beginnings of a synthesis raising questions that range from the personal through to the cultural via the socio-political. It manifested itself as a moment of terror and beauty. The piece was over four rooms. In the primary room, which had originally been the ballroom, I painted the walls silver and installed lights and a sound system. It was a holistic work that people could enter and enjoy. There was also a study devoted entirely to the excellent left-wing broadsheet *7 Days*. Then there was a private room in which I slept, and a fourth room that acted as a social space into which I would invite people to discuss what I perceived then as the primary problematic facing contemporary culture: the alienating gap between the work and the viewer. I think the art world found the work quite difficult to access, because they simply didn't have the conceptual tools. I mean, they would literally look through the door rather than go in.

I'm always amused when you tell me that I would never have understood this work at the time; and I have to confess it's absolutely true. I would have been one of those people looking through the door rather than going in.

But it's also true that local kids would come in and sit down and probably roll up a joint and enjoy it very, very much. So, in a way, there was a dislocation in terms of response. The Gallery House installation was taken down after about a month, but I did salvage a number of the material aspects of the piece, which then lay dormant in suitcases under my bed for about twenty-seven years until Cabinet Gallery eventually convinced me of the viability of re-presenting the work. When I did so, in 2000, I introduced a third word to the title, *Celebration? Realife Revisited*, in a reference to Bob Dylan's 1965 album, *Highway 61 Revisited*. Currently, the work is on show in FRAC Aquitaine. Although it's acquired a great degree of autonomy over the years, it still needs a lot of attention. I suppose, in terms of museology, it would be a good example of what is beginning to emerge as active rather than passive curating, because a lot of love and care goes into the changing of the flowers and the music, and the lighting of the candles. It's a living work. Curiously, when *Celebration? Realife Revisited* was shown a few years ago at the Migros Museum für Gegenwartskunst, Zürich—a city in which my work wasn't well-known—quite a lot of the younger viewers presumed it was a piece by an emerging artist. So, it seems to have retained a certain degree of critical currency, which is heartening.

I think that's wonderful, because it means this important historic moment is still able to communicate today. This brings me to the idea of the temporal fold: the fold of past into present and present into past and present into future. In a recent interview with Dan Fox in frieze*,* *you referred to the invitation you had received to exhibit at the Vienna Secession next year. The fact that you had spent time and made work in Vienna in 1982 led you to observe that the future will, in all probability, "fold itself into the past, the better to accommodate itself into the present." Your work frequently concerns itself with the effervescence of memory. The fabulous installation that you produced for the 5th Berlin Biennial in 2008,* For MvdR, *refers back to two other works:* The Vienna Triptych *of 1982 and the* Warsaw Suite *of 1993.*

What intrigued me upon being invited to show in Berlin's Neue Nationalgalerie—the illustrious, but complicated building designed by Mies van der Rohe that is, in a way, an anathema to the plastic arts because it's all windows—were the marble columns. The columns actually shield air-conditioning units—the roof is a stunning example of freestanding engineering—but they also work as a formal device to break up the space. Given the draconian thinking of Van der Rohe towards the rectilinear and the mechanistic, it seemed the one concession he made to the organic was in the use of marble. I couldn't resist attempting to undermine that "de-feminisation" by transforming marble into a kind of lace. I then sourced a number of original devices that he'd designed for the gallery's inaugural exhibition—including some freestanding, display panels that hung from the ceiling on which were hung a suite of prints—and the piece was completed by curtaining the windows with a fabric patterned with one of my own designs that had been printed by a Swiss textile company in the 1980s. It is worth remembering that Van der Rohe refused to leave his chauffeur-driven car for the original inauguration of the building because he was so horrified by the fact that they'd hung some mesh curtains at the windows. He wasn't the easiest of modernists.

He must be turning in his grave!
To my mind, the building is strong enough to cope with a degree of net curtaining!

Well, now we are going to move on to what I call the performative fold in your work, and which I associate with your awareness of some more "pli" words: the complication, implication, and complicity of the interiorised private person with the exteriorised social and public persona. In the excellent monograph that accompanied your 1983 show "Past Imperfect," Jean Fisher quotes you as saying: "You cannot simply be about you, I cannot simply be about me, my work cannot simply be about my work, simply be." This indicates that your reflexivity at this time was not simply directed inwards towards yourself, but unfolded outwards into a relationship with the spectator, as in Celebration? Realife. *Yet, there's a paradoxical relationship in your work between the private self and the public persona: the extent to which your work shuts out public scrutiny and the extent to which it invites the spectator in—although this is always on your own terms. In many ways you remain quite a private person; even your date of birth has been mystified by your always stating simply that you were born in post-war Paris. There is a certain air of mystery—or is it mystification?—that fascinates but may also repel people. Perhaps you've inherited this from the French Symbolist tradition, which was invested in the implicit and the evocative rather than the explicit.*

There is another important aspect to this performative self: the fold of gender. From early on in your work, you were unafraid to embrace the feminine—the Deleuzian devenir-femme *(becoming woman). You appear to have always been very aware of this artifice of the self as something that was aesthetically constructive. How important were the movements for sexual liberation and feminism in the 1960s in enabling you to engage in this undermining of the dichotomy of sex and gender?*
Although it might seem very naïve now, when I was at the Slade, I spent an undue amount of time going to left-wing meetings to try to understand not just how the world worked, but how to equip oneself with the requisite tools to change the world. I found those meetings tedious in their dogma, their aggression, and their very male mental tyranny. The problem was that there was a dominant culture, which one was skeptical of for evident reasons, and then

there was the drug culture, which was attractive for obvious reasons, but which didn't offer any of the tools needed for change: it was brain-dead, really. And then there were the emerging theories from feminism and from the Gay Liberation Front, and they gave one solace because they recognised the importance of this objective and of the sensual as an extension of that. I wanted to find ways of developing a radical language that took into account senses and feelings, which Marxist theory didn't. I think there were better intellectual discourses occurring outside of the dominant, left-wing forum.

Let's move on to what is, perhaps, the most important fold in your practice: one that I have called the aesthetic/material fold, but that might also be termed the fold between the aesthetic and the artisanal. As witnessed by your 1989 exhibition "Fine and Applied Art" at The Showroom in London—the catalogue for which contained a text titled "On the Dialectic between the Fine Arts and Design" that spoke of the shift from the preoccupation with identity towards anonymity— you have been involved in a conscious undoing of the hierarchical gap between fine arts and applied arts. "One activity will naturally inform the other," you noted, "but they remain intangent and opposite." There's a fascinating essay by Jacques Rancière in The Future of the Image *(2007) entitled "The Surface of Design" that deals with the incongruous boundary crossings and aesthetic commonalities between the poetry of Stéphane Mallarmé and the industrial design of Peter Behrens, and which proves a useful reference for thinking about the boundary crossings between art and design. Rancière describes the "re-invention of the texture of communal existence by drawing lines, arranging words or distributing surfaces"—phrases that are particularly resonant with your work.*
The wonderful catalogue publication The World of Interiors, *from your 2006 show at the Migros Museum für Gegenwartskunst, Zürich, and the concurrent article on your apartment in* The World of Interiors *magazine, celebrate and extend this transgressive fold*

between applied and fine arts. In the above-mentioned text, you wrote that design work is different from fine art in that it is not so much "Pour toi, de moi" (for you from me) as "de nous, pour vous" (from us to you all). Given the co-operative nature of the artisanal, how does this affect your relationship to the ceramicists, textile manufacturers, furniture fabricators, and others with whom you collaborate in the facture of these works?

I had long been fascinated by the implicit hierarchy I encountered within the British art school system, which placed the most "gifted" students in the painting department, followed by the sculpture department, down through a whole hierarchy to textile design, which was at the bottom. So, in part, I was interested in the challenge of questioning certain taboos. But also, in an autobiographical sense, given that my mother had been a seamstress, I'd long been attracted to fabric. When I was offered one of my first overseas solo shows in Lyon, in 1983, it was in a disused factory, which didn't feel all that appropriate. I got talking with the curator and I said, "Well, actually, for me Lyon is all about the silk industry and textiles." And, to his credit, the curator was able to find me one of the last remaining textile ateliers, to which I apprenticed myself for about a month and just imbued myself in that world. Another way of materialising those interests came from trying to furnish my own place in Approach Road, London, in the 1980s. It was a humble housing association space and I didn't have the means to buy anything appropriate, so I was motivated, in a very haphazard way, to make my own furnishings, decorations, and even modest furniture.

Also, I was aware that the dominant question of the 1970s in terms of the visual arts—the post-Duchampian question concerning the status of the object in art—was increasingly resolved, and that this might conceivably lead to another question: whether the artist could adopt a social role by applying his or her skills to design opportunities. This is an ongoing discourse that still interests me.

Next year, I am going to be designing a huge chandelier for a church in France. I see this as an opportunity to respond to another taboo in terms of visual arts practice: compromise. There'll be compromise in terms of available materials, technical skill, budget, and time, but such a project still interests me as a counterpoint to more subjective or, indeed, literary activity.

My show at FRAC includes two dressing tables that were created with the help of the furniture maker Jean-Paul Guy, with whom I have an excellent rapport. I trust him; he understands my aesthetic. If he calls me to say he thinks my design needs to be done differently, I'll usually tell him just to go ahead and change it, which means that on occasion I might actually be surprised by the finished piece. "…In the Cherished Company of Others…" also includes a masterpiece—a *chef-d'œuvre*—made by his father, Émile Guy, in 1937, so there is a kind of continuum, a fascination with a particular practice, which we've lost in fine art.

Let's move on to talk about "…In the Cherished Company of Others…" Would you like to say something about the entrance to the show when it was installed at De Appel?
The show was the result of lengthy dialogue and collaboration with the French curator Alexis Vaillant. Symptomatic of that dialogue is the fact that we decided to forfeit the main entrance to De Appel, which is very ugly and dominant, and were instead able to hit upon this almost hidden staircase, which I suppose is primarily used as an emergency fire exit. Through colour-coding, we guided our public to the back of the building and up the staircase, whereby they entered on the top floor and descended through a number of rooms in which a retrospective of my work was contextualised with pieces by other artists.

There was a piece by Beca Lipscombe, Lucy McKenzie, and Bernie Reid of Atelier. Do you want to say something about that?

We were very happy that Atelier were able to take up our invitation. Their response was intended to serve as publicity for their emerging group practice and it therefore took the form of three posters created using three different techniques by each member of the group. They hope it will publicise the fact that they are, as I understand it, awaiting commission. There were also two small works by Lily van der Stokker. From her art school days, these pieces were, in a way, atypical of van der Stokker, but all the more delightful for that. Then there was a piece by Clémence Meunier who had just left art school the year before in France and whose work had therefore not been shown before. So, the works on display varied extensively in terms of generation and status, but were very carefully chosen in each case.

The show also contains one of your most important pieces, Jean Cocteau, *which was first exhibited at the Norwich Gallery in 2003, but has since undergone wonderful transmutations every time it's been shown.*
In its most recent incarnation in Ostend the work has again mutated to include a later addition, a photocopy of a very beautiful drawing of Jean Cocteau by Marie Laurencin, which makes him look angelic—the very opposite of what he was.

He was demonic, then?
Absolutely!

Your current show at FRAC Aquitaine, includes a piece consisting of a rug and some cushions on the left of the space, and two dressing tables on the right.
The ttle of that work is *Two Dressing Tables, Perhaps for Adolescents,* 2008. I was interested in showing undressed and dressed versions of the table, so that the relationship between the functional and non-functional could be rendered visible. The other work, *A Partial Grammar...* (1984–2008), also presents a very simple visual example

of the labyrinthine negotiating of times past and present that we mentioned earlier: the rug dates from this year, but the cushions were made from the very last remnants of the fabrics I designed in the mid-1980s, and which are now no longer available. So, the contemporary supports a visual referencing of various motifs from twenty years before, which are all brought together in this one work.

Personally, I think it's an absolutely beautiful piece. I'm really looking forward to getting to Bordeaux to see it.
I'm hoping it'll also be shown in London in November as part of the Royal Academy exhibition "Event Horizon."

That's great. Maybe I won't have to go to Bordeaux.
Although, it's an excellent time of year for oysters.

If everything goes according to plan technologically, I have this idea of ending with a very short slideshow of an exhibition called "Summer's Song" that Marc had in 2007 in a deconsecrated synagogue in France. Into this amazing space, Marc released a number of budgerigars...
Canaries, actually.

Sorry, canaries.
And African finches.

And some African finches into this space, so that they were flying around during the course of the exhibition, crapping on the work. But the following is a sequence of slides that, I think, gives a wonderful feeling of this space. And, since these birds were employed, I had the idea of using some of Olivier Messiaen's birdsong transcriptions, his Catalogue d'oiseaux (1956–58), to accompany it.
There is time now, I think, for some questions.

Question: Thank you for such an illuminating discussion. I was wondering whether you might like to comment on another fold in your life: your dual nationality? You live between London and Dijon: What is the relationship between your French nationality and your British residency, and what influence does it have on your work or on your sensibility?

Well, of course, it's central to how I attempt to make sense of things. When I was at art school in London, I was increasingly frustrated by the kind of forced choices that were available. The more ambitious students would look to America as an alternative model, but that never felt right in terms of my own reading and my own thinking. Parallel to that, I was dealing with my personal family past, which is Franco-Polish. I soon became committed to what is, currently, a fading dream: the idea that there may be something that's intrinsically not British and not American, but European. That's partly why I tried living in Vienna and Geneva for a time. It took me a while to conclude that commuting between cultures is the most meaningful option—it enriches my sensibility. It means I have to work twice as hard, but it gives me a certain fluidity: I can benefit from the creative freedom that one feels on the British scene, but also a certain intellectual respect for history that one might better feel in France.

Your practice is nomadic; it's about de-territorialising. Deleuze and Guattari have written: "A path is always between two points, but the in-between has taken on all the consistency and enjoys both an autonomy and a direction of its own. The life of the nomad is the intermezzo."

I think they're absolutely right. The true definition of a nomad is the opposite of Richard Long, who imperialistically tried to conquer the planet. A nomad literally goes from A to B and back again; it's a two-way thing.

Question: Given your experiences at art school, what does it mean for you to teach?

It means many things. I think teaching is an utterly honourable trade. If you look at the American scene, West Coast art differs from East Coast art in that much West Coast art is done by people who came through the art schools there, and continue to feed into the art schools. That kind of continuity, of being able to engage in perpetual dialogue with emerging generations, can only be enriching. Although the current situation seems to be in decline, I would not wish to engage in a critique of art schools in Britain and I'm happy to be able to maintain regular contact with two institutions because it's something I believe in and something that is linked in a very subjective sense to my own time in art school, which was crucial. The progressive London art scene in the 1970s consisted of about 400 people, including the artists. It was tiny! Given there were no places to meet, no locations for exchange, art schools were actually the only possible venues in which one could discuss and clarify one's own agenda. I guess that has left me with a rather romantic approach towards them.

There should be places for convivial exchange, shouldn't there?
Absolutely: bars with ashtrays, and saunas!

I'm all for saunas! Thank you so much, Marc Camille.
Thank you, Roger.

[I. 13]

Fieldwork as Reverie

A/S/N Mutual Press

(2009)

In October 2007, British philanthropist Charles Asprey, in collaboration with British-born art historian and curator Clémentine Deliss, launched the Randolph Cliff residency. Set in a magnificent 200 sq. m Georgian apartment perched on a steep rock face, the flat overlooked the Dean's Bridge and the Water of Leith in the heart of Edinburgh, and offered selected artists a unique natural and intellectual environment. Supported at the time by Edinburgh College of Art, the National Galleries, the University, and of course Asprey, Randolph Cliff ran for five years until 2012. Randolph Cliff's aim was to develop projects beyond the constraints inherent in exhibitions, art fairs, and education. To this end, a select group of international artists were invited to stay in the apartment for a limited period of time. In conjunction with their presence in Edinburgh, public seminars were organised in collaboration with the Edinburgh College of Art and the Talbot Rice Gallery to discuss the conceptual, physical, and legal forms that future research or study collections might take. Additionally, Randolph Cliff has developed a unique collection of ephemera based on initial propositions and blueprints donated by visiting artists, including editions, sound recordings, scripts, plans, photographs, journals, and notes. The Edinburgh College of Art and the National Galleries of Scotland now hold this collection. The artists who participated in Randolph Cliff between 2007 and 2012 include Tom Burr, Frances Stark, Franz Graf, Manfred Pernice, Joseph Kosuth, Dexter Sinister, Joseph Grigely, Marc Camille Chaimowicz, Thomas Struth, and Antje Majewski.

Chaimowicz spent several weeks at Randolph Cliff in 2008. During his stay, he was invited to be interviewed by the postgraduate affiliates to A / S / N, the interdisciplinary Master of Fine Arts course Art / Space / Nature. Led at the time by Scottish artist Alan Johnston at the Edinburgh College of Art, this MFA course was offering postgraduate students from fine art, architecture, landscape architecture, and design the opportunity to study and engage with a wide range of sites from around the world. In 2008, future graduates of this program were: Jacob Bee, Ronald Boer, Valerie Dempsey, Erin Gleason, Florian Graf, Naomi Hennig, Melissa MacRobert, Julia Martin, and Christine Wylie. As a working group, their name was Fieldwork. With Deliss as their consulting editor, they decided to produce a publication featuring "a series of recent conversations with leading international artists who have visited Edinburgh in the past year, as well as anthropologists, landscape architects, and composers." Each of these conversations was to "reveal a complimentary vision of what it means to do fieldwork today, and the stimulating challenges of site-specific inquiry and practice." Chaimowicz was interviewed in the autumn, which was recorded on tape and edited by the A / S / N group, recomposed with the artist, and published in FIELDWORK, a 128-page edition with a print run of 1000 copies, also the first-ever of the A / S / N Mutual Press publications in 2009.

Interested in the concept of "fieldwork" throughout his artistic career [I. 17], Chaimowicz saw this interview as an opportunity for him to reflect on the contexts in which, over the course of his life, he has come to view "fieldwork as research," particularly in his relation-ship to writing and his need for nameless activities. To illustrate the concept of fieldwork, two images were selected accordingly by future graduates of A / S / N in collaboration with the artist. These seminal black and white images included: the artist looking out of the window, Approach Road, London, 1977; and the facade of a restaurant called CAFÉ DU RÊVE, an image the artist had found in Nantes in the early 1980s and used in the dust-cover design of his publication Café du Rêve *from 1985 [III. 11].*

A.V.

• • • • • • • • •

A/S/N: *Marc Camille, have you developed a specific ritual or methodology that bridges working practice and daily life? Can these two domains be separated?*

Marc Camille Chaimowicz: I think it is important that they are separated. Something that is centred to a large degree in subjectivity will be too accessible or obscure if it isn't processed in very particular ways. I think my work is a kind of idealisation in terms of possible models. In the 1970s, when I started, there were no pre-existing models by which to make work, which meant one had to find one's own. Gradually I began to establish a particular working practice, which was pluralistic and multi-formed but always dealt with subjective questioning. It meant that one was working with activities that at the same time were un-named, and that was what was exciting about them. Much of the work was ephemeral. At first it was called "events," then "performance," and later "installation." Then, interestingly, as these activities became recognised, I became more and more frustrated by the very fact that they had become recognised or named.

At that time, I wrote regular criticism on performance for the short-lived magazine *Studio International* edited by Richard Cork. My final column, which never got published, highlighted a fundamental contradiction—namely, that you couldn't actually write about performance because the very principle of that premise was based on a formalised reading of practice. From that I developed a frustration relative to the degree of objectivity, which is needed to write criticism. I felt more and more drawn to writing for myself, to actually including writing within practice. I think that most of us, who write, given that we come from the visual arts, write inordinately slowly. To me, journalism is the antithesis of how I use the written word because the pressure in journalism produces a false urgency.

You use the form of the diary in some of your publications. Is this way of working with text closer to how you want to portrait your work?

Certain forms of writing fascinate me and the diary form way is one, but it is not the only one. If it does feature on occasion then it is, in a sense, a kind of falsehood. I won't actually speak from the diary, but a fictional reconstruction of the diary as a possible arena for reverie. You never really write just for yourself. Subconsciously you want to be read. One needs to find forms by which to structure sensibility. The apartment as personal space has been another form that I've used a lot. Again that has to be processed very carefully otherwise it simply comes across as autobiographical, which may suit someone who is interested in social-realist practice but that's not my intention.

Could you say that these forms portrait the everyday, yet not quite?
I find the everyday so mundane and often so disappointing that one has to go beyond it, but still keep a check on external reality, otherwise one ends up in a totally deluded state. The trick is to tweak the real so that one can transcend it and, in the process, hopefully render it of interest, not simply to oneself but to others too.
I think the photograph that I happened to find in Nantes of the Café du Rêve was a good example of a simple visual form that said everything I wanted to say. It implied a kind of sociability in a place where you get a wide cross-section of people, all dealing with their own solitude. They go to the Café du Rêve for a number of reasons: to pick someone up, or to get drunk, or to find warmth, or to engage in social intercourse. But because the title is *Café du Rêve* it also implies something else: that one can transcend and actually go into reverie. That's a very simple example of what you are hinting at. The everyday in this photograph is not any old café. It has specificity.

You mentioned nameless activities. In some ways fieldwork is an activity that remains nameless or invisible.
I think so. Jean Genet offers a good example here. He found it difficult to make work, i.e. to write, once he'd acquired a degree of visibility. He found mature success rather suddenly because a number of key

players, including the other dandy, Jean Cocteau, took on Genet's writings and started to introduce him to members of the elite and the establishment, which in some ways was a necessary development. At that time, Genet was in deep trouble. There was an obscure law in the French penal system whereby if you were found guilty of whatever criminal act, however minor, on more than five or six occasions you were liable to be given a life sentence. Genet was facing that threat. He was drawn to the criminal world and until his mid-thirties had spent eighty per cent of his life in institutions: an orphanage, a reform house, a prison, and then, I think, four or five years in the army. He became addicted to the eroticism of criminality and risk. But when you're faced with the fact that you may never be free from prison, this becomes something else.

At this point, Genet began to write in a very unusual way, on bits of lavatory paper, on old cardboard, and he hid everything under his mattress. He wrote to make sense of things for himself, because he was imprisoned, because he was not well-connected at the time, and in no way could he presume the probability of finding a publisher. With time, this secret activity became recognised through his manuscripts. Jean Cocteau introduced him to a number of very wealthy patrons who bought these manuscripts. Suddenly he was making a lot of money, which meant that for the first time he was able to get suits made and live in hotels. It also meant that he was increasingly alienated from the fieldwork that had nourished his first writings. Then he had a crisis. He tried other activities such as filmmaking. He produced one masterpiece, which lasts fifteen minutes. He went back to thieving. Eventually Cocteau introduced him to Jean-Paul Sartre who, with others, formed a pressure group that was able to solicit a pardon from the President of France. Jean Genet has become the personification of existential man.

So how would you define fieldwork?
I think I would define it as a kind of freedom. There's a great quote from André Gide: "Poverty is a slave driver. In return for food men

give their grudging labour. All work that is not joyous is wretched, I thought, and I paid many of them to rest. Don't work I said, you hate it. In imagination, I bestowed on each of them that leisure without which nothing can blossom, neither vice nor art." It's perhaps excessively romantic but, as Gide points out, his definition of freedom has to be anchored in the real. He's happy to give people money to live and to free them up to be creative because most work is a kind of drudgery. I guess my definition would be to try to structure one's life so that one has a degree of freedom, which then enables one to resist the pressures of either the market place or categorisation, or a particular way of working. It means that everything is possible, however modest that may be. Sometimes I've just made a model of a piece of furniture out of cardboard and that's enough to enable me to give form to something I need.

Such freedom from external pressures requires a very pronounced ability to improvise and to constantly initiate new contexts and formats for making work.
My very first publication was called *Field-Work*. This would have been in the mid-1970s. It was at the time of my first job at Croydon School of Art. There were some good students there. I felt it would be great if we did an event together, so we met up and did some rehearsals. It was a performance type thing, which we toured to a number of venues.
We showed at a place called Oval House, a community arts centre, which used to be quite good for experimental theatre. They also had their own printing department in the days when one still used the technology, which preceded photocopying. I collated all the sheets of paper myself, and stapled them by hand. We had fun. We used different coloured paper, all low-cost and low-tech. The cover was a reproduction of a filmstrip from the performance: black and white filmstrips of people working.

Would you say that artists produce their own field rather than an existing

field to take notes, describe, and analyse it?
I guess we feel a certain urgency to furnish and furbish our own world rather than respond to the way the world is furnished. In a way, it's a reversal, is it not? I am interested in itinerant workers, in the journeyman, who in previous centuries would go where the work was. Most architecture, as well as stone carvings in graveyards or decorations in baronial houses, has arisen from that movement of skilled people. Take Carouge, which is a small town outside Geneva. It is remarkable for its Italianate architecture and that's simply down to the fact that the great architects and master craftsmen came from Italy via the Alps to Geneva and then moved on to Paris. They stopped in Carouge for many years, settled, and built their own abodes. So you get a moment of Italy by Lake Geneva. The problem with fine art is that it's based on the principle that the artist is God and doesn't compromise, which is absurd because we have to ingest compromise and deal with it in the best way we can.

Once a year or so, I get involved in a public art project of some sort. Often, I will have to compromise because of restrictions in terms of the budget, technical means, and time. You just do the best you can with what's available. I guess that was frowned upon, and instead one idealised the studio as the sacred space where the artist was fully in control. But I don't think that necessarily produces the most interesting work. I don't really have a studio—I have a storage place but I don't really go there to make work. People ask, "Where do you work?" and I never know what to say—on a bus or in bed or in a cab?

Where does one work? I'm enjoying here in this flat at Randolph Cliff in Edinburgh. I've got a photocopier; I have two tables where I can cut and paste and that's a very happy place to be working in. At home in London, I work often on the kitchen table, but it can be distracting—bills to pay, telephones, TV, washing to do. It's a different environment and although I do quite like working at home, there's a kind of intensity and clarity of thought possible here in this apartment that I don't have at home—because it's unfamiliar.

[I. 14]

Marc Camille Chaimowicz Discusses his Exhibition at Artists Space

As told to Lauren O'Neill-Butler

(2009)

In June 1972, Chaimowicz was offered a three-week artist residency in the South West Gallery of the Serpentine, London, over the course of which he designed the immersive installation Enough Tiranny. *Filtered by coloured lights and a soundtrack, and combining references to art history, glam rock, pop culture, and the political news of 1972, this installation was conceived "as a direct response to the political situation in Northern Ireland" [I. 1]. Bringing together over two hundred items, including Christmas decorations, freshly cut flowers, newspapers, a fox fur, a desk lamp, and fairy lights, the installation also featured two pools of water, each with a goldfish and several carp, which Chaimowicz negotiated for free from Harrods and then transported in a bucket, by bus, from the department store to the exhibition space. At the time, Chaimowicz explained, "the installation aimed to bring about new models of collaboration and sociability" while attempting to challenge "the alienation between viewer, artist, and institution." Conceived in a dialectic between the "instinctive / intuitive" and the "general context" [III. 2], Chaimowicz's landmark environment also emphasised the importance of "pleasure" over "work." Presented to the public from 1–23 July [I. 1] as part of the group exhibition "Summer Show 4,"* Enough Tiranny, *which had been conceived as finished, was subsequently stored in cardboard boxes, and lay dormant for over thirty years. Due to a continued interest in the work, Chaimowicz agreed to reopen the boxes in late 2004. While meticulously identifying each enclosed element, he recomposed the installation step by step in close collaboration with Martin McGeown and Andrew Wheatley, the co-directors of Cabinet, London.*

As a result, Enough Tiranny *was back in the spotlight. First presented in "EGOmania," a group exhibition organised by Italian curator Milovan Farronato at the Galleria Civica in Modena (29 January–2 May, 2006), the installation was later included in the highly acclaimed group exhibition "The Secret Public: The Last Days of the British Underground 1978–1988." Conceived as "an attempt to critically re-evaluate Britain's recent past, while also presenting the lasting impact that artists and cultural producers of this period have on the cultural and political fabric of Britain today," this exhibition was named after the Punk culture collage fanzine published by British writer and rock critic Jon Savage and British artist Linder Sterling. Regarding the title of the exhibition, Chaimowicz mentioned that "this historical show shared empathy with a reply from Bob Dylan who had been interviewed by a quasi-reactionary journalist in a live coast to coast interview and who asked aggressively who listens to this stuff. Dylan, looking down: 'I don't know who they are, but they know one another. They are the secret public.'" Conceived by the Kunstverein München (director Stefan Kalmár and curator Daniel Pies), and co-curated by British writer and critic Michael Bracewell [I. 15], and associate curator Ian White (Adjunct Film Curator, Whitechapel Art Gallery, London), the exhibition was first presented in Munich (9 October–26 November, 2006), and subsequently brought from Munich by Mark Sladen in his first act as Director of Exhibitions at ICA, London where it was presented (23 March–6 May, 2007). Due to logistical reasons,* Enough Tiranny Recalled *was only presented at the ICA, while in Munich the artist had reconstructed the interior of the projection room* Here and There, 1979–2006. *Subsequently, the exhibition "Marc Camille Chaimowicz featuring* Enough Tiranny Recalled" *was organised at Galerie Giti Nourbakhsch, Berlin (3 November–15 December, 2007).*

Two years later, Stefan Kalmár emblematically programmed the exhibition "Enough Tyranny Recalled 1972–2009" as his inaugural exhibition as Director of Artists Space, New York, that was on view from 28 September to 19 November, 2009. Conceived the year Artists Space was founded, Enough Tyranny Recalled *was presented throughout the reopened exhibition space after undergoing a significant physical transformation. Led by architects IFAU & Jesko Fezer in collaboration with a group called Common Practice, the* interior transformation of the Artists Space was based on transparency. Taking into consideration a project that American artist Michael Asher had proposed for the space in 1988, all interior walls and all existing lighting were removed. As a result, the installation was displayed in a space that had almost no interior walls and windows without shutters, thus connecting the city to the exhibition. In addition, this was the artist's first solo presentation in an American institution. When the exhibition opened to the public, similar to what had happened in Zürich a few years earlier, the artist recalled, "It was interesting because art students were asking about this "'new young artist.'" After a decade devoted in part to recalling his partially lost environments of the 1970s [I. 7, 11], Chaimowicz felt that "the future will, in all probability, fold itself into the past to better accommodate itself in the present."

A few days before the opening of the exhibition, American writer and editor Lauren O'Neill-Butler contacted Artists Space on behalf of Artforum to find out if the artist had time to answer some questions. Although Chaimowicz was busy fixing the exhibition, he agreed to do so. O'Neill-Butler recalled their conversation as follows:

> "I was the editor of Artforum's Interviews column from 2008 to 2019, and initiated the interview myself. At the time, the column was called '500 Words' and all of the interviews in it were published in an as-told-to format. As for all my interviews, I conducted as much research as possible before we spoke and came up with a series of questions. If I remember correctly, the interview was over the phone while Marc Camille Chaimowicz was installing. It was about 30 minutes long and recorded. It was a wonderful chat—he was so thoughtful and open. I then transcribed the audio (or an online service did, I can't remember) and edited it into the as-told-to statement, which I then sent to Marc Camille, via Artists Space, for

approval or changes. I remember attending the opening a few days later and being blown away by the show."

Published online on 26 September 2009, O'Neill-Butler's "500 Words" included several shots of the installation from 1972.

Seven years later, on the occasion of Chaimowicz's solo exhibition "An Autumn Lexicon" at Serpentine Gallery, London (29 September–20 November, 2016), organised by British curator Melissa Blanchflower, Enough Tiranny *was re-staged as it was in the Serpentine in 1972. Exactly ten years after this installation was first "recalled," noted Chaimowicz, the "scatter environment" he had conceived in 1972 "as a direct response to the political situation in Northern Ireland" had taken a different meaning. Indeed, revisiting and recalling installations that had almost disappeared gave him the opportunity to reflect: "We should resist the tyranny of linear time for one which is much more elusive, labyrinthine, gracious, and, once understood, perhaps even kindly. Once we recognise that it can fold in on itself—wherein, for example, recent events can seem distant and more distant ones seem closer—we then have a greater fluidity of means."*

A.V.

• • • • • • • • •

I wasn't familiar with Artists Space. I don't know too much about the contemporary New York art scene at all, really. My decision to do this show had everything to do with the institution's new director, Stefan Kalmár, who I've worked with before in Munich and London. When he called me with a request to exhibit this piece, I felt as though I couldn't turn him down, even though this particular work takes a while to put into place.

This exhibition is as much about me showing this work as it is about Artists Space inaugurating a new era. It was when we agreed on the show that we also realised that *Enough Tiranny* originated in 1972, the year Artists Space opened. It was last shown in 2007 at the Institute of Contemporary Arts in London, in the context of "The Secret Public," and there it had a dedicated space upstairs. At Artists Space, it will appear in a room that is much more open, as there is now a certain transparency to the gallery.

I never imagined that I'd have to deal with issues of storage or longevity. Everything I made back then was based on the ephemeral. Who would want to revisit all of their earlier work? But in a sense, this show concurs with my skepticism of the forced presumption that time is linear. Perhaps time operates in a different way—a warping that can fold in on itself. Hopefully, given the specificity of the venue, it's like a new work. But it also has a shared protocol, a footprint that returns to its origin.

This exhibition will provide a nice foil to my forthcoming show at the Secession in Vienna, which will comprise new work. There's a comfort in dealing with the known at Artists Space, and it frees me to deal with the unknown at Secession. It's a reversal of George W. Bush's comment in which he said something like "There's new work happening in the old world, and old work happening in the new world."

Enough Tiranny was first shown in the west gallery of the Serpentine in London, which at the time seemed like a posh establishment to young artists. Only weeks before I had exhibited *Celebration? Realife* at Gallery House. These venues were located close to each other in Kensington, so it felt like I was easily transferring issues and sensibilities from one venue to the other, although that wasn't necessarily the case.

Gallery House was a much darker, club-like environment compared with Serpentine, which had traditional hours, a regular staff, and daylight filtering in. But they were opposite sides of the same coin, really. I compensated for the middle-class values inherent in the Serpentine's program. It was tougher, but I had to pare my ideas down.

In terms of reception, the way I was working was alien to an audience that was still presuming to see work on the walls to be negotiated at eye level. Mine was floor-based, scattered. At the Serpentine on a sunny day, people walking through the park might stop by, and they were bemused, shocked, by the work.

In many ways, the young hippie crowd was the most relaxed. They would linger. The drug culture then was charming, more gentle. They spoke to their friends about the work and came back. It became a haven, which I was courting. I was critical of the alienating distance between the work and the viewer, and this is a gap I've continued to review.

One thing I wonder about is whether the work still has a degree of radicality. It was shown several years ago in Zürich, where no one had heard of me. It was interesting because art students were asking about this "new young artist." They presumed youth behind the work, which implies, perhaps, that there is still a critical urgency.

[I. 15]

Adventures Close to Home:
Lucy McKenzie and Marc Camille Chaimowicz in Conversation with Michael Bracewell

Michael Bracewell

(2011)

In March 2011, Edoardo Bonaspetti, then editor-in-chief of Mousse—a bimonthly journal on contemporary art established in Milan in 2006 featuring interviews, conversations, and essays by artists, critics, and curators—invited renowned British writer and critic Michael Bracewell to conduct an interview with Chaimowicz and Scottish artist Lucy McKenzie. "The idea," as Bonaspetti mentioned in his initial message to the writer, "had first come from Lucy." A former music journalist, Bracewell considers himself "a fellow traveller, or a tourist in the arts," and was at the time supportive of the two artists whose work he knew well. He therefore thought that this joint discussion might be a good opportunity to highlight and explore the artists' mutual interest in each other's work. For their part, McKenzie and Chaimowicz were delighted to speak with Bracewell, whom they both considered a key figure in the cultural landscape. As Bracewell reflected:

> "I subsequently met with Marc Camille and Lucy on 14 April 2011 at a hotel in Chelsea, London, called 11 Cadogan Gardens. We recorded the conversation there on my iPhone. This was then transcribed by the people at Mousse, and subsequently edited by Edoardo, Lucy, Marc Camille and myself. There were no major cuts or discussions. The conversation seemed to flow very naturally."

To illustrate the discussion Mousse asked the galleries representing the two artists for pictures from their recent exhibitions. Subsequently selected by the magazine, the images were included without the agreement of Marc Camille Chaimowicz who would later confess, "I wasn't even aware of the publication's release until I accidentally got my hands on a copy," sometime over the autumn of 2011; the magazine was made available in June 2011.

Originally, the transcript of the interview reproduced below was intended to be the first part of a three-stage conversation, which was to take place successively in London, Brussels, and Paris, but which *did not proceed as planned. Indeed, as told by Bracewell:*

> *"A year later, in September 2012, the three of us recorded another conversation at Lucy's apartment in Brussels following a trip to Ostend to see an exhibition there of works by Lucy/ Atelier EB. This conversation was recorded on my phone as a 'Voice Memo' and as I recall the recording was only partially successful. It was transferred to my iTunes but has not been transcribed, as it is only partly audible. Looking at old emails, we had considered discussing, amongst other things, the influences of literature and art education. This second conversation was not for* Mousse *but for our own interest and with a view to possibly putting together a short book of* Three Dialogues. *A further (third) conversation was due to take place in Paris but other events intervened for all of us. There was no agenda of specific subjects in specific cities. The idea was simply to converse. Sadly, none of us subsequently had the time to formalise the project or complete it."*

Published both online and in the print, the discussion was presented as follows: "Lucy McKenzie and Marc Camille Chaimowicz weave a long conversation, aided by the learned and detailed questions of the writer Michael Bracewell. The result is a sophisticated analysis of an art that deftly incorporates territories of design, and the importance of making use of artistic techniques and craftsmanship to combine them in one's poetics."

A. V.

· · · · · · · · ·

Michael Bracewell: *Tell me about this show that you're going to do in Zürich, "Town-Gown Conflict."*
Lucy McKenzie: The show is seven of us, all women who use textiles in their work in one way or another. Some are fashion designers who work with small-scale industry. One person is a tapestry weaver, my friend Beca Lipscombe's mother. A few artists a bit younger than me who use textiles as an inspiration, for instance Verena Dengler, who looks at things like how Abstract Expressionism got domesticated for applied arts. And then, for myself and a couple of the other fine artists, it's just an obscure part of what we do, somehow a component, whether that's writing or embroidery. The impetus was encountering several young male artists who were using things like batik printing because "that's what women do." Or still-lives "like an old lady would do." Women's alternative expressions have always been co-opted as an outsider position. I wanted to instigate a show with textiles that proves how flexible and interesting it is without it just being a symbol of women's work. Because it's not, that's a complete misapprehension.

M.B.: *Do you feel you're trying to depoliticise textiles?*
L.M.: There were enough people I knew who used it in interesting ways. None of the artists are historical. Sonia Delaunay isn't in it. It's contemporary work, just people I know who work with textiles. Combined with being reactive to a perceived position by certain male artists.

M.B.: *How did you become interested in working with textiles?*
L.M.: Specifically through my friend and collaborator Beca Lipscombe. She's a fashion designer, and I became a model for her about ten years ago. I thought the clothes were nice, but a few years later I realised that she made them all in Scotland, and it was all about trying to see what could be done locally. Her position and references were quite unusual, we had some common ground, and slowly we began to work together. In the past I've been very con-

cerned with music, partly informed by doing it myself but mainly by being around people who did it. Now I'm close to her, so it's natural to be excited by textiles. Beca and I were preparing some writing a few weeks ago, and we were considering a loaded and problematic term like "muse," which is often used for women in both art and fashion. As much as we hate the *cliché*, we do function a bit like muses for each other.

M.B.: *I remember once when we very first spoke, we talked about that line that Gilbert and George have always had, "Advance through friendship." And you said that was something you could really acknowledge. Has that been a basis of your work? For instance* Flourish. Ask a friend, ask a friend.
L.M.: Yes, although of course it does feel strange when you have friendships that come to an end. There have been artists I worked intensely with, and now don't have any contact with any more. This is the sad side of it, the lines of where the friendship is or isn't "useful." Not to be callous or take advantage, but you grow up together and at a certain point you begin to want different things.

M.B.: *The Victoria and Albert Museum is doing their exhibition "The Cult of Beauty: The Aesthetic Movement 1860-1900." I went to see it last week. I think it's a very, very good show even though a little bit of it is very familiar. It really struck a chord as far as I was concerned with both of your work. And I wondered about the root both of you as artists work from—a position of aesthetics in that kind of "Aesthetic movement" sense of the word. In other words the cult of beauty, about an art for art's sake, and how do you make that art for art's sake A) derive philosophically, and B) have its place in lifestyle, in what Peter York said in the 1970s about art-directed lifestyles. Is this a lineage that you feel a part of?*
L.M.: My main understanding of the Aesthetic movement comes from the London Weekend Television miniseries *Lillie Langtry*. No, I would place myself slightly to the side of that along with the Arts

and Crafts movement, which attempted to sincerely engage with industry and the real world in general.

M.B.: *So it's about craft.*
L.M.: At the moment, yes. [to Marc Camille] You also make things. From our conversations on this subject in the past, I know that you place what you are doing clearly as art, using craft elements within that, which is not how I staunchly see my work.

M.B.: *And also huge amounts of research into the history of design.*
Marc Camille Chaimowicz: My initial engagement with the misunderstood Arts and Crafts legacy was based on a fascination I had. I was initially drawn to a dialectic between what is named and what is unnamed. It seemed to me that the visual arts are inherently about the artist asking questions, which are inevitably directly or indirectly related to his or her identity. A kind of portrait. Whereas the craft tradition is about the opposite. Certainly from medieval times, craft is made by people whose names are absent from the work, however grand the work might be, stonemasons or otherwise. They aren't asking questions; they are coming up with answers. So in a design sense if we look at this cake stand, for example, it doesn't question anything. A good piece of design—and this probably is, because it's lasted—will say, "I am what I am." It's instantly recognisable for what it is, whereas I think the best visual art often isn't easy to understand on the first take. And that's one of the things that interests me about Lucy's work, what I know of it, is that it is quite elusive. It's got conscious slippage. Whereas design work should not have, in my mind. So in that sense my take on design is an ideological way of counterpointing the inherently elitist nature of visual art practice by—as Beca Lipscombe would probably propose—forwarding oneself as a kind of journeyman who is therefore able to offset any kind of need. If they're called upon by a company to design, for instance, a range of knitwear.
L.M.: Beca has a day job as a co-designer at a cashmere mill in

Scotland. One proposed model is a jumper featuring intarsia devised from a work by Marc Camille. She made a sample using black, and this was an issue because you don't use black in your work, do you, Marc?

M.C.C.: I bumped into Beca recently and said, "Could we maybe attempt charcoal grey?" She said, "Yes, I think we can." But it was shocking. I've never used black. I couldn't use black, not in the way that Matisse could. In fact, when I've used black, when I've given drawings for instance recently to Dovecot Studios, who did an excellent interpretive job of making a rug, I'll always say, with reference to the darkest line work, just go out and buy a bar of ninety percent dark chocolate, and that'll be your colour reference. Black, especially in a rug, would just be too violent.

L.M.: And this is why you don't like Charles Rennie Mackintosh, because of all the black?

M.C.C.: One of the many reasons!

L.M.: You don't like his white rooms?

M.C.C.: I like his architecture. I just have a problem with his furniture design, it seems so aggressive. I get scared in the library at the Glasgow School of Art. Consciously or otherwise, I think it's a profoundly anti-intellectual proposition because his light fittings, though very grand, look just like guillotines. I have this vision of the reader, sitting in studious engagement, finding that his or her head is chopped off by one of Charles Rennie Mackintosh's lights. It's pretty violent.

L.M.: As you ascend to the top of the art school the light is controlled in a certain way so that it seems to get darker, and there are barred grilles like in a prison. Fitting for an art school.

M.C.C.: You didn't actually study there, did you?

L.M.: No, I didn't get accepted.

M.C.C.: Good.

L.M.: I'm really glad I didn't go.

M.B.: *[to Lucy] When you started making work, it seemed to represent a very radical moment. You seemed to be coming at things in a completely different way than your peers. It was almost like you were dealing with a completely different language, in order to say completely different things.*
L.M.: In the context of Glasgow?

M.B.: *In contemporary British art at that time. Which if anything seemed to be slightly lost, wandering between big, peculiar paintings and … Have you always felt that you knew what you wanted to be doing? Are you led by doubt?*
L.M.: As a child my only ambition was to be an art student. To be like those well-dressed 1980s girls that my dad taught.

M.B.: *The only person who's ever said that to me was Brian Eno.*
L.M.: Perfect! No, there's not a lot of doubt. When there is, I make a change. Going to study decorative painting was born out of boredom at what seemed like my trajectory. I wanted to do something else, learn something else, change course, and it worked. But I don't know how much artistic torment is related to personality. I'm not a very doubtful person. I'm rather content.

M.C.C.: I've long admired Lucy. It seems to me that there's less persona about Lucy than there is with other artists. Other artists need to protect themselves because of their doubt, or sense of vulnerability, through a construct that is a kind of shell that protects them as they negotiate the mean, nasty external world. I think that with Lucy there's less of a barrier between the inner and the outer. It's as though she is a fish in water, and there's a kind of ease in the way her questions take form. Different currents have different impacts on different projects. It all feels very natural.

L.M.: It's the way I was brought up. I never thought that I wasn't welcome in the art world because it was just a strand of culture and I was not by default an outsider. I already knew that when I was fifteen. When I was in my late teens and early twenties I did soft pornographic modelling as a summer job, and I remember thinking at the time that it was somehow connected to deciding to be an artist, rather than having a proper job. I didn't know at the time that the reception of this kind of pornographic image would change so much, à la Tom Ford, Terry Richardson, American Apparel, etc.

M.B.: *Do you think the common denominator between both of your motives as artists is an engagement with all the blessings and curses of the romantic? Romanticism? [to Marc Camille] When I saw your show at the Vienna Secession, that was one of the most intensely romantic rooms I think I've ever been in. It was like inhaling talcum powder. It was absolutely astonishing.*
M.C.C.: I guess it was, given the venue, and given my very complex position relative to the Viennese legacy. But I think there was also a high degree of projection that came out of an almost psychotic misunderstanding of what Austria was. There were geographic areas associated with High Romanticism in Germany that were forbidden to me because of my paternal background. In a way it's the antithesis of what Lucy is talking about. With Lucy there's this delightful continuum, this threadlike link, with her father. In my case, within the family home we just could not talk about World War II. So I did a project massively when living in Vienna

in the 1980s, in a highly visual way. And when an invitation to show at Secession emerged, I guess it was the premise on which to return. A kind of thank-you thirty years on, an acknowledgment of the importance that living there had had for my thinking. It was intensely personal, more so than most exhibitions. But it didn't come over as biographical, hopefully.

M.B.: *Samuel Beckett says that an artist is a person who has an inner text that he needs to translate. This idea of the translation out of the personal into the universal is precisely what you achieved with that show. Another thing that I've always felt about both of you—again I'm talking as a generalist, a tourist in the art world—is that you seemed to reconnect with this really refreshing idea of the European at a time when the Scottish scene and the London scene had reached a point of self-satisfaction and safety. [to Lucy] I remember when you started working with Paulina Olowska.*
L.M.: Yes, we found and reinforced in each other a kind of antiquated European-ness, with the romance of being from different sides of Europe.

M.C.C.: That's the most insightful take.

L.M.: Regarding Romanticism, the actual fabrication of my work is extremely dispassionate because I'm using techniques that are purely about procedure. They were taught to people 150 years ago who weren't artists, they were just sixteen years old learning how to make fake wood or fake marble, or how to paint a woman's face the way you should paint it if you have to do it fifty times "round a dado rail." It's as formulaic as Stephen King or Patricia Highsmith, a kind of trick bag. My allowance of Romanticism is placed in how the images I paint, or things I want to make, are chosen. In the past my adolescence seemed to be extremely important to me, but now that I've started making clothes I've been thinking much more about my childhood and my mother. She has a senior position in a domestic violence charity, and brought me up to think I could do anything I wanted. Yet my sister and I were dressed in sweet velvet dresses and we flounced around like Kate Greenaway characters. That for me is very romantic, the double message of feminine whimsy and female empowerment.

M.B.: *Do tell me if I'm barking up the wrong tree, but that seems to come back to this idea of the art-directed lifestyle. There's a part of you that is absolutely fascinated with the idea of the House Beautiful, living as an extension of that.*
L.M.: That's where "The Cult of Beauty" exhibition was very interesting, the section documenting the ridicule of those who tried to "live up to their china." I think that interiors should be truly reflective of the personality, should be formed over years, not predetermined. In Brussels many artists work at home, and their home becomes that reflection.

M.B.: *You did that wonderful series of Nicky Haslam's interiors for Bryan Ferry.*
L.M.: The best way to learn about interiors is to make them, or at least reproduce them, and the same goes for ornament and pattern. What I like with the photos of Bryan Ferry's interior is seeing how a familiar little attic flat is made completely grandiose. *The World of Interiors* magazine, when they were originally published, is a fantastic guide of how to build rooms that combine historical order and human wear. By drawing Bryan Ferry's flat I wanted to get inside it and understand it. You saw all these supporting beams, that the stucco was new, that the classicism had been fabricated out of nothing. And the only way I could learn it was to draw it.

M.B.: *What you're saying is that through studying the photograph and drawing it, you began to realise quite what an act of artifice the whole thing was. It is basically a stage set, and Nicky rolls up and does his thing.*

M.C.C.: It's fascinating too in that there's a kind of transfer of the most traditional if not conservative form of art education. For example when I went to Camberwell College of Arts to do my first degree in painting, we were sent to the National Gallery and told to copy Cézanne, and in so doing hopefully to gain a better understanding of what Cézanne was about. Of course that was brainless, whereas in your case it's conscious. You're directing yourself to a thing that interests you.

M.B.: *Do you feel that that art school copying exercise assisted you?*
M.C.C.: Only in that it strengthened my sense of rebellion! I became more and more contemptuous of tradition in art education. In retrospect I don't regret having chosen to go to a conservative school because at least it gave one values to react against. That seems much more difficult now. Most students are taught that anything goes, and the values are so much more complex. When I was studying, there was implicitly a consensus, and now there isn't. Bad is good, good is bad, where do you site yourself? It's complicated. However we're not here just to talk about art education.

L.M.: Well, I would like to talk about it briefly, because I just became a professor at Kunstakademie Düsseldorf.

M.B.: *The holy of holies in Germany, isn't it? Beuys taught there.*
L.M.: Beuys taught there, and the Bechers. I'm going to try to teach procedural painting because they're mostly still thinking that painting is about emotion, and the moment. I was trying to explain recently that we're always between two poles: academy and tradition at one end, and personal free expression at the other. We're calibrating somewhere between these two points at all times, and an awareness of both is useful. I will introduce decorative painting techniques to them. Some are desperate because they've never been taught anything, and it's exactly what they

want at this point. That's the way it was for me, after years of playing around and doing different things, I knew to go any further I needed to seriously study again.

M.B.: *Robert Hughes writes this extraordinary essay called "The Decline of the City of Mahagonny," and he lambasts American art education in the 1980s, saying that what was being taught was free expression, and then he adds very acidly, "At this no one could fail." Do you feel that your students are feeling similarly starved for substance, that they've had a concept until it's coming out of their ears, but what they actually want is instruction?*
L.M.: Yes, for the ones who want it, I am there. I will teach these techniques and they can interpret them if they want, how they want.

M.B.: *So are you creating your own basic course? What Richard Hamilton did in the late 1950s, beginning with growth and form?*
L.M.: Absolutely. Now I have to make explanatory posters about how wood grows, etc. It will be a completely new fine art course because it promotes artisan-painting techniques. It's satisfying to talk about ideas after you've done something rather than beforehand. When I taught in Salzburg in the summer, the students desperately wanted to talk about everything, and I always had to dampen them down, "We'll talk at the end." We got to the end, and then they said, "We're exhausted, we don't want to talk!"

M.B.: *At the Tate a few years ago you showed this really confrontational painting. Can you tell me about that painting and how you came to make it?*
L.M.: That painting was inspired by the experience of being in an institution called the DESTE Foundation in Athens. I travelled as a friend of some artists who were showing in the city and we were all invited for a fancy dinner there. The dining room was decorated with the Jeff Koons *Made in Heaven* series, so we had to

sit and eat under these images. Over the years I've been in several places like that, with Araki photographs or whatever hanging. I wanted to make a painting that expressed the banal fatigue I feel when this kind of art is used as décor, when we're expected to just accept pornography as a scenic prop in the art world.

M.B.: *Your painting had a very curious feel to it. Its gravitational field was very peculiar. It was sort of explicit and implicit simultaneously. And now that you explain the circumstances, why you made it that makes sense. It freaked people out. Was that deliberate?*
L.M.: Writers like Kathy Acker, Peter Sotos, and Dennis Cooper all combine extremes of repetitive prose and exploitative sex and perhaps I was thinking like that, where the fake wood and marble of the restaurant is the equivalent of Acker inhabiting and using *Great Expectations* in the structure of her novel.

M.B.: *It's an infinitely more shocking work than anything Koons has come up with. Going back to what we were saying about the artisan, about craft, the Koonsian model is the complete antithesis. It's American; it revels in a particular idea of American exploitative and abusive consumerism. I don't think there was an ounce of irony in what you did.*
M.C.C.: I don't think Koons understands irony. His primary agenda is probably world domination. Which is not what Lucy and I are particularly interested in.

M.B.: *Something that came across in your Secession show, and I find it endlessly fascinating, is this dialogue between American glamour and European intellectualism.*
M.C.C.: And it probably works better, does it not, when the energy is toward the East. The great European filmmakers, notably the Italians and Jean-Luc Godard, are drawn to Hollywood, and then they actually make the journey and fail, so I think the distance, the romanticism, the take we have on the West Coast legacy is

safest seen through the hourglass of Europe. I did, incidentally, recently reverse this argument by proposing that for a brief historical moment in the 1940s, architectural California had become more Viennese than Vienna!

L.M.: Certain artists, many in America, for instance Jeff Koons, have massive studios for fabricating their work. The historical model of the Renaissance atelier is invoked to legitimate the overproduction, but in fact it's far more industrial.

M.B.: *There is a fascinating film of Tom Ford interviewing Jeff Koons. He asks Jeff Koons what happens in one of his studios when he is out of town and an artistic decision has to be made, and Koons says, without a flicker of a smile, "Oh, we have management in place." That's probably one of the most articulate, eloquent things that could be said about his practice.*
M.C.C.: That's what made Warhol so European, that self-management. Warhol would be going back at two in the morning, the only person in his entourage who wasn't drunk and hadn't taken any drugs and was therefore able to make work.

M.B.: *And consumed with Eastern European melancholy, anxiety.*
M.C.C.: He would go to Mass with mother every Sunday, as a good Catholic boy does. A very European artist, yet one of the greatest American artists.

M.B.: *Lucy, you spent a long time studying how to make murals.*
L.M.: I went to school just to learn the principles of decorative painting. Fake wood and marble, *trompe l'œil*, perspective drawing, gilding, grisaille, how to prepare surfaces. And the rules of comportment if you're working in someone's house: Don't smoke, don't listen to music, wear a clean coat, if your client is titled make sure to address them by the correct title.

M.B.: *Were you interested in the etiquette?*
L.M.: I just lapped it all up. I loved it all. I loved my classmates. It was a complete holiday in a different universe. There were little tips, like, if you want your work to appear immediately better, wash the windows.

M.B.: *Can't argue with that.*
L.M.: My model for teaching in Düsseldorf is the mistress of that school, Denise Van Der Kelen.

M.B.: *Did you see the exhibition that Oliver Tepel did on the record label "Les Disques du Crépuscule" at Kölnischer Kunstverein? I thought it was one of the best exhibitions I'd ever seen anywhere.*
L.M.: [to Marc Camille] It was the Belgian equivalent of Factory Records, they shared many of the same musicians. Like with Peter Saville at Factory, Benoît Hennebert's designs defined the look and feel of the label. Which was softer, more whimsical than Factory. The label has a completely unique emotional sensibility and is the main reason I moved to Belgium, to understand where that could come from. Oliver Tepel organised the show with many original artworks, and contemporary artists responded to that aesthetic.

M.B.: *I see both of you as being connected to pop in its broadest sense: Lucy with Depeche Mode, for instance. And [to Marc Camille] I keep on waiting for you to make a piece based on Lou Reed's album* Berlin.
M.C.C.: It's probably too late. I might have once done so. I actually saw Lou Reed in Leeds years and years ago. It was a tiny audience, no one knew who he was. And then I saw him many times live in London before he was corrupted by hanging out with Laurie Anderson. And I think about taking up yoga. However, at least he's still alive. I think that the preexisting models I had as a student were so distant from what I was seeking that I was therefore much more greatly drawn to popular music, literature,

or cinema. In my formative years I would have said definitely that even someone as unfashionable as Dylan or Godard or Camus was my true hero, more so than any painter. Therefore rock and pop music were cardinal as a context. There were people who were creative in such a way that they were very elegantly able to negotiate all kinds of class barriers that were inherent in visual art culture in the UK. I remember a tutorial in art school, one of the staff asking, "Do you work to music or not?" Then the question was then asked of the head of the painting school, and in a most snobbish kind of way he said, "I do, but of course only classical music," and we thought, "You asshole."

L.M.: If you paint fake marble to classical music all the lines get too soft and wavy. You stole Manfred Mann's girlfriend, didn't you?

M.C.C.: That's right, I did, actually! That was a coup. At Ealing School of Art, she was studying fashion, of course, which was the coolest course in that particular art school. The things one confesses to in drunken moments! My fascination with that entire cultural scene was extended when Lucy invited me to present work at one of the later Flourish Nights. And Alex, the lead singer for Franz Ferdinand, was me. Before they hit the big time, otherwise there would have been a queue outside the studio, would there not? We needed a figure within a certain age group who was a surrogate for me to actually do the walking for the performance, and Lucy said, "I have a friend who can do it. He's kind of into art. He's a musician. He's slim, he's dark-haired, he moves well." And he was very good. I once stood in for Vito Acconci in New York. And I therefore thought if I ever were to write my autobiography I would call it *I Was Vito Acconci, Franz Ferdinand Was Me.*

M.B.: *That's a great title.*
M.C.C.: Maybe that's all I'd need, just to typeset the title. I wouldn't have to actually write the biography.

L.M.: When you did the group show in Ostend "…In the Cherished Company of Others…" there was a piece, I can't remember the title, the one with the curtain.

M.C.C.: It was the longest title: *We Chose Our Words with Care That Neon-Moonlit Evening; It Was as if We Were Party to a Wonderful Alchemy.*

L.M.: Behind the curtain there were a number of objects—which one was separated from but could view through peepholes—some flowers, a fox fur stole, a fountain. Pinned to the curtain were various photocopies, one of a very sweet looking fox, one of a flyer for a performance of yours.

M.C.C.: From the inaugural show at the AIR Gallery in London.

L.M.: I saw the little flyer and immediately wanted to steal it, like the way one wants a gig poster off a wall. And of course by the end of the opening someone had stolen it.

M.C.C.: It proved to be a trophy of sorts. I reconstructed that piece more ably in Los Angeles, of all places, where it somehow had extra resonance. With Overduin and Kite who were very good. And luckily I did have the original card, since the stolen one had been a photocopy.

L.M.: That overwhelming need to have that flyer proves to me that your work possesses cult status, and you are something of a pop star.

M.B.: *When Afterall published the book* Celebration? Realife, *it was very, very good. It almost reminded me of one of those 33 1/3 books on a WIRE album or something like that.*
M.C.C.: What I like about what we're attempting today … I've

often thought of crossovers between what Lucy does and what I do. It's not related to how the work looks, because our work looks so different. But I think there are many parallels, and one of them surely is that we're committed to an awareness of the implicit dialectic between high and low culture. That's kind of what *Celebration? Realife* in 1972 was about, a fascination with popular culture whilst retaining the specificity and the dynamic inherent to radical visual art practice.

M.B.: *The artist and ceramicist Carol McNicoll once said to me that in the early 1970s there was this notion amongst a certain group of art graduates that you could take ideas from the world of fine art or high culture and apply them to the language of absolute mainstream popular culture, the point being you did it without compromising either. In other words the pop had to remain pure pop and the art had to remain pure art. She designed Eno's peacock feather costume. When he wore it at the Rainbow, she saw fans running to the front and heard these girls screaming, "He's wearing the feathers!" That, for her, was her retrospective at the Tate. Meaning that she'd done it, as far as she was concerned. Is that a sensibility that you can recognise?*
M.C.C.: Very much so. I'm surprised at that particular anecdote because the concept wouldn't have existed then, but Eno was kind of the anorak behind the table full of knobs and wires, and it was the other Bryan who was the peacock. Eno was very much in the background as a kind of scientist-like figure. Almost as a technician.

M.B.: *I think it was all to do with assuming persona.*
L.M.: I've been trying to write about Scottish style in my collaborations with Beca. She was a casual, you know, impeccably worn expensive Italian sportswear, whereas my fashion references came from counterculture and from music. When you headed out of the house in some shredded nightdress and swastika armband you could just tell your mum that that's what the Slits or Siouxsie

Sioux wore and that somehow made it OK. It ushers in extremity for all who need it, at fourteen or fifteen.

M.B.: *I don't want to overload the conversation with Roxyisms, but Eno has this line where he says, "Pop has nothing to do with making music, it's about creating new imaginary worlds and inviting people to join them." I think that that's quite an interesting definition.*
M.C.C.: In working on this amazing book of yours, which as I remember concludes just at the point that they're about to release their first album, the master stroke, were you able to access each Brian as much as the other? So Brian Eno is as important as Bryan Ferry? Because I always felt that the band was in a way a duel between the two, one inherently conservative and one inherently progressive. I invited Eno to give a talk at Maidstone College of Art. Of course it was sold out, and his first line was great. There were people fighting to get in. And he took the mic and said, "You're here because I was in Roxy Music. I'm not." And he went into serious stuff, like cybernetics and logarithms and whatever.
L.M.: They just wanted him to sing some lines from "Baby's on Fire."

M.B.: *He once said he'd made 102 albums, and only two with Roxy. It must be quite difficult. I suppose what I keep coming back to is this idea for both of you of the Aesthetic movement and about the House Beautiful. And about the idea of the perfectly crafted interior, but also that kind of Huysmans-esque mysterious within it. I suppose that in the end for both of you there's an element that you keep in it of mystery.*
L.M.: I don't know if I'm really interested in mystery, but rather a kind of precision. I don't actually make a lot of work, so I try to get it as precise and eloquent as possible.

M.B.: *Given how you work right across media—you've done fashion, performance, painting—would your "ultimate" artwork be to design an entire house, like Lord Leighton's House in Holland Park?*

L.M.: Or Strawberry Hill. What you want of course is the perfect client. You want someone who's going to give you total freedom and an interesting context that leads to something else. People like Henry van de Velde did complete interiors, which also included what the wife of the client should wear. Which may be good art but it is also fascistic. I side with growing naturally, not megalomania.

M.C.C.: Exactly! Because whilst conceptually challenging, this surely need not be rendered material. I think we're more interested in asking questions than in answers. There's an interesting anecdote by Adolf Loos, which is implicitly a critique of his arch-rival Josef Hoffmann. The parable is of a client, a very rich merchant, inviting a most successful architect to build a house. It takes a number of years, and he's very honoured that the architect has deigned to accept the commission, and he's accepted it on the basis that he takes responsibility for everything—the guy's wardrobe, the cutlery, the carpets, as well as the house. On the night of the inauguration there is a great ball, and eventually the last to arrive is the architect, in his cloak. He comes up the steps and the client welcomes him in. The architect looks somewhat displeased, and the client is perplexed, and he says, "Master, what is the problem?" And the architect says, "Your slippers." And the client says, "But master, you designed them with your own fair hand." And the architect says, "Yes, but I designed them for the bedroom. We're in the hall." It's such a great answer. You can't win. That is how fascistic that Hoffmann "take" can become. And you see it today with someone like Norman Foster who bans any architect in his offices from having their own cups. They all have the standard cup; otherwise it would spoil the look of the design studio. That's the legacy. Whereas someone like Le Corbusier was much more relaxed. He designed a housing estate for the workers of one of the Citroën car plants, each unit called a Citrohan. Thirty years later, when Le Corbusier asked to see the estate, to see how well or not the prefabs had weathered thirty years on, he was driven there, and they were getting worried because people had kitsched them up, added trellises, windows, flower boxes. And he was so confident in terms of his own legacy that he found it charming.

L.M.: Cabinet are in the process of building their own gallery. It will be on the corner of the former Spring Gardens pleasure park, so they can think of it like a pavilion, which is a great architectural history to be part of.

M.B.: *It's a very brave thing for them to do, since Cabinet has existed to some extent on its nonexistence. It's impossible to ring them up, and nobody can find the website.*
L.M.: They could be described as being more predisposed to mystery.

M.C.C.: The director of the Hayward refers to them as the Greta Garbo of the art world.

M.B.: *I do rather like the idea of those two existing in some anonymous room somewhere with a couple of packing cases and a telephone. [to Lucy] After the show in Zürich, is there a show coming to London as well, did you say?*
L.M.: Just the showroom at Cabinet of the fashion collection by Atelier in September.

M.B.: *Were you approached by Pringle of Scotland? [meaning, approached as a contemporary artist to lend her face and signature to a product, and sign a contract promising to attend promotional events]*
L.M.: Yes, but I didn't participate. It was through the Serpentine Gallery, and it was not the way I wanted to engage with fashion. Instead I worked on *The Inventors of Tradition*, an independent project in Glasgow about the Scottish textiles industry. After doing the *Beck's Futures* in 2000 those things just seem like anti-ex-

periences. The artist never wins. The chance to do something that isn't a compromise is so slim. But I understand that companies like Pringle have to keep moving to survive. They need to shake off the Alan Partridge image.

M.B.: *The last conversation I had with Malcolm McLaren, he'd been asked by Pringle to do it.*
M.C.C.: Burberry was revamped, very successfully. Again by an outsider.

L.M.: Companies like Etro and Missoni are still in the family.

L.M.: [to Marc Camille] Do you have a dream collaboration you'd like to do?

M.C.C.: Woolworth's would be interesting. Or even Marks & Spencer.

M.B.: *If you're going to go mass, really go mass.*

[I. 16]

Marc Camille Chaimowicz
with Anette Freudenberger

Anette Freudenberger

(2012)

The conversation with Chaimowicz reproduced below took place at the Vienna Secession on 23 January, 2010 at 4 p.m. in the context of the exhibition "Marc Camille Chaimowicz" (20 November, 2009–24 January, 2010) organised by Elisabeth Bettina Spörr, curator at the Secession. Tape-recorded, the conversation was conducted by the German art historian and curator Anette Freudenberger, who subsequently edited it in collaboration with the artist for publication in The Secession Talks: Conversation Exhibitions, 1998–2010, *a 632-page compilation featuring fifty talks by artists whose work was presented at the Secession between 1998 and 2010. Edited by Sylvia Liska, President of the "Friends of the Secession," the book was published in 2012 with the intention of providing "an insight into artistic production with practical educational use."*

Six years earlier, Freudenberger invited Chaimowicz to do a personal exhibition at the Kunstverein für die Rheinlande und Westfalen, Düsseldorf, where she worked as a curator. Entitled "MARC CAMILLE CHAIMOWICZ" (11 September–6 November, 2005), this exhibition took place in a context that was not neutral for the artist. Indeed, as Chaimowicz revealed to Freudenberger at one of their first meetings, "As a child and young man, I was anti-German by distance to paternal historical past." It was therefore impossible for Chaimowicz to take on a project in Germany during his father's lifetime. The exhibition in Düsseldorf was, indeed, a German premiere. Aware of this, Freudenberger became crucial to the artist's understanding of the German situation. When they were both in Düsseldorf, for example, she made sure that Chaimowicz was presented in an appropriate way to a new generation of artists and art producers.

In 2006, Freudenberger moved to Vienna. Upon her arrival, she worked at the Secession for a few months during which she happened to talk about her recent experience with Chaimowicz. Her eloquence about the artist aroused the curiosity of the Secession staff, especially that of Liska, who had met the artist in Vienna in the early 1980s. This is why,

*when the exhibition was officially programmed at the Secession, Liska,
who was also responsible for the exhibition talks at the Secession, suggested Freudenberger for the public discussion with the artist usually
scheduled at the conclusion of each exhibition.*

*During 2009, Chaimowicz visited Vienna several times to prepare
his exhibition, refreshing his relationship with a city that had been
dear to him since the early 1980s. In 1982, Chaimowicz was part of
the Humanic-Artist-in-Residence-Program [III. 9]. At that time, his
involvement with the craft productions of the Wiener Werkstätte and
his engagement with Viennese architecture was an important stimulus for this work. Since then, Vienna has been, he said, "A rare city in
which we can both work and dream." Therefore, when the Secession
invited him to do a solo exhibition, he accepted immediately, with
a long letter/collage describing his relationship with the city in
mind [III. 26] and an exhibition space immersed in a pastel-toned
environment especially designed for the Secession.*

*As a German native, Freudenberger was aware of the differ-
ences between Germany and Austria. Keeping the artist company,
Chaimowicz remembers that "Anette was able to sensitise me in terms
of the local scene, rituals, and the courtesies required of the present
day in the city. I had to engage, not like in the 1980s! Yet another
scary-good aspect of being in Vienna anew." Although Freudenberger
was not part of the Secession staff at the time when the exhibition
was in preparation, she contributed indirectly to it, especially when
it came to securing a loan from Viennese architect Hermann Czech,
whom Chaimowicz wished to involve in his exhibition, in addition
to British artist Simon Thompson. As Chaimowicz recalls: "This
loan was typically Viennese and complex: Hermann Czech resisted,
whereas my request was simply about getting a photographic detail
of a piece of fabric, an anonymous variation of a 1950s upholstery
design that is used on the seats of Kleines Café II, which Hermann
Czech designed in 1973–74." Aware that Chaimowicz held*

Hermann Czech in high esteem, Freudenberger advised him to write a letter telling him how "fantastic" his design for Kleines Café II was, which he did, forgetting to mention his love for the Wunder-Bar that Hermann Czech designed in Vienna in 1975–76, which had made the artist's evenings alone in the crowd "so enjoyable." As a result, the situation was quickly resolved and the enigmatic photographic sample of fabric was presented in the exhibition. Illustrating what the artist calls "the cherished company of others" [I. 11], this anecdote further highlights the genuine complicity between Chaimowicz and Freudenberger that permeates the discussion below. Focusing on the artist's recent exhibitions, including the one in Vienna, their dialogue underscores the fact that even in the context of a solo exhibition, artists do not find themselves in a sociopolitical vacuum sealed off from the outside world.

A.V.

• • • • • • • • •

Anette Freudenberger: *Marc, I remember your major exhibitions in the last years, like in the Migros Museum für Gegenwartskunst, Zürich, the show we did together at the Kunstverein in Düsseldorf, the Berlin Biennale, the most recent show at Artists Space in New York; and you had this fantastic show in De Appel in Amsterdam two years ago that also travelled to Ostend called "…In the Cherished Company of Others…" So, despite your being a very experienced artist, I can imagine it was exciting to receive the invitation to the Secession, especially because you had a residency in Vienna in 1982.*
Marc Camille Chaimowicz: It was good, but it was scary. Kind of scary-good. Because of the history of the Secession and because of my unique relationship to the city of Vienna and because of the really scary nature of the space, which is not easy, especially for someone who tends to deal with understatement and who has a tendency towards wanting to hide. I am aware of the flexibility

of the space and that one could technically have proposed temporary walls to be built or partitions or whatever, but it seemed important to honour the inherent integrity of the exhibition space, which therefore meant finding ways of negotiating something that doesn't afford any kind of intimacy.

The first time I saw some of your artworks was in Berlin in a group show at Galerie Neu curated by your London gallery Cabinet. There had already been those intimate photos on a folded screen and these very peculiar patterns, which are not on paper but are painted with a roller instead. As I grew up in a completely constructed city, where that kind of old-fashioned pre-war decoration doesn't exist at all, it touched me in a quite strange way, like messages from a past that is thought to be hidden tightly underneath the typical clean white ingrain wallpaper. On the other hand, the rollers interested me for technical reasons, because they eliminate the gesture, if you like, the immediate subjective expression and introduce contingency and unavoidable mistakes. In Berlin you applied the colour yourself, right? Here you didn't. How was that?
Acrobatic! Neu is an atypical tall space. I wanted to do it by hand. But in the Secession I had the opportunity of skilled help. What happened here is that we were able, during the period of installation, to transform the gallery space into a temporary studio and as the professional technicians were working on the wall, I was able to work on the panel. It was really a question of getting quite a lot done in a condensed period of time.

The portable, sellable artwork was often connected to a conservative art practice, not only by Daniel Buren. You seem to consider that from a different angle. I would like to know how you deal with the idea of studio-based work in relation to site-specific work and what that might have to do with interiors. You recently published together with Migros Museum für Gegenwartskunst, Zürich, the hilarious artist-book The World of Interiors. *The domestic interior not only constructs the modern subject and raises the question about the private and the political; it is a basic topic of painting as well. A subject that comes along with the emancipation of painting as independent art and with the appearance of the figure of the artist, which reminds me of Vermeer's* The Art of Painting *in the Kunsthistorisches Museum in Vienna, that shows the artist in his studio.*

I think your work has partly to do with this relation between the artist and the space of production, whether it be the studio, the living room, the exhibition space or a carpenter's workshop, and that is already true for this early piece Vienna Triptych, Leaning… and Surrounded by Chorus Girls and Sentinels. *Could you first say something about that piece and the time when it was produced?*

It was done entirely in Vienna by courtesy of Grita Insam, who is with us this evening, who invited me to come and live in Vienna, and offered me a very small bed, but a very big studio. It was a massively important time of reassessment for me. Also the wall patterning originates from then. As yourself I am not from a culture where that form of decoration is practiced. So, it was only in wondering about the city and notably in engaging with public housing that I became more and more conscious of this inexpensive low-tech form of decoration.

But Vienna Triptych… *is not made with the rollers, I see a painted or collaged pattern.*

Those were done by hand. What often happens, I think, in the pursuit of art practice is that we sensitise ourselves to certain things, and then it takes a while before that sensitisation will become manifest, as in a kind of time warp. The rollers were found in Vienna, which for me, in some way, was a fictive city. Vienna in 1982 was a kind of Warsaw, which had been denied for me, for family reasons and cultural reasons, as a result of the legacy of World War II. So, given I would not get to Warsaw, I would in my deluded subjectivity project Poland onto Austria. I therefore imagined possible environments in which my father might have lived, which would have been decorated in that manner. This was quite a slow piece to produce because it meant to me installing a dark room. All those photographs and many more to build up this complex narrative were printed in this provisional dark room.

There are some photos from Vienna, but there are also photos of a space, I would say, it's like a living room, or a flat, or maybe it's a hotel. Were they taken in London?
Well, that's not a question that needs answering, because where the images come from is not important as to how the images are received. If they are received as coming from London, then maybe that is where they might have come from, but they may equally have come from … Trieste.

I was asking about those interiors because they turn up very often in different forms in your work. One has the idea that they show your flat, which must have been used as a studio, if one thinks of the kind of happening-like work you did there. You have invited certain people to sit down in a very formal setting to talk about art in a certain amount of time.
Quite by chance, I recently read a quote by Virginia Woolf. What I found relevant if not to some extent tragic is that she talked very eloquently about that time when she wrote *A Room of One's Own*. It was kind of metaphor for her arguing as a gender-aware person, as an early feminist. Not only would a woman writer need a room of her own, but she would also need money of her own to establish a degree of autonomy, and furthermore, she would need a language of her own. And that's when it gets very complicated, because she was doomed to write in a language, which was not inherently her language, but a male language. And so given that she then argued that the constriction that women writers were then facing is that there was an implicit critical hierarchy whereby for men to write books about war was seen as serious, and worthy of critique, but for women to write about the drawing room or a shop was seen as inferior. So I guess, what that quote was about for me is that—in

a convoluted retort to your question about interiority—it seems to me that interiors of work dealing with the intimate is still often seen as somehow, certainly in socio-political terms, having less merit than work dealing with, say, a bigger subject matter. But it may also be, in terms of art history, that interiors may always be a kind of niche place. I for myself, when studying painting, was very much drawn to a very particular French sensibility, which in retrospect makes more sense now than it might have done then. You know, we are drawn to things we like, and we don't necessarily know why we like them. But now, I can understand better why I was drawn to Edouard Vuillard or Pierre Bonnard, who were not fashionable figures at the time. It's because they were actually dealing with that sensibility.

There is this view on a remembered past, which is partly autobiographical, but there is a quite concrete, constant back-and-forth in time in your work. Vienna Triptych... *is an old piece, whereas most of the pieces you have done for this show are new.*
What was great about the invitation, apart from the invitation, was that it arrived in letterform. And the letter was actually produced on a typewriter, on a letter-headed paper that was signed in ink. Therefore I had a good feeling about this invitation. And I quickly came over, thinking I must meet these people and see the space. At that point it was explained to me that there is a sort of expectation that shows here are primarily to do with current practice or new work. And actually, there are fifteen new pieces, which have not been seen before, which is probably a personal record. But there was an exception, which we discussed at some length in terms of historicising the practice, and that was the opportunity to return the *Vienna Triptych...* to its city of origin. That is the premise of establishing time as an element of exhibition.

People who know your work might wonder what is new. In your practice, there is a constant revisiting of situations like in your famous environment Celebration? Realife *that was suddenly* Celebration? Realife Revisited *in 2000. A lot of works here seem to have been somewhere already, maybe in a different form, like on a photo or as part of an installation.*

My feeling has long been that time is actually not necessarily chronological. I don't think it's linear. I think it folds in on itself. We've all experienced situations in which we have a recall of something that happened a long time ago, which seems actually more current than something that happened six months ago. That's a very simple example of that position. But in terms of implicit dialogues within this whole project there is the letter, which is only a second published letter in terms of a potential book work, recalling the letters from Vienna that was published, I think in 1984, in a book called *Café du Rêve*, which is called "Chorus, a letter from Vienna." So again, this is a kind of retort, relative to using a pre-existent form in the present.

Last year, the building of the Secession was approached several times in a critical way. Paweł Althamer built a tunnel through this building; Katrin Plavčak's white approach was more humourous, she attached a moustache to the facade; and Hannes Zebedin threw a stone through a window. Whereas your site-specific work reconnects with the cultural background, your latest letter opens up a dialogue between your two shows in L.A. at Overduin and Kite and at the Secession, you prepared at the same time, and a dialogue between old Europe and America. You talk about the exodus of people to America and Schindler who left Vienna in 1914 to find a more open atmosphere over there.

There is, here, a portrait of Schindler on the bookshelf. I was fortunate in being able to go to California in April; I had not been to the West Coast before. And I was intrigued, given my historical awareness of this exodus that you refer to, as to whether or not one might propose a historical moment in which there might have been a more Viennese sensibility outside of Vienna, which I think, for a while, might have been the case. I then drew a number of parallels.

That was compounded by the happy good fortune of being able to see a Franz West show in California. I have seen a number of Franz West shows, as we all have, but this was the best show I have seen. When one is sensitised to something, one is sensitised pretty much everywhere one looks. So, given I was thinking of how to deal with this challenge to exhibit at the Secession, wherever I might have been, I might have seen Vienna. We are talking recently about this restaurant, which we like very much, in Los Angeles. And it turns out it's a Viennese guy who happens to run a really good restaurant in California. So, Vienna is everywhere.

Paris as well! The over painted Yves Saint Laurent advertisement happened while you were working in your temporary studio in the Secession.

That's a very specific example where a page torn from a current copy of *Vogue* ends up in the show. Given it refers to a product launched by Yves Saint Laurent, we could then go out and buy the perfume and place it on the dressing table, so it's yet another example of the subtle correspondence, which hopefully functions as a kind of metaphor for dialogue. That is what this whole project means. As artists, we are inevitably doomed to the silence of our own subjectivity. Given that, we yearn for dialogue both literally and metaphorically. In my case, a dialogue may be with somebody who fabricates something, so it's a technical dialogue. Or it might be a dialogue between artworks and time, or between work and space.

You also collaborated with other artists. Paulina Olowska, for example, did a drawing on your wall painting in the show at Galerie Neu, so it became one piece by the two of you, which was probably also about Warsaw. Then, you did this show in Amsterdam, together with the curator Alexis Vaillant. You integrated artworks from friends and artists related to the exhibition context or to the city where the show took place. You did the same here, I think, in a less extended way?

I have done it here in a more economic way, perhaps more precisely.

Simon Thompson and Hermann Czech, for example, were invited. It's very often said that you are concerned with the idea of dandyism. Doesn't that oppose the very idea of collaboration?
I remember once reading an interview with Michael Krebber. They asked him about dandyism, and he said: I am not a dandy, I am an artist. That was a very acute way of taking that question. But I think the issue of fraternity is something that fascinates me and I aspire to. With retrospective shows, which of course this is not, but the one in De Appel was, there often is something sad and false, you know, walking into the top floor of the Tate, and seeing room after room, forty or fifty years of work presented in such a way that it would seem that that person had worked in complete isolation. But hopefully, we all regularly need to step outside of ourselves and make connections. It's something that happens actually much more often in music, which is perhaps a more social practice. Technically, a guest band appears before a main band. The idea of guest appearances is something that I would continue to work with. What we did here is actually better than what we did in Amsterdam. Here we are much more specific, notably in terms of the limited number of invited guests and in terms of the specificity of the work chosen by them.

You have this photograph of Hermann Czech here that shows a textile seat covering. Why did you invite him?
I first encountered his work when living in Vienna. Notably through the bars he had designed, and I became interested. I was also fortunate, when living here, to be introduced to a number of people who had a real sensibility for the historic and present architectural climate of the city.

You said you don't like to be in the foreground, you prefer intimacy. I think this is an idea that Czech is interested in as well. He is anti-

dogmatic, in a way. In her really wonderful text in your catalogue, Silvia Eiblmayr mentions his idea of mannerism, as a possibility to include irregularities. He wanted to react to a given situation and the way a user would utilise it. So there is an openness that offers a sort of participation.
Well, Hermann Czech … we had lunch and we talked and he went off and considered the invitation which he then in time graciously accepted. So, the issue of what he might contribute arose. We talked about the bars he has rendered possible, which miraculously still exist. That's something that is probably rare nowadays. There is a slower time base in Vienna than there is in New York or London. And so, interiors that were built thirty years ago are still intact. Which is kind of great!

Thirty years feels quite contemporary in Vienna. The textile is not in Czech's bar anymore, though. He used it in the 1970s, but it was actually from the 1950s. So it is in itself already a time capsule.
And it was anonymous. We don't actually know who designed that piece of fabric, which I like, given that it concurs with the other pieces of fabric—again from someone unnamed—which were lent by the Museum of Applied Arts in Vienna. Fabric is generally more often unnamed than named. That's something which, in terms of decoration, has interested me for a very long time, that one can establish a dialectic between the self, which is by definition about naming, and the anonymous, which is its opposite. And I think Hermann Czech is also quite interested in that.

We did not yet talk about painting, but I have the feeling this is a show about painting, even if you included only one.
There are more paintings in storage here. With a show of this dimension, if there is the sensibility and the understanding of the curatorial team … I need a degree of time in the space, playing with different things, moving them around, taking things out, putting things in. One tends to bring more than one needs. So, we ended up with just that one painting, that painted board. But I

am happy that you see that the show is dealing with painting. Many of the questions are apparently painterly. Painting is a bit like Catholicism. They say: Once a Catholic, always a Catholic. And I guess, once a painter, probably always a painter.

You have chosen your colours with great care. They are very unusual and elaborate. Where does this palette of colours come from? This one over there looks grey from further away, but if you look closer it's more greenish-yellow with pink; it's post-impressionistic somehow. In your text you talked of a lexicon of colours?
One of the problems we were facing in the '70s—by "we" I would imply those artists that were critical of the values in the dominant culture and that were probably seen as left-wing in their sensibility—and one of the problems that I was facing at that time was that it seemed that a radically engaged practice had an inherently puritanical premise, which manifested itself through denying questions around colour and beauty. The premise then was that beauty and truth were falsehoods and therefore inappropriate and therefore inherent to conservatism. And yet it seemed to me that pleasure and beauty were too important to hand over to the enemy. One had to try to reclaim them back for oneself.

It seems to be a very conceptual approach to questions of painting. For example, when I see your carpets, I think, in every carpet you deal with different premises of painting.
Painting is conceptual. You can't get more conceptual than Barnett Newman. He is a great painter.

At first I had some difficulties with the parasols, because I couldn't relate them to your work. I didn't know that they were not yours but from a designer.
There is a term in the English language, which probably comes from medieval times, the "journeyman." It is a term I like. And I think the journeyman is a tradesperson, a skilled person, who

would just walk from one city to another—it would inevitably have been a man—and he would just go from one client to the next, he would go where the work is. He would respond to commissions. I wanted to do that as well, which has led me to work in a wide range of materials as part of a commitment, as part of the practice of questioning the possible role of the artist. So, I am waiting for those moments, when somebody might call and say, would you be interested in doing this or that? Anastasia Denoux wanted to set up her own business and had decided that the time was right to edit and produce parasols. And I felt, at the height of the biggest economic crash since 1930, there is Anastasia deciding that the world needs parasols. I was charmed by this kind of presumption and included them in the show.

For me, they make the difference between design and art very clear, or between your art and her art, because she applied the patterns on a given form, and somehow it's different from the way you do it.
Absolutely. In the context of this project, she could be seen as just another guest.

In the Vermeer painting that I mentioned, there is a curtain that helps the recipient to enter the painted space. You included a curtain in the Secession show that was originally your contribution for the Berlin Biennale. It somehow supports my impression that we are in a surrounding here, that continuously switches between a real and fictive respectively painted space. It was for the Neue Nationalgalerie in Berlin, which has a higher ceiling than the space here, therefore it folds on the ground.
The curtain is a specific example of the principle of "journeyman." A while ago, maybe in the 1980s, I was approached by this illustrious company in Switzerland; they weave and print fabrics. They invited me to work with them and I was happy to do that. From the many drawings I did a number were selected for production, one of which was this design. When the opportunity of showing in the Mies van der Rohe building in Berlin in the context of the 5th Berlin

Biennial came up and I was offered one corner of that illustrious space, I remembered that Mies van der Rohe, as a sick and elderly man, had been driven in a white Mercedes Benz to the inauguration of the pavilion. Given the rigour of his aesthetic position he was shocked to see that they had hung curtains in order to break the violence of the setting sunlight coming into the glass wall box. He was so angered by this that he refused to leave the car and never saw his finished work. I mean, that's an extreme example of architectural arrogance, is it not? Thinking about the exhibition opportunity and that one could not ignore the magnitude of the venue I figured it would be interesting to answer some of the issues inherent in what is actually a very antisocial building. In terms of its function, it is certainly strange to design an exhibition space, which doesn't have any walls. It is a problematic building. So I proposed a curtain.

But it was not meant to be an exhibition space, when he designed it first. Or am I wrong? He didn't design it for Berlin, the design is older. The original design was a headquarter building for a company in America. Then he radically reviewed the design as a national exhibition space. He even designed fittings by which temporary panels could be hung from the roof structure. So I engaged with the one concession he made, the inclusion of marble columns. They look as though they may be functional, as though they might be holding a roof, but in fact the roof is miraculously self-supporting. Partly, those columns may introduce a sort of verticality; they also function now as cladding for air conditioning and services. In a way they reminded me of Adolf Loos who once said the greatest form of wallpaper is marble. So I then worked with added marble and felt it useful to slow down the latitude between the inside and the outside of the building, through a kind of fabric that is actually made for that and is known in the trade as transparent.

Your dressing table reminds me of Tom Burr's versions he exhibited in the Secession in 2007, though his were much more minimalist. In

Vienna these dressing tables used to be called Psyche *by the way. In your show at De Appel you included a mirror piece by him.*
The Tom Burr piece we borrowed for Amsterdam is a very simple work—it's on two metal legs, pieces of mirror, designed to enable someone dressing to see how the shoes work in the context of the whole. I first saw it in London in a collector's dressing room; it was used as a functional piece. It looks a bit lost in a big exhibition space, until somebody walks past, and then it incorporates or includes the passer in the exhibition. I think it's a great piece. Quite subversive.

Beyond that, mirrors are a subject in painting as well. For example in Velasquez' Las Meninas *or Jan van Eyck's* The Arnolfini Portrait, *the mirror connects the painting space with the space outside the painting and integrates the artist and the beholder. But of course Tom Burr is a sculptor, not a painter, and he surely would not place the furniture so directly in front of the wall like you did.*
My items were designed as functional objects.

How many did you do? I heard that you wanted to use them as models for mass production, such as the wallpaper, for example, something everybody can buy in a wallpaper shop—and that they cease to be artworks as soon as they are out of the exhibition context.
I have certainly not found the means or been introduced to the right people. Even someone who is usually fashionable like Eileen Gray did not see her pieces mass-produced in her lifetime—most of my works have not been realised in higher quantities, with the exception of printed matter, i.e. wallpaper and fabric, which on occasion has been made for the commercial market. That's delightful, but those are the exceptions.

It took a very long time to give art its own legitimisation and to separate it from applied and religious art. Nowadays, it's intermingled again.
Perhaps the separation was too successful and we need to reintegrate more.

Trusting Our Eyes:
A Conversation with Marc Camille Chaimowicz

Clémentine Deliss

(2012)

Since its founding in 1904, the Weltkulturen Museum (Museum of World Cultures)—Frankfurt's renowned collection of non-European artefacts—has made a significant contribution to exploring new ways of combining works of art and ethnographic artefacts, particularly under the leadership of British-born art historian and curator Clémentine Deliss. Indeed, during her tenure (2010–15), the museum's collection (which includes 65,000 ethonographic artefacts from Oceania, Africa, Southeast Asia, as well as North, South, and Central America, plus 120,000 ethnographic photos and films) has been reinterpreted at the intersection of post-colonialism, anthropology, and gender, with the intention of progressively deconstructing the presupposition of homogeneity and timelessness upon which this type of museum is usually based. Among the innovative events developed during Deliss' tenure was the exhibition "Object Atlas. Fieldwork in the Museum" (25 January–16 September, 2012). As Deliss described in the exhibition catalogue: "This unusual form of domestic fieldwork has resulted in an experimental set of new artworks, produced on site and directly related to the ethnographic collections of the museum."

For this exhibition Deliss invited seven artists to Frankfurt over the course of 2011 to develop "fieldwork in the museum." The artists were: Helke Bayrle, Thomas Bayrle, Marc Camille Chaimowicz, Sunah Choi, Antje Majewski, Otobong Nkanga, and Simon Popper. Interested in "fieldwork" from a contemporary point of view [I. 13] and stimulated by a sensitive approach to visual and material cultures, the artists selected objects from the museum's collection while developing their research and project for the exhibition. To facilitate their stay, they could stay at the Weltkulturen Labor, a new building across the River Main in Frankfurt, blending apartments, studios, seminar rooms, a laboratory, and the photographic archive.

Chaimowicz visited Frankfurt three times in April, May, and July-August. At the beginning of the process, he met with the museum's curators, archivists, and librarians, which was, he said, "An enjoy-

able occasion to travel the world in two or three days: one morning in Africa, one afternoon in Oceania … in a very efficient and professional way." Subsequently, Chaimowicz focused on artefacts from Indonesia, Samoa, Amazonas, and Africa, and then developed his own "fieldwork in the museum." His selection of objects was based on floral elements from Indonesia and Samoa, as well as hats, headrests, and belts from Africa, and bark cloth paintings and feather jewelry from the Amazonas region. As a visual response to these artefacts collected in the collection, Chaimowicz produced a new series of vertical wood panels with stencil prints, entitled The Frankfurt Suite.

The conversation with Chaimowicz reproduced below took place in Frankfurt, in the museum director's office, in early August 2011. Tape-recorded, the conversation was subsequently transcribed by the museum's editorial team, and edited by Deliss in collaboration with the artist over email. It was then published in the catalogue of the exhibition Object Atlas: Fieldwork in the Museum, which was published in conjunction with the exhibition. Edited by Deliss and produced by the Weltkulturen Museum in collaboration with Kerber Verlag in 2012, this 508-page bilingual (German and English) publication brought together new commissioned essays, archives, and facsimiles of anthropological texts, and was divided into two parts as follows: the "Expeditions," comprising the seven artist's sections, and "Fieldwork in the museum."

Chaimowicz's section was divided into four parts: the conversation reproduced below; the list of the artist's "laboratory library"; a letter from Roger Cook; and a text on the language of flowers. The artist's "laboratory library," which includes the eight publications the artist consulted during his visits to Frankfurt, reads as follows:

— Bird, Adren J. & Josephine Puninani Kanekoa Bird: 1987. Hawaiian flower lei making. Honolulu: University of Hawai'i Press.

— *Brandon, Reiko Mochinaga & Loretta G. H.Woodard: 2004.* Hawaiian quilts. Tradition and transition. *Honolulu: University of Hawai'i Press.*

— *Brinkgreve, Francine & David Stuart-Fox: 1992.* Offerings. The ritual art of Bali. *Bali: Image Network Indonesia.*

— *Frances, Perry & Leslie Greenwood: 1977.* Blumen der Welt. *Freiburg: Herder.*

— *Gide, André: 1991.* Der Immoralist. *From the French, translated by Gisela Schlientz. (Collected works, twelve volumes; vol.VII/1). Stuttgart: Deutsche Verlagsanstalt.*

— *Kepler, Angela Kay: 1998.* Hawaiian heritage plants. *Honolulu: University of Hawai'i Press.*

— *McDonald, Mary A. & Paul R. Weissich: 2003.* Na lei makamae. The treasured Lei. *Honolulu: University of Hawai'i Press.*

— *Meller, Susan & Joost Elffers: 1991.* Textile designs. Two hundred years of European and American patterns. *Cologne: DuMont.*

Also featured in the catalogue was a 16-page photo-documentation of the artist's studio at the Weltkulturen Labor, including a portrait of the artist showing a stencil sheet in front of his face. The "Letter to MCC" from "Dr Roger Cook, Visiting Fellow, Institute of Germanic and Romance Studies, University of London," is dated 24 September, 2011, and signed "Yours efflorescently, frère fictif, Roger" *[I. 12].*

The artist's section concludes with a text by Vanessa von Gliszczynski, Research Curator at the Weltkulturen Museum, Southeast Asia Collection. Focusing on "The Language of Flowers," this text provides historical and anthropological background to the artist's research. Speaking on the subject, albeit in a more political manner, Cook explains in his letter that "it is not surprising that your selection of ethnographic objects should take a stand against androcentric domination and settle on the ambivalently gendered ephemerality and eroticism of flowers. The floral motifs have always appealed to you as they did for Baudelaire and Genet [Ill. 27] for their not so innocent insolence as fleurs du mal.*" Indeed, Chaimowicz's use of flowers are something of a transitional motif: utterly mundane, yet capable of capturing the ambivalent essence of what is otherwise better left unsaid.*

A.V.

· · · · · · · · ·

Clémentine Deliss: *When you came here, you first visited the storage areas and then objects that you had selected were brought to the Weltkulturen Laboratory.*
Marc Camille Chaimowicz: Yes, and I was really impressed to see how remarkable they are. But I haven't responded in the most obviously descriptive manner. Because of circumstances, and the way I work, I figured out that I wouldn't have the luxury of spending weeks in the Laboratory attempting to come to terms with these artefacts. Instead, I did all the preparatory drawings away from Frankfurt as a means of charging up my creative batteries. Having completed the drawings, stencils were prepared in Burgundy. In the Laboratory, the first creative decisions that I made were basically the ordering of materials and colour choices so we could start straight away. When I came back to Frankfurt to work, I could triple my time with the help of assistants and make the very best use of a concentrated amount of time.

You have a particular approach that enables you to see these objects and somehow create a visual X-ray of them. But the perception of many other artists isn't constructed in that way.
Sure, other artists have a different take on materiality. I uphold the principle of the laboratory. But I resist the fetishisation of the studio. In the past many people have asked me where I work. I can't

answer that question because I work most probably in the back of a cab, in a bar, in bed, or on the Tube. I live in a rich mental mindscape and I've never been a studio-based artist in that sense. I feel trapped in a studio and get restless. I mean this studio at the Weltkulturen Museum is different because it is located in an historical building. And I can pop in and out of the Lab at different times of the day, even during moments of insomnia. This is a great luxury. I have never taken a glass of wine down to the Laboratory out of respect for the objects, but I have taken a glass of wine down to the studio here late at night and really begun to understand what is going on in the work, and prepare the ground for the following day so that my assistants can get stuck in rather than wait for me to dither and fluster about. So the integrated nature of the workspace with apartment, studios, and Laboratory is nearer to how I would normally work in London, where I tend to work in my kitchen.

This is the idea of domestic research and domestic production.
I agree. And I think that in my quest for honesty and position I underplay the importance of the Laboratory at the Museum. It has been valuable to know that it is there, so I can just go and check on the objects. And it is also true that this is a unique project, it is more than a commission. A commission is something that I take on once a year. I have this conceptual position, I like the idea that one can indulge in the medieval tradition of journeymen who responded to a request—be it to carve an angel on a coffin or to travel down to Portsmouth to work on the town hall. This situation in Frankfurt is much more intellectually challenging than the journeyman's commission would be. However, if the request had come from any other director of a similar museum I probably would have declined. I would have said I don't have the qualifications. I don't have the tools with which to meaningfully respond to the commission. The reason that I have been positive and sympathetic has been out of my respect for who you are and how you think and work, rather than to a tradition of the anthropological.

There's a great quote from André Gide, "Poverty is a slave driver. In return for food men give their grudging labour. All work that is not joyous is wretched, I thought, and I paid many of them to rest. Don't work I said, you hate it. In imagination I bestowed on each of them that leisure without which nothing can blossom, neither vice nor art." It's perhaps excessively romantic but, as Gide points out, his definition of freedom has to be anchored in the real, i.e. he's happy to give people money to live and to free them up to be creative because most work is a kind of journey. I guess my definition of fieldwork would be to try to structure one's life so that one has a high degree of freedom, which then enables one to resist the pressures of the marketplace, categorisation, or a particular way of working. That's quite demanding, I know, but it makes for a much more interesting life. It means that everything is possible, however modest that may be.

There are itinerant objects in your selection from the collection. They too have moved around the world. Are they exotic to you? Or have they lost this exoticism?
No, they are absolutely exotic to me and absolutely alien. They entreat me, but I don't pretend to have any understanding of what they are for or why they are here. I guess my initial doubt would be based on a sort of committed cultural anchorage to that which is European. If I were offered the world to travel in with the exclusion of Europe, or Europe with the exclusion of all other parts of the world, I would have no hesitation in choosing Europe, especially if I knew that there wouldn't be enough days left in my life to enjoy the cultural difference between Oslo and Tangiers. I also understand that to some extent we have been constructed through cultural cross-fertilisation.

But what is it that you do when you see an exotic object or an object that is outside of your frame of reference? Take that belt from Namibia in our collection, with its small hanging tortoise. Your work does something to this piece. You are not trying to legitimise its cultural background; you're not trying to be an expert or specialist in African art. So what is it that you are putting together here, and do you need to bring in other objects in order for this process to work?

I think this is interesting. Yesterday we were talking about John Hoyland. He is a good example of someone who out of vanity, I suppose, was very reactionary. I met him a few times, and he was anti-intellectual as many of his UK-based generation are. He had a really good colour sense, was good at drawing, had a good sense of virtual space, but intellectually he was kind of inactive and therefore the work just went round and round in circles. Yet the one thing we can learn from Hoyland is to trust our eyes, to enjoy the world and its material artefacts on a visual level. That has been my motive and my directive on the shopping trips into the stores of the Museum here, which were remarkable.

What do you mean by shopping trips?
You know, like the rich have personal shoppers to help them navigate through the different departments of Harrods. In the Museum stores, the research curators were like my personal shoppers. I asked one expert, what do we have that admonishes the floral? And she said, that's a good one because it's difficult. By definition, flowers are part of the natural sciences. But through a range of different research routes, we found different ways into the floral. So this is an example of the importance of the conduit of the personal shopper and specialist. And although my criteria were very fluffy, they were principally pleasure-driven according to what I enjoyed looking at. So in one case, I selected a sword and some shields, which are objects that I would normally find problematic because of the reference to fighters.

You didn't want to look at weapons?
Right. This was the exception because this shield has been beautifully decorated with this very fine floral motif. That weapon was

made principally for symbolic use by its owner in order to train himself and perform an act of purification. Even if it is a weapon, it has not been made to hurt others. So it isn't a weapon in the classic sense.

It was meant to heal the person who held it.
Yes, to drive away evil spirits.

I am interested in the eclecticism of this collection. The analogy to the shopper is curious because clearly these objects reached Frankfurt through trade circulation, through the exchange of goods, through notions of faith and the actions of missionaries. They were interpreted at certain moments in time and they have been reinterpreted once, twice, three, or four times. But in some cases, interpretations have highlighted certain aspects of the object and omitted others.
Many of these objects elude interpretation. For example, my favourite object is the basket or mask from Angola that was collected in 1941. We don't know what it's really for.

Yet that doesn't stop us from creating a new understanding of it today. It's by no means completed as an object of interpretation.
But that is your job and you're good at it, but I haven't done that. I just draw pretty patterns.

I don't think so. I believe these objects are stored code.
You may be right. With one object, I needed two stencils because it was so elusive. So I've taken two takes on it, whereas with others I've taken only one.

But with your take on this object, you created another metaphor for it.
Yes, I'm hoping this will be visible in the exhibition. We have to agree that in the twenty-first century one doesn't simply make art. One acknowledges differently the making of the work and the exhibition of the work. The exhibition cannot be reduced to

the making. I think this project consists of three parts. The first is the shopping, the second is the hands-on aspect of making, and the third is the presentation of that work of research (although I would avoid this word out of respect to properly trained scientists). So the interface between the codification of the stimulus, the reason or maybe even the excuse, will actually become the work. In that sense the panels that I made here lack that late modernist credo. They are infinite, incomplete, and yet they come into their own in dialogue with the objects from the collection. That is what makes this project meaningful.

What you have produced here and have gifted to the Museum is a new and unfinished prototype that is based on a coded object that is itself unfinished. Different people can add a further production to it. It can't resist being rearticulated or reinterpreted again. It has to offer something or one might as well put it away in a cupboard and not look at it again. With a collection of 67,000 objects, your visual training is very important. That is why you have chosen certain objects and not others.
I bumped into Mona Suhrbier, the Museum curator for the Americas collection, yesterday and she commented very positively on my choice of objects. And I answered, thank you, but my choice has been quite superficial because I don't pretend to have any expertise. And she replied, you know, we anthropologists indulge in that as well! And I thought, good for you! She was reminding me of a greater proximity between us than I would have presumed. Research is necessarily serious; pleasure is fun and what you do on weekends. In visual art practice these two aspects conflate.

For this exhibition, several artists unexpectedly introduced painting as a tool to understand the ethnographic objects. Do you see a connection to painting in your work here too, or are the panels and stencils part of an existing repertoire?
I don't think of these panels as paintings. I use household paints

rather than artists' materials or watercolours. Household paint is inert and mute as a material. It doesn't harbour any painterly brush strokes. In that sense, this is not really painting. It is closer to decoration. Nonetheless, it may be that I have returned to my roots since my first love was painting. The primary reason for working in the way we did here was to establish a resemblance of coherence through the agency of three people, which will hopefully appear as one. There are no individual fingerprints on the work. And here is the analogy to the craftsman. What interests me is this interface between identities, something which motivates much of fine art practice and which comes back to an essential questioning of the self. And this questioning is counterpoised by the anonymous, the way a craftsman works.

Yes. And that anonymity appears by default with these ethnographic objects, as we often don't know who made them, or whether several people made them.
Exactly, like a collective.

Marc Camille Chaimowicz
in Conversation with Connie Butler

Connie Butler

(2014)

Launched in London in 2011, Her Eyes and My Voice *is a publishing project consisting of four volumes produced over a five-year period. Self-published by British artists and editors Connie Butler and Lauren Godfrey under the creative pseudonym of "Vanessa Visual and Virginia Verbal,"* Her Eyes and My Voice *was conceived as "a platform for research into the relationship between the visual and verbal." Rizo printed by Hato Press in a print run of 100, each issue had a specific theme which established and emerging artists were invited to respond with essays, imagery, and poetry. The themes were: "A Relationship in Ekphrasis" (no. 1, 2012); "Performing to Objects" (no. 2, 2013); "Decorative Grammar" (no. 3, 2014); "The Interview Issue" (no. 4, 2016). A5 format and bound together with a rubber band, the four volumes produced vary, yet share a formal language, such as the number of inks used (from one to five), the amount of interior pages (between 56 to 78 pages), papers, typefaces, typography, and layout.*

Between 2013 and 2014, Butler worked part-time as an assistant to Chaimowicz in London. Given the frequency of her meetings with the artist, the artist became aware of her projects. So when she invited him to participate in "Decorative Grammar," the third issue of the project, Chaimowicz immediately agreed to contribute an interview. Conducted by Butler, the interview took place at the artist's home in London over the spring of 2014. Tape-recorded, the conversation was transcribed and edited by Butler in collaboration with Chaimowicz. To encompass the theme of the intersection of pattern and language, the artist proposed illustrating the conversation with ice cream cones, rosettes, and bows, in addition to the drawing of a nude female in a rhombus. Printed in soft mint and pale grey tones, the selected illustrations were loosely arranged on either side of the centred text and repeated in various combinations throughout the section. Moreover, as Butler recalled, "Marc Camille signed off the page layout, colours and artwork layout before printing. The hand-stamped page was conceived by him, who chose the yellow paint used."

At the end of the conversation is a picture of a piece of paper pinned to a corkboard with a quote from British literary theorist and critic Terry Eagleton. Chosen by the artist, this 1990 quote from The Ideology of the Aesthetic *reads as follows: "The avant-garde's response to the cognitive, ethical and esthetic is quite unequivocal. Truth is a lie: morality stinks; beauty is shit. And of course, they are absolutely right … Equally, of course, they are wrong. Truth, morality and beauty are too important to be handed contemptuously over to the political enemy."*

"Decorative Grammar," Her Eyes and My Voice'*s third volume was launched at Gowlett Peaks, London, on 29 July, 2014.*

A.V.

· · · · · · · · ·

Connie Butler: *So our title as you know is* Decorative Grammar *which for us encompasses the crossover between pattern and language, repetitive symbols, alphabets, and glyphs in the hands of the artist decorator. So I thought we could talk about the motifs that appear on the Formica screen commissioned by Focal Point Gallery in 2013 as it was a pattern I helped to colour. How do these motifs arise, why do they keep coming back and how are they organised? We've got rosettes, bows, ice creams...*

Marc Camille Chaimowicz: Rosettes, bows, ice cream cones, books, and a double profile and of course a figure within lozenges. I had a studio at La Cité Internationale des Arts in Paris, and that was very nice. I mean it was frugal, but then residencies often are, you've got a big space with a tiny kitchenette and a big wall, which you can pin things on. An empty space with a big window looking onto the Seine. I was working in the evenings on this in a way I would have worked differently in London, because I could hang long sheets of drawing on a wall and I would fall asleep with

them and wake up to them, a very nice way to work, is it not? I was accompanied by these motifs. Because it was an empty space I could then, with bits of paper and photocopies, cut things out roughly and pin them up and gradually build up the vocabulary and the repeat.
I think that played a useful part in the construction of a long drop that was designed with the probability of a repeat in mind for what was initially to be a curtain for a high window, which must be four metres. So those were the mechanics whereby over a couple of months I could tweak and review, and organise the drawing and the collaging.
Drawing and collaging is what I do a lot, I find it quite therapeutic.

Could you tell me about the figure in the lozenge?
In parallel and fortuitously I'd been thinking about water, for a non-related project to some extent acknowledging the Thames Water Board. This had drawn my attention and indeed my eye to a feature we've all enjoyed in London, something which is part of our environment I guess, which is the fountain on Sloane Square. I had a good look at that fountain again and I was attracted to this 1930s bronze figure holding in one arm an urn which is generating a permanent source of water, and in her other hand is a smaller urn above her head which is more evidently splashing water and gurgling water. It seemed to me synonymous with London somehow as Sloane square is so near to the river. I thought I'd bring that motif in because I was conscious of the fact that the commission was from a new building in Southend, which of course is where the Thames opens out and feeds into the sea. It's the surmise of the Thames. I wanted a degree of specificity with the commission.

I thought it would be interesting to have a number of references that were culturally specific. So there is the water, the ice cream cones are self-evidently synonymous with sea-side culture, the books are specific to the parallel function of the building which is multifunctional being both the university, the city library, and containing Focal Point Gallery.

What about the double profiles?
The profiles of the two heads, or one head silhouetted in shadow were carried through from earlier work, which I had presented in Southend, at the Focal Point Gallery in the precedent building. I'd like to think that it was relevant, as there is the drawn reference to the gaze, to looking in the gallery or indeed the act of reading. The rosettes originate from some very beautiful tiles that I noticed in a fourteenth century Abbey I'd worked in earlier that year in Provence. That particular motif lends itself to repetition. So then it was a matter of completing that particular grammar notably with some roses, some lilies, and some bows.

There is a pair of these Formica screens, because as well as the one which is a permanent work in Southend, there is one here in the studio. I understand one is going to be in your home, so does that mean that one is an art object and one is a piece of domestic furniture?
That is one possible reading, which would fit well with my way of working. There is also another reading; first and foremost, the history of the commission is with buildings of cultural intent, a condition of any grant to that end depends on a percentage of the budget being spent on commission.
In this instance the director Andy Hunt invited three of us. Initially we each had specific briefs, mine was for seating in the lobby area and some means by which to block out the light from the main gallery that is glazed, so it could be easily turned into a projection space. I had initially suggested a system of hinged folding screens, which could be opened and closed relatively instantly. We looked into the technicality of that, but it's a big window and it would have been rather bulky and cumbersome so we elected to work on a curtain, which is what those initial drawings were for, in parallel I had long wanted to work in Formica which is a really interesting

material. So in the meantime the architect started to research that possibility.

We elected to work on fabric, but the director had enough budget remaining to work with Formica anyway on a more domestic screen. I was very happy about that. By reworking that commission, that would have meant topping up my fee, but given that I don't really have access to the technical means of production it seemed to me much more interesting to forfeit the fee and ask for a second screen. So as you rightly point out, two exist, one for occasional use in the Focal Point building and one, which was in lieu of my fee, which will eventually be for personal use.

So that then enabled us to start reassessing quite what visual matter we would use for the screen. It was at that point that I acknowledged the fact that the screen artwork would be very different in terms of materiality from the curtain in that it would be three flat surfaces that folded in on one another. The Formica being flat rather than textile based and therefore hanging with a fold.

The thing about fabric is that motifs and repetition work very differently, notably if it is a curtain but it could also apply to dress fabric, in that it is a lot more forgiving in terms of the mechanistic nature of repetition because fabric by definition folds in on itself. There is no hiding with the Formica; it's more like wallpaper, flat. The simple option would have been to give them the same artwork, but I figured it was much more interesting to actually complicate that iconography by having an overlay in terms of scales and colours which would then imply a much richer form of picture space within the three facets of the screen.

Do you imagine that this interview will be illustrated?
We could have an illustration of the screen. It would only be in two

colours because of the Risograph printing which would be either black and burgundy or black and teal.
That could be nice. We could even generate artwork for it, such as a frieze with a detail repeated? It could be illustrated like a medieval manuscript.

I know that you have used the ice cream cones previously in a wallpaper design, and the bow is also from a wallpaper?
It was, I've used it also in a carpet design. The bow is something, which seemed to mutate as a motif for a number of projects during 2013, and I think we all do that. But one has to be careful; there comes a time when we have to put that on hold and work on something new, otherwise it gets a bit too repetitive.

What would be the danger in something being too repetitive?
I guess that I'd find myself bored. Some artists do repeat themselves and some do it with great applaud. Notably one would think of someone like Giacometti. The mature work was very repetitive, bronze figures and drawings of scratchy lines. The miracle of those is that each time they seem kind of new. I'm not dismissive of repetition, repetition is the wrong word. I'm not dismissive of, say, Morandi, who I adore who pretty much did the same thing throughout a distinguished career. I guess for myself the danger would be that I would lose interest, I need a range … rather like a bumble bee to land on different flower heads to keep myself happy.

This puts me in mind of Gertrude Stein when she said "Repetition is not repetition, it's insistence." Is there an insistence on these motifs' importance, significance, or currency within a pattern?
I guess we have to differentiate between formal repetition in terms of motif or gesture, and a certain type of careerist branding. Many artists establish their own brand and then simply consolidate the brand by repeating that which they have managed to

claim as theirs. That's something that I would have reservations about. The idea of visually repeating something within its own boundaries can work very well ... since we are in the studio I'm thinking for example of this pattern. Have you seen the wooden stamp for that? We could do a page in the book of these stamped patterns?

Good idea.
I love this so much. When I was working on a project at the Weltkulturen Museum in Frankfurt, which meant working with material from an anthropological collection, I was looking at some African fabric with this floral motif on it, which was in a very haphazard way repeated. Luckily the restorer there had been trained as a carpenter, as a cabinet maker. He was called Mr Krabber; I jokingly asked if he would be able to make a stamp of the motif which I drew for him. He did it; he carved it out of hardwood and signed it with his carpenter's sign that incorporates his initials into a picture of a crab.
To use this stamp to repeat the motif endlessly could produce something really quite attractive.

Attractive can be a complex word...
Well this opens up such a range of questions; it makes me think of what Roger Cook said at my open talk in February at the South London Gallery.

About you being a purveyor of pleasure?
He then got back to me by email and said that he wished he had elaborated because he has since acknowledged to himself that the question of pleasure is very complex, and can be quite a radical position to juggle with. He hadn't used that word as a pejorative term in any way but it is for sure in our culture, in terms of radical practice, it would seem contradictory. Especially from a relatively left-wing position, pleasure is something that is falsely and often

problematically associated with the right, with a kind of decadent culture. This is something which will be very interesting to review relative to the huge late collages by Matisse that are about to be shown at Tate Modern. Hopefully these questions will be revisited. It is still contentious, as it was certainly at the time of Matisse.

I think we have found the word "decorative" has been difficult for us as a working title, to overcome our anxiety around its use…
I can understand that. I think if you look at the gender divide, it can be more problematic for women artists to be categorised in that way, because of the history of the decorative arts. I think that what drew me to fabric design was really to do with gender politics, because I had been really shocked as a student to see there was this hierarchy implicit in the courses offered, more so than encouraged. There wasn't any discussion, men were told to go into painting, which was then considered to be the most noble of all practices or otherwise sculpture, and women were directed toward the applied arts be it fabric design, ceramics…

…wallpapers and surface pattern design.
Exactly.

[I. 19]

At the Tip of My Fingers:
Marc Camille Chaimowicz

Eva Fabbris

(2016)

In March 2014, Vincenzo de Bellis—then director of Miart (Milan Art Fair) and Peephole, an art centre operating in Milan from 2009 to 2016—discussed with Edoardo Bonaspetti an exhibition project that would explore the artistic interactions between Chaimowicz and Carlo Mollino (1905–73). Inspired by this artist duo, Bonaspetti, then artistic director of the Triennale di Milano, curator of Triennale Art, and editor-in-chief of the Milanese art magazine Mousse, presented the project to the Triennale's board of directors, who immediately approved it. The exhibition was programmed at the Triennale in 2015.

However, due to a last-minute change in the Triennale's annual program, which was ultimately devoted to "Italian Art," Chaimowicz's exhibition had to be postponed until 2016. In the meantime, the Triennale had agreed that as part of the "Italian Art" year, de Bellis would be the guest curator of Triennale di Milano for the exhibition "Ennesima. An exhibition of seven exhibitions on Italian Art" (26 November, 2015–6 March, 2016). Unfortunately, neither Bonaspetti nor de Bellis knew that at the Triennale di Milano there was a rule that guest curators were only allowed to curate one exhibition. Therefore, de Bellis could not develop his project with Chaimowicz. Bonaspetti was then asked to choose another curator to work in collaboration with Chaimowicz on a new exhibition scenario for the Triennale di Milano.

Over the spring of 2015, Bonaspetti approached Eva Fabbris, a Milan-based art writer and curator, with the idea of working collaboratively with Chaimowicz on an exhibition project for the Triennale di Milano. Although she contacted the artist once the project was confirmed, they met in person several months later. Initiated by Bonaspetti, their meeting took place in a hotel in Paris on 23 October, 2015, at the time of the Art Fair (then FIAC, Foire Internationale d'Art Contemporain). In the course of their conversation, Fabbris invited Chaimowicz to do an "email interview" in Mousse, *explaining that it would contribute to highlighting his two upcoming exhibitions in Italy—"Now and Then…" at Studio Indipendenza, Roma (26 May–10 September, 2016), which was developed by Paris-based curator Eva Svennung; and "Maybe Metafisica" in Milan (14 October, 2016–8 January, 2017). Completed in late 2015, and published in early February 2016, simultaneously in the magazine and online as part of the "Conversations" section, the interview was released far ahead of the exhibition "Maybe Metafisica," which was still being conceived.*

At the time, this exhibition was still in its design phase, and little had been decided. Chaimowicz had been researching "the intriguing architecture of the Palazzo dell'Arte"—home to Triennale di Milano, built between 1931 and 1933—as well as The Mysterious Bath, *a spectacular open-air fountain designed by Giorgio De Chirico in 1973 in Milan's Sempione Park, which had been built in thirty-five days, and consisted of two petrified swimmers, a trampoline, a beachball, a cabin, a large painted swan, a fish, and a fountain, all contained in a curved pool. Chaimowicz was also interested, he said, "in works revealing a formal and emotive affinity with the most oneiric of the historical avant-garde movements: Metaphysical Art, and its artistic heirs." If this research was occupying the artist at the time the interview took place, it is not mentioned in the discussion because it was still underdeveloped. To get round this, Fabbris decided to focus on the notions of spatial ingenuity, semi-privacy of creation, and tactile intimacy, as explored by the artist in his recent projects. Eight months later, however, the artist's research had become visible in the exhibition. As described in the press release, "Starting from Giorgio de Chirico's* Prodigal Son *of 1973, in which a father and son are painted in a bare interior imbued with a surreal disquiet, the exhibition follows a circular path that is characterised by a sense of suspension […] which immerses the viewer in the meditative atmosphere of motionless time."*

Finally, a few days before the opening of the exhibition, Fabbris was appointed curator at the Prada Foundation, Milan, which had an unexpected effect on Chaimowicz. Once the exhibition was installed, they went together to Prada to see the new collections. While the artist was trying on hats, Fabbris was socialising with the staff. Suddenly, she said, "Look at my Uncle! Look at my Uncle! Isn't he fantastic?" As a result, Chaimowicz observed, "The discount at Prada shops has turned immediate!"

A.V.

· · · · · · · · ·

Eva Fabbris: *We shared a few texts and sources in preparation for this conversation. Among them, a note by Sabrina Tarasoff where she speculates "the return to craft methods of making suggests some sort of semi-privacy from the peering eyes of capital." Could you comment on this, from the perspective of your own making methodologies?*
Marc Camille Chaimowicz: I like this quote! Not so much because it could be construed as honouring "craft traditions"—which I don't, as such—but because it acknowledges the "semi-privacy" of making. This resonates for me, in that with regard to objects I invariably proceed, often by the tips of my fingers—with balsa wood, cardboard, and glue—as a way of thinking speculatively (this tactility surely being a form of intimacy), which is therefore the antithesis of "the peering eyes of capital!"

This original dimension of tactile intimacy is something that is intensely present in those works of yours that dance in the realm of the object, that touch on a potential function. These works are necessarily produced by manufacturers skilled in specific materials and processes. Could you describe these collaborations a little? For example, let's stay in a field characterised by a manifestly tactile aspect, ceramics. For your solo show at Galerie Neu in autumn 2014—which also featured pieces by guests Klara Lidén and Manfred Pernice—you made forty vases with Bottega Gatti in Faenza, Italy, a workshop traditionally involved in artists' projects. How did you get on with them? There are no banners, they are disabled, or none is qualified for this location!

Well, given that Davide Servadei—the Artistic Director of Gatti—speaks neither French or English and I don't speak Italian, our dialogue was muted, or at least deferred! I was, however, fortunately accompanied by Marta Fontolan, then my contact at Galerie Neu in Berlin, who was able to interpret, and it was equally helpful that I had previously worked with glazed earthenware in Nevers and Quimper and was therefore familiar with both process and potential. I had prepared for our first visit, introducing myself by means of a portfolio of working drawings and a colour chart, and as Marta was researching possible glazes with a technician, I was primarily using sign language to negotiate possible forms for vases with Davide and a clay "thrower."

I've found that if one shows empathy with craft specificity, the specialist will in turn be attentive to one's agenda (and also that they generally enjoy having their skills put to the test). A working vocabulary was thus proposed and prototypes agreed on; and these, some months later, were duly sent to London so I could then suggest possible corrections.

I guess in a sense, then, this working vocabulary derives from the sensuous tactility you were describing earlier...

This also applied to a range of 3-D items, notably the furniture pieces, since working with maquettes has better enabled me to think three-dimensionally. Or, taken metaphorically, a caress that resonates is invariably a quest!

In your work, this collaboration with manufacturers and realisation of 3-D objects runs parallel to your pictorial practice.

The primary contrast between the practice of painting and this way of working is related to touch, and the absence of it … but this can then be negotiated through the mediation of drawing. And so at Bottega Gatti, a different dialogue, which had begun via linguistic translation, was later extended through the interpretative tool of drawing…

Speaking of your working method, I've been fascinated by your accounts of the time you spent last summer in Burgundy, working in your house together with your assistants…

I've worked regularly with my French assistants, who are therefore familiar with my ways. But this had previously entailed distance: me delegating things, which could be quite predictable and mechanical. Last summer, in Burgundy, we worked differently, at the same time and in the same building (although not in the same space; they were downstairs, where we'd installed trestles, and I was in the studio, on the floor above). They were working on a new panel piece—a version of which is probably to be shown in Rome in May—in a situation that allowed greater potential for dialogue, fluidity, and improvisation. Meanwhile, I was working on a new diptych, *Summer's End*, which was made uncharacteristically quickly, i.e., intermittently completed over three months and perhaps as a result, showing a greater lightness of touch (shown at FIAC last autumn).

Lucy McKenzie recently described a parallel between the "powerful natural materials that are instrumentalised in Marc Camille's work, like marble and fine cabinet makers' wood, as well as their metaphorical counterparts, figures such as Genet, Cocteau and Flaubert. The physical matter, complex and precious in its own right, gets paint rolled onto it and then is stacked, its inherent value overturned. The personalities too, forces of style and intellect—their failures and successes part of their beauty as fissures are in marble and stray bullets in forest rosewood—are interwoven into Marc Camille's conceptual and sensory narrative." In 2013 you conceived the visual matter for the

English edition of The Studio of Giacometti *by Jean Genet. You had already invented and evoked a form of domestic interior for this author in your show "Jean Genet: The Courtesy of Objects" at Nottingham Contemporary in 2011. The book describes Giacometti's studio as a place of intense intimacy between the privileged visitor and the artist...* It was an honour to be involved in this publication, a long overdue English translation of this majestic text. And regarding the visual matter, my approach was based on the premise that a very pretty French edition was, in my view, chronically imbalanced, in that the use of attractive black-and-white photographs of Giacometti's studio were so seductive as to unduly dominate the text. My response was therefore to propose a rebalancing, whereby the text was to be primary and the visual matter accordingly subservient to it. I therefore offered an anti-aesthetic that entailed photographing incidental details of walls, doors, and locks—taken in both Toulouse and Burgundy—and then painting over, scribbling on, scratching and in general, visually "soiling" them. They were then transferred to Japanese paper—the book was designed in conjunction with a wonderful London-based designer, Fraser Muggeridge, who excelled (like the previously mentioned specialists) with insights and liaising.

Architectural elements taken from a specific area, items that define the perimeters of a private space, protections that were used for decades and decades to determine what was inside and what was outside. Something similar happens in Proposal for a rural home. *This piece, which was made for your show at Synagogue de Delme in 2007, is a wooden house with two small, round windows taken from traditional buildings in the region, and it is inaccessible. Your visual intervention in a book like* The Studio of Giacometti, *which is emotionally charged, and very much summons up physical presences (of bodies, of sculptures) moves in the direction of discretion. This makes me think of your earlier performances, when you shared your private space, certain intimate experiences, with the public: for example, drinking tea,*

a subtle stimulation of taste. You gave people the possibility to step in, but not in order to open out, not to voice a loud declaration…
Yes, intimacy, both as bodily manifest, and symbolically—as a mental state—is surely a possible link between exclusivity and its opposite (for example, in paintings as different as those by Vuillard or Morandi!). And furthermore, it is a feature of the kind of understatement, which you allude to…

Could we consider the presence of the canaries in your exhibition at Galerie Neu—the one we mentioned previously, where you showed the forty vases—an emblem of this mental state?
Perhaps! In order to avoid upsetting the forty canaries, the visitors to the work *Forty and Forty …* were let in gradually, only five being allowed in at any one time. This therefore slowed down the experience, establishing a feeling of privilege or a sense of exclusivity and intimacy … the very vivacity of the free-flying birds tended to be countered by the unusually long time that people spent within the work (such was the pleasure and energy established that the gallery staff were rumoured to have been impatient to come in to work). From the perspective of authorship, however, the unpredictable or anarchic behaviour of these tiny birds was such that the usual pictorial control was forfeited or qualified … and the possibility of a pact between the viewer, the live element, and the work was instead perhaps proposed.

Artist of the Month:
Marc Camille Chaimowicz

Nicolas Trembley

(2017)

The interview with Chaimowicz reproduced below was first published in March 2017 in Numéro. *Founded in Paris in 1999 by publisher and editor-in-chief Babeth Djian,* Numéro *is a "leading monthly magazine that offers an avant-garde view of the world of fashion, art and luxury." From its earliest issues, the magazine has linked artistic trends and exhibitions with the cultures of fashion and glamour. Among the many features in the publication is the "Artist of the month." In December 2016, Paris-based art advisor, curator, and contributor to* Numéro, *Nicolas Trembley contacted Chaimowicz to invite him to be featured in the next issue. Usually declining this type of invitation, and although the proposal was not linked to a particular event or exhibition, Chaimowicz accepted. Trembley had confirmed that the process would be quick, and* Numéro *is a magazine that Chaimowicz appreciates, especially when travelling: "In* Numéro, *I like the paper, the photos, etc., and of course, Éric Troncy!"*

As a result, shortly after the confirmation of his participation, Chaimowicz received by email a series of questions to which, as expected, he answered them, in English, in "ten minutes." His answers were subsequently translated into French for publication. Technically, Chaimowicz said, "this was not an interview, but rather a question-naire, which was made for the magazine's broad audience to whom my work was probably being introduced for the first time." Published in both the French and English sections of the magazine, the "Artist of the month" column was introduced as follows: "Since the late 1970s, this Franco-British dandy has been raising pleasure to the status of a core value. Whether inviting the visitor to take tea or mixing furniture, wallpaper and ordinary objects, his pieces are a joyful smash-up of art and the everyday that is a true celebration of the real."
As requested, Chaimowicz additionally emailed the magazine some illustrations to accompany his featured portrait. Among them, an outdoor (Involuntary) Self-Portrait, Ventimiglia, February 6th 2016, *which was reproduced in both the French and English versions of the chronicle. This unintentional outdoors self-portrait depicts the*

*artist looking at the interior of a general store selling magazines, trin-
kets, sweets, and gadgets. Because of the artist's reflection in the store
window, the objects inside the store are reflected on his body, as though
he is made entirely of objects.*

A.V.

· · · · · · · · ·

Numéro: *Where did you study?*
Marc Camille Chaimowicz: My teenage years were spent in Ealing, in northwest London, where I went to the local art school, before doing a first degree at Camberwell and afterwards a second one at the Slade School of Fine Art (these are such different neighbour-hoods, however, that it might almost have been three different cities).

How much did your family background influence you?
I guess hugely … After all, although we didn't necessarily realise it at the time, wasn't 1960s London briefly the epicentre of the universe?

What did it mean for you becoming an artist?
Due to teenage exuberant behaviour, I almost lost my place at art school, and I think it was only then that I understood that to be involved in that world was what mattered to me more than anything else. It was a moment of awareness and the catalyst to creative engagement. What it meant to be an artist then, as I recall, was to be asking questions, dreaming and striving towards a new order through the questioning of boundaries (specifically through the agency of touch).

What's the first encounter with art that you remember?
An Allen Ginsberg reading at the Royal Albert Hall. How incon-gruous is that?! And Jasper Johns at the Whitechapel, as a surrogate

encounter of the legacy of Marcel Duchamp and Henri Matisse.

Is the idea of décor central to your practice, or more architecture?
I spent some concentrated time looking at the work of Carlo Scarpa last summer, and was then reminded that each can complement the other.

In an interview in the 1980s with Stuart Morgan, you said, "Making art itself isn't that interesting." What did you mean exactly by that?
We had talked of my wish to give coherence to the way I lived, and how lifestyle was taking precedence over practice, how the making of work may then flow from that.

Much has been written about sexuality and space—are there texts that have influenced your work?
The implicitly gendered references in the writings of Adolf Loos and the poetics of those of Gaston Bachelard have had influence.

As Michael Bracewell put it so well, you use a pale-palette colour chart with lavender blue, pink, lemon, ivory, oyster, violet, or eau de nil, like a minor fugue. Why this choice of colours?
To which we might add amber, putty, dusky mint, coral, and apricot … I prefer nuance over harshness. Anyhow, primary colours are best kept in primary school.

Literature is important in your work and in your pantheon—we meet Jean Genet, Marcel Proust, Baudelaire, and many other poets. How can you translate poetry into the form of your work?
… to which we could add Flaubert and also Cocteau, who has led me to surrogate forms of portraiture.

Is there anything you would like to make people conscious of through your art?
Pleasure is a core value, both conceptual and aesthetic. It yearns to be seen.

What's your next project?

My Serpentine exhibition will be shown in modified form in New York in 2018. I'm currently working on a new show for the Kestner Gesellschaft in Hanover for next autumn. It's a wonderful Art Nouveau venue that was originally a swimming pool. I'm also working on two commissions, one for an indoor space and the other not...

[I. 21]

A Conversation with
Marc Camille Chaimowicz and Roger Diener

Cristina Bechtler, Fredi Fischli, and Niels Olsen

(2022)

While installing his exhibition "Forty and Forty" with Berlin-based artists Klara Lidén and Manfred Pernice at Galerie Neu, Berlin (17 September–1 November, 2014), Chaimowicz received a call from Beatrix Ruf, then Director of Kunsthalle Zürich. Having purchased his first mobile phone—a Nokia N9—a few days earlier, he was thrilled to use it, and quickly called her back. "A beloved curator smoking non-stop," as Chaimowicz calls her, Ruf was also working part-time as a consultant and curatorial advisor for Swiss Re Next, the new headquarters of Swiss Re, "one of the world's leading providers of reinsurance, insurance and other forms of insurance-based risk transfer." Designed and planned in Zürich by Basel-based Diener & Diener Architects, the Swiss Re Next building was in development between 2008 and 2017. Conceived as a "new and agile workplace concept that fosters collaboration, dialogue and flexibility," the building was to offer "various options for flexible working that enable employees to shape their working day independently and choose the most suitable place to work." As part of this plan, selected visual artists were invited to develop a project in the building, under the curatorial direction of Ruf. Chaimowicz, who likes the idea of injecting art into a workspace, accepted Ruf's invitation to join a meeting in Zürich, and it is here the architect and the artist crossed paths for the first time.

The interior of the Swiss Re Next building consisted of a series of open spaces with small, convertible units called "Think Tanks." These transparent, glass-walled units were for individual work, or work in small groups, and were to be scattered throughout the building, combining intimate areas within larger workspaces. At some point, Roger Diener thought that semi-transparent curtains could enhance the privacy inside the "Think Tanks." When discussing this with Ruf, she immediately thought of Chaimowicz, particularly the fabrics he had produced throughout his career. While in Zürich, Chaimowicz discovered the exceptional scale of the building as well as the "Think Tanks." At their first meeting at Swiss Re Next on Wednesday, 8 October, 2014, Chaimowicz was seated next to Swiss artist Mai-Thu Perret, who was

*also being consulted about the the curtain project for the "Think Tanks."
Chaimowicz did not know her, but over the course of Diener's introduction, he discreetly handed Perret a small piece of paper that read:
"Shall we share one together?" After Diener's "brilliant presentation,"
Ruf described the "Think Tanks" in detail, including their distribution
in the building. At the end of her presentation, the little piece of paper
was back in the hands of Chaimowicz. It read: "Yes!"*

*Back in London, Chaimowicz made four different drawings, one of
which Mai-Thu Perret would later add red dots to. After two years of
work marked by technical meetings during which they "were always
four, like the Beatles," the curtains were finally manufactured in 2017.
Entitled "Zürich," "Monaco," "London," and "Paris," these premium fabrics produced at Cosmo in four-colour ways and in large quantities,
and that come in sixteen different versions, each in four versions, were
installed inside the "Think Tanks" in late 2017.*
*Around the same time, Chaimowicz moved into a new apartment. The
apartment is in an idiosyncratic building that occupies a five-story
mixed-use new-build that stands alone in a corner of the Pleasure
Gardens, on the site of an old pub near by the River Thames in London.
Designed by British firm Trevor Horne Architects, in close collaboration
with Cabinet co-founders Martin McGeown and Andrew Wheatley,
Cabinet's artists, and Charles Asprey who funded the development, the
structure's two lowest floors serve as the gallery exhibition space; above
them are two floors of residential apartments, including Chaimowicz's
flat, while the top floor is dedicated to special events. The artist's
apartment was designed in close collaboration with London architect Stephen Beasley of Manalo &White, whom Chaimowicz considers
to possess "a unique creative approach to problem solving, coupled
with an exceptional empathy towards the client's brief." Although the
apartment was created with an eye for detail, Chaimowicz nevertheless
made his own additions. The walls were left unpainted, with Trompe-
l'œil skirting boards, and the artist's designs were printed on Formica
for the door and cabinetry finishes. The interior design was arranged so*

that there is a view of the trees in the park and city from the bathtub. After forty years in a third-floor apartment in a nineteenth century building in Camberwell with no elevator, moving to such a place was a major change for the artist. Succeeding Approach Road (1974–79), and Hayes Court in Camberwell (1979–2017), Vauxhall Pleasure Gardens in Tyers Street has become the artist's third home in London.

Having spent time with Chaimowicz when he was working on the interior design of his Vauxhall apartment, Beasley was familiar with the Swiss Re Next project. Accordingly, when he heard that Diener would be giving a talk as part of the "Architecture on Stage" lecture series at the Barbican, London, he immediately informed the artist. On 21 May, 2018, Chaimowicz went to the Barbican with his beloved friend, the English artist Nadia Wallis, to attend the lecture. Arriving "faster than expected thanks to Nadia's fast little red car," they found a "decent" area to be able to continue their conversation. Suddenly, a person with a hat interrupted them and said: "Hey! Marc Camille! Hello!" "That was Roger!" Chaimowicz reflected. "He and his wife, writer and editor Maryam Diener, were looking for the lecture room!" Since the conference was about to start, there was no time for them to talk, and Diener invited them to join for dinner after the lecture. They met at St. John Restaurant.
Over dinner, Trevor Horne's idiosyncratic building was discussed, as well as the Chaimowicz's contribution to the building. Diener had heard about the collaboration between Trevor Horne Architects, Charles Asprey, the Cabinet Gallery, and the artists involved. He was delighted to learn more about the project directly from Chaimowicz, who also spoke about his apartment and the large geometric sawtooth windows set in natural oak frames that he had designed for the facade. A few days later, Diener went to Vauxhall to get a better sense of the neighbourhood and see the building in person. He took a grand tour of the artist's home, eventually reaching a concrete wall inside the bedroom. This wall, indeed, was slightly different from the others. When asked, Chaimowicz showed Diener one of his patterned rubber rollers, with

which he had made this "fake patina" wall, and the architect made a connection with the Armadillo House, the project he was developing at the time with his wife in a green enclave on a hill in Basel, and whose developments and contributions are described in the interview below.

Amazed by the artist's apartment as much as he had been by the Swiss Re Next curtains, Diener invited him to design an interior curtain for his Armadillo House. To discuss this further, they began meeting in Notting Hill on Saturday mornings. After a few meetings, the relationship between the Dieners and the artist became more intimate. On one occasion, Chaimowicz showed them a sketch he had made. Based on the initials of the Dieners' first names, it depicted the letters "M" and "R," which the artist skillfully juxtaposed and superimposed in order for them to blend with the rectangular modules of the facade. The Dieners loved it immediately. In the process, Chaimowicz took the bottle of champagne that was on the table and customised it with a marker pen, changing the name "Pol-Roger" to "Pour-Roger." Later, the Dieners invited Chaimowicz to collaborate with them again on the design of Würenlingen house, both inside and outside. Although the artist had been interested in architecture throughout his career [II. 10; III. 9, 23, 26], his collaboration on the Armadillo House was "unique" in the sense that, he said, "I had never been involved to such a degree before."

Inspired by this collaboration between artist and architect, Fredi Fischli and Niels Olsen, a Zürich-based curator and editor duo, went to Armadillo House, knowing that "ordinarily, Diener & Diener Architekten do not build private homes and, even when working on a single building, they tend to map out an urbanist strategy." While walking on the hill overlooking Basel, they discovered the recently completed house come into view. As they described it:

> *"The house stood out like an industrial building in the middle of a residential area. [...] The initial impression from afar is*

that of an automobile repair shop in a Milanese suburb. As you come closer, vertical, concrete slabs subvert this impression [...] Marc Camille Chaimowicz has masked the concrete slabs with a pattern that looks like wallpaper, giving each slab its own colour and motif [...] Since it is only perceived from nearby, Chaimowicz's cladding reinforces the sense of exposed intimacy and makes manifest the subtle interaction of art and architecture. This inversion lends the building a subversive tension, where the basically unbroken facade becomes a subtle travesty of domesticity. No windows have been cut into the patterned wall [...] Instead, the artist signifies the interior by employing the traditional decorative technique of painting walls with patterned rubber rollers—a method used by the Wiener Werkstätte to imitate wallpaper by applying real paint. The soft coat of paint on the harsh concrete foundation is almost like a garment, dressing the raw, shed-like architecture in a translucent light."

Fascinated by the multifaceted nature of the project, on their way back to Zürich Fischli and Olsen decided to contact Cristina Bechtler, who developed the acclaimed book series "Art and Architecture in Discussion" between 1999 and the mid-2010s, thinking it might be of interest to her given the publications she had done previously. For the past few years, she said, "the book series has hibernated, but the enthusiasm of Fredi Fischli and Niels Olsen inspired me to launch a restart." In the aftermath, Bechtler, Fischli, and Olsen joined Diener and Chaimowicz for a late afternoon meeting at Maryam Diener's home in London on 7 September, 2019. Over the course of this tape-recorded meeting the collaboration between Diener and Chaimowicz at Armadillo House was discussed, as well as their respective artistic visions and divergent approaches to spatial arrangements.

This discussion was transcribed and edited by the three interviewers, and then emailed to Diener and Chaimowicz for comments. At the time, the artist was busy finalising preparations for his solo exhibition

"Marc Camille Chaimowicz—Dear Valérie…" at Kunsthalle Bern (22 February–26 July, 2020). Therefore, he did not answer them. In order for them to meet a second time, another appointment was made at the end of February 2020 in London. But due to the pandemic it was cancelled, and the final corrections were made by email. Thereafter, the publishing project lay dormant until the Zürich-based graphic designer Teo Schifferli began designing it in late 2021. A few months later, when the layout was ready, the publication's PDF was emailed to Chaimowicz for final checking. Upon opening the PDF, the artist admitted, "I was OK with it, but not my type of design." Finally, in early summer, he received in London a box full of Marc Camille Chaimowicz & Roger Diener: Armadillo House, *and found out—"delighted"—that the book was published by Verlag der Buchhandlung Walther und Franz König.*

To fully appreciate the dialogue between art and architecture as developed in Armadillo House, the reader can refer to the aforementioned 96-page illustrated monograph whose iconography documents the project from start to finish, including the wide range of materials used by the artist—wood, fabrics, tiles, metal, and glass—and the multiplicity of interior features he designed—from bespoke floor tiles and kitchen panels, to painted cupboards with crystalline glass door knobs, lamps, and the sculptural railing. The very end of text, as it originally appeared, has been edited for this anthology. If, finally, as Fischli and Olsen rightly mention in their preface, "Armadillo House creates an atmosphere of enigmatic tension for its inhabitants," which is certainly related to the fact that, as Chaimowicz says, "I have long felt that my decorative commentary feminised the building," it can be considered a pivotal building, in that it has set a new template for an expression of queerness through architecture.

A.V.

· · · · · · · · ·

Fredi Fischli: *We want to begin with the question: What attracted you to each other's work? What you each do seems very different at first glance, not just your discipline, but the aesthetic as well. Roger, I see your approach to architecture as essentialist or non-expressive, while you, Marc Camille, deal with the notion of ornament, décor, and a certain opulence. We are therefore curious to hear how your—in our opinion surprising—collaboration for the Armadillo House in Basel came about.*
Marc Camille Chaimowicz: Well, we first crossed paths at an event about the new headquarters for Swiss Re, where Roger gave a presentation. I was singularly impressed, not just by how ambitious the project was, but also by the ideology behind the building. For instance, Roger had commissioned a detailed sociological study of the staff at Swiss Re, acquiring insights that informed his design and allowed him to take a very perceptive approach to the building and accommodate its actual day-to-day functions. So, I was intrigued. But it never occurred to me that we might work together. Then I heard that Roger was giving a talk at the Barbican in London. I got there a bit early and was sitting in the lobby when someone called me by my first name. It was Roger, and he was delighted to see me. He asked me to join them for dinner afterwards. When I learned that they were in London almost every other weekend, I invited them to my new apartment in Vauxhall and there he informally mentioned the project for a new house in Basel. I had become more dissatisfied with the pressure of having an international profile and had decided to take a year off, so the timing was perfect. Obviously, I was interested; this was a once in a lifetime opportunity. How could one pass it up?

Niels Olsen: *Just shortly before you had realised a commission in Vauxhall—an intervention in the design of the new building housing the Cabinet Gallery.*
M.C.C.: Vauxhall was quite different. I should first point out that Cabinet designed it themselves. Martin McGeown and Andrew Wheatley basically designed the whole building in consultation

with Charles Asprey, who provided the financial backing, and of course Trevor Horne and his team. So, many people were involved in the building's design with the greatest input coming from Cabinet. I sat in on a few meetings, but I wasn't that directly involved. They wanted three artists to contribute to the design of the building. I was one of them. The others were Lucy McKenzie who did the decorative panel work on the balconies, and John Knight who did this one window on the ground floor—a very subtle, but important intervention that acknowledges the function of the building and enables an architectural feature leading directly into the gallery, like a Barnett Newman "zip." I was invited to design the window frames.

N.O.: *Yes, they have an irregular, angular wooden structure, making each individual window painterly, recalling a modernist tableau.*
M.C.C.: Designing the windows was one reason I got involved. The other was personal. I was looking to move for various reasons, not least health-related, because I knew that at some point I would no longer be able to live where I had lived for more than thirty years—on the top floor of a 1900 building without a lift. This seemed to be a great opportunity to downsize. So I approached the gallery, who were actually interested in having one of their artists live above the gallery. I was fortunate enough to have an architect friend Stephen Beasley help me design the interior space since I was acquiring only the shell of a flat. That was really exciting. I got closely involved in the floor plan, the finishing and the redrawing of the apartment even though I have very little architectural experience.

N.O.: *Was this your first permanent architectural intervention?*
M.C.C.: It certainly was. It was unique in that sense and also because the collaboration was so intense, the fact that we were almost co-authoring a project. I had not been involved to such a degree before.

F.F.: *It would be interesting to hear from you Roger. How would you characterise the Vauxhall building when you first visited?*

Roger Diener: When Maryam and I first approached the building in Vauxhall, it was very clear to us that it was both an interesting and complex collaboration. On the one hand, it was completely different from traditional housing, yet on the other hand, not as spectacular as one might expect from its description. I did not realise, for example, how special the windows were until coming back from the pub one day and seeing the building from another angle. It's a great neighbourhood. There is a little city farm across the street. You feel the neighbourhood spirit; there's energy and an incredible sense of community. In a way, the building, in all its complexity, is an unexpected but elegant response to all of the informally organised structures nearby.

M.C.C.: It is most interesting to walk around the building with Roger because he has a particular eye for public housing, which, as we know, requires great commitment and experience. For instance, in the bedroom of my apartment there is a really wonderful view, which is layered almost like a theatre set; in the foreground there is a great Victorian school building. Farther back there is social housing from the '50s to the '70s and then, in the distant background, there is the twenty-first century—the city of London with the Richard Rogers buildings, etc. So you have three centuries in one view, a wonderful context.

N.O.: *How interesting, when you talk about the building now, you really address it from an urban perspective, how it is situated in the cityscape, but your work is all about the interior, domesticity, and the history of design. Roger, it is obvious from your oeuvre that you have always resisted working in domestic private spaces. I was wondering, what made you decide to focus more on public projects rather than private villas?*

R.D.: An architect's oeuvre has a lot to do with the opportunities that present themselves. As a young architect, you can't be choosy. We were privileged to be commissioned for the subsidised housing project Hammerstrasse in Basel already in the second half of the '70s and this project defined our practice for the first fifteen years. An invitation to an international competition for housing in Salzburg followed and added to our early reputation as architects engaged in housing. At that time Salzburg was a hotspot within the debate on contemporary architecture and all of a sudden, we found ourselves among the likes of such important architects as Luigi Snozzi and Alvaro Siza. Following Salzburg, we were invited to international housing competitions in Amsterdam and elsewhere, mainly based on the transformation of former industrial sites such as factories or breweries. Only later did we become involved in public projects like the extension of the Swiss Embassy in Berlin, but I was always hesitant about the program of private villas. Either you design a house as a strong answer to the program, a signature statement the client might be fond of, or you try to give shape to the specific visions clients have for their house. I was not attracted by either concept. There are still other productive options but they have to be based on mutual curiosity and trust.

N.O.: *In 1995 you and Martin Steinmann published an important book titled* Das Haus und die Stadt.
R.D.: Yes, it actually became a reference book because it was an attempt to discuss urban planning concepts in terms of the potential of urban and architectural design, and included documentation of case studies as well as built projects. This message was proposed at a crucial moment in the debate and therefore the response was quite strong. Such projects imply a certain scale, like university buildings, office buildings, or housing. At that time villas seemed far removed from our practice.

Cristina Bechtler: *So what gave you the courage to build your first private home in Basel?*
R.D.: It was more out of weakness than courage. [Laughter] It was Maryam's influence. She wanted to do it; I was really not prepared.

N.O.: *The way you dealt with this problem is impressive because the area where your house is located is full of relatively conventional villas with gardens in front. Your project has an industrial feel to it. No garden in front, but instead a garage.*

F.F.: *You said that you were always more interested in houses that have to do with work. That's clearly reflected in the looks of this home, which is presumably both for living and working.*
R.D.: Yes, home plus studio appeals to me much more than a mono-functional residential villa. In a way, it's a cross between an elegant Italian villa and a rundown industrial structure. And of course, architecture always has references, an architectural past.
It's a question of composition and has nothing to do with being postmodern or not. In St. Alban-Tal, for instance, we introduced studios on the ground floor even though the composition did not call for them. That was really early in 1983/84. We analysed the area with its late medieval buildings and early industrial paper mills. Our composition included aspects of industrial design combined with the vocabulary of Gothic architecture, but it was less about collage, as Martin Steinmann suggests, but rather about the complexity of composition. It is not just a matter of combining visual experiences but creating a compelling and inseparable whole.

C.B.: *How did you have the courage to hand over important aesthetic decisions to Marc Camille? Did you take decisions together for the design of the Armadillo House?*
R.D.: An artist's work should have a crucial influence on the gestalt of a building. In my experience, those projects in which the artistic work has become prominent have proved to be particularly interesting. So, yes, we took the decisions together as far as the scope and mapping of the artwork for the house is concerned. However, this did not concern the artwork itself. It was, of course, solely up to Marc Camille, and all parts were realised

exactly as he developed and presented them. It starts with the architectural design, with the three-dimensional organisation of a program in space. Design is the foundation of dialogue between artist and architect. The architect is, of course, solely responsible for the function, unless the functional design is also included in the dialogue between artist and architect. But that was not the case with the Armadillo House. I suggested Marc Camille work on the parts of the project where our repertoire as architects was exhausted. His approach not only adds expressive surfaces but also even shapes the architectural space. The overall (in contrast to the specific) nature of the space, the transparency of the space, an important quality for me, would not be destroyed or drowned out. On the contrary. The high walls and floor are transformed into a gentle embrace by the presence of Marc Camille's work, which softens the rawness of their proportions. This illustrates the special challenge of a collaboration between artist and architect. It can only be fruitful if the work of both merges into a whole and yet both parts are able to retain their autonomous form. Finding these fields is the focus of the dialogue. It involves conceptual questions as well as those of the actual realisation of the artistic work as a constituent of the building. The involvement of a prominent artistic work that essentially shapes the design of the building and at the same time ensures the autonomy of architecture and art is also the foundation of dialogue in the projects we have realised with Helmut Federle, first in Berlin for the extension of the Swiss Embassy (1995–2000), then in Basel for the project of Novartis Campus Forum 3 (2002–05).

N.O.: *Marc Camille, I see your ornamental pattern on the facade of the Armadillo House as a reverse side of the interior. The patterns you applied to the raw concrete panels recall tapestries, which are common in old-fashioned interior spaces. Now, it seems as if the volume has been turned inside out and, in an abstract way, the intimate language of the domestic is made public. What made you decide on a patterned facade?*

M.C.C.: It came out of dialogues with Roger and Maryam. What is ironic about this collaboration is that I was so busy that year—I had three solo shows—that I was forced to change the way I work. The dilemma for me is that when I am invited to do a show, people increasingly presume that I will deliver a newly conceived work. This is partly my own doing because I tend to respond specifically to given spaces, I don't recycle old works per se. Given the way I work, this became untenable. I work alone, I don't have a big studio, and I work slowly; I am the antithesis to that American way of working, those production lines producing lots and lots of work with a massive team and assistants. I always put so much effort into a show, like the one at Indipendenza in Rome, and then after six weeks it's gone. I started to question that dynamic and became increasingly interested in working through commissions or on projects that would have a degree of permanence. So, as mentioned, the timing was perfect for me.

But in terms of the outside, my input was relatively small because we were working with pre-existing design decisions. Once again, the idea for the facade arose from conversations with Roger and Maryam during their visit to my apartment in Vauxhall. They went into one of the rooms, actually the most private of the apartment, the bedroom, and Roger noticed straight away that I had added a patina to one of the concrete walls. Of course, that must have rung a bell. But the more recent decisions that we took had to do with the intimate space of the interior and its fabric, the floor, the decorations for the kitchen cupboards, and how to finish off the bedroom. Some decisions were taken about the exterior, the metal gates and the glass ornaments above the window frames. I mean, we were working with quite a wide range of materials. The balustrade on the first floor was a remarkable piece of engineering. What I found particularly interesting about this project was that Roger has so many connections. So, I was able to take short cuts and delegate tasks to the very best craftspeople, something which I am not always able to do.

F.F.: *It would be interesting to learn more about the sources and references that informed your interventions in the Armadillo House. The installations in your exhibitions are often very beautiful, but at the same time, they have an uncanny side to them. Every object is so charged and comes with its distinctive history of which the viewer is unaware.*

M.C.C.: I am pleased you noticed that! From the start I was very conscious of the relationship between Roger and Maryam—so the project was a form of portraiture. In several works around portraiture that interest me, the subject is actually not visible. For instance, Jean Cocteau doesn't appear in the work *Jean Cocteau...* and *The Casting of the Maids* doesn't feature the work of Jean Genet. Yet with the Armadillo House, I see it as kind of a portrait about two people who will use that space as their personal living space.

C.B.: *This is very interesting because you are also known for criticising modernist architecture, for example, as "inhuman." Yet, I would say that Roger falls in the modernist architect tradition.*

R.D.: We spoke openly about these issues, and I share Marc Camille's critique of contemporary architecture, and also modern architecture, for its male-focused gestures. I think that we addressed this issue in Binningen. When you look at those facade panels now, there is a feminine quality to them. They are fabulously fragile and soft—characteristics you would never expect from slabs of concrete.

F.F.: *Marc Camille's subversive intervention triggers thought, raises questions.*

M.C.C.: I think Roger's subtle reference to the subject of gender is very relevant because I have long felt that my decorative commentary feminised the building. Once during a project meeting, I suggested to Roger that he should introduce me as his couturier at the next meeting, since I was, in essence, dressing the building.

R.D.: The paneling with those mere six-centimeter-thick concrete slabs enhances this notion of "dressing." It is apparent that they are organised in such a way that they aren't load bearing. Marc Camille has always shown his pattern-based artworks within interiors. But the second "bell," so to speak, or another moment when the idea for the facade came up, was when I discovered your series of works consisting of panels with different tapestries, propped loosely against the wall. I could easily imagine such works outdoors as well. Quite interesting is that some of your panels have a painted pattern, but others are actually marble plates.

C.B. [to Marc Camille Chaimowicz]: *I remember your exhibition at the Neue Nationalgalerie in Berlin (2008), where you installed your panels leaning on Mies van der Rohe's precious green marble walls. I read this as a critical gesture.*
R.D.: Our intention was to create a facade that almost appears to be a curtain, to have a textile quality to it. This was a perfect fit for Binningen.

C.B. [to Maryam and Roger Diener]: *The two of you hadn't seen the panels in Berlin?*
R.D.: No, I wish we had. You know the first thing Marc Camille said was that he would like his patterns to be visible only as you come closer to the house. At first I thought: "Oh, no I don't want it to be so subtle," but in the end it turned out exactly like Marc Camille suggested.

N.O.: *I would like to come back to the notion of portraiture you mentioned before, Marc Camille. Some of your early installations of interior spaces were dedicated to literary protagonists. Did you also work on Maryam and Roger's project in a narrative manner or is there a literary source?*
M.C.C.: Rather than going back to earlier works, let me speak about the Armadillo House. The process was as follows: Roger would examine the plans and the various proposed requirements

for a period of time, after which I would consider other possibilities and come back to him with some new drawings. Then we would discuss my suggestions, some of which would then be modified in the process. The longer we worked together, the more the process improved. I got to know Roger and Maryam better and better, and my perception of their relationship is reflected in my work. This work is not transferable; it is unique to the two of them. This is what I mean about portraiture being specific.

C.B.: *In this sense, it is a literary portrait.*
M.C.C.: Yes, in a way. Some specificities, like for example my unrealised idea to depict the initials of Maryam and Roger on the facade of the building, actually came from my fabric design of the curtains. Some subtle jokes also appear, like the "Pour Roger" in the textile ornament.

F.F.: *But other people are also involved, not just the two of you.*
R.D.: May I say that Marc Camille's dialogue with Maryam was particularly intense. I was not always part of the dialogue, but the conversations we had with him were very inspiring. They went far beyond choice of fabric or colour. Marc Camille contributed a lot with his French cultural background and that certainly influenced the dialogue as well. There was much to discuss in the designing of twenty-three different floor tiles! [Laughter].

M.C.C.: When I was studying in London in the 1960s—first at Ealing, then Camberwell and then the Slade, three very different schools—the dominant role models were principally minor figurative painters from the "London School." Naturally I disagreed with this premise and looked to the Americans for an alternative. I was skeptical of the conventions in British institutions, especially for ideological but also cultural and personal reasons. Partly because I have no English DNA in my family, I was drawn to the European sensibility as a possible third alternative. The European tradition with its Surrealists, its Symbolists and of course its literature resonated the most for me, and it is in this tradition that I find the majority of my references, especially in terms of literature, film, and the visual arts. I also immersed myself in the Viennese sensibility by choosing to live there for a period of time. England didn't feel like home for me, so I was searching for an appropriate spiritual alternative. I obviously have kind of detached and romantic ideas of Europe, evidenced by the Viennese and Parisian references in Binningen. These two cultural histories are the richest for me to draw upon, especially in the decorative arts. England only has Bloomsbury art or William Morris to offer, and I am greatly skeptical of both, William Morris in particular. So, one must look for alternatives. This is why Roger Diener's contributions are so vital.

[I. 22]

Marc Camille Chaimowicz in Conversation with Nicolas Vamvouklis

Nicolas Vamvouklis

(2022)

Since discovering Chaimowicz's multifaceted work in his solo exhibition "An Autumn Lexicon," at the Serpentine, London (29 September—20 November, 2016), Greek curator and writer Nicolas Vamvouklis had dreamed of collaborating with the artist. Vamvouklis, based on the island of Lesvos, is a curatorial collaborator at Fondazione Imago Mundi, an art foundation based in Treviso that manages a collection, organises exhibitions, and runs a website. In addition, he is the editor of FEATURES, *a section of the foundation's website, which publishes online "interviews that explore inspiring artistic and research stories in contemporary culture." Conceived by Vamvouklis during the pandemic, and launched in November 2021,* FEATURES *has since published monthly interviews with artists, including Simon Fujiwara, Sophie Utikal, Loukia Alavanou, Jeremy Shaw, and Cory Arcangel, among others.*

In April 2022, Vamvouklis contacted the Andrew Kreps Gallery in New York, to see if Chaimowicz would be willing to do an interview with him in FEATURES. *The artist did not immediately accept the invitation. Indeed, as Vamvouklis said, "before proceeding, Marc Camille Chaimowicz wanted to check the questions." Vamvouklis emailed six questions to the gallery, who forwarded them to the artist. "Excellent questions," Chaimowicz replied, which led to a two-month conversation between Vamvouklis and the artist. When Vamvouklis received the artist's responses, he noticed that the last question ("In which ways do you consider your audience when developing new work?") was missing. Although each interview published in* FEATURES *is based on six questions, Vamvouklis decided "not to put any pressure on the artist," but rather "take advantage of what seemed to be like a fantastic opportunity to talk with Marc Camille Chaimowicz," he said. At the end of June 2022, Vamvouklis emailed the Q&A interview to Fondazione Imago Mundi for translation into Italian. The feedback was as follows: "This interview is different from the previous ones, more poetic," probably because the artist's sentences had italics, ellipses, and no end point as for him, "there is no end point in the ideas." To standardise the text, punctuation was inserted.*

[I. 22]

FEATURES #9 *was then published online, in early July 2022, without further modification, accompanied by a selection of old and new works by the artist. The italics and ellipses initially intended by Chaimowicz in this Q&A have been restored in the version reproduced below.*

A.V.

· · · · · · · · ·

Nicolas Vamvouklis: *Marc Camille, you are one of the first artists to merge the realms of performance and installation art. Which were the challenges in creating a new, staged space where the personal becomes political?*

Marc Camille Chaimowicz: The pre-existing ways of practice left him dissatisfied; was he surely yearning for the once halcyon days of the avant-garde?

… intense in his need for radical change, the young man was driven by a longing for a sense of fellowship

… and yet, although possible directions were then signposted, within the emerging counter-culture: as well as in the realms of music and film, it was essentially a matter of finding one's own voice within a new order, or simply of seeking a more personal language, freed from formalism's straight jacket… and such terms as "performance" or "installation" were felt to be an irritant because what was least wanted was to be (re)classified… and it was in this sense that he was then drawn to the *unnamed*…

If I had to describe your shows in one word, that would be hospitable. They blur the boundaries between art and design, private and public, intimate and formal, masculine and feminine. Can you imagine a world without colour? How would that be for you?

You are perhaps familiar with *L'atelier d'alberto giacometti* by Jean Genet?… one of the best texts ever written on art, ever, in which

Genet (for whom he is posing) recalls Giacometti telling him that he once imagined burying life-size bronze figures deep underground—as though belonging to a defunct time—to not then to be found until some distant future when even his name ... would no longer have been remembered! ... such were the musings of two of the finest *existentialist* minds!

but above ground, in the land of the visible, colour of course matters: it would after all be difficult to visualise a bathroom scene by Bonnard or a bunch of flowers by Vuillard in B/W. Jean-Luc Godard's black and white film *Breathless* was transformed in its remake as *Pierrot le Fou*, not simply by the casting of Anna Karina, but by the process of Technicolour!

In the exhibition "Dear Valérie..." at Kunsthalle Bern (2020), in addition to your own artworks, you also presented a photograph by your long-time friend Balthasar Burkhard. Céline Condorelli says that friendship could be charted both as a desirable set-up for working and a dimension of production. What is your idea of friendship?

As, and when concerning a particular person, friendship then becomes *bespoke*... and is more often than not tinted by the tone of complicity or that of implied intimacy...

Although Jean Genet, ever the outsider, professed to have no need of friendship, he would surely have upheld the spirit of fellowship, as measure of fraternal solidarity...

My 2008 exhibition "...In the Cherished Company of Others..." at De Appel, co-curated with Alexis Vaillant, featured many guest artists, as metaphor of fellowship, and included Lucy McKenzie: alongside whom I have since regularly exhibited... as well as having co-authored a number of conversations... We correspond but do not, however, exchange birthday or Christmas cards; our ongoing dialogue is therefore one of a shared fellowship

... by way of contrast to the condition of friendship, which is inherently *exclusive*, the nature of fellowship, both pluralistic and porous, implies a degree of commonality...

… and how about collaborations as part of the creative process? You use an extensive range of media, which means working closely and experimenting with different craftspeople.
… exactly!
I am currently working with two ceramicists (one Italian, one Japanese)—one for an outdoor commission and the other for an edition—and although each project differs, I am equally grateful to each of them for their expertise. I am also overseeing the production of ribbons, this entailing industrial process, as well as having two rugs hand-woven in Mexico… and so a diverse range of media and techniques may be found in my back catalogue: these including tufted wool, sandblasted aluminum and Crystal glass, printed and woven fabrics, tooled bronze, decorated leather, printed wallpaper, lacquered ply, etc., etc., which have, over many years, extended the parameters of my practice (as well, perhaps, as that of my attention span?—because each has had its own specific challenges)…
And yet, although a close dialogue is often implicit, as has been the case with my primary cabinet maker, the premise of collaboration is often as much with the potential of each process or material, as it may be with that of each artisan…

The artist's house organically connects the domestic world or the workplace with the exhibition venue. May I ask which is your favourite spot in your living space?
… at the very start of the lockdown, my bedroom was initially a favoured place (as was surely the case for many others)… whether to read, to be making notes, or drawing birds in flight, which I would enjoy seeing from the window… or but to be engaged in reverie, which… upon waking, remains often so.
… it was for decades otherwise the kitchen table and is now the generous table in my *salon*, from where the view is good and the coffee is of easy reach, as are the bookshelves, … and in the early evening, most often, a Campari soda…

[I. 23]

In the Studio with... Marc Camille Chaimowicz

(2023)

Founded in London in 1925, Apollo is a 90-page monthly art publication. International in scope, each issue features news, articles, and scholarly writing. The magazine, it says, "covers the visual arts of all periods, from antiquity to the present day." Edited by Edward Behrens since 2021, Apollo also has an evolving online platform, which is updated daily with news and reviews, as well as interviews with artists. On the occasion of the exhibition "Marc Camille Chaimowicz: Nuit Américaine," Wiels, Brussels (17 February–13 August, 2023), organised by Zoë Gray, at the time Senior Curator at Wiels [I. 24], Sam Talbot, a London-based PR Agency commissioned by Wiels to extend the exhibition's media visibility, invited Chaimowicz to answer Apollo's regular editorial series "In the Studio with…" This mini-Q&A consists of seven questions about how they work in their studio space, their daily routine and their upcoming projects. Although the questions are slightly different each time, their content and key words are similar to one another. The magazine emailed the questions to Wiels' PR department, which subsequently forwarded them to the artist. What Talbot and Apollo probably did not know was that over the course of his life, Chaimowicz never really had a studio. Indeed, the studio is the exhibition space itself. In the early 1970s, the artist was already declaring, "The very concept of a studio was anathema to a number of us then, and so the streets, and notably the streets at night, were material for the need to contest the dominant cultural value of the time." While answering the questions, however, he thought, "I think it's great… Anyway, my studio is first and foremost in my head." His answers were quicky answered and returned, and the Q&A was posted online on 23 February, 2023. Beyond the immediate satisfaction of responding so quickly to such a short questionnaire, what pleased the artist most was that, from start to finish, there was no human interaction.

A.V.

• • • • • • • • •

Where is your studio?
My studio is first and foremost in my head, but the material realisation of work happens either on a large table in my salon in London or when exhibiting, it happens in situ.

Does your studio practice follow a particular routine?
Only in that each new project determines its particular discipline.

How would you describe the atmosphere of your studio?
Given that it is through the making of work that I come to many self-realisations, I'd say generally, gratifying.

Is there anything you would change about the space?
In an ideal world, I would have the studio close to a 24-hour restaurant or bar.

What's the strangest object in your studio?
There is an acute triangle at one end of my salon, which is currently occupied by an enigmatic and what I presume to be an Aboriginal figure, carved from a piece of dark wood. She is naked, but decorated with earrings and has a wonderful big smile. She is perhaps awaiting to be reclaimed by her owner who left suddenly and without notice, but in the meantime, she makes for wonderful company.

Who is the most interesting visitor you've had to your studio?
Other than my assistant, visitors are generally discouraged, but I did once see, at the height of last summer's heat wave, a sweet little mouse who had somehow scaled the three external walls.

Is anything or anyone banned from your studio?
For health reasons, and somewhat regrettably, smoking is no longer possible…

[I. 24]
Interview

Louisa Buck

(2023)

In early 2023, British art critic Louisa Buck, author and regular BBC radio and TV columnist on contemporary art, contacted Chaimowicz to conduct an interview with him on the occasion of his two over-lapping exhibitions in Continental Europe: "Zig Zag and Many Ribbons," Musée d'art Moderne et Contemporain, Saint-Étienne (19 November, 2022–10 April, 2023), and "Marc Camille Chaimowicz: Nuit Américaine," Wiels, Brussels (17 February–13 August, 2023).

Both based for years in Camberwell, Chaimowicz and Buck met from time to time, especially during the holiday season, and when, sadly, they visited their beloved friend, Welsh art critic and editor Stuart Morgan, in hospital together, before his death on 28 August, 2002. Buck, who has been the London contemporary art columnist for The Art Newspaper *since 1997, was eager to catch up with the artist at Cabinet, London, on 2 February, 2023. The interview began at 9:30 a.m. and thanks to Buck's ability to master time as a radio broadcaster, "she grabbed her helmet and bike, and left the gallery at 10:29 a.m., assuming she had enough information for the interview." Recorded on her mobile phone, the interview was subsequently transcribed and emailed to* The Art Newspaper. *"Truly confident in Louisa Buck's efficient editing," the artist did not wish to proofread the text, which was published online on 10 March, 2023.*

While "Zig Zag and Many Ribbons" was an elaborate museum retro-spective in dialogue with the museum's collection, and within which the artist for the first time pleasurably presented some of his late mother's work [III. 29], "Marc Camille Chaimowicz: Nuit Américaine" brought together three work groups by the artist, including for the first time The Hayes Court Sitting Room *(2023) and* Dear Zoë— Emma Bovary *collages (2020–23), in addition to* Celebration? Realife Revisited *(1972–2000), three environments that "examine intimacy, domesticity, and the desire—or need—to create one's own context," as exhibition curator Zoë Gray put it in the visitors guide. Different in scale and content, these exhibitions nevertheless have one thing in common: a digital approach to "curating" and to installation, including the lighting, which plays a central role in the exhibitions, transitioning "from a dark space of festivities to the half-light of a domestic interior for dreaming, and finally to the filtered daylight of a reading room," as Zoë Gray described it.*

Over the pandemic, Chaimowicz, whose health is quite fragile, stopped travelling. This partly contributed to the digitisation of most of his life for a while, including the two aforementioned exhibitions, which were mounted with the live assistance of Anna Clifford, Chaimowicz's collaborator, who travelled to France and Belgium, assuming the artist's role from the other side of the screen. So, when Chaimowicz met Buck at Cabinet, the latter was delighted to hear this "hugely influential" artist, speaking "so eloquently" about two exhibitions that he had recently installed via Skype and had not seen in person.

Published as part of the "Artist interview" section of The Art Newspaper, *an art journal founded in 1990 by Umberto Allemandi and Anna Somers Cocks, the interview with Chaimowicz reproduced below was an opportunity for the artist to highlight the influences and inspirations behind these two solo exhibitions. The interview includes illustrations of* (Involuntary) Self-Portrait, Ventimiglia, February 6th 2016, *"A self-portrait of Chaimowicz, who readily admits to being more comfortable with portraits of others;" a view of* Celebration? Realife (1972–2000) *as presented in the exhibition "Marc Camille Chaimowicz—Dear Valérie …," Kunsthalle Bern (22 February–26 July, 2020); a 2021 collage from the* Dear Zoë (Emma Bovary collage) *series; a colour photograph of* Emma and Freddie in the Hayes Court Sitting Room, *2022; and finally, a view of the artist's* Art School Levi's *(circa 1960), a skinny and customised pair of jeans that hang on the wall above the artist's 2005 wallpaper* Vase, *as premiered in the Saint-Étienne exhibition. Three days after this interview went online, it was republished in French, as part of* The Art Newspaper's *French edition, 13 March, 2023.*

A.V.

The Art Newspaper: *Each of these two exhibitions span your career in different ways. At Saint-Étienne around eighty of your works dating from the 1960s onwards are combined with thirty or so artworks and artefacts from the museum's collection in a series of environments and mise-en-scènes described as "discrete dramas." What was your aim here?*

Marc Camille Chaimowicz: I've long wanted to do just one museum show in the country of my birth. It's over seven galleries, grandiloquent and it took many years. Because of Covid it was a slow burn. Apart from one or two new works, it largely meant orchestrating pre-existent work and was quite a finely honed, academic exercise. It also gave me the opportunity of showing some of my late mother's work, which I really enjoyed. When, pre-Covid, I visited Saint-Étienne and picked up on their multifarious collection, I had this moment of insight: given that I always like to guest somebody, why not show mother?

What form do your mother's works take?

As a young woman, mother had been instructed to take an apprenticeship as a dressmaker in the couture House of Paquin. She made these beautiful sewn patterns as exercises: they were a kind of *devoir*, a rite of passage. I was touched that she should have given them to me rather than to my sisters—I think she'd picked up on the fact that I was into visual matter and also textiles. I've had them for many years and have been delighted by them. They are a cross between Agnes Martin and Louise Bourgeois. They're fabulous.

By contrast your Wiels exhibition consists of just three works: your post-pop scatter environment, Celebration? Realife *(1972);* The Hayes Court Sitting Room, *which takes the front room of the flat in Camberwell, South London, where you lived and worked for more than four decades and reinstates it as an art installation; and finally* Dear Zoë... *(2020–23), a suite of forty-eight collages that uses Flaubert's*

heroine Madame Bovary as a starting point.
If we were to use categories of genres, one could argue that *Celebration* is a kind of landscape, *The Hayes Court Sitting Room* an interior, and the collages are portraiture. However much we wish to undermine our training and the ubiquitous history of art, I think one is inevitably reined back into those kinds of references.

But at the same time, you have been a pioneer in challenging the categories of art, décor, and design in your practice. Why has this been so important?
It came out of an early engagement with feminist theory. Because it was so male-driven, and black and white, the dominant left-wing ideology seemed as alienating as what it was contesting. Colour was seen as decadent and pleasure as reactionary, and for me that had to be recalibrated. And so domesticity became a sort of metaphor for me. I was also questioning the very function of visual art practice and its implicitly elite role in the canon. Camberwell School of Arts in the 1960s was hierarchical and the applied arts were seen as taboo. I was interested in questioning that, and so in the 1980s I took up volunteering as an intern in one of the last remaining traditional silk design studios in Lille. It completely undermined the hallowed ground upon which painting has always been upheld, and instead you'd do a drawing and the team would try it out. This gave me the confidence to engage in a very wide range of materials with the benefit that I could often use the skill of others. There would be dialogue and discussion, and this continues to the present day.

As well as collaborating with artisans and craftspeople, and "guesting" other artists—ranging from Alberto Giacometti and Pierre Bonnard to Wolfgang Tillmans, Lucy McKenzie, and now your mother—you often also devote entire exhibitions to admired figures, such as Jean Cocteau or Jean Genet. In many ways yours is a very sociable practice.
I was always suspicious of the studio. I felt it was a kind of trap.

And likewise, my current studio in Camberwell, I avoid it religiously. I store things there and I occasionally have people come in and help make work, but I'm still much at my best working on the kitchen table. So deep down there has long been this yearning for a degree of conversation, literally or metaphorically.

You were born in post-war France to a Polish Jewish father and a French Catholic mother, but when your father got work in the UK you moved as a child from Paris to England, first to Stevenage and then to Ealing in West London. Yet, although you grew up in the UK, your French cultural heritage has always played a major part in your work. At Camberwell [art college] the dominant value was a parochial, figurative, Euston Road [School] kind of aesthetic. And, of course, I rebelled against that. As a way of rebelling, one would be drawn I guess to American practice, but large-scale abstract painting was just utterly alien to me. So that drove me back to a European sensibility. I was drawn to a very wide range of artists from Vuillard to Fragonard. But first and foremost it was probably to [the film director Jean Luc] Godard, as well as to literature and French thought, people like [Marguerite] Duras and Simone [De Beauvoir]. The theory came later.

It's interesting that you describe your Dear Zoë... *collages as a self-portrait even though they are inspired by Emma Bovary, whereas the earlier photographs and films in which you physically appear seem more to do with role-playing and tropes for ideas of the romantic, androgynous artist.*
Yes, in a Bowie-like way they are often behind a form of mask. When I was doing live work, I would find a means by which to avoid anything overtly confrontational, so I'd either be in shadow or walking. I'm happier dealing with the portraits of others than I am of my own, and that's partly why I so enjoy working with Emma Bovary.

You had already illustrated Madame Bovary *for Four Corners Books in 2013. Was this recent series of collages, which you began after the first lockdown, a form of personal response to Emma's feelings of entrapment and longings of escape?*

There was almost inevitably a degree of projection and implied symbiosis. During that time I was also processing, editing, and jettisoning a lot of magazines and visual material from Hayes Court and that fed into the Emma collages. Right now, while Emma is in residence in Brussels, I'm giving it a pause. But I think there's still mileage left and I'll probably pick up again afterwards. And then we'll see where that goes.

[II]

CRITICISM

Featuring introductions by Alexis Vaillant

[II. 1, 2, 3, 4, 5, 6]

Studio International

(1976–77)

Launched in April 1893, The Studio, *an "illustrated magazine of fine and applied art," was one of the first art magazines
to adopt photomechanical reproduction. To maintain its
circulation,* The Studio *took a middle-of-the-road path
between visual and applied arts, art history and art news. In
1964, under the impetus of editor GS Whittet and designer
David Pelham, the magazine changed its name to* Studio
International *to expand its influence abroad.*

*In 1968, British writer and editor Peter Townsend was
appointed editor of* Studio International. *From 1968 to
1975, he reinvigorated a tired publication, overseeing its
transformation from a mainstream Britain-centric publication
into a vanguard journal reporting on some of the most radical
artistic art projects in the UK and internationally. Townsend's
editorial focus was on the role of art as a privileged means
of activating social change in relation to the definition of
public space at a time when it was a flashpoint for political
and social contestation. Therefore, when millionaire architect
Michael Spens acquired* Studio International *in 1975, the
magazine was identified as an emancipatory social and cultural media outlet. Shortly after, Richard Cork became the
magazine's editorial chairman. A renowned British art historian, Cork was at the time a broadcaster at BBC Radio 4 and
an art critic for the* Evening Standard. *Upon his arrival at*
Studio International, *he made a radical decision to transform the format of the publication. As Chaimowicz recalled,
"Richard Cork felt implicitly that new activity is something
that he and his fellows were not necessarily able to understand.
He was convinced that only people involved in these areas were
capable of understanding what was happening, and therefore
writing about it." To facilitate this, Cork created six columns
edited by a select group of artists and writers in their twenties: New Music by Michael Neiman; Books by John A Walker;*

Photography by Ian Jeffrey; Performance by Marc Chaimowicz; Video by David Hall; Film Practice by Malcolm Le Grice. "These columns were created with the intention of initiating readers over each issue by means of establishing the beginning of a framework," *Chaimowicz recalled. At the time, in fact, "not so many publications were interested in the emergence or devoted to art's first recognition with an equal value whatever the type of art produced," he admitted in retrospect.*

Over the autumn of 1975, Cork contacted Chaimowicz. They decided to meet in person. During their meeting, Cork explained to Chaimowicz why it would be interesting to have him report on performance in Studio International. *He mentioned, of course, the artist's recent performances and installations that had attracted attention in London and elsewhere, including* Celebration? Realife *(1972) [I. 7; III. 2, 3, 4];* Shoe Waste *[I. 1];* Genug Tyrannei in Graz *(1972);* Table Tableau *(1974). In addition to this, there was also Chaimowicz's involvement in the alternative art scene in London. Among other initiatives, the artist participated in the creation of an Artist Union, which, according to Cork, matched well to the concerns of the magazine.*

As Chaimowicz assumed, "Richard Cork may have been introduced to my work by Caroline Tisdall." An art critic for The Guardian, *Visiting Professor of Art History at the University of Reading, and curator of the exhibition "Inaugural Show" at AIR Gallery, London, June 1975 [I. 2], Tisdall was aware of the artist's interests and no doubt recommended him. At the time, Tisdall, who was also a contributor to* Studio International, *and Cork were interested in how the artists were able to develop social concerns in their work in relation to the community—a topic that Cork would later develop as curator in the exhibition "Art for whom?" at the Serpentine, London (22 April– 14 May, 1978). By the end of 1975, Chaimowicz was con-*

vinced that "the most interesting work of performance at that time was coming from a critique of formalism … addressing two problems: first, the gradual institutionalisation of the practice; second, the fact that the first generation was beginning to be recognised." Conscious of what was at stake in that particular moment regarding performance, Chaimowicz accepted Cork's invitation to report in Studio International, *knowing that his contributions would relate to his interests as an artist and would also align with his interest at the time in non-studio-based practices. Furthermore, although performance art was an important topic in the art world at the time, it still lacked recognition as an activity. Chaimowicz was aware that his reporting could help to promote the practice. In this regard, the performance column for* Studio International *was, he said, "An interesting means for me to clarify the relationship of performer / artist while considering that performance is not a specific field, and that time-based artists can also produce objects."*

Chaimowicz began reporting on performance for Studio International *in late 1975. At the time, he was intrigued by "the possibility of putting ideas in writing in parallel to a practice." Quickly, the artist gained "confidence into using words in a work, which was also recognised with a slight change of name," with his middle name—"Camille"—not being part of his signature from the first report to the last one.*

From January 1976 to March 1977, Chaimowicz contributed six times to the bimonthly publication. Among these, two stand out. The first contribution (Vol. 191, no. 979, January / February 1976) includes a two-paragraph introduction that expresses the intentions of the artist as a reporter. The fourth contribution is not a report per se but an interview conducted by the artist with British filmmaker Sally Potter, whose background is in choreography, music, performance art, and experimental film. Entitled "Women and performance in the UK," the interview was in the "Performance" issue of Studio International *(Vol. 192, no. 982, July/August 1976) on the cover of which is reproduced a photo of Chaimowicz's* Table Tableau *(1974) in relation with Tisdall's text "Brisley and Chaimowicz."*

Apart from these two exceptions, Chaimowicz's reports were standardised in the sense that they were systematically subtitled "Report by Marc Chaimowicz," divided in sections of varying length, corresponding to events that the artist had selected "to inform, clarify, and develop a dialogue regarding cultural experimentation by artists working in and/or with performance," he said. In addition, his reports were illustrated accordingly, including some of his own shots.

Chaimowicz's reports in Studio International *can be considered a selective mapping in real time of the performance scene in London in 1976 to 1977. In retrospect, however, as Chaimowicz said, "on a naïve level, I went very critical. I realised later that I was not objective but perhaps too subjective?" Although, "Richard Cork was a gentleman of editorial manners, committed to editing and rewriting texts, and working closely with the contributors as well as with the graphic designer in every detail," Chaimowicz decided to quit reporting as he was busy with his own work, including the performance* Doubts… A Sketch For Video-Camera and Audience *[I. 3], which was touring Europe. And anyway, he said, "before Richard Cork conceded that he had lost the production, issues were becoming eratic."*

More than three decades later, referring to his role as a reporter to postgraduate students affiliated with A/S/N—the inter-

disciplinary *Master of Fine Arts course Art/Space/Nature at the Edinburgh College of Art*—in an interview entitled *"Fieldwork as Reverie," reprinted in this publication [I. 13], Chaimowicz told them that the sixth report on performance for* Studio International *was not supposed to be the last, but the penultimate:*

> "My final column, which never got published, highlighted a fundamental contradiction—namely, that you couldn't actually write about performance because the very principle of that premise was based on a formalised reading of practice. From that I developed a frustration relative to the degree of objectivity, which is needed to write criticism. I felt more and more drawn to writing for myself, to actually including writing within practice. I think that most of us who write, given that we come from the visual arts, write inordinately slowly. To me, journalism is the antithesis of how I use the written word because the pressure in journalism produces a false urgency."
>
> A.V.

· · · · · · · · ·

[II. 1]

Performance

(1976)

A number of "first-generation" artists working with performance are currently questioning the viability of working under the often unacceptably demanding pressures of a "live" situation. They feel that certainly within the gallery circuit the "zoo-like" situation leads to compromise rather than exploration and development. There is talk of "private" performance, the "piece" or result, the public experience being videotape, sequential photography, a discussion, or whatever. In other words, the performance remains the energy source (private) and the evidence, the "artwork," is public. An international demand for live work as with, say, Vito Acconci would also be a factor. Conversely, a number of groups are acquiring "theatrical" trade experience and seem happy to present a polished show to a passive audience.

There are, of course, still a number of people and groups working in the "alternative theatre, street/events" tradition, some of whom consider themselves "performance" artists, and they are no doubt contributing to the emerging tradition of community arts. Also a few "frontline" galleries, publishers, writers, and even TV producers (traditionally as insensitive as ever) are showing a growing interest in performance work. Some are making real developments possible. As Jonathan Harvey states (see below) the term "performance art" may, like "pop art," have become redundant, the activities and characters within the perimeter being so diverse. As from the January/February issue of *Studio International* this column will, however, attempt to inform, clarify, and develop a dialogue regarding cultural experimentation by artists working in and/or with performance.

Arts Council Report

Whilst on the Arts Council's Administration Course this summer, Jonathan Harvey produced *Problems in Patronage of the "Living Arts,"* an investigation into the relationship between the Performance Art Committee of the Arts Council of Great Britain and artists working with performance. The report is primarily concerned with systems of patronage rather than with performance work. From a sensitive introduction Harvey then plots the complex history from 1968–75 of various arts council committees' attempts to cope with cultural experimentation that could not be handled by the existing panels (visual arts, music, drama, and literature). In his history of an essentially conservative organisation's attempts to relate to "the new and non-categorizable," he makes no reference to FACOP (Friends of the Arts Council Operative), the pressure group of 1968–70, which not only "occupied" 105 Piccadilly but also succeeded in awarding moneys in open meetings organised by the democratic London artists' panel. Arguably this important model may have deserved a chapter to itself.

Back to performance, the main body of the report is given over to the findings of a long questionnaire sent to almost 200 artists working in Britain. Some of the findings from the eighty replies show that:

(a) Half the artists are working loosely in the "theatrical" tradition and half in that of the visual arts.
(b) 70% are ex-art school.
(c) That the most frequent venues were (in order) galleries, arts festivals, theaters, streets, community festivals.
(d) That the majority of artists "were involved in other activities, with performance as one element of their activity, and others with performance work, including other subsidiary concerns." (This appears to be a factor peculiar to this country.)

Paradoxically, although the majority of artists do not specialise, the Performance Art Committee currently seems to. Harvey argues that "a system of funding, which favours a small minority of full-time artists is far from equitable." If he is hinting that a small number of individuals are receiving recurring annual support at the expense of other artists it is a sound point. He adds that

"[...] the terms of reference of the Performance Art Committee are being narrowed and may preclude experimental artists whose work may either have an element of performance or who work in performance occasionally." Here, however, he doesn't mention the Visual Arts Panel, which has, for example, recently given substantial awards to two such artists, Bruce McLean and Paul Neagu, under its awards to artists scheme. Finally, re definitions, Harvey argues that "there is just a whole area of activity, which artists move through or take up a position within, that is so broad as to defy definition." Queries to Jonathan Harvey, tel. 01-987 7585.

Brisley in Poland

Stuart Brisley and photographer Lesley Haslam were working in Poland this summer with *Moments of Decision/Indecision*, a performance piece at Gallery Studio, Warsaw, for six days in August 1975.

"On the first day before the beginning of the work, the figure's head was shaved to reduce the sense of personality and to increase the feeling of nakedness. At the beginning of the work each day the figure was dressed in a greyish shirt and trousers. As soon as the clothes were covered with paint, and were wet, they were removed. When clothed, the figure, although separated by the work, was related to the viewers in the sense that generally he was as they were—dressed in accordance with social requirements. The naked state of the figure induced a more acute sense of distance or separation between the figure and the viewers but a closer relationship between the figure, the wall, the floor, the paint, etc. This sense of distance was required so that a distinction could be made between like circumstances and the circumstances of an art process involving a live person. Bowls of black and white paint were strategically placed on the floor—two bowls of white and black paint placed opposite each other towards the front of the floor area, and two placed towards the wall at the back.

"Each day's activity began with the figure placing one foot in black paint, one in white paint, likewise with the hands. This image established the visual contradiction, which was itself a condition of the work, of which there was no final resolution. After the clothes were removed, the sense of involvement in the process increased. When the paint covered the eyes, and the figure was unable to see for the duration of the work, the order of the 'normal' perceptions of space-distance and gravity was subtly changed. The figure demonstrated this limited sense of a 'release' by attempting to climb the wall, as part of the process of painting the wall. No signs were made in paint by the figure: the images that were left on the wall were largely involuntary marks, made by bodily contact and by chance.

"The collaborator (Haslam) photographed the work at intervals using a flashlight, which also gave a repetitive rhythm to the process. He directed the blind figure, on request, to the front, back, and middle of the space, and to the bowls of black and white paint placed on the floor. The collaborator became the eyes of the figure. The figure sensed the space and distances in which the action took place, in order to change and develop the work. He moved between the floor and the wall, from the floor onto the wall, to the floor, between the black and white areas in the space, from black into white, and from white into black. He changed black areas, into white areas, white areas into black areas and was himself changed from white into black into grey at regular intervals.

"In this work, several paradoxical situations established themselves. The resolution could only take place within those people who came to see it. Given the fact that *Moments of Decision/Indecision Warsaw* only existed in the time/space in which it took place; in order to extend the work beyond that time/space, it was necessary to obtain information and material from the process. The form of information needed (in this case photography) required the collaboration of another person. Such a person should have a specific understanding of the nature of the activity, and be independent in terms of his own ability to be able to make clear decisions in relation to the work in process. The activity itself changes from one state of reality into another. What is revealed through the process of photography are 'moments of decision' selected from the activity by the person using the camera. The long series of changing states of the actual process are termed 'moments of indecision.' The need for collaboration is determined by the notion of the potentiality of a continual process leading from one state of the work to another until the work is finally resolved or dies, e.g. action—photography—film—book. It generates a democratic situation in which there is an interchange of responsibility leading to the resolution of the work in its various forms. This notion of a democratic collaboration is a creative aspect of the process and is influential in determining the form, feeling, and outcome of the original concept." (Stuart Brisley)

Diplomacy

Stuart Brisley's work in Gallery Studio, Warsaw, ended in a curious twist of fate, reversing our accepted understanding of artistic freedom or license. The Poles, by nature both mischievous and courteous, invited the British Ambassador and his wife to the opening action of *Moments of Decision/Indecision*.
The Ambassador then wrote a long and detailed letter of protest apparently to the British Council in London (who were simply responsible for the travel costs). The contents of this letter are not known, but the Poles were delighted to point out that the letter of protest did raise the question of political interference in cultural matters, something that the West has been at great pains to camouflage when presenting art both in the East and West.

Cambridge Circus

The busker outside the Palace Theatre on Cambridge Circus

who plays harmonica and has an aviary of performing budgies (tight-rope walkers, etc.) now includes a little dog in his routine. Balancing on his back legs the dog wears a hat, spectacles, and holds a stick in his mouth, on each end of which is, yes, a budgerigar…

Notes and Rumours

Klaus Rinke will be working and performing at the Museum of Modern Art, Oxford, in conjunction with his show, between 11 and 14 February. The exhibition (January 11–February 15) will be of photographs of those works in which his body is the prime agent (1960–75). At least one special day for art colleges is to be arranged, during which Rinke will be performing and discussing his work. Again congratulations to MOMA (remember Beuys last year).
Charlie Hooker Performance at Robert Self, 17 Queen's Lane, Newcastle, 24 January at 8 p.m.

Going Tornado, the performance piece that is part of Paul Neagu's third stage of self-realisation and last seen as part of his show at the Oxford Museum of Modern Art, Spring 1975, will be developed/performed at the Arnolfini, Bristol, in early March.
The Ting: Theatre of Mistakes, surely last summer's busiest troupe with the Cambridge Poetry Festival in April, *The Street* in July, the performance show in Southampton also in July, six concert performances at the London exhibition in October and Workshops at the Roundhouse in November and December, are next presenting *The Table Piece, Parts 3, 4, 5, 6* at the Melkweg (the Milky Way) in Amsterdam this winter.

Material to be considered for this column should be sent to me, c/o *Studio International*.

[II. 2]
Performance

(1976)

Most of the action recently has taken place within the West Central London area.

Some say that artists are the instigators and are therefore the ones to lead discussion on current ideas: they produce the art so they have their finger on the pulse. The Artists' Sangrams held at Tone Place in Endell Street, WC2 were an example of this argument. Others say that critics and gallery people are the ones now that are setting the pace, that through their decisions of who shows, etc., it is they who construct and define the climate. The seminars at PMJ Self, Earlham Street, in November and the Clement Greenberg forum and lecture at Art Net, West Central Street, in January are such examples. Maybe it shouldn't be so fixed; maybe everyone should take turns at doing things and occasionally swop roles. This is what seems to have happened in January at both the "Festival of Expanded Cinema" at the ICA and at the "Real Space Conference" at the Architectural Association, Bedford Square. (AIR, now at 125 Shaftesbury Avenue, is or was technically an artists' organisation run by artists for artists, but it isn't strictly so now, nor is the new gallery.)
I've no idea what "Sangrams" are, but what happened at Tone Place was clear and went very well. Apparently, John Sharkey, who is a poet and author, had organised poetry readings the year before and decided to extend the idea to visual artists, so he and Rebecca Sharkey invited Susan Hiller, Amikam Toren, David Maclagan, Sue Braden, Richard Bernas, and Tina Keane, raised some money so they could each receive a fee, and began to organise. They then asked around for a venue, but there were always problems so they went back home and had them right in their own front room, as they had done with the poets. And this seems a significant part of the success of the series. After all you can hardly shout at and hit people when you're a guest in someone's front room, with a log fire burning and people passing the nuts and wine and bread and cheese round. The attendance was always small, approxi-

mately thirty-five, which made talking more relaxed. Depending on who was on different people showed up, and afterwards each artist either talked about his work, or presented a "piece," then there was some real discussion. The evenings were intimate and worked very well and the Sharkeys are now working on the transcripts for a book.

The problem was that Tone Place and the PMJ Self seminars were on clashing dates, so I missed Susan Hiller because I was at the Self discussion on the role of criticism, etc. Incidentally, although that particular evening was ruined by an aggressive crowd and left the audience dissatisfied and bitter, it surely shouldn't mean that these discussions shouldn't continue. They are still so rare and maybe they'll get better; perhaps it's because they are so rare that things can go wrong at big meetings. There is so much frustration about and it will take time to catch up with saying what should have been said long ago and to start discussing current issues. So congratulations to Bill Furlong of Audio Arts, and Robert Self, who with others organised the talks and to Caroline Tisdall, for at short notice showing a strong hand at chairing an impossible meeting.

One person I saw at Tone Place was David Maclagan. After showing a short and quick slide sequential piece, *After Image*, there was a break and we then went upstairs for his performance/ritual, *Circle with a Cross-Drawn Inside*. A corner is marked out by a white square of paper on the floor, which is accentuated by lighting. A candle in each corner is lit, Maclagan is crouching in the corner, his back to the audience. Sitting to one side is his reader, Harry Walton. The piece begins with a handclap, at which point Walton begins to read from a piece written by Maclagan. There are four texts each read five times in a cycle of four sections, and within each cycle are five movements. The texts are read evenly, one by one, almost in monotone and work as a strong structure. The first goes like this:

"The blows are everywhere, and suddenly nowhere. This is the colour of mid-day. You cannot grasp the changing shape of its heart-beat. It strikes, again and again.

"This is the shock of what you always knew; the dangerous now. Do not touch it. Let it touch you.

"This is the burning focus of outside in, the sign of sacrifice."

Maclagan turns to face outwards and we notice that his head is bandaged in gauze. He stands up, raises his hands to horizontal, drops them, walks in a spiral towards the centre, turns to face each corner and facing us, slowly unwinds the gauze from his head. For the first time he can "see" and this is a touching moment. A square of gauze is made on the floor and, crouching to collect a black Leichner make-up stick, he draws two lines from each corner to the inner square then a black circle around the centre. He returns the black and collects it, crouching and facing us. He then draws a black cross, a line over his eyes and one down his forehead and over his nose. Slowly he stands, then crouching he takes a sponge of red liquid from a bowl and draws a circle around his face and with scissors cuts the tapes, then stands. He then lies on his stomach, head to far corner with his arms and legs outstretched, gets up and colours an inner circle red, attempts to erase the red with a white powder, does nothing for a while, forms a white cross with the gauze on the white heap of powder and draws red lines from corners to the centre (now white) circle. The lights go out, and he slowly walks to each corner, blows out the candles and bows to the audience.

The piece lasts about an hour but nobody seemed bored and it isn't as "keep fit" as it may sound. I've described it methodically because it seems that in this kind of piece, each action is deliberate and economical. It is elementary and though in practice very complicated he's obviously trying to let the elementary speak. The impersonal showed through the personal like a reverse of the traditional approach to formal work. The actions he was instigating were after a while imposing on him, and the vulnerability of the piece seemed central to his concerns, i.e. he was only naked from the waist up, but this seemed to be because he was too shy to strip rather than narcissism, and anyhow he was very naked in a way. The steady rhythm of the words anchored the piece like a base note, enough to save it from transcending right away, and there were moments when he was obviously in sync with the reading and the text. The Tone Place evenings were informal and small in number so there was usually a lot of quality discussion, but in this case though the piece was meant as a "sketch" or a point of departure for discussion, ironically because it was so complete it sort of preempted it. I didn't feel like saying much, but a number of people did chat for a while... And when I saw the piece again at St. Martin's School of Art the greater formality of that specific context produced a more "polished" piece but no discussion at all. David Maclagan has written a book on creation myths for Thames and Hudson [*Creation Myths: Man's Introduction to the World*], which is coming out later this year, and if it has the dignity and quality of this piece it should be worth reading.

Like Keith Moon, Charlie Hooker is a wee lad who wears big boots and occasionally plays drums, but this is where the similarities end. He performs cerebral works and seems overtly influenced by the New York School of systems music of Steve Reich and co. The second piece of his six-part performance at PMJ Self in December was witty and consisted of four piano performers working each note down the scale and then up with one finger according to pre-determined and constant but various speeds. This is what made it, because although they each did the same thing and began and ended at the same time, the different speeds gave the piece texture and humour. Three pieces were for the four pianos and the others were based on a simple rhythmic idea that was then multiplied and/or elaborated on. For these pieces wood blocks, drums, and clapping were variously used to build up rhythms, and the score was on the floor in the form of a large circular path of coded marks. Watching the performers walking round and reading and hitting their two wood blocks and clapping gave the pieces a sculptural quality, which is lacking in the "frozen" photograph. The clarity of the works was extended by having information sheets available to the audience, which presumably was an attempt to help de-mystify. It was almost as if given the instructions anyone could do it, and apparently Charlie Hooker "found" his performers by advertising in *Time Out*, meeting them for the first time on the morning of the day of the presentation. The price for the simplicity of the pieces was that they often seemed unadventurous. There was nothing unpredictable, and unlike the work of Terry Riley the simple overlaying of sound structures never produced a mantra-like "up." It was as if they stayed on the ground that they grew from: they were without emotion and maybe a little too mechanistic.

Another interesting organisational structure, which people central to an issue organised around themselves was the "Real Space Conference" at the Architectural Association, where one Wednesday afternoon in January Bernard Tschumi and others organised a very intensive program of activity between 2 p.m. and 9 p.m. Each spot was roughly forty-five minutes, and varied from talks by Daniel Buren, Germano Celant, Roselee Goldberg, and John Stezaker to a presentation of past work from the Nice Style days of Bruce McLean and Paul Richards. There were also performance pieces by COUM, Pompes Funèbres, and Eno/Bernard Tschumi's *Discreet Music at the Villa Savoye*. It is to their credit that they tried to integrate or inter-relate art and architecture, and the idea of such concentration was also interesting.

At Garage, Kevin Atherton presented *Double Vision* during the last week in January. For five days there was a performance every hour. He had made a videotape of himself looking around the previous show of paintings by Stephanie Bergman. The soundtrack contained a detailed description of his actions: "[…] move to the next painting, stand to the left, hands in back pockets, move to the next work, head to the right, stand, back a bit, fold arms, reach for a cigarette, light it…," etc. The half-hour performance was an inter-play between past and present. The gallery was bare, the paintings gone, but a black line marking where they were hung was drawn on the walls. The videotape played back last week's activity and with this Kevin used the soundtrack to determine his present behaviour. So concurrently with his video image he … moves to the next painting, stands to the left, hands in back pockets, etc., just like the tape except that he's now looking at a white wall.

The time spent in front of each painting or space starts at about a minute and gradually speeds up to a few seconds, so that at the end of the cycle he's almost running round the gallery. This no doubt relates to his interest in the ritual of looking at art. It's oddly related to Marilyn Halford's film-performance *Hands Knees and Boomsa-Daisy*, recently shown at the ICA in which, in front of the screen, she plays with a filmed image of herself; although her piece was more coy and dramatic, it is more predictable.

Finally, I'm glad not to be a girl art student working in performance or any other area, having just seen that the New Contemporaries selection panel is all male. Even the *Daily Mirror* acknowl-edged International Women's Year, and the Equal Pay and Sex Discrimination Bills, but most of the art world carries on oblivi-ously. Then there is surprise when people get angry. A bad start to the year…

PS If any final year students working in performance would like to have details of their "finals" work in the May/June issue, could you please send me brief information c/o *Studio International* by 25 March.

[II. 3]
Performance

(1976)

Neagu and Rinke are similar. Both in their mid-thirties, they use their bodies in their work. They have both developed a (binary-derived) personalised and refined systems approach to visual and documentation work. Both consistent and highly productive, they perpetuate a male approach in the way they manipulate people and ideas. Both are ambitious and, thanks to Nick Serota, both have had their first major English shows at MOMA Oxford (Neagu in 1975).

Neagu and Rinke are dissimilar. Neagu's work is expansive and inclusive; Rinke's work is reductive and exclusive. Neagu's approach is organic and sensual; Rinke's approach is mechanical and cerebral. For me, Neagu's work is inspirational; it gives. Rinke's takes, it is oppressive. Although Neagu is overtly complex and open-ended and Rinke is overtly simple and closed, because of his horizontal approach the totality of Neagu's work is clearly interrelated, almost hermetic. Conversely, because of Rinke's vertical development, the totality of his work is more fragmented.

Klaus Rinke at Oxford

At the MOMA Klaus Rinke showed on the ground floor for a month, during the last week of which he also had the top floor for two programs of performance and discussion. The exhibition was of work from 1960 to 1975. The earlier pieces were, dare I say it, the more beautiful. They were dark (photographically) and ominously framed in roughly welded blue steel. The later pieces of the better-known performances were more methodical, large and heavily framed in thick wood. The show was dense, about sixty pieces, edge to edge. Approximately 200 images of Rinke.
I am baffled by the assumed importance of Rinke's work. He has done immensely well professionally and has recently been appointed professor at the Düsseldorf Academy of Art. Surely, it is not simply that he's a hard working boy. Maybe it is that hard working boys are working for him, or that I've a mental block.

His documentation work is a little like semaphore, except that semaphore is a language used concisely to communicate messages while Rinke's works seem rather blank and mundane, often bordering on the pretentious. They appear "serious" and "meaningful" but under closer scrutiny are simply illustrative. Although the systems of presentation should presumably function to clarify an attitude external to the statement (about our perception of time/space or whatever), the pattern-making within the pieces (the construction) elevates the organisation of images to the very role of content. Though this would be all right if intended, as with the work of Troostwyk, here it seems unresolved and possibly invalidates the source of the images, i.e. the performances, as well as producing an uneasy relationship between the two.

The performances or demonstrations were professionally staged, methodical, and efficient. Rather as at a concert, he and his assistant Monika Baumgartl presented a "set" of pieces from an existing repertory of work, the last being the "new number." Among the pieces featured were *Mutation* (1970), *Naming by Pointing* (1971), and *Maskulin Feminin* (1970–72). The last piece was for me the most interesting (partly because it wasn't documented downstairs). A five-foot stainless steel gong-like dish that appeared convex was placed centrally on the floor. Rinke then lowered a brass plumb-line that hung dramatically, almost touching the surface. He proceeded to fill this gong (which was in fact concave) with buckets of water, the amount it held being a surprise. Then he stepped back and in an assured and masterly way swung the plumb-line outwards with one gesture. We were left watching the serene rhythm of the weight slowly finding a circular path first outside then inside the metal dish until, suddenly, he stopped it. Before it came to a standstill, it naturally found its centre.

During discussion he stated that if he hadn't stopped it we might have got bored, but he didn't seem concerned with that in the previous pieces in which he was the focus of attention. Equally we might have been given some choice, i.e. to wander about. For me this intervention was more fundamental: it seemed either a lack of sensibility, a loss of faith, or implied a need to control, to dominate.

Paul Neagu and his Generative Art Group at the Arnolfini

In the past six years and as part of the totality of his work Neagu's performances have been, chronologically, *Blind Bite, Horizontal Rain,* and *Going Tornado.* Each has been seen as an autonomous piece either at Sigi Krauss, Neal Street, MOMA Oxford or c/o Demarco in Edinburgh. His grand plan is complex and riddled with paradoxes. Briefly, he has developed an approach to his work within which anything he does fits into his overall scheme. This has enabled him to produce objects, drawings, major sculpture, prints, and performance; all inter-referential. In 1972, Neagu founded the Generative Art Group. Again, it is an organisational structure that reconciles apparently disparate elements into a whole. In its way brilliant, it consists of five "fictional" personages each with their own individual artistic skills and attitudes that can be manipulated as five facets of one totality, i.e. GAG is Neagu (five times) and Neagu is GAG.
In March, Neagu and his GAG presented variations of the above three pieces, for the first time as a trilogy, at the new Arnolfini Gallery in Bristol. *Gradually Going Tornado* was also new in that Neagu worked with four other people; the abstract members of the GAG had for this occasion materialised. Finally, owing to the extensive facilities, Neagu was able to develop his recent interest in manipulating technology (as he would have more traditional materials). The result was a polished presentation of three half-hour parts.
The first stage of Neagu's odyssey is *Blind Bite/Perceptions.* The ground plan is a triangle, the soundtrack *Nocturnal* by Edgar Varese. The film of *Blind Bite* at Sigi Krauss in 1971 is projected while Neagu simultaneously parallels the activity of preparing waffles "for real." The four performers are led in, blindfolded, and are seated and given the waffles. Having eaten them slowly, their

blindfolds are removed, they can see. The two boys then hold up a pole from which hangs a plastic tube, while the two girls look on (black mark here). Neagu then blindfolds himself and swings a scythe round in one dangerous-looking but controlled act, splitting the tube. The area is filled with a cloud of powder. The antithesis of this explosion is the gradual dimming of the lights in sync with the settling of the powder.

The second is *Horizontal Rain/Communication*. The ground plan is four isolated tables or rectangles and the sound is mostly the swing of Count Basie. Images of earlier versions are projected as an intro. One person per table, each engaged in a separate activity: taking photographs, writing, drinking soup, drawing. Neagu in a rectangular moduled suit is coordinating. The development is the gradual moving of each table (or separate element) into one bigger table (or whole), and corresponding attempts at communication begin. The loosest piece, it makes sense in retrospect possibly as a societal model of the individual in a group, whereby rather like the Generative Art Group itself five personalities attempt a complex interaction. The finale is the gaining of attention by a boy who, yoga-like, is gradually impressing the others by achieving the impossible; the bending double of his body until his head is between his feet.

The third stage is *Going Tornado/Assessment*. The ground plan is a spiral and the soundtrack is Varese's *Desert*. Again a slide intro. Materially the simplest, it is the closest to the whole spirit of *Gradually Going Tornado*, and the most overtly allegorical. (The most evocative and beautiful, it is also near-impossible to describe.) Neagu emerges more fully, eventually, to dominate the space, and conversely the other four fade to the role of echoes. Three processes, imperceptibly linked, occur simultaneously. First, he steps out of his jumpsuit and gradually sheds layers of complicated clothing. The floor is littered with them and other remnants. As at Oxford, he shaves, and these normally private acts seem part of a preparation to "face the world." Second, he begins to acknowledge the spiral. Third, a hand-held microphone is spun around a metronome, signalling the beginning of the end. Now, almost naked, he measures, restricts parts of his body, and exercises; and you notice that all his actions are within the visual dynamic of the spiral and the audible rhythm of the metronome. Gradually he begins to spin, then falters, and finally stops. The floor is cleared, and the debris is tied to his body like luggage. Disadvantage is turned to advantage: the weights or "burdens" become counter-weights and help him establish equilibrium as he moves into the centre. The last action is simple, self-contained, and beautiful. He is the focus of our attention but because of his speed we cannot see him clearly. He is out of focus.

Neagu's grand plan is ambitious and his approach so "clever" that it could be counter-productive; one life-long hermetic work? Whatever its executant weaknesses (and in a piece as complex as this, by an artist temporarily working so close to the alien territory of theatre, they were inevitable), I think he just succeeded. Because of its refined and economic use of symbol, his balance between spontaneity and control, his sense of timing and his visual skill, he just got through to produce a more advanced piece than most performance work currently being done in England. There is a chapel at London Airport that Neagu might enjoy: it is quiet, underground, and, of course, multi-denominational.

Troostwyk Tape on Capital Radio

One Saturday night, in late February, those listening heard the following on Capital Radio:
"Modern Modern Modern Routine
'This is an advertisement'
Modern Modern Modern Routine
Modern Modern Modern Routine
Modern Modern Modern Routine.
'This advertisement has advertised the text of a work by the artist David Troostwyk.'"

The advertisement was spoken by a woman in a tense, slightly hurried manner, and the commentary was by an older male voice, suitably flatter. The piece lasted approximately fifteen seconds and throughout the three-hour late-night show—starting at midnight—it was repeated nine times. The idea, the advertisement of that idea, the turning of the idea into a radio commercial, and the repetition of that commercial was the work itself. The broadcast was one of a series of five texts applied to various other forms, all of which are concerned with advertising an idea. Seemingly unconcerned with commenting on advertising as an "evil" socio-manipulative industry, unconcerned with taking a moral position, the success or validity of the piece depended on its ability to encourage the listener to tackle or focus on the nature or structure of the ad itself. In other words, the ad primarily "advertised" or referred to itself. What seemed the issue was that:

a) Troostwyk had chosen to operate within the perimeter of commercial radio (Capital is London's commercial station, the program is "low-brow" middle-of-the-road pop music for night workers and insomniacs) as an artist or private individual rather than as an advertiser with a commercial proposition. He had bought time and yet had not used it to "sell" but rather to promote an advertisement of an idea.
b) He had "annexed" the program itself, i.e. although he only bought approximately two minutes we became aware of structures other than his. He had retrieved time to his advantage.
c) Although he had chosen two simple but highly emotive words as the core of his idea, he had, underneath its overt simplicity, paradoxically produced a highly complex piece loaded with implications.

The broadcasts were within a web of sound ranging from *Go Now* by Manfred Mann and *I Love to Love* by Tina Charles to repeated and pre-taped news on deaths in Northern Ireland. I quite rightly leave the last word to the DJ who, at 1.55 a.m., bravely tackled his odd ad: "It's nice to hear inventive advertising every once in a while, so infrequently do people bother to take the plunge into something inventive..."

Changes in Arts Council policy

The Performance Art Committee has been disbanded. Originally established in 1974, partly as a result of the Experimental Projects and New Activities Committees (1971–74), it was one of the sub-committees of the Art Panel. Its function was to service the needs of "Performance Artists," and in its short but busy life (it handled an annual budget, at its peak, of £45,000), it had a reputation for being accessible and for representing a wide range of interests. The new approach is streamlined. A new steering body, The Special Applications Committee, has been established. It will consist of two members from the Dance, Art, and Music Panels, and one from Literature. Internally, it will be serviced by an officer who will refer to the director of a department. It will engage specialist advisers from time to time to report on the work of experimental artists. Its function will not be to award grants but rather to assess applications that do not easily fit into the existing panel structure. (Hence the mixture of panel members partly co-opted to liaise.) It will then offer detailed advice to the panels that will decide on all grant aid. The Arts Council might have made an announcement sooner than it did. As it was, rumours, disquiet, and alarm grew, producing concern. This led to the "Conference Concerning Performance Art" being held at the ICA in March. Attended by fifty people, it defined its main concerns as:

a) Doubts re lack of information regarding the new structure and their future position.
b) It questioned the validity of the new committee and queried its future criteria.
c) It questioned the Arts Council's current position on Performance.

A shift of attitude re status?

d) It queried current policy on representation.

e) It sought an assurance that, whatever the structure, future needs would be served, and it sought a meeting.

Although the new structure is more logical, and may be fairer "across the board" of experimental work (whatever that is), it obviously needs careful monitoring. (As a specialist advisory body it will equally service all panels, whereas PAC was mainly linked to the Art Panel.) In the short-term performance artists (see Jan/Feb *Studio* for definition) may suffer financially, but then historical factors had put them in a relatively favoured position. What matters, surely, is that whatever structure is adopted, attitudes should be jointly developed towards solving this recurrent dilemma of assessment and of funding awkward and/or unusual work.

Queries to: The Steering Committee, "Conference Concerning Per-formance Art," c/o ICA The Mall, London, SW1. Or: The Secretary, Special Applications Committee, The ACGB, 105 Piccadilly, London, W1.

New Contemporaries at the Acme Gallery

The Acme Housing Association has for three years been providing cheap studio and living space in short-term GLC property in East London. It is now extending its organisational skills to opening a professionally run non-commercial gallery, where else but in Covent Garden? A policy of multi-functional usage has enabled them to offer a helping hand to the New Contemporaries, who were looking for a home. It is the first time the student show has attempted to cope with the strange beast "live work," and details are currently being finalised. Video and film may be shown elsewhere (as are painting and sculpture). Performance will definitely happen from 31 May to 5 June (programs will be available) at The Acme Gallery, 43 Shelton Street, Covent Garden, WC2. Tel: 01 -240 3047.

Women and Performance in the UK:
Sally Potter Interviewed by Marc Chaimowicz

(1976)

Marc Chaimowicz: In England there are more artists working with performance as a part of their activity than there are artists specialising in performance. Do you see specialisation as a basic issue facing women artists right now?

Sally Potter: Work in performance is often hard to define in terms of existing art categories. It has evolved essentially as an anti-specialist area. Some women may have gravitated towards it because traditionally they haven't had much access to highly specialised areas of work; it corresponds to a tendency in their cultural indoctrination to learn how to do a little of everything without taking anything too seriously. But this has paradoxically become strength—women don't have such a vested interest in upholding specialist traditions and so they can be freer to challenge the mystique that surrounds them.

But isn't it true that the most interesting women artists in performance have brought to it skills from existing traditions?

Yes, it's not a matter of denying existing traditions but of seeing how cross-references can be made between them, and how they cannot be divorced from their social and historical contexts.

Would you say there is less of a "male shadow" over performance than over, say, painting or sculpture, leaving women free to make more basic decisions?

Only in the sense that it has a shorter history, otherwise the same constraints apply. A person becoming an artist of any kind has to work in relation to art practice within the dominant cultural mode. Women artists don't have many role models to follow, which creates internal conflicts about working at all. But once started you identify with work that has been done, whoever has done it. At a later stage you realise it's mainly men who have done the work and ask yourself where all the women artists were. Further analysis leads to the understanding that under capitalism most of women's labour has been devoted to the maintenance of basic needs, with some crafts as extensions of that. You have to face the fact that the art practice you have been accustomed to is not universal and abstract; it's a language largely determined by men in a specific social context. So the problem for a woman artist conscious of these issues is how to relate to that male-defined language, and also to find out if there has been a suppressed, hidden, woman-defined language.

What attitudes have you come across within the women's movement regarding women artists?
In my experience women in the movement are more ready to support specific feminist issues, for example the fight against sexist imagery in advertising, than the less tangible fight for a woman-defined art practice. Some political activists don't consider art to be a legitimate front to be fighting on, as if by definition artists are upholding the bourgeois individualist ethic, and a concern with the problems of aesthetics is considered very much a secondary issue. In identifying with these definitions of what is politically correct the women's movement may not have been supportive to women artists in their struggle. But I think the real problem is in the ambiguous area commonly known as "radical" in art. In other words, how to determine what, if any, is the relationship between radicalism in terms of aesthetics and radicalism in terms of political activity.

Given the loaded implications of a term like "radical," is it possible for you to compare performance work by women here in relation to other countries, say, relative to your visit to New York last year?
As a generalisation, performance in New York seemed to have lost all pretensions to being a subversive form; it has become institutionalised and contained by the art world. And as far as I could make out women artists, with some exceptions, were mainly fighting for equal opportunities within the existing art world, rather than for a redefinition of what art, or specifically performance, could be. In England, unlike New York, people have to struggle against rigid categorisation of work to make performances

that refer to more than one tradition, and this gives the work a raw edge, which is kind of exciting. But as yet there is no feminist art practice here. This will change as women in art schools and so on exchange information about their experiences and apply their consciousness to the work, rather than seeing it as an abstract entity separate from the realities of their everyday lives.

Some women work with men in performance, almost as couples. Do you see that as productive?
Women who work with men in a collaborative way, without consciously analysing how the male-female relationship affects the work are going to unconsciously perpetuate male and female archetypes through the work. Women need to work either by themselves or with other women across the board, and that includes the art area, in order to really gain control of the productive process and understand how it relates to them. But there can nevertheless be constructive working relationships, and there can certainly be a useful dialogue with men on many levels. One of which can be a joint struggle against sexist ideology, uncovering how it manifests itself in terms of art. Men have their own particular struggles with the competitive power games they often have to play to survive. In a sense it's in the process of questioning and the commitment to struggle against the dominant ideology—not just cynically using it, getting ambitious within it—that there can be solidarity. We can learn from each other. But in terms of art, women specifically need now to learn from each other, to gain the strength necessary to take hold of art theory and practice for themselves, on their own terms.

And in showing confidence for the next few years in performance you obviously see that beginning to happen?
Women grasping the language for themselves? Yes.

What I found particularly interesting about your Berlin piece was its structural nature and the formal use of the three spaces, subdivided.

But in terms of what I've seen generally, it seems that the formal aspects of performance (and the structural aspects of recent performance) have predominantly been handled by men.
In fact women's concern with structures has often gone unnoticed because the images used have been very potent, thereby diverting everyone's attention. Whereas many men have stripped down their use of imagery until all that is visible is the structure. It is now crucial to make a radical examination of imagery, and *not* to attempt to designify imagery in order to relate only to formal problems. Because in the attempt one is actually going to perpetuate the invisibility of ideology. It's necessary to analyse in what ways images crystallise ideology and to articulate those before one can begin to build a new language, one that is useful to us rather than one which drags us down into a repressive mythology. And I'm talking not just about a re-examination of symbolism and the representational image, but also about a demystification of how our perceptual structures operate in relation to images. The issue of subjectivity and subject matter needs to be confronted rather than avoided. We can learn from the structuralist examination of procedure and process, but I think we also have to make an equally rigorous examination of imagery and how it relates to ideology.

So if there is a basic difference between women and men working in performance, you'd say that difference mainly concerned imagery?
Well, criteria I'd say, criteria from which to work. The important thing at this moment is for women to define for themselves what the valid criteria are and not to accept the criteria that men need to work from, which are the culturally dominant criteria anyway. So it means the redefinition of attitudes, for example to the nature of subjectivity, and specifically to "the personal." One of the major contributions of the women's movement is the understanding that the personal *is* political. Similarly the nature of objectivity and subjectivity and how they are intertwined and affect each other needs to be understood, and this can be worked on in art.

[II. 5]

Performance

(1977)

DAN GRAHAM
ICA New Gallery, 6 August
KEVIN ATHERTON
Butlers Wharf, 21 August

In addition to a small show of drawings and plans of video pieces and installations, Dan Graham presented a performance *Performer/ Audience Sequence* at the ICA New Gallery. The presentation was formal. He stood "centre stage," facing the audience, who were seated on tidy rows of chairs, almost in the tradition of the proscenium arch. The piece was static and in layout implied a return to Brechtian concerns. It was, however, neither theatre nor a lecture but rather a performed extension of his artwork in other media. It consisted of Graham describing or interpreting the double reality of himself and his audience simultaneously with his perceiving that reality. He began by rationalising his current experience: "… my left hand is now in my front trouser pocket, thumb out, the weight of my body is on my right foot, there's tension on the right side of my neck …" and continued almost in monotone and with no emphasis on any particular point, shifting his focus to describe "us" the audience: "the back row is mostly relaxed, possibly bemused, three are smoking, most have a hand to their face, the rows nearer to me are now looking round and the back row is changing its behaviour, becoming stiffer, maybe more self-conscious, someone has just entered the room through the back door, people are looking round…," etc.

Throughout the long piece he switched back and forth from himself to the audience, and this continuous flow gave the piece fluidity. The relentless process of attempting to articulate real time, of keeping it constantly in focus, never losing it, seemed very demanding, especially with Graham having to cope with someone in the audience provocatively qualifying, "talking back," and presumably threatening his concentration. Towards the end the piece lost some of its sharpness and clarity, became generalised and a little vague. As an attempt to demystify the role of the artist in performance this piece was deliberately more accessible and less philosophical than most of Graham's work. But conversely, because of its demanding nature, it depended to a large extent on the fitness and skill of the artist and therefore emphasised Graham's role and authority.

First presented in New York two years ago, it derived from a video work of 1971 in which a girl sat in front of a TV monitor looking at her self-image, which was being taped by a man describing his activity. In *Performer/Audience Sequence* it was almost as if Graham had become the video camera and monitor, recording and playing back the live situation simultaneously. The nearest parallel however might be that in which a political speaker (especially in the US) will "play" with the audience attempting to project him or herself into the audience and vice versa. Thus establishing, with a rhetoric that of course played no part in Graham's performance, a process of cross-identification whereby he or she is simultaneously part of the audience and outside it.

Graham has stated: "Video is a present-time medium. Its image can be simultaneous with its perception by/of its audience (it can be the image of its audience perceiving). The space/time it presents is continuous, unbroken and congruent to that of the real time, which is the shared time of its perceivers and their individual and collective real environments." In this sense the piece was experiential in real time and therefore fundamentally impossible to describe in past-time; i.e. I am in retrospect removed and distanced from a piece, which incorporated the audience structurally, in which the audience was integral and essential rather than external or detached.

Butlers Wharf

As the ships on the Thames get bigger the docks become too small and warehouses, unable to cater for containerisation, become obsolete. When business moves out the artists move in, starting in the late 1960s with St Katharine's Dock on the north side. But St Katharine has now been transformed into a "top bracket" marina and the buildings once occupied by artists and rats have been converted into luxury flats. So the artists have moved either further east to Wapping or south of the river. Given many London artists' almost fetishistic fantasy about the lofts of New York (and presumably the resultant art of that distant culture) the most noticeable difference between Lower Marsh and Lower Manhattan is people, or the lack of them. In SoHo, the lofts are situated in a few blocks busy with residents, shops, bars, galleries, and therefore, lots of people. Here there is a rather foreboding, darkly-lit network of Victorian industrial shells in ghostly Dickensian streets devoid of people.

At 2B Butlers Wharf a group of eight or nine young artists are attempting to "activate" this part of town with a regular program of film, video, and live work. Although similar groups have failed this looks like becoming the first specialist base for performance and related work. Whatever the pros and cons of specialisation, it is positive that some artists are committed enough to work for themselves and others, and to combat the general lack of interest and support in this area. Their efforts could possibly herald a more professional approach towards performance than, with a few exceptions, has been the case both amongst artists and organisers. Butlers Wharf has been running an irregular program for a while, and now aims to "launch" the space with a regular program on Saturday evenings as from this autumn. Artists who would like to show film, video, live work, or work closely related to those areas, should contact John Kippin at 01-928-8501 Ex. 38 (day) or 01-352-4849 (evening).

In August Kevin Atherton presented *Some Features of Support*. The piece began in darkness and as the lights were switched on we saw the ten central white-painted pillars, on each of which was a silhouette, presumably of the artist, painted black. Beginning at the furthest on the right he made his way up, pillar by pillar, towards the audience. He carried a can of cream paint and a brush, painted various marks and daubs on the right-hand pillars, and at the third began to talk. Saying he wasn't sure it was right to speak he generalised about "… the context, the place I work …" and began to elaborate on his actions. Explaining how each pillar appeared the same but was in reality different, unique, and how with the paint marks he was "pointing out these cracks and faults," how the ground plan showed identical pillars but that they were each in fact particular.

He then made his way down the left side again stopping at each pillar, but this time "reversing" the process by transferring the faults and cracks of each one onto his painted body with a stick of black greasepaint. Having worked on, and then from, each pillar he attempted a half-hearted discussion on performance, audiences, private views, the "art crowd," etc., that was too vague to succeed. The wit inherent in the title materialised in the piece and the analogy between the pillars and "human characteristics" was beautifully and lucidly managed. It was the clearest performance of his that I have seen and the first that transcended the basic idea. Just as he had talked of the pillars being more complex and particular than the squares representing them on the ground plan, so this piece, although seemingly authentic to his contextual concerns, was nevertheless more complex than the simple structure on which it was based—thereby logically extending his fascination with the differential between plan and reality. Whether he was equating the "flaws" in the pillars with human characteristics, or humanising the pillars, wasn't clear during his commentary. (The pessimistic equation would be that, ideally, the pillars should have been identical and perfect but in reality were marked, as if with human flaws. The optimistic equation would be that the pillars were each different and particular, that these differences were "human characteristics" and that because of them the pillars had acquired individual and original qualities.) But it was the tentative nature of his talking that, with an element of doubt and vulnerability, gave the piece tension.

More problematic was his attempt at discussion at the end, and it seemed odd that after such an ordered and complete piece he should have assumed the possibility of instant discussion. The very success of the piece rendered discussion superfluous. Maybe the "problem" of the audience, and Kevin Atherton's frustration in attempting to relate to it, is put into perspective by the Dan Graham piece, which had so clearly defined and resolved the audience role by incorporating them within the piece.

London Calling

"London Calling" was a good idea. Sub-headed "A Portfolio of the Performing Arts," it was organised by a number of artist-run organisations and mushroomed spasmodically throughout last summer. September was the turn of the Covent Garden area, and the Artists Meeting Place and Tone Place organised the final program. Lasting two weeks, it was the biggest and the busiest of the series. Neither Tone Place nor AMP has a home suitable for large audiences, so they co-opted The Basement (the usual home of the local youth club) and the Acme Gallery. Each was responsible for one week of activity. Given the nature of a festival intended to focus on interaction and discussion as much as on the actual work, it is impractical and inappropriate to review in depth any specific presentation. Rather, here are brief notes on the live work featured, in running order.

Tom Puckey and Dirk Larsen are Reindeer Werk (see this column, Sept/Oct issue). They work in a self-defined area called "behaviorism" and argue "… a tramp is someone to emulate. His swaying stance alone is a sufficient action. It is enough that he is there, 'being,' rather than involving himself directly with an activity in order to resolve a situation …" Their piece consisted of Puckey and

Larsen quietly, and at first almost unnoticeably, concentrating on one simple action akin to a nervous tick, like repeatedly twitching one arm or emulating a disabled walk, and with much concentration building up a rhythm on that behaviour and its developments. By pushing the threshold of control and the boundaries of what is acceptable as "sane," they were able to build an intense piece that was paradoxically formal and disciplined. Perhaps they found energy within their actions that took them beyond both control and rationality, into an automatic mental/physical state that was self-regulating. It is disarming to see them wander in, dressed in their street clothes and with no equipment or preparation whatever, and begin, just like that. Once the audience had overcome the obvious aspects of the "crippled and the mad" elements of their grimaces, references, and movements, they appeared intent on experiencing a piece that seemed to end only at the point of exhaustion. But assuming they travel beyond the rational to another state, the questions of whether they could take the audience with them remained unresolved.

Tina Keane presented a short piece called *Echoic*, seen before at AFD (Artists for Democracy). She appeared anonymously dressed in a boiler-suit, her face concealed by a circular mirror. All we could assume from the flowing hair and a monologue, presumably from a concealed tape recorder, was that it was a woman. The soundtrack was a collage of sounds, whisperings, and dislocated words and was rather unclear. She wandered tentatively (her eyes covered) within the audience, reaching close to those at the front so they could catch a reflection of themselves in the mirror. The concept of cross-identification with the audience through the device of the mirror at head level was not, however, open to development in a crowded basement where most of the audience were, to her, physically out of reach

A Dialogue by Peter Lloyd-Jones and Michael Upton was a balanced piece. (Beginning late, and therefore witnessed by few people, it was fittingly quiet and discreet). Taking the form of a demonstration, Upton, working to a time clock, would arrange a red ribbon or two red sticks in various configurations on the red floor and afterwards retire. Lloyd-Jones would then configurate sheets of paper, upon which he arranged knives, brushes, a mirror, and some clothes pegs, and also retire. Upton would return and work with the light from a cine-projector, and so on. His gestures and comments tended to be "modernist" and ethereal. Lloyd-Jones' were "classical" and territorial. These two diverse approaches resulted, through equal involvement and understanding, in a harmonious joint work. The dialogue was mute and the silence positive. The specific decisions tended towards pretentiousness and obscurantism but the overall approach to the relationship was lyrical, and it was moving to see two men working well and so understandingly together.

Virgil Calaguian presented *The Stone and Paper Orchestra.* Beginning with a story of his youth in the Philippines, he then gave a demonstration of the stone, paper, and scissors hand-game with the assistance of a local lad. After a relaxed attempt at inducing audience involvement in noise-making with the use of various waste materials, he meandered on to a sketch, which involved him walking on with a suitcase, talking of "opening his mind to find shattered illusions," of dreams, and of his experiences on arriving in England. He then gave a varied slide presentation and, via a sketch about the ominous bourgeois force and the burial of remnants in a box then nailed down and rejected, he finished to the sound of cardboard drums and slides of Red China.

Carlyle Reedy discussed "potential," the poet's role of delineating the void, the peak of perfection occurring within mutuality enterprises, the command of the intuitive process, and establishing anarchy as a criteria. She demonstrated sleep and, with a regal presence, her ease in summoning ghosts. With her experience as poet and artist and her natural dialogue, she held her audience spellbound and brought some magic into one of the few successful seminars.

[Text missing from original publication] include theatre, a proportion of the budget could have produced a small but worthwhile program from the number of European artists doing major work in performance. Instead theatre was well organised but at the expense of performance, which was therefore very much in the second-class position.

The Bologna Arte Fiera in May was held in a similar venue and also featured performances. There, the programming was organised by two commercial galleries, one from Milan and the other from a New York-Venice combine, both running daily programs, one at lunchtime, the other at 6 p.m. The standard was much higher but the publicity was slight and, with work presented only on the stands, the facilities were meagre. There were problems: Hermann Nitsch's intentions of shock and catharsis were in the context completely negated, reduced to a black Hollywood musical (adjacent dealers complained that the noise, and the smell of rotting meat, was driving away custom).

Here in England, maybe because we do not have one, it is argued that art markets are specialist trade fairs, that artists will inevitably find them alienating and should best avoid them. But that does not solve the issue of presenting live work as a significant aspect of current concerns, or the fact that in Düsseldorf 20,000 people visited the fair in two days alone.

The Ting at the Serpentine

Performance hasn't featured at the Serpentine Gallery since a few summers ago when community-art-derived, post-surrealist pieces were annexed to the Bank Holiday fun packages along with the inflatables. Credit therefore goes to Michael Craig-Martin, selector of the "Summer Show No. 5," for inviting The Ting: Theatre of Mistakes to participate alongside other artists and on equal terms; well, almost equal. They weren't quite inside the gallery but rather on the East Lawn. (Performance will have come of age, indoors, in December.)

Ting is an old Norse word for meetings where weapons were left outside a ring of stones. The Ting group consists of three founder members plus a few ad hoc extra performers. During September and October they presented *Homage to Pietro Longhi* on weekends, in total nine times. This piece was basically a descendant of both the piece reviewed by Peter Dunn in this column of the Sept/Oct issue, and of the *Scenes at a Table* that they presented within "London Calling." But for some specific adaptations and general developments it therefore concluded a six-month cycle of one work. Lasting two hours and arranged in five acts, *Homage* is performed by five people, each one responsible for a single act. The order is decided according to the throwing of dice at the start of the piece.

The ground plan is a rectangle, enclosing a table and some chairs. A number of possibilities seem to occur within a conceptual structure, which presumably ensures that accidents or "mistakes" read and become assimilated as intentions. It gradually becomes evident that each person, although behaving autonomously and perhaps arbitrarily, is in fact working according to some order and to codes and signals emitted by the instigator. A number of games, patterns, and recurrent mannerisms emerge within each act like trademarks, and these are built up into layers of cross-reference. Slowed-down songs, fragmented sentences, repeats of body actions, tonal sounds, the sudden freeze of actions, a gasp then a fall, become comments on and for someone else's activity. They wear uniform flying suits but have the option of stripping these to reveal individual clothing, and this metaphor is extended through the tension of order/chaos to that of the individual and the group. Two hours is a long time, and the infuriatingly hermetic and self-referential nature of their working vocabulary can be exhausting to both performers and audience. But in their first appearance this summer, at "London Calling," the sheer intensity of their commitment resulted in a disciplined piece that transcended its source of "exercises" and produced a work of symphonic dimensions that elated their audience. Maybe it was a mistake to undertake nine pieces in succession at the Serpentine. This subjected them to the alien strain of theatrical repertory, with negative results. Work that needed spontaneity slowly disintegrated and gaps appeared. These were filled by the acquired ability of "playing for laughs" and the humour, different from the candour inherent in their work, deflated the necessary tensions. They were, however, honest in their self-criticism and this perhaps reflects a confidence in the rightness of their attitude. They are now talking of making themselves available, as a company with many skills, to be commissioned for works by other artists, and should this materialise it could produce some especially interesting results.

Association of Performance Artists

A new organisation, the "Association of Performance Artists," was set up as a result of a conference held at the ICA on 19 September to discuss "the possibility of organizing collectively to develop a common theoretical base and a practical strategy in relation to the present funding crisis."

The funding crisis referred to is mainly the result of an inadequate system implemented by the Arts Council (the main source of funding for performance artists) since it disbanded its Performance Art Committee. The Special Applications Committee was set up to forward applications that did not fit easily into the four main categories recognised by the Arts Council (Art, Drama, Music, Literature) to the most appropriate panel. In practice, mainly because of the lack of informed representatives on the panels themselves (particularly Art) many applications have been shunted around the Arts Council without any criteria for dealing with them. The net result would appear (from the results of surveys sent out before the September conference) to be that many performance artists have had their funds cut, and would-be applicants are sufficiently baffled by the new system to refrain from applying at all. The Arts Council has maintained its usual position of silence about the whole affair. Only through hearsay did performance artists who were clients of the ex-Performance Art Committee learn of its demise. After their March conference artists requested a meeting with the Arts Council to discuss the new system but this was not granted, and artists were asked to give it a chance. A second request for a meeting has now been made by the steering group of APA, in the light of experience of the failure of the system. It is hoped that the Arts Council is not implementing expected government cuts by cutting off those artists who work on the lowest possible overheads in an experimental and therefore often problematic area, as this would be in direct contradiction to the Arts Council's charter. Cuts to large organisations may simply mean tightening belts. Cuts to individuals or small groups can make it impossible to function.

The "Association of Performance Artists" is working to define the needs and defend the interests of all performance artists (whose work at this time covers a diverse range of ideological and aesthetic positions) and to campaign for adequate and informed representation and funding for this area of work. By facing the social and economic realities of artists' existence and taking an active determining part in changing them, it is hoped that a critical perspective in a wider sense can also develop.

The Steering group is Kevin Atherton, Gillian Clark, Di Davies, Rose English, Paul Fahey, Judith Katz, Jacky Lansley, Sally Potter, and Colin Wood. For details of membership apply to: APA, C/0 147 Knapp Road, London E3, tel. 01-515-4279.

Performance Magazines

Two artist-produced magazines have recently been published: *Extremes*, which featured in *Studio*'s Sept/Oct magazine survey, and a special issue of *Musics*. *Extremes No. 1* is, in my view, disappointingly thin but hopefully later issues will improve. Decide for yourself. Issues are planned to come out every two months and will always be on performance. £2 per annum or 25p + 10p postage per single issue from 197 Fountain St, Morley, Leeds, W. Yorks.

Musics, the experimental music magazine, devoted its September issue (Number 9) entirely to performance. It's a good issue, featuring pieces by John Sharkey, The Ting: Theatre of Mistakes, Finnan McCollum, and articles on Hermann Nitsch and Reindeer Werk. It is more substantial than *Extremes No. 1*, but then *Musics* has had more practice. Available from 48 Hillsborough Court, Mortimer Crescent, London NW6 for 30p + 1 0p postage.

The Drill Hall Arts Centre

Action Space, a volunteer group of artists and performers, has converted a former territorial army headquarters into an arts centre. The Drill Hall is aimed at bringing the arts to a wider public by providing space for rehearsals and workshops as well as public performances. Facilities include music, rehearsal, performance, and exhibition spaces; video, film, photography, and graphics studios; costume making and a cinema. A whole foods café, with drinks available, will be open from 12-2 and 5-10. Membership of £1 a year entitles use of equipment and facilities and reduced entry to performances.

Further information from The Drill Hall, 16 Chenies Street, London WC1, tel 01-637-7664.

[II. 6]

Performance

(1977)

**Furlong/McLean: *Academic Board*
Battersea Arts Centre, December 9–11**

**Paul Neagu: *Hyphen-Ramp*
Serpentine Gallery, December 5–10**

Academic Board: A New Procedure was presented in a theatre, followed a linear narrative, and evidently was pre-rehearsed by a partly professional cast. It is relevant to this column in that it was conceived, produced, and directed by two people usually associated with different practices. The enigmatic publicity simply referred to Furlong/McLean, though neither of them appeared in the production. The varied career of Bruce McLean, sculptor, conceptual joker, Nice Style mastermind, and energetic teacher had taken another turn, this time as designer. Likewise, the editorial skill of Bill Furlong of *Audio Arts* had been adapted to that of playwright.

Visually, the piece was stunning. On entering the theatre the first impression was of a large grey truncated triangle with various attachments: rope, planking, and tubular scaffolding, i.e. McLean's stock materials, and what seemed fairly standard setting for a "body sculpture" piece. But as the cast, tastefully dressed in shades of grey, took their place, the piece metamorphosed into a bird's-eye perspective view of a table with people sitting around it. Or, more precisely, a boardroom table with the chairman at the top. Rather than the tabletop being horizontal, it had been swung 90° so that it was vertically facing the audience.

The publicity handout took the form of an agenda with minutes, committee reports, etc., and the committee meetings structure was the form of the production. Beginning with a long discussion illustrated by obscure diagrams about diagrams, the committee elaborately discussed different procedural methods by which to conduct its business. The meetings then discussed the purchase and treatment of a house for the caretaker of the institution. They brought out various stereotypes of people presumably often found on committees: the pretentious and authoritarian chairman; his careerist and sycophantic right-hand man prone to coughs and grunts of approval; the smug architect, the person with a tendency to sleep; and two people, always overruled, speaking up for "the little man" (the caretaker).

The absurdities of local authority regulations regarding improvement grants, terms of tenancy, etc., were interwoven with the horrors of governmental red tape and the separateness of meetings from the issues on which they profess authority. The long discussion was illustrated with various examples of styling options for the proposed house and garden conversion. The script kept up a steady laughter from the audience with many, no doubt, recognising their own experiences of meeting procedures. Certainly the sense of boredom and frustration, building up to near-hysteria over the minutiae of irrelevant detail, produced from the audience the very English reaction of laughing at one's own foolishness.

The end was predictably the point at which all committee members began to speak simultaneously, thus producing a chaotic barrage of noise. Decisions were not taken, and the moral was that these structures are unable to take them. A different production might have produced an emotionally more disquieting statement; it might have looked more analytically at processes of decision taking or, from the angle of local government, offered a dialectical alternative. Although Furlong/McLean focused on issues of public concern, they identified problems but did not offer solutions. Rather did they operate within the domain of British comedy or quintessential farce.

As part of the "6 Times" exhibition at the Serpentine Gallery, Paul Neagu presented *Hyphen-Ramp*. His week in the North gallery was an attempt to interrelate static exhibits with a performance. The constants were a painting on one wall, a display of drawings placed on shelves on three walls, and *Hyphen-Generator*, a big wood and metal sculpture, placed centrally in the room. The variable was a daily performance of *Ramp*. *Hyphen* is a structure that frequently features in Neagu's vocabulary. Basically, it is an open rectangular frame, standing on two short vertical and one long diagonal leg. There are a number of versions ranging from highly finished to roughly made, but the version here was rough in feel and appeared relatively primitive. *Ramp* originated in 1975, when it was first performed in Aberdeen. It is overtly a simple action: Neagu jumping against or up a wall. It has also featured regularly in his work. This was the first occasion, however, in which the statements were used together.

Hyphen is for Neagu the objectification of his philosophic model, with its ground base, its horizontal platform and, in this instance in the shape of a wire spiral, its level of potential. It has been arrived at dialectically. *Ramp* is more intuitive and is the physical enactment of an attempt to achieve the impossible, i.e. literally to challenge gravity. Perry Robinson, his collaborator, was led, blindfolded, and placed with her back to the wall. After each jump she would mark the place at which she approximated he had hit the wall by "seeing" with her senses. The flux of the piece was the marking of time, with Neagu recording each jump by marking the inside of the wooden sculpture. Time was further structured by the rhythm of a metronome that needed rewinding regularly, thus allowing for resting, and by the 2 p.m. to 4 p.m. advertised duration per day. The performance was concentrated rather than dispersed.

When Neagu jumped, the effect was to push him up and it seemed that he was walking up the wall. The jumps obviously demanded both inner and outer strength, and an awareness of his physical and spiritual limits. When he jumped well it looked animal-like, "half feline–half brute," and the jump then seemed a freeing device whereby he transcended the threshold of control and became one both with his partner and with his intention of becoming "a flying being." At times there was wholeness to the piece close to the sublime state of the final sequence of his *Going Tornado* (see this column, May/June 1976). However, the brute strength involved was evidently exhausting, and he frequently faltered. It was on these occasions that the piece became aggressive and the jumps seemed coarse. This was, no doubt, the result of his obligation to the public to perform daily. Conversely the strain involved in approximately 600 jumps in all sometimes produced a kind of pain that can lead to purification. It also produced a measure of empathy and inter-reliance between him and Perry, which was, I suspect, of surprise and value to him.

During my second visit the strain was so great that he was becoming unable to jump, and so he reversed the roles of subject/object with her. He had adapted the piece according to circumstance without weakening its concept, and this inherent trust in another person is a quality rarely seen in male performance. The temporary change and interdependence also heightened the essentially private nature of the piece, rather like two people working harmoniously in adverse conditions. For a work about fighting gravity or leaving the ground it was paradoxically physical and earthbound, and in this sense uncharacteristic of Neagu's work, which is usually more complex, subtle, and metaphorical. It was also more basic and repetitive, and this may be linked to the generally unresolved issue of presenting performance publicly over a pre-programmed period of time. The very short amount of time given him to install the whole work in a changing show may have also contributed to the tenuous relationship between *Hyphen* and *Ramp*. The wish to challenge dogma of form and to cross-breed types of work is becoming more frequent in performance; and problems posed by such a wish, which partly reflects an attempt to synthesise past with present, were inherent in *Hyphen-Ramp*. Compared with Neagu's installation at the Serpentine Gallery in 1973, which remains one of the delights of their Summer Shows, it was therefore inconclusive. But that earlier piece was the completion of a cycle, whereas this one is obviously symptomatic of a transitional stage and is therefore bound to be less conclusive.

[II. 7, 8]

Art Monthly

(1977–79)

*Founded in London in 1976 as a "throwaway polemical forum"
by the American collector Jack Wendler and British editor Peter
Townsend (former editor-in-chief of* Studio International
[II. 1]), Art Monthly *has been published ten times a year
since October 1976 with the same motto: "To provide informed
coverage on contemporary art and the issues that surround
it." Credited as co-editors, in practice Townsend provided the
publishing expertise and most of the editorials, and Wendler
the financial backing. Although* Art Monthly *had an international scope, its focus was predominately on British art.
Initially printed on cheap paper with few illustrations, the art
journal looked more like a political and literary paper than
an art magazine. Associated with highly politicised debates on
contemporary art, it includes interviews, feature articles, an
editorial opinion column, and news briefings. Other sections
include artist profiles, reviews of artists' books, films, performance, reports from particular events, and a unique art-law
column.*

*By February 1977, Chaimowicz, who was then reporting on
performance for* Studio International, *thought there was
some kind of fundamental contradiction with the magazine
[II. 6]. Instead of hybridising the content and opening the
publication to other disciplines, some formalism was being
repeated. As a result, he thought it was time to quit. To explain
his position and the decision to leave* Studio International,
*he wrote a text, supposedly the last of his to be published in the
magazine. But at the same time,* Studio International *was
facing financial problems, and the issue in which that text was
supposed to be published became impossible to produce. The
magazine went bankrupt, and Chaimowicz's "farewell text" to
the journal remained therefore unpublished.*

When Peter Townsend heard about the situation at Studio

International, *he invited Chaimowicz to contribute to* Art Monthly *with texts on the work of some artists possibly associated with "performance." The two texts reproduced below were written in a moment when the artist became recalcitrant about reporting on performance. According to Chaimowicz, if the first contribution to* Art Monthly *can be considered as "a hire-based text," the second one might be appreciated as a "farewell text to criticism."*

A.V.

• • • • • • • • •

[II. 7]

Nine Works for Tape/Slide Sequence

(1977)

A popular medium in the late 1970s, tape / slide projections were used by those who wanted to show synchronised images with sound. Based on this principle, "Nine Works for Tape / Slide Sequence" was a group exhibition of nine visual and performance artists combining image and sound, including Kevin Atherton, Marc Camille Chaimowicz, David Critchley, Rose English, Bruce McLean, Paul Neagu, Sally Potter, Jacky Lansley, and Reindeer Werk. Presented for a few days in early September 1977 at the Battersea Arts Centre, London, the exhibition was subsequently displayed at the Whitechapel Art Gallery, London, from 21 September to 23 October of the same year. "Nine works for Tape / Slide Sequence" appears to be one of the first projects curated by William Furlong under the name of Audio Arts, *the "contemporary art magazine on cassette" that he founded in London in 1973 and published for over forty years [I. 7]. The nine artists involved in this exhibition were asked to "produce an artwork for slide and tape sequence using up to 10 minutes of sound tape and 5 slides," as William Furlong stated in his text for the special edition produced for the event. Such a production protocol also implied that each artist's tape / slide sequence "was not the documentation of a previously realised event but a new work specifically produced for this project," as William Furlong recalled.*

Chaimowicz conceived, he said retrospectively, "A work for tape / slide that preceded Dream, an Anecdote by Marc Camille Chaimowicz Dreamt in the Winter and Remembered in the Spring of 1977, *which is my first publication [III. 5], which Nigel Greenwood published in October 1977 with £500 that he borrowed from his mum to pay for the printer." As for the slides Chaimowicz selected five photographs from a series made in his studio / apartment in Approach Road, London, in 1977. As for the sound tape, Chaimowicz recorded his voice reading* Dream, an Anecdote *in its entirety, lasting ten minutes. The piece presented in the exhibition was also made available in the form of an edition consisting of a folded box including seventy-one slides on one end, and two cassette tapes on the other, subsequently distributed and marketed by* Audio Arts.

Invited by Peter Townsend to write on performance art in Art Monthly *after his departure from* Studio International *[II. 7, 8], Chaimowicz thought it would be interesting to report on this exhibition even though he was participating in it. Published in the "Art notes" section of the magazine, the text reproduced below was considered at that time by the artist as a "hiring-based text for* Art Monthly." *Signed "Mark Chaimowicz," the piece was written at a time when the artist was becoming skeptical of time-based works. Chaimowicz was interested in the tape/slide format because of the combination of the two formats, which "was one way of continuing to work through time with self-effacement," he said. Accordingly, Chaimowicz reviewed the exhibition from this perspective, praising the initiative as one of the first opportunities to show original artworks being presented to an audience as time-based events, not time-based works. The distinction was important at the time, as the tape/slide sequence allowed the work to be closer to a performance than to a recording. Therefore, as Furlong wrote in "Performance Art or is it?" an article about the exhibition "Nine Works for Tape/Slide Sequence" published in October 1978 in the catalogue* Performance Art Festival, Cultureel Animatiecentrum Beursschouwburg Brussels, *"given the lack of response to non-object art by our cultural institutions and the absence of any recording or archive of time-based work and performance, this tape/slide sequence is a light on the horizon."*

A.V.

• • • • • • • • • •

In September, Bill Furlong, editor of *Audio Arts Magazine*, premiered *Nine Works for TAPE/SLIDE SEQUENCE* at the Battersea Arts Centre. It was then shown throughout October as part of the "Audio Arts Presentation" at the Whitechapel Art Gallery.

After three years of the regular publication of "Sound Cassettes," Furlong felt the need to expand the technical form of the magazine. It is an ambitious project, each "Magazine" consisting of seventy slides, two pulsed sound cassettes, and an information sheet, all packaged in an elegant case. Nine artists were each invited to produce a work using up to ten minutes of sound and five slides. From the onset of the project it was clear that Furlong was interested in original pieces, rather than documentation of previous work. The artists are, in order of the sequence, David Critchley, Sally Potter, Paul Neagu, Bruce McLean, Rose English, Reindeer Werk, Jack Langley, Kevin Atherton, and Marc Camille Chaimowicz. Each is noted for having worked with performance or time-based work, i.e. they are presumably familiar with the inherent nature of working with real time rather than illusionary time. Use of the term "premiered" is not arbitrary to the extent that in attempting to review this presentation I am faced with a dilemma, I imagine not dissimilar to that of someone reviewing a film.
First, many of the works benefit from *being seen* to develop, and would be weakened by being pre-described analytically. Second, because the package was designed to be hired by museums, art centres, art schools, etc., there is a good chance that you will have the opportunity of seeing it at a public screening. I am not therefore specifically reviewing each contribution, or "giving the plot away" but rather briefly discussing the concept as a whole. The range of work, both in nature and quality, is wide. Given the alien form, most pieces are curiously typical of the usual work of each artist. David Critchley's *Rotation* is well chosen as the first piece in that it immediately establishes the criteria of sound and slide. The relationship between them is resolved (as is not always the case). Structuralist in nature, the piece is layer upon layer of sound and of image and is well managed.

Sally Potter's *Speaking In Tongues* is dialectic in structure. She is both within and outside of the piece in that she presents a running commentary on slides and a live recording of her attempt at a dialogue with the public at Speakers' Corner. There she talked of art and feminism; in the piece she records her responses to that occasion. It is typical of her general approach in that it is ambitious and intellectually complex, but perhaps because of the nature of her concerns by definition unresolved and problematic.

Bruce McLean's *National Anthem* is delightful and comes as welcomed relief in a fairly dense fifty minutes. His wit and skill is often best manifested in spontaneity, but in this instance he succeeds marvelously. It would spoil it to say more; just go, see, and listen.

Many of the pieces are self-conscious rather than aware of the medium and become almost academic in their structuralist reverence. Generally, it is those that surmount the form and overcome the intrinsic technicalities that are the more successful. Whatever the success or value of each contribution, the sequence as a whole is important within our conservative climate. It is a serious and adventurous venture by one person who obviously believes in finding new forms for new ways of making art and then distributing them to a broad public. Given the lack of response to non-object art by our cultural institutions and the absence of any recording or archive of time-based work and performance this tape slide sequence is a light on the horizon. There will, no doubt, be many derivative pieces from our art schools, but this is to the good. This was the first, and it is enough to make one believe in private enterprise.

[II. 8]

Problems of Presenting Performance

(1979)

Conceived in May 1977 as a farewell text for Studio International, *Chaimowicz's article "Problems of Presenting Performance" was not published due to the magazine's poor editorial and financial situation at the time. Unexpectedly, two years later, the artist recycled parts of this text, adapting them to current events. Published without illustration in the "Books" section of* Art Monthly *in July 1979, this text, emblematically signed "Marc Camille Chaimowicz" and no longer "Marc Chaimowicz" [II. 1, 2, 3, 4, 5, 6] or "Mark Chaimowicz" [II. 7], is considered by the artist to be his "farewell text to criticism." Combining remarks on a selection of performances and events from 1978 and 1979 with a review of Roselee Goldberg's book* Performance, Live Art: 1909 to the Present, *the text reproduced below was written at a time when Chaimowicz was distancing himself from performance and video, and when "there [was] talk of a major international survey show of Performance in London in 1981."*

First published in January 1979, Goldberg's book was intended to give performance art "historical credibility from that date," as Chaimowicz recalled. Shortly thereafter, this volume was made available in the UK in paperback. Chaimowicz took advantage of this UK release to clarify his current position on performance, both as a performer and as a writer on performance, in the form of a book review.

While admitting that Goldberg's book "was presumably intended to fill a gap," Chaimowicz pointed out its lack of expertise on the current issues in performance art, including "problems of presenting performance." Drawing on his experience in this field during the 1970s, in which he sought to envision a less passive role for the viewer attending a performance [I. 2, 14; II. 7, 9; III. 3, 4, 8], Chaimowicz admitted in 1979 that "performance as a container for practice is by defi-

nition a formalism." Relating his declining relationship with performance to Goldberg's acclaimed publication, Chaimowicz felt "this book should not be considered authoritative." In the early 1970s, Chaimowicz considered performance art to be "an alternative practice" boosting transdisciplinarity within the arts. By the end of the decade, he assumed, "there was a contradiction of writing on performance." Without further clarification on his part, his decision to stop writing about performance or to develop new performances was hardly perceived at the time, as most of his performances were touring Europe and other projects were being prepared.

Referring to "a major international survey show of Performance in London in 1981," Chaimowicz concluded his text by saying: "Timing is a particular factor, as many major artists, not unlike show boxers, have already retired or become punch drunk. Others have developed tangential working methods. It is unrealistic to expect 'live works' from, say, Acconci, Beuys, Oppenheim, and Co.," which coincidentally echoes an experience he had a couple of years before in New York City. Chaimowicz had travelled there for the first time between 1 March to 2 April, 1971. While visiting the cutting-edge John Gibson Gallery, then located 27 East 67 Street, he saw Vito Acconci's solo exhibition "On-Going Activities and Situations," which was presented at the gallery from 27 March through 2 April. In this exhibition, Chaimowicz saw a key placed on a plinth, which was accompanied by a short text, an instruction to "be Vito Acconci for a day."

Ignoring the presumed conceptual nature of this proposal, Chaimowicz took the instructions literally, taking the key to a locker in Grand Central Station, within which he found a simple grey suit, which he promptly changed into, thus enabling him to be Vito Acconci for the day! Later that day, reading The

Village Voice, *he noticed that Acconci was staging a performance that very evening, at a space in Greenwich Village. Still
dressed as the artist, Acconci spotted him and they began to
talk, whereupon Acconci invited him to his home. Chaimowicz
remembers being duly impressed by a completely bare room,
"save for an entire wall covered from floorboards to ceiling …
with shelf upon shelf … of books!"*

*In 1979, at a time when Chaimowicz was distancing himself
from performance and criticism, his remarks on Goldberg's new
publication reminded him of his encounter with Acconci when
they performed at the same time unbeknownst to each other.
Still fresh to him, the encounter in 1971 reminded him of
the "problems of presenting performance." Coincidentally, when
Chaimowicz was writing this text, Acconci, who had stopped
performing around the same time, said, "What I loved about
performance was the fact that presenting and doing were one
and the same." As a performance reporter, Chaimowicz did not
express this in the same words. As an artist, however, he solved
the problem in similar terms, shuttling between the public
and private realms. In the studio/flat [III. 5] he occupied in
Approach Road, London, from 1975 to 1979, Chaimowicz
developed a* gesamtkunstwerk *within which, precisely, "presenting and doing were one and the same."*

A.V.

• • • • • • • • • •

Roselee Goldberg dates the beginning of "performance" as 1909, with the publication of the *Futurist Manifesto,* and in her book* proceeds to give it historical credibility as from the date. But regarding issues of presentation "performance" remains problematic and if no longer *l'enfant terrible* it is still an awkward child, particularly within the context of survey shows. Perhaps because, relative to static work, time-based activity makes particular and specific demands on the artists, organisers, and the public, difficulties arise with attempts to mix the two.

In the first "Hayward Annual" of 1977 there were performances by Stuart Brisley and the Ting: Theatre of Mistakes. Regarding showing and catalogue space they were treated as equal to the other artists—no problem here. In Part One Brisley was remarkably able to sustain intensity each afternoon for three weeks, i.e. half the duration of the show. To stretch the piece further would have invalidated it; he was right to stop when he did. In Part Two Ting worked daily for an hour throughout the six weeks, and as the piece progressed the times of performances changed. A daily visit of an hour was clearly beyond most people's resources and would have proved expensive. In neither case were times broadly advertised, so many of the random public missed them. On a less practical level, the question as to whether these very different pieces worked self-sufficiently on one visit or had to be seen many times remains unsolved, as does the issue of some artists tailoring pieces to suit the situation. In last year's "Annual" I was the only artist working with time-based work and I was well treated regarding my working needs by both selectors and organiser, I felt it inappropriate and liable to lead to misunderstandings to present performances, and chose instead to limit time-based work to a videotape incorporated within an installation.

A new development last year was a subsidiary program of performances by women artists. A small space was allocated both for this and for discussions—performances were presented once or twice, usually on weekends, and tended to attract a separate and specialised public. Its success was limited and it may well have become an awkward precedent.

Plans for this year's "Annual" again include a neutral space for a changing program. A complication, however, is that there are at least three time-based artists in the main body of the exhibition. A number of artists have declined the invitation to contribute to the auxiliary program. They argue that to have accepted these terms would have restricted their contribution and that relative to the main body of the show they would have been reduced to "second-class status." Given the lack of outlets, artists are understandably touchy, if not paranoiac, and it seems over-zealous or both gauche and inept for a selector to have invited people on terms that appear peripheral. But as art making changes and develops, so must ways of showing it; some performances (rather than artists) may not have needed a six-weeks base but, rather clear publicity. The problem therefore seems to be the English fixation with status, the fact that working within group shows is often hell and the difficulty of mixing real time with illusionary time.

There is talk of a major international survey show of "performance" in London in 1981. Skill and sensitivity will be needed to make this both a workable structure for artists and an accessible one for the public, for although this activity is historically reputed to stem from a wish to bring the two closer, their needs have often clashed. Timing is a particular factor, as many major artists, not unlike show boxers, have already retired or become punch drunk. Others have developed tangential working methods. It is unrealistic to expect "live works" from, say, Acconci, Beuys, Oppenheim, and Co.

This was highlighted by a performance by Hermann Nitsch in Vienna in March 1978. The occasion was the International Performance Festival staged as the inaugural show of the Kunstverein. It was rumoured that Nitsch was invited, because of the historical importance of his work, to contribute with film and discussion. Rather he took this opportunity to descend from his baroque castle into Vienna like the return of the prodigal son. With help from a dozen adolescent boys, the performance was a very long and noisy charade of gross overkill resulting in the arrival of a confused unit of the riot police. The local bourgeoisie, many stained by real and pretended blood, were suitably mesmerised. There were, perhaps, parallels with the return of Gary Glitter; dear Gary, however, had a sense of irony. Hermann was deadly earnest, which must be a limitation in show business. Viennese kitsch aside, the Festival remains the most successful survey held in Europe in recent years. Approximately twenty-five artists from Europe and America were involved, mostly showing new works. There was the support of discussions, documentation, and videotapes. Two pieces were presented each evening, and the Café Society, although on the decline, was a bonus, ably hosting, chatting and drinking afterwards and making the Festival accessible. (Hanging round London's South Bank hardly seems magnetic.) There were moments of disorganisation, but these were outweighed by the spirit of the situation.

Problems of presentation are multiplied with regard to documentation, which is possibly why there is little written material on "performance" and its history. *Performance, Live Art: 1909 to the Present* is presumably intended to fill a gap. There are seven chapters, the first five dealing with Futurist, Russian, Dada, Surrealist, and Bauhaus Performance. Roselee Goldberg's definition very broadly includes meetings, demonstrations, and manifestos. There is little attempt to analyse the rise and fall of these movements; rather, the accent is straightforwardly on factual account. Original research is manifest in the excellent Bauhaus chapter. The sixth chapter is on American and European performance from the 1930s to the 1960s. The last, bringing us up to the present, is American-orientated with a New York bias. As with encyclopedias, a listing of names and events can devalue the uniqueness of individual contributions, and descriptions and arguments are brief. The book, written with enthusiasm, is pacy

and well illustrated, but should not be taken as authoritative.
It is odd to see attempts at classifying and organising a rough and
diverse tradition that has, perhaps, as its one common base a long
history of attracting those artists who have rebelled against definitions, and ironic that current radicality is moving away from
form-based structures to content-oriented ones.

* *Performance, Live Art: 1909 to the Present* by Roselee Goldberg,
Thames and Hudson, paperback, £2.95.

[II. 9]

The Staircase Project

(1980)

At the turn of the 1980s, after British curator and historian Sandy Nairne was appointed curator of visual arts at the Institute of Contemporary Arts in London, it was decided that the staircase connecting the two floors of the ICA would be used as an exhibition space for emerging artists. Called "The Staircase Project," this incongruous exhibition space, launched in 1980, had a short life span. It took advantage of the ICA's innovative feminist art program at the time, which included "Women's Images of Men" (4–26 October), "About Time: Performance and Installations by 21 Women Artists" (30 October–9 November); "Issue: Social Strategies by Women Artists" (14 November–21 December), yet was quickly abandoned afterwards.

The first artists invited to show their work together in this stairwell were the young British artists Allan Parker, Rick Rayner-Canham, Helen Sear, and Catherine Seely. Born in the mid-1950s, they had just graduated from the Fine Art Department at Reading University and Middlesex Polytechnic, where, coincidentally, Chaimowicz had been their tutor. The ICA press office contacted the media to increase the visibility of the exhibition. Flash Art, the Milan-based art magazine, had confirmed that a full page would be devoted to "The Staircase Project" in the "Britain" section of the magazine, and that the ICA needed to find a local critic for the review. Just after the opening, Chaimowicz was contacted by someone from the ICA's press department. Given his knowledge of the artists, he was invited to write the article. Although Chaimowicz was done with reporting for the press [II. 8], he agreed to do it. As a former tutor, he said, "Contributing to the emergence of my former students was also part of my job, when appropriate, of course, as intergenerational support." In addition, Parker and Sear had collaborated with Chaimowicz on various occasions such as in photographic series mostly made in the artist's studio/apartment in London in 1978 and 1979 and that the artist continually re-used in his later work [III. 6], perfor-

mance [III. 8, 11c], and text [III. 7]. Therefore, Chaimowicz was aware of their interests and future projects.

Published in November 1980 in the 100th issue of Flash Art, *the text reproduced below was originally signed "Marc Chaimowicz." Illustrated accordingly, it included a portrait of Sear, a photo-work by Rick Rayner-Canham, and the cover of the Flying Lizards'* Summertime Blues *record, featuring a milk splash by Rayner-Canhan. Recalling the work he did together in the late 1970s, Chaimowicz acknowledged in retrospect: "This review was written for them and should therefore be considered a thank you text."*

A.V.

· · · · · · · · ·

Allan Parker, Catherine Seely, Helen Sear, and Rick Rayner-Canham are young artists (each left college within the past three years) eking out a living in this most awkward and expensive of cities. They live in cheap short-term housing and are attempting to continue with their art practice. They typify the more inventive strata of ex-students attempting to live from sources loosely related to their art. This phenomenon is recent in London, which lacks a strong economic trade base, and is a more positive approach than that of living off social security or of dreaming about a now dried-up source of part-time work in art schools.

These artists have shown professionally for the first time in a new space within the Institute of Contemporary Art. Sandy Nairne, recently appointed to run the visual arts there, has opened up the space linking the upper and lower galleries. This inconvenient space (consisting of a hall and an L-shaped staircase), with its ready-made public, is nevertheless to be welcomed. His idea is to offer it to artists to use as they wish for half a year. I was invited to do so and elected to offer this space to the above four people. Parker showed working notes and images toward a film project, this being a change from previous work and a conscious wish to avoid the constrictions of a consistency of production. The film stepped aside from the past decade's obsession with ideology and was based on personal experience, using the suspense story as its form. It was speculative at the time of its presentation, and suited the dynamic of the staircase as a space for work in progress. The notes extended his interest in interiors, atmosphere, and the states of fear and suspicion; the linear narrative was typically detailed, precise, and evocative. His decision to experiment with a new medium seems to both invigorate and substantiate his sensibility and typifies a growing dissatisfaction with over-specialisation.

Seely showed nineteen framed statements, which she considered as one work. Text, photographs, and collage were loosely structured as four interrelating subject-areas—the phenomenon of the staircase, a short story, autobiographical comment, and self-image in relation to advertising. The first piece, comprising a brief speculative text on the staircase as an "exposed and intimate space," was left undeveloped. The short story, an evocative text on the feelings of a woman towards a young boy, written with economy and sensuousness, most successfully incorporated her interest in the male / female axis and that of role reversal. The variety of the remaining pieces was conductive to to-ing and fro-ing and would have been ideally suited to book-form. The show, perhaps over-ambitious in its range, lacked the sublime quality of Seely's earlier drawings and the strength of her work on videotape. This was possibly symptomatic of pressures specific to a first show.

Helen Sear tackled the space directly, treating it almost as a sculptural problem by changing and "cutting" both walls and stairs. The first part of the staircase was cut diagonally with a triangle of carpet. As one turned the corner up to the longer staircase, the steps were again half-covered diagonally, in this instance with wallpaper. The main facing wall was partially papered with a wedge shape of the same pattern. The choice of paper was critical and her solution masterly. She chose a bold green floral pattern which, with skillful use of green lighting, established a highly particular presence, taking the work beyond formalism and giving the space a sense both of wit and of ambiguity. An anonymous through-space was transformed so as to seemingly heighten an arch and other architectural detailing, creating a simultaneous sensation of transposing one elsewhere, perhaps back to the sunlit park of St. James' immediately outside the building. Her decision to work in a contextual way and her gamble in dealing totally with the treacherous nature of this space resulted in a most effective show.

Rayner-Canham studied photography before going to art school. His approach to this now common currency is therefore at one remove, yet he is unusually conversant with both its technical range and its history. He has developed and built a motorised camera that produces what he terms "parallax prints." The image is recorded along a vertical plane over time ranging from seconds to a minute. The distorted result, in his own words, can be considered as "a graph with the vertical as space and the horizontal as time, recording movement through the plane, the structure and speed of this movement determining the image produced." Whatever the intentions, however, the results were constricted. His photography of movement gave rise to a uniform distortion of figures and lots of vertical lines. Inventiveness of method was not always equalled by content.

The final works were five small photographs, each of the same woman within a coastal townscape. They were frankly romantic, making good use of high shadow and exuding moods raging from timelessness to discreet drama and expectancy. He seemed to know both town and woman well. They were anti-classical in that, whereas photographers are taught to compose angles within the image to suit the frame, he instead shaped the frames according to the angles within each image. The results have wit, elegance, and economy, and subtly continue to query mainstream criteria.

[II. 10]

Architecture Is Not Art

(1989)

The London-based magazine World Architecture *was launched in the spring of 1989, printed and published by Grosvenor Press International Ltd in Hong Kong, and produced by Design Analysis International. As "The Official Magazine of the International Academy of Architecture (IAA)," the editorial board of this prestigious publication included Pierre Vago, Carl Aubock, Vyacheslav Glazychev, Dennis Sharp, and Georgi Stoilov. Star architect Norman Foster served as consulting editor, and Jonathan Glancey and Peter Dormer as co-editors.*

A 100-page colour publication, World Architecture *was billed at the time as a "cutting-edge architectural journal published six times a year." In June 1989, Dormer, who had already written about Chaimowicz's work in various journals, invited the artist to contribute to the magazine in the form of a text on an architectural subject of his choice. A few weeks later, Chaimowicz sent his contribution to Dormer who replied, "The text is too long." Instead of shortening his writing, Chaimowicz kept the first part of his text as a manifesto of sorts, published for the first time a few months earlier [III. 15]. As a result, the two parts of this text differ from each other, both in form and content. While the first deals with Le Corbusier's Catholic Chapel at Ronchamp, France, the second is a reflexive statement on the relationship between the fine and the applied arts. Entitled "Architecture Is Not Art," and published in the third issue of* World Architecture, *Chaimowicz's text was featured on the cover alongside "Richard Meier," "Frankfurt Mixes Art With Mammon," and "Architecture Rises in the East." Published in the second half of the magazine, it was introduced as follows: "In this essay, the artist and designer Marc Camille Chaimowicz explores the distinctions between sculpture and architecture and art and design, and challenges the idea that architecture is art; architecture is constrained by responsibili-*

ties, art is not." The first part of the text includes three different outdoor views of Le Corbusier's Chapel at Ronchamp that were chosen by the artist, while the second part includes seven furniture pictograms, including Desk on Decline *(1982–83),* Chest *(1983),* Table de Conversation *(1986),* Zed Stool *(1984–87),* Screens *(1986–88),* Telephone Couch *(1983), and* Loxos Crystal Vase *(1989), elegantly reproduced in bright red throughout the text.*

Recalling the way his text "Architecture Is Not Art" was composed, Chaimowicz declared, "My initial ambition was to write a text in three-parts on three architects: Mies van der Rohe, Robert Mallet-Stevens, Le Corbusier. However, due to a short deadline, my initial plan had to be reformulated." Before submitting his contribution to the magazine, the artist decided to focus on Le Corbusier, arguing that calling the Chapel at Ronchamp a "sculpture" is to misread the building. In so doing, Chaimowicz had Robert Mallet-Stevens in mind. According to him:

> *"Mallet-Stevens was marginalised by Le Corbusier who saw him as a decadent bourgeois: a situation that would have surely been different if Mallet-Stevens had lived in another country than France. As a result, Mallet-Stevens was underrated, whereas he was certainly more open than the others to fashion, craft, cinema, stained-glass; he has even built a casino!"*

Therefore, without mentioning Mallet-Stevens in his text, Chaimowicz "took a position," he said, "by reaffirming some basic principles of modernism … currently under such attack," while exploring the distinctions between sculpture and architecture from his own point of view. Chaimowicz's interest in Mallet-Stevens dates back to the mid-1970s, when he lived from 1975 through 1979 in a studio / apartment in Approach Road, London [III. 5], a space of radical subjectivity where he deliberately did not draw a distinction between his working process, the finished object, and daily life, that he "reconfigured like a film set on the art of living with objects, and idealised through its photographic organisation." Ultimately, Chaimowicz's infatuation with Mallet-Stevens also emanated from the "Four Rooms" group project at Liberty's, London (10 February—10 March, 1984), an exhibition on interior architecture and design, which put the artist in relation with "the phenomenology of furniture and of the traditional antipathy between architect and designer—between the manipulator of space as container and the producer of objects that inhabit this space," as he put it in his "Letter to Michael Regan" from 1984 [III. 10].

As mentioned above, the second part of Marc Camille Chaimowicz's "essay" in World Architecture *is a recycling. Adapted from a letter written in 1987 by the artist to the French art historian Hubert Besacier, this text was first revised in the spring of 1989, and was published inside a double-folded card produced in conjunction with the artist's solo exhibition "The Fine and the Applied Arts," The Showroom, London (22 March—16 April, 1989). In the process of revision, the original letter lost its primary characteristics and took the form of an artist's statement on the relationship between the fine and the applied arts. That version of the text is republished as a facsimile in this anthology [III. 15]. Recycled again a few months later by the artist as part of his contribution to* World Architecture, *the text this time did not use the layout originally conceived by the artist nor the seven thematic subdivisions that structure his written piece, certainly because these design peculiarities were hardly compatible with the immediate graphic clarity desired by the journal.*

A.V.

Part 1: On not dismissing Ronchamp as "sculpture"

A common response, still, to Le Corbusier's Chapel at Ronchamp
is to refer to it as *sculptural*. Thirty-five years on it is as though
the shock and the loss of adequately descriptive words that this
remarkable building still promotes is such that the only possible
defense is to relegate it to that easy area for all that, which is controversial or ungraspable—the visual arts.

This reflex—if we cannot immediately describe a thing, it must
be art—is misleading. Moreover it is a false criticism. Even more
important, the confusion between "art" and "architecture" and
"architectural decoration" can lead even master architects astray.
Consider: the one detail at Ronchamp to have poorly suffered
time's test is the decorative enamel work on the main entrance
doors. Here Corbusier was trying to assert himself as an "artist"
and it is here that the master falls into pastiche. The wish to
present himself as an artist resulted in work which now looks arbitrary, minor, and dated.

Calling Ronchamp "a sculpture" is a misunderstanding because the
chapel surely asks to be confronted, not as an icon but as a working
building—one in which the issue of function is central. A church
is complex and cross-layered in its function and meaning. With
Ronchamp even the use of the radical "free style" cast and sprayed
concrete raises questions about which authority Corbusier felt
himself responsible—God perhaps or was it to himself as architect? The "free style" use of the concrete meant it was subservient
to Corbusier's will but leaves us undecided as to whose glory the
result is intended to celebrate. And today are the pilgrims primarily religious or cultural?

To relegate Ronchamp to the merely formally inventive (that of
abstract sculpture) is to deny the issues of service and function. In
a secular age it is too easy to dismiss what and who a *church* serves.
Does Ronchamp serve God, and serve the congregation and the
spiritual pilgrim?

The chapel and its attendant outbuildings were commissioned not as a parish church but as a site of pilgrimage and study, therefore to function beyond the vernacular and to be used by the faithful, by those devout enough to have tackled inner skepticism.

There is no dead space within the building, the whole space is alive but to even differentiate between inner and outer space is perhaps academic because with its masterly siting and its external pulpit used for the many outdoor celebrations of mass the plasticity of the building is confirmed.

Unlike architecture, art is speculative, and the artist deliberately, necessarily courts failure. The architect, being responsible to other people, has no right to court failure. He or she must seek resolution. The chapel at Ronchamp is utterly resolved and, like all successful buildings, Ronchamp's success is largely the consequence of intelligent negotiations and real, worldly problem-solving of a kind that do not often impinge upon the artist. These "negotiations" include vital if banal matters such as drainage as well as the geology of the site, the structural possibilities of the materials, and the constraints of safety and cost, and the limitations of the engineers and builders. So much is, in the literal sense, out of the architect's hands and yet the architect is responsible.

Unlike a sculpture, a building, to succeed, must be well made—if not, it lets people down. Whereas with art there is much that is successful, which is yet "poorly made."

Artists have no desire for an actual client, they are in this sense not of the world, but detached. The designer works in the constant desire for a client or according to an external brief. The architect exists only fully by courtesy of the client. Architects being worldly should therefore have conceptual modesty. Whatever the size of their ego, practice, or status they after all produce results that will be used, modified, tampered with, re-painted, and sometimes demolished … and for which they are well rewarded. In contrast, artists need conceptual arrogance (it is after all often all they have). What art can have is a sense of the "enigmatic"—the artist has a

license to find the ungraspable, the irresponsible, the non-account-
able, and the non-unitarian. The enigmatic has no place in the
department store or in the design of a telephone. In architecture
and design we expect—indeed rely upon—the familiar. This need
for the recognisable applies as much to a railway station, a café,
or a chapel, or one's home. Of course, this criterion of familiarity
need not preclude the new—indeed the worth of any radical re-
ordering or re-definition is that, in any given culture, it introduces
innovation in such a way that the unknown, the not-before-seen
can somehow seem typical or familiar … in good new design one
is startled by recognition.

Part 2: On the dialectic between the fine arts and design

I have adapted the following from a letter I wrote to Hubert
Besacier, which I revised in 1989. I have kept the spirit of the letter
because it is in conversation that one often resolves contradictions.

*"The craftsman is responsible to his material, the architect to his client …
the artist is responsible to God."* Adolf Loos

I am intrigued by your argument that there is no essential difference between my fine art and design activities… Because whereby
this applies to the level of commitment to each activity, in that
I make no hierarchical distinction between working, say, on a
painting, a book, a silk scarf, or a piece of furniture, I nevertheless
instinctively feel that there are differences, which are more than
qualitative and perhaps to do with motivation … or is this merely
a cultural response?
Whenever engaged in various design projects—whatever the
possible aesthetic closeness—my relationship to this work feels
somehow different. It is as though it comes from a different part
of me … that I am calling upon other faculties and that although

I may be just as engaged I nonetheless feel more objective and detached.

This variance is probably in part due to the slow time base of such projects, with their frequent delays … and the greater objectivity resultant of those technical intermediaries as producers and manufacturers … which in turn can lead to design changes … and therefore to a shift in the relations of responsibilities…

But I think the fundamental difference to be roughly this:

That as artists we work and produce primarily for ourselves … that I do so for myself and, the Other … who, real or imagined, is the object of my desire, the one I want to seduce, to offer myself to … be seduced by. That when making art I am therefore, metaphorically, both privileged and handicapped by a desirous condition … a sort of state of grace, within which I am beyond any sense of obligation, responsibility or of conscience … other than from those terms that are specific to that intimate complicity—and thus exclusive.

Design work therefore differs in that it is not so much for myself and the other, not so much *"Pour toi, de moi"*… as *"de nous, pour vous,"* that given it includes the skills of others'.

A shift of emphasis is thus established from the singular to the plural and logically so, in that one is dealing with multiplicity, with the "editioning" of objects, with the "production" of wallpaper or fabric…

If my mainstream work is rooted in matters of identity … in the quest of the self (and its ideal) and therefore in a problematic, then within the poetics of design it is as though there is also a shift *away* from the self towards the selfless … (that which is free of any problematic) the nameless, the anonym, and perhaps the platonic… And on this path leading away from the unique there also lies a shift … from the intimate and towards the anonymous.

One activity will naturally inform the other but they remain in tangent and opposite… It is this contact, which stimulates me … and within which, rather than extend my fine art aesthetic, I can *complement* it with design. I enjoy the dialectic.

A fire extinguisher, a coffee pot, an armchair, or a jug are each imbued with instant meaning… They tell us what they are, and what they do … in a way that the mute, enigmatic painting does not. Design gives us answers, Fine Art poses questions. We *take* meaning from Design … and *give* meaning to Fine Art.

[II. 11]

A Letter From Paris…

(2013)

Chaimowicz met Dan Fox in the mid-1990s while Fox was a student at the Ruskin School of Art and Drawing in Oxford. From that point on, they began a playful dialogue about art, music, and curating that continues to this day. This dialogue has occasionally led to publications, public lectures, and interviews [I. 11]. So, when Chaimowicz received a letter in early 2013 from Fox inviting him to contribute to a survey on "curating" that he was editing for frieze, the London art magazine where he worked as editor and staff writer, Chaimowicz immediately agreed to be included. After clarifying the context of the survey with Chaimowicz, Fox emailed him on 4 February, 2013, with "A letter from Paris…" in the subject line. This email letter was thereafter added to by Ed Atkins, Nick Mauss, Tom Nicholson, Paulina Olowska, Slavs and Tatars, and W.A.G.E. (Working Artists and the General Economy) and published in April 2013 in the 154th issue of frieze.

Also invited to participate in this survey was the French artist Daniel Buren, as an opportunity to reassess his seminal statement from 1972 "Exhibiting Exhibitions." Published the same year that Chaimowicz conceived his floor-based "post-Pop scatter environments" Celebration? Realife [I. 7; III. 2, 3, 4] and Enough Tiranny [I. 14], the use of that text in frieze "forty-one years later!" as a preface to a survey about "curating" involving a small selection of (young) artists, seemed to Chaimowicz "somewhat outdated." In that text, indeed, Buren complains that individual artworks were being reduced to the status of mere dots of colour in a curatorial Gesamtkunstwerk. First published in the ring-bound catalogue of Harald Szeemann's 1972 "documenta 5," part of the statement reads: "The subject of exhibitions tends more and more to be not so much the exhibition of works of art, as the exhibition of the exhibition as a work of art."

Featured on the cover of frieze *under the title "Artists on Curating," Fox's survey on "curating" was introduced as follows:*

> *"Second only, perhaps, to the white-hot temperatures of the art market, the rise of the curator has been one of the most discussed developments in art over the past 15 years. The growth of the profession has wrought profound changes on how we think about exhibitions and what institutions can be. It has helped networks of artists to grow, and has shone a light on the overlooked and under appreciated. It has also assumed ministerial power in art-industry war games, and has—in Europe and the US, at least—taken over from television production as the sensible option for nice middle-class youngsters wanting a career in the arts. No other word or phrase from the professional lexicon of contemporary art has leaked so quickly into widespread popular usage as 'curating.' When it's not celebrities 'curating' your lunchtime sushi box or clothes shops 'curating' your summer sock collection, curating is the motor of power and discourse in exhibition making. For the most part, the conversation about curating has largely been dominated by curators. (The many who freelance as critics have also altered the nature of such basic staples of art writing as exhibition reviews. But that's another story.) ..."*

In order to both pre-calibrate the contributions of the seven invited artists and artist groups, and to facilitate the overall editorial process, Fox asked the participants the following four questions:

> *"How do they feel about their role in the discourses of curating?*

What do they think about their work being placed in themed exhibitions or biennials, or in the context of new exhibition formats and experiments in display?

Are they happy to engage in dialogue with curators when shaping exhibitions, or do they feel instrumentalised, their work put at the service of someone else's interests?

How do artists who curate—and there are many—feel about their position in relation to professional curators?"

Although Chaimowicz thought these questions were essential, he did not recycle them into his letter to Fox, which was subsequently published in the magazine without any changes. Letter writing, Chaimowicz confessed in retrospect, generally offers "access between the objective and the subjective, and a conscious way not to be academically active," especially in the context of a publication like frieze.

Furthermore, each artist's contribution was divided in three parts, namely the written contribution, a current biography and one exhibition view of an exhibition they curated. In the case of Chaimowicz, the illustration was a detail of Jean Cocteau, 2003–2012, which was presented at the time he wrote "A letter from Paris…" in the exhibition "A Bigger Splash: Painting After Performance" (14 November, 2012– 1 April, 2013), a group exhibition considering the impact of experiments in performance, theatricality, and masquerade on expanded approaches to painting from 1950 to the present day, curated by Catherine Wood, Curator of Contemporary Art and Performance, Tate Modern, London.
In the end, a collage by Chaimowicz was published on the cover of frieze. Featuring "male objects chosen with care,"

this originally A4 collage made from various printed adver-tisements from different eras, is airily organised around an outdated storefront in Dijon called "Articles pour Cadeaux" (Gift items)——"You know, the kind of store that looks closed, as from another time, yet stays open until the owner dies"—— which serves as a backdrop for several images of items, including two bottles of perfume, three partially wound geo-metric ties, a rectangular Rolex watch with black a leather strap, and a Mont Blanc fountain pen. Working at the time around a multifaceted portrait of Emma Bovary and the pro-vincial manners, Chaimowicz felt that "these objects are linked to the idea that they could have been gifts from Emma B. to Rodolphe B." This "curated collage," which echoed the issue's main feature, namely "Artists on curating," actually belongs to a series of 250 works that Marc Camille Chaimowicz conceived to "illustrate" the exceptional 536-page volume Madame Bovary by Gustave Flaubert—Illustrated by Marc Camille Chaimowicz *that Four Corners, London, published in March 2013 [III. 28].*

A.V.

• • • • • • • • •

Dear Dan,

A time was such when curators preferred the inanimate… They were more at ease with objects, things, artworks … than they were with people. Artists were just as suspicious … and, more at ease with a drink, were often aggressive. At once both patronising yet over reverent … the curator's positioning towards artists has long been one of ambivalence … in their turn artists felt misunderstood—were often arrogant or paranoid … or both. Small wonder then, that there was a common mistrust…

Performance went some way to redressing this … of necessity—we were after all working in real time—and there was nowhere to hide … it may indeed have precipitated a climate change … because some form of dialogue between artists and curators, generally with some urgency, had now become a necessity. Of course, artists still drink too much, but now as often than not in the company of the curators … and so begun the realisation that we might yet, after all, be sharing a common agenda… So it is no mere coincidence that this keyword, "performance," should now feature in both the titles of two current Tate exhibitions in which my work is included: "A Bigger Splash: Painting after Performance" at Tate Modern, London, and "Glam! The Performance of Style" at Tate Liverpool.

Is it not curious that the showing of my more anarchic installation *Celebration? Realife Revisited* (1972–2000), in Liverpool, should have arisen from the more traditional route of a simple loan request…?

My contributions to the Tate Modern show—*Jean Cocteau…* (2003–12), *J&J* and *After Image* (both 2012)—were, however, the result of a protracted yet focused dialogue with the curators which, in turn, shaped my contribution and procured work thematically specific to the exhibition. So, whilst the axis of the curator curating work from the artist remained this was nonetheless symptomatic of a new sensibility, which now took one from awkward imbalance to greater parity…

You may recall a brief exchange we had recently in London. Well, I am now writing from Paris where I am preparing for the exhibition we spoke about, to be held at the Musée d'Art Moderne de Paris/ARC this autumn. I have been invited to be artistic director for "DECORUM" and I shall be working principally with the curator Anne Dressen and architect Christine Ilex on the staging of more than 100 carpets, rugs, and tapestries by modern and contemporary artists…

Ranging from the "Primitive" to the "Conceptual," these are to be displayed in a variety of ways … I elaborate as the resultant show will emerge from a uniquely close collaboration between curator, artist, and architect … I shall be dealing with issues—once deemed outside of an artist's remit—as diverse as the means of display, patternation and the use of wallpapers, the designing of motifs for Axminster, décor as back-drop, the mapping of a floor plan, and so on. And, given that much of the work to be shown oscillates between fine and applied arts, between high and low culture, a degree of slippage will surely mirror emerging shifts of museological emphasis?

… Initially somewhat tentatively, we are now, with greater aplomb, developing a shared language by which to elaborate on a possible scenography, and it seems that as we move from the mechanistic to the complicit, so we may be heading towards … possible Baudelairean harmonies … I hope this goes some way to meeting your request, and meanwhile look forward to seeing you soon,

Amicably yours,

Marc Camille

[II. 12]

Jean Cocteau... A Letter to Wolfgang Tillmans, 9 December, 2013

(Pending a possible future publication)

In 2012, Chaimowicz's life-sized installation Jean Cocteau…, *[I. 8] was featured in the group exhibition "A Bigger Splash: Painting After Performance," Tate Modern, London (14 November, 2012–1 April, 2013). Curated by Catherine Wood, Curator of Contemporary Art and Performance at Tate Modern, London, the exhibition, titled after David Hockney's stunning 1967 painting of the Los Angeles heat brushing against the cool blue water of a swimming pool, aimed to explore the impact of experiments in performance, theatricality, and masquerade on expanded approaches to painting from the 1950s to the present day. This was the seventh time in nine years that* Jean Cocteau… *had been on view. Originally conceived in 2003 in Norwich as "a furnished interior that obliquely references [Cocteau's] poetics," this major theatrical yet fantasy study-cum-bedroom, which fictionalised a three-dimensional portrait of Jean Cocteau without any of his work being included, is composed of artworks and objects by Chaimowicz meticulously combined with a perfect selection of works by other artists, most of which were produced long after Cocteau's death in 1963.*

From its second iteration in 2004 at Angel Row, Nottingham, the installation began to morph slightly, either because a piece was no longer available for loan and had to be replaced, or because Chaimowicz opportunistically added a new contribution, such as the portrait of young Cocteau by Marie Laurencin as a surrogate in 2008. In addition, there was the Andy Warhol work that was borrowed from a local collection every time the installation was displayed and was therefore each time different. When the installation was exhibited at Tate Modern, Chaimowicz felt that Tom of Finland's untitled and undated drawing of two black motorcycle cops buggering a white guy, which had been part of the installation since 2003, had become "kind of redundant with time." Moreover, the private collector who had "so generously lent it to us every time since 2003 was keen on having it back permanently." As a result, Chaimowicz set out to find "a work that celebrates sexuality."

The previous year, the artist had been in contact with German artist Wolfgang Tillmans about the exhibition "Marc Camille Chaimowicz—Jean Genet… The Courtesy of Objects," a major exhibition project in three acts Chaimowicz developed in different versions at The Gallery, University College of the Arts, Norwich (19 April–21 May, 2011) [Ill. 27]; Nottingham Contemporary (16 July–2 October, 2011); Focal Point Gallery, South end on Sea (13 February–24 March, 2012), involving guest-artists responding to Genet's writings. On the occasion of the second act, Chaimowicz contacted Tillmans to introduce him to the project. While telling him about his desire to include "photos of young men for Jean Genet" in the exhibition, Tillmans "immediately" made the connection with three of his photos, and suggested he come to the studio to see them. As Chaimowicz recalled:

> *"It was, as usual in East London, a very calm Saturday morning. It was just the two of us at his studio. We sat around a table, and Wolfgang showed me the prints. It was fascinating for me to see how his work is organised. Probably due to his past in the world of fashion and music, each print was codified and numbered. The 'client' has just to choose the supports. Either a slide or a projection, or a print. In the case of a print, the dimensions are S, M, L. Once this is decided, the assistants can take over the situation, and Wolfgang can move on, go out and dance! With Wolfgang, the creative moment is one of choice, and order."*

The three photographs that were selected that day were subsequently included in the Nottingham exhibition.

A year later, having learned that Chaimowicz was looking for "a work that celebrates sexuality" in relation to Jean Cocteau…, *Tillmans, who was familiar with the curatorial approach developed by the artist in this installation, suggested that he include* like praying (faded fax) *(2005). "That was quick. I was put in touch with the studio, and since each photograph is digitised, like in fashion, I only had to decide on the size of the print. Of the three sizes offered, I chose the smallest." After the print, the photo was loaned to Chaimowicz by Maureen Paley, Tillmans' gallerist in London, and subsequently hung in* Jean Cocteau, 2003–2012 *at Tate Modern, London.*

Following this new component, it was time for Chaimowicz to determine the "final composition" of his installation. To do so, he consulted with Martin McGeown and Andrew Wheatley at Cabinet, London, in late November 2012. Coincidentally, Fiorucci Art Trust, London, which was about to open an exhibition space in Sloane Avenue, London, was interested in acquiring this work for its collection. It was therefore necessary for them to draw up a definitive information sheet on the work and to set a price for it. As a result, the availability of several artworks needed to be confirmed, including Tillmans' like praying (faded fax).

Technically, this photograph is a small horizontal photomechanical reproduction, or laser print, of a faded fax, itself a print of a photograph, depicting a naked young man in profile crouching in a prayer-like position. Emphasising the faded aspect of the fax, the photo functions as a "filter," highlighting a process that might both increase contrast and damage the quality of the image. At the same time degraded and as delicate as a pen and wash drawing, this photograph evokes, moreover, the vanished memory of a situation seen or encountered. Both touched by the "implicit impact" of the photograph on "the reading of the work" and hurried by the imminent acquisition process of his installation, Chaimowicz wrote an email to Tillmans on 9 December, 2013 with "Jean Cocteau…" in the subject line. In this letter, he questions the availability of this photograph while "much hoping that it might, conceivably, now be included as a permanent element in Jean Cocteau…" *Shortly thereafter, Chaimowicz received a call from Tillmans who "generously" offered to make* like praying (faded fax) *permanent to the installation. Pleased that the work was available, and particularly honoured by Tillmans' response, Chaimowicz said in retrospect, "In many ways, this image was a gift to the installation; and furthermore, it is unique."*

This previously unpublished email letter from Chaimowicz to Tillmans from 2013 is included in Trois Inventaires— *the visual and textual inventory of all the Jean Cocteau, Jean Genet, and Emma Bovary materials that the artist has developed over the past twenty years. In that anthology, this "letter to Wolfgang Tillmans" is paired with other text materials, including among others a transcript of Roger Cook on Jean Genet and a commissioned text by the Nouveau Musée National de Monaco Chief-Curator Célia Bernasconi about "Cocteau in Monaco." Co-edited by Marc Camille Chaimowicz and Anna Clifford, in collaboration with Swiss-American London-based graphic designer Zak Kyes,* Trois Inventaires *is pending a possible future publication.*

A.V.

· · · · · · · · · ·

Dear Wolfgang,

When *Jean Cocteau…* was last shown at Tate Modern (in "A Bigger Splash") it was augmented by *like praying (faded fax)*, 2005, which has been graciously lent by Maureen Paley, and it is upon her suggestion that now I write.

Perhaps built on the metaphoric premise of Cocteau's renowned sociability, one aspect of this work is that it incorporates a guest list of works by other artists … which would seem to fall into either one or two groupings—those works included in one showing only and those which have become permanent—and thus now in a company including Marcel Breuer, Tariq Alvi, Andy Warhol, Giacometti, and Marie Laurencin (in surrogate form)…
Given the work has been shown—in varied forms—eight times in public institutions, and that it has recently been acquired by a private collector, Cabinet and I are currently in the process of determining its definitive composition.
We are so touched by the tone given to it by the recent inclusion of your piece, by its implicit impact on the reading of the work, that we are much hoping that it might, conceivably, now be included as a permanent element in *Jean Cocteau…*
We are aware of the highly limited edition number of this work—and of the probability that it may therefore no longer be available—but we are nonetheless hoping that there may be a version—perhaps *hors serie* or some such equivalent—which could conceivably be made available?
If so, it would give *Jean Cocteau…* greater clarity and depth and I cannot think of a finer way by which to complete this key work…

My fondest wishes,

Marc Camille

[III]
TEXTS

Featuring introductions by Alexis Vaillant

[III. 1]

Assumptions—Specific Work-Pieces

(1971)

In late 1970, Sigi Krauss met with young post-graduate artist, Marc Chaimowicz, in London. At the time, Krauss, as Chaimowicz put it in a telephone conversation with the German writer Tom Holert on 14 August, 2006, was "an enthusiastic, if slightly disorganised intuitive, a 'chance taker.'" At the time Krauss was running a commercial space combining a frame store and an art gallery at 29 Neal Street, Covent Garden, London. Intrigued by the artist, the gallerist invited him to stage his very first solo exhibition, "Sweetness" (11 March–2 April, 1971), for which a large part of the gallery floor was covered with silver-painted shoes, while several objects were displayed behind a net. Enthralled by this exhibition, Krauss subsequently arranged the artist's first solo show outside London, which took place at Vaughan College, University of Leicester, in November of the same year.

A few days before the opening of "Assumptions—Specific Work-Pieces" in Leicester, the artist made a 14-page "self-published publication," which can be seen as a foreshadowing of Chaimowicz's long-term interest in "publishing as a significant exhibition space." Described retrospectively by the artist as "the most coherent trace of the Leicester project, where three-dimensional works were displayed on the floor in a large, whimsical 1960s building corridor," this black and white, stapled A4 Xerox combined images and texts, and was edited entirely by the artist. The iconography that Chaimowicz selected for the publication is emblematic of his interests at the time. It includes photo-documentation of his "purpose-built" works as well as his "landscape shoe-pieces," both developed at the turn of the 1970s. Also included are two photographs of Covent Garden Market taken by British photographer Bob Young, at the time a close friend of the artist, as well as a newspaper image of bootless skinheads "disarmed" by police in Farrington Street, when Rockers and Mods would travel by train to the *coast over the weekend; a recent press clipping by acclaimed British art critic Guy Brett about "Sweetness," the artist's exhibition at the Sigi Krauss Gallery; as well as two texts from 1971, which the artist arranged by mixing quotations with cut-outs, classified ads from the period, newspaper jokes, and awkward sentences from his notebooks.*

While dealing with "the Culturally Urgent" [III. 18], a subject Chaimowicz has considered part of artistic life since he was a student at the Slade School of Art, the 14-page set reproduced below can be seen both as a springboard for (re)invention—a canny reminder that what might seem lost or ephemeral can prove as provocative as anything that manages to survive— and as a mindscape that somehow anticipates the political DNA of the artist's "scatter environments" from 1972: Enough Tiranny *[I. 1, 14] and* Celebration? Realife *[I. 7; III. 2, 3, 4].*

A few months later, this self-published Xerox was reproduced in facsimile in #1 Schmuck—*subtitled "Schmuck Presents Real Schmuck"—a 64-page unnumbered A4 fanzine mimeographed in various colours, whose name means "penis" in Yiddish and "idiot" in American slang, that was published by the independent publishing house Beau Geste Press from 1972 to 1976. Based on a farmhouse in Cullompton, Devon, Beau Geste Press—whose name Beau(tiful) Geste comes from Gestetner, the brand name of the stencil / multiplying machine the publisher used—was founded in 1971. Initiated by Martha Hellion and Felipe Ehrenberg, two Mexican artists who came to England in the wake of the 1968 student movement in Mexico, Beau Geste Press and its zine* Schmuck *later developed in collaboration with British artist and art historian David Mayor, graphic designer Chris Welch, and his partner Madeleine Gallard. Together they quickly formed a decisive network of production, reflection, participation, and dissemination in the international interrelationship of avant-garde artists of the early 1970s.While preparing the first issue of* Schmuck, *they felt that Chaimowicz's Xerox, of which they got a copy from Krauss, was eligible for* Schmuck, *which they envisioned as "a vehicle for the artists to present their ideas and their art (when the two don't overlap!)."*

Published twice in four months, first as a photocopy in November 1971 in Leicester, then as a photocopy duplicate in March 1972 in #1Schmuck, *this very first text-collage by the artist subsequently disappeared for over five decades. The version reproduced below is the result of a scanned copy of the 1971 Xerox, whose original size (A4) has been adapted to the dimensions of this publication.*

A.V.

• • • • • • • • •

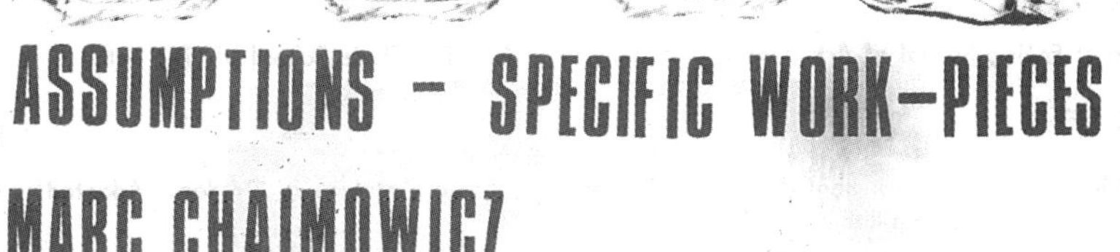
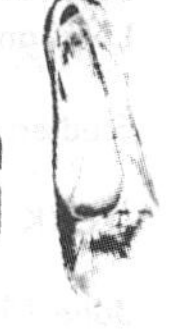
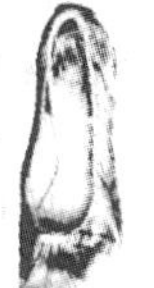
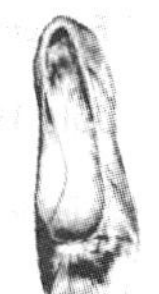

ASSUMPTIONS — SPECIFIC WORK-PIECES

MARC CHAIMOWICZ

VAUGHAN COLLEGE   UNIVERSITY OF LEICESTER

st. nicholas' circle leicester

8TH NOV TO 24TH NOV 9 AM – 9·30 PM SAT TILL 6 PM

talk-discussion nov 11th 7 pm

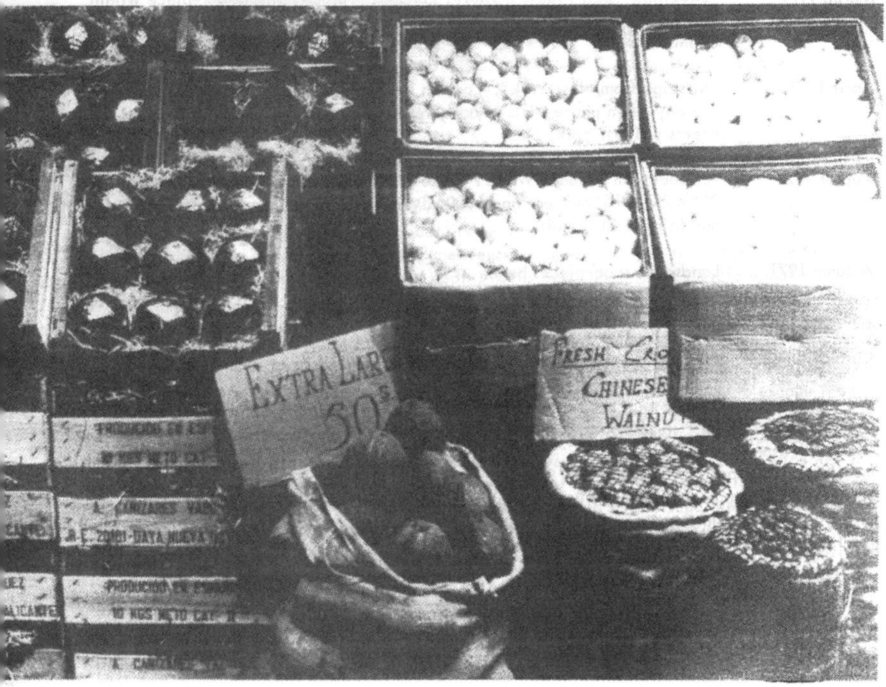

Born Paris between 4th and 5th Republics.
Lives and works in London.

Studied at Ealing School of Art, Camberwell School of Art, The Slade School of Fine Art.

WORK SEEN

June 1969   "Environments Reversal" Camden Art Centre, London, in Garden, 'Adapted'
                   Living Room.

June 1969   Devised "Random-Landscape-Approximation" Theatre Event seen in nine places
                   including above Exhibition.

July 1969   "Five Young Artists" Greenwich Art Gallery.

January 1970   "Banquet" Camden Art Centre in conjunction with P. Carey. Purpose-built
                   sculpture 24' x 20'.

February 1970   Staged events on Victoria Underground Line (documented).

July 1970   City of London Festival. Purpose-built shoe sculpture and sound.

Summer 1970   Shoe Waste? Pieces on various river Thames sites, London.

November 1970   Devised "Field-work" an indeterminate theatre-event. Words and performance
                   by students of Croydon School of Art. Performed in nine various places
                   including Royal Court Theatre Festival (See case-book).

March 1971   "Sweetness" Sigi Krauss Gallery, London. Purpose-built work-piece within
                   total Gallery space and continuous sound assistance of Bob Young and Arts
                   Council.

April 1971   "Message from New York", Camden Festival, London. Messages painted every
                   two days from phone calls of daily response to delights and horrors found in/on
                   streets of New York.

August 1971   Art Spectrum London "Waste? Piece 3" enclosed environmental installation
                   25' x 25' x 15' real car and 1000 silver shoes. Continuous sound - strobe light
                   and fairy light circuit.

Autumn 1971   Landscape shoe-pieces begun.

Currently teaching at Croydon and Maidstone Schools of Art and visits at other schools.

With emphasis on group interaction/communication work via a hybrid of methods/techniques
from encounter group + re-sensory awareness techniques and the co-operative alternative to the
competitive ----
manifested in experimental workshops focusing on practise of group dynamics, creativity potential,
re-defining/integrating roles of artist/audience, nature of expression/communication, the
I-us-you axis, media usage and leading to physical realization often in group forms (courses +
results documented).

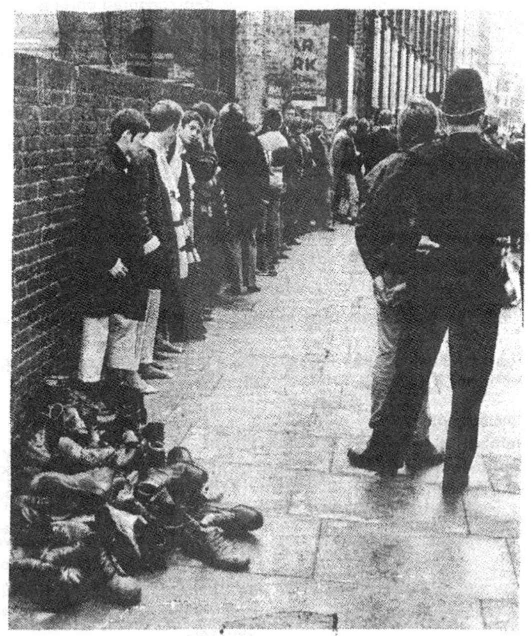

Disarmed . . . police line up the bootless skinheads in Farringdon-street.

I am within the present world situation/crisis as person, artist, teacher --- my identity must be
seen as a micro-personality of a macro-identity --- as such my art is interdependent on my. life
is interdependent on my teaching is interdependent on my identity --- the artist is not before his
time, rather he is immersed (at degrees of depth) in his own epoch --- I therefore make an art
that manifests aspects/obsessions of my place/time, specific to socio-historical environment ---
"static" work is the "quiet" aspect of performance work --- in the search for honesty, meaning
or transcendence an art of doubt --- transient --- not trusting memory which distorts but from
personal experience --- by starting with the real that it may lead to the intangible rather than
to try to make the intangible real --- that is clear about chaos --- that hopes to escape from
mystification guised as sophistication --- the one hope is to return to the basic to the simple ---
transcending to a subjective source --- but the present objective conditions are furthering the
cause of subjectivity --- to find the simple is most complex --- enough grandiloquence --- if
the simple seems corny that's not my problem --- the artist can kid himself no longer --- if we
are after qualitative rather than quantitative change he can no longer separate himself from the
social structure --- parallel to self-responsibility he must re-acquire a social contract --- we
must cancel our illusionary sense of power --- the artist will only help to clarify the negative
irrationality through others successfully parallel to the teacher and politician --- so let's drop
our crazy alley that we may re-integrate these three aspects of man within each individual.
Marc Chaimowicz   Feb. & L 71

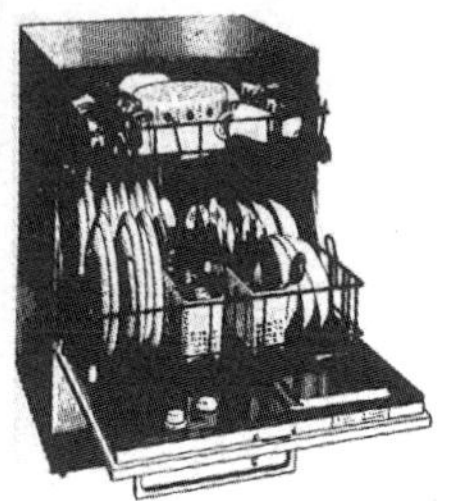

Notes relating to this show, Nov 1971.

Real/adapted objects found in the city
after show thrown away
general - detached - secondary

History/personal objects part of day to day
after show returned
specific - personal - primary

Working process is to re-assess and re-define general persona/work language --- which is then
adapted for realization according to specific nature of working/showing context ---

A work-piece is therefore affected by its context and in turn activates that context.

The context is affected by nature of its audience which in turn affects work.

Cancel exclusive use of memory as
distorts and via mental acrobatics
becomes unreliable and untrustworthy ---
but rather from subjective experience.

Everything starts from subjectivity, and
nothing stops there. Today less than
ever. R. Vaneigem p.6 Black Book 1

Witness
experience
involve

Selection of objects instinctive/intuitive ---
conditioned & influenced by personal & general
context & controlled/uncontrolled landscape
then adapted/personalised & edited for specific
context.

Involvement rather than detachment,
to be inclusive rather than exclusive.

No real more real than real --- only the
super-real or surreal --- and that becomes
rhetorical --- and unreal ---

Begin with the real the tangible --- once
seen it might lead to the intangible.

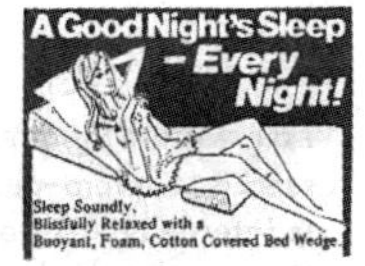

If work has real/trust ---
trust comes from experience ---
experience is subjective ---
reality is experience ---
reality is subjective ---

Experience is elusive ---
rarely real ---
reality is elusive ---
rarely experienced ---

Does not act purely through reason and argument,
but also through feeling and suggestion... "in this
way the emotionally suggestive or the purely
rationally persuasive may predominate as means
of communication" P.14. on Brecht Ernst Fischer
"The Necessity of Art" Pelican A632.

... what started as subjection by force soon became 'voluntary servitude', collaboration in
reproducing a society which made servitude increasingly rewarding and palatable. The
reproduction, bigger and better, of the same ways of life came to mean the closing of those
other possible ways of life which could do away with the serfs and the masters with the
productivity of repression.   p.12. Herbert Marcuse 'Eros & Civilization' Sphere Books.

Although my indoor static work has been intrinsically dependant on stringent control of working area ---
the physical restrictions at Vaughan College i.e. lack of light control, free access, lack of structural
control, of sound control etc. are not real limitations nor lead to compromise as physical manifestation of
intent is influenced by the physical context which affects reclization ---

So work is the inter-relationships between specific context (work-show area) -
artist persona - general context which affects both artist and spectator i.e. artistic
and socio-historical climates.

That which distinguishes surrealism from the artistic movements
which preceded it is its determination to minimise the fragmentation
of consciousness... P.17. Patrick Walberg Surrealism Thames and
Hudson.

and manifested by
manipulating/adapting
found/history objects

To adapt
   affect
   activate

The real to lead to the intangible rather
than to try and make the intangible real

Existing
situations

Adapted
Activated

Not simply for aesthetic reasons but primarily because of
socio-political and philosophycal factors.

Work is seen in a context, born in a context, grows out of one general context (artists place/time)
and a more specific context (artists personality/personal work development etc) which in turn may
be consciously affected by a general context (artists place/time, heritage, environment) which to
the artist may become specific etc.

It is therefore unreal to simply transplant one reality i.e. art work into a
context without pre-adaptation of that reality to that context.

Only work/reality on a primary level can be trusted - experienced - witnessed.

But out of context and adapted become symbolic? More real? The
choice/adaptation, + the witnessing transforms concepts into experience?

Nothing at this point can be
permanent ---

...Socio-political factors establish
a precarious fragility in which
permanence as a.microcosm of our
civilization is impossible ---

And trust/real situations elusive ---

The issue is to see.

Subjectivity is elusive.
real/trust is elusive ---

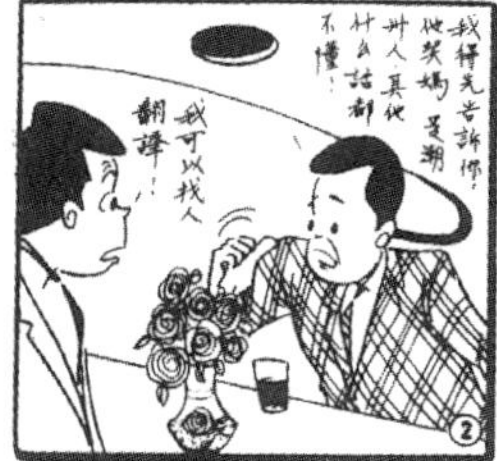

Photographs and assistance Bob Young
Thanks and acknowledgements to
D.J. Rice, M.A. Warden, Vaughan College
University of Leicester
East Midlands Arts Association

To this end the work here is purpose-built specific to
its context,non-permanent --- non-saleable or
profit-making ---

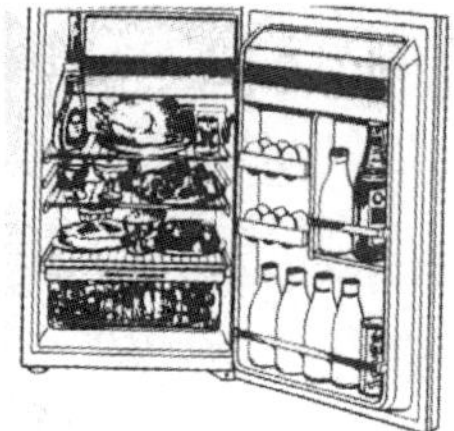

Art can no longer be wholly built on private and introspective
preoccupations --- spectator/witness/participant? Function/role has
to be re-defined ---

People art life cannot be made/exist in a vacuum --- yet most art seems
unrelated to people *** life but only to art, art about art, rhetorical,
linguistic, hermetic, vacuous --- a microcosm of this repressive fragmentory
society.

The audience factor is abstract and possibly the root of a general problem --- on a general cultural
level (why art, what for) and on a specific one (can the wish for private to become public, work) ---

Empty symbols or agent of
change?

Necessary for artists to help shatter the myths, false traditions and fake
relationships ---
to rebuild a human art
possibly fundamentally different to history art and
reversed from present functions.

The artist has the degree of choice and the responsibility
to counter-act this constrictive and repressive process.

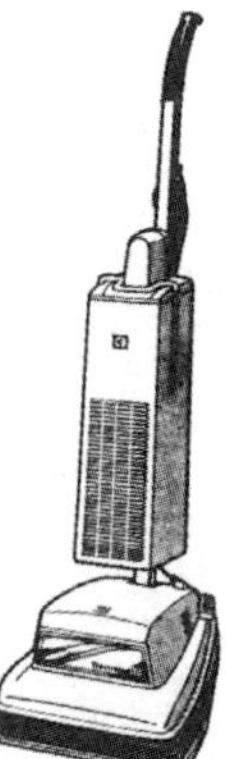

He was rebelling against "Retinal Paintings"... saying "I was interested
in ideas not merely in visual products..." Re. Marcel Duchamp P.52
"DADA" K. Coutts-Smith Studio Vista 48.

Generally a cultural empasse? --- maybe ---
and let the polemics rage on ---

Radical polemics and change are needed to re-define a viable
social role ---

--- enable man to reverse the direction of progress, to break the
fatal union of productivity and destruction, liberty and repression ---
to learn the gay science of how to use the social wealth for shaping
man's world in accordance with his life instincts, in the concerted
struggle against the purveyors of death --- p.11   Eros & Civilization.

In one sense this show is simply an interim
statement ---

Making work that has relevance to something
more than self & friends i.e. general as well
as local relevance is difficult if not impossible ---
the wish for a general, less local (and less
definable) context may in itself be irrelevant ---

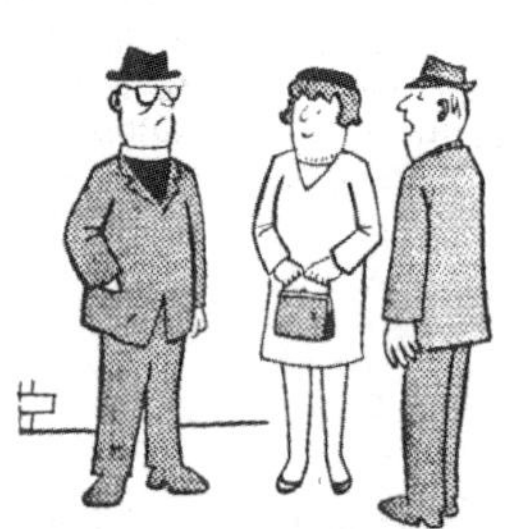

--- due to historical factors art has been separating itself more and more from mainstream issues --- it mostly doesn't measure up ---

And is less and less relevant to the majority of the people ---

--- it is not the issue to build a "working class culture" ---

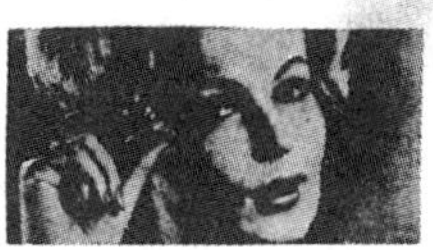

A paradox riddled with middle class paternalism.

Or of building "protest political art" often a highly marketable industry ---

And yet this assumed breakdown is resultant of a destructive class structure ---

Which conditions us all, containing the artist who produces fragmentary contextless products, often irrelevant except to the artist, the good taste squads and the investment speculators.

A holding operation?

It would be false to assume that (m)any artists have begun to tackle at depth the issue of function ---

Or that (m)any are interested ---

Or that solutions can emerge without the basic restructuring of our society --- and then of its culture.

Or questionable high taste prestige motives ---

And certainly so in the present condition of split class and split needs ---

The criminal produces an impression now moral, now tragic, and renders a 'service' by arousing the moral and aesthetic sentiments of the public... He interups the monotony and security of bourgois life... P. 167 'Karl Marx' writings Pelican 563

Consumption witnessed adapted

An artist IF of his/her time will produce work of our time ---

Reducing art and its inherent subversive potential to help affect change to the role of culture pawns manipulated by profit-motives.

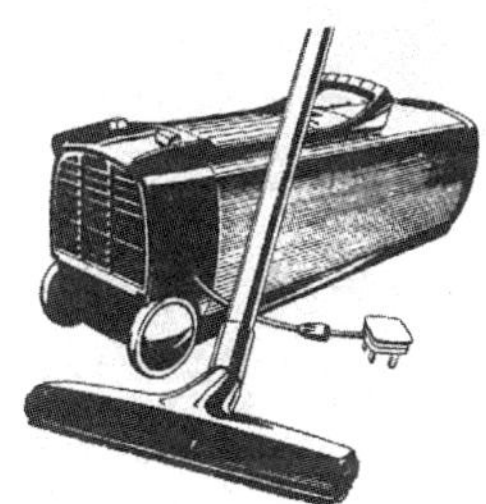

Rather than manifest present fragmentation artists can refute this role and work towards re-integrating the artist - politician - teacher; the id-ego-super ego aspects, of man within each individual ---

And this implies fundamental redistribution of power ---

Ordinary? Nature of these objects make them elusive ---
Ordinary? Nature of ordinary daily life makes it elusive ---

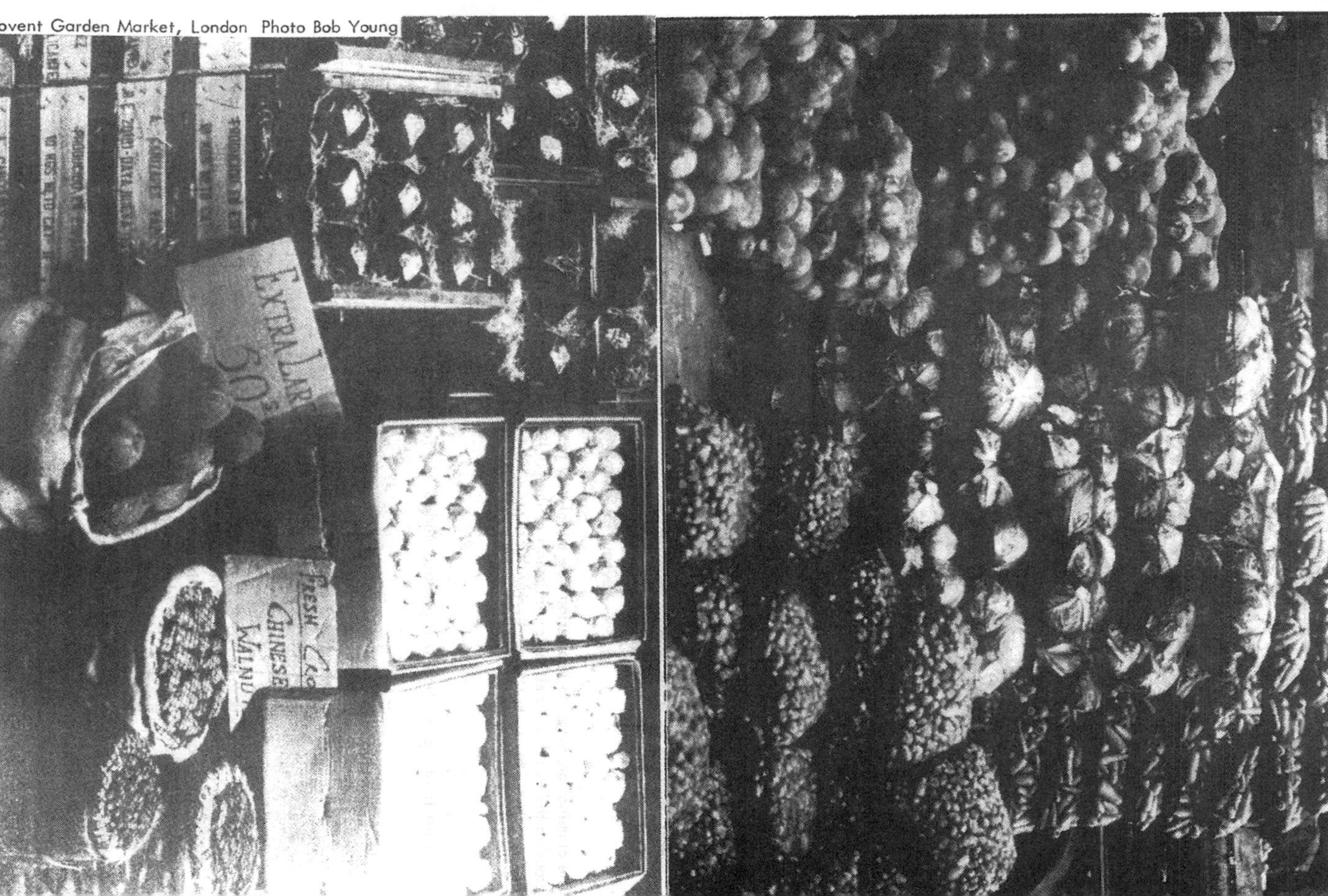
ovent Garden Market, London Photo Bob Young
EXTRA LARGE
50
FRESH CROP
CHINESE
WALNUTS

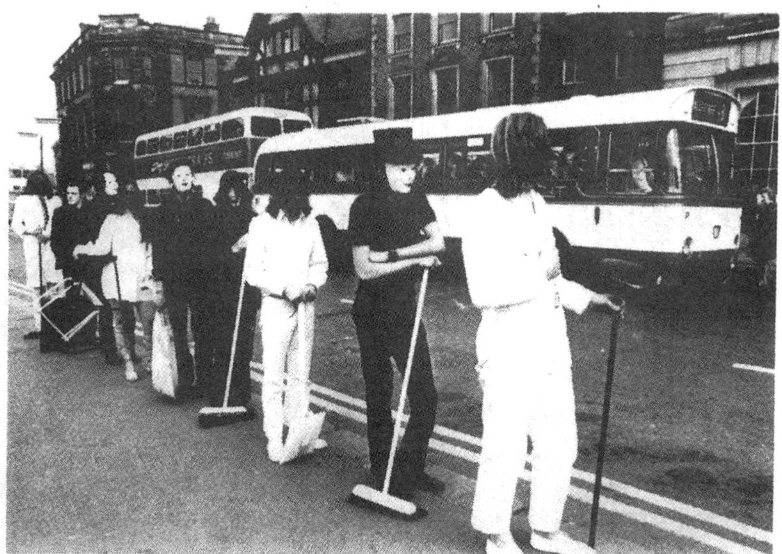

Part of city centre piece on three locations with students
of Derby Art School   May 71

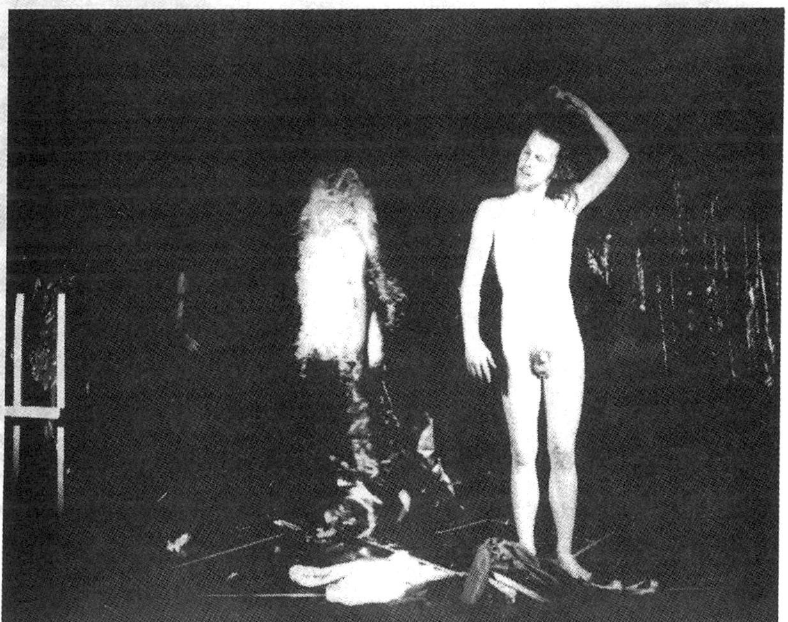

MAIDSTONE SCHOOL OF ART FINE ART Photo John Chandler

Part of Supper/Performance derived from a six month workshop...
researching person work, group creativity and to re-defining
an expression/communication matrix. Performed various venues

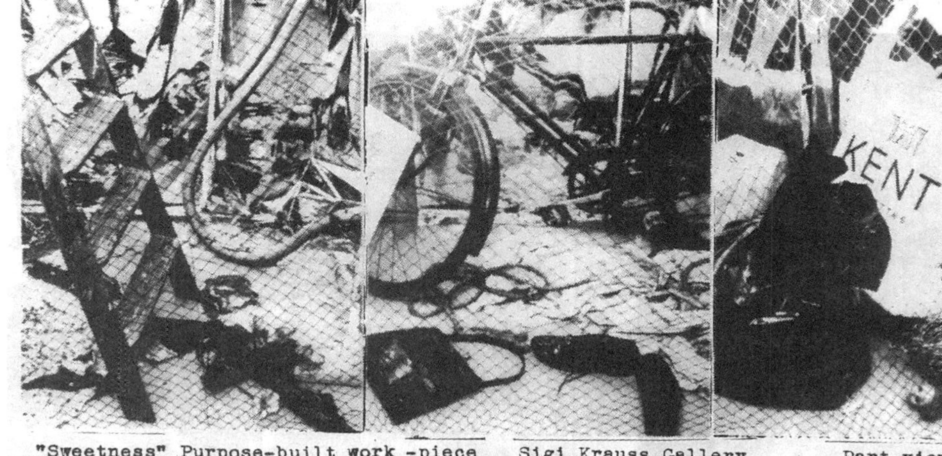

"Sweetness" Purpose-built work -piece   Sigi Krauss Gallery   Part-view of sectional installation inner room

Marc Chaimowicz
Sigi Krauss Gallery
Guy Brett

The Sigi Krauss Gallery has an ordinary frontage on the street. The young artist Marc Chaimowicz has made striking use of this in a kind of environmental college he has set up there. After passing a shop selling luxury glassware you glance in at the open door of the gallery, and there in very dim light the whole floor is littered with cast-off shoes; every conceivable kind of footwear. All are painted silver.

Shoes, unless they are lined up in pairs, soles on the ground, like parked cars, are an image of confusion and waste. They have no owners, but they are full of human associations. They seem to communicate a sense of disorder and vulnerability very readily. In the back room of the gallery, where daylight is allowed in, Chaimowicz has arranged two displays: a wall of colour advertisements from women's magazines and, behind a screen of netting, some used hardware such as a bicycle and a vacuum cleaner. These are there possibly because, in contrast to the shoes, they seem unaffected by human use.

Chaimowicz is an ex-Slade student who devises theatre pieces and events. His kind of cautionary art demands a simple effect, and he has the visual refinement to bring this off without overstatement. But this kind of work has a basic limitation. In seeking an atmosphere, a mood, it isolates a fragment of experience and expresses it in terms of another fragment.

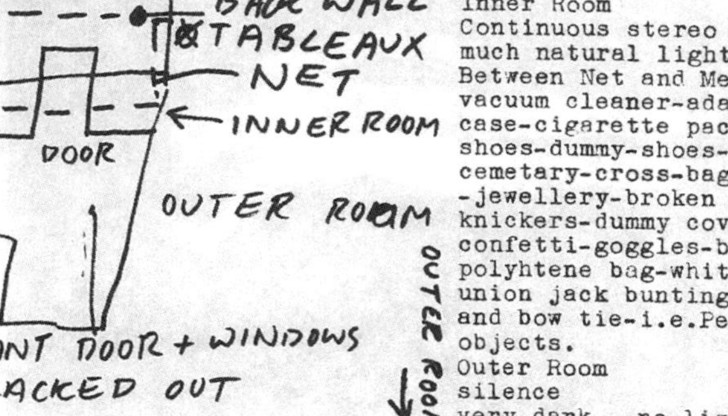

Inner Room
Continuous stereo sound collage
much natural light & spots
Between Net and Melanex-steps-
vacuum cleaner-adapted bike-suit-
case-cigarette pack-handbad-dress
shoes-dummy-shoes-dolly head-rope-
cemetary-cross-bag of dirty washing
-jewellery-broken glass-my girls
knickers-dummy covered in sheet-
confetti-goggles-broken doll-black
polyhtene bag-white silk scarfe-
union jack bunting-white waistcoat
and bow tie-i.e.Personal history
objects.
Outer Room
silence
very dark - no lighting - scattered
shoes.

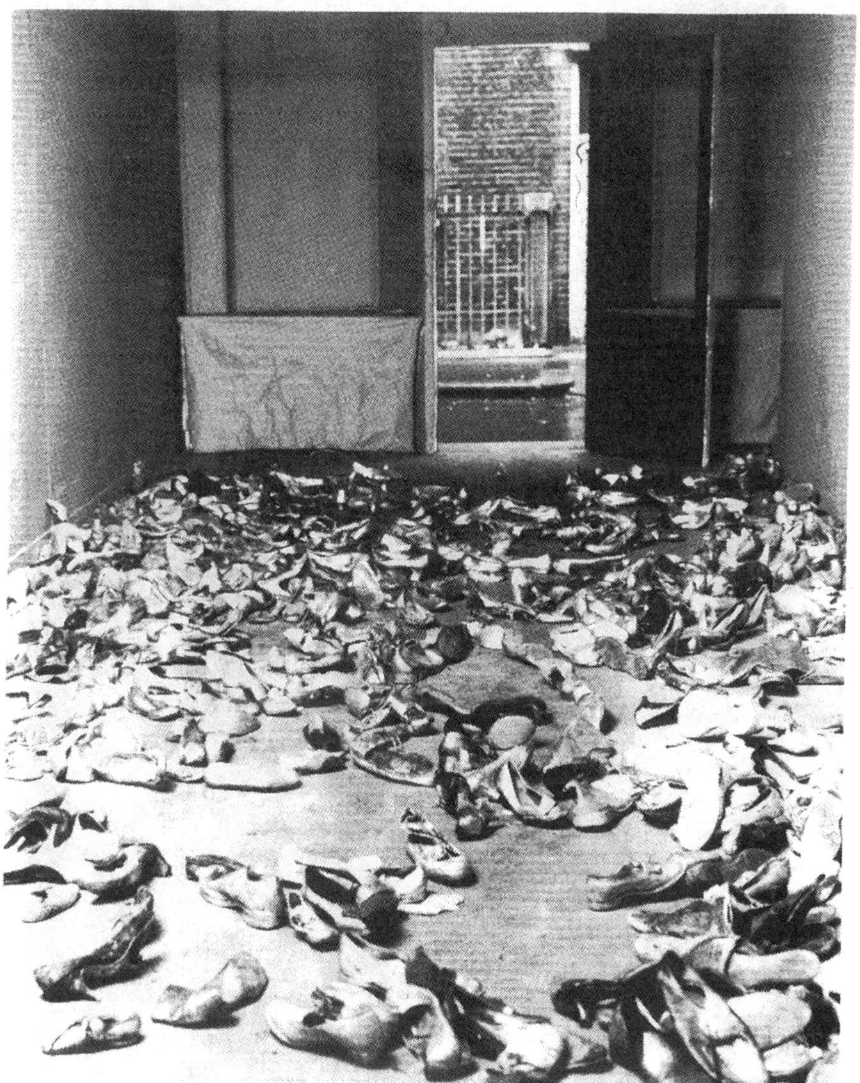

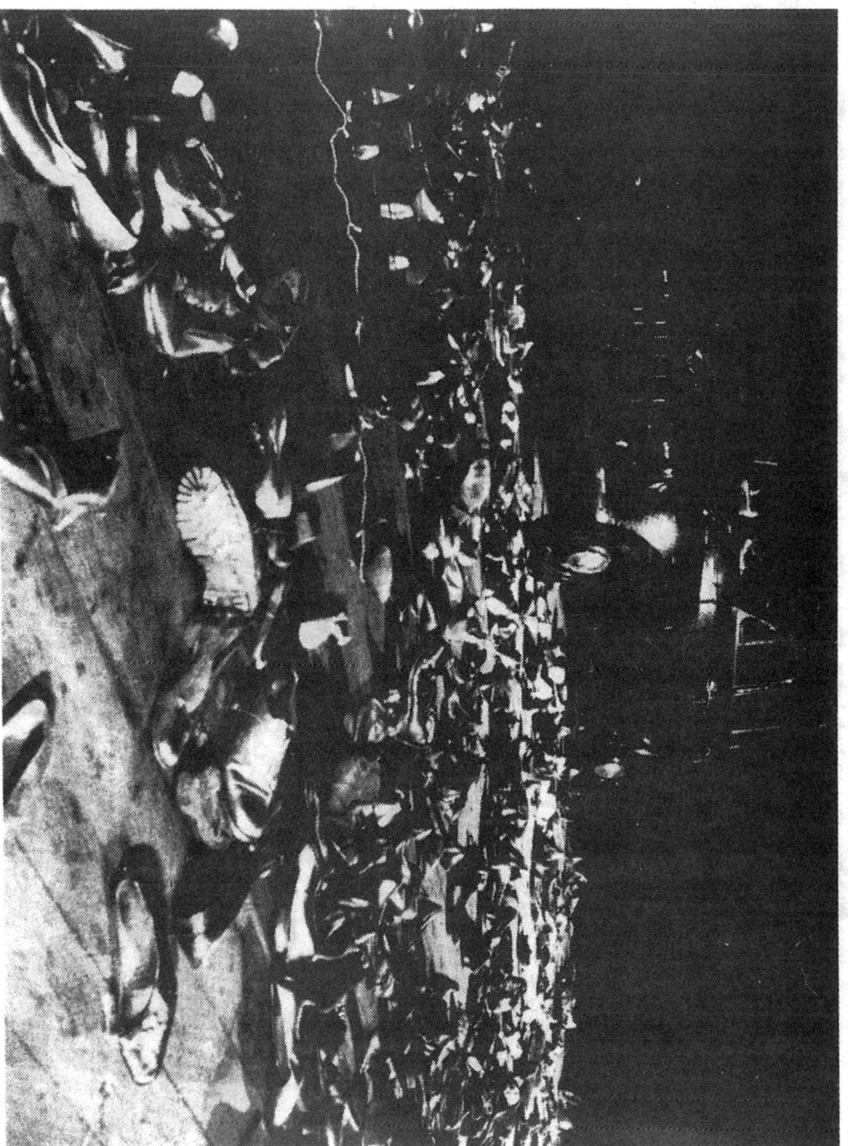

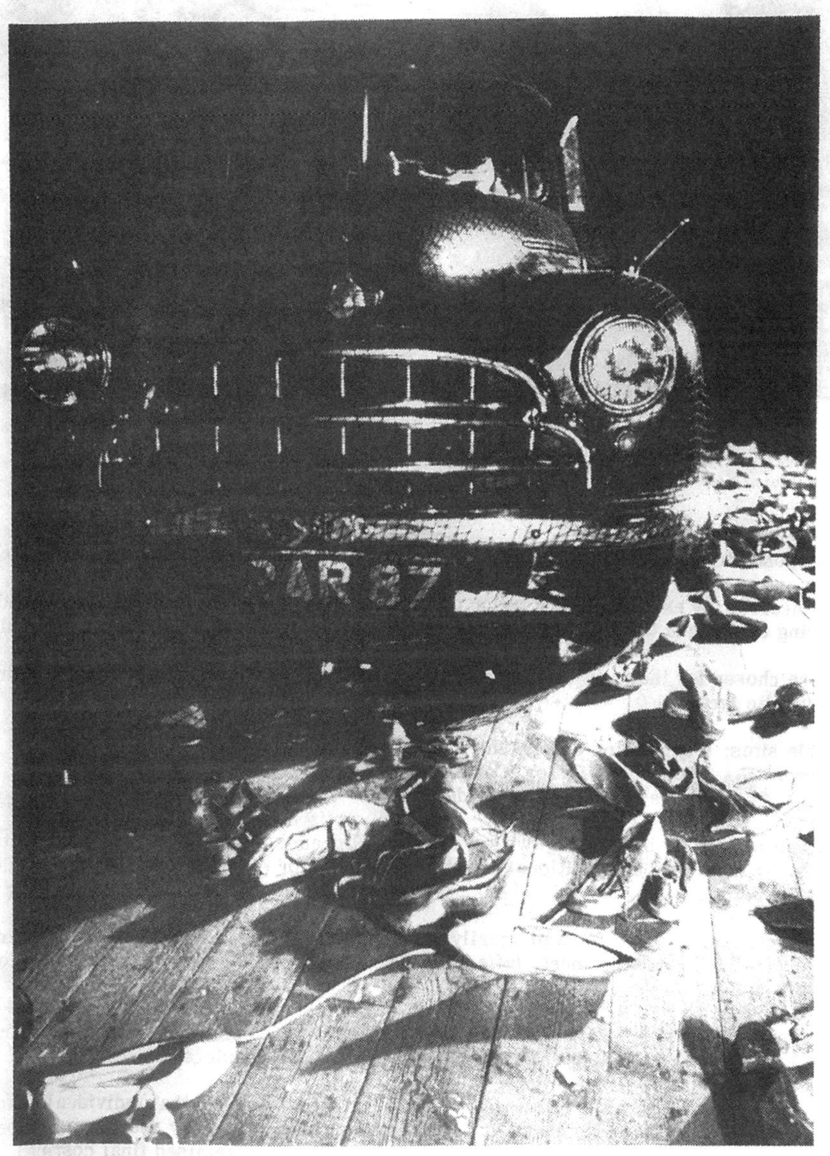

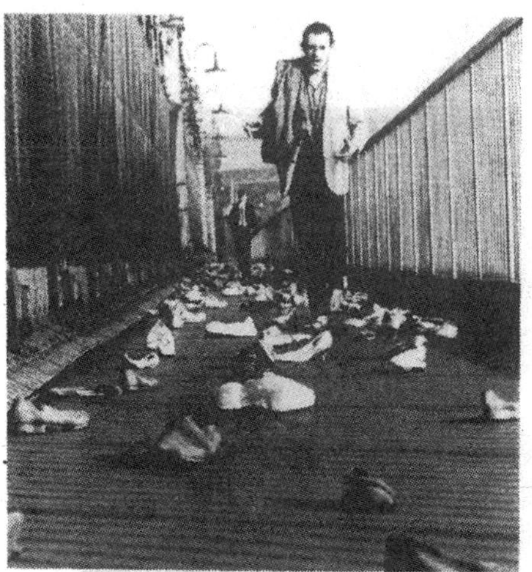

Hungerford Bridge '70

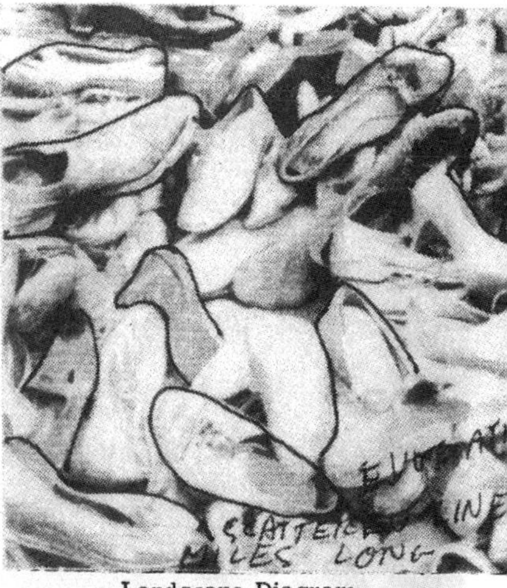

Landscape Diagram

Dear................

PROPOSAL

It is proposed to set up a dialogue between art-work, the natural environment and a large, random, non-selective audience with the possibility of inducing a quiet, static based experience.....by extending work begun on various river sites, London '70...... and scattering continuous lines of worn shoes sprayed silver over miles of public moorland.

Sites are chosen for their artistic suitability and for their close proximity to large industria eities (public factor)

Probable sites: West Riding of Yorkshire (Leeds-Bradford)
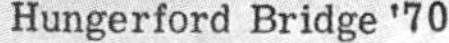
        The Rhonda Valley (Cardiff)
        Newcastle Moor (Tyneside)

                                    artistic
The proposal aims at by-passing two key traditional/premises; (a) The indoor, selective audience, gallery (b) The traditional artist economic factor of one to one i.e. the single patron/sponsor.

These pieces will be sited for a primarily accidental, non-selected audience, a non-art public and will be non-permanent, (affected by weather, passers-by etc.) non saleable and non-profit making ....

Approximate costing re purchase of worn shoes (approx 2000 per mile) silver paint, transpo hire, spray equipment hire, printing and mailing etc. is £50 a piece.

Rather than a single sponsor a democratic sponsorship is proposed that individuals each giv a pound. This will help cover costs and includes the mailing to every sponsor a numbered documentation print/sheet (photographs + statement, map and itemised final costing)

The number of sites used is accordant to sponsor response

Art interest can go beyond words and help activate culturally dormant terrain.
....
Copies + related information available, cheques, etc. to M. Chaimowicz, 36 Earlham St. WC2

[III. 2]

Celebration Realife Ikon Gallery March 1972

(1972)

Whilst completing his MA at the Slade School of Art in London (1968–71), Chaimowicz decided to give up painting, and began making "purpose-built" works and "landscape shoe-pieces" [III. 1], attempting to confront socio-political issues through Situationist-type events [III. 18]. In early 1972, he was invited by Jeanette Koch to spend a few days "in residence…" at the Ikon Gallery in Birmingham, where she worked at the time as gallery manager. The Ikon Gallery was then located in Swallow Street, in the Old Town Mortuary. During his short stay there, Chaimowicz created Celebration Realife, *an immersive light and sound installation that included a multiplicity of objects and artefacts scattered across the floor in a seemingly random display, evoking an abandoned party. The exhibition was on view for five days, from 7 to 11 March, 1972. Two weeks later, the installation was re-staged in the exhibition "3 Life Situations" [III. 3, 4], the inaugural exhibition produced for Gallery House, London (29 March–15 April, 1972). Considered finished, the installation was subsequently retired by the artist after its presentation, precluding its potential future and preservation until it was revisited in 2000 [I. 7].*

Created in close proximity, Celebration Realife *has been perceived as the antechamber of* Celebration? Realife, *whose extensive photographic documentation made it useful for referencing [III. 3]. In 2005, however, Chaimowicz recalled in* Celebration? Realife Revisited, *a key monograph dedicated to the revisitation of the piece, that the Birmingham exhibition was "bearing little formal resemblance to the later fully expanded project." As the artist recounted in retrospect:*

> *"March 1972 was a hectic period … I was young, things were moving quickly, and everything was done*

at the last minute. I came to Birmingham with some stuff in my bag, "found" some extra detritus there. And that was it! At the same time, I received a phone call from Sigi Krauss, who had just been offered the keys of a beautiful building in South Kensington, in which he could do whatever he wanted until the construction plans were confirmed. In a way, Gallery House was created in one day! The Birmingham exhibition was expanded in London renamed Celebration? Realife, *including this time a question mark. It's a bit like theatre plays, they are created in the provinces where they are experimented, and then, afterwards, they are staged in the capital."*

For the duration of the show in Birmingham, Chaimowicz lived within the domestic space he had created, offering visitors cups of tea and friendly conversation.

In 2005, speaking about the Birmingham installation, the artist said, "This work was nonetheless of value, perhaps as a working drawing. It notably introduced, as methodology, the presence of the artist within the work. A modest publication affirmed emerging principles." Conceived by Chaimowicz while he was in Birmingham, this "modest publication," as the artist described it, is a black and white, folded Xerox A3 collage that Chaimowicz considered at the time to be an "exhibition guide." The publication was made available to the public for five days on the occasion of the exhibition, but it disappeared and was never made available in print again, until this publication. Distributed around the outline of an interior space with a mirror ball hanging low near the floor and three wall projector locations facing it, Chaimowicz's multiple sentences can be seen as a mind map, an essay, a to-do list, and an intuitive program concerning, among other things, the scale of a performance, the presence of the artist within an exhibition, the mutual and subjective relationship of artist and audience to specific and broader contexts.

To share its graphic specificities, the original Xerox from 1972 has been scanned and reproduced below in facsimile, reduced to the proportions of this publication.

A.V.

· · · · · · · · ·

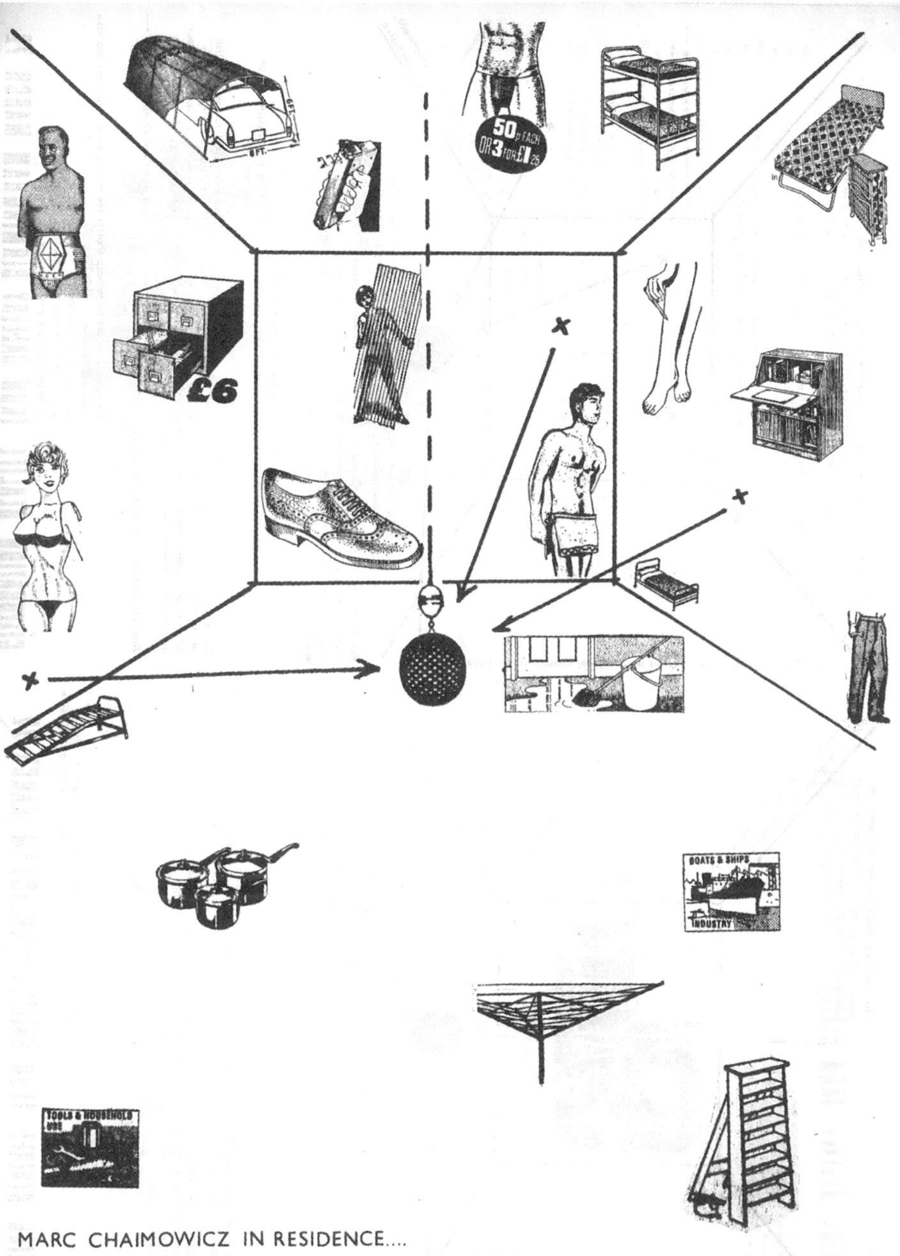

MARC CHAIMOWICZ IN RESIDENCE....

CELEBRATION REALIFE IKON GALLERY BIRMINGHAM MARCH 72

Open daily 11a.m.—6p.m.   Closed Sunday & Monday   SWALLOW STREET. MARCH 7 8 9 10 11

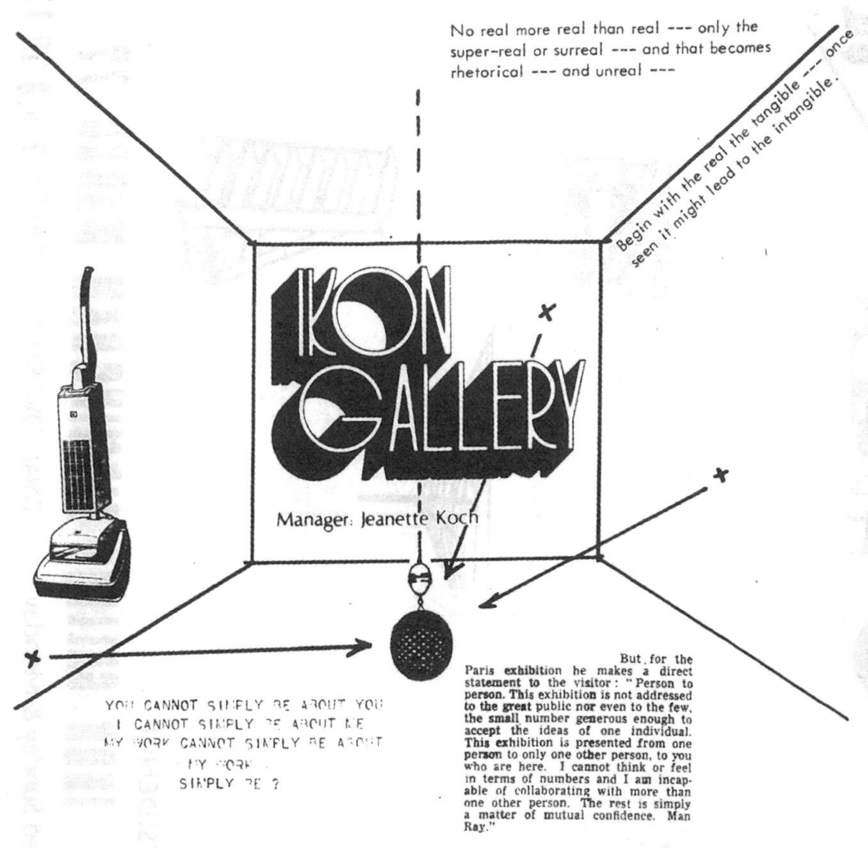

.. the artist as related to life rather
than to art. For these reasons, he will be in residence during his
exhibition, using the Gallery as a working situation rather than a
showcase.
This current work entails the day to day change of a subjective
response to the Gallery and the local environment, using found and
adapted objects and sound, and leading to audience response/partici-
-pation situations:

CELEBRATION REALIFE IKON GALLERY BIRMINGHAM MARCH 72

Working process is to re-assess and re-define general persona/work language --- which is then
adapted for realization according to specific nature of working/showing context ---
A work-piece is therefore affected by its context and in turn activates that context.

The context is affected by nature of its audience which in turn affects work.

It is therefore unreal to simply transplant one reality i.e. art work into a
context without pre-adaptation of that reality to that context.

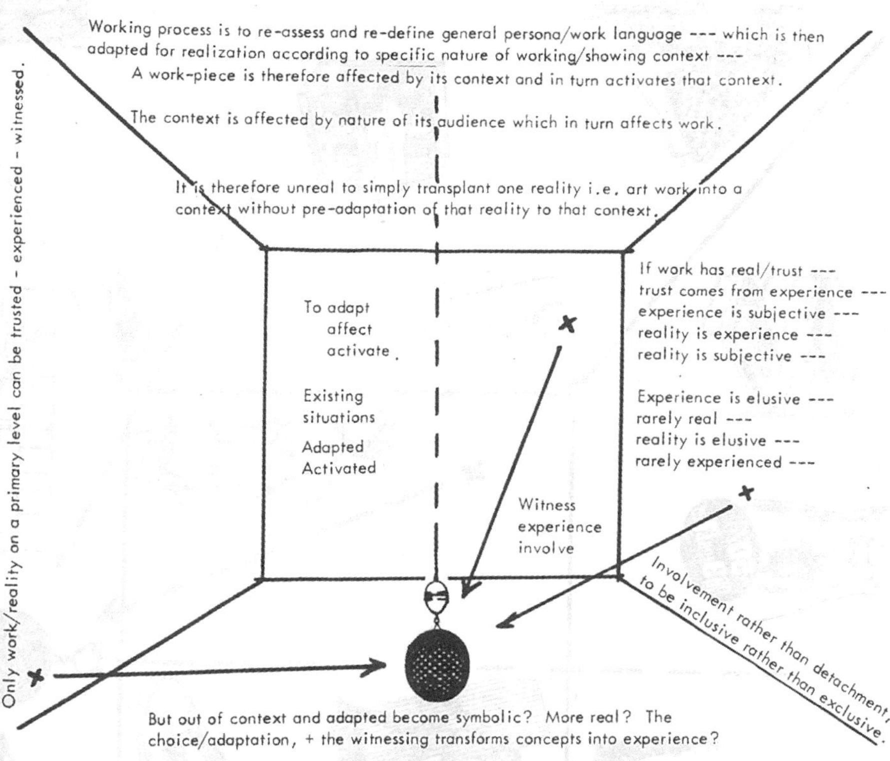

But out of context and adapted become symbolic? More real? The
choice/adaptation, + the witnessing transforms concepts into experience?

People art life cannot be made/exist in a vacuum --- yet most art seems
unrelated to people *** life but only to art, art about art, rhetorical,
linguistic, hermetic, vacuous --- a microcosm of this repressive fragmentory
society.

The artist has the degree of choice and the responsibility
to counter-act this constrictive and repressive process.

Nothing at this point can be
permanent ---

...Socio-political factors establish
a precarious fragility in which
permanence as a microcosm of our
civilization is impossible ---

Rather than manifest present fragmentation artists can
refute this role and work towards re-integrating the
artist - politician - teacher; the id-ego-super ego
aspects, of man within each individual ---

And this implies fundamental redistribution of power ---

And trust/real situations elusive ---

Necessary for artists to help shatter the myths, false traditions and fake
relationships ---
to rebuild a human art
possibly fundamentally different to history art and
reversed from present functions.

CELEBRATION REALIFE IKON GALLERY BIRMINGHAM MARCH 72

So work is the inter-relationships between specific context (work-show area) -
artist persona - general context which affects both artist and spectator i.e. artistic
and socio-historical climates.

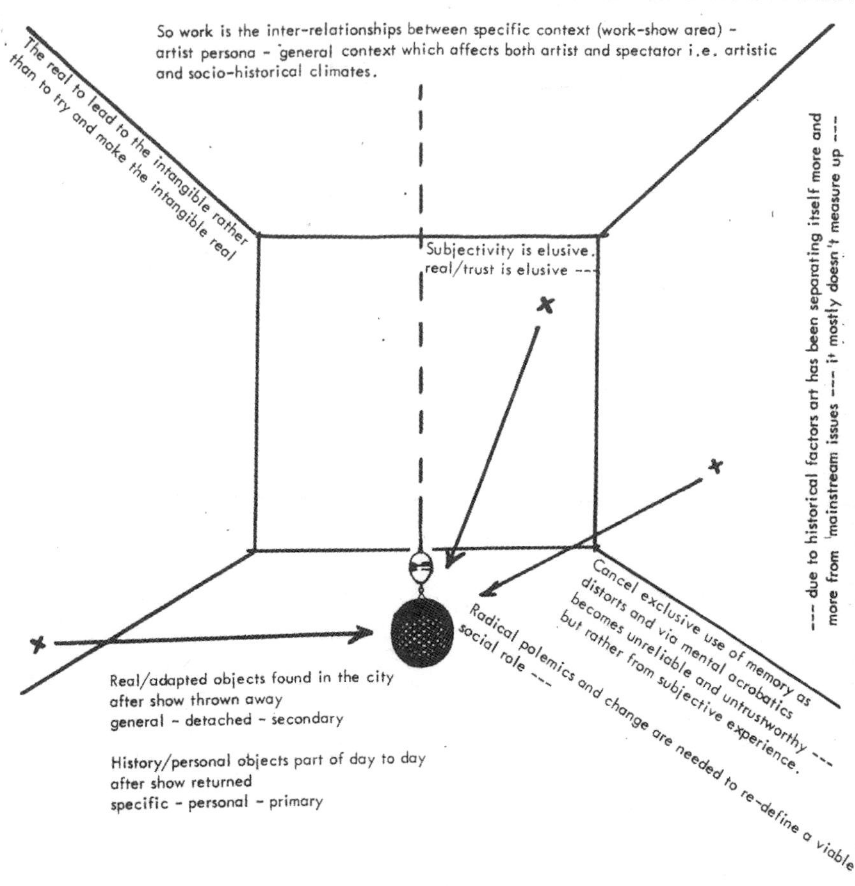

Selection of objects instinctive/intuitive ---
conditioned & influenced by personal & general
context & controlled/uncontrolled landscape
then adapted/personalised & edited for specific
context.

Work is seen in a context, born in a context, grows out of one general context (artists place/time)
and a more specific context (artists personality/personal work development etc) which in turn may
be consciously affected by a general context (artists place/time, heritage, environment) which to
the artist may become specific etc.

CELEBRATION REALIFE IKON GALLERY BIRMINGHAM MARCH 72

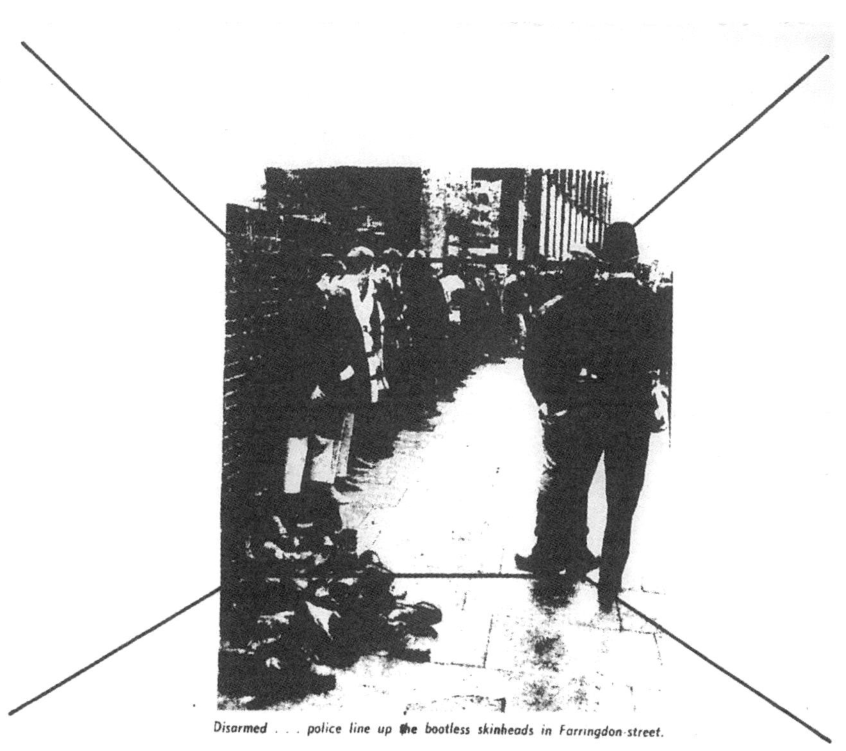

Disarmed . . . police line up the bootless skinheads in Farringdon-street.

I am within the present world situation/crisis as person, artist, teacher --- my identity must be seen as a micro-personality of a macro-identity --- as such my art is interdependent on my life is interdependent on my teaching is interdependent on my identity --- the artist is not before his time, rather he is immersed (at degrees of depth) in his own epoch --- I therefore make an art that manifests aspects/obsessions of my place/time, specific to socio-historical environment --- "static" work is the "quiet" aspect of performance work --- in the search for honesty, meaning or transcendence an art of doubt --- transient --- not trusting memory which distorts but from personal experience --- by starting with the real that it may lead to the intangible rather than to try to make the intangible real --- that is clear about chaos --- that hopes to escape from mystification guised as sophistication --- the one hope is to return to the basic to the simple --- transcending to a subjective source --- but the present objective conditions are furthering the cause of subjectivity --- to find the simple is most complex --- enough grandiloquence --- if the simple seems corny that's not my problem --- the artist can kid himself no longer --- if we are after qualitative rather than quantitative change he can no longer separate himself from the social structure --- parallel to self-responsibility he must re-acquire a social contract --- we must cancel our illusionary sense of power --- the artist will only help to clarify the negative irrationality through others successfully parallel to the teacher and politician --- so let's drop our crazy alley that we may re-integrate these three aspects of man within each individual.
Marc Chaimowicz   Feb. 1971

[III. 3]

First Floor

(1972)

In early 1972, the German Institute, a large house in 50 Princes Gate, in Exhibition Road (opposite Imperial College), South Kensington, London, took over the adjacent mansion, formerly the property of the Mormon Church, in view of connecting the two townhouses and thus expanding the Goethe-Institute. Instead of waiting until construction plans were confirmed, the Institute's director, Klaus Schulz, turned to the London-based German framer and gallerist Sigi Krauss to organise an exhibition and event program in this six-floor empty building. Although Schulz was familiar with the Krauss Gallery in Covent Garden, both the German Government and the German Institute were unprepared for the radical program that was initiated at Gallery House. As described in the press release issued in March 1972:

> *"The house will be able to accommodate three or four one-man exhibitions running concurrently and will have a cinema where films by artists can be seen. Behind the gallery is a terrace with a private park, which will pro-vide an excellent opportunity for outdoor work by artists. There will also be a bookshop for any catalogues, books and magazines not readily available in London […]. The aim of the gallery is to remain flexible to the needs of both artists and public thereby fulfilling an important function as a focal point for art activities."*

Despite a minimal operating budget, Gallery House quickly became the enfant terrible *of the London art world. However, despite its social and cultural impact, the German Institute closed it in July 1973. Although the closure was abrupt and contested, "the building had to be vacated. No alternative space was offered. The experiment was effectively terminated," as German writer Tom Holert put it in his monograph* Celebration? Realife *(London: Afterall Books, 2007, p. 28).*

"3 Life Situations," Gallery House's inaugural exhibition, took place from 29 March through 15 April, 1972. It consisted of three one-man exhibitions running concurrently on three floors of the gallery by London-based artists Stuart Brisley (ground floor), Chaimowicz (first floor, hosting Celebration? Realife*), and Gustav Metzger (second floor). According to Krauss, the three artists were at the time "linked by their socio-political concerns" in a context that had changed significantly after 1968 but remained a vivid and unresolved issue four years later. Laconically, Chaimowicz said at the time that* "Celebration? Realife *was representing the 'sensuous' level, sandwiched between Gustav Metzger's 'cerebral' upper floor, and Stuart Brisley's 'visceral' ground floor." According to the exhibition floor plan annotated by the artist, the first floor was divided into four interrelated spaces named "piece contemplative," "tea + coffee social discussion," "7 days reading room study," and "rest sleep (private)" that provided a variety of spatial and atmospheric options to the visitor. Conceived as an attempt to function as "a social space,"* Celebration? Realife *aimed to foster "experience rather than understanding." Composed for everyone to "feel good" and relaxed in this laboratory-like exhibition, which was rocked by the music of David Bowie, The Who, Janis Joplin, Bob Dylan, or Lou Reed [I. 1], these notes touch on the alchemy by which the exhibition as a "situation" might take shape in the fragile and contingent act of the visit.*

In April 1972, Jean Fisher, the acclaimed British writer, spent time within the exhibition, which she later described in Past Imperfect. Marc Camille Chaimowicz 1972–1982 *(Liverpool: Bluecoat Gallery et al., 1983, p. 7) as follows:*

> *"The largest of the artists' rooms: previously an elegant ballroom, was transformed into a contemplative work room for the senses. Natural light was excluded in favour*

of theatrical spotlight with strobes and filters whose colours were refracted and dappled across the silver walls and grey floor by three slowly revolving mirror globes suspended from the ceiling. A string of fairy lights traced a course across a floor mapped out as a landscape of scattered objects: cheap beads, a fancy dress mask, a clown's conical hat, flowers, miniature of Rodin's Kiss, a bust of Beethoven, barbed wire and underwear, and other items of sentimental value, of "low" taste, or simply incongruous. This space underwent small day changes according to audience response.

Adjacent to this were three other rooms. One of these the artist had nominated as a relaxing 'domestic and social' space where he hoped '… to begin to relate the work back with the guest to its original sources, i.e. cultural and socio-political factors this building, and to demystify creativity.' In contrast to the impersonal atmosphere of the conventional gallery, guests were made to feel welcome with offers of coffee, and invitations to discuss issues arising from their reaction to the work. There was a further room called 'space for the mind,' containing copies of the radical magazine 7 Days [21 issues 1971–1972, engaging with semiotics, psychoanalysis, situationism, and structuralism], and a private room, inaccessible to the public, where the artist slept throughout the duration of the show."

The fact that Gallery House was open 24/7, contributed to creating a "life situation." Chaimowicz, based at Gallery House for seventeen days, welcoming the visitors, and in general inviting public involvement, contributed to redefining participatory artistic strategies, questioning obliquely the role of the artist as one issue at stake in Celebration? Realife, while reframing the white cube as a surface furnished for and by the artist. The artist also expanded on the idea that any space could be an exhibition space—as any domestic space already represented objects reflecting the history, habits, and taste of its inhabitants—offering room for display, music, and performativity. As a result, the myths surrounding this piece turned it into an important reference point, which, in this particular case, was reinforced by the presence of the artist within the installation [III. 4].

For the exhibition, Gallery House produced Newsheet / 1, *a photocopied four-page leaflet, made available to the audience. Inside, each artist was offered a page to design. "First Floor" is Chaimowicz's contribution to the leaflet. Conceived at the same time as the installation, this collage brings together images of recent works by the artist as well as a plate taken from* Silver Surfer *and a 1968 self-portrait "adapted" in February 1972. In addition, four numbered notes claiming their own open-endedness of* Celebration? Realife *in an "inconclusive time" are published on the right side of the page as in a column. Separated by the sources of the images appearing in black frames, these fragments, which were intended to give directions to the visitors, were also published to invite them to reflect upon the social and ideological conditions of the work as a means of visibility and collaboration [III. 4]. This collage provides a first-hand account of a moment when art began to develop as a collaborative and relational practice as a way to invigorate the social function of art in a post-1968 art context.*

Reproduced below in facsimile, Chaimowicz's contribution to Gallery House's Newsheet / 1 *has been scaled down from its original A4 size to the dimensions of this publication.*

A.V.

• • • • • • • • •

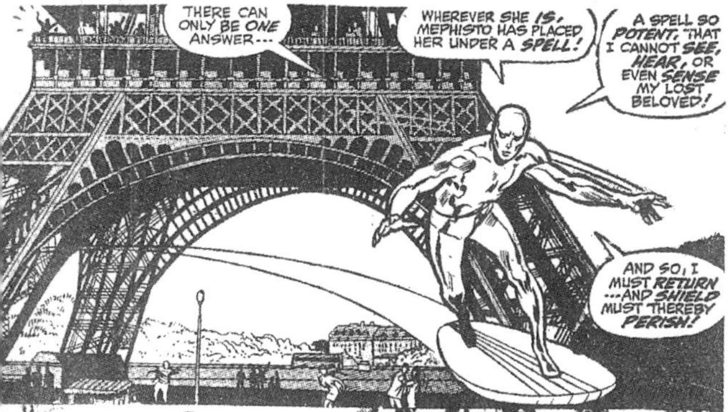

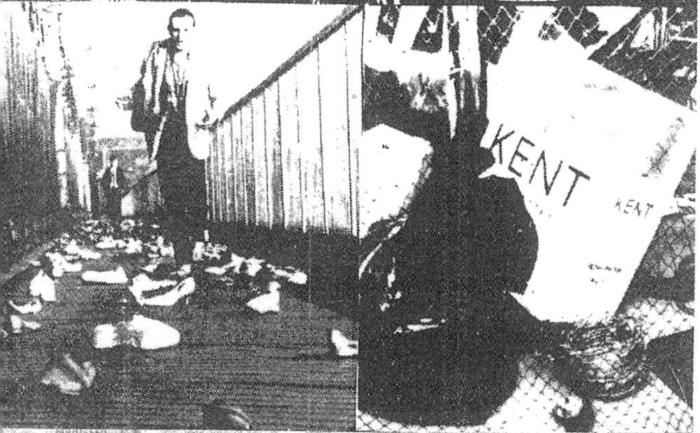

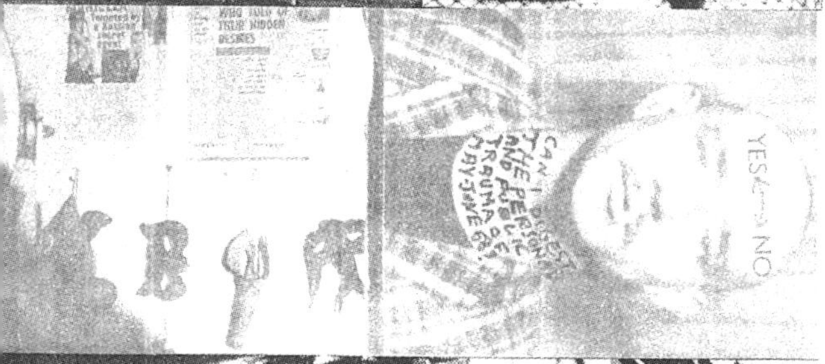

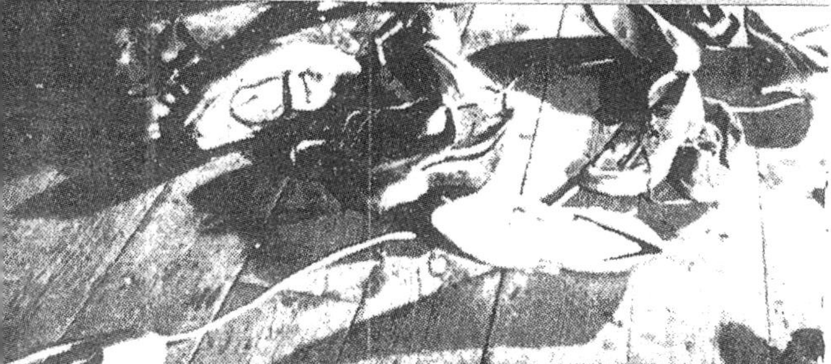

surrealism and politics didn't marry--- only flirted,
we are the bastard children of art and politics --

First Floor

in residence --- marc chaimowicz

selected biography related to this show

born + primary educated? paris works and lives in london studied? ealing, camberwell and slade school of art

silver surfer issue17

n.b.1.
this show should not be mistaken as a conclusive statement --- we live in chaos and an inconclusive time --- if art part reflects our time it will by necessity be non conclusive --

landscape shoe-piece 3 june '70 part-view "sweetness" sigi krauss gallery march '71

n.b.2.
no more than five people in working area at any one time please --- a waiting area with tea coffee and biscuits is available --- thank you

part-view celebration realife ikon gallery birmingham march '72, self-portrait photo '68 adapted feb '72

n.b.3.
should there be any queries regarding the show, possibility of collaboration, please ask attendant, thanks.

waste? piece 3 london spectrum aug '71

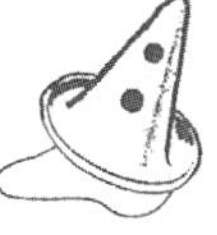

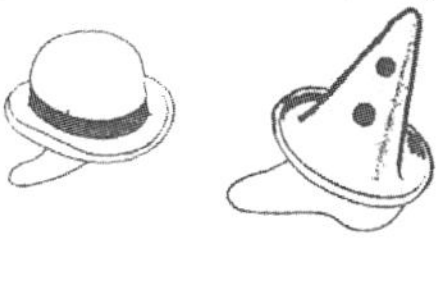

n.b.4.
---as with the macrocosm, this microcosm is ever visibly changing/ developing throughout the show --- your presence visibly affects this process

[III. 4]

Progress Notes

(1972)

On the occasion of the exhibition "3 Life Situations," Gallery House London (29 March–15 April, 1972), an A3 information sheet folded in two was produced, comprising separate statements by the three exhibiting artists: Stuart Brisley, Marc Camille Chaimowicz, and Gustav Metzger. This photocopied leaflet, Newsheet / 1, *was made available to the public from the start of the exhibition. Entitled "First Floor," Chaimowicz's contribution was a black and white collage, in the style of a zine, with juxtaposed images and fragments of text [III. 3]. Shortly after the opening, Chaimowicz felt that this "exhibition guide" needed some "degree of clarification." He therefore wrote "Progress Notes," a typewritten A4 handout dated "Mon. 3 April," which was thereafter photocopied and inserted into* Newsheet / 1. *Reproduced below, this text clarifies the artist's notes from "First Floor," while providing opportunities for the visitor to negotiate and reflect on their own role when hanging out in the exhibition.*

In order to link the two texts, the artist reused the organisational plan of "First Floor" in "Progress Notes." Accordingly, "Re N.B.1," which refers to "n.b. 1," takes the side of "experience VS understanding." Re N.B.2 introduces the visitor to the "de-icing factor" intended to "demystify creativity." Re N.B.3 promotes "participation and collaboration." Re N.B.4 encourages the visitor to relax and "feel good" about the "work patterns and response patterns" that constantly emerge along the exhibition. Advocating for experience, these progress notes further aimed to activate "the conditions under which subjectivity and intersubjectivity are open to change and development," as German writer Tom Holert said in Celebration? Realife *(London: Afterall Books, 2007, p. 11). Although* Celebration? Realife *was a crazy, anarchic work for 1972, Chaimowicz recalled, "People did get it. And kids from the neighbourhood were simple: they sat down, listened … and some of the audience was questioning the presumed relation between art and life. So, writing some extra notes about how to behave within this exhibition was more symptomatic of a feeling than of an actual necessity."At the time, "Progress Notes" was received like a "blast," he said. "This was not the English way that an artist may write parallel to art."*

As described in "Progress Notes," Chaimowicz arranged the site, ensuring that there was "no intended hierarchy of importance" between the rooms in which the exhibition was distributed. These exhibition rooms had names. Among them was "7 days," a reading and study room in which the twenty-one issues of 7 Days *were made available to visitors. Founded in March 1969,* 7 Days *was a radical socialist newspaper with no party allegiance or editorial sermonising, nor did it have an editor-in-chief; in March 1972,* 7 Days *went into "suspended animation" while funds were sought for a relaunch that never materialised. There was also the "Coffee room," or "waiting room," a room designed for social discussions. The third was the "work-piece room" dedicated to the contemplative piece* Celebration? Realife. *Finally, the artist used the "Rest sleep (private)" room to rest. This division was significant for the visitor, who could "hang out" in the exhibition. Quoting the artist in 2007, Holert said (in op. cit., p. 25) "Chaimowicz recalls the notorious presence of people smoking dope, drinking tea or coffee, and eating biscuits, spending hours at the table in the 'waiting room.' In so doing, visitors were supposedly experiencing what he called at the time the 'de-icing factor.'" If the exhibition space did indeed function as "a social space," this was most likely facilitated by the artist's physical presence within the exhibition 24/7.*

In April 1972, Jean Fisher, the British anthropologist and art writer, spent time in the exhibition. On this occasion, she observed the artist, whose attitude she would later describe in Past Imperfect. Marc Camille Chaimowicz 1972–1982 *(Liverpool: Bluecoat Gallery et al., 1983, p. 9) as follows:*

> *"His presence in the space was continuous but not in the conventional role of the performer in relation to an audience: his rather undefined multiple role of 'housewife,' 'host,' 'guide' and 'creator' was an attempt to avoid fixed relations and to explore the possibility of an alternative identity for art."*

While seeking to create an immersive experience, the artist formulated in his associated notes key concepts about both performance and the presence of the artist in the exhibition. Anticipating his performances from the second part of the 1970s such as Table Tableau *(1974),* Doubts … A sketch for video camera and Audience *(1977),* Shift *(1978), and* Partial Eclipse *(1980) [I. 2, 3; III. 8, 11], "Progress Notes" further announced the artist's relationship to performance as explored in the performance reports published in magazines between 1976 and 1978 [I. 2, 3; II. 1, 2, 3, 4, 5, 6, 7]. For obvious reasons, when* Celebration? Realife *was "revisited" in 2000 [I. 7], it was clear that the artist would not be on site 24/7 as he had been in 1972. As a result, the contemplative piece presented in 1972 in the so-called "work-piece room" became the "installation" we know today.*

Finally, through this open-ended exhibition and associated notes, the artist gently expressed in 1972 a resistance to both physical interaction and socio-cultural context. At that time, Chaimowicz was already in the nuance and the in-between regarding the "legacy of the psychedelic counterculture of the late 1960s—the ethos of anti-capitalism collaboration and 'total participation'," as Tom Holert summed up in 2007 (in op. cit., p. 71). When the time was of radical things, Chaimowicz was already more libertarian and socialist. Indeed, both the sensuality of the exhibition at Gallery House London and the artist's position regarding the cultural context immediately set him "apart," compared with the works and aspirations of Brisley and Metzger, the two other artists presented in the exhibition. Furthermore, as the exhibition was very well received, Celebration? Realife *boosted the fledgling career of the artist who, at the age of twenty-five, was considered as "one of the most important figures in the British high-subculture of the time": a phrase frequently used in the artist's biography. Shortly after, Chaimowicz was invited by the Arts Council of Great Britain to develop a new project at the Serpentine Gallery, London, where he conceived* Enough Tiranny *[I. 1, 13]; an immersive and politicised "scattered environment," in which some parts of* Celebration? Realife *were recycled and radicalised.*

A.V.

. . . .

… every aspect of this piece, *Celebration? Realife* is no more or no less important than any other … this applying to the three rooms (7 days room—coffee room—work-piece room) to the on-going work and to the various people's response patterns … there is no intended hierarchy of importance.

Points of clarification

re N.B.1.
self-evident … patterns of old and new are emerging and being strengthened … the workroom in part and at different times is supporting, for experience rather than understanding … sickness and health … plus.
re N.B.2.

the number of people is controlled, though most often is self-regulating, because of the need for quiet, contemplative choice … re the response of guests it seems more productive to allow oneself to be drawn into experiencing the complex levels of contradiction paradox and activity … this piece if complex, is also evocative and seductive … that being the part of the nature of the room … before adaptation to the current purpose it had a certain sanctity, maybe to do with its original function as a ballroom … the feedback is accordant to the time and energy that guests give, e.g. there's a right spot for every person … sitting or standing, etc., it's a matter of finding it … and when found I'm told things happen … or, one minute in the room produces merely a one minute response.

<u>The de-icing factor</u>
the intention remains that guests have the choice of resting and taking coffee with or without the people responsible for the show … this can lead to dialogue and dialogue has and can lead to collaboration … the implications are, to help people feel good, to begin to relate the work back with the guest to its original sources, i.e. cultural and socio/political factors outside this building, and to demystifying creativity.

re N.B.3.
what of participation? In no publication relating to this or any other of my work has this word been used. I am critical of it on technical grounds and prefer the term collaboration … participation art has tended to disrespect "the audience" by its tendency of treating everyone similarly and thus reducing people to a uniform role … unless people are treated as individuals, when faced with the assumption that they are expected to "respond?" they are often bound to feel inadequate and a false feeling of inadequacy will lead to two possible response patterns … that of the "shy introvert" withdrawing into him/herself or that of the "aggressive extrovert," manifesting that aggression, both stemming from the same falsely induced feeling of

inadequacy … rather from dialogue and personal contact the possibility of collaboration on an individual and original basis can occur … the fact that here the most common response is private and contemplative and that most guests do not feel the need to physically affect the situation but rather to mentally involve themselves is understandable and acceptable.

re N.B.4.
visually plus … self-evident … work patterns and response patterns are constantly emerging…

[III. 5]

*Dream, an Anecdote by Marc Camille Chaimowicz
Dreamt in the Winter and Remembered
in the Spring of 1977*

(1977)

From 1974 to 1979, most of Chaimowicz's work revolved around his personal studio flat in Approach Road, Bethnal Green, London. An idealised refuge from the external world, this two-floor apartment, which the artist would later consider "…Both a dream space and a physical space…" was used by him for a quiet domesticity propitious to self-inquiry and creativity. This is the "Approach Road" period. Characterised by the artist's intense interest in interior artifice and quest for "living well," this period testifies to the decadent singularity of the artist's expansive inner vision, while meditating on the simultaneity of life and dreams in his work. When Chaimowicz was an art student at Camberwell College of Arts in the late 1960s, teaching was based on the principle of "suffering for your own work." The artist remembers: "You had to be poorly dressed, unshaven, get drunk as often as possible, while dealing with the post-68 context." Intuitively, Chaimowicz reversed this dialectic: instead of suffering for his own artistic practice, "trying to live well became the priority," as he told British-American Berlin-based writer Kirsty Bell in a phone conversation in November 2011. This changed his relationship to artistic practice as well as to daily life. As Kirsty Bell mentioned in "Marc Camille Chaimowicz's Provisional Interiors," (Parkett, *Vol. 96, 2015, p. 23), "Chaimowicz could play out alternative notions of cultural identity, expand ideas of creative activity, and establish an androgynous zone for its production." At that time, Chaimowicz thought of himself as an "image-maker." Giving rise to an important photographic series that he would re-use in later works [I. 13, 17; III. 6, 7, 8, 11], he also elaborated a piece called* Dream, an Anecdote by Marc Camille Chaimowicz Dreamt in the Winter and Remembered in the Spring of 1977, *which explores the self within an interrelationship of image and text. Also known as* Dream, an Anecdote, *this text-work echoes, to some extent, the artist's early 1970s collages [III. 1, 2, 3] and announces some of the texts [III. 6, 8, 11] and artworks he produced at the turn of the 1980s.When the well-regarded British gallerist and publisher Nigel Greenwood—a graduate of London's Courtauld Institute of Art, who launched the career of emerging artists such as Gilbert & George—discovered, in Bethnal Green, the text and images associated with* Dream, an Anecdote, *it struck him Chaimowicz should turn it into an artist book.*

Founded in 1969, Nigel Greenwood's gallery worked internationally with conceptual artists through the 1970s and 1980s. Describing the context in which the gallery developed, Nicholas Serota, then Director of Tate, noted in an obituary published in The Guardian *on 21 April, 2004:*

> *"In the early 1970s the number of galleries in London committed to showing international developments in contemporary art, and especially European art, could be counted on the fingers of one hand. Nigel Greenwood Inc Ltd was one of the four. Alongside the Lisson, Situation and JackWendler, the gallery of Nigel Greenwood, who has died aged 62, played a crucial part in introducing the work of emerging artists to the then small audience for contemporary art in London [. . .] Nigel Greenwood was determined that his practice should be 'to make history, rather than to record it,' observing in a characteristic aside that the choice was made, 'rather than dig around in dusty old archives looking for yet more laundry bills of Michelangelo.'"*

From the early 1970s, Nigel Greenwood Inc Ltd soon played a key role in the presentation and distribution of artist books. In this regard, an exhibition of Ed Ruscha's book works, which was organised at the gallery in 1970, was followed in 1972 by the landmark exhibition "Book as Artwork" that was mounted at the gallery by British curator Lynda Morris and Italian curator Germano Celant. These two key exhibitions reinforced

Nigel Greenwood's emphasis on publishing and distributing artists' publications, as did the subsequent establishment of the Nigel Greenwood Bookshop, which became an integral part of the gallery's operations.

So, in the late summer of 1977, when Greenwood and Chaimowicz met in person after several missed appointments, their discussion, which naturally focused around fine art and publications, took on a life of its own. At that moment, the artist had just recorded himself reading a text for a ten-minute two-part piece combining slides and audiotape together for "Nine works for Tape / Slide Sequence"—a group exhibition featuring the work of nine visual and performing artists commissioned by William Furlong from Audio Arts *[II. 7].When Greenwood saw it in the studio, he liked it very much, but could not afford it. Nevertheless, determined to engage with the artist, he offered him "a little support" in another form and said, "Let's do it as a book!" As the work for* Audio Arts *was to be exhibited prior to the publication's release, Chaimowicz titled it* Scenes from a Forthcoming Novel.

At the time when Chaimowicz composed this work, he was withdrawing from the public view as performance had become problematic to him [I. 3; II. 8]. A couple of years later, Jean Fisher would argue in Past Imperfect. Marc Camille Chaimowicz 1972–1982 *(Liverpool: Bluecoat Gallery et al., 1983, p. 29) that "the artist was in the need to reassess that aspect of the more traditional view of the creative process which was based on the production of an art object." Indeed, at that time, Chaimowicz was searching for something that he couldn't find in the real world, namely his personal concerns, which he knew would have to be externalised. Echoing that quest,* Dream, an Anecdote *features the transcription of a dream "he" had at Approach Road, in which this place is destroyed and rebuilt. Looking back on this key work from*

1977 in 1995, Chaimowicz told French writer Alain Coulange [I. 6] that at the time he composed Dream, an Anecdote, *he said, "Writing and its relationship to the photographic image enabled me to externalise my personal concerns."* Approach Road *is a custom-designed environment in which the artist converged the precision of a gallery installation with the DNA of a work-in-progress within which he simultaneously lived. Instead of a hidden sanctuary away from the world, this carefully configured environment was made permanently ready to be filmed or photographed—like an interior portraying its sole inhabitant. As Bell summed up in 2015 in the essay mentioned previously:*

> *"In 1974, the artist moved into a ground-floor [plus basement] flat on Approach Road in London's Bethnal Green, in a row of tear-downs rented to artists on a short-term basis. One of his first acts there was to perform* TABLE TABLEAU*, alone, without an audience, as a means of marking the territory with his own aesthetic and performative intentions. For him, the home was not a pragmatic shelter for the mundane daily tasks of sleeping, washing, and eating but rather a host to inaction, reverie, and the workings of imagination. Rather than divide the two-floor apartment into studio and living space, as did many of his artist neighbours, Chaimowicz dedicated both to living, while radically reorienting his ideas of what 'making art' could encompass. Rejecting the traditional assumption that art should redeem the sufferings of daily life, he decided instead to focus on the basic qualities of life itself…"*

Greenwood was particularly receptive to this interior that the artist developed "as a sensibility." Therefore, over the course of their meeting, Greenwood invited Chaimowicz to take part in the forthcoming group show "… Additions to New Editions …" at the gallery (18 October–5 November, 1977). Alongside new editions by artists Bill Beckley, Ger Van Elk, Joel Fisher, John Walker, Chaimowicz presented "a new book plus new additions," as mentioned on the invitation card. Three black-and-white photographic juxtapositions of himself in his interior, hand-tinted with watery-soft hues of grey, soft green, pink, and silver in playful free gestures that dapple to wooden frames were presented on a wall. And Dream, an Anecdote *that Greenwood had just produced in a limited print run of 500 copies "thanks to mum's money," recalled the artist in retrospect, was "elegantly presented" on a shelf at the gallery entrance for sale.*

Over the course of the 36 horizontal pages making this book (15 × 19 cm), the artist plays with the two meanings of the word interior—interior meaning the domestic interior, and interior meaning one's inner life—which the juxtaposition of text and image entertains. Not reproduced below, the images used by the artist in this book are small square illustrations showing details of his studio flat, as well as a partial view of the kitchen in which Chaimowicz sits and smokes. As with Café du Rêve *[III. 11], or* The World of Interiors *[III. 22], it is necessary to consult the original publications.*

Linking Approach Road *to* Dream, an Anecdote, *Bell noted in 2015 that the artist has set up a live situation resembling "a low-budget Des Esseintes—the anti-hero of J.-K. Huysmans's* À Rebours *(1884)—who self-consciously invented a domestic realm as a stage for a solo, unwitnessed performance of everyday life." Echoing this hypersensitive neurotic and aesthete, Chaimowicz wrote* Dream, an Anecdote *at a time when, he said, "many artists were developing photo-based work, all was black and white since the colours were for painting, which was reactionary, and the colours were fiction." Minimal yet sensual, this low-key publication in black and white and decadent green crystallises the relatively intuitive state of mind the artist was in at the time. As he put it in retrospect, he was "increasingly drawn to the premise that all cultural constructs are inherently fabricated." As a result, in his attempt to culturally construct his identity within* Approach Road, *the artist had the intuition that this anecdote "dreamt in the winter and remembered in the spring of 1977" should be written in the third person, not the first. This enabled him, at the time and subsequently, to constantly refresh his distance from the self, and thus to steer clear from the biographical. This is undoubtedly why this "modest publication" is, in his words, "of great implication."*

A.V.

* *Performed in 1975 within* Approach Road, *this approximately fifteen minute duration performance, which the artist performed in public first in 1974 at Garage Arts in London, and subsequently across Italy in 1976 and on BBC TV in 1977 for five minutes, is described by Jean Fisher in* Past Imperfect. Marc Camille Chaimowicz 1972–1982 *(Liverpool: Bluecoat Gallery et al., 1983, p. 12) as follows: "A partially drawn curtain in the corner of the space reveals a dressing table and a chair. The artist enters, sits in the chair, and leans motionless on the tabletop with his head in his arms and gazes at his reflection in a mirror on the facing wall. His back, marked by a long diagonal scar, is to the audience who sees his face, made up in various colours, only as the reflection in the mirror. Objects are scattered on the table top: lighted candles, a bundle of letters tied with a ribbon, a vase of flowers, a half-consumed drink, an ashtray with cigarette butts, and an*

*assortment of trinkets. Flowers decorate the wall, and a vase
of gladioli and a fox fur lie by the figure's feet. The piece is
accompanied by the soundtrack of a violin solo whose composition was based on a story told to the composer, Conal Shields,
by the artist. The performance is concluded by the artist's exit
from the space."*

· · · · · · · · ·

*"The night dream (rêve) does not belong to us. It is not our possession.
With regard to us, it is an abductor, the most disconcerting of abductors:
it abducts our being from us. Nights, nights have no history. They are not
linked one to another. And when a person has lived a lot, when he has
already lived some twenty thousand nights, he never knows in which
ancient, very ancient night he started off to dream.*
*Paul Valéry says that he believes dreams are formed 'by some other
sleeper, as if in the night, they mistook the absent person.' To go and be
absent from the house of beings who are absent, such is precisely absolute
flight, the resignation from all the forces of the being, the dispersion of all
the beings of our being. Thus we sink into the absolute dream."*
—The Poetics of Reverie, Gaston Bachelard

Although he was often away and did not feel the need to be at
home on a regular basis his studio flat was very special to him…
A home to flirt with, a place to play at domesticity, perhaps reminiscent of his childhood days, playing with his sisters in their Paris
apartment…
And the more he was away so the more magical and necessary
it became… In one sense it was when away from it that he was
most at home…
The lease was short term and he would soon have to move but he
had decorated it to his taste and attempted to keep it tidy, to wash

the windows regularly, to water the plants, to house clean…
The lounge was a haven of peace and tranquility, the water fountain soothing and seductive… Keeping the curtains closed, it was here that he could shelter from the external world, it was here within this privacy that he gathered energy for his spirit and re-acquired contact with his self.

As at the terrace of any anonymous provincial café, so here he could sit alone for hours, daydreaming and wandering, dwelling on ills and pleasures and on how personalities were affected by inner and outer worlds…
Whilst staying with a friend on one of these frequent occasions of being away, he dreamt of his returning here… And he was stunned by what he saw…

As I walked into the lounge it was unrecognisable… The man and the woman from upstairs were busily dismantling the room… They had a team of boys who were steadily destroying this installation… The folding imitation bamboo table had collapsed and drinks had splattered onto the pale grey walls… The arch had fallen and was broken, the circular chrome and mirror table lay on its side, its contents strewn across the mid-grey floor… The pale green curtains were ripped letting in the violent sunshine…

The fountain seat was in pieces, leaving the water to happily find its own level… The pink glass sidelights were broken and dangling from the wires… The mementoes and artworks were generally thrown around as were the various mantle-piece bric-a-brac… The statuettes were broken and, with the chairs and vase of flowers, were lying askew on the floor... He assumed that in the dream he did not take it too personally or that he chose not to become involved with this wrecking of his home, because he remembers politely asking the man,

"You do this sort of thing regularly, I mean you and your team go to a lot of houses to do this sort of thing! Are you from the Council, maybe this is to do with government policy or part of a standardisation plan?" I received no reply and so opened the grey adjoining doors and wandered into the bedroom. Here the situation was much the same... Floorboards ripped out, the mirror smashed, my wardrobe of clothes and the collection of records thrown around, the pale grey walls with the hand-stenciled green motif seeming rather incongruous amid this scene of organised chaos...

By this time the space had become a far larger place and had metamorphosed into a cross between these two rooms and the installation that I had presented at Gallery House in 1972...
And the team of boys was equally busy, within this bigger space, gradually stripping it bare and methodically establishing their code of disorder... Turning this private world into a shell, into nothing but a ruin.

I went downstairs to the cream and red kitchen... There they were having a tea break and presumably resting after such hard work... The woman offered me a cup of tea, she banged the teapot on the table top, she was obviously an accomplice to this violation, to this rape but I remember noticing a small tear drop in the corner of her eye … and at this point he woke up.

He did not feel particularly responsible for this dream, nor did he remember being unduly upset... Perhaps he knew that this place oddly both in England and yet elsewhere, remained still untouched and undisturbed... Or maybe it was that he enjoyed it, having become two... Both a dream space and a physical space...

[III. 6]

Here and There…
Notes Towards a Preface, London 1978

(1978)

In 1976, the Hayward Gallery in London decided to stage an annual exhibition of British art. The stated aim of these exhibitions was to "present a cumulative picture of British art as it develops." Each year, a small group of artists or critics would select the artists accordingly. The selection committee for the "Hayward Annual '78" included five female artists, namely Rita Donagh, Tess Jaray, Liliane Lijn, Kim Lim, and Gillian Wise Cioboratu, who invited Chaimowicz to take part in the exhibition. Displayed throughout the gallery as well as the outdoor sculpture courts, the exhibition ran from 23 August through 8 October, 1978. Organised by British curator Catherine Lempert, the exhibition, which brought together twenty-three artists, was conceived with an overtly political goal in mind to "bring to the attention of the public the quality of the work of women artists in Britain in the context of a mixed show." American critic and curator Lucy Lippard contextualised the "Hayward Annual '78" in her introductory essay, saying that the exhibition had its roots in a feminist protest against the exhibition "The Condition of Sculpture" at the Hayward Gallery in 1975, which featured thirty-six men and only four women. Following this exhibition, Liliane Lijn proposed a historical exhibition of women's art to the Tate, who later passed it on to the Arts Council. Although the Arts Council didn't take on Lijn's proposal, they invited her to bring together an all-female selection committee for the second "Hayward Annual" in 1978.

As one of the seven male artists invited to take part in the exhibition, Chaimowicz was allocated a two-room space in which he conceived Here and There… *an installation whose title indicates a concern with the interrelation between the private world (here) [III. 5] and the gallery space (there), where the installation was presented to the public. Like an entrance, the first room was furnished with a stool, a mirror, a dresser with a welcoming vase of flowers, beside which were installed three small tinted framed studies (Self Portrait... Qualified, 1977; Interiors... Qualified, 1978; Still Life... Qualified, 1978) trapped like specimens floating between the glass and the patterned wallpaper. In the adjacent room, seventeen tastefully coloured and patterned plywood panels leant lopsidedly against light grey painted walls in a seemingly casual manner, as if temporarily stored there, with their edges overlapping. They had large square photographs depicting domestic scenes set in Approach Road pasted to their surfaces. In a confined adjacent space was a fifteen-minute videotape, in colour and black and white, of a pre-recorded tape of the same interior entitled Partial Views of an Interior, 1978, with the soundtrack of a continuous fountain.*

The Hayward Gallery was "then prestigious," admits the artist in retrospect. "I was aware of the issue to elaborate a text in connection with Here and There..." Written before the exhibition was set up, this text reproduced below consists of notes recorded in the third person singular masculine, similarly to Dream, an Anecdote [III. 5]. Like a reverie, this text suggests a dialogue between two places, namely the idealised domestic interior space (here) and the almost aggressively neutral gallery space (there), two spaces at the junction of which the installation designed by the artist in the "Hayward Annual '78" articulates. Characterised by a mood of quietude and serenity, this text further includes remarks on undefined places, moments of inaction and versatile memories, while depicting a space that is "alien in its correctness, distant in its estrangement."

Considering writing "more vulnerable than works of art," the artist subtitled his text "Notes toward a preface" to emphasise that it had been written before the installation to which it refers had been set up. Jean Fisher would later suggest in

Past Imperfect. Marc Camille Chaimowicz 1972–1982 (Liverpool: Bluecoat Gallery et al., 1983, p. 34) that these "notes toward a preface" could also be seen as "a reverie perhaps about memory itself. Or about the imaginative process, through which a glimpsed image acquires an identity in language." Displayed in the exhibition space as an A4 single-sided page, this text was also printed in the catalogue published by the Arts Council of Great Britain in conjunction with the exhibition, on a double spread page over two photographs showing the interior of the artist's studio flat in Approach Road.

This text was subsequently translated into French and reproduced in the catalogue for the exhibition "Un Certain Art Anglais...," ARC, Musée d'Art Moderne de Paris (20 January–12 March, 1979), a group exhibition devoted to the multiplicity of conceptual and perceptual artistic practices in Britain in the 1970s. The text was also translated into German and displayed as a freestanding A4 single-sided page in the exhibition "Marc Camille Chaimowicz" [III. 9], Galerie H Air, Vienna, Spring 1982. Finally, the original Xerox from 1978 was reproduced as a facsimile in Marc Camille Chaimowicz's The World of Interiors *in 2007 [III. 22].*

A.V.

• • • • • • • • •

"… As at the terrace of any anonymous provincial café, so here he could sit alone for hours, daydreaming and wandering, dwelling on ills and pleasures…"

He thought of the Hayward Gallery, of the odd rooms with no windows or doors, neutral spaces with no identity, not really rooms at all…

Sitting in his lounge, this temporary truce between the ideal and the real, he dwelt on change…

How it is not possible to transfer his reality to another without this act of transference affecting that reality… How the transference of an experience qualifies that experience… How an idea, once subjected to change, is no longer that idea, how its purity is violated, modified…

He thought of black and white, … critically, and in this instance preferred greys and silvers, sometimes hazy as a Venetian dawn and sometimes crystalline… Greys that seem to annex a depth of nuances and colours, in a sense not really greys at all but greys that in their handling have become more than a mix of two extremes, rather, a new breed…

… and so with many false polarities…
He thought of here and there of this and that… (the fact that he was doing precious little passively…)

He read Samuel Beckett on Marcel Proust "… He deplores his lack of will until he understands that will, being utilitarian, a servant of intelligence and habit is not a condition of the artistic experience…"

Hints of past cultural battles perhaps, between the German and the French…
Within this space, alien in its correctness, distant in its estrangement…

… He recalled it…

As sometimes reproachful, with a quality of abandonment … at times deliciously formal as with traditional hotel rooms… Sometimes sullen as adolescence, moody as delinquency…

The fountain screened out external noise establishing a particular silence … as with a well-matched duel, so the light of the mantelshelf lamp countered the daylight filtering in through the pale green curtains… As if natural light needed the qualification of electricity…

… within this intimacy he felt complete…

I realised that this space, seemingly so singular, was infinitely composed…
Still as to appear timeless, was fluid and prone to change…

And here, where possibilities of action seemed inappropriate, a multitude of activities were possible…

[III. 7]

Screens…

(1979)

To coincide with "Screens...," Chaimowicz's first personal exhibition at Nigel Greenwood Inc Ltd, London (31 October–24 November, 1979), the gallery produced a black and white announcement card (19 × 11.8 cm) designed by the artist, printed on both sides. On one side of the card, a short untitled text signed "MCC '79" is printed. Reproduced below, this text provides a quick overview of the artist's interest in the folded-screen, the subject of his 1979 exhibition at the gallery. Written at a time when Chaimowicz's relationship with the ideal space and refined décor of Approach Road *began to seem "...deliciously close to a state of entombment...," this text is an attempt to contextualise the artist's need to escape this aestheticised interior, as well as the solitude and state of languor inherent to it. Echoing this, the exhibition included three coloured hand-stenciled freestanding screens in three, four, and five panels, with either straight or angled top edges, whose surfaces are enlivened with black and white square photographs. Hand-tinted in pastel colours, these screens depict a charismatic young couple evolving in the artist's studio flat in Approach Road. In an unpublished interview with a member of the Tate Gallery staff (8 January, 1983) Chaimowicz said, "in the most overt sense manifested with ambiguity, screens being something which both reveal and conceal," they inaugurated a process of de-hierarchisation that the artist would meticulously develop over the course of the 1980s, aiming to dissolve the modernist boundaries between "sculpture" and "painting," "artist" and "designer," "fine" and "applied" arts [I. 6; II. 10; III. 9, 10, 15] as well as notions of "good taste."*

On the other side of the announcement card is the exhibition information, with two horizontal black and white photographs showing a young solar couple. First, the couple is entwined. Second, she and he are seated in two identical armchairs, seen from behind, looking towards a large double-leaf closed door, whose brilliant white paint reflects the daylight entering the room. Below the second photograph, the title of the exhibition—"Screens…"—is reproduced in small characters. The identity of the protagonists is revealed—like on a screen—on the other side of the card, in a thank you line at the end of the text. They are Helen Sear and Allan Parker [II. 9], two young British artists, who have just graduated from the Fine Art Department at Reading University and Middlesex Polytechnic, where, coincidentally, Chaimowicz had been their tutor and with whom he developed multiple photographic series, including this one.

The screen is a domestic piece, which can create a temporary space anywhere, in private or in public. It is a structure that Chaimowicz explored in his work in the late 1970s and across the 1980s. First, in 1979 in the exhibition "Screens… ." Second, in the exhibition "Maquettes…,"Nigel Greenwood Inc Ltd, London (10 December–30 January, 1982), where five screen models were presented on glass shelves with symmetrical wall mirror plates to make the other side of the folded screen visible, in addition to "Le Désert,"an artwork consisting of eighteen single and one double sheet of card, supporting photographs collaged onto decorative backgrounds of the artist's own design, and in places accompanied by short texts, which the artist would use in 1985 as the first chapter of his most ambitious published project Café du Rêve [III. 11]. Third, in the exhibition "Autour de Cinq Paravents," Musée des Beaux-Arts, Dijon (26 September–14 November, 1987), where the artist displayed five mid-century style curved partition screens, painted on canvas on one side, and inlaid with exotic woods on the other, also the starting point for a long-term collaboration between Chaimowicz and Guy HF, a French cabinet-making company based in Bourbon-Lancy, in the Burgundy Region.

In the previous decade, the artist experienced the formal structure of the folded-screen from a metaphorical point of view, *interfering with human relations in public and private. First, as a curtain in* We Choose Our Words with Care, That Neon Moonlight Evening; It Was As If We Were, Party to a Wonderful Alchemy *(1975) [I. 2]. Second, as a projection screen in* Doubts… A Sketch for Video-Camera and Audience *(1977). Third, as a wall panel in* Here and There… *(1978) [III. 6].*

Sent by post, the announcement card published for the "Screens…" exhibition was also available at the gallery for the duration of the show. Visitors were therefore able to read the artist's text in the exhibition, while experiencing in public a formal structure developing a discourse on intimacy and inter-individual relations within the gallery.

A.V.

•••••••••

Not simply … decorative or functional, flaunting yet obliterating their own identity, screens are hybrid. Within a room they may be awkward, taking up much space, or self-effacing, folded and hidden. Their protection is illusory and because they are itinerant, their offer of privacy is qualified…

Their liaison … clandestine, decorative, and problematic … partial in appearance … held moments of entirety, intimacy, and estrangement…

His search … for a particular perfection was becoming stifling, constrictive … a feeling deliciously close to a state of entombment … and his foray outside of that condition held an immediacy tantamount to that of a reprieve…

…thanks to Alan Parker and Helen Sear without whom…

[III. 8]

Partial Eclipse...

(1981)

Late 1979, when Chaimowicz left the studio flat he had occupied in Approach Road since 1974 [III. 5], which "was rumoured to be coming to an end" the artist recalls in retrospect, he found a cheap flat to buy in Hayes Court, a red-brick mansion block on Camberwell New Road, in Southeast London. Here, as British-American Berlin-based writer Kirsty Bell put it in "Marc Camille Chaimowicz's Provisional Interiors" (Parkett, Vol. 96, 2015, p. 25), "he replicated his Approach Road interior, with the same colours, patterns, and furnishings, even repeating the same arrangements. In the brief period before this re-creation, however, he used it as the stage set for a series of black and white photographs. This became the basis for Partial Eclipse…," *a languid performance addressing the tension between the need for solitude and for company. First staged on 15 March, 1980 at the ICC—Antwerp's Internationaal Cultureel Centrum, the first public institution of contemporary art in Flanders—*Partial Eclipse… *was subsequently performed live by the artist until the end of 1982.*

At the turn of the 1980s, the announcement of a new performance by Chaimowicz caught the attention of the artistic community, eager to reconnect with him after his Approach Road period. Furthermore, as suggested by the title of the performance, rumours were circulating that the artist might soon be retiring from performance art. Anticipated as key, Partial Eclipse… *was immediately programmed in cultural venues across Europe and Canada throughout 1980 and 1982. To help promote the event, the artist was asked to provide information concerning the performance. Anticipating that each venue would subsequently require more or less the same thing, he wrote a note, which was first included in the press kit of De Appel, Amsterdam, where* Partial Eclipse… *was performed on Friday the 25 April, 1980, at 9 p.m.*

This note reads as follows:

> *"To describe* Partial Eclipse*... would be inappropriate. Suffice to recall that there were one hundred and sixty images, in approximately twenty sequences (mostly black and white), projected onto a screen with a dissolve unit so that each image flowed into the next. A man [Marc Camille Chaimowicz] interrupted these images by walking in a figure of eight, behind and in front of the screen, qualifying the images both in actuality and shadow. This passivity was countered by a woman [Helen Sear] sitting in front of the screen, who read a text in twelve sections. Background was* Discreet Music *by Brian Eno. The piece lasted for about forty minutes."*

To this description it could be added that the upbeat sound of Metropolis *by Kraftwerk opens and closes the performance; that the performer smokes a cigarette, whose smoke is caught in the light of the projector to create a "filmic" quality; that the performer wears a jacket, which is removed within the opening minutes of the performance, in order for the light coloured shirt to act as a secondary screen for the slide projection, incorporating his body into the images shown.*

The twelve sections of the script were completed in 1979. An integral part of the performance, this text was read as a monologue by then-emerging Welsh artist Helen Sear [II. 9; III. 7]. Her voice that everyone comes to think of as standard, genderless, complete, performed this text between March and June 1980, successively in Antwerp, Amsterdam, and Munich. Then, in order to make the performance easier to tour, her live reading was replaced with pre-recorded voiceover reading. As mentioned above, for each performance, an information sheet was photocopied to announce the event, as well as providing the audience with a bit of content. These last-minute photo-

copies usually included the artist's note above, as well as a selection of texts from the twelve sections of the performance script. As the artist wished at the time, this helped him to "let the text go," at least for three years.

Among these informative sheets, a luxurious three-panel folder leaflet (22.6 × 20.4 cm) was produced by Tate Britain (then Tate Gallery) where Partial Eclipse… *was performed in the Duveen Galleries, as part of the "Artists and Performance" exhibition, which ran from 22 September to 11 October, 1981. Referring to the artist's diary, the chronology of the performance was as follows:*

"September 23 / Text check.
September 27 / Technical check.
September 28–29, PE Tate, 4.30 pm
October 5, PE Tate, 4.30 pm"

To mark the occasion, a three-panel folder (22.6 × 20.4 cm) was printed by the museum. Designed by the artist, this luxurious leaflet printed on thick cream paper in shades of pale yellow, dust peppermint, and grey—"a reservoir of nuance and colours," according to him—combines script samples and black and white square photographs hereby juxtaposed in accordion fashion. Composed with extreme care and precision, the selected photographs are razor-sharp, as if to emphasise the importance of every gesture or moment. Representing flowers and cacti, details of furniture and interiors, as well as recumbent bodies suggesting a post-coital calm, these semi-autobiographical images make no real distinction between the working process, the finished object, and the observable rituals of daily life. Echoing the artist's highly staged sense of tableaux creating a scene between image and text, this three-panel folder was made available to the public in the museum until the end of the exhibition. For its part, the performance script was first published in its entirety in "Partial

Eclipse, a performance"[III. 11c], one of the seven chapters of the artist's 181-page book Café du Rêve *[III. 11], which was first published in May 1985.*

A.V.

· · · · · · · · ·

Sitting in his lounge, this temporary truce between the ideal and the real, he dwelt on change… How it is impossible to transfer his reality to another without this act of transference affecting that reality… How the transference of an experience qualifies that experience, how an idea once subjected to change is no longer that idea, how its purity is violate, modified…
from Third Section

Of the two travellers it seemed one was fragile or delicate, the other strong
… One assertive, one withdrawn … which was which was unclear, or rather, they were within one condition… As one acquired clarity, so the other lost focus…
from Fourth Section

The impossibility of possessing a feeling or sensation in its entirety … that as memento or reminder, the most acute or quintessential definition of another, is that of smell; more than a letter, lock of hair, or photograph, for both pleasure and recollection … that it is perhaps its elusiveness that makes it tantalising and missed most when separated or travelling…
from Seventh Section

His walk has detachment, is both casual and flamboyant. Oblique and qualifying image with rhythm and interruption in actuality and shadow … the notion of privacy is a characteristic,

as is a sense of ambiguity… Feelings oscillate from idea to mood, from elegance and décor to neo-metaphysic sensibility… Should these words be taken as sensuous, as didactic, perhaps as metaphor… Are these characters an extension, or fabrication and invention, … experience qualified and a fiction, both idealised and simultaneous…
from Eighth Section

The pale green walls have both of a hint of dust and peppermint… The white patterning reminiscent of many things, for some, melancholy or the graciousness of a lost age, for others, echoes or the unity of timelessness, shadows intertwine in mute dialogue with illicit sunlight, a flirtation which heightens the tranquility.
from Ninth Section

Of shared pleasures in silent dialogue at times wicked and at times pure, of whispers as punctuation… We later talked of many things, found a pace that was mutual and, of course, avoided accountability…
from Tenth Section

His search for a particular perfection was becoming stifling and constrictive, a feeling deliciously close to a state of entombment, and his foray outside that condition held an immediacy tantamount to that of a reprieve.
from Twelfth Section

They talked of shared moments and of plans… Not separating fact from fantasy, savoured a mutuality Florentine in its logic, transcending the mundane, establishing profundity… The feeling of complicity delightful, then later paradise.
Thirteenth Section

[III. 9]

Rare Is the City in Which
We Can Both Work and Dream…

(1982)

At the turn of the 1980s, Chaimowicz travelled frequently to Vienna, where his work was shown on several occasions. This included the solo exhibition "Hier und Dort," Galerie nächst St. Stephan (13 March–24 March, 1979), in which the artist presented several slide projections together with a pendulum and 1905 furniture by Austrian architect and designer Josef Hoffmann, as well as the group exhibitions "Extended Photography. The 5th International Biennial," Secession (22 October–22 November, 1981), and "Paris 1960–1980: Panorama der zeitgenössischen Kunst in Frankreich," Museum des 20. Jahrhunderts (now Belvedere 21), from 14 May to 25 July, 1982. These frequent stays were important to him, not only because of the city's rich cultural context, but also because of the cultural environment in which he began to deal with his paternal legacy [I. 16]. The Slavonic aspect of Vienna made him fantasise the social and cultural environments in which his father could have established himself as an academic. From there, Chaimowicz drew a parallel between his father, who was in Warsaw in the 1940s, and himself in Vienna in the 1980s: "a projection of the Slavonic onto Vienna," which, he admitted in retrospect, bore an uncanny resemblance to "a psycho-pattering situation."

In February 1982, Horst Gerhard Haberl, initiator of the Humanic-Artist-in-Residence-Program in Vienna, approached Chaimowicz and suggested that he come and spend several months in Vienna in the spring of 1982. Horst Gerhard Haberl had thought of him to inaugurate that artist-in-residence-program because three years earlier, in Graz, when he was director of Galerie H., which he had founded in this city in 1973, he had seen the artist perform Doubts… A Sketch for Video-Camera and Audience *(1977–1979) [I. 3], which had a positive impact on him. He had seen in this performance "the simultaneity of a double reality" that he wished to be able to infuse into the artist-in-residence-program, and that Chaimowicz might, perhaps, contribute to activating from the outset.*

The artist stayed in Vienna from 31 March to 30 May, 1982. Both artistically and individually, this nine-week stay in Vienna was crucial to him. Chaimowicz also admitted in retrospect that it was "a return to childhood." Not only because of the paternal legacy, but also because, not speaking German, he found himself in a situation of de-socialisation, being almost alone 24 / 7. As a result, the artist developed many works.

Over the course of his stay, indeed, Chaimowicz finalised a written piece entitled "Le Parc…" illustrated with black and white photographs. This text depicts a specific urban setting, which offers the protagonist consolation. Designed by the artist, "Le Parc…" was published in English in the newspaper Österreichischer Kulturservice in April 1982. Conceived as "a sullen wistful narrative," it would subsequently be reprinted as Chapter 2 of Café du Rêve *[III. 11b], a 181-page artist book composed of texts by the artist, designs, drawings, and photographs, co-published on 9 May, 1985 by the Galerie de France and Editions du Regard, Paris, and republished in London in September of the same year by Thames and Hudson [III. 11]. Furthermore, Chaimowicz wrote "Chorus, a letter from Vienna" [III. 11d], an illustrated text that encapsulates the artist's Viennese experience. In addition, he deeply engaged with the craft products of the Wiener Werkstätte and Viennese architecture, which provided him with important stimuli that he is still imbued with today. Collected, in part, in the letter mentioned above, these stimuli linked to architecture and design in Vienna, and would be reconsidered by the artist from a socio-political angle in "A letter, transcribed" [III. 26] on the occasion of his 2009 solo exhibition at Secession.*

On 28 May, Galerie H. Air, the exhibition space linked to

the Humanic-Artist-in-Residence-Program, was inaugurated. On that occasion, the new works by Chaimowicz were pre-sented. For the first time, Vienna Triptych, Leaning… and Surrounded by Chorus Girls and Sentinels… *(1982), was shown. Comprising six glass panels, painted photo-graphs, and eight gloss painted wooden panels (1.80 metres high, approx. 6 metres long), this key work, displayed leaning upright against the gallery wall, intersperses decorated painted panels ambiguously positioned between abstract painting and interior decoration, with glass panels featuring square black and white photographs that evoke fugitive contents and views of Vienna. This formal reduction to a two-dimensional plane is paradigmatic for the artist's development towards works and spatial compositions characterised by a condensed formal aesthetic, which would distinguish the artist's furniture, fabrics, and curved partition walls from the mid-1980s [III. 10], as well as the multi-coloured patterns of* Café du Rêve.

Also included in this exhibition was North Africa Song, *a nine-page collage piece depicting "a return to the French romance with its colonial past: a tone poem of touristic views and joyful arabesques," as Jean Fisher put it in* Past Imperfect. Marc Camille Chaimowicz 1972–1982 *(Liverpool: Bluecoat Gallery et al., 1983, p. 47). Conceived as a light counterpoint to "Le Parc…" [III. 11b], that collage piece would later be published as Chapter 3 of* Café du Rêve. *Containing no text, that chapter is therefore not included in this anthology.*

In conjunction with this exhibition, a 16-page "poor image quality" stapled leaflet (26 × 21 cm) was produced by the Humanic program. Designed by Chaimowicz, this "small illustrated pamphlet" includes a short introduction by Horst

Gerhard Haberl, a text by the artist, and a few illustrations documenting his new works. Written in Vienna, the text reproduced below was originally published on a double-page spread, in English on the left-hand-page and in German on the right. Displayed inside accordion-tilted squares, the text was surrounded with animated curved patterns designed by the artist and covering the double spread page. Addressing his complex relationship with Viennese architects and designers such as Adolf Loos and Josef Frank, this text briefly features the versatile premises of the artist's interest in both architecture with sculpture quality [I. 21; II. 10; III. 11d, 23] and applied and decorative arts in relation to fine arts [III. 9, 15]. With apparent lightness, this text anticipates the artist's interest in creating a holistic and aesthetic environment in which socio-political upheavals and the search for the pleasure principle might converge.

If Chaimowicz was inspired by the "enlightened patronage," which is inherent to the city, his stay in Vienna took place in great solitude. Gradually, however, a sense of community emerged from the context. Thanks to the cafés and bars where the artist used to spend time at night, he "was able to absorb some of the sociability of the city." So, when he returned to Vienna in 2009 for his solo exhibition at Secession, the first sentence of the text reproduced below, written twenty-seven years ago, remains relevant: "Rare is the city in which one can both work and dream…"

A.V.

• • • • • • • • • •

Rare is the city in which we can both work and dream … and here in this city: grand, mysterious, to a stranger relaxed, I have been able to do both… And yet, have we not each, on occasion, sat in a café or bar of a distant land only to think "Why travel when I can equally well be bored at home?"

… There was an element of risk to this new experiment… (I might, after all, have merely wandered about the city, restless or enjoyed its splendid diversions, exclusively) but also one of trust. And it was this aspect of enlightened patronage, which I found conducive to creativity…

We each have our churches… And here mine has been the seventeenth century Jesuitenkirche by Andrea Pozzo. My café was the Prückle (décor and furniture by Oswald Haerdtl, 1954) and I have especially enjoyed the Wunder-Bar (interior by Hermann Czech, 1975) both for its ambience and clientele. I arrived with, predictably, Josef Hoffmann as a hero (but although a fine designer of furniture have found his building disappointingly two-dimensional) and am leaving having discovered the excellent work of Josef Frank, been singularly impressed by Adolf Loos, and having for myself confirmed the genius of Otto Wagner…
… If it is a happy artist that works well, then in this enchanting city prone to melancholy and gaiety, I have worked well…

[III. 10]

Extracts From a Letter to Michael Regan

(1984)

In 1983, whilst working as a curator for the Arts Council of Great Britain, Michael Regan came up with the idea of an exhibition which would take the form of interior rooms, each one designed by a prominent British artist. Among the artists Regan approached was Chaimowicz, who agreed to take on the commission. The result was an immersive room, painted in a unifying blue-grey tint, (entitled thirty-nine years later Rachel and Graham*), combining modernist influences with new furniture pieces. The other artists involved in the exhibition were Anthony Caro, Richard Hamilton, and Howard Hodgkin.*

The exhibition "Four Rooms" opened in London in the winter of 1984, not in a public gallery but in the department store Liberty's of Regent Street, causing a stir in the art-press and catching the imagination of the public. "With the course of the time, the exhibition can seem provocative as this was fine arts from the State," recalled Chaimowicz. "However, the context was interesting since it was quite easy for the department store to find sponsors, and pay a lot for new productions, which predates the PPP System (private/public) that is common in the UK, from prisons to railways." The exhibition was presented in London from 10 February through 10 March, 1984, and subsequently toured under the supervision of the Arts Council of Great Britain at Central Art Gallery, Wolverhampton (7 April–12 May, 1984); Southampton Art Gallery (26 May–8 July, 1984); Newport Museum and Art Gallery (21 July–25 August, 1984); Aberdeen Art Gallery (8 September–7 October, 1984); Mappin Art Gallery, Sheffield (20 October–18 November, 1984), and finally was toured by the British Council as a key visual exhibit, in 1986, as part of The Adelaide Festival, Adelaide, South Australia.

The youngest artist to take part in this exhibition was Chaimowicz.When he was contacted, he had in mind a "room based on an amalgam of many low-cost European hotel rooms … from a turn-of-the-century sensibility." In his room, with no specific title at the time, were presented eight new works by the artist developed in relation to architecture and the domestic environment, including:

> *– A grey-painted prototype of a curved partition screen that would later be developed with a carpenter in 1986–87;*
> *– An oblique blue-grey wall box measuring approximately 170 × 130 × 60 cm, inside of which was continuously back-projected a sequence of slides "crystallizing a probable narration between Rachel and Graham, as in a picture-story" which was shot by the artist in a warehouse in East London, where his environment for "Four Rooms" was provisionally constructed;*
> *– Stained glass window (23 × 152 cm) produced by John Stevens in 1983—at once an ode to Liberty's and a modernist reference to the spirit of "The Charter of Athens"—which is today inserted into one wall of the artist's apartment in Tyers street, London;*
> *– Desk… On Decline, a 213 × 73 × 61 cm desk made in 1983 with medium density fibreboard finished in extra matt grey lacquer produced by Pearl Dot Workshops, London;*
> *– Chest of Drawers, a 188 × 66 × 58 cm piece of furniture produced in 1983 with medium density fibreboard finished in extra matt grey lacquer and leather handles;*
> *– A prototype of Sofa, a 147 × 61 × 165 cm couch in wood produced in 1983, including upholstery by Duresta and lacquer work by Pearl Dot Workshops, London;*

– Stool, a 55 × 35 × 30 cm tubular frame with stove enamelled finish produced in 1983 by Haley Sharpe Associates, Leicester;

– Sideboard, a 230 × 110 × 90 cm corner console made in Birdseye maple veneered plywood with exposed edges, finished in clear lacquer Perspex, produced in 1983 by Pearl Dot Workshops, London, upon which was displayed a tiny bouquet of orange and yellow daffodils in a 12.5 × 12.5 cm vase with a "Moonstone" glaze designed by Keith Murray in 1933, produced by Wedgwood. In addition, also displayed in the room, was a plywood chair from 1934 by Alvar Aalto, a tube lamp from 1935 as well as Tour de Nesle, *a 200 × 200 cm wool rug designed circa 1920s, both by Eileen Gray, and a glass table lamp signed on the glass V. de Wigger.*

As listed above, Chaimowicz's participation in "Four Rooms" was developed with craft companies and artisans, which proved to be decisive in the artist's work. Ten years later, indeed, he would tell Alain Coulange [I. 6], "The particular setting of 'Four Rooms' enabled me to imagine an 'alternative' model: I realised that I could assume a certain social role by occasionally embracing the area of the applied arts." By inquiring into the "boundaries" of social norms such as public and private and interior decoration and architecture, as in the studio flat he had on Approach Road, London, between 1975 and 1979 [III. 5], the furniture pieces he conceived in the early 1980s crystallised his ideas "on the dialectic between the fine arts and design" [III. 15] that he would synthesise in 1987 in his eponymous text. Furthermore, this room anticipated his interest in having works by other artists included in his exhibitions, a curatorial dynamic which he would experiment with further from the early 2000s, on many occasions [I. 8, 11; II. 12]. Following that logic,

Chaimowicz emblematically reproduced a view of his room at Liberty's of Regent Street on the front side of the invitation card for "Jean Cocteau, a project by Marc Camille Chaimowicz," Norwich Gallery, Norwich, in 2003, in which, for instance, Sofa, *1983, was inserted.*

Chaimowicz's participation in "Four Rooms" was complemented by the sale, at Liberty's, of works created for the exhibition. First, Garden Dusk, *a hand screen wallpaper printed by John Perry & Sons in two colour ways—beige on grey and green on beige—and produced by Coles Wallpapers. Second, that of* Neon Lines, *a cotton and resin fabric produced in four colour ways—blue, yellow, grey, beige—by Warner & Sons Limited, a British company known for supplying exceptional upholstery fabrics woven from the finest silk since 1870. In addition to the works produced by the artist in relation to the exhibition, those two also confirmed the artist's interest in the possible crossover between fine art and design.*

Although, quite exceptionally for an exhibition of this time, a scenography firm designed the walls dividing the spaces allocated to each artist, Chaimowicz subsequently had to split up his "room" due to storage problems, with the result that its elements disappeared over time. As for the furniture pieces listed above, they were later presented independently from each other in various contexts and refabricated in some cases. In October 2007, at the Frieze Fair in London, Cabinet sold to the Alexander Schröder Collection a detailed, large-scale 3-D model of the installation that Chaimowicz had kept with him since 1984, the last trace of his participation in the "Four Rooms" exhibition, which had hardly ever been shown before, and a large ektachrome, which was included in Gallery 2 of the Saint-Étienne exhibition "Marc Camille

Chaimowicz. *Zig Zag and Many Ribbons…"(19 November, 2022–10 April, 2023) [III. 29].*

In conjunction with the 1984 exhibition, a 28-page illustrated catalogue entitled Four Rooms: An Arts Council touring exhibition *was produced by the Arts Council of Great Britain. Sold for £2, this publication edited by Michael Regan includes an introduction by English critic and prolific writer Reyner Banham, who was best known at the time for his theoretical treatise* Theory and Design in the First Machine Age *(1960) and his 1971 book* Los Angeles: The Architecture of Four Ecologies. *For their part, each of the four artists involved in the exhibition were offered a double page section inside the publication. Chaimowicz decided to publish some "Extracts of a letter to Michael Regan" with whom he is not sure of having really corresponded—"probably not." The epistolary format was, the artist said in retrospect, "a symptomatic way to make cohesive various issues linked to my contribution to 'Four Rooms,' yet in a fictional form," which, incidentally, the word "extracts" in the title both reinforces and leaves open to other content. Written in Paris in September 1983 for publication, this text is an opportunity for the artist to "re-affirm some basic principles of modernism … currently under such attack…" While reflecting on "the traditional antipathy between architect and designer—between the manipulator of space as container and the producer of objects that inhabit this space," Chaimowicz extends his observations to "those masters, perhaps androgynous, whose genius, partly, was surely the overcoming of this dichotomy; Frank Lloyd Wright, Eileen Gray, Adolf Loos, Le Corbusier, and perhaps Mallet-Stevens."*

Although the last paragraph of the letter is enclosed in quotation marks, it is left unattributed. Taken from Gaston

Bachelard's The Poetics of Space *(1957), the quotation
addresses the notion of "reverie" or "daydreaming," which the
artist has been exploring in his work since the mid-1970s as a
creative space between work and dream. Throughout his career,
Chaimowicz has often referred to this book, which examines,
through literary images, the imaginary dimension of our relationship to space, focusing on the spaces of intimate happiness
[I. 8, 15, 16; III. 5, 6, 22c, 22d]. Moreover, by speculating on
how imagination fills a space with spirit and meaning and,
conversely, how space evokes fantasy, feeling, and memory in
the imagination of its occupant, this book was decisive for the
artist in his approach to the exhibition space as a possible
site for a conversation with its occupant, something that the
fictional aspects of his emblematic participation in the "Four
Rooms" exhibition, as well as the casting of objects characterising it, publicly initiated.*

A.V.

· · · · · · · · · ·

Dear Michael,

You may recall my first intention, that of the film project… It
now seems like such a long time ago! We talked then of architecture and of language, unsure as to which was the fictive. We
talked more of *a* cinema than of a film, because having no actual
wish to film I was free then to start wherever … and chose to
begin at the end, finding as location for an imaginary premiere a
fine if dilapidated cinema in Deptford, intriguing chiefly for the
relationship of the facade to the body of the building.

We were constructing a false or reversed history, and then talked of a scenario between the protagonist, whose home I was to be designing, and his accomplice, or perhaps of a frozen moment on an imaginary film set, a single frame in three dimensions.

We talked of the phenomenology of furniture and of the traditional antipathy between architect and designer—between the manipulator of space as container and the producer of objects that inhabit this space. Then of those masters, perhaps androgynous, whose genius, partly, was surely the overcoming of this dichotomy; Frank Lloyd Wright, Eileen Gray, Adolf Loos, Le Corbusier, and perhaps Mallet-Stevens.

I then travelled, and we lost touch but gradually, and perhaps as a happy accidental echo of history, my ideas are acquiring a rationale ... and as I hope you will see from these drawings the interior has become simpler, purer, more lucid ... as the narrative has become tangential, the drama understated, so the room seems to emerge proper, and in her own right as of central or equal character...

If previous interiors, their aesthetic based on an amalgam of numerous low-priced European hotel rooms, were turn-of-the century in their sensibility, and largely comment on the actual or the found, then this interior is a constructed space set firmly in the twentieth century. And, incidentally, what good fortune it is that I am able, in all modesty, to reaffirm some basic principles of modernism, currently under such attack...

Its location is in the centre of an imaginary city—a hybrid of parts of Paris, London, and Vienna—and yet closest to the sea. It is on one corner of an apartment, on the fourth or fifth floor and on a street junction overlooking both a railway terminus and a market. It is by implication therefore both here yet elsewhere ... and although issues of function (both of the artist and from the

objects) are queried, the nature of the room is consciously free of
role and non-specific … hence, perhaps, within its purity, a sense
of ambiguity or of disquiet…

Enough sophistry… I have recently come upon the Villas of Pliny.
Have you heard of these? Caius Plinius was a diplomat in ancient
Rome who is chiefly remembered for his eloquent letters … and
especially for those describing in great detail his country Villas
in Laurentinum on the coast of Tuscany. In order to entice his
friends, Pliny describes the locales, the extent of the grounds and
gives a room-by-room account of function, characteristic, and ori-
entation of each space. But because no archaeological trace of the
Villas has been found, whether they were ever built remains a
mystery. They have become mythic … and since the Renaissance
a standard pedagogical model and basis of countless reconstructions. What is charming is that notwithstanding the extraordinary richness of descriptive detail in the letters, each interpretation is so different. Due perhaps to the lack of any ground plans
and of a total dependency on the written word each generation
seems to have projected its own values and aspirations… Does
this not therefore undermine the presumed objective exactitude
of words? And yet … is it *because* of words that they were built
that these villas have outlived those built but of stone?

"How concrete everything becomes in the world of the spirit
when an object (a mere door) can give images of hesitation,
temptation, desire, security, welcome and respect!…
And then, onto what, toward what, do doors open? Do they
open for the world of men, or for the world of solitude?"

Paris, September 1983

[III. 11]

Café du Rêve

(1985)

In response to the pressure resulting from the media and social attention paid to his early performances and "scattered environments," Chaimowicz began to think of "alternatives." Reluctant to perform in public as early as 1973, he also sensed at the time there was a growing institutionalisation of installation art. While distancing himself from the realm of performance, however, he did not completely abandon performance art overnight. In the second part of the 1970s, Chaimowicz actively reported on performance in art magazines such as Studio International, Art Monthly *and* Flash Art *[II. 1, 2, 3, 4, 5, 6, 7, 8, 9], while preparing* Partial Eclipse *[III. 8, 11c], which he performed across Europe and Canada from March 1980 to December 1982, thus acting out in person his own* eclipse *from the world of performance.*

Coincidentally, at the end of 1974, Chaimowicz was given the opportunity to move into a four-room apartment over two floors in Approach Road, Bethnal Green, London. The bulk of his work would be made in two rooms (sitting room and bedroom) until the end of the decade. Testifying to the singularity of his expansive inner vision of interior space, and blending the seductions of a greenish-grey domestic environment offering unexpected twists and turns with a refreshing sense of decadence, the five years the artist spent in this studio flat enabled him to meditate on the simultaneity of life and dreams jointly developed in his work [III. 5, 6, 7]. During that period, Chaimowicz produced a large body of photographic series that he disseminated as "illustrations" in some of his texts [I. 13, 17; II. 7; III. 6, 7, 8, 11c, e] and works [III. 6, 7, 11c]. When Nigel Greenwood, the British gallerist and publisher of the time, visited the artist in Bethnal Green in early September 1977, he was struck by the multiplicity of interactions between text and image featured in his work. And when the artist showed him the work that was to be premiered in the forthcoming group exhibition "Nine Works for Tape / Slide Sequence" [II. 7], Chaimowicz remembers Greenwood saying "Let's make a book of it!" Designed by Chaimowicz in just a few days, the 16-page publication Dream, an Anecdote by Marc Camille Chaimowicz Dreamt in the Winter and Recalled in the Spring of 1977, *was published in early October 1977 by Nigel Greenwood Inc Ltd Books, London, and presented as part of the group show "… Additions to New Editions …" at Nigel Greenwood Inc Ltd, London, from 18 October through 5 November, 1977. Combining image and text with no hierarchy between the two, this work of art in book form enabled Chaimowicz to lay the intellectual and sensitive foundations of the "alternative" to performance art that he was seeking at the time. The possibilities inherent in this "humble and uncanny" book, which the artist would later link to those of the screen, struck him so much that he soon embarked on, as he would acknowledge in retrospect, "a new book adventure with no clear goal," the result of which was* Café du Rêve *in May 1985.*

In an unpublished interview with a member of staff at Tate Britain (then Tate Gallery) on 8 January, 1983, following Tate's acquisition of Le Désert… *[III. 11a] from Nigel Greenwood Inc Ltd, London, where the work had recently been shown in the exhibition "Maquettes…" (10 December, 1981–30 January, 1982), Chaimowicz discussed the origins of* Café du Rêve:

> *"I suspect I remember a kind of frustration with certain forms of work… one of which was performance … the performances I did were invariably very introspective. I was intellectually and philosophically drawn to the need [to work] in that kind of a direct manner but I would tend to retreat into myself by working obliquely and time*

and space seemed more appropriately translated into the physicality of the book ... the actual activity of turning even a page, the privacy of the book, the form of the book fascinates me... I think there are a number of roads that led to the book ... one was to do, oddly enough, with some screens... I did a show for Nigel [Greenwood] at the end of 1979 [III. 7]. I did three screens, in the most overt sense manifested with ambiguity, screens being something which both reveal and conceal... which have a back and a front... which can be stored away easily enough or brought out ... I found books, a logical extension of screens in a formal sense..."

Designed by the artist in collaboration with a London-based typographer and a typist, Café du Rêve *is structured like a diary that travels between the desert, the park, and the hotel room. Embodying the singular itinerary of an epistolary journey, this artist book (21 × 26 cm) is based on non-linear reverie and daydreaming explorations that reflect the artist's identity in a suspended time of sorts.*

Reflecting on the start of the project, Chaimowicz recalled: "I was inspired by 1930s magazines such as L'Oeil *or* Documents, *in which anthropology and ethnography are treated both textually and visually." In the early 1980s, Chaimowicz also had in mind Man Ray's image-sequences and photo-essays, two forms of visual storytelling that take the viewer on a narrative journey. And so, as the project developed, the artist specified in retrospect, "I was coordinating a work of art in book form, I was not curating it. I don't like that word!"*

Conceived independently from each other between 1979 and 1985, the seven chapters in Café du Rêve *differ from each other in length, size, topic, typography, design, and number of pages. Combining texts, notes, postcards, advertisements, Xerox paper, acetate, silkscreen, and photographs that sometimes interact with drawings from textile prints, the chapters are organised as follows:*

1. "Le Désert..."
2. "Le Parc..."
3. "North Africa Song"
4. "Partial Eclipse, a Performance"
5. "Chorus, a Letter From Vienna"
6. "Liaison"
7. "Le Select..."

Each chapter has its own specificity, internal structure, mood and variation. While Chapter 1 documents a work process, Chapter 2 evokes a pastiche of nineteenth century writing, Chapter 3 deals with the non-verbal, Chapter 4 is a performance script, Chapter 5 unfolds a threatened narrative, Chapter 6 explores an imaginary liaison, and Chapter 7 invokes the hotel's "ubiquity" in the form of a letter. Intended for publication, only one chapter—"North Africa Song"—is not reproduced below as it contains illustrations only. With the exception of "Le Parc..." [III. 11b], which was first published in April 1982 in English as a centrefold in the Austrian newspaper Österreichischer Kulturservice [III. 9], the other chapters were first published in Café du Rêve.

Discussing the editorial structure of the book on 8 January, 1983, in the above-mentioned unpublished interview with a member of staff at Tate, the artist states:

> *"It's difficult for me to be explicit. I suppose if one were to use a contemporary metaphor I would in a way see it not unlike the memorable albums by groups, by rock*

groups for example, that I have high regard for … each group I've liked has produced one or two albums, one or two have perhaps produced more, which are so good that each track has the potential of being a successful single."

This book, the artist would confess in 1994 [I. 5], "was conceived like a record, whose every chapter was a song." The editorial structure of Café du Rêve, *as Jean Fisher describes in* Past Imperfect. Marc Camille Chaimowicz 1972-1982 *(Liverpool: Bluecoat Gallery et al., 1983, p. 47), "does not present sequential time, but an oscillation back and forth— the possibility of a timelessness—where to open at any page is to find a single and unique moment of reflection." To specify this, she suggests "this book is the vessel which, like Marcel Duchamp's* Boîte-en-valise *[1936–1941], embodies the territory through which the artist has travelled." Describing in greater details the interplay between image, text, and design that characterises this travelogue involving a retrospective examination of several years' work, Fisher stated two years before the book went to print:*

> *"The mood is one of quietude and serenity, a deliberate lack of incidence which allows the image to act as a screen onto which can be projected the fantasy and drama of the 'other scene' relayed by the text. It is a strategy of interlocution between two textual spaces which was subsequently developed through* Here and There *[III. 6] and* Partial Eclipse *[III. 8, 11c] but become finally realised in* Café du Rêve…"(in op. cit., p. 30)

Conceived like an auto-fiction scrapbook with no narrative link albeit a graphic and visual continuity, Café du Rêve *invites the reader to experience a fiction of one's self—perhaps that of the artist as a writer. However, as Chaimowicz told*

Philippe Cuenat in 1987 [I. 4], "the aim of Café du Rêve *was to produce a book that was not founded on the myth of the artist but would help to redefine the framework in which an artist can work and reach out to an audience." Combining micro-details and universal experience,* Café du Rêve *is a multi-faceted work of art, which the six chapters reproduced below without their original iconography or stunning design in nicotine grey, ivory, smoky yellow, beige, and menthol tones partially reflect. This is why, as with* Dream, an Anecdote, 1977 *[III. 5], or* The World of Interiors, *2007 [III. 22], the artist's two other highly crafted artist books, we recommend that you refer to the original publication.*

How did such an amazing book project come about, both editorially and financially? In preparation for the group exhibition "Un certain art anglais…," Musée d'Art Moderne de Paris (20 January–12 March, 1979), in which facets of conceptual and perceptive artistic practices in Great Britain in the 1970s were presented, Chaimowicz, whose work was featured in the exhibition, met Catherine Thieck, the exhibition coordinator. From their first working meeting, they immediately hit it off. A year later, Thieck left the museum to become the director of Galerie de France. Founded in Paris in February 1942, Galerie de France was identified in the early 1980s as a pioneering art gallery that promoted Paris-based artists such as Pierre Alechinsky, Victor Brauner, Hans Hartung, as well as, in the 1960s, North American artists, then unknown in France, such as Willem de Kooning, Franz Kline, Robert Motherwell, Jackson Pollock, Ad Reinhardt, and Mark Tobey. In 1981, at Thieck's instigation, the gallery relocated to 54, rue de la Verrerie, two blocks away from the brand-new Centre Pompidou. At the time, the gallery was famously supported by André Rousselet—a 1980s business tycoon, founder of Canal+ TV, CEO of the G7 Cab Company, and close friend of the recently elected French President François

Mitterrand—who not only enabled Thieck to continue developing the gallery estate, but also to implement a new program involving some of the artists of the day. In the spring of 1982, Thieck met with one of her good friends, Gabriella Cardazzo, the co-director of the Galleria del Cavallino in Venice and Milan, who had just returned from a trip to London where she visited the artist in preparation for his forthcoming solo show "Marc Camille Chaimowicz" at the gallery in Venice (23 October–16 November, 1982). Cardazzo was so impressed by the artist's new works on paper that she advised Thieck to see them in person, mentioning at the same time that the artist's project was to bring them together in a single volume. As a result, Thieck, who had planned to go to London in the near future, contacted the artist and suggested a visit. On the spot, Chaimowicz showed her his recent works on paper and introduced her to the book project, which immediately won her over. As Chaimowicz later reflected, Thieck said, "I know someone who could make it happen." Before leaving the artist, Thieck invited him, as he put it, "to do a one-shot solo exhibition . . . like a museum show, but in a gallery." Back in Paris, Thieck contacted José Alvarez, founder of the Editions du Regard in Paris in 1978, to tell him about Chaimowicz's book project she wished to publish to coincide with his forthcoming solo exhibition at the gallery. Sometime later, on closer examination of the publication project, José Alvarez was struck by the synergy between the editorial concept and the aesthetic qualities of the book. The deal was done and the book's production began. The artist recalls: "Although the six first chapters of Café du Rêve *were progressively hand-delivered in a small aluminium case, which I still have, to Editions du Regard every time one was ready, in the end, nobody read anything. The good thing, fortunately, is that from start to finish, there was no interference." At the same time, Alvarez contacted Thomas Neurath, then Managing Director of Thames & Hudson in London, who agreed to take part in the project. Printed in Milan on*

29 March, 1985, this 181-page volume was co-published by Galerie de France and Editions du Regard, Paris, and Thames & Hudson, London. The difference between the two publishing houses can be seen on the dust jacket, title page, and colophon page of each copy.

Oscillating between indeterminacy and distance, the fiction that runs through Café du Rêve *fuels a travelogue that can be seen as "the record of a journey through the time and space of memory and experience which nurture creative life," as Jean Fisher put it in 1983 (in op. cit., p. 47). As an echo, and probably because* Café du Rêve *is the artist's first major publication, he dedicated it to his parents, with whom, perhaps, the cover image is also linked.*

Reproduced on the book jacket and cover, a small square black and white photograph of a 1950s crêperie restaurant called "Café du Rêve" provides the book its title. The artist found the picture in Nantes, following a break-up with his lover at the time. The timeless photograph is printed on small, multi-directional curved patterns of colour drawn on a burgundy background. In 2009 [I. 13], Chaimowicz discussed the purpose of this image:

> *"I think the photograph that I happened to find in Nantes of the 'Café du Rêve' was a good example of a simple visual form that said everything I wanted to say. It implied a kind of sociability in a place where you get a wide cross-section of people, all dealing with their own solitude. They go to the 'Café du Rêve' for a number of reasons: to pick someone up, or to get drunk, or to find warmth, or to engage in social intercourse. But because the title is* Café du Rêve *it also implies something else: that one can transcend and actually go into reverie ... The everyday in this photograph is not any old café. It has specificity."*

*This photograph might explain why Matthew Higgs, Director
of White Columns, New York, once mentioned to the artist that
he once found a copy of* Café du Rêve *in a second-hand book
in San Francisco … in the cookery section!*
Café du Rêve *was first presented at Galerie de France from 9
May to 15 June, 1985, in conjunction with the exhibition of
the artist at the gallery. On this occasion, the artist had superimposed books on top of the other, like an endless column "à
la Brancusi." Displayed in the gallery lobby, this stack of books
was complemented by copies of the book, which were made
available to the public for both consultation and sale. Four
months later, the Thames & Hudson copies of* Café du Rêve
*were first presented at Nigel Greenwood Inc Ltd, London, as
part of the exhibition "Marc C Chaimowicz, recent paintings
and sketches" (18 September–19 October, 1985). After* Café
du Rêve *was presented twice in the same year, and although
it was inconceivable at the time to produce an autonomous
work in book form, recalls the artist, "I was asked if I'd be interested in doing a French version of the book. Why not, I replied,
without really understanding the need. And I immediately
specified that the paper I had in mind for this possible edition
was scritta paper…" which, given the book's specifications, was
probably meant as a way of saying: "Yes, but no thanks!"*

A.V.

[III. 11a]

Le Désert…

(1985)

Produced in 1981, Le Désert... is an original work whose panels are dated and numbered by the artist and signed "Marc C.C. 81." Pairing images and short typescripts, plus a final two-page text on decorative pages, "Le Désert..." is also the first 24-page chapter of Café du Rêve *to be completed. Jean Fischer described it in* Past Imperfect. Marc Camille Chaimowicz 1972–1982 *(Liverpool: Bluecoat Gallery et al., 1983, p. 47) as "a journey within a journey that pivots around the repeated image of a French postcard illustrating date palms in a desert." At the time of completion, the artist was also working on Chapter 2 ("Le Parc..."), Chapter 3 ("North Africa Song"), and Chapter 4 ("Partial Eclipse, a performance").*

Presented in the exhibition "Maquettes...," Nigel Greenwood Inc Ltd, London (10 December, 1981–30 January, 1982), along with five folded-screen maquettes, the first version of Desk on Decline *[Ill. 10, 15] and* Pyramid, Le Désert... *was purchased in January 1982 by Alan Bowness, then Director of the Tate Britain (then Tate Gallery), thanks to the "Grant-In-Aid" allowing the museum director to purchase artworks outside the museum's commissions. As a result, the work entered the museum collection right after the purchase, which subsequently gave rise to a fully detailed catalogue entry published in* The Tate Gallery 1982–84: Illustrated Catalogue of Acquisitions *(London: Tate Gallery, 1986), later made available online on Tate's website. According to this catalogue entry, in which both the artwork and the chapter are described in relation to each other and duly contextualised, it is said that:*

> *"When acquired by the Gallery, [Le Désert...] consisted of 18 single and one double sheet of card, supporting photographs collaged onto decorative backgrounds of the artist's own design, and in places accompanied by short texts. After acquisition, all but the title page were framed in pairs, on*

the instruction of the artist. At five intervals throughout the sequence, a collaged sheet has been paired with a blank sheet."

For this reason, although originally comprising 18 plates as a work of art, the chapter comprises 24 pages, which includes blank and title pages.

From the beginning of the project, the artist placed "Le Désert…" at the opening of Café du Rêve. *With a title borrowed from a short 1950 text by Albert Camus, who at the time felt the hostile emptiness of the desert to be the ideal place to depict the characters in his novels, a place where man feels like an alien with no chance of happiness or hope for the future, Chaimowicz, by contrast, explored it thirty years later in an essentially optimistic acceptance of the imperfection of "real life", probably inspired by one of his first "scattered environments"* Celebration? Realife *(1972) [III. 2, 3, 4]. "Le Désert…" explores a dilemma. As a journey into an imaginary desert, this chapter immediately suggests the possibility of an escape into solitude. However, as late Welsh art critic and editor Stuart Morgan put it in 1983 in "Marc Camille Chaimowicz: Design for living," published in* Past Imperfect. Marc Camille Chaimowicz 1972–1982 *(Liverpool: Bluecoat Gallery et al., 1983, p. 63), "The desert is less a physical space than a mental construct." Therefore, as the work unfolds, notes Morgan, the artist takes us beyond "the extremes of isolation and the quest for perfection and the resulting engulfment, toward an essentially optimistic acceptance of the imperfection of 'real life.'" As if to underline this point, the artist would later speak of the desert "as a temporary truce between the ideal and the real." Placed at the beginning of the book, "Le Désert…" also acts as a preface to* Café du Rêve.

A.V.

For Angelo B

"I understand the need to frequent the marketplace ... but miss the chances of going into the desert."
—Cardinal Hume, Thames Television 1981.

How do you think it feels

How do you think it feels
When you're speeding and lonely
Come here baby
How do you think it feels
When all you can say is if only

If only I had a little—
If only I had some change
If only, if only, only
How do you think it feels
And when do you think it stops?

How do you think it feels
When you've been up for days
Come down here Mama
Hunting around and always—ooh
Cause you're afraid of sleeping

How do you think it feels
To feel like a wolf and foxy
How do you think it feels
To always make love by proxy?
How do you think it feels
And when do you think it stops?
When do you think it stops?

From *Berlin* Lou Reed 1973
Sunbury Music Ltd.

"Oh, Michael! Every joy is always awaiting us, but it must always be the only one; It insists on finding the bed empty and demands us a widower's welcome."

"Oh, Michael! Every joy is like the manna of the desert which corrupts from one day to the next; It is like the fountain of Ameles, whose waters, says Plato, could never be kept in any vase…"

Tunis! The quality of the light here is not strength but abundance. The shade is still full of it. The air itself is like a luminous fluid in which everything is steeped; one bathes, one swims in it. This land of pleasure satisfies desire without appeasing it, and desire is sharpened by satisfaction.

Poverty is a slave driver; in return for food, men give their grudging labour; all work that is not joyous is wretched, I thought, and paid many of them to rest. 'Don't work,' I said, 'you hate it.' In imagination, I bestowed on each of them that leisure without which nothing can blossom— neither vice nor art.
—André Gide, *The Immoralist*

The desert…

No longer carrying other keys but his own, he walked lightly and
well…
Accounts settled, he then tackled the clearing of his garden …
and to his surprise,
realised that in his zeal, had rid himself not only of the
overgrowth, but also of
plants and buds … of future promises…

The horizon was awesome in its vastness

… he recalled the desert…

Consider whether the passionate are consumed by passion, the
powerful ruined by
power … the hedonists wasted by pleasures, the submissive by
subservience … that
those who court silence, forfeit the benefits of dialogue…

He now took orders from no one, was no longer accountable…
Alone, impulsive and carefree, he realised that he had, in his daring,
inadvertently achieved a state casual
only in appearance, and close to suffocation in effect… Because the less
his needs, the
fewer were the demands made of him and the greater his retreat,
the more infrequent the enquiries…

He was now left in peace but the price had been harsh
and in his quest for the
absolute, was appointing himself his own executioner…
What had begun as an
infatuation with choice, now left him with her opposite…
Noting it better to travel alone than in false company,

he reconsidered the desert…

as magnet to those who seek truth, mirror of serenity,
as image of openness and context for privacy,
mirage and oasis, cacti and hyena,
as quiet illusion of sullen staticity…
as cruel wasteland, fierce desolation, unforgiving and extreme…
The black texts of the nomads echoing a deep silence,
both of wonder and fearful…
wanton and sensual as in French literature,
a colonisation, body to the Parisian mind…
as sublime in appearance yet shifty as any urban drifter…
sanctuary to the spirit, haven of amorality…

he remembered the Cardinal*

reconnected the telephone, glanced at his correspondence …
dressed and was last
seen walking, well and lightly, towards a land of discourse and of
dance, of
intoxication and gaiety…

* Editor's note. Cardinal Hume was the surprising and radical appointment by the Holy See to Westminster in 1976. Plucked from a sheltered life as Benedictine student, monk, then Abbot at Ampleforth Abbey, he reintroduced progressive thought, and therefore doubt into the Church, thus qualifying a moribund and reactionary order with timely relevance.

[III. 11b]

Le Parc…

(1982)

Chapter 2 of Café du Rêve, *"Le Parc…" was completed in 1981. At the time of its completion, Chaimowicz was also working on Chapter 1 ("Le Désert…"), Chapter 3 ("North Africa Song"), and Chapter 4 ("Partial Eclipse, a performance"). Pairing image and text, "Le Parc…" depicts a specific urban setting that offers the protagonist consolation. The only chapter in black and white, "Le Parc…" evokes a pastiche of nineteenth century writing, in which images serve as visual interludes to the text.*

First published in April 1982 in Österreichischer Kulturservice *no. 11 as a double-sided centrefold in conjunction with Chaimowicz's artist residency at the Humanic Program, Vienna [III. 9], this newspaper centrefold was subsequently made available at Galerie H. Air, the exhibition space linked to the residency program, where the artist exhibited new works until the end of June 1982. Divided into three columns interrupted by 14 black and white photographs, this newspaper page was designed by Chaimowicz. Three years later, "Le Parc…" was published in* Café du Rêve *in a classic 27-page layout, also designed by the artist. It is the only text in* Café du Rêve *that is paginated. Each page features a thin black line framing the centred text, printed in large type, imparting the chapter with a literary feel. As in the previous version of "Le Parc…," the same fourteen black and white photographs are used and distributed along the text as follows:*

> *The first flight of steps of an eighteenth-century French circular staircase*
> *The two angle-towers of a three facades building*
> *A nineteenth century glasshouse*
> *A nineteenth century provincial park*
> *A weeping willow looking at a water canal in a provincial park*

An empty bench in a ninetheenth century provincial park
A Georges Vieljeux container ship at the dock
A negative outdoor photograph of a liner
The facade of "Le Navigator" restaurant
The outdoor sign of "Les Mirages" bar-grill
A child seeding doves and pigeons in a provincial park
A nineteenth century provincial park
An ancient commercial sign that reads "VOYAGE"
A child running in a provincial park

"Le Parc…" was never exhibited as a work of art. After its second publication in 1985, the artist considered it more of an "illustrated text for two voices." When the artist was invited to deliver a lecture in Adelaide, South Australia, where the "Four Rooms" exhibition was on view at the time as part of the Adelaide Festival in 1986 [III. 10], Chaimowicz used "Le Parc…" as a script for a live presentation. For the first time, he experimented with reading this text "in the company of a distinguished English woman with an excellent accent, living in Adelaide for a very long time." Both visual and spoken, this presentation brought together a narrative read by two voices—male and female—in addition to the projection of black and white slides, as in the printed version. As a result, since 1986, "Le Parc…" has become the script for an illustrated reading accompanied by a slide show. This reading has been subsequently performed in various contexts, such as the Städelschule, Frankfurt am Main, on 20 June, 2012. On this occasion, Chaimowicz reactivated "Le Parc…" by giving voice to himself and his collaborator at the time, the unforgettable Capucine Perrot. Seated next to each other, they read together while twenty-six black and white slides were projected.

Originally conceived as "a sullen wistful narrative," the park Chaimowicz depicts throughout his text is also a melancholic refuge from the noise of the city, a place where we can dream of a journey. Through the dual text / image space that structures the narrative, the artist traces a perimeter that not only makes the border of image and text porous, but also acts as a reflexive lining between worlds, that which is "seen" in the photographs and that which "sees" in the text.

A.V.

· · · · · · · · ·

I recently dreamed that we shared the same thoughts, that I echoed your sentiments.

HERE … the apartment is on the fifth and top floor in the very heart of the city, and overlooks the clock of a church steeple… This location is in a sense unique, being simultaneously within the city and yet distanced or apart from it. On the other floors are dressmakers' workshops, and though I am alone, by evening the closeness of other buildings in this eighteenth-century quarter strengthens an illusion of being party to a thriving, albeit abstract community… The clock presides over the routine and thus the convention of urban life.

In their neutrality, these rooms are fitting as a retreat from the sickness of the metropolis, and this city is as conducive as any to my convalescence…

An aura of self-importance is manifest in the numerous legal, civic, and cultural buildings, many still functioning. Some, symbols of faded economic might, like the Stock Exchange, have either been adapted with sanguine pragmatism, or are obsolete. All are opposed by broad and equally imposing tree-lined avenues…
There is a smugness common to many provincial centres that have acquired within their region (often through a dubious history) a sense of self-righteousness … a certain self-consciousness, insufferable for being so serious and so stuffy or dusty as to be claustrophobic.

But owing to the closeness of the sea, coastal winds carry the dust elsewhere, and blessed as it is with a port, these limitations are qualified…

And it is to my increasingly frequent visits there, that I accredit my recovery…

Yesterday, I woke up by the sea…

Yesterday, I or we … woke up by the sea.

THAT IS, I awoke at first having no idea where I was … and how delightful are those first few seconds of unknowing … but how unfortunate then that they are generally accompanied by a headache or a hangover…

Then, as my lulled reflexes vainly attempted reason, so my eyes tried to focus. But it was very bright in that strange room, and outside, beyond a large plate-glass window, the sun nearing its zenith shone with ferocity. Gradually I deciphered a foreground that was of sand … a beach merging into sea and then sky… Drawn to this unlikely image, I wished to enter its picture frame, and so, with trepidation, stepped out onto a balcony… An arc of deserted beach startled me. It was as though a forgotten and exotic postcard had slipped from the pages of a long discarded book…

This wide and gracious beach, untrammelled yet reserved, was born a star in this resort of grand hotels, pine woods, and pavilions … its majestic curve only interrupted by the harbour, which is where we had breakfast at the solitary open café…

And this town … doubtless bleak and ghostly in winter, in summer crowded yet exclusive … might have been then, on this out of season day, faintly ridiculous … just the pleasure ground of the privileged—boarded up and dormant … however due to the perfect weather it was tranquil and idyllic, and, like an unexpected gift, the more remarkable for its improbability…

And soon, perhaps due to its charm as we strolled through it, casual and carefree, what had so recently seemed startling, now by appropriation became ours and natural…

Our departure was as impromptu as our arrival, for it seemed that my three companions had engagements later that afternoon … but we had enjoyed this act of spontaneity, this detour, and I especially had enjoyed spending some time in company. The girls, Isabelle driving, sat in the front. Jeannot and I sat in the back… As the return journey unfolded, so various landmarks seemed familiar … but only occasionally, and then as if in reverse…

We were of course returning by our earlier route, but with the strong light and heat, and given that we were tired (albeit perceptive), this reversal seemed not merely one of direction or even of an opposite, but one of contrast—as a negative is to a photograph … or akin to a sheet of photographic paper submerged in a tray of developer … and as an image when being developed slowly appears, acquiring clarity … so I recalled…

THE lengthy drive on a dark and deserted motorway, the white roadside markers effecting a soothing rhythm… Then in the distance as if placed there for (our) diversity, a vast petrochemical plant—all tubes and towers and glittering lights. A proud and whimsical symbol of progress and industry, fleetingly grand as a cathedral and curiously optimistic…
Then to reflect that in daylight, this same plant would become its own opposite, and seen in reverse conditions, would look desolate, brutal … ominous…

… How I had spent the afternoon at the port and had watched the arrival of a large ship then noticed the distinctive smell of the sea … and remembered, given that we were some sixty kilometres upstream, this maritime taste was unusual and perhaps a matter of climate … that it was usually

accompanied by a sense of quiet drama concurring with the arrival of ocean going ships—when regally, attended by their tugs they are guided to their moorings… It seemed that these giants, temporarily harnessed, brought their recent history with them … in silence and with some mystery … and their legend…

… And later met Jeannot in a local bar where the floor is of small mottled grey mosaic with a geometric intrusion of dark red, and the curved counter is of stained veneer with a worn but functional aluminium top, the lip bulbous, a little dull, the tables echoing this odd but customary combination—each leg joined to a curved foot decorated or protected with aluminium trim…

THEN on to a busy corner café on the square, by contrast a hectic noisy meeting place in which no one settles … where we had a drink with Marie Claude and were later joined by Isabelle. How an evening that had begun casually seemed to be acquiring purpose… The four of us, feeling gregarious, restless, and decisive, went on to a pretentious bar, then to a charming if dilapidated club… And each of us by now quite drunk, were entertained by the delighted owner, who perhaps stimulated by our youth, or perhaps because we were her only customers, happily recounted anecdotes from her show business past and danced with us… Then, eventually, we found ourselves at my favourite bar by the docks…

Which is where we settled … my friends first with caution, then won over by alcohol and circumstance, with abandon… In this no-man's land where they gather—the North African, the alcoholic, the whore, the pimp, the transient and bankrupt … the cowboys, cavaliers, sailors, nancy-boys, and paranoiacs—where all believe themselves to be outsiders, but in fact belong beyond language. By their very presence they inescapably become parties to a truce … where they could be themselves, yet live out any fantasy (yet, in presuming an audience, were wrong, as nobody much cared and this location was therefore a private place—as home is)

... Here, our evening, from hybrid and amorphous beginnings, had taken a form within which we relaxed into complicity. Thus we found it natural— then the police, nonchalantly, as if by habit, cleared the bar—to extend our purpose ... choosing to drive on to the coast...

EARLIER today, after our return ... strolling aimlessly about the city, not so much lost as drifting, I wandered down an arcade that led into a pleasant residential square of fine if uniform townhouses, within which there was a park...

Its formal layout consists, on each of the longer sides (upon which the eighteenth-century terraces actually back), of two rows of plane trees and gravel paths, and on the shorter ends, of tall iron fencing with double gateways. A central avenue with cast iron benches and lamp standards, also features an equestrian statue and a fountain ... there are conical bushes, well-kept flowerbeds, and a dark green caretaker's hut...

Its occupants are ordered, tidy, seemingly local, as mannered as the park ... and sitting there, I was captivated by its conventions—so mundane and so ordinary; its modesty—so elusive and seductive ... by qualities so intangible as to be startling—a feeling matched only by my surprise...

Where the caretaker sweeps, children play, parents chat, nannies watch. Where the elderly take the air or walk the dog... And where the occasional passer-by sitting to read or day-dream is tolerated, yet as any stranger to an established club, does not generally linger ... perhaps feeling unwelcome, or excluded by a discipline uneventful but demanding—within which the habitues seem to have a timetable of exchange, intrigue, and relaxation...

And yet I felt strangely drawn to this alien and enigmatic place ... willingly succumbing to its ease. It had become a temporary sitting room and with its classical appeal, reminiscent of Mies van der Rohe's Barcelona chair—spacious, grand, supremely comfortable

… I have returned a few times—usually (because of the capricious weather) after a spring shower—to find it glistening wet, its smells profuse … and glowing … almost bashful…

Remembered … a classic Chinese side-table in the Victoria and Albert Museum, so fine that within the abundance of the collection it is hardly noticed or is mistaken for a museum fitting. Made of deep subdued mahogany, the rightness of its proportions and the usage of material is such—its quality being so understated—that it becomes, in its perfection … invisible…

Here, I realised that the sadness of loss is not so much a matter of sentiment as of function… That we dwell upon recent memories—reconstructing an image and savouring moments wonderful—because we suspect that their vividness (and their meaning) will fade with time … first distorting, then receding, and finally, involuntarily, disappearing… As significant chapters in our lives end—often through our own doing—so we re-live them … first from a sense of loss, then respectfully and later, fondly … that we may then be free to live on sweetly or to dream, and in the future have access to an even clearer image that we can call upon with generosity. In the exclusivity of sadness we recall loss that we may then forget … and thus be free to live our future…

IT IS commonly held that to drift is to avoid … that to travel without reason is escapist … that we travel without purpose in the forlorn hope that we may resolve or out-distance our problems, lose our cares … although these—like a dumb but faithful dog—have a habit of staying close…

Yet it is possible that an alien landscape, in which we see more clearly than in a familiar one, may in its simplicity—beyond offering solitude—afford us, as a new mirror, an unfamiliar view of ourselves, revitalising in its candour, and from which we might (Oh optimism!) dare contemplate futures and possibilities…

I have no way of knowing to what extent I was responding to the park, seemingly so generous, or how much I myself was bringing to it—projecting in silent dialogue upon its sympathies ... it was, perhaps, a surface through which images broke and coalesced ... the bar the previous evening—wanton and exotic ... then, the beach— pure and brutal...

But when I returned there in early evening and sheltering from the rain, the light changing, enjoyed the novelty of its emptiness ... and brought to it sunshine, imagining its shadows and flirtations ... I was startled then gradually enveloped by a sum of feelings ... complete and exact ...
in which I felt at one, both with my self and with my surroundings ...
in which I recognised the vindication of my travelling.
Realising that this was to be my final visit to the park, I submitted to a sense of intimacy exacting but sublime, in which I was momentarily ... free of desire...

Editor's note: The protagonist, on his many visits there, did half-heartedly take a few snapshots ... but perhaps due to poor weather was unsuccessful ... the park, ever coy, had eluded him ... photographs of another park have been used instead ... but that is another story...

[III. 11c]

Partial Eclipse, a Performance

(1985)

Addressing the tension between the need for solitude and for company, Partial Eclipse… *is a languid performance, which Chaimowicz performed from March 1980 to December 1982 in various venues across Europe and Canada. In a note written in April 1980, he states:*

> *"To describe* Partial Eclipse… *would be inappropriate. Suffice to recall that there were one hundred and sixty images, in approximately twenty sequences (mostly black-and-white), projected onto a screen with a dissolve unit so that each image flowed into the next. A man [Marc Camille Chaimowicz] interrupted these images by walking in a figure of eight, behind and in front of the screen, qualifying the images both in actuality and shadow. This passivity was countered by a woman [the then-emerging Welsh artist Helen Sear] sitting in front of the screen, who read a text in twelve sections. Background was* Discreet Music *by Brian Eno. The piece lasted for about forty minutes."*

To this description it could be added that the upbeat sound of Metropolis *by Kraftwerk opens and closes the performance; that the performer smokes a cigarette, whose smoke is caught in the light of the projector to create a "filmic" quality; that the performer wears a jacket, which is removed within the opening minutes of the performance so that the light coloured shirt acts as a secondary screen for the slide projection, incorporating his body into the images shown. According to Jean Fisher in* Past Imperfect. Marc Camille Chaimowicz 1972–1982 *(Liverpool: Bluecoat Gallery et al., 1983, p. 24), "*Partial Eclipse… *transplants an intimacy and a subjectivity into a formal and neutral public space, and presents us with dualities: passive/active, private/public, real/represented."*

Chaimowicz conceived that work as his ultimate performance. Performed over three consecutive years, it resulted in a production of simple informative sheets. Usually photocopied, and subsequently sent by post and made available to the audience on site, their content was mainly based on quotations from the artist's performance script. As a result, although this script was completed at the end of 1979, only snippets of it circulated between 1980 and 1982 [III. 8].

In 1981, while working on Chapter 1 ("Le Désert…"), Chapter 2 ("Le Parc…"), and Chapter 3 ("North Africa Song") of Café du Rêve, *the artist set about customising the script of* Partial Eclipse… *with a selection of images taken from the slides projected throughout the performance, with a view to a new chapter. Conceived when the artist was leaning away from the field of performance, this work, a 29-page collage pairing text, image, and graphic design, was completed in 1984. Including the performance script in its entirety, "Partial Eclipse, a performance," the fourth chapter of* Café du Rêve, *made the text public when the book was released in 1985. This version of the text is reproduced below.*

When the artist put an end to his performing activities in December 1982, after presenting Partial Eclipse… *at the Museum of the Twentieth Century (now Belvedere 21) in Vienna, little did he know that exactly twenty years later,* Partial Eclipse… *would be re-enacted in Glasgow, "re-incarnated" in Berlin, and performed again at Tate Britain. Accompanying this second life, the script circulated again, both as a transcript of a work that had its own autonomy and as documentation.*
Occupying a transitional state between two meanings of interior—interior meaning the domestic interior, and interior meaning one's inner life—and refracted through layers of

language, sound, image, and live presence, Partial Eclipse... *crystallised a situation that, over the years, acquired a cult following from a younger generation of artists and cultural producers, who were ready to experiment again at the turn of the 2000s [I. 7]. Contributing to this momentum, Scottish artist Lucy McKenzie [I. 15] politely urged the artist to revive* Partial Eclipse... *as part of her 2002 "Flourish Nights," a series of summer events taking place "amidst the Baudelairean decay of Flourish studios and the Victorian wood panelled sumptuousness of Sloans Bar in central Glasgow," as commented in* Kneel, Mullholand: Drive! *in May 2003. Removed from the performance world, Chaimowicz suggested that to replace him, McKenzie find someone "in their thirties, approx. 1 metre 75 tall, who should not be wearing spectacles (but can be wearing contact lenses)." A few days before* Partial Eclipse... *was performed again publicly, McKenzie called the artist and said, "I've got a surprise for you!" The surprise, indeed, was that Alex Kapranos, lead singer and lead guitarist of Scottish rock band Franz Ferdinand, would be performing* Partial Eclipse... *in place of Chaimowicz. This not only recreated the event within another person, but also turned the performance into a trans-generational tribute recalling the earlier Vito Acconci moment in New York in 1971 [II. 8], leading Chaimowicz to state that "I was Vito Acconci and Franz Ferdinand was me!!" It was at this point that* Partial Eclipse... *became a repeatable work, taking its script with it. Propelled into the future like a time capsule,* Partial Eclipse... *was subsequently "re-incarnated" by the artist who has performed* Partial Eclipse... *live for the first time since December 1982, at Galerie Giti Nourbakhsch, Berlin, on Friday, 12 November, 2004, at 6 p.m. and 9 p.m., and on Saturday, 13 November, 2004, at 6 p.m., once again proving a hit with the younger generation. In both cases, the pre-recorded script was broadcast throughout the performance.*

Partial Eclipse… *was thereafter programmed as part of "Tate Triennial 2006: New British Art," Tate Britain, London (1 March–14 May, 2006), curated by Swiss curator Beatrix Ruf [I. 21]. At the same time, albeit independently from this event, Cabinet Gallery, London, produced a boxed set (40 × 60 × 10 cm). Comprising 160 35mm Kodak Elmo slides divided in two round slide trays, two CDs containing the audio tracks needed to stage the performance, including the upbeat* Metropolis *by Kraftwerk as well as the voice reading the twelve sections script and* Discreet Music *by Brian Eno, and the performance script signed "Marc C. Chaimowicz" and numbered by the artist. Renamed* Partial Eclipse…1980–2006, *this boxed set was edited in five copies and signed "Marc C. C. Spring 2006." The following year, one of them was acquired by Tate Britain. From then on, as the artist noted, the work became "more of a space for performance than an installation inside which to perform." Meanwhile,* Partial Eclipse… *had indeed acquired historicity, as did, logically, its performance script.*

Five years later, Tate Britain organised the group show "Has the Film Already Started?" (27 June, 2011–26 February, 2012). Presented in a newly refurbished suite of contemporary galleries, this exhibition, which was conceived as an atmospheric installation, aimed to highlight the role of set design and performance in British art from the 1970s to the present day. Featuring works by artists from three generations, including among others Genesis P-Orridge, Mike Nelson, Cerith Wyn Evans, Cosey Fanni Tutti, Marc Camille Chaimowicz, David Musgrave, Enrico David, and Cathy Wilkes, the exhibition sought to trace how the history of performance and related ideas came to occupy a defining place in the art of the last thirty years. Co-curated by Lizzie Carey-Thomas, Katharine Stout, Claire Wallis, and Andrew Wilson, at the time Curators of Contemporary British Art at Tate

Britain, the exhibition brought together arrangements of objects that could be considered as performance settings. In addition, a performance program was devised. "Each Saturday afternoon at 3 p.m.," Partial Eclipse… was presented in an environment where the audience could sit and watch slides projected onto a screen. The exhibition room also featured folded screens, painted panels, and on occasion, a subtle performance physically surrounded by the words of the performance script, which had been wall-displayed. For the first time at Tate Britain, a performance work was integrated within the displays. As Acatia Finbow, then-doctoral researcher, asserts in a 2016 "Case study" dedicated to the long story of Partial Eclipse… *following its acquisition in 2007 and reactivation by Tate Britain in 2011:*

> *"This demonstrates Chaimowicz's aspiration to present a performance which adheres as closely as possible to his 'original' intention, even after a lapse of thirty years. There is an implication within this that although Chaimowicz has embraced the repeatability of the performance, demonstrated by the creation of this set of instructions, he does not automatically accept that it could be changed; each iteration, although spatially and temporally different, has common elements which should not be compromised."*

Throughout that eventful story, the script reproduced below remained identical to its original version. Completed in 1979, performed live in 1980, recorded in 1981 and thereafter broadcast, circulated in bits and pieces between 1980 and 1982, illustrated and crafted by the artist into the autonomous chapter of a book published in 1985, then made available as part of a case box in 2006, this text finally reappeared on the walls of a museum in 2011, documenting the performance outside its presentation time. Although it has accompanied the many twists and turns of the artist's endless partial eclipse for over fifty years, the text below has remained noticeably unchanged since its inception in 1979.

A.V.

. . . .

Performance with 160 slides in twenty sequences and text either read live or pre-recorded by Helen Sear, duration approximately forty minutes.

In the corner of a darkened room stands a projection screen and a simple wooden chair. As the images are projected on the screen, the artist walks at a steady rhythmic pace in a figure of eight behind and in front of the screen and the chair. His body both "absorbs" fragments of the image and throws a shadow on the screen as it interrupts the projector's path of light. As they softly dissolve into each other, the predominantly grey-toned images present us with the familiar iconography: details of an interior, its objects, glimpses of figures engaged in activities, flowers, fruit, a coiled snake, reflections, filtered light, and shadows. This quasi-narrative is complemented by the woman's narration which, like the images, refers speculatively to objects, moments in a relationship, recollections of a place, or a journey which may have special significance.

The upbeat sound of Metropolis *by Kraftwerk opens and closes the performance, which is otherwise accompanied by the contrasting ambient* Discreet Music *by Brian Eno.*

Jean Fisher, 1983, *Past Imperfect. Marc Camille Chaimowicz, 1972-1982.* Published by Bluecoat Gallery, School Lane, Liverpool, The Orchard Gallery, Orchard St., Londonderry, John Hansard Gallery, The University, Southampton.

"… a haunting and impressive experience"
—Roger Cork, *The London Evening Standard*, December 1981

"… The warmth of his work comes from his ability to approximate, through a variety of media, the experience of a private conversation."
—Mick Hartney, *Art Monthly*, no. 53, 1981

"… We were embarrassed, bored, fascinated, yet not one walked out."
—Hetty Einzig, *Sunday Times*, 6th December, 1982

"… experience is a fiction and art a dream…"
—John Roberts, *Artscribe*, no. 32, 1981

"… Again one is held in thrall…"
—Thomas Lawson, *Artforum*, December 1981

Editor's note: Based on the working script of a performance developed and presented during 1980-1982 this is the one chapter of *Café du Rêve* not originally conceived as book material… Yet, given that this performance established the artist's interest in the inter-relationship of text to image, in the unfolding of a fragmented narrative—it is perhaps a prelude… *1984*

Anonymous   Neutral   Temporary   Ideal   Real
Violated   Modified   Fragile   Delicate   Strong
Assertive   Withdrawn   Unclear   Lost   Hazy
Crystalline   False   Precious   Harmonious
Classical   Transient   Quintessential   Reminiscent
Illicit   Carefree   Adolescence   Delinquency   Search
Reprieve   Casual   Sublime   Florentine   Mundane

As at the terrace of any anonymous provincial café so here he
could sit alone for hours daydreaming and wandering, dwelling on
ills and pleasures…

He thought of museums, of odd rooms often with no windows or
doors, neutral spaces with no identity, not really rooms at all…

Sitting in his lounge—this temporary truce between the ideal and
the real, he dwelt on change…

How it is impossible to transfer one's reality to another without
this act of transference affecting that reality…
How the transference of an experience qualifies that experience,
how an idea once subjected to change is no longer that idea, how
its purity is violated, modified…

from third section

Of the two travellers it seemed one was fragile or delicate, the
other strong…
One assertive, one withdrawn…

Which was which was unclear, or rather, they were within one
condition…
As one acquired clarity, so the other lost focus…

Much time is spent in description, within sensations … in shifts
of mood, and in ambiguity … so rare scenes of activity, occasional
moments of action, seems as incongruous as scars on delicate
flesh…

…dwelling on ills and pleasures…

from fourth section

He thought of black and white, critically…

And in this instance preferred greys and silver, sometimes hazy as
a Venetian dawn, sometimes crystalline … greys that seem to tap a
reservoir of nuance and colour … in a sense, not really greys at all

… greys that in their handling have become more than a mix of
two extremes … have become a new breed…

He thought of many such false polarities … of here and there,
of this and that … of the fact that he was doing precious little,
passively…

…in shifts of mood, and in ambiguity…

from fifth section

He thought of the tyranny of words … the luxury of thought, the
necessity and delight of reverie … of the aesthetics of solitude, of
the symmetry of their liaison, once harmonious and classical in its
proportions…

Turned a corner, the clouded evening sky rich in its variety…
Walking past the concert hall, the Palace of Justice, the Museum,
he thought of previous orders and of ruins, of sunsets and of
dawns… It seemed to him that to give attention to detail was all
that remained to be done…

…and sometimes crystalline…

from sixth section

The impossibility of possessing a feeling or sensation in its
entirety…

that our conception of an idea or a wish can only be partial—at
best approximated through time—sequentially…
that as memento or reminder, smell provides the most evocative
and quintessential definition of another—more than a letter, a lock
of hair, or a photograph for both pleasure and recollection … that
perhaps its elusiveness makes it so tantalising and missed most
when separated or travelling…

rich in its variety…

from seventh section

His walk has detachment—is both casual and flamboyant …
obliquely qualifying the image—in actuality and shadow…

The notion of privacy is a characteristic as is a sense of
ambiguity…

are these a woman's thoughts or comments from a man?

are the characters fictive … or an extension of experience qualified,
then idealised…

There is no discrepancy … images oscillate from the evocative to
the literal, from idea to mood, from décor and elegance … to the
metaphysical…

Speculative and incomplete in content—in form both hermetic and
resolved…

…for both pleasure and recollection…

from section eight

The room is silent save for the ticking of clock. The pale green wall
has a hint both of dust and of peppermint… The white patterning
is reminiscent of many things. For some—melancholy and the
graciousness of a lost age.

For others—timelessness and echoes of classical unity. Shadows
intertwine in mute dialogue with illicit sunlight—a flirtation that
heightens the tranquility… The door is opened, and he leaves
this space—active in his absence … recalling that nothing is as it
seems…

…from elegance and décor … to the metaphysical…

from ninth section

The letter read,

*My eagerness to join you was justified, as was my impatience, so firstly,
thank you for your hospitality…*
After the other guests had gone I was silent in your company…
*At first we treated one another as strangers, formally and with caution,
later becoming accustomed… We talked, drank, and often laughed … the
time spent with you was carefree and relaxed.*

*We made small talk of joint acquaintances, and of course, a little of
ourselves—idly passing the time with pleasantries that countered moments
when I lusted for you … found you irresistible … was drawn to your
physicality…*

*I can recall the warmth of you, your taste and smell … holding and
caressing you … intimate… Anticipating you finding me, at first with
delicacy and almost hesitant, later hard and fully with impatience and
urgency … of undressing one another, of intertwining limbs, dampness and
activity…*

*Of shared pleasures in silent dialogue at times wicked and at times pure,
of whispers as punctuation…*

*We later talked of many things, found a pace that was mutual … and, of
course, avoided accountability…*

…melancholy and the graciousness of a lost age…

from tenth section

Within this space, alien in its correctness, distant in its estrangement, he recalled some of its many facets… As sometimes reproachful with a quality of abandonment… At times deliciously formal as with traditional hotel rooms… Sometimes sullen as adolescence, moody as delinquency…

The fountain screened out external noise establishing a peculiar silence … like a well-matched duel, so the light from the mantleshelf lamp countered daylight filtering in through the pale green curtains … as if natural light needed the qualification of electricity,

Within this intimacy he felt complete…

I realised that this space seemingly so singular and infinitely composed—still as to appear timeless—was fluid and prone to change… And here, where possibilities of action seemed inappropriate, a multitude of activities were possible…

…of shared pleasures in silent dialogue…

from eleventh section

In search for a particular perfection was becoming stifling and constrictive,
A feeling deliciously close to a state of entombment.

And his foray outside that condition held an immediacy tantamount to that of a reprieve…

…reproachful with a quality of abandonment…

from twelfth section

Chapter Five is of the senses,* both of rain and of sunshine, of whispers and of touch…
then later of the heart, of enveloping myself in thoughts of you…

Sitting on the terrace they might have been in Italy … their previous evening had been relaxed … casual and sublime they had talked of shared moments and of plans … not separating fact from fantasy…

Had savoured a mutuality Florentine in its logic, transcending the mundane, establishing profundity

—the feeling of complicity … delightful. Then later … paradise…

…an immediacy tantamount to a reprieve…

from thirteenth section

* This reference is incidental and does not refer to the structure or pagination of *Café du Rêve*.

As at the terrace of any anonymous provincial café,

Of the two travellers it seemed one was fragile or delicate,

He thought of black and white, critically…

Of the aesthetics of solitude

More than a letter, lock of hair, or photograph,

His walk has detachment—is both casual and flamboyant,

The room is silent save for the ticking of a clock,

The letter read… My anticipation in joining was well founded, as was my impatience,

Within this space, alien in its correctness, distant in its estrangement,

His search for a particular perfection was becoming stifling and constrictive,

Chapter Five is of the senses, both of rain and of sunshine, of whispers and of touch…

Presented at:

First version, live reading
Internationaal Cultureel Centrum, Antwerp, 1980
De Appel Gallery, Amsterdam, 1980
Städtische Galerie, Munich, 1980

Second version, pre-recorded tape
Parachute Festival, Montreal, 1980
Nigel Greenwood Inc Ltd, London, Wapping, 1980 *by invitation*
The Tate Gallery, London, 1981
Comportement Environnement Performance, Lyons, 1982 *by invitation*
L'Atelier, Grenoble, 1982
AMAM / Touring Balance, Geneva, 1982
The Basement, Newcastle upon Tyne, 1982
Museum of the twentieth Century, Vienna, 1982

[III. 11d]

Chorus, a Letter From Vienna

(1985)

Originally handwritten on stationary from the Hotel Kärntnerhof Wien, "Chorus, a Letter From Vienna" was composed by Chaimowicz during his residency in Vienna in 1982, as part of the Humanic Program [III. 9]. Encapsulating the artist's Viennese experience at the time, this letter was subsequently typeset and illustrated for publication as Chapter 5 of Café du Rêve *in 1985.*

Initially titled "Correspondence..." the artist felt this title was too generic. By calling the letter "Chorus," he introduced fiction into it. This chapter of Café du Rêve *borrows its textual and visual aesthetics from the Parisian interwar period, particularly the academic and formal literary magazines of the time, such as* Les Nouvelles littéraires, La Nouvelle revue française, Europe, *or* Documents, *whose editorial programs based on a "modern classicism" allowed them to publish the best authors of their time while contributing to the regeneration of the French novel, sociology, and anthropology. This chapter of* Café du Rêve *borrows its dramaturgy from that of the photo-novel, in which the correspondence between lovers is commonly fuelled by an elusive desire crystallised in photographs. Although the original 13-page letter on stationary paper is not illustrated, its 22-page published version includes moody photographs of buildings in Vienna and Venice, city views, and faded coloured patterns inspired by Viennese designer-architects. These photographs are Polaroid: surely then chosen for their instantaneous quality, implicit to travel, they visually interact with text. Opening on an oblique sample of the handwritten letter, Chapter 5 features a square black-and-white photograph from the early 1980s in which the artist's hand is seen writing on a table surrounded by writing props including a tiered translucent pen holder, an ink bottle, a blotter holder, and an ashtray. Meticulously orchestrated, that table display (featured on the cover of this book) suggests that the codes of writing are just as important for the artist as the written word and the meaning induced by the act of writing.*

Referring to the four cities closest to the artist's assignments—Paris, London, Venice, and Vienna—"Chorus, a Letter From Vienna," as Jean Fisher put it in Past Imperfect. Marc Camille Chaimowicz 1972–1982 *(Liverpool: Bluecoat Gallery et al., 1983, p. 49), refers to "a paradox of presence and absence that seeps insistently through the artist's work, for a while a letter offers a remission of solitude to the receiver, it also signals the absence of a writer." Addressing the artist's committed relationship with Viennese architects and designers such as Adolf Loos and Josef Frank, as well as with the craft products of the Wiener Werkstätte, this text in letter-form briefly introduces the versatile premises of Chaimowicz's interest in architecture with sculptural qualities [I. 16, 21; II. 10; III. 23, 26]. Collected in part in the letter reproduced below, these stimuli from the 1980s would later be reconsidered by the artist from a socio-political angle, for example in "A letter, transcribed" [III. 26], which the artist wrote for his solo exhibition at Secession (20 November, 2009–24 January, 2010). Both written to "J"—a fictitious recipient, or perhaps the artist himself?—twenty-seven years apart, these two letters present similarities and differences based on meticulous sources, the second being an extension of the first. Designed solely for* Café du Rêve, *"Chorus, a Letter From Vienna" has to date not been exhibited, either as a book chapter or as a handwritten letter.*

A.V.

• • • • • • • • • •

Dear J,

As itinerant workers we go where the work is … and yet, at some time has not each of us sat in a bar or café in a distant land, merely then to ask of ourselves: why travel when I might just as well be bored at home? Rare therefore is the city in which we can both work and dream … happily, here in this complex and effervescent city I am able to do both … Living almost the life of a monk—albeit of a gracious order—I have developed the semblance of a routine … so although I often lose myself walking about the city—the better to enjoy and discover it—I have nevertheless established my own landmarks…

We each have our churches—here mine is the discreet renaissance Jesuitenkirche built by Andrea Pozzo. My café is the Prückle whose excellent décor and furniture are by Oswald Haerdtl (1954), and in which it is especially pleasant, on Sunday mornings, to read the foreign press… And in late evening, as now, I particularly enjoy the Wunder-Bar (interior by Hermann Czech, 1975), where a mix of conversations, seemingly in many dialects, becomes an abstract background—a free space most conducive to thought and reverie … an ambience queried only occasionally—but then the more shockingly—by the sound of an English record … by that which is recognisable.

These brief sorties during which I enter in imaginary dialogue with Vienna's citizens, are like late morning shopping, a welcome interruption from the routine, demands, and isolation of my studio. We are humbled in a foreign place when we cannot speak the language, and even the simplest of tasks can seem awesome. Through the temporary loss of familiarity and social placing we become anonymous… Thus disadvantaged, we are perhaps not so much emasculated … as effeminised … and surely these apparent

forfeits are also assets—our greater vulnerability makes us more aware. With the loss of an identity we become freer to observe—more receptive to a multitude of sensations ... to innuendo and to detail ... and it is perhaps these—a subversion of the form and practice of tourism—that comprise our true souvenirs...
In anonymity we extend our senses ... and the greater our detachment, so the more lucid is our overview... And in this bar where I am already on occasion acknowledged by some of its habitues, this temporary paradox ... of handicap becoming privilege, seems the more precious...

I shall probably be visiting Venice soon. There is no finer time to do so than winter, and my favourite way of travelling there being by train, there is no better departure point than Vienna.
The night train leaves around midnight. A couchette cabin to oneself is preferable, and even at short notice, the guards are usually open to the most reasonable bribes... In addition to Calvino's *Invisible Cities* I will take Rossetti's translation of *La Vita Nuova* by Dante... And after crossing the causeway, the delight of stepping down from the train at Santa Lucia still half asleep, to stall or prolong pleasure with a light breakfast at the station buffet ... and only then to venture out in disbelief onto the suddenness of the Grand Canal and the Rialto bridge.
This is the only correct introduction, because until one has succumbed to its singular way this discreet and ethereal city is prone to appear vague and particularly ungraspable. This first view from the wide station steps holds it framed almost as though it were two-dimensional...
And if it is best to arrive by the morning train—which provides instant aural contact and offers a specific visual picture—then the loveliest way to leave it is at dusk and from the airport ... to slowly enjoy the panorama ... the silent distancing. After days of floating to the curiously comforting drone and vibrations of the vaporettos, to be in a plane does not seem so very different.

London, Vienna, Venice! Each once so portentous and omnipotent but now so much diminished ... bewildered—like aristocrats stripped of privilege... And how odd that of these three graces it should be Vienna—having suffered the greatest trauma—that now seems the least troubled, the best recovered, and the most decorous. Could this not be due in part to her inherent ambiguity and duplicity?

To follow the Ringstrasse—this magnificent leafy boulevard—and to witness its monumental civic buildings is to invoke Vienna as it was but one hundred years ago—the modern capital of the Austrian Hungarian Empire ... the Vienna of the Dual Monarchy. This mid-nineteenth century reconstruction encircling the city is a splendid exercise in historicism ... the product of a conscious eclecticism in which buildings symbolically reflect their roles: Faith is embodied in the Neo-Gothic Votivkirche of the City Hall; democracy in the Classicist parliament; Art and Science in the Neo-Renaissance of the Imperial Opera House, the Court Theatre, the Museums and University... A planning achievement matched only by Haussmann's Paris, and one which with a new Imperial Palace and the incorporation of numerous Baroque marvels, becomes a more than fitting symbol for the Habsburg Empire— then the most brilliant cultural centre of Europe.

Vienna's past power is thus commemorated... Its atmosphere has perished ... yet there is still sometimes an ominous quality here—a sense that all is not what it seems—that beneath its superficial hedonism there lies, beyond melancholy ... a darker aspect.
In parallel with the above aggrandisement was an insufferably ornate and sentimental residential architecture. What had begun as planning degenerated to the servicing of bourgeois pretensions...
And apparently, as Vienna's population increased—as though many were magnetised by its brilliance—there grew a multiplicity of social ills; a housing crisis, corruption and censorship, moral

hypocrisy, bureaucratic and courtly stagnation... Yet still the myth of Vienna as the charmed City of Dreams persisted ... as did the extravagance, the joie de vivre, and the waltzes ... and the Ringstrasse, in its glittering falsehood, remained an image of achievement. Because the emerging problems were never publicly admitted, so there arose a sense of duplicity... Habsburg society escaped further from the harsh reality, into make-believe, artifice, and illusion ... constructing a fraudulent but scintillating facade, behind which was despair, impending chaos, and disintegration—a dying Nobility ... the collapse of an empire ... the unacknowledged emergence of a proletariat...

This then is one preface to the twentieth century ... to the city of Karl Kraus and Adolf Loos, Mahler, Rilke and Schönberg, Otto Wagner, Hoffmann and Moser, Kokoschka, Freud, and Wittgenstein ... the very cradle of Modernism!

My dear J, Do not imagine that I am suffering from a surfeit of history... Just as intuition precedes reason so I have discovered much here by happy accident and only later has detail come to my attention. But in Vienna some awareness of history is inescapable ... in the grandiloquence of its buildings and in its psyche, the glory of Austria's recent past still intrudes. It exists both as a mental construct—of which many of its inhabitants seem particularly conscious—and in actuality... When I sit in the Café Sperl, for example, my thoughts tend to oscillate between their own subjectivity and a memory seemingly rooted in the surroundings. As though a gentle but insistent aura pervades this now dilapidated place, prompting me to recall that it was once the regular meeting place of Otto Wagner, Josef Hoffmann, Kolo Moser, even the enigmatic Adolf Loos...

And likewise in the Museum Café I cannot help but note that it was built by Loos in 1899, and that this was the year Wagner completed Vienna's railway stations, Mackintosh the Glasgow

School of Art, C.H. Townsend the Whitechapel Gallery in London … and that here a year later, Freud was to publish his *Interpretation of Dreams*.

Indeed throughout this city, cafés were once the fertile meeting ground between the public and private. Those Viennese subjected to grossly overcrowded housing were forced by circumstance to take refuge in such places—here to live out much of their lives—to receive their mail, to eat, even to shave, to court, and to marry… And from the pretensions of insufferably claustrophobic middle-class homes it was also the cafés that a precocious young intelligentsia escaped, there to establish their particular groups and forums…

If then the cafés once appeared to symbolise a relaxed and carefree existence of easy gossip, slow waltzes, and cream pastries—the very image an increasingly anxious city was eager to project— these enchanting institutions were also the product of a grim reality…

I arrived here predictably with Hoffmann as a hero, intrigued by Loos, and ignorant of the range of Wagner… Hoffmann's furniture is remarkable for its simplicity, inventiveness, and wit, as is his cutlery. His buildings are a disappointment, remaining rather two dimensional, and he is perhaps better in Brussels, where he was more able to exercise his true talents as a catalyst and impresario. Wagner has been a revelation. The greatest pioneer of the nineteenth century, he was able to extend his influence into the twentieth. The range of his output was colossal, extending— as father of the Wiener Werkstätte—from furniture to city planning, and including transport systems, railway stations, civic engineering, homes, and churches…

The Post Office Savings Bank of 1904 is rightly his most renowned building, which with its sense of light and space, its integrated furniture and fixtures, and its audacious use of new materials, remains an achievement that still looks splendidly modern.

Marvelously fluid, it is a synthesis of thought with love for detail and finish. Its main hall, although not vast, feels very grand and must surely be the most beautiful of the early twentieth century. My favourite building however is his earlier Am Steinhof Hospital Church just outside and above the city. An exercise in bravado, its detailing is wonderfully simple … the cool tiled interior is so functionalist as to be almost clinical—the floor indeed being at a slight slant that it may be washed more easily. Spatially fluid, it feels pure and oriental. Outside its high cupola with flanking towers is presumably a wicked pastiche of the hectic and over ornate St. Charles', which it overlooks.

If you should visit, avoid the American Bar by Loos now frequented by call girls and their clients … shifty and depressing, its customers trashy ornamentation. Knize, the men's outfitters, retains a sense of exclusivity, and the houses Straser, Steiner, and Moller are intriguing although externally stern and unfortunately not accessible.

A discovery has been Josef Frank, who built some assured yet charming houses in the International Style and was responsible for the Werkbundsiedlung building of 1930—a remarkable model estate of workers' homes. It brought together the work of many local architects including Loos, Haerdtl, and Frank as well as Lurçat, Haring, Neutra, and Rietvelt—each designing low-cost detached or terraced dwellings usually in ferro-concrete. Now somewhat dilapidated it is slightly Toy-Town, but here illusion and facade— subject to some recent tenant *improvements*—were finally laid to rest … and the whole remains a wonderful testimony to Modernism.

By contrast and on a much grander scale are the mighty municipal estates of the late twenties built by the socialist administration, of which Karl Marx-Hof is the supreme example… With vaulted gateways, towers, and the skyline of a mythic liner, it conveys a monumental effect—a hybrid of medievalism and Russian constructivism. Its entrances have great steel porticoes, used during battles between fascists and communists as protection for its tenants—Symbolism becoming function…

In "Red Vienna" municipal institutionalism became a political motif central to a party strategy of which a vast housing program was the most outstanding achievement. These super-blocks then stood defiant … as citadels… With their nurseries, shops, health centres, and enclosed squares, they were grand and isolated … enclaves within enclosures…

Remind me to tell you one day about the evening of my opening … of noticing—my friends gathered around—that here are two kinds of people; those who to succeed at all must travel incessantly, and, perhaps the truer Viennese, those who remain, forever dreaming … of my personal Mahler recital and of the barmaid … of Demel, The Spanish Riding School, the brick gasworks, the Woods, the Belvedere and Schönbrunn Palaces…

[III. 11e]

Liaison

(1985)

When Gabriella Cardazzo, co-director of Galleria del Cavallino, Venice, visited Chaimowicz in London in the spring of 1982 to discuss his forthcoming solo exhibition at the gallery (23 October–16 November, 1982), the chapters of Café du Rêve *that she discovered in his home [III. 11] were of great interest to her. As she turned the pages of "Liaison," which was still in progress, she immediately wanted to present them in the exhibition as a work of art. Still unfinished at the time of the exhibition, only part of it was shown in Venice. Once the exhibition opened, the artist went back to London and continued to develop the text, which turned out to be the longest one in the book. Initially, "Liaison" was intended to be Chapter 2 of* Café du Rêve, *but due to an internal rhythm that became easier to perceive as six other chapters were completed, "Liaison" was finally published as Chapter 6.*

Comprising seven sections, this chapter, as Jean Fisher describes it in Past Imperfect. Marc Camille Chaimowicz 1972–1982 *(Liverpool: Bluecoat Gallery et al., 1983, p. 47), "represents six stages of an imaginary affair and one ideal which are explored in five different ways: the literal, the metaphorical, as interiors, words and drawings. Each of the stages of this fictional liaison has its onset text and, as in 'Le Désert…' [III. 11a], there's a shift in the decorative ground, moving from a delicate filigree to a more physical sensuality." Spanning 44 pages, "Liaison" combines six slightly different types of design that interact with square black and white photographs mostly arranged in accordion fashion throughout the chapter. Successively depicting a young couple, a train corridor, the artist's worktable with his hand visible, writing, and two intertwined bottles of oil and vinegar, these photographs often juxtaposed with a multiplicity of the artist's faded patterns, bring to life the imaginary affair depicted throughout the chapter.*

For the launch of the Thames & Hudson edition of Café du Rêve *at Nigel Greenwood Inc Ltd, London, in the exhibition "Marc C Chaimowicz, recent paintings and sketches" (18 September –19 October, 1985), material relating to the book was displayed alongside copies presented on shelves. This included 3 studies for Liaison 9/11, 1982–1985, each consisting of black and white photographs enhanced with oil paint smears and ink on paper in a painted artist's frame (13.5 × 18 cm), a section of* Liaison, *and bookmarks designed by the artist. Although parts of* Liaison *were subsequently exhibited in various exhibition contexts, the work itself has never been shown in its entirety until now.*

A.V.

• • • • • • • • •

VERTIGO

TENDERNESS

AND BEYOND…

GENEROUS	HOPEFUL
PASSIONATE	TRUSTING
ADVENTUROUS	MAGICAL
DELUSION	NEGLECT
DISSENT	CONFLICT
RETRIEVAL	DOUBT…
PARANOIA	CONFUSION
MISERY	DESPAIR…
SENSUALITY	ORDER
SPLENDOUR	LOGIC
MEANING	PERFECTION…
CASUAL	CAREFREE
DETACHED	FLIRTATIOUS…
PROVOCATIVE	INNOCENT
PLAYFUL	OPTIMISTIC…
TANTALISING	MAGNETIC
RITUALISTIC	EXHAUSTING…

Each would have denied any conscious intent, arguing that their presence in the bar was simply good fortune, and that they never stayed for long… Yet any interested observer would have noted the frequency of their visits, the cheerfulness of their manner, and perhaps the increased attention each took of their wardrobe and one of another…

Detached casual and carefree—theirs was a chance encounter…

The first few weeks were those of innocence, neither admitting to any complicity … then with some joy and surprise discovering shared characteristics intended to draw them together, but in fact compensating for major differences … then finding nicknames—a baptism … the manifestation of a shared language—intimate and exclusive…

… Each then appointing the other, without their knowledge, as agent for their feelings … each introducing fate, first as an ally, then as an alibi…

Then gladly forfeiting habits and landmarks … submitting sensually to the other … irresistible … co-director and co-star in a half-happy drama—each act consuming, and prone to end in exhaustion.

And in that rare moment when they begin to reach beyond mere spontaneity, daring, with the other in mind, to construct shared futures and possibilities…

So fierce in its defiance as to be brutal, yet pathetic as are the vanquished, the setting sun glowed low over the bay… And stunned by a cruel light—a mix of source and reflection abruptly flattened by the large plate glass windows of the airport

lounge—I saw you for a moment only as a frozen silhouette …
but vividly… And ironically you became then a living metaphor
of what in the past you had reproached me for constructing—
an outline within which I projected too definite an image
… one inappropriate not for being constructed but for being
unattainable…

A silence is broken by the ringing of a telephone… But first, imagine…
A marvellous social occasion… It is early evening—there is access
to a summer's garden. Here are friends, some new faces, many
acquaintances… We are free to wander, to exchange gossip and
share news, contribute to the discourse … to laugh and chatter,
perhaps preen or flirt a little…

To drink and relax, content simply to witness the range of quiet
dramas … To talk of the future, settle arrangements … be
entertained, inquisitive, provocative. A gathering therefore buzzing
with potential within which we may easily choose our own pace,
then enjoy its sophistication and variety. And yet, preoccupied, we
sulk … we are restless, vague, and withdrawn. Abruptly—we leave
… then if questioned, invent a reason—an urgent appointment
perhaps. *furtive*, we feign purpose…

If our usual social pattern and habits are a mirror to that which in
any given season we have become, then this mirror is now fading …
losing its silver … and its utility. Rather than reflect, it obscures. The
gilt flaking, it acquires the look of an antique—or should the image
be static, its edges blurred—that of an early photograph. An instant
is relegated to a frozen image, then becomes a relic or memento.
Thus detached, we are vividly aware of the present becoming past,
and although seemingly driven on helpless toward no rendezvous,
we are in fact shaping decisive landmarks in our personal history…

Long listless days pass by uneventfully … our behaviour is slovenly and erratic, our daily life disintegrating…

We forgo commitments, cancel appointments, adjust plans…
But if this amorphous condition recalls that of the drifter, it is as an opposite—because we do not so much seek a space open, as one empty … and closed. A private space containing the object of our obsession…

a telephone

In such chaos we clear room for solitude within which we may then be free … to dwell on the other…

The silence is broken by the ringing of the telephone. Its tone is ominous, erotic, tantalising. Startled, excited, dismayed, heart palpitating we prepare to answer … hoping it will not be a reminder of the glittering scene so recently left yet now so distant, or merely an acquaintance … and nervous with anticipation, wishing, willing it to be the subject of our yearning … reason for our departure … object of our desire.

What had begun as casual and flirtatious was acquiring purpose … as if whilst simply and hedonistically enjoying the company of the other, they had each in their gradual submission inadvertently developed—alongside intimacy—an emotional requirement, and shockingly … a dependency… A bonding … of pleasures, wants, of common reference and anecdotes, of shared memory and of language…

They had become inseparable—their reciprocal affection becoming almost a need … then to establish itself into a pattern of exchange. The more of themselves they gave to the other, then in part to reside there, so the more they sought the other out, that they might there find themselves…

But because there was almost coldness still within the formality of their various encounters, this closeness of theirs was as thrilling with quiet drama (and as ritualistic) as those meetings between dealer and client in any illicit trafficking…

Yet in contrast to such transactions, that function upon and demand clear static roles, they had no code by which to decide which role each would adopt for their reunions. It was as though each was the dresser or the cloakroom attendant of the other, and that both were oblivious of the production or the locale…
And if the frisson of lawlessness was absent, then taking its place was an unknowing close to vertigo…

They were now seen less often by the crowd, with which they had once shared a common ground … which had once drawn them by its exoticness, and in which they had been advantaged— each becoming central figures much liked for their style and humour … eventually to abuse it as camouflage. They now seemed disinterested there, and withdrawn. It had become merely a backdrop … and a liability.

Wary of stereotype, they now lived by intuition and qualified instinct … relegating nobility to the imperial lion … preferring the ways of the misappropriated—the fox and the hyena.

They were sharing the daylight hours … and yet often feeling restricted and dissatisfied…

The night was more gracious to them, and more subtle … And if they had first met in the city's evenings, it was within the night's welcome that their romance developed. They felt at ease within its tolerance … as though the space of the night and its many ante-rooms—the bars and clubs, music venues and dance halls, the contrastingly empty streets and parks—offered them the comfort of a retreat from the harshness and sobriety of the day … and greater possibilities…

Feeling less constrained by convention, each was then the better able to challenge reason and presumption. She, in rebellion with innate femininity, by being *such a tomboy*—and he, oppressed by the tedium of masculinity, *such a she*… And further, in finding such complementary predilections they could now interchange their roles…

Within the night's exclusivity, ambivalence, and tinsel glamour, they were freer to enjoy and extend their ambiguity…

Free of intermediaries and preoccupied…
they were defiantly living out an order
that circumstance and history,
in ignorance of its reserves,
had declared bankrupt or made redundant.

What had begun as refreshingly as fine drizzle on a warm spring evening, became as invigorating as a sudden shower in high summer, then developed into a storm of force and splendour. A trickle had become a flood … but although threatened they held their ground, not through bravado, but through the fascination of their predicament—transfixed … like nocturnal rabbits held by car headlights.

Like wet crystal glass, all around them seemed to sparkle and to acquire clarity. He gained from her a sense of the physical and the immediate, and she from him some of the ways of reverie... Critical, and a loner by habit, he was fascinated by the disruption of an aesthete calm, and by her intrusion—alien, provocative, and disarming. In turn she was charmed by the novelty of his sophistication, by his attentions and flattery—then the more able to respond to his tenderness and persistence with generosity.

Both were now buoyant with self-assurance, and in turn willful and assertive—passionate and moody... Notions of time and place were redefined... They were living in the present, and yet the clearer the outside world appeared, so the more it receded... In becoming less threatening and less important, it became more … distant...

This then was a high point—each captivated by the other and revitalised, it seemed that all was possible...

Most evenings they take a stroll by the sea, where
the day's heat is met by the evening breeze,

usually beginning with a drink at a beach bar—empty by this time, and about to shut. It is as though they use the sanctuary as a vantage point from which to check, as foxes might, that the beach is finally empty, safe, … and theirs.

Then following the line of the short from a beginning to an end. From the stone wall of the harbour to a large rock formation separating—as if it were a custom post—their beach from another … of much the same look, but to them, elsewhere and foreign.

Their walk is similar each evening, and held, as though by mutual consent, mostly in silence and at some distance apart—she choosing the water's edge, and he, barefoot also, the dry sand… Their pace is natural and leisured—the stopping often to treasure-hunt for shells, he tending to lose himself in reverie… She, choosing the setting sun for companion, he, the ascending moon… And is in the beauty of the changing sky. Thus engrossed, each continues to observe the other by instinct and for reference … for without the other, neither could so enjoy their walk.
The light is beginning to fade…

this then is their meeting ground

… and their happiness. Because regardless of the day's events, whether relaxed, passionate, or fraught, and despite the promise of the night, it is as though this ritual is a truce—temporarily platonic … a shared journey in an imaginary childhood—trusting, adventurous, and magical…

The night is closing in. Reaching the end of the beach they re-unite, refreshed, and as friends simply … then to begin a slow climb up terraces of semi-tropical shrubbery—returning to the peopled world.

The twilight over, the evening beach is theirs no longer. Yet, dark and again empty—ever benevolent—it offers them a new intimacy to take with them for a while…

and perhaps until tomorrow…

She felt lost … he felt hurt—both were sad … neither could understand.
The Summer's folly had seemed so easy, infatuous, and carefree…
Both delighting in the absence of commitment, overtly disclaiming any responsibility, yet each demanding of the other—as if needing for excitement the challenge of a forceful personality. One had seemingly set the pace, nervous but elated—the other, both encouraging and deflecting, was obliquely masterminding. Each revelled in being wanted by the one they desired.
And how tender, adventurous, and assertive were those first nights, that often stole long into their day…
They had indulged in an attempt to regain the innocence and the intensity of adolescence—a condition, which originally they had been restless to forget.

They had enjoyed power but avoided accountability
and earlier, feeling trapped and dissatisfied by the facts of their lives, each had attempted with the other to live out a joint fiction.
We lose ourselves in the other. In the hope that, rejuvenated, we may there … find ourselves…
If each was once a figure of fantasy for the other—an image of desire—in each possessing the other they had begun to live out a shared fantasy.

Engrossed, consumed, and elated they had then falsely equated the other person—cause of so much pleasure—with the solution to their cares...
And had conveniently forgotten that to ignore problems is not to lose them ... such problems, like unopened bills ... remain...

They could not therefore see that the losing of themselves in the other was mere illusion, that over investing in the other was foolish, and that to internalise their many problems—and their rebellion—into this liaison, was to court disaster...

The appeal of the wanton and illicit is short lived and impossible to maintain—is liable to cease as abruptly as it began, then to seem tedious...
And now, at a kind of slowing down, and with for the first time some attempt at an assessment, they did sense a vague change... *As if the appeal, the intoxication—once so sensuous and electric—was waning...* It was in fact that their affair was no longer audacious or controversial ... it had become accepted, both publicly and privately ... thus losing its fascination as unorthodox—its value as taboo. *By becoming acceptable it had lost its meaning...*

Although they were as yet unaware, their achievement was also their failure ... *in becoming normalised their liaison had become factual ... and was no longer fictive.*

It was now acquiring many of those very traits that had first propelled them together ... *(had they not once escaped from the factual and mundane, into the unreason of the other?)*

Still hopeful (and lustful), they struggled on, ominously mixing past with present to retrieve something close to happiness.

Yet they were uneasy … their behaviour was increasingly erratic … and as if by instinct or a tacit understanding they now often stunned one another.

As their problems surfaced, so did a build up of external debts… As though in their half-hearted attempts to escape from their conflict they had opened an outside door, then to be startled by an accumulation of detail that had—as might vegetation in an unkempt park or garden—gained much ground through neglect…

There was now between them a false or exaggerated closeness … and an increasing distance. She, feeling inadequate, became demanding and aggressive—he, feeling threatened, became distant and withdrawn.
He grew agile in avoiding confrontation—she sought it out as fuel—needing its tangibility and drama as much as he took comfort in solitude … *she monopolised their assertiveness—he their exclusivity … if in the past they had identified the other as the source of their pleasure, each now held the other responsible for their misery…* Paranoid and confused … in having bypassed reason, or dismissed it, they could hardly now appoint it as agent of their salvage… It was to them as useless as is a neglected religion when called upon in despair…

And perhaps their final echo of defiance was that in still disclaiming failure, they could not see it to be also … their success…

The manner of their journeying is relaxed. If they had once hurried to cover the country—impatient to reach its southern point—they now linger, finding a richer and more sensual pace ... happy to discover the by-ways and the customs of its corners and its limbs... To savour its cuisine, share its literature, marvel at its scenery... To enjoy its railway and its stations, its town squares, boulevards, and Grand Cafés... To be inspired by the magnificence of its Metropolis, its renaissance splendours, its medieval heritage ... by the shade of village evenings the withdrawn beauty of its lakes, the drama of its rivers, the mysteries of the silent countryside...

And the more they extend this continuous journey the more intimate they become, so the greater is their understanding ... and their affection...

Once awestruck by the grandeur of the capital—finding there a focus of the country's will and intellect—then seduced by its vistas ... they now see the soul to be in the amalgam and splendour of the whole... In furthering their sympathies for this shared scenery, complex and varied yet complete
—for this aesthetic discourse—
so they become one with the landscape...

it is as though this voluntary journey—seemingly asymmetric and free of any conscious plan—has nevertheless a sense of order ... a logic and a meaning ... by which the pleasure of their travelling is thus enhanced *... as is the prospective joy of their return.*

… by simple good fortune, theirs was a chance encounter

each introducing fate, first as an ally, then as an alibi…

*… gladly forfeiting habits and landmarks and how tender,
adventurous, and assertive, were those first nights…*

… this then was their meeting ground … and their happiness

*… losing its fascination as unorthodox—its value as taboo
there was now between them a false or exaggerated closeness …
and an increasing distance…*

*… pathetic as are the vanquished, the setting sun glowed low
over the bay.*

*… In furthering their sympathies for this shared scenery—for
this aesthetic discourse…*

[III. 11f]

Le Select…

(1985)

As Café du Rêve *was being finalised, Catherine Thieck insisted that the artist develop a final chapter in relation to the city of Paris. In just a few hours or days, the artist wrote a letter to "M," a fictitious or real enigmatic recipient, on the stationary of "Le Select" where he used to stay, in connection with the preparation of the exhibition. Located at 20, rue du Temple, a two-minute walk from Galerie de France, it was easy for him to come and go. Written in blue ink, the letter is illustrated with pen-and-ink sketches of stars, hearts, and other Chaimowiczian motifs, as well as polaroids of Paris showing a hotel room key among numerous papers and an ashtray, Parisian hotel entrances, 1980s floor and wall tiles, a melancholy view of a Parisian backyard, an Art Deco fountain-sphinx, rue Mallet-Stevens in the 16th arrondissement, details of a Parisian bistro chair, and a pink water lily floating in dark green water. This 11-page illustrated letter was then photographed and inserted into the book at the last minute, making it, as the artist says in retrospect, "an almost chapter."*

In "Le Select," Chaimowicz asserts the seductive power of the transition that characterises any stay in a metropolitan hotel room. For him, the hotel room is first and foremost an image of passage. In hotels, as he put it, "we are aware of future and past occupants … Our arrival is the testimony of an absence…" This particular "ubiquity" of the hotel appeals to him insofar as it permits anonymity. Typical of the in-between that characterises hotel lobbies, where contemplation and reflection can constantly interfere, "Le Select" also sums up the artist's attraction to the hotel as an inverted image of home, in the sense that the hotel welcomes all those who go there to meet no one. If staying in a hotel doesn't bring him perspective or an escape from everyday life, it may refresh the distance he maintains with himself, which he can, in turn, explore as a reverie. Chaimowicz wrote this letter in a hurry. To make it easier to read, the text has also been published as a single-page typed postscript at the end of the chapter. Finally, as if to link the end of the book to another journey, the artist inserted at the end of Chapter 7 a small, stylised advertisement, probably from the 1930s, promoting the Paris-London train journey via Dieppe and Newhaven, thus signifying, as in the letter below, that he would return and leave again, "happy simply to have made myself available..."

A.V.

· · · · · · · · ·

Dear M,

My current hotel room has imposing double doors that promise a suite of some grandeur... Actually, its width barely exceeds that of the doors, and it has those odd proportions common to the many sometimes-charming conversions of the inter-war period. It still manages to be more than merely a wardrobe, and its dimensions are extended by a view that annexes the prominent skyline and the courtyard below...

I need not describe it further—the essence of such hotels being a ubiquitousness in which we may aspire to anonymity. Convention discourages personal mementoes, and anyway the invisible hand of the chambermaid is a corrective to any idiosyncrasy. The metropolitan hotel room is foremost an image of passage and transition. We are conscious of past and future occupants... Our arrival is the witnessing of absence....

I recall… Once, journeying in from the airport … as the
city became more tangible, I realised that although it was
then synonymous with B we had nonetheless lost touch.
I remember that my initial feeling of bewilderment soon
became one of defiance … and in that light I welcomed the
pleasures of autonomy…

My travelling was wistful … and urbane… I had left one
city to free myself from engagements only to resurrect
or construct others. The hope of an accidental reunion
persisted… I longed to catch sight of B perhaps purposeful …
or in a crowd … I exploited the reticent streets, savouring a
curious tension between the vivid and the remote, eventually
descending into the busy Metro, which in turn became
eroticised … the vacant crowd personifying both my wishes
and our estrangement.

HAUNTED * SOMETIMES * REGRETS * PERHAPS

(1986)

*Recipient of a Hille Fellowship in 1985 [I. 4], Chaimowicz was able to stay in Geneva over the winter and spring seasons of 1985–86, where he was offered an artist's studio in the city centre. One day when he was out walking, Chaimowicz passed by the Centre genevois de gravure contemporaine (Centre d'édition contemporaine; CEC since January 2001). Once there, he met the new co-directors of the place, the young Swiss artists Paul Viaccoz, Anne Patry-Chenu, and Marie-Claude Ruata, who cordially invited him to develop a project with them. Chaimowicz began working at the Centre genevois de gravure contemporaine in the autumn of 1985. After becoming familiar with the techniques of engraving and lithography with the help of engravers working on site, Chaimowicz produced a portfolio (56 × 37.5 cm) comprising four watercolour-enhanced prints and a text entitled "HAUNTED * SOMETIMES * REGRETS * PERHAPS" both engraved on Arches paper 250 gsm, and thereafter presented in the gallery space of the Centre genevois de gravure contemporaine, from 13 November, 1986 to 6 January, 1987, in conjunction with the exhibition "Marc Camille Chaimowicz. Œuvres récentes," Galerie Éric Franck, Geneva (13 November, 1986–3 January, 1987).*

The text reproduced below in facsimile mixes remarks on artisanal techniques as experienced by the artist in Geneva, and melancholic words describing his state of mind throughout this creative process. Although the focus is on the materials themselves, confronting their weight, substances, texture, and construction, it is fully counterbalanced by metaphor, reference, and expressive narrative. This text was also reproduced as an illustration in the interview that Swiss art historian Philippe Cuenat conducted in French with the artist in November 1986 that was thereafter published over Spring 1987 in the architectural magazine Faces *[I. 4].*

A.V.

HAUNTED * SOMETIMES * REGRETS * PERHAPS

Merely four words...which beyond their specificity and perhaps their melancholic feel, can nevertheless appear almost heroic... and which for me—in half as many years—thus re establish some sense of possibility...

Genève ◦ Adelaide ◦ Sidney ◦ Bombay
London ◦ Paris ◦ Dijon ◦ Montreal

Words which, other than in a handful of personal letters, from as many impersonal cities, are the first to have acquired some tangibility... Albeit introduced—as though by night time stealth—by being scratched in reverse, firstly through a black varnish, then into copper plate,

REGRETS * PERHAPS * HAUNTED * SOMETIMES

. . . to be then reappropriated by the alchemy of this most contradictory of mediums . . . of curious tensions between the laboured precision of engraving, and the urgency of the acid bath o o o o o o o o o o o between the violence of a steel point digging into flesh like copper . . . to then potentially procure such subtle and delicate results . . .

Four words that could almost be
the destinations on the crossroad
sign post of yet another junction . . .

PERHAPS * REGRETS * SOMETIMES * HAUNTED

or perhaps the chapter headings of some imaginary or future noveletto . . .

[III. 13]

Restlessness in the Belgian Congo

(1987)

In the mid-1980s, German-born, American-citizen, London-based artist Sharon Kivland was dating a good friend of Marc Camille Chaimowicz's. For her solo exhibition to be held at Kettle's Yard Gallery, Cambridge in 1987, Kivland asked her boyfriend to test the waters to see if Chaimowicz would agree to write a text about her work in the 20-page publication to be produced as part of her exhibition. At that time, Chaimowicz was unaware of her work and had no feeling for it, "probably considering it problematic." However, foreseeing that she would insist despite his radio silence, he had to develop diplomatic strategies to avoid her. As expected, she pestered him and finally managed to arrange a meeting to present her work and commission a text, the artist recalled, "with no brief in terms of subject or approach." Their meeting took place over the winter of 1987 at the National Gallery, London, and was followed by an uninterrupted series of messages on the artist's answering machine. From then on, Chaimowicz confessed, "the only way out for me was to write an article about her work, and, at best, to search for ideas we possibly had in common." Rather than focusing on what was going to be exhibited, the text creates a middle-level starting point from which to approach an artistic practice by a subtext commentary on the subject, defying the assumption that interpretation should originate in the mirror of the work itself. Kivland, who is a "proud person," the artist recalled, found the text "brilliant!"

Published on the occasion of the first iteration of Kivland's exhibition at Kettle's Yard Gallery, Cambridge (30 May–12 July, 1987), which subsequently toured to Chapter, Cardiff (18 July–9 August, 1987) and Usher Gallery, Lincoln (18 July–31 August, 1988), the exhibition catalogue was enti-tled The Conversation at Pleasure in Sickness, *and featured an introduction by then Kettle's Yard Gallery curator Hilary Gresty and the essay reproduced below. If this text somewhat reflects the kind of conversation they might have*

*had at the National Gallery in 1987, it is neither particu-
larly knowledgeable nor enthusiastic about Kivland's work,
and it is certainly not working in the service of. As the artist
knew from the outset, "this text would never have made her a
better artist."*

A.V.

· · · · · · · · · ·

When in London, earlier this year, I can remember two consecutive suppers. Firstly, roast duck on a Tuesday—deliciously roasted
in honey, and informally prepared at the home of friends in
Battersea... Then, on Wednesday, a splendid pheasant, formally
cuisined, according to a Normandy recipe by Sharon Kivland.

I can visually recall the locations... The Battersea home is positively cluttered with bric-a-brac. Much of it of French origin;
branded water, jugs, and ash trays—deco lamps in various stages
of repair—old toys—enamelled advertising—items of plastic, and
oddly, much ephemera, postcards, labels, imaged paper bags,
empty cheese boxes... A disordered yet cheery chaos—an image
of anarchic bohemia. And what distinguishes this home is both
the amount of things *around* and the quality of an obsession ...
culminating in some sense of a whole ... a sort of Franco-rustic
as seen by English eyes ... procuring a resultant image of casual
charm and comfort ... and in a rather British way, establishing
a welcoming informality, which encourages sociability. Sharon
Kivland's flat in Lewisham, although crowded, is not cluttered
... it is ordered. Its high profile décor consists of various objects
presented as *collections*... These are principally: plastic souvenir
snow storms—black ceramic heads—religious artefacts—tin animals—white jugs—'50s bric-a-brac—rustic scenes in plaster, and
seaside memorabilia.

These seemingly discordant objects are each placed within their groupings, as though anthropologically. The first impression is that of a private collection or of a somewhat idiosyncratic study... Unlike a museum however it feels strangely ambiguous. It merely has a *sense* of order later qualified by a certain tension... The underlying feeling is somewhat ominous ... and thus not a particularly relaxing space, it is in its oddness and formality, thought provoking. Although these objects are mainly of English origin they seem, perhaps due to the manner of their presentation, strangely alien: England as seen through European eyes? And whatever the trendy look of '50s funk, or '60s *moderne*, they are in their sullen quietude here, bereft of charm... The overriding feeling is indeed one of anxiety...

I am perhaps overemphasising this collection, and Sharon Kivland had probably good reason to despair of the role it has taken on within the general perception of her work—as manipulator of kitsch. It has become to her somewhat of an albatross ... and yet that collection *does* exist and did once feature strongly in her work...

Looking and alone in this sitting room I first recall the Battersea home and realise that there the objects have been wrenched from their origins—then to be cherished, as trophies are, and in manner not dissimilar to that of the Fauves towards Africa ... that is colonised and then re-appropriated aesthetically... Then thus emasculated they are projected outside of an aesthetic framework—towards the spectator in a provocative and playful manner ... indeed that they only now exist ... courtesy of our presence, and according to what life we re-invest in them.

There is in Sharon Kivland's case, no such identification... The very reverse is the case, in that her relationship towards the artefacts is truly subjective. She was born in the mid-'50s, its artefacts are to her normal rather than exotic, they for her are to recall her childhood, *she has loved those things* ... and has said that she's "attracted to the cheap, not from sadness but from joy" and later that "I don't want to collect anything that anyone else would think worth having..." No wonder, therefore, that she should feel both troubled and ambivalent. How would you like *both* your childhood and the *matter* of your labour (mis)appropriated by yuppies driving up to Camden Lock in their BMWs, there to spend merely the *spoils* of their labour.

Intrigued ... and alone in her sitting room I sense that this is no aesthetic pastiche, no shrine to the bizarre, that this location has too great a sense of gravity—and of purpose—to be merely trendy... Yet its purpose eludes me still...

It is as though the real activity occurs in spite of us ... as though these regimented and inanimate artefacts realise themselves ... in our absence... And gradually, within the severity of their regimentation, these ominous objects reveal themselves to me ... to become, of all things, mortars and shells, grenades and rockets ... whatever... *This* is their true function! I am now in no sanctuary, no arty bazaar, but in a veritable arsenal ... and as barrack boys lack credibility when parading ... and realise themselves only when active ... that is, in bars and clubs or fields of war... So here, these objects had this far eluded me—by their good behaviour... I cannot specify the exact nature of Sharon Kivland's battleground and will not further extend the metaphor beyond asking: whose uniform— if any—does she wear? Partisan, Loyalist or that of the Resistance? And is she with her much updated weaponry—attempting to ... "subvert dominant ideology?" Probably ... (Sharon Kivland takes a rare collectivist position in her ongoing commitment to curatorial work; and in supporting other artists believing them to be "a force for radical change.")
If there is a credible sense of unease in the home, there is one of

positive disquiet in the work ... and as Sharon Kivland talked of and around it: of how it is perceived (response being *party* to it, it *matters* to her)—of current (French) modes of thought—of mutations and ambiguity—of pleasures and disease and abundance—of cultural displacement, unknowingness, and sickness—of "having nothing to do with British culture"—of the fallibility of language—of phantasmagoria, strangeness, and the eccentric—of puns and photographic jokes—and much of oddness and the absurd...

It seemed ironic that someone as literary should in her practice refute narrative and I detected a yearning for a pre-wise state that would enable her to tell us ... the stories she would like to, yet given her skepticism regarding language ... cannot.

Then, as she described various characters pictured in her work as ... "angry and shouting people ... sick, tired and thirsty—unfulfilled, ugly and not very nice—fierce and unpleasant, not people you would like to meet—rather grasping..." So a second image came to mind ... that of Belgium! Firstly, these characters became part of the crowd, or joined the rabble in Ensor's magnificent painting of Christ entering Brussels. And secondly, the problematic which is Belgium, its Surrealist tradition from Magritte to Broodthaers. Its simmering radical tensions ... its crisis of language and (thus?) cultural identity... But enough of these hallucinations...

The dilemma ... seems to hinge around the fact that in sharing a post-war sense of disillusionment ... for a cruel and faceless age, Sharon Kivland has acquired the sophistication with which to negotiate the bleakness of the landscape ... but in so doing had to forfeit ... both the romantic and the heroic ... (presumably all the more dubious to her for being male constructs.)

Dispossessed ... she laments this loss, hence perhaps her emphasis on the absurd ... (here seen in dialectical opposition to the heroic!)

But other than seen historically—or indeed rejected (as by Camus), can the phenomenon of absurdity be opposed by something other than the heroic? and placed beyond it into a radical now? An awesome task, but truth wins through … and Sharon Kivland has the capacity to produce images … of intolerable splendour.

[III. 14]

On Orange … As Torture … From a Text in Embryo

(1988)

Co-founded in February 1980 in Marseille by French writer Liliane Giraudon and French poet Jean-Jacques Viton, Banana Split *is a literary review whose editorial selection marked the poetic field of the 1980s. Designed to run for ten years, the twenty-seven issues produced over this period were experienced by the editors as "a kind of shooting star."* Banana Split *was a magazine of poems and texts often published as typescripts, translations, and interviews, which, with a provocative taste for mixing contents and people, borrowed its title from "the stupid name of an internationally famous dessert." Printed on an ever-changing range of coloured papers,* Banana Split *had an artisanal touch, typical of the pre-computer era. Printed on a "large and noisy Xerox machine," the magazine comprised mimeographed texts, a stapled spine, and images roughly printed on offset paper. Favouring immediacy,* Banana Split *aimed to reduce the gap between author and reader. With a print run of between 200 to 500 copies, depending on the issue, the journal (21 × 29.5 cm) was inexpensive, and undoubtedly boosted by its title, which, as Chaimowicz put it in retrospect, "was announcing the desire for an inedible dessert." An active laboratory of the present,* Banana Split *was also open to sculptors, musicians, and writers, as well as to all forms of contemporary poetry, until its dissolution in December 1990.*

Chaimowicz was invited to contribute to Banana Split *at the instigation of Alain Coulange, a French writer from Marseille, in whose company Chaimowicz felt confident [1.6]. However, unfamiliar with poetry,* Banana Split *was not really a place for him. Nevertheless, appreciating the idea of delving into the "subjective and symptomatic of the emotional condition aspect of writing," recalling the context, Chaimowicz began to write a text in the autumn of 1987. The writing process was slow and did not satisfy him, and the situation became "quite embarrassing" as the deadline approached. Chaimowicz had to deal therefore with a pressure he was not used to—being accustomed, as he recalled in retrospect, to a state that "predates instant communication, and therefore operates more readily with written correspondence and outside pre-existing circuits." Thus produced "under pressure," his text for* Banana Split, *which, according to the artist, is "a sort of amalgamation of different types of information," became a torture on orange paper, which the artist included in the title of "text in embryo."*

Designed by Chaimowicz, the text layout consists of one black frame per page, within which the text is surrounded by a multiplicity of Chaimowiczian motifs edged in black. This five-page text was inserted in the centre of the 178-page issue, alongside contributions by Octavio Paz, Christian Boltanski, Pascale Monnier, and Olivier Cadiot, among others. Unlike the other contributions, which are page-numbered, Chaimowicz's contribution is announced in the table of contents on pages "A, B, C, D, E," which do not exist. On receiving the magazine, the artist conceded, "the orange colour is too weird to be worse!"

A.V.

· · · · · · · · ·

Editor's note: The protagonist is wintering in the Rocky Mountains of Western Canada … his lover is enjoying the last of the summer sun in Southern Australia. There is, between them, a considerable correspondence. At this point in the narrative he is in the reverie … of writing … to her, for her.

There is an inoffensive wooden pole (as surveyors might use) directly in view from his window—but which he now tries to avoid—of plain wood, i.e. beige. It is topped in a fluorescent orange. Orange … whose violence is that of the hollow ground razor blade, whose shrillness is perhaps based on what it lacks, because as a hybrid it has neither the softness of yellows nor the warmth of red (which, if it can match in force, it cannot in its passion).

The colour of emptiness … its cry is one of loss. Orange is then the hollow cry of impotence.

(It is controversial because it can repel and attract… Take the Marigold, it attracts the slug, yet what aphid—that destructive little pest of most flora—will ever have the courage to eat away the tender bud of this flower?)

Lacking both gentleness and true visibility it was anathema to La Belle Ecole and is now generally feared and avoided by painters.

Lacking in authority, it is a bastard child, sickly and mean spirited; and rather than being dependent on a gang, as is the bully, it is the loner … prone to delinquency. (The hyena laughing alone and desperately.)

The skill then of Matisse, and also of Bonnard, is that they have each in their own fashion understood this. They knew, as master colourists, that colour cannot truly ever exist alone … that it is always ultimately a matter of relationships.

And their genius is such that, more than being merely co-opted or fostered, this orphan colour has by them been … adopted … and so re-socialised.
And once thus rehabilitated, it is then able to flaunt its marginal origin, its uniqueness—but now with defiance rather than surliness—with a new confidence, bravado, and vigour.

He was, anyhow, recently vacantly staring out of the studio window, his mind on him and her, when…

Oh horror, that silly little stick all of a sudden became… Her (triggered doubtlessly by an image from a recent letter, by a casual, provocative but now intolerable reference) … her … in 39 degrees and wearing nothing but a saffron shirt! (It was here freezing still.)

And this set off a whole chain of associations but principally the vivid recall of one specific afternoon;

… A begun languid bedroom time in which they were each progressively undressing the other … and of a particular moment, when caressing one another—each now semi-dressed and semi-aroused—she giving him a look began as fleetingly quizzical, then mercurially to acquire a hint of wickedness … exuding sexual appeal … reach for a kiss, now generous, lustful, desirous … free of ambiguity. And preceding that time in which
he found his favourite place…

Becoming aware then of a combination of colours somehow remarkable… Of the hues of her flesh ranging from an ivory of her stomach, through light umbers to a soft sienna on her breast, then of the warm beige of her satin top, all to a backdrop of the dusty pale green bed cover…

Then to realise that these colours were each in correspondence, charged, eroticised, by a perfect note, by the vibrancy of the orange of her satin underwear … which completed this aesthetic and galvanised it, taking it from the pleasurable to the sublime.

And he thought then that this colour play, should it have been possible to single it out from the bliss of their caresses—on which it was of course dependent—could only then possibly have been matched, in its harmony and perfection, by the very sensuality, by the erotic mutuality … from which it derived.

And it was for a moment exquisite then, as though they were within a hybrid yet living … late Bonnard interior.

Such now for him is the torturousness of Orange.

On the Dialectic Between the Fine Arts and Design 1987

(1989)

The text reproduced below comes from a letter written originally by the artist in 1987 to French art critic and scholar Hubert Besacier. The two men had been conversing since the mid-1980s, meeting in Dijon when Chaimowicz visited students at the École des Beaux-Arts. Tired of speculating about the promiscuity of painting, furniture, sculpture, and motif in his work, the artist felt it was time to attempt to clarify these interactions and decided to set them out in a letter to Besacier.

Revised two years later, the letter was designed by the artist and illustrated accordingly, including in the lower section pictograms of his furniture pieces from the 1980s. Organised around seven themes, this text, the artist reflected, "kept the spirit of the letter, because it's in conversation that one often resolves contradictions." Conceived as "a trace" of the artist's production over the decade and of his ongoing conversation with Besacier, this text was first printed in 1989 on the inside of an announcement card (21 × 25 cm) produced for the exhibition "Marc Camille Chaimowicz: The Fine and The Applied Arts," The Showroom, London (22 March–16 April, 1989). Printed on thick grey paper, this announcement was printed in two different versions. One was mass-produced in black colour, while the other was produced in very small quantities, and features reddish-brown elements. In addition, the one with the largest print run is marked "Published to concur with an exhibition held at the gallery," which is not the case with the other card. Over time, and because only few people knew about it, the card with the red-brown elements proved to be extremely rare. Beyond these editorial details elaborated by the artist, "On the dialectic between fine arts and design" began to circulate publicly in March 1989.

Founded in 1983, The Showroom is a non-for-profit art gallery that displays site-specific works by emerging artists. Underused in the second half of the 1980s, British curator and art writer David Thorp was commissioned to reorganise the venue, then located in Bethnal Green. As director of The Showroom from 1988 to 1992, he developed an exhibition program that made it one of London's most interesting experimental galleries of the late 1980s. Chaimowicz's solo exhibition was one the first exhibitions Thorp organised. At the time, he was convinced of the need to show recent developments in Chaimowicz's work. Over the course of the decade, the artist had produced wall-paper, textile design, furniture, and painting—most of which was eschewed by the fine art establishment as "decorative"—contaminating each other. Thorp intuited that the artist had forged a left-leaning practice, whose camp, seductive, and erotic dimensions merited public discussion. As British-American Berlin-based writer Kirsty Bell wrote (Parkett, Vol. 96, 2015, p. 20), "bringing together the social space of the gallery with the solitude of the home, Chaimowicz consciously contaminates the fine arts of the former with the decorative arts of the later, until there is no division between the two." The 1989 exhibition and text are among the first public steps in this direction.

At the time, Chaimowicz ironically considered "On the dialectic between the fine arts and design" to be "the premises of a manifesto," knowing that, in the British context, the artist admitted from a distance, "people are suspicious of dogma with a few exceptions, including Karl Marx, who actually wrote his manifesto in London!"

The text reproduced below was subsequently used by the artist as the second part of the essay published in the autumn of 1989 in World Architecture *[II. 10]. The following year, it was reproduced as a facsimile in* To Give and To Take Meaning… Fine and Applied Art: Marc Camille Chaimowicz 1986–1990, *a 64-page bilingual English-French monograph co-published by The Showroom and the Musée de Cosne-Cours-sur-Loire, where the London exhibition ran from 13 July to 16 September, 1990.*

A.V.

ON THE DIALECTIC BETWEEN THE FINE ARTS AND DESIGN

"The craftsman is responsible to his material, the architect to his client . . . , the artist is responsible simply to God" Adolf Loos.

I am intrigued by your argument that there is no essential difference between my fine art and design activities . . . Because whereby this applies to the level of commitment to each activity, in that I make no hierarchical distinction between working, say, on a painting, a book, a silk scarf or a piece of furniture, I nevertheless instinctively feel that there are differences which are more than qualitative and perhaps to do with motivation . . . or is this merely a cultural response?

Whenever engaged in various design projects — whatever the possible aesthetic closeness — my relationship to this work feels somehow different. It is as though it comes from a different part of me . . . that I am calling upon other faculties and that although I may be just as engaged I nonetheless feel more objective and detached.

This variance is probably in part due to the slow time base of such projects, with their frequent delays . . . and the greater objectivity resultant of those technical discussions with such intermediaries as producers and manufacturers . . . which in turn can lead to design changes . . . and therefore to a shift in the relations of responsibilities . . .

But I think the fundamental difference to be roughly this:

That as artists we work and produce primarily for ourselves . . . that I do so for myself and, the Other . . . who, real or imagined, is the object of my desire, the one I want to seduce, to offer myself to . . . be seduced by. That when making art I am therefore, metaphorically, both privileged and handicapped by a desirous condition . . .

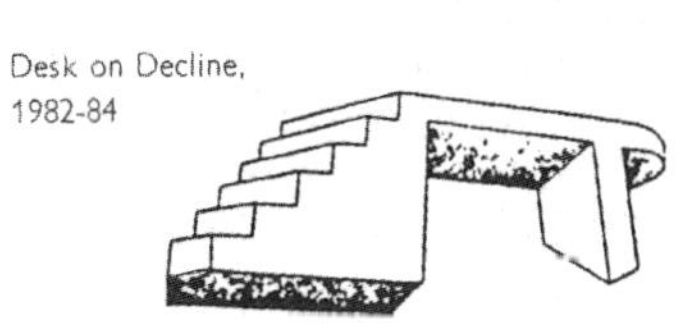

Desk on Decline, 1982-84

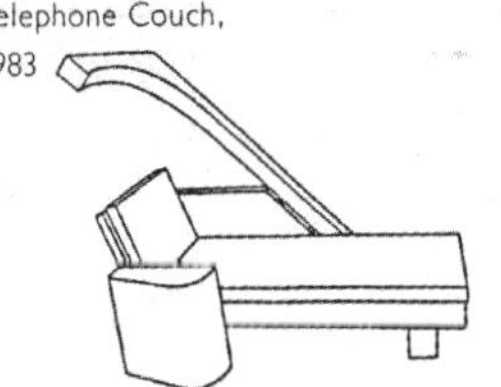

Telephone Couch, 1983

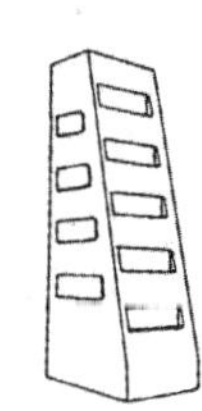

Chest, 1983

ront cover: Innuendo No. 3 1985-86

a sort of state of grace, within which I am beyond any sense of obligation, responsibility or of conscience . . . other than from those terms that are specific to that intimate complicity — and thus exclusive.

Design work therefore differs in that it is not so much for myself and the other, not so much *'Pour toi, de moi'* . . . as *'de nous, pour vous'*, that given it includes the skills of others'

FROM OURSELVES — FOR OTHERS

MULTIPLICITY

A shift of emphasis is thus established from the singular to the plural and logically so, in that one is dealing with multiplicity, with the *'editioning'* of objects, with the *'production'* of wallpaper or fabric . . .

If my mainstream work is rooted in matters of identity . . . in the quest of the self (and its ideal) and therefore in a problematic, then within the poetics of design it is as though there is also a shift *away* from the self towards the selfless . . . (that which is free of any problematic) the nameless, the anonym, and perhaps the platonic . . . And on this path leading away from the unique there also lies a shift . . . from the intimate and towards the anonymous.

THE ANONYM

One activity will naturally inform the other but they remain in tangent and opposite . . . It is this contact which stimulates me . . . and within which, rather than extend my fine art aesthetic, I can *complement* it with design. I enjoy the dialectic.

SPECIFICITY

A fire extinguisher, a coffee pot, an armchair or a jug are each inbued with instant meaning . . . They tell us what they are, and what they do . . . in a way that the mute, enigmatic painting does not. Design gives us answers, Fine Art poses questions. We *take* meaning from Design . . . and *give* meaning to Fine Art.

MEANING

From a letter of 1987 to H. Besacier, Revised 1989.

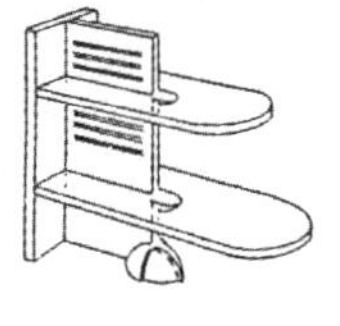

Table de Conversation, 1986

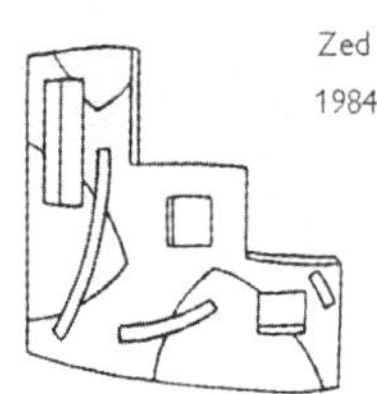

Screens, 1986-88

Zed Stool, 1984-87

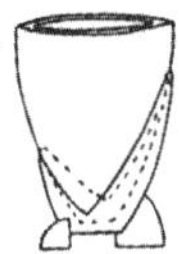

Loxos Cristal Vase, 1989

[III. 16]

The Drawings Done Away...

(1993)

In 1991, Chaimowicz was invited to hold a solo exhibition at the Centre for Contemporary Art Ujazdowski Castle, Warsaw. Having previously declined all invitations to exhibit his work in Poland, he accepted this one as a tribute to his Polish father, who was at the time hospitalised in London. For "The Warsaw Suite" (12 March–15 April, 1993), Milada Ślizińska, curator of the exhibition, proposed that Chaimowicz produce a new publication, similar to Vocabulary… Jan 87 →. *Published in France in 1990, to coincide with four exhibitions of the artist's work held between April and June 1990 in Lyon and Nice,* Vocabulary… Jan 87 → *is a 36-page book (11 × 15.5 cm) consisting of 47 scanned drawings made by the artist between 1987 and 1990, and "chosen arbitrarily" by him from his sketchbooks. When Ślizińska suggested the idea of a second volume of "vocabulary," featuring a selection of sketches made by the artist in Warsaw between 1991 and 1993, Chaimowicz took it up immediately.*

Conceived and designed by the artist in parallel with the exhibition, Vocabulary… Vol. 2 *is a 44-page publication (11.5 × 16.5 cm) comprising 47 colour drawings scanned "probably at the beginning of scanning," assumed the artist in retrospect, and reproduced to scale. Arranged in a loosely chronological order, these drawings are divided into three groups: first, the drawings made in July 1991, when the artist first visited Poland; second, the drawings made between the artist's first and second visits to Warsaw; third, the drawings made in September 1992, to which have been added the same drawings based on the artist's memories of this stay. The three groups are separated from each other by endpapers featuring black and white motifs similar to those on the works shown in the "The Warsaw Suite" exhibition. The result is that, page after page, recurring elements appear, making visible some elements of the artist's "vocabulary."*

At the end of Vocabulary… Vol. 2, *small notes by the artist are collected in English and translated into Polish. In the notes reproduced below, the artist evokes both the role that sketch-books have in his daily life and the "curiously relaxed, connected and … familiar" relationship with Warsaw, a city that is deeply linked to his family origins, especially to his father, and that he was discovering at that time. The sketch of the artist's father's face, drawn from memory after he visited him in hospital, is emblematic of this period. Reproduced as the frontispiece to Vocabulary… Vol. 2, this sketch, entitled "In Memory of my Father born in Wloclawek," interacts with the notes published at the end of the volume and reproduced below, in particular when the artist presents meditations on the theme of "separation" and "detachment" in relation to Warsaw, just as his father was passing away. Regarding the sketch of his father's face, the artist said, "I'd never done anything like this before. My brain scanned it, and the resulting resemblance is quite disturbing." Chaimowicz never returned to Poland thereafter.*

A.V.

· · · · · · · · ·

The drawings done away from home, and therefore when away from the studio, tend to be richer and more intense, i.e. more complete (My books become the primary creative space) and the work in them NOMADIC.

Ideas and notes, i.e. generally the written, exist in different formats. "Vocabularies" are of the visual order. "… moments of pleasure," and "the focal point where the mental and visual can collude, coincide and take form."*

By their very nature of being intimate carnets they procure signs, motifs, and speculation which exist outside of censorship … and therefore of usual value judgments. They are often worked on in ambiguously public yet solitary places … stations, trains, airports, cafés, hotel rooms. Beyond helping to reconnect with myself and to make some sense of the external they can inform later work.

Volume One was selected by an editor. Regarding *Volume Two*, I have been selective on the basis of either the most arresting, resolved, or revealing…

From Notes of 5 July '91
Warsaw was so vivid and intense that my week seemed to cover an eternity of feelings, dislocated memories, borrowed fictions, and reconstructions.

… how anxious if not a little paranoid I was about this, my first trip to Poland. (by which) I wasn't so much transformed—not so much upon leaving a different person—but more so, as though touched … perhaps by the invisible yet weighty hand of history… The better (then) to recognise unknown aspects with which I can now contemplate some (genetic) restoration.

****

In the infantile phase of self-development and the subsequent separation from the body (of the mother) how much do we progressively project our fantasies and sense of self on the outside world? And is development measured by the ability to glide over the landscapes (or to master the urban)? i.e. for detachment? Then—to reconstruct our self-chosen mental contexts. This perhaps being one role of creativity and therefore why I was whilst in Warsaw able to feel, on occasion, curiously relaxed, connected, and … familiar.

* Hubert Besacier, "A privileged moment…" in *Marc Camille Chaimowicz, Vocabulary… Jan 87 →*, Vol. 1, 1990.

[III. 17]

On the Everydaynessness of Things

(1996)

In 1996, after almost two years away from artistic activity, Chaimowicz was invited to hold an exhibition at Interface, a not-for-profit organisation based in a private apartment in Dijon. Founded by French cultural producer Frédéric Buisson in 1992, Interface was initiated to support artists in their early development both logistically and financially. In 1996, the organisation began to involve established artists. Emblematic of this turn is Chaimowicz's solo exhibition "Au quotidien des choses" ("On the Everydaynessness of Things"), which ran from 21 September through 19 October, 1996.

Like any other artist-run space, Interface operates in the art world without grandiloquence. Enthralled by "the pleasant modesty of the context," an empty one-bedroom apartment in a small 1950s building, Chaimowicz choreographed his "humble" exhibition into three moments. In the entrance hall, a cane with a painted knob and two wine glasses are on display. In the living room, a white-painted wall shelf, entitled On the Everydaynessness of Things "contained" *features domestic-size objects and sculptural forms covered in paper and hand-decorated with paint by the artist. In the bedroom, a white-painted wooden table featuring objects covered in paper is installed in a corner roughly painted on the wall by the artist. Next to the table, two simple wooden chairs leaning against each other, one topped by a worn white sneaker, are surrounded by small sculptural pieces scattered across the floor. Entitled* On the Everydaynessness of Things "extended," *this domestic environment functions in the apartment as an arena, defining a space within another. The exhibition marked a turning point for Chaimowicz. Not only because he presented covered objects with paper or paint, which he subsequently used for the aesthetic formation of an artwork or installation, but also because he demonstrated that "under a decorated surface, objects remain functional stuff," which, as an artist's statement echoes Chaimowicz's furniture sculptures of the 1980s [III. 15] as well as the objects and paintings he exhibited in 1994 in his solo exhibition "Paintings and Objects" [I. 6] at Le Consortium, Dijon. Moreover, by coating the objects in something else, Chaimowicz keeps their raw material veiled while satisfying our ambivalent desire for depth and surface in relation to (art) objects, which the artist pins down into three emblematic "species" of the mid-1990s.*

A few days before the end of the exhibition a folding hardback leaflet was produced, "thanks to an almost overdue financial support of two institutional partners!" the artist recalled in retrospect. Printed in red colour on a thick yellow paper, this tiny exhibition souvenir (12 × 15 cm) comprises illustrations of the two works exhibited, as well as a short text by French art critic and scholar Hubert Besacier written for the occasion, as well as the text reproduced below. Written in English in September 1996, and subsequently translated into French, this text, conceived like a program, was published only in French. The English version below is therefore published for the first time.

Written in one night after the exhibition was open to the public, this text is based on elements from a correspondence between the artist and Besacier. Conceived as a synthesis about the objects presented in the exhibition at Interface, the text is divided into three parts, referring to three "species" of objects—"AUTONOMOUS, HYBRID, alien or MUTANT"—whose specificities are described by the artist in an attempt at classification. Throughout this text, the artist emphasises the opacity of objects—or at least the right to stake one's claim to it.

A.V.

… There is to be a diversity of objects or things, and their providence is from London, Burgundy, and Athens.
Some retain their identity, whatever plastic treatment they may have endured, whilst others now only exist by courtesy of the collective…

They would seem to fall into three species:

The first are whole, in that they are recognisably of the everyday. These are the AUTONOMOUS objects. Once functional, they now seem to enjoy their ornamental role, and whatever the conditions, they hold their identity and innocence … intact.

The second are HYBRID and hint at having once being related to the first. They are imbued with the memory of function yet, in their wholeheartedness have become, in their practical sense, irretrievable. Their circumstance is now within the cultural.

The third are alien or MUTANT. They were never of the everyday… Yet if they seem, in their strangeness oddly familiar is this not because they would appear to have wandered into this context from a more familiar order; that of painting? Yet, in so doing, acquiring three dimensionality. And so, as might season partygoers upon finding themselves by accident at the wrong party, these, of all the objects or things, nevertheless, are perhaps the most at ease!

[III. 18]
Statement

(2000)

Taking its title from Harald Szeemann's seminal 1969 exhibition "Live in Your Head: When Attitudes Become Form," the exhibition "Live in Your Head: Concept and Experiment in Britain, 1965–75," Whitechapel, London (4 February–2 April, 2000), was conceived with the aim of re-examining the artistic legacy of the 1960s and 1970s, and attempted to clarify points of origin of a formative generation in British art. Initiated and curated jointly by Clive Phillpot, a British art writer, curator, and librarian, and Andrea Tarsia, an Italian-born, London-based curator, the exhibition, in fact, documented a crucial period of change in British art, during which the supremacy of painting and sculpture was challenged with long-lasting results, particularly the more ephemeral and remote practices that flourished during this legendary period.

Conceived as "an essential guide to the period," the 175-page black and white publication produced to coincide with the exhibition is the first since the 1970s to focus specifically on conceptual and experimental art in Britain between 1965 and 1975. Gathering the work of sixty-four artists, including John Latham, Gustav Metzger, David Medalla, Art & Language, Susan Hiller, the Boyle Family, Richard Long, Kay Fido Hunt, Marc Camille Chaimowicz, Margaret Harrison, Mary Kelly, as well as more extreme projects, the publication was intended to be a source book. Divided into four sections, the book includes texts and essays by Michael Archer [I. 7, 8], Rosetta Brooks [III. 3], Catherine Lampert, Clive Phillpot, and Andrea Tarsia, as well as a lively illustrated chronology of social and cultural events in the period 1965–75, and a section devoted to the artists, each of whom has a double-page spread. Chaimowicz's double-page spread includes the "Statement" reproduced below, a portrait of the artist on the cover of Art and Artists, *December 1973 [I. 1], three reproductions of work, and biographical and bibliographical information.*

Dated 1999, the artist's short "Statement" briefly describes the context in which, in the early 1970s, Chaimowicz took up a political position, attempting to "integrate ideas of the counterculture with practice." Written almost thirty years later, this statement is supported in the publication by illustrations that include Table Tableau *(1974),* Celebration? Realife *(1972) [III. 2, 3, 4], and* We Chose Our Words With Care, That Neon-Moonlit Evening *(1975) [I. 2]. In addition, three quotations chosen by the artist from previous publications are reproduced alongside each illustration. For example, next to* Table Tableau, *in which the artist shows his bare back lying on a table next to a mirror, a lit candle, flowers, and cigarettes, we read "Unlearn 'art'. Unlearn 'artwork'. Unlearn 'closure'. Unlearn 'public' and 'private'. Finally unlearn 'man' (Stuart Morgan, "Under the Sign of Saturn," Nigel Greenwood Gallery, 1987)." The illustration of* Celebration? Realife *is accompanied by a quote by Caroline Tisdall from* Studio International, *Vol. 192, no. 982, July/August 1976, to the effect that "Chaimowicz's* Celebration *was light to this darkness. In place of the isolated framed individual he tentatively offered a sense of integration." Finally, to accompany a shot of* We Chose Our Words With Care, That Neon-Moonlit Evening, *the artist chose a quote by Jean Fisher. Taken from* Past Imperfect. Marc Camille Chaimowicz 1972–1982 *(Liverpool: Bluecoat Gallery et al., 1983, p. 5), the excerpt reads:*

> *"This is an art of pleasure, of the self that strives for a purity of expression and a perfect harmony uncontaminated by the discordant noise of the outside: an art in whose exquisite formality, however, there yet resides a restless and unquiet spirit. For it is a sensibility antithetical to New World vigor, one that is introspective, and*

deeply embedded in the French tradition that gave rise to Proust, Gide, Camus and Genet: a psyche born in the evening shadows of a culture ancient and possessive."

By supplementing illustrations to illuminate the work's reception in retrospect, the past links to present and the present to the past. And, at the same time, Chaimowicz was making a similar movement, overseeing, between past and present, the "revisitation" of Celebration? Realife *[I. 7], Cabinet, London (9 June–29 July, 2000).*

A.V.

· · · · · · · · ·

I got to Ealing art school in 1963, a year after Pete Townshend of The Who. By 1968 I was graduating in painting in Camberwell and encountering the tutor's wrath by absconding to Paris (as though from A Calling) to *Les Evénements* in May. Nonetheless that year I was offered a place at the Slade School. It was from there that I dealt, in my own manner, with the Culturally Urgent.

There seemed then to be three options…

The first, and the dominant, was to busy oneself in the studio. The second, and "in the now" and then probably the "coolest" was to drop out.

The third, and perhaps the most complex and audacious, was to try to integrate ideas of the counter-culture with practice. This was naturally my choice … and was why I was drawn away from the claustrophobia of pre-existent forms towards activities that were as yet unnamed or ill formed … like an emergent language.

[III. 19]
Aléa

(2003)

When Chaimowicz was working in Agey, Burgundy, in the pied-à-terre he occupied in the conciergerie of a castle, the young French artist Jocelyn Saint-André used to assist him from time to time. Chaimowicz didn't know much about him, except that he was a graduate from the École des Beaux-Arts in Dijon. Nevertheless, he was always happy to spend some time in Agey with him and his dog Aléa. Because of this proximity, Saint-André assumed around the spring of 2003 that Chaimowicz would be delighted to write an article for the forthcoming bilingual 48-page monograph on his work that he was preparing. This monograph was to be published in September 2003 by Interface, a non-profit organisation based in an apartment in Dijon [III. 17], where Saint-André had presented several works the year before. Sharing this idea with Chaimowicz, the latter in return proposed a studio visit the next time he was in Dijon. This happened a few months later, in July 2003. On this occasion, Saint-André introduced Chaimowicz to his work as well as to the monograph project, which was in process. That day, Chaimowicz discovered that the contributors involved in this publication were people he knew personally: Jean-Philippe Vienne, then Director of the École des Beaux-Arts in Dijon, French artist Guillaume Mansart, and Burgundy-based American socialite Sherry Thévenot.

Wishing to be courteous to the publisher, and because Saint-André had noticed that his dog drew Chaimowicz's attention, he suggested that he contribute to the monograph on an allegorical level, and therefore write a few lines about his dog instead of his work. "Aléa was boyish," recalled Chaimowicz, her surname was "Tomboy." Truly blown away by the agility of this "jumping dog" with long black hair, Chaimowicz decided to translate Aléa's art of movement into words. Interacting metaphorically with Saint-André's artistic approach, this text reproduced below, was written by the artist in one sitting, simultaneously in English and French, in August 2003. Subtly interfering with "the clean and the dirty," "the general and the particular," "the vertical plane and the seemingly gravity free," Chaimowicz has developed unexpected analogies between Aléa's art and that of her owner. "Aléa was so difficult to photograph," Chaimowicz said in retrospect, "the photographic portrait of her published alongside the few lines I wrote for Jocelyn was uncredited. It seems that no one has been able to identify who took the photo!" In this photo, indeed, opposites attract. As the maxim seems to be proving true, the dog is standing outside on the ground, a tennis ball between her paws, probably ready for the next jump. Is the veil between Aléa's energy and the art of Saint-André thin or thick? As Diana Vreeland, the influential Harpers & Bazaar *and* Vogue *fashion editor put it in the 1960s, "The eye has to travel, and colour does just that. It takes you on a journey. One dash—of fuchsia or deep green—can make a dog sing."*

A.V.

• • • • • • • • •

Aléa arrives full of energy and is soon wholeheartedly engaged in her favoured pastime, which entails running at high speed in chase of her new tennis ball. She is sure footed as she runs over the parched uneven earth and, as might a silkscreen printer when pulling a print, she skims the surface in one single non-stop move. Her rapport to the ground seems effortless…

The new ball is soon sullied, its once anodyne and neutral surface acquiring through use, through wear and tear, (albeit imperceptibly) a discreet specificity. This *interface* between the general and the particular would seem to fascinate her owner Jocelyn Saint-André.

… She suddenly leaps into the air, this acrobatic jump is *Aléa* at her finest or, (to quote Guillaume Mansart), at her most noble. She is now some 90° to the ground, i.e. on a vertical plane and seemingly gravity-free. Her muzzle wide open, she suddenly catches her ball in mid-air. It is a vertiginous moment to behold.

[III. 20]

Notes Regarding "Concertina"

(2005)

Following the acclaimed "revisitation" of Chaimowicz's Celebration? Realife in 2000 [I. 7] and the dazzling re-enactment of Partial Eclipse… *in Glasgow in 2002 [III. 11c], it was clear that a younger generation of artists and cultural producers had a keen interest in the artist's work. Building on this momentum, the Berlin gallerist Giti Nourbakhsch, who met the artist in Zürich mid-June 2002 on the occasion of the opening at Migros Museum für Gegenwartskunst of the exhibition "St. Petrischnee," convinced Chaimowicz to "re-incarnate"* Partial Eclipse…, *which the artist performed in person at the gallery on Friday, 12 November, 2004, 6 p.m. and 9 p.m., as well as on Saturday, 13 November, 2004, 6 p.m. This event sealed the premise of a fruitful collaboration between Chaimowicz and Nourbakhsch, the latter began to represent the work of the artist, whose first solo show at the gallery—"Concertina"—was presented from 25 June to 30 July, 2005.*

For the exhibition, the artist decided to "compress a time base of thirty-five years into one experience." To achieve this, he brought together old and new works in the same exhibition space. Created for the occasion, Two Speed Staircase *was installed obliquely in the centre of the gallery space. Made of Carrara marble weighing "2 1/2 tonnes!"* and almost touching the ceiling at a height of around four metres, it was surrounded by 200 silver-spray painted shoes scattered across the floor.* Shoe Waste? Piece *dates from 1971 [III. 1, 3]. Three years before it was repeated at Galerie Giti Nourbakhsch, the installation was reactivated for two weeks (2–14 July, 2002) as an off-site project on the paths and bridges of the canal network around Birmingham's Brindleyplace, c/o Ikon Gallery, Birmingham [III. 2]. Displayed in 2005 inside the gallery,* Shoe Waste? Piece *functioned in "Concertina" as a "temporal fold" linking a clandestine past to the present and vice versa. Originally unpacked as part of "Sweetness," the artist's first solo exhibition, Sigi Krauss, London (11 March–2 April, 1971),* Shoe Waste?

Piece *was completed with Bob Young's black and white photographs documenting Chaimowicz's "shoe-waste landscapes" from 1971 [III. 1]. Dated 1971–2005, these five framed photographs were presented at the gallery as an edition.*

When Chaimowicz arrived in Berlin a few days before the opening of "Concertina," he was struck by this "massive piece of stone in the gallery," and immediately thought it might be "fortuitous to draw a parallel with the new Bentley!" He walked around it, sat in front of it, and scattered the silver-painted shoes across the floor, before writing a few notes about the exhibition. Taking the exhibited pieces in context and time, these spontaneous notes were subsequently submitted by the artist to the gallery as "a proposal of text for this piece, with no format in mind." At the instigation of Giti Nourbakhsch, the text was printed on an A4 sheet of paper with the gallery letterhead. Turned into a press release signed by the artist, the text reproduced below was then sent by email, fax, and post to the gallery's mailing list, and was made available to the public over the course of the exhibition.

A.V.

** In 2007, Chaimowicz was invited to be part of Anyang Public Art Project, APAP, Korea. Under the artistic direction of Seoul-Based curator Sung Won Kim and co-curated by Seungduk Kim and Franck Gautherot of Le Consortium, Dijon, the second APAP was inaugurated in Pyeongchon and Anyang on 20 October, 2007. It consisted of forty-six new commissions by both Korean and internationally renowned artists, among which thirty-two are permanent. As described in the press release, "APAP 2 was held under the theme of 'Appropriate, Regenerate, Transform,' centring around the parks and the city centre of Pyeongchon in order to regenerate the identity and environment of the city, and to transform the urban environment."*

For his part, Chaimowicz envisioned that KIOSK, originally a model for "A Structure for an Individual in Society," be made in concrete. Designed in the early 1980s, KIOSK was first a drawing and a small cardboard model until the artist suggested in 1994 that the life-size KIOSK be manufactured in wood so that a person can actually fit in, jointly to the exhibition "Peintures & Objets," Le Consortium, Dijon (10 September–15 October, 1994) and Le Quartier, Quimper (22 October–31 December, 1994) [I. 6]. To develop the concrete and steel version of a place where intimacy and social function might intersect in public space, Chaimowicz travelled to Seoul. He visited Hakun Park, and chose the location for KIOSK. During that trip, he also provided several technical drawings, from which that "Space for an Individual" began to be produced in a combination of three different colours. A year later, far from any contingencies linked to that project, Chaimowicz received, he said, "a very heavy, yet not so big wooden crate," which, apparently, had caused considerable pain to the three deliverymen who brought it up to his third floor apartment in Camberwell, London. After inspection, Chaimowicz opened the crate and discovered, baffled, that it was full of concrete coloured samples. At first thinking this "beautiful palette" was a joke, he stressed out, anticipating how difficult it would be for him to carry this mass of cement out of his apartment. Dumbfounded that "people are able to send concrete by plane," that day, unexpectedly, his 2.5 tonnes Two Speed Staircase from 2005 came back to his mind, this time as a bad trip.

··········

The principal space of my first solo show, "Sweetness," at the Sigi Krauss Gallery, London 1971, consisted of an empty room save for the floor, which was filled wall to wall with once discarded shoes, now painted silver.

(I had, earlier, enacted *Shoe Waste? Piece* in agitprop and thus clandestine fashion on various sites above and beneath the River Thames.)

Plans for *L'Escalier à deux vitesses* arose whilst on scaffolding, thirteen metres from the ground, to execute the commission to paint the ceiling of the chapel *L'Hôtel-Dieu* at Cluny in 2003. If this Commande Publique was to be permanent, the exhibition at *Les Ecuries de Saint-Hugues* that summer was temporary, and consisted of a suite of autonomous 3-D works, which were each grounded. Of these, the *Two Speed Staircase* was the biggest and, at over four metres, also the tallest. Almost touching the ceiling it was therefore perhaps a visual link between the terrestrial and celestial…

(A domestic version had earlier been proposed within an integrated design solution for a friend's London studio flat—and was later prototyped as a quasi-functional feature within the *Jean Cocteau* interior of 2003 in which, whilst *implying* ascendancy, it also functioned as a unit for display.)

Concertina shown at the Galerie Giti Nourbakhsch, Berlin, June 2005, is the first time these two aspects of *Repertoire* coexist, in time and space; it thus *compresses* a time base of thirty-five years into one experience. As with the *Deleuzian temporal fold* which negotiates the fold of time, the past folds into the present, and the present into the past. It is also the first occasion in which I have used Carrara marble (2 1/2 tonnes!), its inherent nobility perhaps here heightened by the pedestrian nature of *reclaimed* shoes.

This then is background; I leave a multiplicity of possible readings to you and your audience.

[III. 21]

Central Line…

(2006)

In 2006, Chaimowicz was commissioned by the South London Gallery, London, to consider a work in relation to a group show entitled "Around the World in Eighty Days" in co-production with the ICA, London. Presented simultaneously in both venues from 24 May through 16 July, 2006, and displayed according to the eighty days of Jules Verne's novel, forming a timeline that begins at the ICA and finishes at the South London Gallery, this exhibition, Chaimowicz recalls, "was designed to gather UK-based artists born outside England, who were invited to respond to a Jules Verne's classic nineteenth century novel..." Based on an idea by Jens Hoffmann, then Director of the exhibitions at the ICA, and jointly co-organised by Margot Heller and Kit Hammonds, at the time respectively Director and Curator at the South London Gallery, the exhibition focused on "the growingly internationalism of the London art world while considering art, history and the social construction of places, spaces and identities from both a global and a local perspective."

Each of the nineteen participating artists (Jananne Al-Ani, Alexandre da Cunha, Marc Camille Chaimowicz, Godfried Donkor, Ivan Grubanov, Mona Hatoum, Runa Islam, Janice Kerbel, Oswaldo Maciá, Rosalind Nashashibi, Uriel Orlow, Zineb Sedira, João Penalva, Hiraki Sawa, Raqib Shaw, Yinka Shonibare, Erika Tan, Francis Upritchard, and Nicole Wermers) were sent a hard-cover copy of Jules Verne's eponymous book, from which they were invited to "either exhibit a new piece that has been especially conceived in response to the novel, or present an existing work that relates to a theme or topic outlined by the narrative." In the press release issued some time before the exhibition opening, it is specified that "regardless of having read the book or not, the very idea of circumnavigating the globe within a limited and pre-determined time frame conjures myriad thoughts, questions and possibilities around the mode of transport, the route to be followed and importantly, as

Phileas Fogg discovered upon his return, the method of time-keeping to be used."

As a contribution to the exhibition, Chaimowicz submitted the text reproduced below. Designed by the artist on two A4 sheets, this piece was presented at the South London Gallery on an adjustable plywood bookstand (28 × 44 × 28 cm) that the artist designed in 2005–06 for his long-time friend Roger Cook [I. 12]. As Cook was about to retire, the art department at the University of Reading consulted Chaimowicz, who also taught at Reading, to help determine what would be the most appropriate farewell gift for his colleague. Knowing that Cook particularly enjoyed reading lying down, he offered to design this adjustable plywood bookstand, which he engraved with the words "Pour mon frère fictif" (For my Fictive Brother), the work's title. Installed on a museum plinth, this adjustable prototype for the bookstand made it easy for visitors to the exhibition to read the artist's text.

Inspired by the title of Jules Verne's book, this text takes us to the London Underground, precisely on the "Central Line," where the artist relates a real-life experience. While travelling on this line, two men seated next to him were wearing hats, as Chaimowicz always does when in public. So, with ease, reflected the artist, "we made eye contact and talked about … our respective hats!" Illustrated accordingly, the text originally includes the three hats the passengers were wearing that day—namely an Islamic-style Albakaram cap, an English tweed cap, and the artist's Trilby hat—which together do indeed evoke the "growingly internationalism of the London (art) world" that both the ICA and the South London Gallery set out to highlight. Instantly linking three different cultures on the tube as if in a hatbox, the artist later showed the text as, he said retrospectively, "the preface to a work for the exhibi-*

tion." Made available for reading only for the duration of the exhibition, this text is reproduced below for the first time.

Some time after the opening, "Artists + Friends" were invited to The Reform Club, a private members' club located on the south side of Pall Mall in central London, to celebrate the launch of Around the World in Eighty Days, "a publication conceived as a travel book, reader and exhibition catalog." Marc Camille Chaimowicz attended the party. He recalls, "The venue was impressive." However, given the tight budget allocated to the artists for that exhibition, the artist thought perhaps "the show should have been taking place only in that Club."

A.V.

** Chaimowicz acquired this grey felt hat at the Chapellerie Fourcroy, Dijon, in the early 2000s. A few weeks after his purchase, he noticed the hat was slightly too tight on his head. Therefore, he returned to the shop, where the "serious" saleswoman offered to enlarge his hat accordingly. As a result, Chaimowicz left the hat to her, and asked for a receipt in return. Upset, the saleswoman told him, "Sir, I never forget the hat, neither the client!" There again, the artist felt the charm of provincial manners, and, by extension, the ruin of Emma Bovary.*

· · · · · · · · · ·

Travelling back from Oxford he felt as ever pleased to be back in town, there to meet associates for drinks…

Both engagements had gone well… Such are those days, which

result in that satiated condition… Mix of exhaustion and a sense of startled relief which, when tempered by drink, can conclude in a sense of lightheadedness.

Making his way home he boarded a westbound Tube—at that time after the commuter rush and West End crowds but before the exit of pubs and restaurants—at which the network is uncommonly quiet. But for three passengers the two facing rows were free. On his side sat a good looking couple, both dressed in traditional Islamic manner… The bearded young man was wearing a beautifully decorated Albarakam skull cap.

… Just as the misanthrope may permit himself the occasional foray into the sociability on the premise that it be with strangers and thus free of recourse … or perhaps as measure of his sense of well being (yet in the fore knowledge that he was to alight at the next station) so he inverted protocol, made eye contact and spoke…

"Nice hat!" he said to the young man who … somewhat startled, smiled, and replied, "Do you think so?" "Yes, it really suits you" … and was told, "Yours is pretty good too."

After this briefest of exchanges and on seeing the third passenger—perhaps a chartered accountant, wearing a Barbour jacket and checked cap—he then proposed, "His is pretty good too" … and this chap, probably aspirant to Reform Club membership and doubtlessly feeling inclusive, now joined in by suggesting that the headscarf of the young woman's Chador, was also pretty good.

The protagonist rose, wished the strangers a splendid evening and on leaving the train reflected on the currency of Wim Delvoye's concept of the glocal…

[III. 22]

The World of Interiors

(2007)

Struck by the historical relevance of Chaimowicz's work and its generativity, Heike Munder, Director of the Migros Museum für Gegenwartskunst, Zürich, invited the artist to participate in three consecutive group shows at the museum between 2002 and 2004. First, in "St. Petrischnee" (15 June–8 August, 2002), where Celebration? Realife Revisited *(1972–2000) [I. 7; III. 2, 3, 4] was presented following its recent acquisition by the museum. Then, in "The Future Has a Silver Lining" (28 August–31 October, 2004), co-curated by German art historian and curator Tom Holert, where* Partial Eclipse *(1980–2003) was presented [III. 11c] following its acquisition by the museum in 2003. Finally, in "It's All an Illusion: A Sculpture Project" (12 June–8 April, 2004), where three sculpture works by the artist dating back from three different decades were shown. Following on from this, Munder invited Chaimowicz to do a retrospective exhibition at the museum in 2006, coinciding with the period when the artist's work was being rediscovered by a younger generation of artists and curators, and adopted as a significant reference point and role model.*

At the end of 2005, Marie-France Boyer, Associate Editor, Paris, of the sumptuous British interior and decoration mag-azine The World of Interiors, *contacted Chaimowicz with a view to reporting on his "artist's home." Located in a red brick mansion block on Camberwell New Road, South London, this third-floor apartment was then rumoured to be a one-of-a-kind London home. Honoured by this proposal from a magazine he has consulted extensively since its creation in 1981, the artist immediately accepted the invitation, and a meeting with the photographer was subsequently arranged. Accustomed to reporting on interiors, Chaimowicz was aware that, as an artist, he would undoubtedly be asked to pose in one of the rooms of his apartment for the magazine. As he had already observed, "artist homes" are an exception in interior magazines, insofar as the portrait of their inhabitant is often included in the feature: "To ostensibly give a glimpse of the artistic practice," unlike reports devoted to other interiors, which are "free of people, to allow the reader to idealise the photographed spaces." Chaimowicz was told that the article would be published in the April 2006 issue of* The World of Interiors, *coinciding with both his participation in the third Tate Triennial, Tate Britain, London (1 March–14 May, 2006) and solo exhibition "Zürich Suite," Migros Museum für Gegenwartskunst, Zürich (8 April–18 June, 2006).*

On the day of the shoot, photographer James Mortimer came to Hayes Court with two assistants. It was decided to shoot the apartment in natural light, which is not so easy in winter. A little intrusive and slow, the process took longer than expected. "It was," recalled the artist, "one picture, one morning!" So in the end, it took three days to document the entire apartment. Although Marie-France Boyer was behind the story, she did not make it to the shoot. When she saw the photographs, she freaked out, probably because this interior seemed difficult for her to embrace all at once, and subsequently asked Chaimowicz if he would write an "artist's statement" to accompany the photos, instead of the article she was supposed to write. A few days later, the artist sent the text to her. As soon as she received it [III. 22d], she passed it on to the magazine's editor-in-chief, who turned it down as "too intellectual," and further asked, "Is the artist an Existentialist?" As a result, Boyer ended up writing a text based on the photographs of the apartment, which she never saw in person. In the few lines preceding her article, the apartment is described as "a home that is not quite sure what it's meant to be. A paean to 1950s cinema? A home to landmark art and design? A quaint remnant from the 1970s?" Despite colour photographs attesting to the existence of the central hallway, main bedroom, kitchen, and living room, the seven-page feature was entitled "This is not a flat." As expected, the selected photographs and the accompanying text describe the artist's interior. Among the items featured are the artist's own designs (hand-printed wallpaper and soft furnishings), iconic pieces by Eileen Gray or Otto Wagner, the spectacular red-and-cream-painted kitchen complete with a charming red-and-cream "Peeress" gas stove by Parkinson Cowan, and artworks by Nadia Wallis, Andy Warhol, Jeffrey Camp, or Keith Milow, to name but a few. No doubt this is more than a flat. As British-American Berlin-based writer Kirsty Bell would appropriately describe it ten years later in "Marc Camille Chaimowicz's Provisional Interiors," (Parkett, Vol. 96, 2015, p. 23), Chaimowicz's apartment is akin to "a low-budget Des Esseintes—the anti-hero of J.-K. Huysmans' À Rebours (1884)—who self-consciously invented a domestic realm as a stage for a solo, unwitnessed performance of everyday life." As the sole inhabitant of the Hayes Court apartment, Chaimowicz experienced the interior as a metaphor for presenting real life through the filter of art, in a kind of Lynchian day-for-night environment crystallising an indirect and vibrating portrait of himself.

Unsettled by this semi-lit reverie-inducing domestic interior, Boyer felt it necessary to ask the artist a few questions about the period in which this apartment played with. In one breath, the artist replied to her: "I wanted to capture the nostalgia of the 1940s in the late 1970s, but now with these walls, there is nostalgia for the 1970s, since the place has hardly changed since that time." By designing his apartment as a portal through time, Chaimowicz suggested a camp way of considering the domestic texture of his flat between artifice and irony, of which decoration can only be one aspect. After Chaimowicz moved to Tyers Street, Vauxhall, London, in 2016 [III. 21], the apartment remained unoccupied. In early 2023, however, the apartment entered a new temporality as most of its living room was packed and shipped to Brussels, where it was rearranged into an installation at Wiels, Brussels, on the occasion of the artist's solo exhibition "Nuit américaine" (17 February–13 August, 2023). Encouraging seated contemplation, the now entitled Hayes Court Sitting Room (1979–2023), is a recreation that, as exhibition curator Zoë Gray states in the exhibition guide, "proposes a subjective and provisional experience, rather than the static, authoritative 'museumification' typical to preserved artist's studios and houses." She argues that "to enhance this fictional aspect of the work, Chaimowicz staged what he describes as 'a fast-forwarded photo sequence of two people, as yet unnamed, animating the work in what may be presumed to be a liaison…' The resulting photographs, shown here, function for the artist as the twenty-first-century activation of a twentieth-century interior."

Testifying to a new stage in the history of his lavish yet austere Camberwell New Road interior, this rearrangement of the sitting room into an exhibition space, together with the photographs taken on site before the furniture was shipped to Brussels, gives the appearance of a time machine, whose artistic use over four decades goes far beyond the decorating issues supposedly addressed in interior design magazines. In early April 2006, the issue of The World of Interiors came out. Curious to see the feature on his apartment, Chaimowicz picked up a copy. At that time, he was completing the installment of his solo exhibition "Zürich Suite," featuring an emblematic selection of works from the early 1970s to the present day. Flipping through the magazine, Chaimowicz had the intuition that it would be much better, he said, "to reproduce a magazine than to consume it." Since the exhibition catalogue project initiated by Munder had not yet taken shape, the timing was spot-on. Known for his recalcitrance to conventional exhibition publications, and given that *two small "monographs on artist" were still available at the time, it seemed, the artist admitted, that "a third monograph didn't seem necessary unless it is an autonomous book."*

With the magazine in hand, Chaimowicz began exploring the possibility of deconstructing it with a view to producing a catalogue in magazine form. Using the April 2006 issue of the magazine as a template for publication seemed appropriate in relation to the retrospective exhibition he had just conceived as a series of "interior" rooms—"interior" meaning the domestic interior as well as interiority of one's inner life—in reference to the decisive role this notion had played in his work since the mid-1970s. As a result, Chaimowicz opted for a radical reworking of the issue, as a possible basis for original artwork and documentation. As a reference monograph, this project immediately aroused the collective enthusiasm of the publisher (Migros Museum für Gegenwartskunst), distributor (JRP-Ringier, then headed by Lionel Bovier), and graphic designers (Lehni/Trüb) alike. Lehni/Trüb, a then-new Zürich-based design studio, had just been hired by the Migros Foundation to design the museum's publications throughout 2006. According to Chaimowicz's 2006 diary, a first meeting took place in Zürich with Urs Lehni and Lex Trüb on Thursday, 2 March, 2006. At the end of this meeting, the artist felt "lucky" to be collaborating with them. When they met again a month later, this time with a specific project, "things just clicked," as Chaimowicz recalled. From there, the publication was painstakingly designed over eighteen months. The result of a creative dialogue between the artist, the museum director, and the designers, the publication nonetheless underwent a particular process. As told by the artist: "There was a mutual fascination, both traded and age-based, between the generations. Urs and Lex were fascinated by the discrepancy between cutting and pasting with scissors, as well as by the presence of shadows, etc., in view of their refined understanding of graphic design." As a result, the artist said, "every page was discussed in terms of what should be cleaned up and what shouldn't." In the same spirit, the cover issue provoked lively debate. Among the options were "a commercial cover contaminated with advertising, and a pristine version for subscribers with a wrap-around band," recalls the artist. In the end, the idea of using the cover image of the April 2006 issue of The World of Interiors *was replaced by a view of a London interior. Taken on 4 April, 2007, this photograph shows an elegant and comfortable master bedroom in which a diptych painting by the artist is on the wall behind the bed. At the end of the volume, the same image is reproduced, this time including Charles Asprey and Justine Adlington at home with their child Badger.*

Looking back over thirty-five years of work, the publication includes paintings, installation views, sculptures, collages, furniture, decorative objects, drawings, and designs by the artist, as well as photographs of his domestic interiors, subtly interacting with advertisements for upholstery fabrics and furniture from the original edition. As for the texts, Chaimowicz included a facsimile of his first artist's book Dream, an Anecdote by Marc Camille Chaimowicz Dreamt in the Winter and Remembered in the Spring of 1977 *(1977) [III. 5] as well as a reprint of "Here and There... Notes towards a preface, London 1978," a text that was first published in the* Hayward Annual '78 *exhibition catalogue [III. 6].*

In addition, four previously unpublished texts were included [III. 22a, 22b, 22c, 22d], three of them written for the occasion [III. 22a, 22b, 22c]. Printed either in chestnut colour or black, these single-page texts are reproduced below without their accompanying illustrations. Written between 2006 and 2007, the texts include a preface [III. 22a], the portrait of a bedroom by Eric Ravilious [III. 22b], the unexpected juxtaposition of a 1950 sculpture by Alberto Giacometti, and Marshall McLuhan's TV theory as a "cool" medium [III. 22c], and the above-mentioned rejected artist's statement from 2006 [III. 22d]. Also featured in the publication are press clippings from other magazines. Ranging from a Mafia godfather's den and Keith Richards' living room to articles on Eileen Gray, these selected inputs interact with the artist's work. Peppered with references to Cocteau, Proust, Flaubert, Gray, Genet, Giacometti, and punctuated by quotations from contributing art writers such as Roger Cook, Alex Farquharson, Tom Holert, Barry Schwabsky, and Catherine Wood, this appropriation of the glossy pages of a world-class interior decoration magazine furthermore contains "reproduced reproductions," which help reinforce the work's ambiguous disciplinary status as a monograph in magazine form.

As indicated on the contents page, the artist's World of Interiors *is divided into sixteen sequences, each with a section title and a punch-line subtitle, so that the publication's organisation reads as follows:*

> *"12*
>
> *WALLPAPERS & CARPETS*
> *How an aesthetic may court anonymity … to then become a backdrop for the day-to-day.*
> *26*
> *THE WARSAW SUITE*
> *The unique status of easel painting is hijacked by contemporary concerns.*
> *42*
> *SHOE WASTE?*
> *From gutter to museum, the once worn or abject are aestheticised.*

178

WHEN IN LONDON… [III. 22d]

182

THE PASTEBOARD PALACE

During the 1930s, Chick Austin transformed the Wadsworth Atheneum in Hartford, Connecticut, from a fusty provincial museum into a cultural trailblazer.

201

MADAME BOVARY

A masterpiece of 19th century literary portraiture prompts a visual retort.

207

(ONE OF) FOUR ROOMS, A SOPHISTIC EXERCISE

How, in 1984, a couple intervened within an artwork, in order to complete it through visual narrative."

Consisting of two separate volumes produced jointly by the museum, and presented in a pale pink cloth hardback cover elegantly embossed in silver, the publication was released in October 2007. The two volumes contrast with each other. Whereas the artist's World of Interiors *comprises 216 glue-bound pages (including 225 colour illustrations) printed in offset on glossy paper (21 × 26 cm), the "Index to* The World of Interiors*" is a stapled booklet of 24 pages (12.3 × 21 cm) printed in chestnut-coloured monochrome offset on uncoated white paper [III. 22e]. From the outset of its release, this printed object aroused keen interest; immediately considered a must-have, this magazine-facsimile-monograph was subsequently awarded "The most beautiful Swiss books 2007" by the Swiss cultural federal office, and quickly became a cult object. Considered one of the greatest artist's books of our time, Chaimowicz's* World of Interiors *sadly disappeared from distribution fourteen months after its release, adding to the book's cultural status.*

On 11 July, 2008, Chaimowicz received a "cease-and-desist" letter from a London attorney's office on behalf of The Condé Nast Publications Limited of Vogue House, owner of The World of Interiors. In this letter, the artist was informed that a legal action was put in motion concerning his recent book commissioned by the Migros Museum für Gegenwartskunst due to alleged copyright infringement, with the publishers threatening to sue for the unauthorised use of the magazine's trademark. The demand of Condé Nast was that all the copies (only 1,500 printed) remaining in distribution be returned and destroyed, and to cease any copyright material taken from the magazine, although there is no commercial gain for the artist. Chaimowicz was shocked. He was deeply concerned that a major corporate power was bearing down on him and was eager to clarify his intentions. In response, he wrote a compelling letter to Jonathan Newhouse, then Condé Nast's head of international operation, in the hope that he would reverse his legal department's decision. Dated 29 September, 2008, the letter, in which the artist skillfully explains his intentions regarding this in no way defamatory or libelous artist book, went unanswered.

Corresponding with lawyers, Andrew Wheatley, co-director of London's Cabinet Gallery, heard that the magazine had received complaints from advertisers about the "defilements" of their advertisements, and explained that "if the artist had asked permission ahead of publication that would have been the sensible route." To that, he perceptively retorts, "Marc Camille Chaimowicz's book would not have looked the way it did if every advertiser was complicit and retained power of veto." With nearly two years of work and the publication on hold, Wheatley recalled that "the smart action would have been for Condé Nast to embrace Marc's exquisite volume and send each advertiser a free copy, stating that it had won the most lauded Swiss Graphic Design Award—something that could only be achieved via the sensibilities of an artist such as Marc Chaimowicz. Hardly likely that any single WoI ad would achieve the same!" Despite the arguments— from appropriation in art and the homage to The World of Interiors*—Wheatley reflected that "there was stunned silence as the editor had no counter-response. Even the magazine's Arts correspondent, Charlotte Edwards, thought it exquisite," but to no avail. Allegedly, the book was reportedly withdrawn from sale on 9 December, 2008, making it a very scarce and sought-after artwork.*

A now hard-to-find classic, Chaimowicz's World of Interiors *is described online as "a rare and out-of-print publication." Rarely seen, though much discussed, this legendary book has been the subject of insistent demand for public presentation as a documentation of a work. In 2016, two original copies of the publication were dismantled, and the individual sheets displayed floor-to-ceiling on a gallery wall as part of the exhibition "Marc Camille Chaimowicz: An Autumn in Lexicon," Serpentine, London (29 September–20 November, 2016), organised by Melissa Blanchflower, then curator at the Serpentine. Either too high or too low, many pages documenting the work were unfortunately difficult to read.*

Interested in touring the exhibition at the Jewish Museum, New York, Kelly Taxter, then Curator of Contemporary Art at the museum, travelled to London to view the show and finalise the exhibition tour with the artist. On discovering this wall installation, she immediately suggested that the artist build a long, bespoke cabinet complete with inclined glass cases, to provide viewers with suitable conditions for viewing this detail-filled documentation of work. The vitrines were installed in "La Bibliothèque" (The Library), one of the five exhibition rooms in "Marc Camille Chaimowicz: Your Place of Mine..." at the Jewish Museum, New York (16 March–5 August, 2017).

Dismantled and displayed in this way, the work was presented as documentation for a few months. Mapping a landscape of reflections on crucial aspects of the artist's "interior" sensibility and interests, this unbound work of art, as curator Kelly Taxter puts it in the exhibition booklet, could be seen up close: "A window onto his creativity and … a guidebook to his practice."

In response to constant requests to view this work in magazine form, the "complete work" was finally made available online by Cabinet Gallery in 2020, as part of a documentary dossier dedicated to the artist. This online documentation of a destroyed work of art does not include, however, the associated "Index to The World of Interiors." *Reproduced below [III. 22e], this index is essential for in-depth consultation of the work's online documentation. Comprising iconographic and bibliographic information, as well as commentary by the artist on his work, this methodical index, which highlights the way in which the original magazine was simultaneously deconstructed and reconstructed by the artist, also makes transparent its passage from a workplace to that of a work of art. The resulting work not only disrupts the hierarchies of cultural and social values inherent in magazine culture, where everyday life, lifestyle, art and design, private and public interact like a readymade, but also dazzlingly crystallises the way Chaimowicz has been exploring authorial voice, queerness, witty interiors, art forms, gender, and fiction in his work and his writing since the early 1970s.*

A.V.

[III. 22a]
Preface

(2007)

Initiated in April 2006, Chaimowicz's World of Interiors *was published a year and a half later, in October 2007. In the process, the artist felt it necessary to include a cautionary "preface" explaining how and why such a project came into being. To spark curiosity and draw the reader in, Chaimowicz explains how* The World of Interiors, *which he has long held in high esteem and which has given him great pleasure, inspired this project, particularly with regard to the photographic treatment of the range of aspirational fantasies encouraged by the interior views published in the magazine, which he sees as a possible link between lifestyle and fiction. Based on a facsimile of the April 2006 issue of* The World of Interiors, *the volume produced is, as the artist wished, "an autonomous work of art." Although it had the look of a magazine from start to finish, some parts of the 216-pages are closer to a book. Such is the case of the text reproduced below. Deliberately entitled "preface" rather than "editorial," which would have brought it closer to the magazine lexicon, it was written by the artist at the end of the process, around June 2007. Standing alone at the beginning of the volume, it was originally printed in chestnut colour, and positioned in the centre of the page.*

Providing the reader with an idea of the theme and scope of the publication, the text highlights the difference that exists in world-class interior decoration magazines, between, on the one hand, the interiors that are photographed "free of occupants [...] to distance the day-to-day and thus to accentuate various possible fictions," and, on the other, the "artist's homes," which, according to artist, "invariably feature the artist [...] as though these are seen either as extensions of their work or might in some fashion elucidate insight." Linking his long-standing interest in interior design to the environments staged as fictional spaces in interior decoration

*magazines, Chaimowicz finally suggests in his "preface" that
the publication of his work may reflect his home and his art,
which, in turn, might challenge our daily behaviour towards
interiors.*

A.V.

· · · · · · · · ·

In contrast to the fleeting pleasure of drifting through the department store, which similarly offers up experiences chaptered for our attention, the magazine surely affords us a greater latitude of critical investment…

The very act of purchase enables us to be judgmental and as we drift from page to page, probably avoiding text and feigning disinterest … we are both held enthralled by some images and conversely drawn to the dubious pleasure of dismissing a plethora of bad taste and poor design decisions taken…

In common with more pedestrian generic magazines, the domestic spaces featured in *The World of Interiors* are invariably free of occupants… This not merely affords the stylist greater scope to rearrange, to distance the day-to-day and thus to accentuate various possible fictions—it more importantly enables the readers the better to project themselves into a range of aspirational fantasies…

The exception is that of artists' homes which invariably feature the artist. It is as though these are seen either as extensions of their work or might in some fashion elucidate insight…

[III. 22b]

Farmhouse Bedroom

(2007)

In autumn 2003, Chaimowicz visited the retrospective exhibition of British artist Eric Ravilious, considered by some to be one the greatest British watercolourists of the twentieth century. Curated by Alan Powers, "Eric Ravilious: Imagined Realities: a centenary exhibition" (23 October, 2003–25 January, 2004) was presented at London's Imperial War Museum to mark the centenary of the birth of the artist, who died prematurely on an air-sea rescue mission off Iceland, while on assignment as a war artist. The exhibition featured more than ninety watercolours, as well as examples of Ravilious' outstanding work as a decorative designer and wood engraver of the 1930s. Although Chaimowicz was familiar with the work, he greatly appreciated the exhibition. In particular, the years of engraving, which accustomed Ravilious to discerning underlying patterns and bending his subjects to the service of symmetry, rhythm, and composition. Chaimowicz also paid particular attention to the watercolours featured in the exhibition. A medium of choice for the artist, watercolour allowed Ravilious to bring an "innocent eye" to English rural subjects such as greenhouses, watering cans, the quiet countryside, peaceful gardens, and farmhouse interiors, while drawing inspiration from contemporary innovations, albeit with a consummate mastery of the traditions on which he had chosen to stamp his mark, thus teasing out the strands of his formal language.

To coincide with this exhibition, Lund Humphries, London, reissued Freda Constable and Sue Simon's The England of Eric Ravilious *(1982), a 104-page paperback in which the artist's water-coloured England reveals itself as a country of gently rolling hills, where calm and beauty are threatened by the growing storm of an imminent war. It is through this book that Chaimowicz turned his attention to Ravilious'* A Farmhouse Bedroom *(1939). Part of the Prints, Drawings & Paintings Collection, Victoria & Albert Museum, London, this original watercolour drawing depicts a bedroom with a double bed and a chair, and a hallway to the right. In this example, the pattern in the wallpapers, carpets, and rugs is contrasted with the plainness of the bedspread. The curves of the iron bedstead and the wooden bedside chair also contrast with the linear shape of the room. In* A Farmhouse Bedroom, *the sober bedstead battles to hold its place against a cacophony of carpet, wallpapers, runners, and rugs. Even the ceiling bows down like a sagging mattress. Such a combination inspired Chaimowicz, who saw in it, he says, "a space that functions as a screen, eventually allowing the viewer to symbolically enter a welcoming interior." Flipping through the pages of the aforementioned monograph, Chaimowicz linked Ravilious' watercolour interiors to the interiors seen in decorating magazines, in that both are free of people.*

Accustomed, he says, to the "exquisite dishonesty of interior design magazines," which routinely organise and photograph interiors without any people present and therefore facilitating the reader's projections, Chaimowicz intuitively appropriated a reproduction of A Farmhouse Bedroom *from which he created a new work. The result was a horizontal triptych, comprising two reproductions of Ravilious' exhilarating, confining, and strangely suggestive bedroom, as well as a one-page text. While the watercolour on the left remains intact, the one on the right has been enhanced with marker pens, suggesting other shades of colour, and complemented by a black and white photograph in the right-hand section of the drawing. Showing a person on the telephone in the hallway of Chaimowicz's studio flat in Approach Road, London, in the late 1970s [Ill. 5, 7, 8], this photograph brings a human presence to Ravilious' character-free watercolour. In-between these two visual elements was the text, reproduced below. Written in autumn 2006, this text focuses on Ravilious' watercolour interiors. By emphasising the difference between the imaginary interior, which instantly functions as a screen for a projected space (the watercolour), and the interior photographically fabricated to serve the idealisation of the projected space (the magazine), the artist provides a concrete example of how interiors might embody an active fiction of the self. To fully appreciate the visual context in which the text below was first published, reference should be made simultaneously to the "Index to* The World of Interiors*" reproduced below [III. 22e], as well as to the corresponding individual sheets forming part of a documentary dossier devoted to the artist on Cabinet's website.*

In the 1930s, Ravilious exhibited his watercolours three times in London. Responding to the last exhibition in 1939, Jan Gordon noted in The Sunday Times *that the artist managed to make every subject he painted "appear as something magic, almost mystic, distilled out of the ordinary everyday." Among the works exhibited that year was* A Farmhouse Bedroom. *Neither entirely comfortable, nor merely pretty, but undeniably "distilled from the ordinary everyday," this windowless room with no represented access caught Chaimowicz's eye to such an extent he associated it, in his triptych, with "the frisson which can be felt on firstly entering a hotel room wherein anonymity may hold a promise of impending drama…" suggesting that, although Ravilious' interior watercolour is absent of people, it might arouse envy and awe, not just projection.*

A.V.

• • • • • • • • •

Of the interiors drawn by Eric Ravilious, which I have seen, *A Farmhouse Bedroom* of 1939 is the one I prefer. His manner of description is such that there is a little pictorial depth—the bed is visually almost flattened—as to become graphically integrated within the picture plane and thus close to the language which might, at the time of its making, have been referred to as *Orientalist*. I am nonetheless drawn to further embellish the bedspread … and to do so in such decorative fashion that—as a well-tendered flower bed sits with perfection within a municipal garden—so to further integrate it within the whole…

I am however equally tempted to challenge an inherent contradiction which hinges on the neutrality of the image surely at odds with its location… For all its charm, apparent innocence, and visual resolution, the work remains nonetheless mute and melancholic… Because other than with the frisson which can be felt on firstly entering a hotel room wherein anonymity may hold a promise of impending drama, within the domestic realm—and all the more so in the gentle setting of rural England—a well made bed in an empty room can seem incongruous and museum like… And as here, when lacking in signification more ominously perhaps metamorphose into the image of a tombstone within a mausoleum. (A historian may indeed suggest that, given its providence, it was a prophetic image of war looming…)

It is therefore as if the Ravilious is yearning to be *peopled* in some fashion … and prompting a potential scenario wherein the interior is *habituated* by a figure perhaps in the act of reading, reverie, or some other possible pastime… I am therefore proposing that it be completed or resolved by narrative potential.

[III. 22c]

Giacometti Meets Marshall McLuhan…

(2007)

The text reproduced below was first published as part of the 14-page section entitled "Giacometti" and subtitled "Or how, unbeknown to the artist, a work of 1950 is re-interpreted." Small (29.5 × 53.5 × 9.4 cm) and visually striking, the work referred to in this subtitle is Alberto Giacometti's famous painted bronze Figurine dans une boîte entre deux boîtes qui sont des maisons *(Figurine in a Box Between Two Boxes That Are Houses) (1950), which Chaimowicz had the opportunity to see again in the early 2000s. At the time, he saw it as a "new currency." From a distance, the empty volume in which the walking figurine stands seemed to him similar to a television screen, albeit in bronze. Although it is open, this central part of the sculpture emphasises the constricted nature of the figure's movement, boxed-in, before and behind, and so unable to move. Struck by this composition, Chaimowicz subsequently associated his vision with the crossover talent of Marshall McLuhan, who coincidentally declared in 1962, "TV is two-dimensional and sculptural in its tactile contours." Such "new currency" deserved its own text: "When Giacometti Meets Marshall McLuhan…"*

Produced in six copies for the artist's solo exhibition at Pierre Matisse Gallery, New York (12 December, 1950–6 January, 1951), Giacometti's work was received at the time as a brilliant combination of vacuity and vulnerability, characteristic of Existentialism between "being and nothingness," to quote the eponymous title of Jean-Paul Sartre's 1943 book. By 1966, when Giacometti passed away, a younger generation was looking the other way, seeing in the artist's work something quite alien or absurd. Chaimowicz, who was still an art student at the time, remembers feeling a kind of "fictive urgency" in Giacometti's last period, which he would associate years later with his first steps into the art world. Chaimowicz experienced this "fictive urgency" first-hand, such as in 2011, when he choreographed several of Alberto Giacometti's "walking men" that were presented in his solo exhibition "Jean Genet... The Courtesy of Objects" [III. 27] at Nottingham Contemporary (16 July– 2 October, 2011). "It's really 'something' when you have to install several of them in a single exhibition room...," recalled Chaimowicz. Getting so close to Giacometti's sculptures brought back a distant anecdote to the artist's mind. At the end of the 1960s, Chaimowicz went to a party at the Royal College of Art, London, in the pre-fab containers dating from World War II. In the toilets, scrawled amongst various anodyne graffiti and phone numbers was a phrase which caught the artist's eye: "Giacometti ate spaghetti."

The "Giacometti" section of The World of Interiors *from which the text reproduced below is originally taken includes several illustrations linking McLuhan's time with that of Giacometti. To fully appreciate this section, reference should be made simultaneously to the "Index to* The World of Interiors*" [III. 22e] and to the corresponding individual sheets forming part of a documentary dossier devoted to the artist on Cabinet's website. "Giacometti Meets Marshall McLuhan..." is printed on a double-spread page organised as follows: on the left-hand page, the text is arranged in a single column, opposite which is a photocopy of Giacometti's* Walking Man. *At the bottom of the text is a sketch by Chaimowicz of Giacometti's 1950 small sculpture, from which the walking figure is excluded. Enhanced with light brown marker pen, the sculpture does, indeed, look like a television set. On the right-hand page, a 2002 postcard of Giacometti's 1950 sculpture is superimposed on a two-colour photograph showing a group of metal chairs with thin legs in the Jardin du Luxembourg, Paris, in 1961. This photograph is taken from a French illustrated diary that once belonged to Chaimowicz's father. As noted in the "Index to* The World of Interiors*" [III. 22e], "It is incidental that the photograph is from a time which predates multinational*

*car production ... The cars: Peugeots, Citroëns, a Simca, and a
Renault, were all French built," at the time when "Giacometti
meets Marshall McLuhan."*

*Immersed among some of the industrial emblems of the 1960s,
Giacometti's* Figurine dans une boîte entre deux maisons *might be considered, as suggested by the artist in his text below,
"a codex for the television age." Stripped of the anxiety and
solitude that won this sculpture so much admiration in the
1950s, Chaimowicz points out that "once read as a surrogate
television set this would give the work new currency ... and
thus offer another perspective on* modernity." *By visually
linking the central part of Giacometti's 1950 sculpture to
a television screen, itself suitably associated with McLuhan's
name, this text by Chaimowicz not only wraps the sculpture in
another historical sequence, radically modernising it, but also
addresses the specificity of the "interior" in which the figurine
finds itself walking, inserting itself into the main theme of the
publication in which it is reproduced.*

A.V.

· · · · · · · · ·

What distinguishes Giacometti's standing figures from those walking is that of time implied... Yet both manifest vulnerability and doubt and are thus true to the existentialist lexicon...

Invariably solitary, these figures now read as surrogates of post-war Europe ... that of the isolated self-yearning for some placement, within the wastelands of reconstruction ... and if bronze would seem the very antithesis of Existentialism is it not because these works were cast of this semi-precious metal that they tenaciously resist time—as does perhaps that erstwhile philosophy?
Our reading of them has changed nonetheless. Alienation is now mainstream and beyond their probable intentions they now seem rootless and somewhat lacking of purpose ... no longer radical they may appear faintly absurd, as can the heroic... They have thus settled, with a degree of elegance into the canon of mid-twentieth century art.

What distinguishes his *Figurine dans une boîte entre deux maisons* from the above is—beyond the semblance of habitat—perhaps an element of fictional urgency ... if much of his work functions as a mirror we are here placed more so in the role of voyeur... Then to delight in any number of possible scenarios... Do the two buildings imply duplicity ... is the figure ominously engaged or simply and in all innocence, homeward bound? The readings are boundless...

An alternative if fortuitous reading might however be that of a codex for the television age ... once read as a surrogate television set this would give the work new currency ... and thus offer another perspective on *modernity*.

[III. 22d]

When in London…

(2007)

In late 2005, Marie-France Boyer contacted Chaimowicz with the idea to write on the "artist's home." A long-time contributor to The World of Interiors, *Boyer had, as one profile described, "an unerring eye for the eccentric and elegant [...] bringing quirky beauty to* The World of Interiors *since 1983. Always on the look-out for the 'unexpected or complicated,' [she] often finds herself in the less-travelled realms of the aesthetic landscape." In preparation for the photo shoot, Boyer kindly asked Chaimowicz to be at his home on the day. Unsurprisingly, Chaimowicz was invited to take centre stage and pose, leaning against the central fireplace in his Camberwell sitting room, looking out of the window.*

Although Boyer was behind the story, she did not make it to the shooting. When she saw the photographs from which she had planned to write her article, she was confused, probably because this interior seemed difficult for her to embrace all at once, and subsequently asked Chaimowicz if he would write an "artist's statement," instead of the article she was supposed to write. As soon as she received it, she passed it on to the magazine's editor-in-chief, who turned it down as "too intellectual," and further asked, "Is the artist an Existentialist?"

A few months later, while installing his solo exhibition "Zürich Suite" at the Migros Museum für Gegenwartskunst, Zürich (8 April–18 June, 2006), Chaimowicz bought a copy of the recently published April 2006 issue of The World of Interiors. *While leafing through it, he came across the feature and noticed that Boyer ended up writing a few lines about the apartment, which she had not seen in person. Entitled "This is not a flat" the feature was subtitled in the magazine's contents "The Camberwell home of artist Marc Camille Chaimowicz unsettles Marie-France Boyer, adrift in a Daliesque daydream." As he continued to leaf through the magazine, it occurred to him that "it would be better to reproduce a magazine than to consume it." This led Chaimowicz to imagine a monograph in magazine form conceived from the facsimile of the April 2006 issue of* The World of Interiors, *in which his "artist's home" was already reviewed. By inserting the text rejected by the magazine the previous year in the exact place where it should have been published, the artist actively regains control of his text, while clearly conferring a ready-made dimension on the facsimile on which his editorial project is based.*

Written in early January 2006, "When in London…" was first published in October 2007 as part of the artist's book The World of Interiors. *Printed on a single page, in two chestnut-coloured columns, the text describes the artist's "interior" as a long-term project, both as a place of inspiration and a constantly evolving testing ground for ideas since the mid-1970s. Reproduced below, this text summarises Chaimowicz's long-term relationship to the interior, which, as he puts it, is "simultaneously the catalyst of his art and its resultant form." From a contextual point of view, this text must be seen as the author's re-appropriation of a commissioned piece initially rejected and finally inserted in its exact place, thus shedding light in retrospect on its earlier rejection. To fully appreciate this editorial context, reference should be made jointly to the documentary dossier devoted to the artist on Cabinet's web page, as well as to the corresponding page of the "Index to* The World of Interiors" *[III. 22e] describing the section it belongs to. Banned from distribution by Condé Nast as of December 2008 [III. 22], the text below is therefore the only one currently available in hard copy.*

A.V.

• • • • • • • • • •

... home is a top floor flat in a red brick mansion block, some ten minutes south of Tate Britain, and conveniently close to the Eurostar terminal in Waterloo.

And yet, surely as with all manner of relationships, wherein attitude is affected by precedent and the past, thus impacts on the present. Its template was first developed in the mid-1970s, in London's East End, where for five years a dilapidated council-leased house was transformed into the semblance of a home. Driven by what he then felt to be culturally urgent: the questioning of gender roles and the perceived need to redefine what art might be, his elected method was that of decoration and his chosen aesthetic perhaps loosely based on that of modest Parisian hotel rooms, the better, within, to engage in philosophic reverie...

At a time of relative design innocence, in which England was then free of TV driven trends-anxiety, two floors of an Edwardian terrace thus became a cross between home and existential laboratory, salon and perhaps show room. Leased on the premise that it be converted into a working space, i.e. all strip lighting and white walls, this flirtation with "tradition," this blurring of boundaries was—by Artworld criteria of the time—nonetheless seen as contentious. After all, even dabbling with decoration was frowned upon, dilettantism challenging the work ethic was not generally approved of ... and such play with "conventional" values was thus paradoxically seen as radical.

Appearances can belie and it did by default generate much artwork, mostly photo-based, the stenciled wallpapers and handmade fittings serving as backdrops. Objects were placed with still life exactitude as vanitas, while a sacred mood pervaded the carefully regulated environment. Understated moments of the everyday were staged or ritualised, framing a make believe of beauty and critique which allowed the idea to take hold. Being neither quite public nor private, however, the space existed in limbo, somewhere between the world of ideas of art and the interior life of the artist, and this "home," both real and metaphorical, was therefore simultaneously the catalyst of his art and its resultant form.

One such example was *Here and There*. Thirteen 8 × 4 feet stenciled panels were provisionally leant against soft grey and pale green gallery walls. They displayed a rhythmic assembly of black and white photographs depicting cropped scenes of the domestic interior: evocative rather than descriptive, fragmentary rather than exhaustive, poetic rather than factual—artificed and subjective the enterprise was the obverse of documentation. An accompanying text elaborated on the process of transferring a reality from one location, the private, to another, the public, and how meanings and readings were implicitly qualified by this procedure. Shown at the Hayward Gallery in 1978 and as *Ici et Là* at ARC in Paris in 1979, it fortuitously echoed his dual-citizenship, which was later to be developed as of central concern.

Bethnal Green however felt somehow so exclusive, and this experimenting with inner space became claustrophobic, feeling increasingly like a state does to entombment. Indeed, *Dream, an Anecdote,* a small book published in 1977 by Nigel Greenwood (WOI May 2004), prophesised its demise: it was time to leave.

He'd long favoured apartments, surely as some reminder of a Parisian childhood. This inner London Borough, though settled, felt more cosmopolitan and this flat therefore had potential, yet on acquisition lay dormant for many months, at least domestically. It was first used, or rather was initiated, as a set for a "photo-roman" like project. Its empty rooms suited the photo shoots, now involving two young characters, and the space was thus first inhabited as fiction. The images, in the manner of a fragmented narrative, were then mounted on decorated folding screens. These were metaphors both as a structure of that which is concealed or revealed and as an object which is both functional and non functional i.e. furniture and/or artwork. The hinges, seemingly incidental were thus both technically and symbolically pivotal, the very agent of time folding in on itself…

The previous aesthetic was gradually transposed, now concluding in some coherence perhaps as an imaginary amalgam set in a composite of Paris, London, and Vienna … by implication, therefore, both here yet elsewhere…

The first two rooms are currently the study and library. The floor plan is castellated, each room therefore having one truncated corner, save for the sitting room, which perhaps heightens its sense of formality. Also the largest, it is the one invariably kept tidy and functions as reception room for meetings or conversation, the laying out of works on paper, a particular reading (i.e. sitting upright on the Otto Wagner chair), but mostly as oasis, or lieu for contemplation…

Understated visual incidents punctuate this apparent neutrality as with the RICARD carafe: a work by Richard Hamilton which actually reads RICHARD, or the incidental photograph of Jean Cocteau's hands which twenty years on was to conclude in a project based on the construction of an imagined bedroom become study for the artist/poet.

The backbone of the flat is the corridor, often used for that activity which follows reverie and can precede creative action … that of gentle pacing. It also leads to the kitchen, the epicentre of the apartment, which offers the best view, the light is good, its sunsets can be spectacular. Its colour scheme was prompted by the red and cream Parkinson Cowan Peeress gas stove, to which was added a dusty peppermint green, for spring-like energy. If the stand-alone items are the antithesis of built-in culture there are nonetheless original cupboards and these shelter the visually unacceptable white goods. Although currently canary free, it has more often than not been animated by a flurry of free flying birds.

Little has changed in twenty years, save for plumbing and this sense of stasis within this mental construct has the better enabled him to direct a creative restlessness towards extending a vocabulary of means and of materials in his art practice… The exception is surely the bathroom, and its wall painting is an echo of an emergent aesthetic which includes experimentation with translucent resins, decorative stove enamelling, self-drawn wallpapers, and cellulose finishes for a sixteenth century rural building in Burgundy … which opens out towards the future…

[III. 22e]

Index to *The World of Interiors*

(2007)

On seeing the first draft of Chaimowicz's The World of Interiors, *Heike Munder suggested including a list of works to make it clear that the publication was an artist's book. Anticipating that such information might visually and conceptually disrupt this 216-page masterpiece devoted to the artist's irresistible versatility for interior classifications, the graphic designers advised instead to produce a separate index that would provide page-by-page information to the reader without interfering with the content, while positioning the publication as an artist book. Painstakingly conceived in the summer of 2007 by the artist, in collaboration with Valérie Knoll, then an intern at the Migros Museum für Gegenwartskunst, Zürich, and editorial coordinator of the book project with Raphael Gygax, then curator at the museum, the "index" became a project in its own right. Designed by Urs Lehni and Lex Trüb, the small booklet reproduced below was printed alongside the other volume, at the end of September 2007, in chestnut-coloured offset monochrome on uncoated white paper. As a result, each copy of Chaimowicz's artist book came with a stapled 24-page (12.3 × 21 cm) booklet entitled "Index to* The World of Interiors" *that was made available through the museum. Also produced by the museum, this remarkable "index of works" meticulously lists the contents of the publication to which it refers, noting every visual or textual contribution, every modification or "correction" made to the original magazine, which served as a template for the artist. In addition, the index shows that the artist "read" the original magazine as a readymade: first, with scissors and glue, then with a scanner, two computers, and two graphic designers.*

To contextualise the editorial project, the "Index to The World of Interiors" *includes an introduction by Heike Munder. Written in collaboration with the artist and Valérie Knoll, this introduction reads as follows:*

"Glossy magazines such as the English World of Interiors, from a unique category in the great flood of publications. New trends are proclaimed, old ones celebrated, lavish-photo series are staged, and the content is often rivaled by equally lavish advertisements. Exquisite furniture, objects and wallpapers appear as actors in a theatrically charged still life, awakening desire and inciting playful annoyance or delight at what may be deemed good or bad taste.

Elements of the applied arts and interior design play a central role in the works of Marc Camille Chaimowicz. Hierarchies and opposites, such as form and function, art and craft, representation and abstraction, are somehow succinctly subverted in a seemingly nonchalant way offering non-traditional potential. Thus the personal is invariably a discreet distance proposed in the neutral exhibition space, overlaid with texts, wallpapers, carpets and furniture. Out of this a mood is generated, somewhere between coolness and intimacy, which has the potential of perpetual variation and possible revivals.

This artist's book has been produced in the context of the Spring 2006 retrospective exhibition 'Zürich Suite,' staged at the Migros Museum für Gegenwartskunst. Around the time of the exhibition, a feature on the artist's London apartment appeared in the April edition of The World of Interiors. *This coincidence, together with the artist's unease about the fetishisation of the catalog format, led to the idea of using that magazine edition as a template for an alternative artist's project. Page for page, the central principle of collage and bricolage was used until the issue was transformed. Through text and image, as well as painterly interventions, Chaimowicz has com-*

mented subjectively on the original pages '… resulting perhaps in a conditional truce between two divergent aesthetics—personal practice … and magazine culture' in palimpsest-like manner, and in so doing a rich cosmos of references has been proposed. The reader is thus invited to peruse the artist's commentary and digressions but, above all, to enjoy the reading process."

As in the original index, the above introduction is preceded by a quotation. Selected by Munder in collaboration with Chaimowicz, this quotation sums up the artist's interest in interior design as a space "prone to change." Taken from his text "Here and There… Notes towards a Preface, London 1978" [III. 6], the selected quotation refers to the studio flat in Approach Road, London, where the artist lived until 1979 [III. 5], and about which he wrote: "I realised that this space, seemingly so singular, was infinitely composed … Still to appear timeless was fluid and prone to change…" By linking his late 1970s interior (meaning both the domestic space and the inner life) to his mid-2000s exhibition and publication, Chaimowicz blurs the boundary between the space of the museum, interior decoration, and self-projection. In doing so, he not only links one century to another, but provides his "world of interiors" an aesthetic and political horizon.

When the book was presented, dismantled, in two exhibitions in London and New York eight years after it was withdrawn from sale [III. 22], the "index" was neither mentioned nor made accessible. Is this because the pictorial work predominated at the time? To this question, the artist replied, "Like magazine culture, interior design magazines are mainly about pictures and names … The text part is secondary."
In response to the many requests to consult this extraordinary 216-page work, Cabinet Gallery decided to include the com-

plete contents of Marc Camille Chaimowicz's The World of Interiors *as part of a documentary dossier dedicated to the artist. Based on a selection of works from the gallery archive, this dossier has been made available on the gallery's website since March 2020. Although this web page provides access to the visual documentation of the work, the "Index to* The World of Interiors*" is missing. Testifying to Chaimowicz's subjective/objective relationship with magazine culture as a readymade, this "index" makes transparent the editing of the work to which it refers, while making palpable the stages in the artist's appropriation of a decorating magazine, from a workplace into a work of art.*

A.V.

• • • • • • • • •

THE WORLD OF INTERIORS

Cover   Initial image from *The World of Interiors*, April 2006,
          replaced with view of a London interior taken on April 4th, 2007.
          Photograph: Andy Keate.
Inside   Hand-painted page.
1   Initial magazine page with collage.
2–3   Initial magazine page with collage of photograph from an
          unspecified French women's magazine.
4   Initial magazine page replaced with artwork by the artist.
5   Inside title.
6   Initial magazine page replaced with artwork by the artist, 2006.
7   Preface [III. 22a].
8   Initial magazine page replaced with artwork by the artist, 2006.
9   Contents.
10   Initial magazine page with collage.
          LEFT HAND COLUMN: Initial magazine page.
          RIGHT HAND COLUMN: Initial magazine page and text:
          Schwabsky, Barry, "Marc Camille Chaimowicz," in: *Artforum*,
          January 2006.
11   Initial magazine page with collage.
          Tracing paper with postcard of *Morandi's Studio*, City Museum
          Bologna.
          Photograph: Luciano Calzolari.

WALLPAPERS & CARPETS

12–14   Initial magazine pages replaced with samples of
          a wallpaper design, commissioned from the artist and produced /
          edited by The Art of Wallpaper, Norwich, 2005.
15   Initial magazine page replaced.
          Marc Camille Chaimowicz, *Wallpaper*, commissioned from the
          artist and produced / edited by The Art of Wallpaper, Norwich, 2005.

Installation view at Kunstverein für die Rheinlande und Westfalen, Düsseldorf, 2005.
Photograph: Achim Kukulies.

16   Initial magazine page replaced with study for a wallpaper design by the artist, 2006.

17   Hand-painted magazine page.

18   Initial magazine page replaced with photocopy from: Miller, Duncan, *Interior Decorating*, The Studio Publications, London / New York, 1948.

19   Initial magazine page replaced with collage.
        Tracing paper and photograph of detail of a seventeenth century French interior, including painting *Sad Phone Call*, 1988–1990, by the artist.

20–22   Initial magazine pages replaced with samples of wallpaper designs, commissioned from the artist and produced / edited by Wallpaper by Artists, Dijon, 2006.

23   Initial magazine page replaced with working drawing (see page 25).

24   Initial magazine page replaced with collage.

25   Initial magazine page replaced.
        BACKGROUND: Working drawing.
        INSERT IMAGE: Marc Camille Chaimowicz, *Desk... on Decline*, 1982–2003, MDF, cellulose lacquer, 75 × 214 × 61 cm, and *Carpet*, 1992, tufted wool, 277 × 231 cm, realised by Tisca, Châlon-Sur-Saône.
        Installation view at Kunstverein für die Rheinlande und Westfalen, Düsseldorf, 2005.
        Photograph: Yun Lee.

26   Initial magazine page replaced.
        BACKGROUND IMAGE: Detail of Marc Camille Chaimowicz, *Wallpaper*, commissioned from the artist and produced / edited by Wallpaper by Artists, Dijon, 2006.
        Photograph: David Poissenot.
        INSERT IMAGE: Marc Camille Chaimowicz, *Wallpaper*, 2006 (for details see above).
        Installation view at Migros Museum für Gegenwartskunst, Zürich, 2006.
        Photograph: A. Burger, Zürich.

27   Initial magazine page replaced.
BACKGROUND: Working drawing. Marc Camille Chaimowicz,
Winter's End, 1994, detail from *The Warsaw Suite* (for details see below).
INSERT IMAGE: Marc Camille Chaimowicz, *The Warsaw Suite*,
1993–1994 (thirty-two decorated plywood panels, on some of which
thirteen easel size paintings—six being diptychs—are placed).
Installation view at Migros Museum für Gegenwartskunst, Zürich, 2006.
Photograph: A. Burger, Zürich.
Collection FRAC Bourgogne.
The thirteen paintings were realised between 1991 and 1994:
Somnolence, oil, charcoal and Indian ink on paper, 61 × 46 cm.
Between, oil on canvas, 61 × 46 cm.
Glance, oil on canvas, 61 × 46 cm.
Varsovie, oil on canvas and wood, 61 × 92 cm.
Sad Phone Call, oil on canvas, 61 × 92 cm.
Study for Placing, oil on canvas, 61 × 92 cm.
Preface, oil on canvas, 61 × 92 cm.
The Delicate, Challenged, oil on canvas, 61 × 46 cm.
Early Days, oil on canvas, 61 × 92 cm.
Awaiting, oil on canvas, 61 × 46 cm.
Winter's End, acrylic, charcoal, and pastel on wood, 61 × 46 cm.
To Draw, oil, chalk, and charcoal on wood, 61 × 92 cm.
For P.B, oil on canvas, 61 × 46 cm.

These paintings are each duplicated, one on canvas and one on
board, as simulacrum—one being hung on the gallery walls, perhaps
in mimicry of the traditional mode. The work is completed by two
benches (drawn by the artist).
The panels are lent, in a *seemingly* provisional or casual manner,
expanding in response to any given exhibition space. It is not possible,
from any one single viewpoint, to see a painting and its duplicate.
The sensation of a *double-take* can thus only reveal itself as time unfolds.

The various painted decorative patterns on the plywood panels and
the paintings displayed upon them focus on the tense relationship
between the bourgeois value system of the nineteenth century and
that of today. Translated into art historical discourse, painting and the
current use of the concept of the installation are critically opposed to
one another. The individual paintings hint at bourgeois modernist taste
and lose their effect and uniqueness due to accumulation and uniform
appearance, which emphasise the character of the installation. The
behaviour code of contemplative observation within museum spaces
is destabilised by the portable, freely moveable panels, and further
contradicted by the innocent presence of the archetypical museum
seating, which, in itself, invites contemplation.

28–29   Initial magazine pages replaced.
        BACKGROUND: Working drawing.
        INSERT IMAGE: Marc Camille Chaimowicz, *The Warsaw Suite* (for
        credit details see index for page 27).
30–31   Initial magazine pages replaced with photographed details of *The
        Warsaw Suite* (for details see index for page 27).
        Installation view at Migros Museum für Gegenwartskunst, Zürich,
        2006.
        Photograph: A. Burger, Zürich.
32   Hand-painted magazine page with collage.
33   Initial magazine page with glassine paper.
34–35   Initial magazine pages replaced.
        BACKGROUND IMAGE: Photograph of maquette for Marc Camille
        Chaimowicz, "Four Rooms," Liberty's Regent Street, London, 1984.
        INSERT IMAGE LEFT: (left to right) Marc Camille Chaimowicz, *Laura
        Street, for Georgy*, 1987, marquetry, oil on canvas, 200 × 225 × 15 cm,
        and *Man Looking Out of Window, for S.M.*, 2006, black and white
        photograph on aluminium, 180 × 120 cm (from a photograph taken in
        Approach Road, 1975–1979, see page 36).
        Installation view at Migros Museum für Gegenwartskunst, Zürich, 2006.
        Photograph: A. Burger, Zürich.

Courtesy of the artist and Cabinet, London.
INSERT IMAGE RIGHT: (left to right) Marc Camille Chaimowicz, part
view of *Partial Eclipse...*, 1981, black and white and colour photograph,
text, gouache, hand-coloured photocopies, colour ink.
A chapter for the publication *Café du Rêve*, published in 1985.
Marc Camille Chaimowicz, *Desk... on Decline*, 1982–2003, MDF,
cellulose lacquer, 75 × 61 × 217 cm.
Marc Camille Chaimowicz, *Arch*, 1977, MDF, cellulose lacquer,
166 × 385 × 16 cm.
Marc Camille Chaimowicz, certificate in the form of a technical
drawing for *Desk... on Decline*, 2004, screen print on paper and black
and white photograph, 76.5 × 100 cm.
Installation view at Migros Museum Für Gegenwartskunst, Zürich, 2006.
Photograph: A. Burger, Zürich.
All works courtesy of the artist and Cabinet, London, with the
exception of *Arch*: Collection Charles Asprey, London.

36 Initial magazine page replaced.
Marc Camille Chaimowicz, *Approach Road*, 1975–1979,
black and white photograph.
Courtesy of the artist and Cabinet, London.

37 Initial magazine page replaced with text from: Cook, Roger,
"A Sense of Tact," in: *Miser & Now*, No. 8, London, 2006.

38–39 Initial magazine pages with collage from *The Guardian*, date
unspecified.

40 Initial magazine page replaced with artwork from Marion Thibault,
Untitled, 2004, original work: 121 × 200 cm, adapted for this
publication. Marion Thibault was a student at l'École Nationale
Supérieure des Beaux-Arts de Dijon.

41 Untouched magazine page.

42 Initial magazine page replaced.
Marc Camille Chaimowicz, "Sweetness," 1971, partial installation
view at Sigi Krauss Gallery, London, 1971.
Photograph: Bob Young.
Courtesy of the artist.

43   Initial magazine page replaced.
         Marc Camille Chaimowicz, *Shoe Waste?*, 1971–2005, one of
         five black and white photographs, hand impression silver gelatine,
         39.9 × 23.5 cm.
         Photograph: Bob Young.
         Collection Migros Museum für Gegenwartskunst, Zürich.

44–45   Initial magazine pages replaced.
         Marc Camille Chaimowicz, *Shoe Waste? Piece*, 1971–2005–2006,
         once-worn shoes, silver spray, dimensions variable.
         Installation view at Migros Museum für Gegenwartskunst, Zürich,
         2006.
         Photograph: A. Burger, Zürich.
         Collection Migros Museum Für Gegenwartskunst, Zürich.

46   Initial magazine page replaced.
         Marc Camille Chaimowicz, *Shoe Waste? Piece*, 1971–2005–2006.
         ON WALL: *Shoe Waste?*, 1971–2005, five black and white
         photographs, hand impression silver gelatine, 24.9 × 40.3 cm,
         21.5 × 40.3 cm, 29.7 × 36.5 cm, 40.3 × 27.4 cm, 39.9 × 23.5 cm.
         Installation view at Migros Museum für Gegenwartskunst, Zürich,
         2006.
         Photograph: A. Burger, Zürich.
         Collection Migros Museum für Gegenwartskunst, Zürich.

47   Initial magazine page with collage.

48   Initial magazine page with collage.
         LEFT HAND COLUMN: Initial magazine page.
         RIGHT HAND COLUMN: Collage with insert image, *Prototype for
         One Metre Chair*, 1994, by the artist.

49   Initial magazine page with collage.

50   Initial magazine page replaced with collage.
         INSERT IMAGE: Photograph of detail of *Villa Savoye* in
         Poissy, France, by Le Corbusier and Pierre Jeanneret, 1929–1931.
         Photo credit: Versailles, Mediathèque de l'École Nationale
         Supérieure d'Architecture.

The colour index, *blue céleste, ocre jaune, sienna*, is that, and only
that, requested by the master architect for a choice of interior walls
in the *Villa Savoye*.

The contemporary advert on the corresponding initial magazine
page, for a luxury fitted kitchen, typifies the residual effect of his
aesthetic, and thus perhaps the dubious consequence of its legacy...

51   Untouched magazine page.

52   Initial magazine page replaced with blank page.

53   Initial magazine page replaced.
          BACKGROUND: Artwork by the artist.
          INSERT IMAGE: Two polaroids taken by the artist.

The two polaroids by the artist were taken as part of research for
Pendulum Polaroids, a project organised by *The Laboratory* at the
Ruskin School of Drawing and Fine Art, Oxford, in association with
the Maison Française, Oxford, in 2000. One photograph is a detail
from *La Mosquée*, the other from a private apartment on the rue
Saint-Séverin, both in Paris 5ème.

54–55   Initial magazine pages with collage.

56–57   Initial magazine pages replaced.
          LEFT HAND PAGE: Photograph featuring "Müller House," Prague,
          by Adolf Loos, view of ladies' room, 1930.
          RIGHT HAND PAGE: Photograph featuring "Müller House,"
          Prague, by Adolf Loos, view of living and dining room, 1930.
          Both photocopies from: Safran, Yehuda / Wang, Wilfried, exhibition
          cat., *The Architecture of Adolf Loos*, Arts Council of Great Britain,
          1985.

58   Initial magazine page replaced with photocopy featuring "Müller
          House," Prague, by Adolf Loos, view of hall through stairway from
          vestibule, 1930, from: Safran, Yehuda / Wang, Wilfried, exhibition
          cat., *The Architecture of Adolf Loos*, Arts Council of Great Britain, 1985.

59   Initial magazine page replaced with a photocopy featuring "Wittgenstein House," Vienna, view of stairs and elevator shaft on second floor, 1928, from: Leitner, Bernhard, *The Architecture of Ludwig Wittgenstein. A Documentation*, New York: University Press, 1976. Photograph: Ing. F. Kunz, Vienna.

60   Initial magazine page with artwork commissioned from Nadia Wallis, 2007 (see also pages 111, 115, and 117).

61   Initial magazine page with collage.

DREAM, AN ANECDOTE (1977)

62   Initial magazine page replaced with text from: Fisher, Jean, *Past Imperfect. Marc Camille Chaimowicz, 1972–1982*, co-published by Bluecoat, Orchard, John Hansard Galleries, UK, 1983.

63–82   Initial magazine pages replaced with reproduction of the Artist's book *Dream, an Anecdote*, London: Nigel Greenwood Inc Ltd Books, 1977. This work [III. 5] has been repaginated for this publication.

65   Initial magazine page replaced with text from: Bachelard, Gaston, *The Poetics of Reverie. Childhood, Language and the Cosmos*, Boston: Beacon Press, 1971.

83   Initial magazine page replaced with artwork by the artist.

HERE AND THERE

84–86   Initial magazine pages replaced with text from: Fisher, Jean, *Past Imperfect. Marc Camille Chaimowicz, 1972–1982*, co-published by Bluecoat, Orchard, John Hansard Galleries, UK, 1983.

87   Initial magazine page replaced with text from: Chaimowicz, Marc Camille, "Here and There... Notes Towards a Preface, London, 1978." (This text [III. 6] was originally conceived as integral to the work and remains so in all subsequent presentations of *Here and*

There and *Hier und Dort*).

88   Initial magazine page replaced.
Marc Camille Chaimowicz, *Here and There*, 1978, plywood,
emulsion paint, black and white photographs, 244 × 122 cm each.
Installation view at Hayward Gallery, London, 1978.
Courtesy of the artist and Cabinet, London.

89   Initial magazine page replaced.
BACKGROUND IMAGE: As index for page 88.
INSERT IMAGE: Marc Camille Chaimowicz, *Here and There*, 1978,
plywood, emulsion paint, black and white photographs,
244 × 122 cm each.
Installation view at Migros Museum für Gegenwartskunst, Zürich, 2006.
Photograph: A. Burger, Zürich.
Courtesy of the artist and Cabinet, London.

Thirteen boards, most of which have large dry mounted black and
white photographs of interior views from *Approach Road*, featuring
either domestic activity or decorative detail. Painted boards of
various tones (silver, pale green, two greys). The piece is completed
by a text specific to the work (enlarged and wall mounted). The
boards are provisionally placed within their own dedicated space,
one wall of which is painted pale green.

HIER UND DORT

90–91   Initial magazine pages replaced with text from: Fisher, Jean, *Past
Imperfect. Marc Camille Chaimowicz, 1972–1982*, co-published by
Bluecoat, Orchard, John Hansard Galleries, UK, 1983.

92–93   Initial magazine pages replaced.
Marc Camille Chaimowicz, *Here and There*.
Installation view of slide version at Tate Britain, London, shown
within the "Tate Triennial 2006, New British Art," curated by
Beatrix Ruf. Featuring furniture designed by Marcel Breuer and

manufactured by Isokon Plus, London.

94–95   Initial magazine pages replaced.
Marc Camille Chaimowicz, *Hier und Dort*.
Installation view of slide version at Kunstverein München, 2006,
shown within the exhibition "The Secret Public. The Last Days of
The British Underground 1978–88," curated by Stefan Kalmár and
Michael Bracewell.

A principle inherent to this work is that *hereness* is materiality
defined by the usage of vernacular or culturally specific furniture...
Its initial presentation in Vienna therefore incorporated furniture
designed by Josef Hoffmann.
The Tate presentation incorporated furniture designed by Marcel
Breuer when working in London for the design company, Isokon Plus.
Consistent with this principle was the use of furniture designed by
a local architect, Josef Hillerbrand (1892–1981), in the version shown
at the Kunstverein München in 2006.

96–97   Untouched magazine pages.
98   Initial magazine page with collage.
99–100   Untouched magazine pages.
101   Initial magazine page with collage.
102   Untouched magazine page.
103   Initial magazine page replaced with photocopy from: Miller,
Duncan, *Interior Decorating*, London / New York: The Studio
Publications, 1948.
104   Initial magazine page replaced with photocopies featuring a set by
Mallet-Stevens for Marcel L'Herbier's *Le Vertige*, 1925, from: *Rob Mallet-
Stevens. Architecte*, Brussels: Archives d'Architecture Moderne, 1980.
105   Initial magazine page replaced with photocopy featuring vestibule
and entrance in Mallet-Stevens' house, from: *Rob Mallet-Stevens.
Architecte*, Brussels: Archives d'Architecture Moderne, 1980.

106   Initial magazine page replaced with text from: Farquharson, Alex, "Des Esseintes As Curator," in: *Le Voyage Intérieur, Paris-London,* Espace Electra, Paris-Musées, 2005.

107   Initial magazine page replaced.
BACKGROUND: Artwork by the artist.
INSERT IMAGE: Marc Camille Chaimowicz, *Jean Cocteau,* 2003–2005–2006, mixed media.
Installation view at Migros Museum für Gegenwartskunst, Zürich, 2006.
Photograph: A. Burger, Zürich.
Courtesy of the artist and Cabinet, London.

The framed work on the outer wall is a poster produced by Cinema City, Norwich, on the occasion of a special screening of Jean Cocteau's *Blood of a Poet* and *La Belle et la Bête* on October 12th, 2003. Held in conjunction with the first presentation of *Jean Cocteau* at Norwich Gallery, which featured a conversation between Marc Camille Chaimowicz and the art historian Krystof Fijalkowski. The poster, as an index of Cocteau's contribution to an avant-garde cinema, was subsequently incorporated into the work when later presented in Nottingham and Zürich, thus implicating an exhibition chronology of the work *within* the work.
"Time to move to the bedroom, no ordinary bedroom this, but the reimagined boudoir of a perverse poet: *The Cocteau Room.* A poster for his film *Le Sang d'un Poète* (1930) awakens expectation. We are not disappointed by this third reconstruction, presided over by Warhol's diamond dust portrait of Joseph Beuys, a magnificent addition to one's memory of the other two. Other surprises await. This is a room in which to make discoveries, a room full of ambivalent objects to intrigue, to set imaginations free."
— Cook, Roger, "A Sense of Tact," *Miser & Now*, No. 8, London, 2006.

108   Initial magazine page with collage.

109   Initial magazine page replaced.
        BACKGROUND: Artwork by the artist, 2006.
        INSERT IMAGE: Marc Camille Chaimowicz, *Jean Cocteau* (detail),
        2003–2005–2006, mixed media.
        Installation view at Migros Museum für Gegenwartskunst, Zürich,
        2006.
        Courtesy of the artist and Cabinet, London.

110–117 Initial magazine pages replaced.
        BACKGROUND IMAGE: Hand-coloured drawing by the artist,
        2006–2007.
        All photographs: A. Burger, Zürich, with the exception of pages
        110 and 117.

110   INSERT IMAGE FEATURING: Marc Camille Chaimowicz, *Jean
        Cocteau* (detail), 2003–2006, found French eighteenth century bed
        and hand-painted bedspread.
        Andy Warhol, *Joseph Beuys*, 1980, colour serigraph with
        diamond dust on black paper, 112 × 77 cm.
        Collection Migros Museum für Gegenwartskunst, Zürich.
        Stephen Buckley, *Alnwick*, 1986–1988, oil on canvas on wood,
        45 × 45 × 8 cm.
        Courtesy of Stephen Buckley and the artist.

111   INSERT IMAGE FEATURING FROM LEFT TO RIGHT:
        Paulina Olowska, *Untitled (Beside Blank Canvas)*, 2002, oil on
        canvas, 175 × 124 cm.
        Courtesy of the artist and Cabinet, London.
        Nadia Wallis, *Tablecloth on a Round Table*, 2004, table, canvas and
        gloss paint, table: 77 × 60 × 60 cm, cloth: 200 × 50 cm.
        Courtesy of the artist.
        Francis Picabia, *Visage de femme penché en arrière*, approx. 1939–
        1941, pencil on paper, 33.5 × 26 cm.
        Courtesy Hauser & Wirth, Zürich, London.
        All other material by the artist.

112   Initial page replaced with hand-coloured drawing by the artist,
        2006–2007.
113   INSERT IMAGE FEATURING: Tom of Finland, *Untitled*, 1985,
        pencil on paper, 57 × 47 cm.
        Private Collection, London.
        All other material from the artist.
114   INSERT IMAGE: Marc Camille Chaimowicz, *Jean Cocteau*
        (detail), 2003, *Two Speed Staircase*, 187 × 180 × 42 cm.
        All other material by the artist with the exception of M.S.
        (unknown artist), *Untitled (Dandelions)*, 1952, tile.
        Collection Migros Museum für Gegenwartskunst, Zürich.
115   INSERT IMAGE FEATURING IN FOREGROUND: Marc Camille
        Chaimowicz, *Jean Cocteau* (detail), 2003–2006, including *Desk on
        Decline...* (maquette), 1981–1984, plywood, paint, 181 × 95 × 92 cm.
        Collection Alexander Schröder, Berlin.
116   INSERT IMAGE FEATURING: Marc Camille Chaimowicz, *Jean
        Cocteau* (detail), 2003–2006, found French eighteenth century bed
        and hand-painted bedspread.
117   INSERT IMAGE FEATURING: Marc Camille Chaimowicz, *Jean
        Cocteau*, 2003–2006, including Marcel Breuer, *Isokon Long Chair*,
        edited by Isokon Plus, 1936.
118   Initial magazine page with collage.
        LEFT HAND COLUMN: Initial magazine page.
        RIGHT HAND COLUMN: Blank collage.
119   Initial magazine page with collage.
120   Initial magazine page replaced with page from: *British Vogue*, No.
        2339, Volume 157, June 1993.
        Photograph: Corinne Day.
121   Initial magazine page replaced with page from: *British Vogue*, No.
        2399, Volume 164, June 1998.
        Photograph: Lord Snowdon.

Two London interiors (portraits)

When Corinne Day's fashion shots featuring Kate Moss first appeared

they attracted controversy for "promoting" *Cocaine Chic* or encouraging
anorexia amongst *youth*. More recently Moss, with her contentious
choice of boyfriend (the dysfunctional Peter Doherty) and her allegedly
drug-fuelled lifestyle, has sustained a controversial image. She remains
highly popular however, and her earnings have increased.
Peter Mandelson, once called the *architect* of New Labour, has the
dubious honour of having being forced to resign not once, but twice,
from Cabinet Office. He is now European Union Commissioner in
Brussels.
These two London portraits can thus be seen as the notorious
photographed by the illustrious.

122   Initial magazine page replaced.
        BACKGROUND: Working drawing for bookstand.
        INSERT IMAGE: Marc Camille Chaimowicz, *Pour mon frère fictif*,
        prototype for bookstand, 2005–2006, plywood,
        each 28 × 44 × 28 cm.
        Installation view at Migros Museum für Gegenwartskunst, Zürich,
        2006.
        Photograph: A. Burger, Zürich.
        Courtesy of the artist and Cabinet, London.
123   Initial magazine page with collage.

FARMHOUSE BEDROOM

124   Initial magazine page replaced.
        Insert image from: Constable, Freda / Simon, Sue, *The England of
        Eric Ravilious*, Hampshire: Lund Humphries Publishers Ltd, 2003.
125   Initial magazine page replaced with text [III. 22b] conceived by the
        artist for this publication, 2006.
126   Initial magazine page replaced with reworked image from
        magazine page 124.
127   Initial magazine page with glassine paper.

128   Initial magazine page replaced.
        BACKGROUND: Glassine paper *Gris perle*.
        INSERT IMAGE: Postcard of Félix Vallotton, *Jeune femme se coiffant*,
        1900, Musée des Beaux-Arts, Dijon.
        Photograph: Hugo Maertens, ©Musée des Beaux-Arts, Dijon.

129   Initial magazine page replaced.
        BACKGROUND: Translucent glassine paper.
        INSERT IMAGE: Postcard of Marc Camille Chaimowicz,
        Partial Eclipse..., 1980–2003.
        Collection Migros Museum für Gegenwartskunst, Zürich.

130   Initial magazine page replaced.
        BACKGROUND: Photocopy of a photograph by the artist, 2006,
        with glassine paper.
        INSERT IMAGE: Photograph by the artist, 2006.

The insert image is of the courtyard of the Musée Nissim de
Camondo in Paris 8ème. The backdrop is of a building site at
London's Aldwych. Given their quasi-theatrical and intimate
nature each highlights those semi-enclosed outdoor spaces that can
nonetheless conjure up the feeling of an interior, the most notable
of which are to be found in Venice...

131   Initial magazine page with glassine paper.

CELEBRATION? REALIFE

132   Initial magazine page replaced with an illustration, as frontispiece,
        from Jullian, Philippe, in: Proust, Marcel, *Remembrance of Things
        Past*, Vol. 7, translation by Scott-Moncrieff, C.K., London: Chatto
        and Windus, 1967, with glassine paper.

... and if an urban built perfection of this phenomenon is Venetian, its
literary equivalent can surely not be equalled by the start of *Cities of*

the Plain, in which for eighteen pages and more Marcel Proust exquisitely draws an analogy between the notorious encounter—and courtship—of Jupien by the Baron de Charlus ... and the possible yet improbable likelihood of the pollination, by a bee, of a potted orchid put out to bathe in the sunlit confines of the courtyard of l'Hôtel de Guermantes.

133 Initial magazine page replaced with glassine paper.

134 Initial magazine page replaced.
Marc Camille Chaimowicz, *Celebration? Realife Revisited*, 1972–2000–2006, mixed media.
Installation view at Migros Museum für Gegenwartskunst, Zürich, 2002.
Photograph: FBM-Studio, Zürich.
Collection Migros Museum für Gegenwartskunst, Zürich.

135 Initial magazine page replaced with text from: Holert, Tom, *Celebration? Realife*, London: Afterall Books, 2007.

"Marc Camille Chaimowicz's ground breaking installation *Celebration? Realife* was originally created for 'Three Life Situations' at Gallery House London in 1972. The work is a strange hybrid of a scatter environment, a theatrical stage and a performance piece. Meant as a critique of modernist objectivism, *Celebration? Realife* is also a consciously messy and ambivalent reaction to the clean conceits of Conceptualist and post-minimalist tendencies.

Tom Holert argues that with *Celebration? Realife*, Chaimowicz makes a strategic and important meditation on the changing role of the artist, who in this defining work simultaneously becomes art director, stage designer, choreographer and participant. *Celebration? Realife* probes the relationship between art, design, popular culture and performance at a moment when these disciplines, genres and milieus hardly ever met. Holert shows how this influential work inventively anticipates and helps to define an important and increasingly popular tendency in art."

— Holert, Tom, *Celebration? Realife*, London: Afterall Books, 2007, publisher's note, back cover.

GIACOMETTI

INSERT IMAGE: Postcard of Alberto Giacometti, *Figurine dans une boîte entre deux maisons*, 1950, bronze, Paris: Centre Georges Pompidou, Musée national d'art moderne, 1982.
Postcard: ©Adagp, Paris 2001 and Éditions du Centre Pompidou.

The graphic backdrop is from a French illustrated desk diary of 1961, once belonging to the artist's father. It is of incidental detail that the photograph is from a time which predates multinational car production... The cars: Peugeots, Citroens, a Simca, and a Renault, were all French built.

163   Initial magazine page with collage.

164   Initial magazine page replaced.
        BACKGROUND: Glassine paper.
        INSERT IMAGE: Photocopy featuring "E.1027" exterior from:
        Rowlands, Penelope, *Eileen Gray*, San Francisco: Chronicle Books
        LLC, 2002.
        Photograph: Eileen Gray Archives, London.
        Courtesy of Peter Adam.

"And the peculiar name of the house? Its origin is touching, and
less impersonal than it seems. It is made up of the lovers' initials
intertwined and, with the exception of the E for Eileen, given
numeric equivalents—J being the tenth letter of the alphabet, B the
second, and G the seventh."
—Tinniwood, Adrian, in: Beazley, Michale (ed.), *The Art Deco
House, Avant-Garde Houses of the 1920s and 1930s*, New York:
Watson-Guptill Publications, 2002.

165   Initial magazine page replaced with page from a non-specified
        French interior magazine.

166   Initial magazine page replaced with photocopy featuring living
        room of "Tempe à Pailla," Castellar, France, from: Rowlands,
        Penelope, *Eileen Gray*, San Francisco: Chronicle Books LLC, 2002.
        Photograph: Eileen Gray Archives, London.
        Courtesy of Peter Adam.

167   Initial magazine page with collage.

168   Initial magazine page replaced with photocopy featuring Eileen
        Gray, age 92, in her rue Bonaparte apartment, 1970, from:
        Rowlands, Penelope, *Eileen Gray*, San Francisco: Chronicle Books
        LLC, 2002.
        Photograph: Eileen Gray Archives, London.
        Courtesy of Peter Adam.

169   Initial magazine page with collage.
          INSERT IMAGE: Eileen Gray, *Block Screen*, 1923, V&A Images,
          estate of Eileen Gray.

THIS IS NOT A FLAT

170–171   Initial magazine pages replaced with text from: Wood, Catherine,
          "In use: An Essay on the Work of Marc Camille Chaimowicz,"
          in: exhibition cat., *Marc Camille Chaimowicz*, Kunstverein für die
          Rheinlande und Westfalen, Düsseldorf, London: Koenig Books, 2005.
172–177   "The Camberwell home of artist Marc Camille Chaimowicz
          unsettles Marie-France Boyer, adrift in a Daliesque daydream," in:
          The World of Interiors, April 2006.
174   Untouched magazine page.

          The credits on the original page merit correction: The painting by Nadia
          Wallis is oval, not circular. The Eileen Gray chrome table is featured on
          the preceeding page, this one is anonymous and was acquired from a
          hatters in Brixton covered market at some time during the 1970s (... such
          is the dubious pleasure of the retrospective perogative ...).

178   Text [III. 22d] solicited from the artist by *The World of Interiors*, then
          rejected by the editor for being too "intellectual."
179   Replication of magazine page 177 now featuring a postcard of Pierre
          Bonnard, *Nude Before a Mirror*, 1933, Galleria Internationale d'Arte
          Modena, Venice.
180   Initial magazine page replaced with artwork by the artist.
181   Untouched magazine page.

THE PASTEBOARD PALACE

182   Initial magazine page with collage.

INSERT IMAGE: Postcard of Édouard Vuillard, *Portrait de Bonnard*, 1930–1935, glue paint on paper, Musée d'Art Moderne de Paris. Photograph: Jacques Le Chevallier, ©Photothèque des Musées de la Ville de Paris, 1997, ©Adagp, Paris, 1997.

183 Untouched magazine page.

184–185 Initial magazine pages with collage.

186 Initial magazine page with collage.
INSERT IMAGE: The *Moule Madeleine* is an engraved illustration from: Maillard, Louis, *La Cuisine de famille*, Geneva: Albert Kündig, 1893.

187 Initial magazine page with collage.
INSERT IMAGE: Poster illustration, from: *Une expérience moderne–le Comité Nancy-Paris 1923–1927*, Paris: Fage éditions, 2006.

188 Initial magazine page replaced with page from a non-specified German design magazine.

189–190 Untouched magazine pages.

191 Initial magazine page with collage.
INSERT IMAGE: Chair by Jean Prouvé.

There are a number of central pillars shared by platforms 16-17, 18-19, and 20-21 at La Gare d'Austerlitz in Paris. Of steel and aluminium, they differ from others yet such is their circumstance—and state of deterioration—that they are destined to remain essentially unnoticed. Yet, on further examination, however for all their modesty the coherence of their design is such as to manifest the singularity of a higher order... These are said to have been designed by Jean Prouvé.

192 Initial magazine page with collage.
INSERT IMAGE: Photocopied detail from: Sharp, Dennis / Benton, Tim / Campbell Cole, Barbie, *Furniture by Pel, 1939. Practical Equipment Limited and Tubular Steel Furniture of the Thirties*, London: The Architectural Association, 1977.

193 Initial magazine page with collage and drawn intervention.
INSERT IMAGE: photocopied detail from: Sharp, Dennis / Benton,

Tim / Campbell Cole, Barbie, *Furniture by Pel, 1939. Practical Equipment Limited and Tubular Steel Furniture of the Thirties*, London: The Architectural Association, 1977.

194   Initial magazine page with glassine paper.

195   Initial magazine pages replaced with photocopies from: Smithell, Roger (ed.), *Better Homes Book*, London: News of the World, date unspecified.

196   Initial magazine page replaced with photocopy featuring "Highpoint 1," London, by Lubetkin, Bertold & Tecton, from: "AR'30s." A special issue of *The Architectural Review*, Volume CLXVI, No. 993, November 1979, London: The Architectural Association.

197   Initial magazine page replaced with photocopy featuring "10 Palace Gate," London, by Wells Coates, from: "AR'30s." A special issue of *The Architectural Review*, Volume CLXVI, No. 993, November 1979, London: The Architectural Association.

198-199 LEFT-HAND PAGE: Initial magazine page replaced with photocopy featuring Otto Wagner's Main Hall of the Austrian Postal Saving Bank, 1904–1906, Vienna, from: Smith, C. Ray (ed.), exhibition cat., *Vienna Moderne: 1898–1918. An Early Encounter between Taste and Utility*, Houston: Sarah Campbell Blaffer Gallery, 1978.
Photograph: Austrian Photo Archives, Vienna, 1978.
RIGHT-HAND PAGE: Initial magazine page replaced with photocopy featuring a detail of Waterloo International Terminal, London, by Nicholas Grimshaw, from: Jodidio, Philip, *Contemporary European Architects*, Volume III, Cologne: Benedikt Taschen Verlag GmbH, 1995.
Photographs: top: Arcaid / Richard Bryant, bottom: Nicholas Grimshaw.

In contrast to the phenomena proposed on page 130 these spaces, as with the Turbine Hall at Tate Modern feel closer to the external… If roof-glazed and subject to light and climate as are many

Metropolitan stations, Norman Foster's Great Court at the British
Museum, some gallerias in Milan and Naples or Parisian nineteenth
century passages, they surely propose a hybrid status, perhaps that of
the *intex-terior*.

200   Initial magazine page with collage.

MADAME BOVARY

201–202 Initial magazine pages replaced.
BACKGROUND: Artwork by the artist, 2007.
INSERT IMAGE: Photocopied book cover and page from: Flaubert,
Gustave, *Madame Bovary*, Penguin Classics.

203   Initial magazine page replaced with artwork by the artist with
collage, 2007.

204   Initial magazine page replaced with collage and text on a magazine
page from *The World of Interiors*, November 2006, featuring the
Muzeum Josefa Hoffmanna, Brtnice, Moravia, Czech Republic.

205   Initial magazine page replaced.
BACKGROUND: Stationery of the Hôtel le Moderne, Menton.
INSERT IMAGE: Photograph of the lobby at the Hôtel le Moderne,
Menton, taken by the artist.

206   Initial magazine page replaced with photocopy featuring "Maison
Motherwell," East Hampton, United States, by Pierre Chareau, 1948,
from: Vellay, Marc, *Pierre Charreau, Architecte Meublier 1883–1950*,
Paris: Rivages, 1986.

(ONE OF) FOUR ROOMS, A SOPHISTICATED EXERCISE

207   Initial magazine page replaced.
BACKGROUND: Wallpaper commissioned from the artist and
hand screen-printed by John Perry & Sons Ltd, London, for Coles

Wallpapers, 1993, for the Arts Council of Great Britain exhibition "Four Rooms," first shown at Liberty's Regent Street, London, 1984.
INSERT IMAGE: Marc Camille Chaimowicz, installation view of *Four Rooms*, 1984, mixed media.
Postcard published by the A.C.G.B in 1984.
Photographer: John Badminton.
208-209 Initial magazine pages replaced.
BACKGROUND: Wallpaper conceived for the exhibition "Four Rooms" (for details see above).
INSERT IMAGE: Eight slides that were on display at the "Four Rooms" exhibition (for details see above.)

In 1983, Anthony Caro, Richard Hamilton, Howard Hodgkin, and Marc Camille Chaimowicz were, in conjunction with a luxury London store, invited to each design a room of their choosing. Integral to the room proposed by the artist was an oblique three-dimensional form housing a back projection screen which, as well as providing a light source, showed a continuous sequence of slides fading from one to the next. These illustrated details of the room and activities of a couple within it, thus proposing a dialogue between the real and the fictive and the possible "narrative" perception of the space, now become set. From this sequence slides: 2–3–8–10–31–49–54–93 are here reproduced.

210   Initial magazine page with transparent insert image.
211   Initial magazine page replaced with advertisement commissioned from Lucy McKenzie, 2007.
212   Initial magazine page replaced with photocopy from a page of the Isokon Plus brochure.
213   Initial magazine page replaced with cover of *Cornerhouse Publications*, Autumn 2006.
Cover image: Marc Camille Chaimowicz, *Study for Central Line*, 2006.

Photograph: Andy Stagg.
Courtesy of the artist and Cabinet, London.

214   Initial magazine page replaced with advertisment by the artist
for Hennessy Cognac, published in various English magazines,
Autumn 1984.

215   Colophon.

216   Initial magazine page replaced with photograph of Charles Asprey
and Justine Adlington at home with young "Badger" on April 4,
2007.
Photograph: Andy Keate.

Unless otherwise stated all centred commentaries are by the artist.

[III. 23]

Re B.B.5 For MvdR

(2008)

At the end of 2007, Chaimowicz was approached by Adam Szymczyk and Elena Filipovic, the co-curators of the up-and-coming 5th Berlin Biennial "When Things Cast No Shadows" (5 April–15 June, 2008). At the time, Polish-born curator Szymczyk was director of the Kunsthalle Basel, and American-born curator and writer on art Filipovic was based in Berlin. Both had the intuition that the biennial should take place both day and night, in different venues around the city:

> *"In our choices, [they said], we hoped the visitor would move throughout Berlin, but not necessarily towards buildings whose histories are manifest in their peeling paint or picturesque state of ruination. Instead, we wanted to work with very distinct possibilities for display and interaction with artworks, proper to each venue. For instance, the implications of imagining a part of the exhibition in the Neue Nationalgalerie, built by Mies van der Rohe in 1968, could not escape us. The museum, now a landmark, was commissioned as a political and aesthetic response from former West Germany towards the East. The vast transparent exhibition hall open to its surroundings runs counter to more traditional concepts of museum display in which art objects are isolated and enclosed within windowless (at best sky-lit) rooms, a practice that later resulted in the white cube's dominance as an exhibition site."*

When Chaimowicz learned from Giti Nourbakhsch—his gallerist in Berlin—that Szymczyk and Filipovic wanted to commission him to create a site-specific installation at the Neue Nationalgalerie—Mies van der Rohe's landmark building, which illustrates the architect's longstanding concern with flowing, open spaces—he immediately accepted.

A long-time admirer of Mies' work as an architect and a furniture designer [I. 16, 21; II. 10; III. 11b], Chaimowicz was also a connoisseur of the Neue Nationalgalerie to which, he said, "I was attached to the building itself." Considered one of the most perfect statements of Mies' architectural approach, the upper pavilion of the Neue Nationalgalerie is, in fact, a precise composition of monumental steel columns and an overhanging roof plane with a glass enclosure. The simple square glass pavilion is a powerful expression of the architect's ideas about flexible interior space, defined by transparent walls and supported by an external structural framework. The possibility of developing an artistic project in such a building immediately inspired the artist. As a result, a couple of months later, Chaimowicz proposed a site-specific installation in three parts for the Biennial.

Entitled For MvdR *(2008), the large-scale installation the artist had in mind first featured materials similar to those used by the architect in the building, namely marble and granite, but decorated and complemented by acrylic, printed fabric, ink, and paper. Responding to the architect's complex aestheticisation of materiality, form, and function, the proposed installation consists of eight large-format panels (2.8 metres high) set against the building's solid marble cladding and covered in colourful patterns, resembling fragments of a wall covered in wallpaper. In fact, the works were marble slabs (decorated with acrylic paint), which, according to the artist, establish "a dialogue between the 'authentic' (natural) but decorative surfaces of the building's interior and the nineteenth and twentieth century traditions in the decorative arts which modernist ideology sought to downgrade."*

Curtain (for MvdR)*, the second part of the installation, consists of a transparent curtain that creates a corner space in the* *exhibition area. This piece of fabric, designed in the 1980s by Chaimowicz and edited by Creation Baumann in Langenthal, Switzerland, was reproduced and suspended in the exhibition from ceiling to floor to accentuate the soaring vertical lift operating in the modernist building, while paying homage in a different context to a gauzy waterfall of blue fabric. The piece was presented afterwards at the Secession, Vienna, partly on the floor, as the ceiling was lower than in Berlin, in the artist's solo exhibition "Marc Camille Chaimowicz" (11 November, 2009–24 January, 2010) [I. 16; III. 26]. In the corner delimited by the curtain, seven framed, hand-printed silkscreens (91 × 72 cm each) were presented. This second corner, the third part of the installation, featured enlarged pictures from the artist's recently published book,* The World of Interiors *[III. 22], installed on two hanging panels originally proposed by Mies for displaying painting.*

The text reproduced below is the result of a correspondence between the artist and Nourbakhsch over the winter of 2008, with the preparation of Chaimowicz's commission for the 5th Berlin Biennial as the backdrop. Reproduced below, these "working notes" refer to developments in For MvdR. *Anticipating their importance, Nourbakhsch suggested that the artist print them on A4 paper and make them available to visitors in the gallery, during and after the Biennial. While providing a backdrop to the "interior dress" the artist created in the western corner of the Neue Nationalgalerie's interior space, these "working notes" also shed new light on Mies van der Rohe's camp architecture as referred to by the artist in his text in the following words: "The organic veining of the dark green onyx marble cladding of the two service columns."*

A few years later, Chaimowicz came across an anecdote concerning Mies, according to which, on 15 September, 1968, the day of the building's inauguration, which featured an exhibition of Piet Mondrian, Mies arrived in front of the building and reportedly refused to get out of the car. He was apparently indignant and traumatised by what the artists had done inside his pavilion, which he could see from the car. When Chaimowicz reinstated For MvdR *in his solo exhibition "An Autumn Lexicon," Serpentine Gallery, London (29 September–20 November, 2016), he told exhibition curator Melissa Blanchflower that the installation he had made in 2008 for the 5th Berlin Biennial was "a critique of Ludwig Mies van der Rohe's attitude, which is rigorously dogmatic and very fixed and inhuman. And with this remarkable building of his in Berlin, the one concession he made to the rectilinear were these pillar like units clad in a very organic material in a quartz marble, and so I thought I'd qualify that by decorating it which of course would have been anathema to the master…" Indeed, if the star architect to whom the "working notes" below are dedicated was "traumatised" by Chaimowicz's site-specific ambition "to 'dress' the western corner of the Neue Nationalgalerie's interior space, in which he may have read an 'effiminization' [I. 21] of the building" that subverted its macho logic, he and Chaimowicz would no doubt have agreed that, as the architect said, "God is in the details."*

A.V.

· · · · · · · · ·

I am proposing to "dress" the western corner of the interior space of the Neue Nationalgalerie by means of firstly two materials, one inherent to the building: that of finished marble, and one not: that of a "transparent" printed fabric.

I am intrigued by seemingly the one concession Mies van der Rohe made to the non-linear or mechanistic, i.e. by the organic veining of the dark green onyx marble cladding of the two service columns.

I am therefore proposing to extend and "qualify" this imposing feature by the provisional leaning of a number of marble and granite slabs—each approx. 280 × 100 cm—against one face of the western column. These are of a range of colours from the almost white CARRARA GIOIA to the almost black PORTORO. They are further visually enriched by decorative repetitive pattern … marble perhaps tuned to lace?…

Regarding the four corner windows, I am forwarding the premise of "domestication" by dressing them with a printed net fabric of my design commissioned and edited by Creation Baumann in Langenthal (in the 1980s?)

(These propositions may have been read by Mies as "effeminisa-tion" and thus perhaps as threatening to the implicitly masculine nature of his practice, but I see my intervention more as a process of compliment, resolution, and of possible historical synthesis.)

Having identified the original proposal by Mies for suspended panels upon which to exhibit painting, I am proposing that two, in their initial dimensions, be reconstructed … and upon these to show monoprints and a new suite of large prints based on artwork conceived from my recent publication *The World of Interiors*.

[III. 24]

Dear Stefanie Kleefeld and André Rottmann…

(2008)

Co-founded in 1990 by German critics and art historians Isabel Graw and Stefan Germer, Texte zur Kunst *is a key publication on contemporary art. Published four times a year, this Berlin-based, thematically oriented art journal features essays, interviews, and roundtables, usually completed by critical reviews. Focusing on the "areas of art, institutional critique, feminism, media criticism and theory of subjectivity," as its web page puts it, each issue of* Texte zur Kunst *"addresses culture-sector questions relating to contemporary art, socio-political theory, and cultural policy from an art historical and sociological perspective."*

Attentive to cultural issues and artistic trends, the editorial team of Texte zur Kunst *dedicated its 71st issue (September 2008) to the topic of "artists' artists," a theme that extends its sphere into "the interaction between artists, curators, critics and market players." According to Graw, Stefanie Kleefeld, and André Rottmann, the issue's co-editors:*

> *"Artists' artists [is a term that] designates largely unknown artists who are passed on as 'insider tips' to galleries and curators by colleagues, or are integrated in artworks in the form of quotes or references [...]. 'Artists' artists' have the aura of those recommended by experts but whom the market and the established institutions have hitherto failed to notice."*

Designed with this in mind, the list of contents includes an international roundtable on "referentialism in contemporary art," and commissioned texts from renowned critics and curators Diedrich Diederichsen, André Rottmann, Stefanie Kleefeld, Daniel Birnbaum, Sabine Breitweiser, and Jay Sanders in conversation with New York gallerist Mitchell Algus. In addition, a "survey" entitled "For Every Time Its Artists" features contribu-

tions from nine artists. Conceived to illustrate the "high esteem in which (certain) figures are held by other artists, while market success and institutional recognition usually commence only posthumously," as the three editors put it in their "Preface," the "survey" included written contributions by Cosima von Bonin, Tobias Rehberger, Danh Vo, Nina Könnemann, Christian Philipp Müller, Lawrence Weiner, Rosalind Nashashibi, Marc Camille Chaimowicz, and Florian Pumhösl.

Kleefeld and Rottmann approached Chaimowicz at a time when his pioneering work was once again discussed and considered highly influential by a younger generation of artists and curators: a situation in some ways facilitated by several key exhibitions the artist created over the decade, including among others "Celebration? Realife Revisited" in 2000 [I. 7], "Marc Camille Chaimowicz. Zürich Suite…" in Zürich in 2006 [III. 22], the 5th Berlin Biennial "When Things Cast No Shadows" [III. 23] and "…In the Cherished Company of Others…" in Amsterdam [I. 11] both in 2008, the latter still in place when Kleefeld and Rottmann contacted the artist. Whereas at the time, the post-war artist attested to a position at the expense of being "rediscovered" by the public, as Diederichsen put it in his text "Showfreaks and monsters" in Texte zur Kunst, *Chaimowicz's artistic profile emerged in 2008, at least for those who (re)discovered his work in the 2000s, as that of an "artists' artist" in the making for a younger generation of artists, which the following decade has confirmed.*

In July 2008, Kleefeld and Rottmann called Chaimowicz to invite him to take part in the "Survey" they were working on at the time. As it was "super urgent," the artist agreed on the spot. Over the course of the conversation, the editors introduced Chaimowicz to the issue and told him, as described in their "Preface," that they had found "two aspects in the model of the 'artists' artists'——the potential of being closed off to market events as well as the precondition for a 'hype.'" At the time, Chaimowicz was enjoying a summer retreat in his concierge lodge [III. 19] in a nineteenth century château in Agey, Burgundy, without any access to a computer or internet connection. Although he confirmed his participation in the "Survey," he recalled, "I became more and more anxious to respond to Stefanie and André in a meaningful manner. I even thought of remaining anonymous…" So, at the last minute, on 24 July, 2008, he wrote a one-page letter, faxed it to them and immediately forgot all about it. Sometime later, Kleefeld and Rottmann contacted him again to suggest that his faxed hand-written letter be scanned and published in the journal, the artist recalled, "as a facsimile in the form of a fax, like an image." Suggesting that the "artist's artist" he had thought of for the "Survey" ultimately does not fit in the categories and classifications of the editors, Chaimowicz mischievously deconstructs in his letter their argumentation explaining point by point the reasons why his choice of artist for the "Survey" will, as a name, remain "anonymous."

A.V.

•••••••••

Burgundy , July 24th

Dear Stefanie Kleefeld and André Rottmann,

Thank you for youre invitation
to contribute to the autumn issue
of "Texte zur Kunst"

I have given due consideration to
youre request... but the dateline
approaches and I find myself,
as yet, in a quandry

... allthough I do have an artist
in mind this person would seem to
site themselves outside of the
two categories...
(is it that youre schema is that
of a false polarity or, more probably,
that it is inherent to the process of
classification that these, in turn,
fragment to produce further possible
categories ?)

Whatever, my choice of artist, who
is singularly gifted chooses currently
– and seemingly for the foreseable
future – to stand outside of practise,
and thus wishes to remain anonymous

I can but honor this position and
regret to be unable, on this occasion,
to be of more use,   My very Best wishes
          Marc Camille Chaimowicz

[III. 25]

Lukas Duwenhögger, "The End of the Season (Cabinet Gallery, London)"

(2008)

Seeking information about the major site-specific installation [III. 23] that Chaimowicz created for the 5th Berlin Biennal "When Things Cast No Shadows" (5 April–15 June, 2008), New York-based art critic Lloyd Wise, then Assistant Editor at Artforum, *contacted the artist in June 2008 to discuss with him about his installation at the biennial. A few months later, the artist received an invitation from* Artforum *to contribute to their "Best of" issue, which takes stock of the past year every December. Chaimowicz was asked to participate in a section entitled "The Artists' Artists. Their favourite exhibitions of 2008," involving an international group of fifty-seven artists, who were asked "to find out—as* Artforum *put it—which exhibitions were, in their eyes, the very best of 2008." For the second time in two months, Chaimowicz was solicited by leading international publications to respond to the concept of "artists' artists" [III. 24]. Once approved, the artist was emailed the question "What was the best show you saw last year?" to which he was kindly asked to reply "ASAP" in a limited quantity of words.*

Instantly, an exhibition came to mind. "In the spring of 2008"—Chaimowicz said retrospectively—"I had been truly captivated by the particular type of heat emanating from 'The End of the Season,' Lukas Duwenhögger's exemplary solo project at Cabinet." Enquiring about reviews from the gallery, Chaimowicz was surprised to find that, despite the magnitude of the exhibition and the inspiring singularity of this Istanbul-based German-born artist, who is as much a painter as a designer and a fabulist, there was none. "This really reinforced my intention to 'best of' the exhibition in Artforum," *he said. At the time, Chaimowicz was in Ostend, where he was installing the second iteration of his touring exhibition "…In the Cherished Company of Others …" at Mu.Zee (27 September–15 December, 2008) [I. 11] and did not have much time to devote to it. Coincidentally, Phillip Van den Bossche, the then museum director, mentioned Lukas Duwenhögger's* The Celestial Teapot *over dinner with Chaimowicz who, at exactly the same time, was supposed to be writing his note for* Artforum. *It was clear that this "celestial teapot" had impressed them both. That piece is a proposal for a memorial site for the persecuted homosexuals of National Socialism in Berlin. Built in 2007 by Werk 5 for Documenta 12 in Kassel (16 June–23 September, 2007) as a highly crafted model of a latticework watchtower upholding a humanised copper camp teapot of improbable height, Chaimowicz was delighted to discuss it in more detail with Phillip Van den Bossche, after seeing it in person at Cabinet, "perfectly presented," alongside two scale drawings for* The Celestial Teapot *and a colourful painting entitled* The Celestial Teapot (cross section) (2007). *In return, Van den Bossche told Chaimowicz that to have it built "as a maritime monument in Ostend would be an incredible feat..."*

As mentioned in his "Best of" text, the second work, which impressed Chaimowicz in the exhibition is The End of the Season (2007–08): *a gaudy painting of a slim Mediterranean young man, reclining in purple and yellow swimming shorts next to a sleeping dog by the sea, which is dazzlingly described in the text below as "a pastiche of devotional painting featuring a young man seated with a dog, perhaps as surrogate lover." Due to the limited length of the text and its later nature, this text could be considered a "teaser" for a past exhibition, possibly to be looked at again in the future. Three years later, Chaimowicz said, "When I was in search of young men for 'Jean Genet,' ["Jean Genet... the Courtesy of Objects," Nottingham Contemporary, Nottingham (16 July–2 October, 2011)], this painting by Lukas Duwenhögger was on my radar, and we managed to have it featured in the exhibition."*

To illustrate his "passionately subjective micro-text," Chaimowicz suggested Artforum *use Duwenhögger's painting* The Celestial Teapot (cross section), *accordingly. Four years later, the same painting was reproduced on the cover of* Afterall Journal *31, Autumn / Winter 2012, in which British art historian and writer Roger Cook's text "Lukas Duwenhögger: [Homosexual] Signs" was published. In this text, Cook, a longtime friend of Chaimowicz [I. 12], traces a parallel between Jacques Rancière's theory of disagreement and queer theories of difference, and also discusses Duwenhögger's embodiment of a specifically queer experience of dissent in an aesthetic form that transcends any categorisation as "homosexual." All points to which, in his own way, Chaimowicz wished to draw attention upon in 2008.*

By all accounts, Chaimowicz's short text about Duwenhögger's "The End of the Season" in Artforum *remained the only one available until 15 July, 2022. On that date, i.e. fourteen years after the exhibition, Duwenhögger published a text about his 2008 exhibition, written especially for his web page and illustrated accordingly. Both a contextualisation and a documentation of the exhibition, that text addresses the queer spirit of the socio-sexual signs present in "The End of the Season," whose subversive political horizon Chaimowicz had hinted at in 2008.*

A. V.

• • • • • • • • •

I recall a highly crafted maquette of a lattice watchtower upholding a humanised copper teapot of improbable height, which thus seemed quasi-celestial... Its provenance was that of a proposal, for a memorial for the city of Berlin, to the homosexuals lost to Nazism. It was thus both a work and a proposition for a work too contentious to have been commissioned. Nonetheless, its very strangeness and wit are what gave it conceptual and ethical viability. A flotilla of riches—including a pastiche of devotional painting featuring a young man seated with a dog, perhaps as surrogate lover—concluded an exemplary project.

[III. 26]
A Letter, Transcribed

(2010)

At the end of 2008, Chaimowicz was invited to stage a solo exhibition at the Secession, Vienna. Eager to imagine a project there, and thrilled to reconnect with that "rare city in which we can both work and dream…," as he said in the text he wrote in 1982 during his stay in Vienna as part of the Humanic-Artist-in-Residence-Program [III. 9], he immediately accepted the invitation. In preparation for his exhibition, he visited Vienna several times in 2009. These trips were an opportunity for him to meet pimps of the Viennese art scene, as well as esteemed artistic personalities with whom he had already collaborated in the past, including German-born Vienna-based curator Anette Freudenberger, who invited Chaimowicz to do an exhibit at the Kunstverein für die Rheinlande und Westfalen, Düsseldorf, in 2005 [I. 16].

Returning to Vienna provided the artist with important stimuli, which he recycled in the works created or selected for the Secession show. Entitled "Marc Camille Chaimowicz," this exhibition, curated by Elisabeth Bettina Spörr, took place in the main exhibition hall of the art venue from 20 November, 2009 through 24 January, 2010. In an eclectic collection of masterfully designed and crafted objects, ranging from asymmetrically cut carpets to individual parasols for dandies, oversized hanging curtains and wallpapers, the exhibition was completed by others' work, including Viennese architect Hermann Czech—whom Chaimowicz holds in "high esteem"—and British artist Simon Thompson. This trans-generational approach to curating reveals the continuity of the European artistic and historical milieus, which the artist has links with in Vienna and elsewhere, while underlining the fact that even in the exhibition context, artists do not find themselves in a socio-political vacuum sealed off from the outside world. Indeed, comprising a mixed-media installation of objects designed and handcrafted by the artist and bearing the stylistic imprint of fin-de-siècle Jugendstil, *consumer objects from mid-century Los Angeles and international modernist architecture and design, the exhibition established interconnections between Los Angeles and Vienna, some of which were compiled by Chaimowicz in a 13-page letter to "J." presented in the exhibition on a wall in enfilade, each page shown under glass.*

Reproduced below, this letter was originally handwritten on the stationery from two different hotels where the artist resided in 2009, the Roosevelt in Los Angeles, where Chaimowicz stayed in mid-April on the occasion of his solo exhibition at Overduin and Kite, Los Angeles (26 April–30 May, 2009) as well as the Steigenberger in Baden-Baden, where he stayed for a few days in July to supervise the installation of Jean Cocteau *(2003–09) [I. 8], presented in the group exhibition "Entre deux actes—Loge de comédienne," organised by Iranian-born Berlin-based artist Nairy Baghramian in close collaboration with late French designer Janette Laverrière at the Staatliche Kunsthalle, Baden-Baden (25 July–28 November, 2009). Concurrently illustrated with small cloud photographs of Vienna's Café Prückle, architectural drawings of the Secession, and views of the artist's recent exhibitions, this letter conveys impressions of contemporary Los Angeles as the artist prepares his solo exhibition in Vienna. Beyond the anecdotal coincidences—Viennese chefs at Los Angeles restaurants, or the exhibition "Franz West, To Build a House You Start with the Roof: Work, 1972–2008" that was on at the Los Angeles County Museum of Art (12 March–7 June, 2009), for instance—the author cites the presence and works of famous Austrian-born artists and architects like Richard Neutra, Adolf Loos, and Rudolf Schindler, who were integral to and directly influenced by the Viennese Secession and Wiener Werkstätte. Spurred by increasing Austrian conservatism in the 1920s and 1930s, each made their way to Los Angeles as part of, the artist writes, "the broad and endless stream of exiles, each generally travelling on one-way tickets." Oscillating between reverie and real life, Vienna appears and reappears in this period, Chaimowicz says, "in myriad form or as chimera—to haunt and envelop us (the conceptual distance between Wittgenstein's Vienna and, say, the death of Michael Jackson is daunting—yet today's cultural overload purports to such mental juggling…).*"

The letter's content is partly based on Chaimowicz's "Chorus, a letter from Vienna." Handwritten in Vienna in 1982 on the stationary of Hotel Kärntnerhof Wien, this illustrated letter to "J.," which sums up the artist's Viennese experience at the time, was first published in 1985 as Chapter 5 in the artist's second book Café du Rêve *[III. 11d]. Written twenty-seven years apart, these two letters written to "Dear J."—a fictitious recipient, perhaps the artist himself?—present similarities and differences based on meticulous sources, the second being the extension of the first.*

The letter reproduced below was first published in 2010 to coincide with the exhibition at Secession, as part of the artist's accompanying publication A Folio for Secession. *Conceived by Chaimowicz, and edited by Elisabeth Bettina Spörr, this "folio" was published by the Secession, and produced in cooperation with La Piscine – Musée d'art et d'industrie André Diligent, Roubaix, where, at the same time, the solo exhibition "To furnish…, Marc Camille Chaimowicz" was presented (21 November, 2009–21 February, 2010). As announced on the folder flap, the 34-page cream card portfolio (20.8 × 27 cm) contains:*

> *"a letter*
> *some patterns*
> *a text and*
> *exhibition views"*

Rather than chronicling something that has already happened, the publication instead proposed an openness to re-arrangement, whose editorial work and writing would be seen more as an assemblage or editing, with the pages slipped freely into the folio. The contents of the publication are as follows: a facsimile of a handwritten letter on headed notepaper in various formats; six patterns drawn by the artist, printed on card; an essay by Austrian academic and curator Silvia Eiblmayr entitled "Marc Camille Chaimowicz Vienna Revisited…?"; a brochure containing "exhibition views." To make the handwritten letter easier to read, it was typed and reproduced in two columns on the front of an A4 page subsequently entitled "A letter, transcribed."

On the night before the opening, the Friends of the Secession held their yearly fundraising dinner in honour of Chaimowicz. "If you are the artist showing at the Secession in the fall, you are invited to curate the dinner, from the lighting to the food," the artist explained in retrospect. To prepare this dinner, Chaimowicz was put in touch with the caterer in charge, at the Metropol Hotel, where he also had a room. Introducing himself, Chaimowicz impulsively complimented a butler about his jacket. In the afternoon, he dropped by the hotel, went up to his room and noted, inspired, that three identical jackets in different sizes had been made available to him, graciously, in the bedroom wardrobe. And so, to everyone's surprise, Chaimowicz appeared that evening in the crowded hotel lobby of the hotel wearing the same jacket as the staff. He wore it throughout the banquet, thus refusing to categorise himself, preferring instead to sustain the tension of ambivalent determination between waiter and guest of honour. Extending this theatrical dialectic into the present day, the artist sometimes wears this long jacket at home, especially when newcomers show up. With this propensity to joke and destabilise, Chaimowicz reminds us what

*Jean Genet—a writer Chaimowicz was at the time curating
a project about [III. 27]—said about theatre, namely, that
making theatre can bring the dead back to life.*

A.V.

....

Dear J,

Uneasy with the breakfast options, I earlier tentatively ventured
out onto Hollywood Boulevard … there to witness a scene of
utter devastation … the barren street was cordoned off, there
was much detritus strewn, as were smashed and burned out
cars, in the mid-distance was a crowd busying itself with more
wreckage. It took me a while to focus on a film crew, then to be
told that a sequel of *Aliens* was being filmed… That I am in Tinsel
town was that afternoon confirmed when—on being advised that
sunlight is a good remedy for jet-lag (if not of a sense of cultural
displacement) I cautiously ventured down to the hotel pool … to
there witness lightly clad bodies, each aspiring to perfection … a
swarm of tattooed boys and leggy nymphets sipping drinks and
each narcissistically feigning indifference, sunbathing or posing
languidly at the Tropicana Bar. The D.J. had rediscovered Jim
Morrison—for which there can surely be no more fitting setting—
and the smell of sun tan lotion tinged with that of wafting dope
completed a sense of relaxed abandon … and yet … for all this
hedonic posturing, I could also sense anxieties manifest, tension,
rivalries, and deals—not all above board—in the making…

I returned to my spacious hotel room, and to the more familiar
solace of drawing … and from this fractured perspective
continued with drawing a partial view of Olbrich's Secession

building, which will potentially be endlessly mechanically repeated … thus turning architecture into lace?

It is one of a number of new motifs, which are intentioned to complement an existing lexicon of patterns once used as a low cost substitute to wallpaper and originating in the early twentieth century European vernacular. Many of which, incidentally, I had acquired when living in Vienna. I am thinking of integrating them—of punctuating the once anonymous with the more subjective—by these of my own making… Lisa Overduin and I went to see the Franz West show at LACMA and what a delight it was… Although compact it was broad in range and masterfully installed, the best of his I've seen. For all his mannered dysfunctionalism the work emerges as visually knowing, his wit is such that although once a "bad boy," as with the waywardness of a precocious adolescent, so his posed vulgarity now reads as conditional… In contrast to the brit pack, generally so lumpen and literal, his work is generous, his palette Viennese Warholian … and he seems conscious of the art around him…

There's an interview in the excellent catalogue … it seems he grew up in Karl-Marx-Hof, which I referred to in my last letter and about which he's somewhat cryptic, stating that it was then "…full of aged Nazis…" (!)

It is given that as we focus on any particular subject, so that subject is liable to appear and reappear—in myriad form or as chimera—to haunt and envelop us … (the conceptual distance between Wittgenstein's Vienna and, say, the death of Michael Jackson is daunting—yet today's cultural overload purports to such mental juggling…)

A favourite restaurant here is Ammo, which is run by Benedikt who is from Vienna, and, after chatting, mentioned that they'd lived close to Secession where it was referred to as "Cabbage head"… I am therefore sensitised to Vienna's after image … there are connections beyond the anecdotal and it may seem an exaggeration to suggest that pockets of L.A. were once more Viennese than Vienna… yet such was the exodus of radical thinkers, and such were the opportunities that this equation is surely plausible…

What I am proposing is that the fractured continuum of history was such that the true spirit of Viennese Radicalism was, in the 1920s and 1930s largely transposed to California…

Dear J, do not dismiss this as incongruous, both early nineteenth century Vienna and early twentieth L.A. were fast expanding and each offered dreams and material advancement to a broad and endless stream of exiles, each generally travelling on one way tickets.

Vienna's progressive milieu and intelligentsia was then largely Jewish as was their clientele—and was feeling increasingly constricted by the stiffening conservatism of Austria … even before the advent of war such was the feeling of despondency that they were drawn to the "free" world and Los Angeles, by contrast, offered them, beyond an idyllic and sensual climate, endless opportunities… Potential patronage would seem as abundant as were desert cacti…

Rudolf Schindler left Vienna for New York in 1914 … and arrived in L.A., aged thirty-two, in 1920. The Hollywood film industry was in its infancy … it was as though Adolf Loos' (himself an advocate of American energy and pragmatism) Chicago Tribune Tower had cast a benevolent blessing over the West Coast… His friend Richard Neutra, with whom he had studied under Loos, later joined him and they set up a joint practice but later fell out…

As exemplar of International Modernism I had been more familiar with Neutra but here Schindler is a revelation … of the two he is the greater by far and closer in both spirit and manner to Loos. Uncompromising, he built to small budgets and thus often with humble materials, his buildings have not generally weathered well. There is something provisional and speculative about his work, perhaps in accord with a young state then in such flux…

After the pomposity of the Ringstrasse how liberated here he must have felt.

By contrast Neutra appears tame and, well, the more bourgeois… Indeed the current late Neutra building available for sale is his Singleton house of 1959, on Mulholland Drive and it seems somehow appropriate that it is being sold for twenty million dollars by coiffure par excellence to the stars, Vidal Sassoon. It is inferred that when Philip Johnson visited L.A. whilst researching for his groundbreaking exhibition at MoMA, R. Neutra was negative of Schindler's work to the point of betrayal. Schindler was thus excluded from exhibiting and consequently forfeited a key showcase for future possible commissions. Johnson is rumoured to have later regretted this but irrevocable damage had been done. Schindler's status is being revised yet such is architecture's horror, and our loss, that he was thus marginalised and doomed to remain local to Southern California. It would seem that deceit and duplicity, those very traits Karl Kraus had so valiantly contested had—alongside hope, vision, and genius—also travelled from the malevolent Mother Country to the New Land…

What ever would Sigmund have made of this? And what a film script this could make… Can you imagine Bruno Ganz and Dennis Hopper as the protagonists?… Which naturally begs the question as to who would play the villain…

I should now prepare for my exhibition; the likelihood of showing *Vienna Triptych* … leaning … of 1982 is probable. Wishing to honour the remarkably open space so radically conceived by Olbrich in 1898 the show will be primarily floor-based and will feature work mainly as yet unseen … including new asymmetric carpets, a bookcase, and, yes, some parasols…

To evidence the principle of fraternity—an issue on which I should, at some later time, wish to elaborate—it will include contributions by a select number of guests…

Dear J, should this letter reach you I would love to see you in Vienna, the Gala Dinner is on Wednesday the 18th of Nov. and the private view the following evening.

Yours as ever Mcx

P.S. I returned to the poolside, now on weekday evenings … to find it transformed and now reminiscent of Schindler's description of California as an "earthly paradise."

Protected from the desert chill by generous steel braziers, the water and palm trees lit—the hotel hubbub muted, I particularly recall one scene … that of a father and daughter alone in the pool and utterly absorbed in a free form-like duet … a scene of tenderness and innocence, it nonetheless reminded me of those knowing yet touching paintings by Michael Andrews of his young daughter at play in a small river in East Anglia…

P.P.S. I enclosed a detail of the work shown at Overduin and Kite.

[III. 27]

Jean Genet in Norfolk

(2010)

Straddling the literary and visual arts, Chaimowicz began scattering references to writers in his work in the 1970s. In addition to emblematic figures such as Marcel Proust, André Gide, Albert Camus, Gustave Flaubert, to whom he paid direct or indirect homage for years, the famous poet of revolt Jean Genet—orphan, thief, prisoner, army deserter, vagabond, and prostitute, who turned brutal experience into sexually fevered poetry—exerted a lasting influence on the artist. Resistant to categorisation, Genet impressed Chaimowicz early in his career, particularly on subjects that create relationships with wider social systems, such as politics or the economy of the self. The first mention of Genet in his work dates from Celebration? Realife *(1972) [III. 2, 3]. Among the supporting sources is* The Balcony. *In this 1956 play, first translated into English in 1960, Genet ironically associates Western society with a luxury "brothel," a place where bodies are exchanged for money, where trompe-l'œil and illusions reign supreme, in the form of a funeral farce where the man who laughs knows that all is lost. In an oblique echo of this, or perhaps unconsciously, Chaimowicz often used the term "brothel" to describe his 1972 "scattered environment."*

Whether direct or indirect, Chaimowicz's references to Genet's texts and persona are manifold in his work. When, for instance, he began working with "screens" [III. 6, 7, 10], both as a concept and as furniture, exploring the intersections between public and private in the second half of the 1970s, references to Genet's play The Screens *(1961) is evident. First performed in public in 1966, four years after the end of the Algerian war, this subversive and highly political play, which deals with play and illusion through the use of screens, activates new potentialities for staging. Indeed, the multiplicity of their uses on stage ultimately implies that the main subject of the play is not only war or colonisation, but above all the scenic process, itself facilitated by the in-betweenness of the screens on which the actors draw and move from one side to the other, from life to death.*

A few years later, a quotation from Genet's The Thief's Journal *(1949) was used emblematically as the frontispiece to Jean Fisher's book* Past Imperfect. Marc Camille Chaimowicz 1972–1982 *(Liverpool: Bluecoat Gallery et al., 1983), the first monograph devoted to the artist's work. This quotation, which somehow orients the publication, reads as follows:*

> *"I remained on the alert to seize those vagrant moments which seemed to me in quest, as a lost soul is in quest of a body, of a consciousness to register and feel them. Having found it, they cease: the poet drains the world dry. But if he offers up another, it can only be his own reflection. When, in the Santé Prison, I began to write, it was never because I wanted to relive my emotions or to communicate them, but rather because I hoped, by expressing them in a form that they themselves imposed, to construct an order that was unknown (above all to me too)."*

In another vein, there's the theme of the flower. Omnipresent in the writings of Genet, flowers are also frequent in the work of Chaimowicz. From Celebration? Realife *(1972) where a freshly cut bouquet in a vase is displayed on the floor, to the artist's interiors, flowers are part of Chaimowicz's artistic and social environment. Since the 2000s, Chaimowicz has developed numerous works that include flowers [I. 17; III. 22]. A recurring motif in his work, the use of flowers undoubtedly intersects with* Our Lady of the Flowers *(1943) and* Miracle of the Rose *(1946), two early novels by Genet which, as in the work of Chaimowicz, are the interface of a latent duality opposing a frequent use of commonplaces to a transgression of the norms that govern them. As Chaimowicz rightly points out, Genet is named after a flower in French. Indeed, "[…] antithesis to the cultured rose, the* Genet, *a humble and hardy plant, is happy to exist in the uncultivated wild."*

In 2011, Chaimowicz paid direct homage to Genet by integrating the writer and poet's charge, legacy, and mythology into his own work into a three-chapter exhibition entitled "Marc Camille Chaimowicz. Jean Genet… The Courtesy of Objects." It was early in the research process for this exhibition that Chaimowicz wrote the text reproduced below. In this exhibition, Genet becomes the subject of a masterful scenography presided over by Chaimowicz in response to his writings. Exploring themes derived from Genet's life, this exhibition in the form of a loose portrait also includes in its storytelling important figures such as the French philosopher Jean-Paul Sartre, author of an essential biography entitled Saint Genet, Actor and Martyr *(1952) in an attempt "to prove that genius is not a gift but the way out that one invents for oneself in desperate cases" as well as David Bowie, who wrote the song "The Jean Genie" in the autumn of 1972, and whose lyrics speak of someone who "sits like a man but smiles like a reptile," and which became the lead single to his 1973 album* Aladin Sane. *Initiated by British curator Lynda Morris, professor at Norwich University College for the Art, where the exhibition ran from 19 April to 21 May as part of the Norfolk and Norwich Festival 2011 "well-funded" program of events, this project shares similar curatorial mechanisms to those of "Jean Cocteau…"—"a project by Marc Camille Chaimowicz featuring Marcel Breuer, Stephen Buckley, Enrico David, Cerith Wyn Evans, Alberto and Diego Giacometti, Tom of Finland, Isokon, Marie Laurencin, Paulina Olowska, Nadia Wallis, Andy Warhol," which, likewise, was developed in collaboration with Lynda Morris seven years earlier [I. 8] at Norwich Gallery, Norwich School of Art & Design (11 September—25 October,*

2003). A long-time friend of the artist, Morris knew of his deep interest in, and admiration for, the life and work of Genet. She was aware that he wanted to create a set for a play inspired by Genet's The Maids *(1948), a play about two servants who rebel against their mistress, which he was discussing with Stefan Kalmár, then director of Artists Space, New York [I. 14]. As soon as Norwich Gallery's participation in the Norfolk and Norwich Festival 2011 was confirmed, Morris called Chaimowicz and said, "Let's do the show!" Following this, two exhibition partners confirmed their interest in the tour, which, after discussion with the artist, developed into a three-chapter project.*

In Norwich, new works by the artist were presented in a sober installation flirting, like the exhibition's subsequent incarnations, with the form of strange and exquisite domestic interiors that offer a mental image of a space Genet might wish to inhabit. The exhibition also included two works carefully selected by Chaimowicz: one by British artist Tariq Alvi, the other by Scottish artist Andrew Cranston, both of them provoking interiority and solitude.

Presented at Nottingham Contemporary from 16 July to 2 October, 2011, Part Two was conceived in collaboration with Alex Farquharson, then Director of Nottingham Contemporary. Featuring works by other artists, the exhibition included six major sculptures and paintings by Alberto Giacometti from the 1950s, including a painted portrait of Genet, and several furniture pieces designed in the 1930s. It also included Lukas Duwenhögger's The End of the Season, *2007–08—a gaudy painting of a slim Mediterranean young man reclining in purple and yellow swimming shorts next to a sleeping dog by the sea, which Chaimowicz dazzlingly described in* Artforum *in 2008 as "a pastiche of devotional painting featuring a young man seated with a dog, perhaps as surrogate lover" [III. 25]. Mathilde Rachet, whom the artist had tutored the year before at the Art*

School in Dijon, presented a video work related to Genet. Finally, after "looking for men for Genet,"Wolfgang Tillmans suggested that Chaimowicz include like praying (faded fax) (2005) [II. 12] in the exhibition.

Part Three was presented at Focal Point Gallery, Southend-on-Sea, from 13 February to 24 March, 2012. This iteration featured new works by the artist, including the complete set of collages conceived as a tribute to Genet, which Andrew Hunt, at the time Director of Focal Point Gallery, described in the press release as follows:

> "Divided into four quartets, these seventeen new images—the fourth quartet contains an anomaly resulting in five pictures—comprise pictorial elements taken from mainstream fashion advertising and newspaper supplements such as How to Spend It and Country Life, some of the highest subscribed publications by prisoners in British institutions. This is a phenomenon the artist would like to envisage in relation to Genet's own time in prison. Perhaps in an imagined contemporary scenario, the writer and his friends might find themselves studying similar adverts, features and country houses in preparation for their release back into mainstream society."

In addition to the artist's works, the exhibition at Focal Point Gallery featured two works. On the one hand, British writer, musician, and frieze editor Dan Fox [I. 11] was commissioned by Chaimowicz to score the soundtrack for The Casting of the Maids (2011), the artist's first ever-video work. On the other hand, Tariq Alvi's screen print A Poster for a Library (1995), depicting a naked man reading a book with an erection, was shown again, this time in the art centre's own library. Finally, as Hunt summed up in the press release for the exhibition at Focal Point Gallery, Chaimowicz's trilogy attempted "to avoid the *dogma of left-wing ideological practice with an accent on the central themes of the artist's work, namely the enacting of alternative performative and aesthetic strategies that address artifice and the real within a social and political context," which the pending publication* Trois Inventaires (Three Inventories) *[II. 12] should account for in detail.*

A few months into the process, Lynda Morris told Chaimowicz a story about Genet that inspired the text reproduced below. In the 1960s, Genet had come to Norfolk, East Anglia, for the wedding of his young protégé Jacky Maglia—the stepson of Genet's lover Lucien Sénémaud—whom he had encouraged to desert from the French Army, leading him across Europe. Later, the lad fell in love with Jacqueline, a young Englishwoman who shared Jacky Maglia's love of fast cars. Their marriage took place in Norfolk in 1964, with Genet as best man. Because of Maglia's youthful passion for stealing cars, Genet, whose writing career was by this time very successful, sponsored him as a racing driver, and later bought him a Lotus Elan as a wedding present. Interweaving Genet's tone with that of Chaimowicz, the text below leads to an exquisite anecdote taken from the 1964 Church registry, which Chaimowicz, in turn, was quick to tell everyone about. Having caught wind of this anecdote, the art journal Picpus *suggested the artist write a text about it, which was also supposed to help publicise his forthcoming exhibition in Norwich.*

Founded by British patron and collector Charles Asprey [I. 13, 21] in 2009 over lunch with British curator, writer and co-editor Simon Grant, Picpus *is an A6 quarterly (10.5 × 14.8 cm), which folds out to a single A2 sheet manifesto / poster (60 × 42 cm) in the tradition of the pamphlet or fly-poster, with no actual cover. Etymologically* Picpus *is* Pique Puce, *fleabite. The name, as Charles Asprey put it in an interview with Jeremy*

Leslie on magculture.com, 6 February, 2023, has its origins in the work of Scottish artist and Concrete Poet Ian Hamilton Finlay. He said, "One of Finlay's themes was the French Revolution and Picpus *takes its name from a cemetery in Paris where Robespierre buried the victims of his Terror and where he himself ended up when the Counter-Revolutionaries got to him." Distributed free of charge in bookshops and art galleries,* Picpus *has been printed by Aldgate Press in Tower Hamlets, London, since the winter of 2009 at a rate of 4,000 copies per quarter. Designed by a team at Studio ARD—Chuard and Nørregaard, London, from an original design by London-based German artist Christian Flamm, which includes the flea logo, the masthead, and a bespoke alphabet,* Picpus *therefore has an artist-designed brand identity that is uniquely theirs. All these specific features for a free quarterly make* Picpus, *according to Asprey in a 2009 statement, "part of a long tradition of small, independent British arts journals and periodicals that attempt to fill a gap left by mainstream arts publications like* Coterie *(1919–21);* Ray Magazine *(1926–27);* The Apple *(1920s) and* ZG magazine *from the 1980s."*

Chaimowicz wrote this text in late summer 2010. At that time, he was in Agey, Burgundy, where he had planned to stay for three weeks to work, and occasionally, stop smoking. Over the period, he said, "I had to reorganise myself under strong medication, which, as a collateral effect, made 'Jean Genet in Norfolk' my first nicotine free text." Back in London, he emailed the text to Picpus, *suggesting to use a photograph of a Lotus Elan car (1962–73) designed by Colin Chapman as an illustration.* Picpus 4 *was published in Autumn 2010.*

In preparation for the exhibition, Chaimowicz reread Miracle of the Rose. *Composed in 1943 while Genet was still interned at La Santé prison, this book depicts scenes from his adolescence, which blend with his experience as a thirty-something prisoner, harbouring erotic homosexual desires for his fellow inmates.*

Against this backdrop of constant surveillance, where some prisoners have their feet enchained and their hands handcuffed, an intimate, anti-materialist description towards the end of the book focuses on Harcamone, a criminal on death row, in the following terms:

> *"Harcamone stood up very cautiously. He did not know whether the night was dark, for his entire existence was being lived at the incandescent centre of a raw white light. He approached the door, holding up his irons, but hardly had he taken three or four steps when the irons opened and fell to the floor noiselessly. Harcamone did not fluster. He must have been used to the courtesy of objects."*

Impressed by this scene in which death sentence and liberation converge on "the courtesy of objects," Chaimowicz felt it necessary to include this notion describing an intrinsic transformation of the relation to objects in the very title of his exhibition, knowing that prison recontextualises, or perhaps clarifies, the role of objects for Genet. Indeed, as Genet described in his book:

> *"The objects here in jail have been worn out by my eyes and are now sickly pale. They no longer mean prison to me, because prison is inside me, composed of the cells of my tissues. It was not before long after my return here that my hands and eyes, which were only too familiar with the practical qualities of objects, finally stopped recognising these qualities and discovered others which have other meanings."*

Without having a predetermined theory on the subject, Chaimowicz used "the courtesy of objects" intuitively, saying in retrospect that "it implies to lose objecthood," which, once linked to artworks as objects in an exhibition, becomes fiercely political. Once published, Chaimowicz recycled a copy of Picpus, *which he installed on top of* Prie-Dieu, *2011, a functional wooden kneeler with a custom-made fabric kneeling cushion designed by the artist in 2011.*

In 2012, the London-based publishing house Grey Tiger Books developed a new edition of The Studio of Giacometti. *Following the exhibition by Chaimowicz in which Genet and Alberto Giacometti were brought together again in a spectacular way, the publisher contacted the artist to find out if he would be interested in illustrating this publication containing a new English translation by Phil King of Genet's ground-breaking essay recounting his experience of having observed Giacometti at work from such close proximity. As a fan of this book that was first published in 1963, Chaimowicz considers Genet's 1958 essay to be a fundamental text on the creative process. As a result, he immediately accepted the invitation, while making his recent Genet-related collages available to Grey Tiger Books for publication. Delighted by the artist's spontaneity and commitment, Grey Tiger Books invited him to give artistic direction to the volume, to which, according to the publisher, "he brings a perfectly-pitched sense for where meanings derived from text and image may work into tertiary areas of finesse and appreciation." Designed by Fraser Muggeridge and Zoe Anspach in London, this 72-page (20.4 × 14 cm) softcover edition of* The Studio of Giacometti *was published at the end of 2013 and sold out within months.*

The multiplicity of links that Chaimowicz has wittingly established throughout his career with (the work and life of) J Genet, among which the above and the text reproduced below, will no doubt continue to be deciphered.

A.V.

• • • • • • • • • •

Jacky Maglia loved cars, Jean Genet, in his fashion, loved Jacky Maglia. Jacky was the stepson of Genet's lover Lucien Sénémaud who had married Jacky's mother. Genet was generally attracted to heterosexual men, often delinquents or pretty criminals … and Jacky stole cars (probably to win Genet's favour). Genet actively encouraged Jacky to take up motor racing and managed his fledging career. They grew very close, later travelling widely together and covertly entering the U.S. (from where Genet was banned) to cover the 1968 Chicago Democratic Convention.

Fame and critical success were sudden and violently echoed by financial gain. Genet was at one point Gallimard's highest earning writer. This having the converse effect in that the more rich and famous he became, the less he was able to write. For so long the outsider and now a literary celebrity it was as though he felt alienated from his own unique and cherished sense of alienation...

One notable concession to material wealth however was the forsaking of his customary leather blouson for that of ready-to-wear suits, and to now occasionally staying in luxury hotels such as the LUTETIA (where he'd surely once frequented German soldiers?). But he did spend big money … on others, financially helping current and past lovers and setting them up in business (there was, in South West France, as recently as the late 1990s a functioning car repair shop called "Le Garage Saint Genet" which was run by Lucien S.). He had houses built for the latter Lucien, Mohamed El Katrani, Ahmed, and others, perhaps wishing on them a lifestyle denied him, that of domesticity. A room for his personal use was invariably allocated, but he rarely used it, preferring when visiting to stay in local modest hotels.

By this time, Jacky had met an English girl who loved fast cars and decided he wished to marry. And so, with Genet's blessing, they both travelled to England, where Genet stayed a while in

Norwich and where he bought Jacky a customised LOTUS sports car. Although the marriage did not last, proof of his somewhat incongruous venture into the conservative heartland of East Anglia is to be found in a 1964 Church registry entry. The marriage was witnessed by the bride's father who stated his occupation as policeman, and Jean Genet who stated his as … thief.

[III. 28]

One Evening…

(2013)

As short-listed in Marc Camille Chaimowicz, Celebration? Realife Revisited *(London: Koenig Books; Dijon: Frac Bourgogne, 2005, p. 44-45), Gustave Flaubert's first novel,* Madame Bovary. Provincial Manners *(1857) is among the twelve literary references that contributed to the creation of the artist's cult "scattered environment" Celebration? Realife [III. 2, 3]. In addition to Chaimowicz's long-standing interest in Gustave Flaubert's oeuvre, his interest in "Emma"—"the best incarnation of provincial life," as he put it retrospectively with a touch of sarcasm—crystallised in 2013, taking the deft form of a 536-page (21 × 27 cm) illustrated paper-back of* Madame Bovary, *published by Four Corner Books, London. This new work, in which Chaimowicz created an illustrated design for the Flaubert classic* Madame Bovary, *is preceded by two works from 2012. The first,* Emma…, *a screen print on fabric intermingling ribbons, grapes flowers, and ice-cream cones (104.6 × 79.1 cm), was produced by Atelier E.B, Edinburgh, Brussels. The second,* For Emma, *a silkscreen print with collaged shape (35 × 51 cm) revisiting the artist's* Here and There *(1978) [III. 6], was produced by Artlead, Belgium. The two editions, circulated at the same time as the Four Corner Books publication, quickly sold out.*

Founded in 2003 in London by Richard Embray and Elinor Jansz, Four Corners Books developed several series among which is the "Four Corners Familiars." As described on the publisher's web page, this series focuses on "artists' responses to classic novels and short stories with the idea to provide a fresh look at the tradition of the illustrated novel." Interested in the work of Chaimowicz, whose three-chapter exhibition "Jean Genet… The Courtesy of Objects" [III. 27] received attention in Britain and overseas at the time, Embray and Jansz invited the artist to imagine the next volume in the "Familiars" series. Later, Jansz and Chaimowicz met in London. Over the course of their meeting, the artist explained to her that the possibility of repacking and reworking an existing text was inspiring. "When I received this exciting proposal," he recalled, "I first made the connection with Flaubert, then with Bovary. I am still struck by the fact that Emma had a strange crossover life, and suddenly died having been strangely confronted with contemporary life." Chaimowicz therefore suggested that Four Corners Books work from Gustave Flaubert's bestseller Madame Bovary, *which he would illustrate accordingly.*

Two years later, Flaubert's Madame Bovary *with art by Chaimowicz and design by John Morgan was published by Four Corners Books in March 2013. "Lavishly illustrated with over 250 images created for this volume by Marc Camille Chaimowicz," as described by the publisher, the publication comprises photographs, collages, and found objects disseminated along the 536 pages, which somehow shadow Emma Bovary's attempts to escape the banalities of provincial life. Design wise, the novel is "set in a new typeface, specially commissioned [...] based on fonts in use in France in the 1800s, from which John Morgan Studio developed a new typeface, Berthe, named after Emma Bovary's neglected child." Finally, the edition features the first English translation of Flaubert's book by Eleanor Marx-Aveling, Karl Marx's youngest daughter, as published in 1886 by Vizetelly & Co., London.*

In addition, Chaimowicz suggested including a supplementary text in the publication. Printed separately on the same paper and in the same font as the book, this page was then inserted in each copy. Reproduced below in facsimile, the text by Flaubert was originally part of Madame Bovary. *However, when the novel was published in instalments in the* Revue de Paris *between October and December 1856, its co-founders deemed it prudent not to print this part (like many others), which might be considered too erotic and immoral, and give rise to a lawsuit. Removed from the manuscript, this scene was not published, either in the* Revue de Paris *or in the first edition of* Madame Bovary. Provincial Manners, *published in two volumes in April 1857 by Michel Lévy Frères, Paris.*

Seven years after Flaubert's death in 1880, Charpentier, Paris, published the first edition of Correspondence. *Comprising 4,000 letters from Flaubert addressed to over 300 people, this correspondence shed light on, among other things, the progression of* Madame Bovary's *narrative. Some of these letters contain fragments censored in 1856, which Flaubert later recycled in his correspondence. Such is the case of the text reproduced below. Indeed, taken from a letter to Louise Cholet, Flaubert's mistress, this passage describes an erotic climax between Emma and Léon. Separated from the original text since 1856, it was physically reintegrated into Flaubert's volume in 2013 by Chaimowicz. To this end, the fragment was published as a one-page supplement, using the same paper and font as in the book stating: "Please insert at page 159. It is at this point in the narrative that Flaubert edited out this passage, included here to give the reader the option of re-introducing it" exactly where it was 160 years earlier.*

Both enriching and commenting on Flaubert's novel, Chaimowicz's reintroduction of this almost lost fragment of text actively operates on the site of the book's story. This erotic passage does not activate the distance between dreams and reality, as it is always said about that book, but rather testifies to Emma Bovary's transgressive ingenuity as a response to boredom. Indeed, in this carriage sex scene, the emptiness of her still-warm glove penetrated by another hand suggests a welcome encounter. Struggling against the inevitability of the immobility fermenting in her life, and against a narrow existence from which she seeks to escape through consumerism, seduction, and the world of the imagination, Emma Bovary, as a modern anti-heroine with no place in society, grabs hold of any hint of an opportunity, to the point of death.

The research undertaken by the artist as part of this book project lastingly reinforced his fascination with Emma Bovary. Following this, two "depictions" of Emma Bovary have taken place in solo exhibitions of the artist. The first was in the exhibition "Marc Camille Chaimowicz. Dear Valérie...," Kunsthalle Bern (22 February–26 July, 2020) curated by Valérie Knoll, at the time Director of Kunsthalle Bern. Then, in a second phase, another room dedicated to Emma Bovary was set up in "Marc Camille Chaimowicz: Nuit Américaine," Wiels, Brussels (17 February–13 August, 2023) curated by Zoë Gray, at the time senior curator at Wiels. Each of the two exhibitions featured a room devoted to "Emma B." Entitled "Portraiture," the room in Bern was painted in shades of pink porcelain showcasing artefacts and everyday objects such as silk ties, underwear, letters, and beauty accessories where fiction and reality come into one. The room also featured a thick multi-coloured curving-shaped rug that was presented on the floor, with the name "Emma" on it. Starring Jean Cocteau, Alberto Giacometti, NJW, Andy Warhol, and Jules Cantini, the room crystallised the artist's first steps towards the rise of the portrait of a fictional character existing in reality.

In the summer of 2020, Chaimowicz began developing a new series of collages linking, as Zoë Gray says in the Brussels exhibition guide, "Emma's longings to recent experiences of containment, social isolation and the desire to escape." Produced during the pandemic until the end of summer 2023, this suite of forty-eight A4 collages was scanned, and emailed fortnightly, one after the other as "visual letters" to Gray until the end of the exhibition at Wiels. Entitled "Dear Zoë"—a reference to the artist's longstanding art of correspondence—forty of these were actually shipped to Brussels and presented in the exhibition (a further ten were produced and emailed to Gray fortnightly during the run of the exhibition), mounted on oblique platforms designed by the artist and fixed to the four sides of concrete pillars partially painted in Chaimowicz's colours, from lavender and tangerine to cream and sage tones. As a result, "Emma B." remained active in the artist's mind for almost ten years without interruption. As in Brussels, however, the production turned more systematic due to the "monologue" correspondence format with Gray. Receiving them fortnightly, she observed that:

> *"As his source material, he used fragments from magazines, literary prints, and reproductions of work by other artists focused on the domestic domain, woven together with his own drawings and patterns. Many of the collages feature luxury items cut out from the Financial Times' magazine 'How to spend it' (a publication that Emma would have simply adored!), which connect her consumerist desires with our own era's attempts at distraction-through-expenditure."*

Entitled "Dear Zoë (Emma Bovary collages)," these duly dated collages include handwritten notes such as "Dear Zoë… Emma dreaming of California," "Dear Zoë… Emma feels tired and longs to sleep yet wants to stay awake," or "Dear Zoë… Decisions, decisions, which tie will Emma give Rodolphe?" ensuring enough decadence for the A4 surface of each collage. Has Emma become real through the filter of art? Is "Emma B." a projection of what could be his self-portrait today? Maybe in the sense of Flaubert's famous assertion, "Madame Bovary, c'est moi!" Whatever the case, and given the artist is uncomfortable with portraits of himself [III. 22], he told Louisa Buck in

2023 [I. 24], "I'm happier dealing with the portraits of others than I am of my own, and that's partly why I so enjoy working with Emma Bovary…"

Between 2013 and 2023, the artist developed what he calls "a deferred portrait" of Emma Bovary. Comprising 300 collages published in 2013, as well as the text reproduced below and one exhibition room in Bern (Kunsthalle Bern) and Brussels (Wiels), the artist depicted, as he stated, "the portrait of a fictional character, which exists in person." This "deferred portrait"—perhaps an indirect portrait of the artist—is at once camp, erotic, political, subversive, and seductive. Its possible pending publication in Trois inventaires *[II. 12] might enable us to fully appreciate the diversity of its political decadent charge.*

A.V.

· · · · · · · · ·

Please insert at page 159. It is at this point in the narrative that Flaubert edited out this passage, included here to give the reader the option of re-introducing it.

One evening at the chemists Mme Bovary, whilst sewing, let drop a glove. Leon pushed it beneath the table, and when all were asleep, crept down on tiptoes to retrieve it, and then returned to his bed.

It was a yellow glove, with small creases, the calf skin of which seemed more greatly raised at that part above the thumb where the hand is at its fleshiest.

Leon, blinking, recalled Emma's buttoned wrist actively engaged in a multiplicity of various functions. He sniffed it. He kissed it. He slipped the four fingers of his right hand into it, then, his mouth upon it, fell asleep.

[III. 29]

An "Open Letter" to Aurélie Voltz

(2022)

Appointed General Director of the Musée d'art moderne et contemporain de Saint-Étienne in October 2017 (MAMC+), Aurélie Voltz contacted Chaimowicz following a conversation she had in 2017 with Marie Canet, a French art writer, art teacher, and independent curator, who was working on an essay about the artist. Following this conversation, Voltz thought it might be interesting to combine a solo presentation of the artist's work at MAMC+ including the production of a monograph based on the essay by Canet. She thought that the opportunity to bring the artist's ideas into dialogue with the museum's collection and Saint-Étienne's industrial past would undoubtedly result in a truly polyphonic examination of his work from the early 1970s to the present day. A year later, Chaimowicz travelled to Saint-Étienne to visit the museum and discuss the potential of such a project. As the meeting progressed, and once the visit to the museum was over, Voltz gave him a "carte blanche" to develop a project across seven consecutive rooms of the museum, a total floor area of 1,000 sq. m, which he choreographed into a retrospective of his own. After having "long wanted to do just one museum show in the country of his birth," as the artist told Louisa Buck early 2023 [III. 24], the exhibition "Marc Camille Chaimowicz. Zig Zag and Many Ribbons…" was presented from 19 November, 2022 through 10 April, 2023.

Following his first visit, Chaimowicz spontaneously wrote "An 'Open Letter' to Aurélie Voltz," describing the "choreography" of a possible exhibition in the museum. This typed letter was subsequently emailed by the artist to the museum director. Like any other "open letter" this one—really a model of an exhibition synopsis for artists and curators—did not expect a response. However, given its early position in the process and its stimulating clarity, somewhere between mind map and detailed exhibition plan, it could have served as a starting point for curatorial discussion, which did not eventuate—due to the pandemic, the exhibition was postponed, and all development halted.

Back on track in mid-2021, the exhibition was developed mostly digitally between London, where the artist was preparing the exhibition together with his assistant Anna Clifford, and the museum staff in Saint-Étienne, where the exhibition was solely treated administratively. In the end, the exhibition comprised a selection of seventy works from the early 1970s to the present day, plus thirty from the museum's collection, and many ribbons produced in collaboration with Neyret, a century-old company from Saint-Étienne. Knowing that he could not be on site in person due to the post-pandemic situation, Chaimowicz made himself available over the installation period, Skyping with Anna Clifford, who represented him in Saint-Étienne. For the first time in his life, Chaimowicz was unable to see his own exhibition. However, although he installed it via Skype, he was able to discuss image, object, pattern, colour, and light in great detail with those who had visited it in person.

In the run-up to the opening, the artist suggested including the "open letter" in the exhibition press kit, arguing that this curatorial outline would complement the press release and accompanying illustrations. Divided into seven sequences corresponding to the actual divisions of the gallery space where the exhibition was presented, this "open letter" had the double function at the time of the show as an exhibition outline and a guide to the exhibition. However, as it was written four years before the exhibition, we can now rightly consider it a "time capsule."

A.V.

· · · · · · · · ·

Dear Aurélie,

… you can but too well imagine how keen I am to be returning
to the museum, to be working on the exhibition, or more
accurately, to be seeking it materialise … yet deferred time
will perhaps have enabled Anna and I to the better fashion our
proposal: its look, structure, and constituent parts?

The floor plan is to be a sequence of eight galleries, akin, perhaps,
to eight tracks of a vinyl album, the titles are to be Zig Zag, One
plus One, L'entrepôt, Rachel et Graham, Beaux-Arts 1, Beaux-
Arts 2, du Textile, and End game / Saint-Étienne.

The exhibition will reveal the unfolding of new configurations of
the given from my work, now to be peppered from items chosen
from the Museum's excellent holdings…

<u>Zig Zag</u>:

by way of acknowledging that the Museum is one of both Fine Art
and Design the exhibition begins in Gallery One with selected
objects (other than works by Matisse and Picasso) ranging from
an oven dish and once worn Levi's, to portable radios… which are
essentially domestic or by nature of the everyday

As might children in the proverbial sweet shop, it has been a pleasure to have been greatly spoiled for choice, and all the more so
given Anna and I have been preparing for the exhibition during the
lockdown and have therefore been reliant on extensive print and
digital catalogues of the Museum's external stocks (an exercise not
dissimilar to that of Internet shopping)

… and so the stone is set: that of a proposed dialogue not simply between my work and the inert structure of the museum: as Host Institution, but now also with elements of its holdings

One plus One:

By way of contrast Gallery 2 is of a single word, which will consist of screens painted on the three walls—one of which is to be the two colours and remain mute—on the other two walls *A Partial View of an Interior* 1979 is to be projected in different time…

L'entrepôt:

Within a medley of furniture is RR 126, a freestanding stereo unit designed by Castiglioni and produced by Brionvega in 1967. Brion, a successful industrialist, was a close friend of Carlo Scarpa, and his wife, Onorina commissioned Scarpa to design them a final resting place and Memorial…
The result Brion Cemetery in San Vito D'altivole was to become probably the grandest personal memorial since ancient Egypt and surely Scarpa's grandest architectural project. An example of the RR 126 was in the personal collection of David Bowie … and this gallery also includes a drawing of the teddy bear, *David Bowie* by Nadia Wallis.

Rachel et Graham:

Gallery Four echoes a work initially shown at Liberty's London in 1984, which no longer exists … consisting of a set-like "interior," it was animated by a slide sequence featuring two friends, Rachel and Graham, who posed within the work of a fictive *Photo Roman* like sequence of slides, which were then continuously back projected within the work…

<u>Beaux-Arts 1</u>:

… such are presumptions and misunderstandings: I had been invited to present a solo show at the Centre for Contemporary Art in Warsaw … at this post-Communist but pre-E.U. time they however had hardly any budget and certainly nothing for the shipping of works … it was therefore proposed that the British Council could cover travel costs and that the Centre be essentially offering hospitality … invitations were based on the premise that invited artists would be Conceptual in practice … this travelling to Warsaw simply with schemas for exhibition in their top pockets,

I was at this time however re-investing in the practice of painting … hence the dilemma … the solution was accordingly for me to take twenty-six easel sized works—as hand luggage—on a number of return flights to Warsaw … and once there to decorate thirty-two decorative boards upon which some of theses small paintings were to be shown…

<u>Beaux-Arts 2</u>:

Stuart's Way

Stuart Morgan was, without question, the most brilliant critic of his generation.

… prior to gentrification, the grass mounds at Vauxhall Pleasure Gardens, come night fall, would become a danger field, a gay badlands … which Stuart would regularly frequent (to have there, on the occasion, found trouble).

Whilst Martin McGeown was finishing a beautiful video recording of the 2020 exhibition, *Paintings...* we were seeking a possible title...

I had previously suggested that a path leading from Cabinet Gallery (at which the exhibition had been presented) might be dedicated to Stuart's memory and Martin recalled this ... and so this is why the video—to be shown in Gallery 6—is so called *Stuart's Way...*

<u>du Textile</u>:

Cascade

The showing of fabric is challenging and a way of doing so, as initially tested at the Consortium Museum, Dijon then developed at the Kunsthalle Bern is to be shown in Gallery 7.

... samples of two fabric designs, woven at Paradiso Tendaggi, Como, in a range of colour ways, are hung in layered overlap in such a manner as to perhaps visually suggest the effect of a cascade...

Also to be shown is a further sample from the Magnum Opus by Marie Tailhardat

... this being a loose leaf collection of exquisite sewing exercises made by my late mother form her days when an apprentice dressmaker at the Haute couture house Paquin in Paris...

<u>End game / Saint-Étienne</u>:

Saint-Étienne was once known for its heavy industries including that of mining, as well as for its textiles and bicycle production,

… it remains the world centre in the region and production of ribbons

Variously embroidered, printed or woven, these fulfil the requirements of a discerning clientele ranging from the military, the High Church, the institution of the Légion d'Honneur, etc, as well as for luxury brands, including those from the spheres of fashion, make-up, and perfumery.

[IV]

BIBLIOGRAPHY

Entries list first publications of texts and are arranged chronologically within each section.

[I] TRANSCRIPTS OF INTERVIEWS

[I. 1] – Mackintosh, Alastair. "Three Approaches: Alastair Mackintosh Examines the Career of Marc Camille Chaimowicz." December 1973. *Art & Artists* 8, no. 9: 26–31 (ill). (Cover)
[I. 2] – Jones, Ben. "Interview." January/February 1976. *Artscribe*, no. 1: 8–9 (ill).
[I. 3] – Kontovà, Helena. "Performance Is Like a Perfect Day: Interview with Marc Chaimowicz." October/November 1978. *Flash Art*, no. 84/85: 13–14 (ill).
[I. 4] – Cuenat, Philippe. "Impressions: Interview with Marc Camille Chaimowicz." Spring 1987. *Faces, Journal d'Architecture*, no. 5/6: 65–70 (ill).
[I. 5] – Roudier, Jean-Michel and Troncy, Éric. "Interview with Marc Camille Chaimowicz." Autumn 1994. *Documents sur l'art*, no. 6: 86–89 (ill).
[I. 6] – Coulange, Alain. "Conversation with Marc Camille Chaimowicz." In *Marc Camille Chaimowicz Peintures & Objets*. Dijon: Le Consortium; Quimper: Le Quartier, 1995, 73–80 (ill).
[I. 7] – Archer, Michael and Furlong, William; McGeown, Martin; Wheatley, Andrew. "Marc Camille Chaimowicz Interviewed at Cabinet on July 26, 2000." September 2000. *Audio Arts* 19, no. 1 & 2: side A. Also in *Untitled*, Autumn/Winter 2000, no. 23: 8–10 (ill). And in *Celebration? Realife Revisited*. Dijon: Frac Bourgogne; London: Koenig Books Ltd, 2005, 99–101 (ill).
[I. 8] – Archer, Michael. "1000 Words: Marc Camille Chaimowicz Talks About *Jean Cocteau*, 2003." February 2004. *Artforum* 42, no. 6: 110–111 (ill).
[I. 9] – Hatfield, Jackie. "Interview with Marc Camille Chaimowicz." 21 November 2004. REWIND Artists Video, Duncan

of Jordanstone College of Art & Design, University of Dundee.
www.rewind.ac.uk

[I. 10] – Wood, Catherine. "A Certain Simplicity of Means, True Luxury of Life: 7 Questions For Marc Camille Chaimowicz." December/January 2006–07. *Metropolis M*, no. 6: 56–62 (ill). (Cover)

[I. 11] – Fox, Dan. "'…In the Cherished Company of Others…' by Marc Camille Chaimowicz: A new work is a retrospective, of sorts." October 2008. *frieze*, no. 118: 274–277 (ill).

[I. 12] – Cook, Roger. "A Personal Grammar of Means." In *Frieze Projects, Frieze Talks, 2006–2008*. London: Frieze Publishing, 2009, 228–239.

[I. 13] – A/S/N Mutual Press. "Fieldwork as Reverie." In *Fieldwork*, edited by Clémentine Deliss. Edinburgh: A/S/N Mutual Press, Edinburgh College of Art, 2009, 16–22 (ill).

[I. 14] – O'Neill-Butler, Lauren. "Marc Camille Chaimowicz Discusses his Exhibition at Artists Space." 25 September 2009. *Artforum* (ill). https://www.artforum.com/columns/marc-camille-chaimowicz-discusses-his-exhibition-at-artists-space-192210/

[I. 15] – Bracewell, Michael. "Adventures Close to Home: Lucy McKenzie and Marc Camille Chaimowicz in Conversation with Michael Bracewell." Summer 2011. *Mousse*, no. 29: 54–64 (ill).

[I. 16] – Freudenberger, Anette. "Conversation with Marc Camille Chaimowicz." In *The Secession Talks, Exhibitions in Conversation 1998–2010*, edited by Sylvia Liska. Cologne: Verlag der Buchhandlung Walther König, 2012, 588–599 (ill).

[I. 17] – Deliss, Clémentine. "Trusting Our Eyes: A Conversation with Marc Camille Chaimowicz." In *Object Atlas: Fieldwork in the Museum*, edited by Clémentine Deliss. Frankfurt am Main: Weltkulturen Museum; Berlin: Kerber Verlag, 2012, 201–206 (ill).

[I. 18] – Butler, Connie. "Marc Camille Chaimowicz in Conversation with Connie Butler." July 2014. *Her Eyes and My Voice*, no. 3: 7–17 (ill).

[I. 19] – Fabbris, Eva. "At the Tip of My Fingers: Marc Camille

Chaimowicz." February/March 2016. *Mousse*, no. 52: 54–59 (ill).
[I. 20] – Trembley, Nicolas. "Artist of the Month: Marc Camille
Chaimowicz." March 2017. *Numéro*, no. 181: n.p. (ill).
[I. 21] – Bechtler, Cristina and Fischli, Fredi; Olsen, Niels. "A
Conversation with Marc Camille Chaimowicz and Roger
Diener." In *Marc Camille Chaimowicz & Roger Diener: Armadillo
House,* edited by Cristina Bechtler, Fredi Fischli, and Niels Olsen.
Cologne: Verlag der Buchhandlung Walther und Franz König,
2022, 31–83 (ill).
[I. 22] – Vamvouklis, Nicolas. "Marc Camille Chaimowicz in
Conversation with Nicolas Vamvouklis." July 2022. *Features #9*
(ill). www.fondazioneimagomundi.org
[I. 23] – "In the Studio with… Marc Camille Chaimowicz." 23
February 2023. *Apollo* (ill). www.apollo-magazine.com
[I. 24] – Buck, Louisa, "Interview." 10 March 2023. *The Art
Newspaper* (ill). https://www.artnewspaper.fr/2023/03/13/marc-
camille-chaimowicz-remet-en-question-les-frontieres-entre-art-
decoration-et-design

[II] CRITICISM

[II. 1] – "Performance." January/February 1976. *Studio International*
191, no. 979: 66–68 (ill). Also in *Towards Another Picture, An
Anthology of Artists Writings (1945–1977)*, edited by Andrew Brighton
and Linda Morris. Nottingham: Midland Group, 1977, 86.
[II. 2] – "Performance." March/April 1976. *Studio International* 191,
no. 980: 188–190 (ill).
[II. 3] – "Performance." May/June 1976. *Studio International* 191, no.
981: 37–39 (ill).
[II. 4] – "Women and Performance in the UK: Sally Potter
Interviewed by Marc Camille Chaimowicz." July/August 1976.
Studio International 192, no. 982: 33–35 (ill). (Cover)
[II. 5] – "Performance." January/February 1977. *Studio International*

193, no. 985: 11–15 (ill).
[II. 6] – "Performance." March/April 1977. *Studio International* 193,
no. 986: 137–38 (ill). Also in *Towards Another Picture, An Anthology of
Artists Writings (1945–1977)*, edited by Andrew Brighton and Linda
Morris. Nottingham: Midland Group, 1977, 85–86.
[II. 7] – "Nine Works for Tape/Slide Sequence." December/January
1977–78. *Art Monthly*, no. 13: 34.
[II. 8] – "Problems of Presenting Performance." July 1979. *Art
Monthly*, no. 27: 14.
[II. 9] – "The Staircase Project." November 1980. *Flash Art*, no. 100:
56 (ill).
[II. 10] – "Architecture Is Not Art." Autumn 1989. *World Architecture*
1, no. 3: 74–77 (ill).
[II. 11] – "A Letter From Paris… ." April 2013. *frieze*, no. 154: 135–
136 (ill). (Cover)
[II. 12] – "*Jean Cocteau*… A Letter to Wolfgang Tillmans, 9
December, 2013." In *Trois inventaires*, edited by Marc Camille
Chaimowicz and Anna Clifford in collaboration with Zak Kyes.
London: Cabinet Editions (pending a possible future publication).

[III] TEXTS

[III. 1] – "Assumptions—Specific Work-Pieces." November 1971.
Leicester: Vaughan College, University of Leicester, St. Nicholas
Circle. Xerox, n.p. Facsimile. Also in *#1 Schmuck Presents Real
Schmuck*, edited by Felipe Ehrenberg, Martha Hellion, and David
Mayor. Cullompton: Beau Geste Press, March 1972, n.p.
[III. 2] – "Celebration Realife Ikon Gallery March 1972." March
1972. Birmingham: Ikon Gallery. Broadsheet, n.p. Facsimile.
[III. 3] – "First Floor." March/April 1972. In "Inaugural Show '3
Life Situations,' Gallery House London, 1972." *Newsheet,* no. 1.
London: Gallery House, n.p. Facsimile.
[III. 4] – "Progress Notes." 3 April 1972. Typewritten handout, n.p.

[III. 5] – *Dream, an Anecdote by Marc Camille Chaimowicz Dreamt in the Winter and Remembered in the Spring of 1977*. London: Nigel Greenwood Inc Ltd Books, 1977, n.p. (ill). Also as a facsimile in *The World of Interiors*, Zürich: Migros Museum für Gegenwartskunst, 2007, 63–82.
[III. 6] – "Here and There… Notes Towards a Preface, London 1978." In *Hayward Annual '78*. London: Arts Council of Great Britain, 1978, 70–71 (ill). Also in *Un Certain Art Anglais…* Paris: ARC, Musée d'art moderne de Paris, 1979, 53–54 (ill); *The World of Interiors*, Zürich: Migros Museum für Gegenwartskunst, 2007, 87.
[III. 7] – "Screens… ." London: Nigel Greenwood Inc Ltd, 1979. Announcement card, n.p.
[III. 8] – "Partial Eclipse… ." London: Tate Publishing, 1981. Brochure, n.p. (ill).
[III. 9] – "Rare Is the City in Which We Can Both Work and Dream… ." In *Marc Camille Chaimowicz Humanic Artist in Residence, Vienna, Spring 1982*, Wien: Galerie H Air, 1982, n.p. (ill).
[III. 10] – "Extracts From a Letter to Michael Regan." In *Four Rooms: An Arts Council touring exhibition*, London: Arts Council of Great Britain, 1984, n.p. (ill).
[III. 11] – *Café du Rêve*. Paris: Editions du regard – Galerie de France; London: Thames and Hudson, May 1985 (ill).

    a. "Le Désert…" 9–33.

    b. "Le Parc…" 35–61. Also in *Österreichischer Kulturservice*, April 1982, no. 11, n.p. (ill).

    c. "Partial Eclipse, a Performance" 73–101.

    d. "Chorus, a Letter From Vienna" 103–123.

    e. "Liaison" 125–168.

    f. "Le Select…" 169–180.

[III. 12] – "HAUNTED * SOMETIMES * REGRETS * PERHAPS." 1986. Geneva: Centre genevois de gravure contemporaine / Centre d'édition contemporaine. Typeset cover page from a portfolio. Facsimile.
[III. 13] – "Restlessness in the Belgian Congo." In *The Conversion*

of Pleasure in Sickness: Sharon Kivland. Cambridge: Kettle's Yard, University of Cambridge, 1987, n.p.

[III. 14] – "On Orange … As Torture … From a Text in Embryo." January/May 1988. *Banana Split*, no. 22, n.p. (ill).

[III. 15] – "On the Dialectic Between the Fine Arts and Design." Easter 1989. London: The Showroom. Brochure, n.p. (ill). Also in Autumn 1989. *World Architecture* 1, no. 3: 76–77 (ill). And in *To Give and To Take Meaning… Fine and Applied Art: Marc Camille Chaimowicz 1986–1990*. London: The Showroom; Cosne-Cours-sur-Loire: Musée de Cosne, 1990, 14–15 (ill). Facsimile.

[III. 16] – "The Drawings Done Away… ." In *Vocabulary… Vol. 2*. Warsaw: Centre for Contemporary Art, Ujazdowski Castle, 1993, n.p. (ill).

[III. 17] – "On the Everydaynessness of Things." Dijon: Interface, 1996. Brochure, n.p. (ill).

[III. 18] – "Statement." In *Live in Your Head. Concept and Experiment in Britain 1965–75*, edited by Clive Phillpot and Andrea Tarsia. London: Whitechapel Gallery, 2000, 57 (ill).

[III. 19] – "Aléa." In *Jocelyn Saint-André*. Dijon: Interface, 2003, 14 (ill).

[III. 20] – "Notes Regarding 'Concertina.'" June 2005. Berlin: Galerie Giti Nourbakhsch, "Concertina," press release.

[III. 21] – "Central Line… ." Spring/Summer 2006. London. ICA, South London Gallery, "Around the World in Eighty Days," exhibited text, n.p. (ill).

[III. 22] – *The World of Interiors*, edited by Heike Munder. Zürich: Migros Museum für Gegenwartskunst, October 2007 (ill).

      a. "Preface" 7 (ill).

      b. "Farmhouse Bedroom" 125 (ill).

      c. "Giacometti Meets Marshall McLuhan…" 150 (ill).

      d. "When in London …" 178 (ill).

      e. "Index to *The Word of Interiors*," supplement to be inserted within each publication, n.p.

[III. 23] – "Re B.B.5 For MvdR." Winter 2008. Berlin: Galerie Giti Nourbakhsch, press text.

[III. 24] – "Dear Stefanie Kleefeld and André Rottmann… ."
September 2008. *Texte zur Kunst*, no. 71: 135. Facsimile.
[III. 25] – "Lukas Duwenhögger, 'The End of the Season' (Cabinet
Gallery, London)." December 2008. *Artforum* 47, no. 4: 103 (ill).
[III. 26] – "A Letter, Transcribed." In *A Folio for Secession*, edited by
Elisabeth Bettina Spörr. Vienna: Secession, 2010, n.p.
[III. 27] – "Jean Genet in Norfolk." Autumn 2010. *Picpus*, no. 4, n.p.
(ill).
[III. 28] – "One Evening… ." Supplementary text by Marc Camille
Chaimowicz, to be inserted at page 159, in *Madame Bovary by
Gustave Flaubert—art by Marc Camille Chaimowicz*. London: Four
Corners Books, 2013. Facsimile.
[III. 29] – "An 'Open Letter' to Aurélie Voltz." Autumn 2022. Saint-
Étienne: MAMC+ / Musée d'art moderne et contemporain, "Marc
Camille Chaimowicz. Zig Zag and Many Ribbons…," press kit, n.p.

MARC CAMILLE CHAIMOWICZ
WRITINGS AND INTERVIEWS

Published by Sternberg Press

Editor
Alexis Vaillant

Design
Sanghon Kim

Copyediting
Tom Melick

Proofreading
Naomi Riddle

Rights Clearance
Margot O'Sullivan

Printing
Tallinn Book Printers, Estonia

ISBN
978-3-95679-651-7

© 2025 Marc Camille Chaimowicz, Alexis Vaillant,
Publishers, Interviewers, Sternberg Press

All rights reserved, including the right of reproduction
in whole or in part in any form.

Distributed by The MIT Press, Art Data, Les presses du réel, and Idea Books

Credits

Front Cover
2022 © Marc Camille Chaimowicz

Photos
2021 © Anna Clifford (9)
2022 © Marc Camille Chaimowicz (13)
2023 © Marc Camille Chaimowicz (10)
Courtesy Centre d'édition contemporaine, Genève © Sandra Pointet (547)

Translations from French to English
2022 © Martyn Back (64–75)
1995 © Nissim Marshall (87–101)

Copyrights ©
1971 by Vaughan College
1972 by Ikon Gallery, Gallery House
1973 by Art & Artists
1976 by Artscribe; Studio International
1977 by Studio International; Art Monthly; The Nigel Greenwood Gallery Archive, Tate Archive, London
1978 by Flash Art; Arts Council of Great Britain
1979 by Art Monthly; The Nigel Greenwood Gallery Archive, Tate Archive, London
1980 by Flash Art
1981 by Tate Publishing
1982 by Galerie H Air
1984 by Arts Council of Great Britain
1985 by Editions du regard; Galerie de France
1986 by Centre d'édition contemporaine
1987 by Faces; Kettle's Yard, University of Cambridge
1988 by Banana Split
1989 by World Architecture; The Showroom
1993 by Ujazdowski Castle
1994 by Documents sur l'art
1995 by Le Consortium; Le Quartier
1996 by Interface
2000 by Audio Arts; Untitled; Whitechapel Gallery
2003 by Interface
2004 by Artforum; REWIND Artists Video, Duncan of Jordanstone College of Art & Design, University of Dundee
2005 by Galerie Giti Nourbakhsch
2006 by Metropolis M
2007 by Migros Museum für Gegenwartskunst
2008 by frieze; Galerie Giti Nourbakhsch; Texte zur Kunst; Artforum
2009 by Frieze Publishing; A/S/N Mutual Press, Edinburgh College of Art; Artforum
2010 by Secession; Picpus Press
2011 by Mousse
2012 by Secession; Verlag der Buchhandlung Walther König; Kerber Verlag; Weltkulturen Museum
2013 by frieze; Four Corners Books
2014 by Her Eyes and My Voice
2016 by Mousse
2017 by Numéro
2022 by Verlag der Buchhandlung Walther und Franz König; Fondazione Imago Mundi
2023 by Apollo; The Art Newspaper

Every effort has been made to contact the rightful owners with regards to the copyrights and permissions. We apologise for any inadvertent errors or omissions.

This book is published with support from
Andrew Kreps Gallery, New York
Gaga, Guadalajara, Los Angeles
Galerie Neu, Berlin

The editor would like to thank

José Alvarez
Michael Archer
Charles Asprey
Véronique Bacchetta
Cristina Bechtler
Edward Behrens
Kirsty Bell
Vincenzo de Bellis
Marius Bolduan
Edoardo Bonaspetti
Phillip Van den Bossche
Michael Bracewell
Louisa Buck
Frédéric Buisson
Connie Butler
Emma Capps
Anna Clifford
Alain Coulange
Philippe Cuenat
Clémentine Deliss
Ann Demeester
Helen Dickman
Maryam Diener
Roger Diener
Richard Embray
Eva Fabbris
Alex Farquharson
Fredi Fischli
Mario Flecha
Dan Fox
Anette Freudenberger
William Furlong
Franck Gautherot

Liliane Giraudon
Melissa Goldberg
Zoë Gray
Phoebe Greenwood
Raphael Gygax
Christina Henneke
Sorrel Hershberg
Tom Holert
Elinor Jansz
Ben Jones
Stefanie Kleefeld
Valérie Knoll
Helena Kontovà
Andrew Kreps
Zak Kyes
Nadia Lauro
Urs Lehni
Christian Liclair
Sylvia Liska
Adam Lockhart
Chiara Longhi
Chris McCormack
Martin McGeown
Corie McGowan
Lucy McKenzie
Fernando Mesta
Julia Michalska
Amalia Mills
Eva Moller
Lynda Morris
Lucy Mounfield
Liz Mulholland
Carter Mull

Heike Munder
Dylan Naylor
Philip Newcombe
Giti Nourbakhsch
Niels Olsen
Lauren O'Neill-Butler
Tommaso Pagani
Alexandra Papadopoulou
Capucine Perrot
Naomi Polonsky
André Rottmann
Jean-Michel Roudier
Beatrix Ruf
Domeniek Ruyters
Katharina Schneibs
Alexander Schröder
Antonio Scoccimarro
Benjamin Shepard
Elisabeth Bettina Spörr
Polly Staple
Kelly Taxter
Catherine Thieck
David Thorp
Nicolas Trembley
Éric Troncy
Lex Trüb
Nicolas Vamvouklis
Aurélie Voltz
Nadia Wallis
Thilo Wermke
Andrew Wheatley
Catherine Wood
Thibaut Wychowanok

Sternberg Press
71–75 Shelton Street
London WC2H 9JQ
www.sternberg-press.com